ASPECTS OF GREEK HISTORY
750–323 BC

Aspects of Greek History 750–323 BC: A Source-Based Approach offers an indispensable introduction to the central period of Greek History for all students of classics, from pre-university to undergraduate level. Chapter by chapter, the relevant historical periods from the age of colonization to Alexander the Great are reconstructed. Emphasis is laid on the interpretation of the available sources, and the book sets out to give a clear treatment of all the major problems within a chronological framework.

This new edition brings the book up to date with the latest scholarship and includes a more detailed study of Sparta, Delian League and the Athenian Empire, expands the range of sources examined, and offers an extended discussion of the growth of Athenian Imperialism towards Samos, Mytilene and Melos.

It includes:

- A critical discussion of the lives, works, usefulness and reliability of the main literary sources: Thucydides, Herodotus, Xenophon, Plutarch, Diodorus and Aristotle
- Numerous quotations and references from these and other sources, including inscriptional and archaeological evidence, accompanied by a critical analysis of their worth
- Maps, a glossary of Greek terms, and a full chapter-based bibliography.

Aspects of Greek History is an invaluable aid to note-taking, essay preparation and examination revision.

Terry Buckley has retired from full-time teaching, having held the post of Head of Classics at Camden School for Girls and Roedean. He was also for many years a member of the J.A.C.T Ancient History Committee.

ASPECTS OF CLASSICAL CIVILISATION

ASPECTS OF GREEK HISTORY 750–323BC
A Source-Based Approach
Second Edition
Terry Buckley

ASPECTS OF ROMAN HISTORY 81BC–AD14
A Source-Based Approach
Mark Everson Davies and Hilary Swain

ASPECTS OF ROMAN HISTORY AD 14–117
Richard Alston

CLASSICAL LITERATURE: AN INTRODUCTION
Edited by Neil Croally and Roy Hyde

ASPECTS OF GREEK HISTORY 750–323BC

A Source-Based Approach

Second Edition

Terry Buckley

Routledge
Taylor & Francis Group

LONDON AND NEW YORK

First edition published 1996 by Routledge
This second edition published 2010 by Routledge

2 Park Square, Milton Park, Abingdon, Oxon OX14 4RN

Simultaneously published in the USA and Canada by Routledge
711 Third Avenue, New York, NY 10017

Routledge is an imprint of the Taylor & Francis Group, an informa business

© 1996, 2010 Terry Buckley

Typeset in Goudy by Taylor & Francis Books

British Library Cataloguing in Publication Data
A catalogue record for this book is available from the British Library

Library of Congress Cataloging in Publication Data
Buckley, Terry, 1946-
Aspects of Greek history 750-323 BC : a source-based approach / Terry
Buckley. – 2nd ed.
p. cm.
Includes bibliographical references and index.
1. Greece–History–To 146 B.C. 2. Greece–History–To 146 B.C.–
Historiography. I. Title.
DF214.B78 2010
938–dc22
2009030559

ISBN10: 0-415-54976-0 (hbk)
ISBN10: 0-415-54977-9 (pbk)
ISBN10: 0–203-86021–7 (ebk)

ISBN13: 978-0-415-54976-9 (hbk)
ISBN13: 978-0-415-54977-6 (pbk)
ISBN13: 978-0-203-86021-2 (ebk)

TO MY BELOVED FAMILY

SUE, ERIKA AND SEAN

CONTENTS

CONTENTS

CONTENTS

CONTENTS

CONTENTS

MAPS

PREFACE AND ACKNOWLEDGEMENTS

As a teacher of J.A.C.T. Ancient History, Section A topics (i.e. military and political) for the past twenty years, I have been acutely aware of the need for a textbook which, first, not only covers a historical period or theme in sufficient depth, but also is structured in such a way so as to help students to take notes, write essays and revise for the most commonly set 'A' level topics; second, includes a large amount of source evidence either in direct quotations or specific source references; finally, encourages students to become aware of the limitations of the literary evidence – both in particular historical instances and generally in the main literary authors – and thereby develop their critical faculties for historical analysis. At present there are three kinds of reading material for 'A' level students: the standard Ancient History textbooks which cover social, economic and cultural themes, and therefore do not treat political and military topics in sufficient depth nor supply sufficient primary source material for critical study as required by modern 'A' level Ancient History syllabuses; the specialist articles and books which assume a high degree of in-depth knowledge and, very often, a fluency in Greek and Latin; and source books which, although quoting in English many of the more inaccessible primary sources, provide insufficient explanation for the average 'A' level student to have a full and coherent understanding of their relevance to a particular topic. Therefore it has been the main aim of this textbook to fill this perceived gap in order to meet the examination needs of current 'A' level Ancient History students.

I am also very aware of the continually increasing curricular and pastoral demands that are being made upon teachers and that, more than ever, the time for preparation of lessons is being drastically squeezed. Therefore, in addition to a general bibliography at the end of the book, I have stated at the end of each chapter the specific articles and the relevant chapters of the books that I found the most useful and informative – hopefully, this will save valuable time for hard-pressed teachers. Furthermore, this will be an aid to the more able 'A' level students who wish to research a given topic more widely. Finally, it is also hoped that this book will be of use to 'A' level Greek students, when reading a Greek historian as a set-book, and to the increasing number of 'A' level Classical Civilization students who need to place writers such as Aristophanes in their historical context.

Finally, my sincerest thanks are owed to a number of people and institutions: first and foremost, to Dr Paul Cartledge of Clare College, Cambridge, whose constructive criticism, constant encouragement and friendly support throughout the last two and a half years have earned my eternal gratitude; to Andrew Wallace-Haddrill, who recommended me to Routledge when this book was first proposed; to Richard Stoneman and his staff at Routledge for their unfailing kindness and courtesy; to J.A.C.T. for their kind permission to use quotations from Lactor 1 *The Athenian Empire*; to my former 'A' level students at Camden School for Girls and at Roedean whose unstinting enthusiasm for Ancient History made teaching such a joy and helped me to shape my approach to this book; and finally, to my long-suffering family who have tolerated the full spectrum of my moods, ranging from exhilaration to despair, according to how well each chapter was progressing or not. Writing is a lonely pursuit, and so I look forward to a welcome return to the companionship, the shared endeavours, the banter and fun of the staffroom and the classroom.

Terry Buckley

PREFACE TO THE SECOND EDITION

I am grateful to Routledge for giving me the opportunity to write a second edition of my book. Apart from correcting typographical errors and some less-than-clear sentences, it allows me to do three things: first, to bring my book up to date in line with current research, especially with regard to the latest thinking on Sparta; second, with regard to the new AS and A2 Ancient History syllabuses in the OCR Classics Suite, to add to and re-organize the relevant chapters, especially concerning the fifth century, so that students can answer the source and essay questions in the AS 'Greek History from original sources', and have added a new chapter (Sparta, the Peloponnese and the Outbreak of the Decelean War, 421–413) so that there is a full continuity of events for the A2 'Greek History: conflict and culture'; third, the arrival of the fourth edition of LACTOR 1: *The Athenian Empire*, with its new organization and changed translations, necessitated a major updating of the relevant sections and quotations.

Once again I am deeply indebted to Dr Paul Cartledge, A.G. Leventis Professor of Greek Culture at Cambridge University, for reading all my new material and offering helpful criticism and advice – obviously all opinions expressed are mine alone. He is a very busy academic in great demand, yet he always found the time to help me in my endeavours – a great guy. Second, I'd like to thank my wife, Sue, who also read my drafts and offered many suggestions to iron out some of the verbal infelicities in my prose. I would also like to thank the London Association of Classical Teachers for granting me permission to use quotations from their publications. Finally, I would like to thank Matthew Gibbons, Lalle Pursglove and Andrew Watts at Routledge for their support and patience. I am now looking forward to a long rest from my labours, including pottering around the ancient Greek sites that I have not yet managed to visit, clutching Pausanias in my left hand and hopefully a cold lager in the other!

Terry Buckley
July 2009

ABBREVIATIONS

AE	*The Athenian Empire*, Lactor 1, ed. 4
CAH	*Cambridge Ancient History*
CQ	Classical Quarterly
FGrH	F. Jacoby, *Die Fragmente der griechischen Historiker*, Berlin and Leiden, 1923–
GHI	M. N. Tod, *A Selection of Greek Historical Inscriptions*, vol. II, from 403 to 323 BC, Oxford, 1948
G & R	Greece and Rome New Surveys in Classics
IG	Inscriptiones Graecae, Berlin, 1873–
JHS	Journal of Hellenic Studies
ML	R. Meiggs and D. M. Lewis, *A Selection of Greek Historical Inscriptions to the End of the Fifth Century*, Oxford, 1969
OO	The Old Oligarch, Lactor 2
SEG	Supplementum Epigraphicum Graecum
YCS	Yale Classical Studies

1

THE MAIN LITERARY SOURCES

The works of six literary sources (Aristotle, Diodorus Siculus, Herodotus, Plutarch, Thucydides and Xenophon) have provided the main evidence for the narrative of this book. The lives and careers of these six sources have been given (as far as it is possible to gather such information) in order to make students aware of the chronological gap – sometimes very considerable – that can exist between the occurrence of events and their recording in writing, a gap which often provides time and opportunity for the continual adaptation and 'improvement' of the original description of events and individuals' motives in accordance with the prejudices and interests of the writers. In addition, the source's family background is given, because this will often reflect the social and political circles, in which he usually mixed and gathered information, and which consequently were bound to exercise some influence on his interpretation of events, especially when there were two conflicting versions arising from opposite ends of the political spectrum. Most of this chapter, by the very nature and title of this book, has been concentrated on their weaknesses as historical sources, using the stringent criteria of modern historical scholarship. This is not to deny the authors' very fine literary qualities, but current Ancient History examination syllabuses demand not only a knowledge of the sources but also a critical awareness of their limitations and defects. With regard to the other sources used in this book, there will be brief comments on them as they make their appearance in the text.

Aristotle

Life and career

Aristotle was born in 384 at Stagirus (or Stagira), situated in Chalcidice, but moved to Athens in 367 in order to become a pupil of Plato at his Academy. When Plato died in 348/7, Aristotle was not appointed to succeed him and decided to leave Athens, spending time in Mysia in north-west Asia Minor and later at Mytilene on the island of Lesbos. In 343/2 he accepted the

1

invitation of Philip of Macedon to become Alexander the Great's tutor. In 335, Aristotle returned to Athens, where he founded his own philosophical school, known as the Lyceum after the sacred grove of Apollo in which it was situated; but upon the death of Alexander in 323, he was forced to leave Athens, due to the threat of prosecution, which arose from the very strong anti-Macedonian feeling that existed in Athens at that time. He retired to nearby Chalcis on the island of Euboea, and died in 322.

Athenaion Politeia

Modern scholarship is divided in its opinion about the authorship of the *Athenaion Politeia* (Constitution of the Athenians), which will be referred to as the *Ath. Pol.* in this and subsequent chapters. One group of scholars (e.g. Rhodes, the principal modern commentator) believes that the *Ath. Pol.* was composed by one of Aristotle's students, and does so on a number of grounds. In the first place, there are stylistic differences between this and Aristotle's other extant genuine works. Second, the differences in historical information, when this work is compared to Aristotle's *Politics*, strongly suggest the two works were not written by the same hand: for example, *Ath. Pol.* 8 states that Solon changed the method of election of the top public officials by removing the Areopagus' right of appointment and replacing it with the use of lot from an elected short list; whereas the *Politics* states that Solon made no change to the people's right to elect these officials (2.1273b–1274a). Third, the *Ath. Pol.* contains some information that is so drastically wrong that a writer of Aristotle's stature could not (it is argued) have been responsible for it: for example, Cimon is described as a young man, just beginning his public career, when Ephialtes passed his reforms in 462/1 (26.1), whereas in reality he was in his fifties and had been the dominant Athenian politician throughout the 470s and 460s. Finally, this work was only one of 158 such Constitutions, and it is very unlikely that Aristotle would have had the time to write all of them, in addition to his many other works. Therefore it is probably the work of one of Aristotle's students, but was attributed to him, because it was the traditional custom to assign all the works produced in his school under his direction to Aristotle himself.

Opponents of this view (e.g. Moore) believe that Aristotle did compose the *Ath. Pol.*, rejecting the arguments above. Stylistic differences can be explained by the fact that this sole surviving Constitution is a different genre from Aristotle's other works. There are also many marked similarities in historical information between the *Ath. Pol.* and the *Politics*, and in particular both works share similar political views – a distaste for extreme democracy and an approval of moderate oligarchy. In addition, Aristotle may have acquired more information and consequently changed his mind between the composition of the *Politics* (probably c.336) and the *Ath. Pol.* (c.332–322). It also does not follow that Aristotle the historian can maintain the same standards of quality as Aristotle the philosopher and natural scientist (which he primarily was). Finally, Aristotle would have received help from his students in the composition of the *Ath. Pol.* (and the other Constitutions), which would explain some of the differences and make the view that he was the author of so many works more convincing.

As there is no possibility of resolving this issue, the *Ath. Pol.* will be attributed to Aristotle throughout this textbook for reasons of convenience. The *Ath. Pol.* is divided into two main sections: the first (1–41) is a historical review of the development of the Athenian constitution, from the earliest times to Aristotle's own day, and is subdivided into eleven parts to represent the eleven major changes in the history of the constitution, which are summarized in chapter 41; the second (42–69) is a detailed account of the workings of the democratic constitution in Aristotle's day.

There is considerable scholarly dispute with regard to the sources that Aristotle used to compose the historical part of the *Ath. Pol.*, ranging from those who believe that Aristotle relied principally upon one source, i.e. Androtion, one of the fourth-century Atthidographers, who wrote an 'Atthis' (history of Athens), to those who believe in a multitude of sources or, at least, more than one source. Those who hold the latter view suggest that Aristotle made use of some or all of the following sources: Herodotus, especially his account of the tyranny of the Peisistratids (14–15, 19) and of the years 510–508, i.e. the expulsion of the tyrants to Cleisthenes' legislation (20.1–3); Thucydides, with regard to the murder in 514 of Hipparchus, brother of Hippias the tyrant (17–18), and the oligarchic revolution in 411 (29–33); the Atthidographers, especially Androtion, whom he mentions by name in his chapter on ostracism (22); the pamphleteer Stesimbrotus, who wrote in the late fifth century about Athenian politicians, and the historian Theopompos, whose *Philippica* (a history centred on the exploits of Philip of Macedon) included two digressions on Athens – both were hostile to Athenian democracy, and their influence can possibly be detected in the anti-democratic tone in parts of the *Ath. Pol.*; the politically partisan writings of the late fifth and early fourth centuries, such as published law-court speeches (e.g. of Andocides and Lysias) and political pamphlets (e.g. the so-called 'Old Oligarch', a critique of Athenian democracy, written some time in the Peloponnesian War and attributed to Xenophon); official documents, preserved in the state archives, such as the 401/0 formal reconciliation between the democrats in Athens and the oligarchs in Eleusis (39); and finally poems, especially those of Solon (5, 12). However, there is general agreement about the sources for the second part of the book, which deals with the Athenian constitution in Aristotle's day: the state archives, and Aristotle's and/or his students' attendance at all the relevant functions and ceremonies that took place in the fourth-century democracy.

One of the main weaknesses of the historical section of the *Ath. Pol.* is the apparent failure of the writer to conduct his own thorough research. He relied mainly on those writers who had already written a detailed account of the events that were relevant to his work, and used any evidence that they had quoted without feeling the need to do further research. A good illustration of this is Aristotle's account of Solon (5–12), which has many similarities with Plutarch's *Life of Solon*, including the quoting of his poems, and this strongly suggests that both writers were using an earlier common source. When Aristotle found a clash in his sources, he usually reacted in one of two ways. In some instances, he states his preference for one version, but arrives at this verdict, not by a careful and systematic study of the available evidence, but by what seemed more reasonable. For example, there is his belief that Solon could not have behaved dishonourably – making a huge profit from his own insider knowledge of his planned 'Seisachtheia' ('Shaking-off of Burdens') – because he behaved so honourably in the rest of his reforms (6.2–4).

His alternative methodology was to combine the conflicting sources, which often results in confusion. His attempt to combine Herodotus' account of Peisistratus' three periods of tyranny with a chronology, probably supplied by an Atthidographer, results in Peisistratus' third period of rule – his longest and most successful (547/6–528/7) – lasting less than a year (15.2–3). In a similar fashion, much of his account of the assassination of Hipparchus in 514 is based on Thucydides. However, having begun chapter 18 with a description of Hipparchus' character and thus apparently preparing the reader for Thucydides' narrative about his rejection by and insult to Harmodius, Aristotle switches to another source, resulting in the immediate disappearance of Hipparchus from the story and his replacement by Thessalos, another of Peisistratus' sons (18.2). Such problems could have been avoided if Aristotle had bothered to research his material more thoroughly, and then made an informed choice between the contradictory sources.

The other aspect of the *Ath. Pol.* that needs careful attention is the political bias that runs through the historical section, namely the writer's support and preference for moderate oligarchy, and his dislike of radical democracy. In this context, he can praise Solon because he does not believe that Solon passed his reforms in order to produce the later radical democracy (9.2); and also the regime of the Five Thousand which, replacing the narrowly oligarchic rule of The Four Hundred in 411, vested political power in those of 'hoplite' status and above (33.2). In fact, this second example provides another feature of Aristotle's approach to his sources: his readiness to repeat an opinion, which he found in his sources, that coincides with his own political views – in this instance, the opinion of Thucydides (8.97). By contrast, like most fourth-century philosophers and intellectuals, he is scathingly and unfairly critical of the so-called 'demagogues' and their achievements throughout the rest of the Peloponnesian War after Pericles' death in 429 (28.1–4).

Even with these reservations, the *Ath. Pol.* is an excellent source, both in its own right and for preserving other sources that otherwise would be lost to the modern historian. Its publication in 1890 has supplied new factual information on Cleisthenes' reforms in 508/7 (21) and on Athenian internal politics from Cleisthenes to the eve of the Persian War (22). In addition, it has provided an alternative account and viewpoint of important fifth-century constitutional changes: a favourable and sympathetic treatment of Ephialtes' reforms (25.1–2); and the oligarchic version of the events of 411 revolution (29–33). Moreover, he gives the modern historian an insight into how a fourth-century historian set about resolving historical problems and disagreements in the sources. But most important of all is his detailed record of the day-to-day working of Europe's first and most famous democracy – a unique literary work.

Diodorus Siculus

Life and career

Very little is known about Diodorus, but he is believed to have been born c.90 BC in Agyrium in Sicily (hence 'Diodorus Siculus', Diodorus the Sicilian). He was writing in the turbulent, last years of the Roman Republic (c.60–30 BC), and died at some time in the Principate of Augustus (27 BC – AD14).

Bibliotheke

Diodorus' work was oddly titled *Bibliotheke* or 'Library of World History', which consisted of 40 books from earliest times to Caesar's Gallic War (54 BC). Although a number of his books exist only in fragmentary form, Books 11–17 have survived in their entirety, and cover the years 480–323. Book 11 gives an account of the Persian War (480–479), Themistocles' career in the 470s until his death, the early years of the Delian League and the First Peloponnesian War (462/1–446/5) to 451. Book 12 narrates the end of the First Peloponnesian War, the causes of the Peloponnesian War of 431 to the Athenian preparations for the Sicilian Expedition (416). Book 13 covers the Sicilian campaign (415–403), the oligarchic revolution in Athens (411), the Ionian War, culminating in the defeat of Athens (413–404). Book 14 is mainly concerned with events in Sicily, but does include the rule and overthrow of the 30 Tyrants in Athens (404–403), the military campaigns of the Spartan king, Agesilaos, in Asia Minor (396–394), the Corinthian War (395–387), and ends with the Peace of Antalcidas (also known as the King's Peace – 387/6). Book 15 deals with the Spartan 'hegemony' (386–379), the recovery of Thebes and its defeat of the Spartans at the battle of Leuctra (379–371), and the Theban 'hegemony' of the 360s. Books 16 and 17 are devoted to the careers of Philip of Macedon and Alexander from their accessions to their deaths (359–336 and 336–323, respectively).

The unusual title of Diodorus' work and his inclusion among the list of compilers by Pliny the Elder (*Natural History*, the Preface 24ff.) give us an insight into the nature of his literary work. Using the histories of earlier writers, he wrote 'epitomes' or 'summaries' of their works, although he was different from the usual writers of epitomes in that he did not merely condense the original work. Instead he often selected specific events or episodes, and then either paraphrased them or included verbatim sections from the original. This method of composition has been deduced by comparing Diodorus' text with other surviving fragments of earlier historians (Hornblower, *Hieronymus of Cardia*, ch. 2). For example, Diodorus' account (12.60–62) of the campaigns of Cimon, from the capture of Eion to his crushing victory over the Persians at Eurymedon (470s–c.469), is very close to the description and order of events in a series of fragments (FGrH 70 F191), which are most probably the history of Ephorus, a Greek writer of the fourth century, much admired and used by Diodorus. Such comparisons or checks with other surviving fragments, especially as they occur in widely differing parts of the *Bibliotheke*, confirm that Diodorus' method of composition and treatment of his sources consisted in following very closely one main source at a time, but to supplement it with additional material.

As a result, Diodorus' worth as a historian is usually (but not always, as he is capable of being inefficient, careless and confusing in his own right) dependent on the quality of his chosen original source for a specific period. It is generally agreed that Diodorus, in Books 11–15 (480–360), mainly follows the history of Ephorus. Ephorus of Cyme (c.405–330) composed a *History of Greece* in 30 Books from the so-called Dorian Invasion in the Dark Age to 341. He was allegedly a pupil of Isocrates, the well-known rhetorician, and consequently his historical writing was greatly influenced by rhetoric. The result of this was twofold: first, a stirring and stimulating presentation of historical events became more important than their factual accuracy; second, history became a medium for moralizing, highlighting the noble and ignoble behaviour of famous men as a lesson for future generations.

It is a feature of Diodorus' handling of his sources that he adopts their approach to historiography and repeats their moral judgements, which can lead to superficial and biased reporting. There is doubt concerning Diodorus' source for Book 16, but his generally favourable picture of Philip of Macedon suggests that he may have used Theopompos, another alleged student of Isocrates, who wrote the *Philippica*, a universal history in 58 books, centred on the exploits of Philip of Macedon from 359–336. Diodorus appears to have based Book 17, his account of the career of Alexander, on the Greek Cleitarchus, the source for the 'vulgate' tradition (see beginning of Chapter 27).

Diodorus has a number of failings, especially in his dating. It is not known what system of dating Ephorus used, but his arrangement of historical events 'kata genos' (by subject), i.e. as self-contained mini-topics, covering a number of years (see FGrH 70 F191 above as an example), strongly suggests that it was not based on the annalistic (yearly) dating system of Thucydides. But Diodorus, while keeping to Ephorus' subject-matter approach, has attempted to superimpose such a dating system, giving the relevant Athenian archon and Roman consuls for each year, as well as the number of the Olympiad every fourth year. This has led to arbitrary and erroneous dating, and is consequently unreliable. For example. Diodorus devotes the whole period from 474–471 to events in the west (11.51–53), as though nothing was happening in the Greek world; but then he gives a long and detailed account of Themistocles' first trial at Athens for treason, his ostracism, his exile in Argos, the second accusation of treason, his flight to northern Greece and later to King Xerxes in Persia, and finally his death (11.54–59) – all these events, covering many years, are grouped under the year 471/0 (see Chapter 11). In the same way, he crams all of Cimon's successes from the capture of Eion, the first recorded action of the Delian League forces, to the battle of Eurymedon into the year 470/69 (11.60–62). It would seem that the availability of these time periods, since he had already allocated the previous three years to events in the west, was Diodorus' sole criterion for inserting the above events into these two years. Furthermore, if he had no information for a particular year, he had no qualms about moving something from elsewhere that was not too far away in time: for example, the Spartan debate about regaining the hegemony of Greece by force from the Athenians is dated to 475/4, although 478 seems a more likely date for such a discussion (11.50).

Diodorus' narrative can also reflect the pro-Athenian bias of Ephorus. As a result, previously unheard-of Athenian victories suddenly appear, and recorded defeats become military successes. For example, at the beginning of the First Peloponnesian War, Thucydides records the Athenians' first defeat at the battle of Halieis and their subsequent naval victory at Cecryphaleia (1.105.1). However, Diodorus' account has an unnamed Athenian victory, followed by an Athenian victory at Halieis, as well as at Cecryphaleia (11.78.1–2). The ultimate source of these battles and the rest of the events of the 'Pentecontaetia' (479–431), via Ephorus, may be Hellanicus of Lesbos, whose history of this period was criticized somewhat unfairly by Thucydides for its brevity and chronological inaccuracy (1.97.2). Thus, where there is disagreement between Thucydides' and Diodorus' versions of the same events in the fifth century, it is a good working principle to prefer Thucydides' account. Nevertheless Diodorus, if used cautiously, does fill in some of the gaps in Thucydides' own brief digression on Athens' rise to power in the Pentecontaetia (1.87.6–118).

Diodorus' worth as a historian improves from 411 onwards, when Thucydides' history comes to a sudden end, especially for the period 411–386. The reason for this is that Ephorus' (and therefore Diodorus') source for this period is a historian, to whom modern scholarship has given the name 'the Oxyrhynchus Historian' because the 1,200 surviving lines have been discovered on papyri at Oxyrhynchus in Egypt. This historian has employed a rigorous and analytical approach to his subject matter, similar in many ways to Thucydides'; and his account is not only different from and thus independent of Xenophon's, but also usually superior. Although the surviving text covers chiefly the events of 396–395, its quality is illuminated by a direct comparison with Xenophon's treatment of this period. For example, Xenophon, in his narrative of Agesilaos' campaign in Asia Minor in 395, is mainly preoccupied with Agesilaos' personality (e.g. his shrewd handling of Lysander – 3.4.7–10) and with scenes that provide for dramatic or colourful treatment (e.g. Agesilaos' conference on the grass with Pharnabazus – 4.1.29–39). By contrast, the Oxyrhynchus Historian dismisses all such material from his work, but concentrates in Thucydidean fashion on Agesilaos' military campaign, thus revealing (which Xenophon was trying to hide) his lack of any substantial victories. In addition, the Oxyrhynchus Historian gives a clear insight into the rivalry of competing political factions in various states, and its effect on those states' foreign policy.

As a result, Diodorus' account of Greek affairs in Books 13 (after 411) and 14 (404/3–387/6) is a useful corrective to Xenophon's pro-Spartan bias, and provides more information about events in northern and central Greece than Xenophon's, which is more concerned with happenings in the Peloponnese. The Oxyrhynchus Historian's work probably ended with the Peace of Antalcidas (also known as the King's Peace) in 386 and so coincided with the end of Diodorus' Book 14. It is not known what sources Ephorus (and thus Diodorus' Book 15) relied upon for the period 386–360, which dealt with the gradual rise of Thebes to a position of pre-eminence in Greece (see Chapter 25). However, Diodorus' narrative is particularly useful, as it provides an account of the exploits of Epaminondas, the great Theban statesman and general, and confers well-deserved praise upon him (15.39.2; 15.88), which Xenophon deliberately omits, as Epaminondas' success was achieved at the expense of the Spartans.

Thus Diodorus is a useful source for the fourth century, since, despite his weaknesses, he provides access to a tradition that differs from that of Xenophon, and also gives a better understanding of events in the wider Greek world than the narrow and parochial Xenophon.

Herodotus

Life and career

Most of the evidence for Herodotus' life comes from the *Suda*, a Byzantine historical and literary encyclopaedia, written about the tenth century AD. His date of birth was 484 BC, according to Aulus Gellius (15.23), but this was probably derived from the calculations of Apollodorus who dated a man's birth to 40 years before a famous event in his life – in Herodotus' case, his decision to become one of the founding citizens of the new colony of Thurii in southern Italy, established in 444/3. He was born to upper-class parents in Halicarnassus, a city in south-west Asia Minor, and thus moved in aristocratic circles. As a young man he became involved in politics, clashed with Lygdamis, the tyrant of Halicarnassus, and was forced into exile in Samos. Later he took part in the overthrow of Lygdamis, but did not return to his home. Instead he chose to travel to Egypt, to Tyre, down the Euphrates to Babylon, to Scythia and to Greece; he lived for some time in Athens, where he gave recitations of parts of his History. In 444/3 he left Athens to settle in the newly founded pan-Hellenic colony of Thurii, where he probably stayed until his death at some time in the 420s, although it is possible that he may have revisited Athens.

The History

Herodotus introduced his work by stating that his narrative was a result of his 'Historie' (Research/Enquiry), thus providing the name for this genre of literature. His work was divided (but not by Herodotus) into nine books. Book 1 contains the rise and fall of Lydia under Croesus (7–94); the story of Persia and the Persians, including the emergence of Cyrus (95–140); and the successes of Cyrus over the Ionians and the Babylonians, and his defeat and death at the hands of the Massagetae (141–216). Book 2 covers the accession of Cambyses to the Persian throne and a description of the geography and history of Egypt (1–182). Book 3 continues with the conquest of Egypt by Cambyses (1–38); the rise and fall of Samos under its tyrant, Polycrates (39–60, 120–28, 139–49); the death of Cambyses, the accession and reforms of Darius in the Persian Empire (61–117); and Darius' conquests in the west (including Samos) and his recapture of Babylon (120–58). Book 4 is based mainly around the history, geography and ethnography of the Scythians (1–82) and Darius' campaigns against them (83–144); the last section is a similar treatment of Libya, including the foundation and history of Cyrene, and its conquest by the Persians (145–205).

Books 5 and 6 set the scene for the Persian War: the military operations of Megabazus in Thrace and Macedon (5.1–27); the Ionian Revolt of 499–494 (5.28–6.41); the renewed advance into Thrace and Macedon (6.42–48); and the battle of Marathon in 490 (6.94–123). Book 6 also includes a brief history of Athens in the late sixth century, covering the fall of the Peisistratids in 510 and the reforms of Cleisthenes in 508/7 (6.55–73), and the attempts by the Spartans to interfere in Athens' new constitution (6.74–96); and the foreign policy of Cleomenes in the last decade of the sixth century and in the 490s (6.49–84). Books 7–9 cover the Persian War of 481–479: the accession of Xerxes in 486, his decision to invade Greece (7.1–19), his preparations and advance to the Greek borders (7.20–137); the counter-preparations of the Greeks and their occupation of Thermopylae (7.138–71); the battle of

Thermopylae (7.196–239), and the preliminary events and the sea-battle at Artemisium (7.175–95, 8.1–25); the build-up to and the battle of Salamis (8.27–96), and its aftermath, including the retreat of Xerxes (8.97–139); the events leading up to the battle of Plataea, the battle itself, and its aftermath (9.1–89); and finally the battle of Mycale and the second revolt of Ionia (9.99–106).

As is the case with Thucydides and Xenophon, there is scholarly disagreement about the order of composition of the books in Herodotus' *History*. This is further complicated by his wide-ranging approach to historiography, since he includes so much geography and ethnography. On the one hand, there are the 'separatists' who hold alternative views: either Herodotus began writing as a geographer and ethnographer, having planned originally to publish the early books (e.g. Book 2 on Egypt) as independent works, but gradually developed into a historian, composing a history of Persia and then proceeding to a history of the Persian War (e.g. Jacoby); or Herodotus' first composition was the Persian War in Books 7–9 and at a later date he wrote the earlier books (e.g. How and Wells). On the other hand, there are the 'unitarians' (e.g. Myres) who believe that Herodotus always planned from the beginning to write a full history of the Persian War, and that the geographic and ethnographic sections of his work are only carefully planned digressions from the main historical theme, which he had conceived on a far broader scale than the narrow concentration on politics and warfare of Thucydides. As there is insufficient evidence to prove either case conclusively, it must remain a matter of speculation. However, most scholars do agree that Herodotus must have gathered all the relevant data for his *History* before he finally settled in Thurii in 444/3, and it is possible that he wrote his work there in the order that has come down to us.

Apart from his own personal observation, Herodotus made use of four kinds of source material: oral, literary, epigraphical and archaeological. It is generally agreed that most of Herodotus' evidence came from oral informants, such as the men who had fought in the battles of the Persian War (see Chapter 9); the priests in Egypt who explained the background to the monuments and dedications in their country; upper-class Athenians and Spartans who related the stories about their family traditions and involvement in affairs of state; and Persian nobles who had knowledge of the political situation and decision-making in the Persian king's court. As regards literary evidence, Herodotus made extensive use of the poets, such as Homer (2.116 on Helen of Troy's stay in Egypt and Phoenicia), Hesiod (2.53 about the origins, appearances and powers of the Greek gods), Solon (5.113 and his praise of Philocypris, the ruler of Cyprus) and many others. There has been scholarly disagreement about his use or non-use of prose writers, but the weight of modern opinion inclines towards the view that, if Herodotus did acquire some of his information from such a source, Hecataeus of Miletus, the Ionian geographer and statesman, was his sole source, but even then he was not used extensively except possibly for Book 2. Finally, Herodotus included epigraphical evidence, although he needed a translator for the foreign languages that he encountered: official Persian documents from which, for example, he derived his account of the Persian 'satrapies' or provinces (3.89–97); temple records such as the oracular responses of the Delphic oracle, e.g. the two oracles given to the Athenians on the eve of the Persian War (7.140–41); monuments such as the tombs of the Scythian kings (4.71) and of the Greek dead at Plataea (9.85); and inscriptions such as the honorific epitaph for the Spartans who held the pass at Thermopylae (7.228). Herodotus is justly praised for the amount and diversity of his source material, but one of the two major criticisms levelled against him concerns his use of this evidence.

Herodotus did not glibly believe all that he was told, and his own words show that he had at least established basic (albeit unsophisticated) criteria for assessing the reliability of some of his evidence:

> I myself feel obliged to write down the things that have been told to me, but under no obligation at all to believe them.
>
> (7.152.3)

Where there were conflicting traditions, he does on occasion show a willingness to express openly or imply his preference for one version, for example, the stories about the origins of the Scythians and how they came to possess Scythia (4.12), and about the means by which the Arabian king supplied water to the troops of Cambyses, the Persian king, so that they could cross the desert in order to attack Egypt (3.9.2). On many occasions, however, he simply narrates the divergent stories and leaves it to the judgement of the reader to decide, such as the conflicting account of the Therans and the Cyreneans about the role of Battus in the foundation of Cyrene in Libya (4.154).

Far more damning is his over-reliance upon Athenian sources and his frequent failure to recognize the presence of obvious prejudice and partisanship in their accounts. This is particularly obvious in his description of the actions in the Persian War of those cities, which later in the fifth century became either allies or enemies of Athens. As a result, the Corinthians, who became hostile to and were the main enemies of Athens in the First Peloponnesian War (462/1–446/5), are given a very unfair press: their admiral, Adeimantos, is portrayed throughout the naval campaign of 480 as corrupt and cowardly (8.5), and is accused of leading the rest of the cowardly Corinthians in flight at the battle of Salamis (8.94). However, he does at least record the claim of the rest of the Greeks that the Corinthians played a leading role in the battle (8.94).

In the same way, Herodotus' treatment of those states that medized (i.e. joined the Persian side) during the Persian War is shaped by their later relations with Athens. Argos and Thessaly are treated very leniently, even though the Argives had refused to join the Greek cause, preferring a policy of neutrality (and friendship, according to some Greeks) with the Persians (7.150–51) and had even warned Mardonius, the commander-in-chief of the Persian army, of the Greek army's advance into central Greece against his forces (9.12.2), while the Thessalian nobles had taken the leading part in inviting the Persians into Greece (7.6.2, 7.130.3; 9.1), and all the Thessalians medized as soon as the Persians reached their borders, proving to be very supportive of and most useful to Xerxes (7.174). It is clear that their decision to become allies of Athens in c.461 against Sparta and the Peloponnesian League was instrumental in their generous treatment by Herodotus. By way of contrast, the Thebans are particularly vilified, even though they sent 400 men to Thermopylae, had medized under duress and claimed later that a powerful narrow oligarchy had been the sole supporters of this pro-Persian policy (Thucydides 3.62). Herodotus is contemptuous of the 400 Thebans, highlighting their half-hearted support and eagerness to surrender, and stresses that medism was widespread (9.87) and welcomed among all the Thebans (9.40, 9.67). Once again it is Athens' long-standing hostility towards Thebes and the Boeotians, which continued throughout most of the fifth century to the end of the Peloponnesian War (404), that shaped Herodotus' attitude towards them.

The second major criticism of Herodotus is his inability to identify and analyse the real causes of political events, concentrating instead on the personal motives and activities of certain individuals. Thus Cleisthenes' decision in 508/7 to carry out his tribal reforms, which did so much to break the regional power of the Athenian aristocracy and to establish democracy in Athens (see Chapter 7), is said to have been motivated and influenced by the same reasons as his grandfather's, who changed the names of the tribes in Sicyon because he despised their ethnic origin (5.68–69). In the same way, the causes of the Ionian Revolt in 499 are ascribed to Aristagoras and Histiaeus: the former, because he needed to protect himself from Persian wrath after his failure to capture Naxos, as promised; the latter, because he was home-sick for Ionia and believed that a revolt would persuade King Darius of Persia to release him from Susa in order to deal with it (5.35–36). In a similar fashion, the internal history and foreign relations of Sparta from 520–490 are mentioned in passing, while Herodotus concentrates on the lives and careers of the Spartan kings. A good example is the long section on Demaratus' dethronement in Sparta (6.61–70): Herodotus gives Cleomenes' desire for personal vengeance as the main cause – Demaratus had refused to support his policy against Athens and Aegina – but does not explain in depth the foreign policy issues facing Sparta, and the alternative options that split the two kings so vehemently and their reasons for supporting such policies.

Herodotus is also criticized for a lack of understanding of military tactics and strategy (see Chapter 9 on the Persian War for a full discussion); and for giving such major prominence to the continuous intervention of the gods in the affairs of men, thus accepting that they had played a very important part in the shaping of history. Some allowance can be made for Herodotus, since sources such as temple records and the collections of oracles were bound to emphasize the involvement of the supernatural. However, Herodotus appears to hold the same traditional, conservative religious beliefs as the majority of Athenians, such as those who welcomed Ephialtes' democratic reform of the aristocratic Council of the Areopagus in 462/1, but would have been alienated if its religious powers had been severely curtailed (see Chapter 13), and those who were deeply upset and frightened by the mutilation of the Hermae in 415 (see Chapter 21). Herodotus had no doubt that the gods revealed their will to men in dreams or omens, and especially through seers and oracles. Furthermore, he is happy to accept, without a hint of scepticism, any tale of the supernatural, such as the story of the successful defence of Apollo's temple at Delphi by the gods against a Persian attack (8.37–39), and of the rumour which crossed the Aegean Sea, informing those Greeks who were about to fight at the battle of Mycale of the victory at Plataea on the same day (9.100). Herodotus is also open to the criticism of being unwilling to search for a historical explanation of an event when a religious one was available. Thus, although he was aware of all the political and military reasons that directly influenced Xerxes' decision to invade Greece, Herodotus preferred to stress at length that Xerxes and Artabanus, who had previously convinced the King by rational argument that a full-scale invasion of Greece was unwise, both radically changed their minds through the influence of a dream from the gods (7.12–15).

Even with these important defects, there is considerable merit in Herodotus' *History*, especially as he was forging a new genre of literature. The scope of his work is far wider than the narrow concentration of Thucydides on politics and warfare, and thus is more in tune with the interests and subject matter of modern historiography. In addition, he lacked the ingrained prejudice and contempt that most Greeks felt for the 'Barbaros' (Foreigner), and thus he genuinely praises the naval and engineering skills of the Phoenicians (7.23.3, 7.44, 7.99.3), and the monuments of the Egyptians and Babylonians (1.93.2), and even acknowledges the Greeks' debt to foreign countries, such as the derivation of the Greek alphabet from Phoenicia (5.58), coinage from Lydia (1.94) and the measurement of time from Babylon (2.109.3). Even more remarkable is his generous and favourable assessment of the Persians – their justice (1.137), their high regard for truthfulness (1.138.1), their loyalty to the king (8.118.3) and their courage (9.62.3). But perhaps his greatest achievement was to prove that history, whatever its subject matter, could be written with charm, humour and panache.

Plutarch

Life and career

Plutarch was born probably in AD 45–50 in the Boeotian town of Chaeroneia in central Greece and died soon after AD 120. He came from a wealthy, cultured family, whose deep roots covering many generations ensured its high standing in local politics: Plutarch himself held a succession of public posts at Chaeroneia. As a young man from such an upper-class background, he naturally went to Athens where he studied under the philosopher Ammonianus, which greatly influenced his approach to his literary works. He spent most of his life in his hometown, but he travelled to Italy and Rome where he lectured and taught. His circle of friends in Rome included men of consular rank, such as Mestrius Florus, whose name was adopted by Plutarch's family when they gained Roman citizenship, and Sosius Senecio, to whom Plutarch dedicated his *Parallel Lives*. Such powerful and influential patronage, encouraged by Plutarch's great respect for Rome and by his belief in the partnership of Greece and Rome, brought tangible rewards in the form of honorary consular rank, and possibly the procuratorship of Achaea. In the last years of his life Plutarch served as a priest of Delphi.

The Parallel Lives

The surviving biographical works of Plutarch consist of 22 pairs of *Parallel Lives*, in which the lives and careers of an eminent Greek and Roman were described individually and then usually concluded with a formal 'Comparison' (four pairs of *Lives* lack a Comparison, possibly lost in transmission), and four single *Lives*. Plutarch's decision to compose dual biographies was clearly influenced by his desire to show that the generals and statesmen of Greek history had an equal claim to fame as their Roman counterparts; and by the ease that this structure allowed for comment on and judgement of the moral worth of their characters (see extract below).

The loss of the first pair of *Lives* (the Epaminondas and Scipio) is especially regrettable since it is most likely that Plutarch explained his method of composition and purpose in the first of the series. However, in some of the other *Lives*, he does give us an insight:

> If I do not record all their [i.e. Alexander's and Caesar's] most famous achievements or describe them in full … I ask my readers not to find fault with this. For I am not writing history but biography, and the revelation of virtue or vice is not usually to be found in men's most outstanding deeds, whereas minor events, sayings and witticisms may reveal more of a man's character than battles with countless casualties, the battle-arrays of the greatest armies and the sieges of cities.
>
> (Plutarch, *Alexander* 1.1–2)

In fact, by modern standards, Plutarch is more of an essayist than a bio-grapther, since the primary aim of his work is not to give a full account of men's lives and careers, but to inspire later generations to emulate their virtues (and sometimes to avoid their vices) by his portrayal of their char-acters (*Pericles* 1–2). As a result, this moral purpose, which permeates and underpins the *Lives*, shapes Plutarch's approach to the material for inclu-sion, resulting in selectivity, distortions, omissions and a marked fondness for anecdotes. Thus the use of Plutarch for historical purposes has to be undertaken with great care, since his own disclaimer in the above quotation and his statements elsewhere about the overriding moral function of his work give the modern historian clear and ample warning. However, although it is necessary to be critical of Plutarch when using him as a his-torical source, it should be remembered that he was not claiming to be a historian.

Four main weaknesses can be observed in Plutarch as a historical source: first, his careless and casual approach to chronology; second, his frequent inability to make an accurate judgement of the quality and reliability of his earlier sources, especially when they are in conflict; third, his failure to understand the political conditions of the fifth and fourth centuries in Greece, which were so different from his own political experiences under the Roman Empire in the late first and early second centuries AD; and fourth, his avoidance of any attempt to assess the effects and historical importance of his subject's deeds and policies.

With regard to chronology, it is clear that Plutarch had little interest in being accurate and systematic – detailed narrative histories were available to those readers who desired such knowledge (*Fabius* 16.6) – because the por-trayal of a specific aspect of a man's character demanded only 'examples'; therefore the inclusion of deeds from different periods of a man's career at this point in the *Life* for this exemplary purpose was far more important than an account of these deeds in strict chronological order. An illustration of this is in chapters 18 and 19 of the *Life of Pericles*: in chapter 18, Plutarch chooses to highlight Pericles' caution as a military commander and his determination to avoid Athenian casualties, citing as an example his warn-ing to Tolmides, the impetuous Athenian general, before the Athenian defeat at the battle of Coroneia in Boeotia in 447. As this is now the appropriate moment to show the effectiveness of his style of generalship, chapter 19 is devoted to Pericles' most famous military successes – his campaign in the Thracian Chersonese, probably in 447, but not necessarily later than the battle of Coroneia; and then his expedition to the Corinthian Gulf *c*.454, which was earlier the two aforementioned campaigns. Furthermore, when he does provide chronological information, he is una-ware of the historical problems that this can cause for modern scholarship. For example, he informs us that Cimon, who was ostracized for ten years in 462/1, was recalled after five years (*Cimon* 17.8–18.1; *Pericles* 10), but makes

15

no mention of how great Cimon's political influence was in Athens and what his foreign and domestic policies were from 457–451 before his final campaign against the Persians in 450. Clearly Plutarch lacked this knowledge of Cimon but did not take the trouble to find out; at least he did not resort to invention, like some other historians, in order to conceal his ignorance.

Concerning his use of sources, Plutarch produces a wonderful array in the *Lives*, and does show some critical judgement of their worth – for example, his rejection of Craterus' statement that Aristides was convicted of bribery and died in exile on the grounds that Craterus produced no documentary evidence in support, which was his usual practice (*Aristides* 26); his recognition of Thucydides' excellence and his scathing criticism of Timaeus as sources for his *Life of Nicias* (*Nicias* 1). He was also aware of the difficulty of acquiring a truthful account from his sources, owing either to the lapse of time between the occurrence of the events and their narratives, or to the bias of writers who were contemporary with the events described (*Pericles* 13.16). However, his judgement of his sources is not based upon any clearly defined and carefully evaluated historical criteria, but upon his own instinct and good sense. As a result, he often fails to assess the relative merits of his sources when they are in conflict, merely putting both accounts side by side with no attempt to resolve the disagreement or suggest a preference. Thus the deaths of Nicias and Demosthenes in 413 after the failure of the Sicilian expedition are presented either as an execution by the Syracusans, according to Thucydides and Philistus, or as suicide, according to Timaeus, a historian of the late fourth and early third centuries (*Nicias* 28.5), whom Plutarch had previously condemned as a historian.

There was a vast difference between the worlds of Classical Greece and the Roman Greece of the first and second centuries AD, separated by four to five hundred years. Plutarch was very much a product of his times: an upper-class Greek, living affluently and safely in a small Roman province, who easily accepted as the norm the political conditions that prevailed in Rome under the emperors Nerva and Trajan. Living at a time when political freedom was severely restricted, Plutarch had no understanding of the rough and tumble of Athenian public life, the prosecutions of important men, the nature of political comedy and the existence of political pamphleteers. As a result, he usually takes this evidence at face value, leading to a crude stereotyping of fifth-century Athenian politicians – either as the decent, honest, army-supporting, popular-with-the-allies conservative (e.g. Aristides), or as the devious, dishonest, navy-supporting, imperialist demagogue (e.g. Themistocles). In the same way, Plutarch's lack of experience of the genre of political comedy often results in either his implicit acceptance of the comic poets' statements, such as their claim that Pericles intervened on the side of Miletus in its conflict with Samos in 440 because Aspasia, his live-in lover, was Milesian (*Pericles* 24.1; 25.1); or giving serious historical

16

consideration to their humorous and biting satire, such as his treatment of Pericles' alleged political problems and his consequent refusal to revoke the Megarian Decree as a cause of the Peloponnesian War (*Pericles* 31–32 – see Chapter 18). Because of Plutarch's lack of political insight, it is necessary to be aware of this distortion in his portrayal of individuals and the political context in which they lived and operated.

Finally, Plutarch never fully appreciated the lasting effects of men's actions and policies on future generations. The best example of this weakness is his failure to recognize the greatest and most long-lasting achievement of Alexander the Great: the creation of the conditions for the development of the Hellenistic Age (*c*.330–30 BC) which, on account of the opening up of the Orient to the Greeks, enjoyed a dramatic flourishing of literature, learning, art and science, and had a profound effect upon the development of Rome and the west. A further illustration is his failure to appreciate the effect of Cimon's naval policy in the 460s on the Athenians and their relations with the rest of Greece until the end of the fifth century. He acknowledges rather superficially Cimon's role in turning the Delian League into the Athenian Empire (*Cimon* 11), but fails to realize that his aggressive foreign policy of crushing the League allies was the main cause of the Spartans' and their allies' fear of Athens and the source of the ongoing conflict between the two superpowers throughout the century. Instead, Plutarch exonerates Cimon by stressing his glorious exploits against the Persians, and puts the blame firmly on the later demagogues and warmongers (*Cimon* 19), even though he frequently used Thucydides as a source, whom he admired greatly and who specifically identified the growth of Athenian imperial power and Sparta's resultant fear as the truest cause of the Peloponnesian War (*Thucydides* 1.23).

Despite these reservations Plutarch is a valuable source, especially for the fifth century from 478. Without his *Lives*, our knowledge of the Pentecontaetia (the 'Fifty-Year Period', 478–432) would be even more limited, consisting solely of a few statements in Herodotus, the brief and highly selective digression of Thucydides (1.87.6–118.2) and Diodorus' confusing and often inaccurate account. Furthermore, he fills in the background of the last third of the fifth century by including biographical detail of some of the leading politicians, as well as the irreverent and mocking criticisms of comic poets and political pamphleteers, all of which Thucydides deliberately omitted on the grounds that it had (in his opinion) no relevance to the political and military history of the period. There are also occasions when Plutarch can be justly praised for displaying historical ability, such as his treatment of the battle of Artemisium in the Persian War in 480 (*Themistocles* 7.5–9.2): he makes use of Herodotus' definitive account, but concentrates on Themistocles' role; adds extra information from Phanias of Lesbos, the late fourth-century philosopher and historian, about Themistocles' handling of the Athenian opposition to his strategy; includes some lines of Pindar, the fifth-century Theban lyric poet, about how Athenian morale was greatly boosted by their experience of fighting at close quarters with the Persian fleet; and finally quotes the official epigram on display outside the temple of Artemis in Thessalian Olizon.

Plutarch's breadth of knowledge and his inclusion of such a wide variety of historical, literary, oratorical, philosophical and epigraphic sources make him a very important and useful asset to modern scholarship.

Thucydides

Life and career

Thucydides was probably born in the 450s: this can be deduced from his statement that he lived through the whole 27 years of the Peloponnesian War, being at an age to understand what was happening (5.26), and by his tenure of the generalship in 424 (4.104) for which post the minimum age was probably 30. He was the son of Oloros, and this fact is evidence that he was probably related by blood both to Thracian royalty and to Cimon, the dominant aristocratic Athenian politician of the 470s and 460s (see Chapter 11), whose grandfather was also called Oloros; and also to Thucydides, son of Melesias, the relation of Cimon, who provided the main opposition to Pericles in the 440s (see Chapter 18). Thus Thucydides came from an aristocratic background. Furthermore, Thucydides informs us that he had the right to work the gold mines in that part of Thrace, which would have also ensured that he was a rich man (4.105). It is important to bear this in mind, since this upper-class background would have coloured his political views and exercised some influence on his writing.

Thucydides was an Athenian citizen from the deme of Halimous, and was present in Athens when the plague struck in 430. Although he contracted the disease (2.48.3), he managed to survive, unlike Pericles and many other Athenian citizens (see Chapter 19). In 424 he was appointed as 'strategos' (general), one of the ten posts that were open for election annually. However, it was his misfortune to be ranged against Brasidas, one of Sparta's best military commanders, and his failure to save Amphipolis, the strategically most important city in Thrace, from falling into the hands of the Spartans resulted in his exile from Athens for 20 years (5.26). Nothing is known of the rest of his life. It would seem likely that he spent some time on his Thracian estate at Skapte Hyle, which is on the mainland opposite the island of Thasos. However, he must have travelled extensively to acquire the necessary information for his history (as implied in 5.26), and returned to Athens in 404 at the end of the Peloponnesian War, when a general amnesty for all exiles was decreed – one of the terms imposed upon the defeated Athenians. He probably died around 400 or very early in the 390s, although a recently discovered inscription from Thasos raises the possibility that Thucydides may have lived several years into the 390s.

The Peloponnesian War

Thucydides' work is now known as *The Peloponnesian War*, although he himself gave no title to his composition, and uses more than one name to refer to this war. The history is divided into eight books (but not by Thucydides), and relates the progress of the war from 431 to 411, where it suddenly breaks off. Books 1–5.24 deal with 'The Ten Years' or Archidamian War (431–421), culminating in the Peace of Nicias in 421. However, Book 1 (2–19) also includes a brief historical account of Greece from earliest times up to his own day – the so-called 'Archaeology' – in which Thucydides sets out to prove that the Peloponnesian War was the greatest war in Greek history; and to stress the important link between sea-power and imperial success. In addition, Thucydides provides the so-called 'Preface', in which he outlines his historical methods and his explanation of the outbreak of the Peloponnesian War (1.20–23); narrates the events at Corcyra and Potidaea, which were the publicly expressed causes of complaint against Athens in 432 (1.24–65); recounts the debates in Athens and Sparta that led to the declaration of war (1.66–88; 1.118–25; 1.139 to the end); and includes two digressions: first, the so-called 'Pentecontaetia' ('The Fifty Years'), in which Thucydides gives a very brief and highly selective account of the development of Athenian power from the end of the Persian war to the outbreak of the Peloponnesian War (1.89–118); second, the story of Cylon, who attempted to become the tyrant of Athens in the seventh century, and the downfall of Pausanias and Themistocles, the most famous of the Greek leaders in the Persian War (1.126–38).

Book 5.25 to its end deals with the period of 421–415, when the Athenians and Spartans were officially at peace by virtue of the Peace of Nicias, but both sides regarded it as a phoney peace and did their best to harm each other. This section of Book 5 includes the so-called 'Melian Dialogue', which gained its name from an actual dialogue between representatives of Athens and of the island-city of Melos on the issue of whether Melos, which claimed to be a neutral state in the war, should give in to Athenian demands and join the Athenian Empire against its will (5.84–113). Books 6 and 7 give an account of the ill-fated Athenian expedition to Sicily in 415–413, which resulted in total defeat for the Athenians and the renewal of the war by the Spartans and their allies. Book 8 deals with the early years (413–411) of the rest of the war (413–404), which is called either 'The Decelean War', after the occupation of this fort inside Attica by the Spartans, or 'The Ionian War', since most of the military action took place in this theatre of war. It is most probable that death prevented Thucydides from completing his history of the Peloponnesian War, but he does mention the final defeat of Athens in 2.65 (when he reviewed the conduct of the whole war under Pericles' successors) and in 6.15 (when he comments on the military ability of Alcibiades and how its absence in the last years of the war brought ultimate defeat).

It would seem from Thucydides' own words that his original aim was to give a full and comprehensive account of all the military and political events of the war:

> I have recorded the events of the war one after another, as they happened, by summer and winter.

(Thucydides 2.1)

This would explain the many repetitions in his history, and especially the excessive recording of minor and historically unimportant details, such as the fact that Anactorium contributed one ship to the 150 ships that the Corinthians led against Corcyra in 433 (1.46). However, such a massive amount of material led Thucydides to limit his scope in favour of selectivity, i.e. recording only 'the most noteworthy items', although he states this explicitly only once in his work when describing the Athenians fighting in Sicily in 426 (3.90). As a result there is a constant tension in Thucydides' work between his desire to record everything fully and his practice of selecting and concentrating on key events or individuals that act as archetypes or prime examples of typical behaviour in the war. Thus the lengthy, detailed description of 'stasis' (civil war) in Corcyra (3.70–81) is used by Thucydides as a typical example of the internal revolutions that broke out throughout Greece between democrats and oligarchs, thus allowing him to generalize about this phenomenon in the section that immediately follows (3.82–84) and thereby removing the need to repeat himself later in his history – the exception being the Athenian stasis in 411, which is related in detail because it had a major influence on the Athenians' conduct of the war. In the same way, Thucydides' detailed picture (or caricature) of Cleon as the archetypal 'demagogue' – the Mytilenean debate (3.36–40), the Pylos command (4.27–29), the Amphipolis campaign (5.6–10) – led him to gloss over Hyperbolus' career and his ostracism in probably 416, mentioning it only in a contemptuous aside when he was assassinated in 411 (8.73).

Opinions differ about when Thucydides wrote his account of the war: the 'unitarians' (e.g. Dover) hold the view that the whole work was written over a short period after the end of the Peloponnesian War; the 'analysts' (e.g. Hornblower) believe that the work was written over a long period, with some books that covered a later period of the war being completed before the book describing earlier events, i.e. Books 6 and 7 (the Sicilian Expedition, 415–413) being completed before Book 5 (421–416). What can be said for certain is that Thucydides began to take notes, at the very least, from the very beginning of the war in 431 (1.1.1) to its end in 404. This can be proved conclusively, although his history breaks off in 411, by several references to Athens' defeat at the end of the war – Pericles' obituary and the mention of the Persian intervention in the war on the Spartan side (2.65.12); the so-called 'Second Preface', in which Thucydides dismisses the

Peace of Nicias as a genuine peace and states his intention to continue writing his account of the war from 421 to the collapse of Athens (5.26); and his short digression on Alcibiades' excellent generalship, but also on his wayward character, which led the Athenians to entrust the conduct of the war to others who brought ruin to Athens (6.15).

Thucydides' greatest quality is the intellectual rigour that he brought to his work in his attempt to discover the truth about the events that he described:

> With regard to the facts of the events that took place in the war, I have made it my principle to report them, not through learning of them from the first person I happened upon, nor from what seemed probable to me, but after investigating with as much accuracy as possible each event, in which I myself participated or in which other eye-witnesses were directly involved.
>
> (Thucydides 1.22.2)

This statement, however, must be taken on trust, since Thucydides does not name his sources, but the integrity of his work has been accepted by modern scholarship. There are numerous occasions when it can be safely assumed that Thucydides received accurate information from an oral source: for example, Demosthenes, while bringing reinforcements to the beleaguered Nicias in Sicily in 413, stopped at Anactorium where he was joined by Conon, the Athenian commander at Naupactus, who asked him for some extra ships (7.31); Thucydides could not have learned this from Demosthenes, who was put to death soon afterwards at Syracuse, but very likely from Conon, who was on active service from 410–407 in the North Aegean, close to Thucydides' home in Thrace. Nevertheless, some caution must still be exercised even when using Thucydides, since he himself admits that eyewitness accounts were not always trustworthy, either through partisanship or through faulty memories (1.22.3). In addition, it is not known how many oral informants were interviewed for each event, nor their social background and political allegiances – Thucydides' very critical view of Theramenes, the 'moderate' oligarch in the 411 revolution (see Chapter 23), has most probably been influenced by the account of one of the exiled 'extreme' oligarchs, who bitterly resented Theramenes' role in the overthrow of The Four Hundred, the narrow oligarchy that governed Athens for almost four months in 411 (8.89).

In the same way, care must be taken when Thucydides attributes motives to various individuals in his history, especially as he explains them so confidently, rarely admitting doubt – the sole instances of Thucydides' uncertainty concern the Spartan king Archidamus in 431 (2.18.5; 2.20.1) and the Persian 'satrap' (provincial governor) Tissaphernes in 411 (8.46.5; 8.56.2–3; 8.87). Thucydides seems to have used three methods in his attribution of motive. The first and the most reliable method was to gain information directly from the individual concerned or from that man's close associates, for example, Brasidas' motives in 424 at Megara (4.70.1; 4.73.1–2) and at Amphipolis, where his Athenian opponent was Thucydides himself (4.120.2; 4.124.4). The second method was his deduction of motive from the behaviour or action of the individual, or from the attitude of the individual to the situation in which he played a part, for example, Demosthenes' motives in 426/5 when he led the Acarnanians to victory over an army of Peloponnesians and Ambraciots (3.107.3; 3.109.2; 3.112.4). The third and most unreliable method was Thucydides' assumption of motive, based on his own assessment of the individual's character: for example, there was no way that Thucydides could have known or discovered the motives of Cleon, his political enemy, when he took part in the second debate about the Spartan forces on Sphacteria in 425 (4.27–28); nor the motives ascribed to the four individuals most involved with the Peace of Nicias in 421, i.e. Cleon and Brasidas who allegedly favoured the continuation of the war, and Nicias and Pleistoanax who allegedly desired the Peace (5.16–17).

The thorniest problem in using Thucydides as a reliable historical source concerns the authenticity of his speeches. He described his methodology as follows:

It has been difficult for me to remember the exact words that were spoken in the speeches that I myself heard, and for those who brought me reports of other speeches. Therefore it has been my method to record the speeches which I thought were the most appropriate ('ta deonta') for each speaker to give in each situation, while keeping as close as possible to the general sense of what was actually said.

(Thucydides 1.22.1)

Unfortunately, there is an inherent contradiction in the last sentence, since the inclusion of 'which I thought were the most appropriate' ('ta deonta') in his speeches is in apparent conflict with his inclusion of 'what was actually said'. Consequently there exists a whole spectrum of scholarly opinion on this issue, ranging from those who believe that all the speeches were invented by Thucydides, to those who believe totally in their authenticity, with many other scholars taking a position somewhere between these extremes. There are without doubt certain speeches whose authenticity does seem very suspect: the Corinthian speech (1.120–24) to the Allied Congress at Sparta in 432 contains many points and suggestions, such as borrowing money from Olympia to lure away Athens' foreign soldiers by offering higher rates of pay, which are precisely 'answered' by Pericles in his speech to the Athenians in Athens (1.140–44), although he obviously could not have heard the Corinthian arguments. On the other hand, Pericles' last speech to the Athenians, in which he set about raising their morale, after they had suffered the destruction of their property twice and the outbreak of the plague, has the ring of truthfulness about it (2.60–64). In reality, there is no absolutely reliable method of assessing how far Thucydides adapted, added to, or even invented the speeches in his history. However, if a doctrinaire approach to the speeches as a whole is rejected, and if each speech is judged individually on the criteria of 'how likely was Thucydides to acquire an accurate report of the speech?' and 'how far does the speaker stick to the point in hand?', in much the same way as his attribution of motive is to be judged (see above paragraph), then it is possible to make selective use of them.

From the historian's point of view, Thucydides' account of the Peloponnesian War has two serious weaknesses: his (lack of) coverage of Persian involvement in the war, and his limited and superficial treatment of economic factors in the war. With regard to Persia, Thucydides acknowledged the key role that Cyrus, the Persian king's son, and his money played in the defeat of Athens, but only in his brief summary of the war after the death of Pericles (2.65.12). However, numerous embassies were sent by Sparta (4.50.2) in 'The Ten Years' or Archidamian War (431–421), and it seems very likely that the Athenians signed a treaty of eternal friendship in 424/3 with the Persian king, which they broke by sending aid to the rebel satrap, Pissouthnes, and later to his son, Amorges, between 421 and 411 (see Chapter 22). Such an ill-considered provocative policy, especially as a major Athenian force was away fighting in Sicily and the Spartans had renewed the war in 413 by occupying Decelea, ultimately brought disaster to Athens by drawing the Persians into the war on the side of the Spartans. Yet Thucydides barely mentions this aspect of Athenian foreign policy, and it is reasonable to presume that Thucydides only recognized the importance of Persia too late, and died before he could rectify his error.

With regard to his treatment of the economic factors in the war, although he knew of their importance (1.80.3–4; 1.141.3–5; 3.13.6; 6.34.20) and even lists some of Athens' financial resources in 431 (2.13.2–5), his failure to give either the total of Athens' annual income or the total expenditure for one or more years gives us no insight into the real value of those financial resources. Furthermore, he does not inform us of the changes in the levels of income that came from allied tribute, even ignoring the dramatic increase from 600 talents to roughly 1,500 talents in 425 as a result of the decree of Thoudippos (see Chapter 16), unless he did not wish to praise the so-called 'demagogues' for solving Athens' economic problems in the mid-420s, which Pericles had failed to foresee.

Nevertheless, even with the reservations stated above, Thucydides is by far the best of our literary sources, and where there is a direct conflict in the evidence supplied by him and by other historians, his version is to be preferred, due to his great desire and effort to find out and to give an accurate account of historical events.

Xenophon

Life and career

Xenophon was born in the very early years of the Peloponnesian War, possibly *c*.428/7, and his family background was upper class – his keen interest in horses and horsemanship suggest membership of the class of 'Hippeis' (Knights). If this is so, then he may well have shared the same political outlook as portrayed in Aristophanes' *The Knights*, who had an aristocratic contempt for the so-called demagogues; and it may explain in part his dislike of Athenian democracy, and his respect for and praise of Sparta's well-ordered and hierarchical society. The main sources for his life and career are his own works and a section in Diogenes Laertius' third century AD *Lives of Philosophers* (2.49–58). His education followed the traditional pattern of an upper-class Athenian with its emphasis upon athletic training. However, at some point in his teens he came under the influence of Socrates who, as Xenophon would have us believe, improved his intellect and shaped his moral outlook. He probably played his part in the defence of Athens in the very last years of the Peloponnesian War, and possibly in the political upheavals in the immediate aftermath of Athens' defeat in 404.

In 402, he decided to join the large Greek mercenary force, which formed a contingent in the army being assembled by the Persian prince, Cyrus, in his Spartan-backed bid to seize the Persian throne from his hated brother, Artaxerxes II. In 401, at the battle of Cunaxa, around 50 miles north-west of Babylon, Cyrus threw away his victory by his impetuous personal attack upon his brother that brought about his death on the battlefield. The purpose of the expedition had died with Cyrus, and the Ten Thousand, as the Greek force came to be known, were stranded in the depths of the Persian Empire. Their plight was made even more difficult by the treacherous assassination of their generals. In the event, Xenophon was chosen as one of the generals, whose task it was to lead this mercenary army as it fought its way back to the Black Sea and then the Aegean. This return journey is recorded in Xenophon's *Anabasis* (March Up-Country), to which there are scattered references in this textbook.

After their successful return to the Aegean and some mercenary service in the pay of a Thracian king, Xenophon and part of the Ten Thousand joined the Spartan forces that had been sent out purportedly to liberate the Asiatic Greeks from Persia, first under Thibron (400), then Dercylidas (399–397) and finally King Agesilaos. This was the first time that the two men had met, and Xenophon soon formed a very high opinion of Agesilaos' ability, which praise was amply rewarded by the Spartan king's patronage. The outbreak of the Corinthian War in 395 (see Chapter 24) led to the recall of Agesilaos and Xenophon to defend Sparta. The presence of Xenophon at

Agesilaos' victory in the battle of Coroneia in 394 over the forces of the Quadruple Alliance, an anti-Spartan coalition of Greek states including Athens, may have been the occasion of his formal exile from Athens on a charge of Laconism, i.e. being pro-Spartan (Xenophon, *Anabasis* 7.7.75). However, his exile may have been passed earlier in *c.*399 on a charge of medism, i.e. being pro-Persian through his military involvement with Cyrus (*Anabasis* 3.1.5).

In 394, Xenophon settled in the Peloponnese with his wife and two sons, first in Sparta, and later on an estate at Scillous in Triphylia, just south of Olympia, which was given to him by the Spartans (*Anabasis* 5.3). Later his two sons underwent, allegedly on the advice of Agesilaos (Plutarch, *Ages.* 20.2), the Spartan 'agoge' (education system) which allowed them to become members of the class of 'trophimoi xenoi' (Spartan-raised foreigners). It is very likely that his exile was formally lifted after the Peace of Antalcidas in 386, but it seems that he preferred the delights of Scillous. However, the devastating defeat of the Spartans in 371 by the Thebans at the battle of Leuctra and the re-acquisition of Triphylia by Elis as a consequence forced Xenophon to move. The remaining years of his life, on the basis of his literary works, seem to have been spent in Athens, which in the 360s had joined Sparta in an anti-Theban alliance, and in Corinth where the ancient tradition claimed that he died *c.*354.

The Hellenica

Xenophon's *Hellenica* (Greek Affairs) covers the period from 411, where Thucydides' history abruptly breaks off, to 362, and is divided into seven books. Books 1–2 cover the Ionian War (411–404) to Athens' surrender; the rule in Athens of a narrow oligarchy, known as the Thirty Tyrants (404–403); and the restoration of democracy and the end of the Athenian civil war (403). Book 3 gives an account of the Spartan campaigns in Asia Minor under Thibron (400), Dercylidas (399–397) and King Agesilaos (396–395) against Persia with the alleged aim of liberating the Asiatic Greeks from Persian rule. This book also relates the formation of an anti-Spartan alliance between Boeotia and Thebes, and the defeat of a Spartan army at Haliartus in 395, which was the opening battle of the Corinthian War (395–386/7 – see Chapter 24). Book 4 deals with the recall of Agesilaos from Asia Minor (394), and the land and naval campaigns of the Corinthian War.

Book 5 covers the period from the King's Peace (or Peace of Antalcidas) in 386, which, with Persian backing, made the Spartans the undisputed leaders of Greece, to 375. Then Xenophon recounts the exercise of power by the Spartans from 386–379: their defeat and dismemberment of Mantinea (385); the imposition of a narrow pro-Spartan oligarchy on Phlius in the Peloponnese (381–379); the seizure of Thebes by treachery (382); and the dissolution of the Chalcidian League (379). He also records the gradual erosion of Spartan power from 379–375 at the hands of the Thebans, after they regained their independence in 379 (see Chapter 25). Book 6 deals with the growing power of Jason of Pherae in Thessaly (375), but records his assassination (370) and the subsequent events in Thessaly over the following two decades. There is also the increasing rapprochement between Athens and Sparta through their mutual fear of Thebes. In addition, this book narrates the battle of Leuctra in 371, when the Thebans destroyed the myth of Spartan military invincibility forever, and the first Theban-led invasion of the Peloponnese and Laconia (370/69). Book 7 covers the events and political developments in the Peloponnese throughout the 360s, beginning with the alliance between Athens and Sparta (369), and the second invasion of the Peloponnese by the Thebans at the request of the Arcadians, Argives and Elis (369), and ending with the battle of Mantinea (362), in which all of the major Greek states and their allies were ranged on either side.

There is no agreement among scholars on the date(s) of the composition of the *Hellenica*. The extreme 'unitarian' view maintains that the whole work was composed as a unit at some time after the battle of Mantinea in 362 and even well into the 350s, since Xenophon mentions the assassination of Alexander of Thessaly (358) and the succession of Tisiphonus (6.4.35–37). The extreme 'analyst' view holds that as many as four separate chronological sections can be identified within the work. However, the general consensus of scholarly opinion falls between the two.

Xenophon, unlike Thucydides (1.22.2), does not inform the reader of his methodology in gathering information from his sources, but it is likely that it was based upon his own eyewitness experiences and the reports of his circle of friends. The vivid and detailed accounts of certain events, such as the civil war in Athens in 404–403 (2.4.138), and the campaigns of the Spartans, especially Agesilaos, in Asia Minor from 400–394 (3.1.3–2.20; 3.4.5–29; 4.1.1–28), supply convincing evidence that he was present on these occasions. With regard to his other sources, the bias, the partisanship and the concentration on Peloponnesian affairs throughout his work strongly suggest that the Spartans themselves and the upper-class, pro-Spartan, pro-oligarchic supporters of Agesilaos were Xenophon's chief sources of information, and that Xenophon decided that their version of events was sufficient for his needs. These were the very men who, according to Xenophon, 'were concerned with the best interests of the Peloponnese' (7.4.35; 7.5.1), such as 'the owners of landed property [in Mantinea] ... who, because they were governing in an aristocratic government and were rid of the annoying demagogues, were pleased with what they [the Spartans] had done' (5.2.7), i.e. the breaking-up of Mantinea into four or five villages and the imposition of a pro-Spartan, oligarchic government in 385.

There is much to enjoy and appreciate in the *Hellenica*, provided that it is viewed as the 'memoirs of an old man' (Cartledge, *Agesilaos*, p. 65) rather than as a work of history, using Thucydides' and modern historical standards as the criteria for assessing Xenophon's worth as a historian. However, for the purposes of this historical textbook, these must be the criteria employed. Consequently, Xenophon's *Hellenica* must be criticized for its blatant bias and its remarkable omissions of events of the greatest historical importance.

Xenophon's bias is most obvious in his favourable treatment of Sparta and his hostile attitude to Thebes. He dwells at excessive length on minor victories of the Spartans, for example, the 'Tearless Battle' in 368 against the Arcadians (7.1.29–32). But he belittles major Theban successes, either by totally ignoring or hardly mentioning them, for example, the liberation of the Messenian 'Helots' and the (re)foundation of Messene in 369; or by presenting them in an unfavourable light: for example, the Theban invasion of Laconia (370/69) up to the very outskirts of the city of Sparta (previously believed to be impossible and therefore deeply humiliating for the Spartans) is portrayed as tentative, fearful and deliberately avoiding any clash with the Spartan hoplites (6.5.27–32), while the Theban destruction of Sellasia, a major Spartan outpost which was strategically important for the defence of Sparta, is narrated in eight words (6.5.27). Xenophon is strongly critical of the Spartans (as opposed to individual Spartans) on only two occasions: their illegal and unprovoked seizure in 382 of the Cadmeia, the citadel of Thebes (5.4.1); and his reporting of the Athenian Autocles' critical speech about Spartan imperialism (6.3.7–9). In the rest of his work, he finds no problem in presenting some of Sparta's more disreputable actions in the most favourable light: for example, the King's Peace of 386, by which the Spartans sold out the Asiatic Greeks to Persia in return for the undisputed hegemony of Greece, is portrayed as an honourable peace that brought peace between Athens and Sparta, and ensured the independence of Greek cities – the Spartans are even given the honorific title 'champions of the peace' (5.1.34–35).

Xenophon's major omissions can usually be explained as other examples of his bias. The rise of Thebes, from a position of extreme weakness after the dissolution of the Boeotian League in 386 to its victory over the Spartans at Leuctra in 371 and to its pre-eminence in Greek affairs, is mentioned in a brief and piecemeal fashion, and no explanation is offered. Even more damning is the failure to give an account of the careers of the two dominant generals and statesmen of the 370s and the 360s, the architects of Thebes' greatness, Epaminondas and Pelopidas (see Chapter 25). Both men receive their first mention, and then only in passing and in a bad light, much later than their political and military successes warranted: Epaminondas in 366, when he failed to achieve his objectives in Achaea in his third invasion of the Peloponnese (7.1.41–43); and Pelopidas in 367 in the Theban mission to the Persian king, which failed to bring about the Common Peace that Pelopidas so greatly desired, since it would have brought great advantages to the Thebans (7.1.33–40). Other very notable omissions include the formation of the Quadruple Alliance (Athens, the Boeotians, Argos and Corinth) that fought the Spartans in the Corinthian War, and destroyed their imperialist ambitions with regard to the Asiatic Greeks; the foundation of the naval Second Athenian League in 378/7, whose ostensible aim was to prevent further breaches of the Peace of Antalcidas by Sparta; the liberation of the Messenian Helots, the (re)foundation of Messene in 369, and the foundation of Megalopolis as the federal capital of the new Arcadian League between 370 and 368 – all deeply humiliating for the Spartans.

A further criticism of Xenophon, which is also levelled at Plutarch (see above), is his excessive concentration on personality for moralizing purposes. Agesilaos in particular is constantly portrayed as the ideal leader, since, apart from the conventional qualities of a good general, he also possessed piety and desired so much to destroy the Persian Empire (e.g. 3.4.3) – two things that especially appealed to Xenophon. As a result, Xenophon rarely misses an opportunity in his narrative to display Agesilaos' qualities as a leader by his words and action. An excellent example of Xenophon's praise for the Spartan king also includes his moralizing about what should be the ideal pursuit of mankind, both of which are contained in the section about Agesilaos' military preparations for his campaign in 395 against the Persians:

> Indeed Agesilaos made the whole city, in which he was staying, a sight worth seeing; for the market-place was filled with all kinds of horses and weapons for sale, and the copper-workers, carpenters, smiths, leather-workers and painters were all making weapons for war – as a result one would think that the city was really a military workshop. And one would also have been encouraged at seeing another sight there – Agesilaos in the front, followed by the other soldiers, wearing garlands while returning from the gymnasia and dedicating the garlands to Artemis. For where men show piety to the gods, practise the arts of war, and prepare themselves to obey orders, surely that place is filled with high hopes for the future!
>
> (Xenophon, *Hellenica* 3.14.17–18)

Agesilaos is clearly the living embodiment of all that is morally desirable in mankind. Other leaders receive praise (although not as much as Agesilaos) due to their moral qualities, even if their contribution to warfare is negligible or even ends in failure: for example, there is the lengthy eulogy of Hermocrates who, while leading a small contingent of Syracusan ships and thus playing only a small part in the Ionian War (413–404) against Athens, was deposed as general and exiled by the Syracusan government (1.1.27–31); and the admirable portrayal of Callicratidas, the Spartan commander in charge of the Peloponnesian fleet, who is depicted in his two speeches as a loyal and obedient Spartan, and as a pan-Hellenist strongly opposed to the despised Persians (1.6.5, 1.6.8–11) – yet his fleet was utterly defeated at the battle of Arginusae (406).

The final major criticism of Xenophon the 'historian' is his inability to provide an effective analysis of the events in his narrative. Thus he provides no perceptive reasons for the shattering Spartan defeat at Leuctra in 371, preferring to attribute it to divine punishment for the illegal seizure of the Cadmeia (the citadel of Thebes) in 382 by the Spartans (5.4.1), rather than recognize the brilliant new tactics of the Thebans under Epaminondas and provide an explanation for the drastic diminution of Spartan manpower, which was also a major cause of their defeat. In the same way, Xenophon totally fails to understand the significance of Athens' rejection of an anti-Spartan alliance with the Arcadian League, Argos and Elis in 370 – it led the triple alliance to appeal to the Thebans, who voted to become their allies (Diodorus 15.61.3) and launched their first devastating invasion of the Peloponnese in 370/69. In fact, Agesilaos' ineffective campaign in 370 against the Arcadians, which Xenophon does describe at length and in glowing terms (6.5.11–21), led directly to Epaminondas' invasion and the subsequent curtailment of Spartan power during the 360s.

2

THE CAUSES OF COLONIZATION IN ARCHAIC GREECE

The great age of Greek colonization is associated with the period of time that stretched from the second half of the eighth century to the first half of the sixth. Greek colonies were sent out westwards to Sicily and southern Italy, even as far as the south coast of France and the east coast of Spain; eastwards to the Thracian coast, the Hellespont and all around the shores of the Black Sea; and southwards to Cyrenaica in modern Libya on the north coast of Africa. There had been an earlier period of Greek colonization during the Dark Ages (1200–900BC) after the fall of the Mycenaean civilization in the twelfth century: the so-called Ionian and Dorian migrations. According to tradition, the Dorians under the leadership of the sons of Heracles, who had been exiled from Mycenae, returned to Greece to regain their inheritance by force, which resulted in the Ionians seeking refuge from them by crossing the Aegean Sea and settling in Asia Minor; but it was not on the same scale nor as well-organized as this later expansion. The end of the Dark Ages ushered in an era that witnessed the rediscovery of long-range travel by sea, widespread trade around the Mediterranean, the re-introduction of writing and the rise of the Greek 'polis' or city-state. The eighth century (799–700) was a time of remarkable economic growth, with agricultural development bringing about a general increase in the level of prosperity, especially for the aristocracy, whose political control over their own polis was based on their tenure of the best and the largest amount of land, as well as their ability to defend the state from external threats. Land, especially in a pre-coinage age, was the most valuable of all possessions because it was the sole guarantee of permanent wealth. However, the eighth century also saw the rise of serious social problems in Greece, which were linked directly or indirectly with the land.

Scholarly opinion in the past has been deeply split over the causes of colonization: whether it was land-hunger, arising from over-population, or trade that was the primary cause. These stark alternatives have proved to be unsatisfactory when all the evidence is considered, especially with the growth of archaeological excavations in colonial sites. In addition, there is a need to clarify what is meant by 'trade' before it can be offered as a motive for colonization: whether it is a search for foreign markets for the state's own exports, or a search for vital resources which the state lacks and can import. It is also vital at the outset to make a clear distinction between a colony ('apoikia') and a trading station ('emporion'), both of which are present from the eighth century. The colony was an independent city from the start, founded at a particular date and by a public act, which had its own government, laws and foreign policy, and whose inhabitants were citizens of the colony and not of the mother-state. The emporion was by contrast a strictly commercial trading post, which was formed spontaneously by traders from different Greek city-states, even by non-Greeks. However, even this clear distinction could at times be blurred: Herodotus refers to the Milesian colonies on the north shore of the Black Sea as emporia (4.24).

Shortage of land

Modern scholarship (e.g. Murray) now inclines to the view that land hunger, arising from over-population, was the chief cause of archaic colonization, especially at the beginning of that period, but that trading considerations were important in many colonial foundations and predominant in a few. The Greeks themselves saw colonization as a cure for land-hunger and over-population. Plato in the Laws explicitly states that colonists were sent out like a swarm of bees to relieve the pressure of land-shortage (708B) and later in the same work refers again to colonization as a means to resolve over-population (740E). Thucydides also reflects this belief:

> For they, especially those who had insufficient land, made expeditions against the islands and subdued them.
>
> (Thucydides 1.15.1)

The chief colonizers were Corinth, Megara, Achaea, Chalcis, Eretria, Phocaea and Miletus, which were all coastal towns (or had a coastline as in the case of Achaea) with fertile territory, but were prevented from expanding due to natural obstacles or by powerful neighbouring states – hence the need to expand overseas. Thus the first colonization in the west was directed towards the fertile grain-growing areas of Sicily and south Italy. Chalcis in Euboea founded Naxos (734), Leontini (728) and Catana (soon after Leontini); Corinth founded Syracuse (734); and the Achaeans founded in southern Italy Sybaris (720), Croton (c.710) and Metapontum (c.700). The Chalcidians and the Eretrians of Euboea were the most active in colonizing the northern Aegean in Chalcidice (which takes its name from Chalcis) and the Thracian coast. Megara founded Chalcedon (c.687) and Byzantium (c.660) on both sides of the entrance to the Black Sea; and Miletus was particularly active in founding colonies around the Black Sea.

It is clear from literary and archaeological evidence that there was a major problem of over-population in the second half of the eighth century. The shortage of fertile, cultivable land in mainland Greece and the tradition of dividing up land equally among male heirs were causing major social and economic problems: there was insufficient land to absorb and support the growing population, and the increasingly smaller inheritances of land were threatening to reduce many small landowners and their families to poverty. Although an increasing number of Greeks were engaged in trade, the vast majority in the eighth century made their living from agriculture. Aristotle mentions the five main ways of gaining a living: pastoral farming, hunting, piracy, fishing, but even in the later fourth century:

> the largest class of men live from the land and from the cultivation of the fruits of the earth.
>
> (Aristotle, Politics 1.1256a)

It was for this very reason that the possession of sufficient arable land in order to provide a reasonable standard of living for their populations so dominated the thoughts of the city-states and their citizens; and these same considerations were uppermost in the minds of the Greek colonists, who were willing or compelled to undertake the arduous and dangerous task of finding a new home overseas in order to acquire the cultivable land that was not available at home. Corinth was renowned for its citizens' commercial enterprise, but the founding of Syracuse (733) was achieved under the leadership of Archias and his followers, who came from the inland village of Tenea; and they, being farmers not seafarers, were primarily concerned with Syracuse's agricultural potential.

There is also a contemporary literary source who gives us an insight into the social and economic difficulties of that time: Hesiod of Boeotia writing around 700 BC. However, it must be noted that he is only describing the internal conditions of Ascra, his own village in Boeotia. Even so, when his evidence is combined with that of Solon of Athens, writing around 600 BC (see Chapter 5), and when an allowance is made for regional variations, it is conspicuous that both writers constantly emphasize that the lack of sufficient arable land was the main source of their society's problems, and it is reasonable to assume that the same troubles were being experienced throughout most of central and southern mainland Greece. Hesiod's *Works and Days* begins with the partition of the land that took place between himself and his brother Perses after their father's death. It is from this literary work that we learn of the tough, difficult demands that were faced by small to medium-small landowners. One of the most important pieces of advice that Hesiod gives is:

> Let there be only one son to support his father's house; for thus there will be an increase of wealth in the home.
>
> (Hesiod, Works and Days 376–77)

This confirms the pressure that was being felt by the growth of population which was fast outgrowing the capacity of the land in the polis to support its increased numbers.

Hesiod is also a valuable source for a secondary cause of colonization: the tendency of the ruling aristocrats to govern in their own selfish interests and to increase their large estates at the expense of the vulnerable small landowners. He complains about the behaviour of his brother, who has gained the larger share of the inheritance, and reveals the injustice that was being endured at the hands of the aristocrats who sat in judgement:

> But let us resolve our dispute here with the true judgement which comes from Zeus and is the best. For we have already divided up our plot of land, but you seized and carried off the bigger part by greatly flattering the bribe-devouring kings [i.e. aristocrats] who want to judge such cases.
>
> (Hesiod, *Works and Days* 35–39)

These 'bribe-devouring kings' would also play their part in encouraging colonization, since it removed those who were struggling to make a living and whose discontent might be forged into a political weapon against their rule, as was often to happen under the tyrants (see Chapter 3). As each colony also had a founder ('oikistes') from the mother-state, usually an aristocrat, this also helped to remove a potential leader of the discontented.

Archaeology also reveals that there was a large increase in the Greek population in the second half of the eighth century, contemporaneous with the colonizing movement. In Attica, the number of datable graves per generation shows a dramatic increase when the Dark Ages and the ninth century (899–800) are compared to the eighth century (799–700). From 1000 to 800 there is little variation in the number of graves per generation, but from 800 to 700 there is an increase by a factor of six. This would suggest that the population of Attica may have increased four-fold in the first half of the eighth century, and doubled again in the second half of the century. This evidence is not conclusive in itself, as it might reflect an increase in the death-rate through natural disasters, for example, water shortage or famine; or it might reflect a change in burial customs. However, when it is combined with the other evidence of this period, the most convincing interpretation seems to be a sudden growth in the population of Attica, as was happening in the rest of Greece.

The best written evidence for the cause of colonization and for the process by which a colony was founded comes from the history of Cyrene on the north African coast, which was colonized by settlers from the island of Thera (modern-day Santorini). Herodotus (4.150–59) records two oral accounts of Cyrene's foundation, one from the Therans and the other from the Cyreneans; and there is also a fourth-century inscription from Cyrene (ML 5), which grants equal citizenship to resident Therans in Cyrene in accordance with the original agreement made between the two cities at the time of the foundation of Cyrene (c.630), and which purportedly includes the original seventh-century decree of the Theran Assembly and the oath of the settlers. The original seventh-century decree does appear, in essence, to be authentic, although there have probably been some adaptations to the original in the intervening centuries. Thus there are three detailed accounts of Cyrene's foundation and, although there are differences and variations, as would be expected from alternative oral accounts of the same event, the outline of the story is consistent.

Thera was a small volcanic island with some fertile land, ideal for vines but limited in extent. The problems of over-population came later to Thera than to mainland Greece, in the second half of the seventh century. The Theran version of the story begins with the priestess of Apollo at Delphi ordering the Therans to send a colony to Libya. Knowing of no such a place, they ignored the oracle to their cost (4.151) as a seven-year total drought immediately followed. When the Delphic priestess repeated her order, the Therans then set themselves the task of discovering the location of Libya and, having achieved this, they decided to send out a colony:

> The Therans decided to send out men, with brother being chosen by lot from brother and with men chosen from all seven villages, and to appoint Battos as their leader and king. Thus they sent two fifty-oared ships to Platea [an island off the Libyan coast].
>
> (Herodotus 4.153)

The Cyrenean version concentrates on the life of Battos, but still includes the Delphic oracle as the initiator of the command to settle Libya (4.154–55). Both accounts agree on the sequel:

> After this the Therans sent Battos away with two fifty-oared ships. These men, having sailed to Libya, did not know what else to do, and thus sailed back to Thera. But the Therans attacked them as they came to land and did not allow them to come ashore, but ordered them to sail back again. Under such compulsion, they sailed back again and settled the island that lay just off Libya, whose name, as has been said before, was Platea.
>
> (Herodotus 4.156)

After living there for two years with little success, they moved to mainland Libya upon the instructions of Delphi; in the seventh year, they finally moved to the site of Cyrene which was situated on steep cliffs, with a difficult access to the sea, but with very fertile plains behind the city: clearly agriculture and not trade was the primary motive for choosing this site. In time the colony grew more prosperous than its mother-state, especially when health-giving silphium was discovered, grown and exported throughout the Mediterranean from the sixth century onwards.

The main stimulus for the Therans to found Cyrene, according to the above tradition, was the seven-year drought, which must have produced famine on the island. However, it can also be deduced that Thera was facing a potentially more dangerous problem: the difficulty of feeding its growing population in the future. It was this long-term threat to the city's survival that led to the need for drastic action to protect the community. The citizens passed a decree compelling each family with two (or more) sons, from all the seven villages, to send one of them chosen by lot to the new colony. The inscription in Cyrene, recording this seventh-century decree of Thera, is exceptionally tough in ensuring that its conditions were met:

> Whoever refuses to sail, having been sent out by the polis, will be liable to the death penalty and his property will be given to the people. If anyone harbours or conceals him, whether it be a father protecting a son or a brother protecting a brother, he will suffer the same penalty as the one who refused to sail.
>
> (ML 5)

The removal of one son from every family with two (or more) male heirs clearly shows that the Theran family plots of land were now so small that any further sub-division would have led to starvation for the next generation of farmers. Having already made the fateful original decision, the Therans were in no mood to compromise and receive back the disillusioned colonizers: they drove them away by force. This hostile action was mirrored in the treatment of Eretrian colonists who, having been expelled from their colony at Corcyra by the Corinthians, were prevented by force from returning to their original home by the Eretrians themselves. They were forced to found a new colony at Methone in Chalcidice, acquiring in the process the nickname of 'the slung out' (Plutarch, *Moralia* 293b). That such a close-knit, agricultural community as Thera had to resort to initial compulsory enlistment and subsequent violence is a clear testament to the massive problems of land-shortage and over-population that were afflicting many cities in the eighth and seventh centuries, and confirms that the main motive for the colonizers was the acquisition of agricultural land overseas.

The importance of trade

Nevertheless trade did play a significant role in the foundation of colonies. It was the search for vital commodities (such as metals) and luxury goods, both greatly desired by the ruling aristocracies, that opened up the Mediterranean after the Dark Ages. This led to traders establishing trading posts in the east and the west, especially on the frontiers of a great power, thereby giving them access to foreign markets. The most important trading post (emporion) in the east was at Al Mina at the mouth of the river Orontes in northern Syria. It was founded just before 800 by Phoenicians,

Cypriots and, as has been established from pottery on the site, Euboeans. Iron from south-east Asia Minor and luxury goods from Mesopotamia, Phoenicia and Egypt flowed into Al Mina, where they were crafted into attractive ornaments, and were transported for trade with Greece and the west. In a very similar fashion, Chalcis and Eretria together founded a trading post (although it may have been intended as a colony) around 775 at Pithecusae on the bay of Naples (modern-day Ischia). This was at the southern edge of the area dominated by the Etruscans who were, in their own right, rich in metal, but also controlled the trade in tin and amber that came from Britain and the north. Thus there was a trade route stretching from the near east to the Etruscans in the west via Al Mina and Pithecusae: many Egyptian scarabs and seals from north Syria have been unearthed at Pithecusae.

It is clear that these traders were the essential precursors of the colonizing movement, since it was their information about the location of fertile agricultural sites, gained from their overseas trading, that gave the colonizers the confidence to seek a new life in a foreign land. However, there are certain colonies where the evidence points to trade rather than land as the main cause of their colonization. Some of the inhabitants of Pithecusae moved later to the mainland opposite and founded Cumae, which was reputed to be the oldest Greek colony in the west. The existence of sufficient cultivable land to support the population, which was not the case at Pithecusae, was clearly an important reason for Cumae's foundation. Nevertheless, its close proximity to the Etruscans and the deliberate decision to ignore fertile land that was still abundantly available for colonization in Sicily and southern Italy strongly suggest that the on-going trade in metals with the Etruscans was a decisive factor in its siting. Zancle (later Messana and then Messina) was founded in *c.*730 by the Chalcidians from Euboea; but, because of the shortage of cultivable land, its foundation can only be explained by the need to control the straits of Messina and the trade route to Pithecusae. This lack of agricultural land led Zancle to send settlers a little later to found Mylae, 20 miles to the west. Having taken possession of one side of the straits of Messina, it made sense to tighten their control by founding, with the help of Messenians and Chalcidians from home, Rhegium on the other side on the Italian mainland. In the same way, the expulsion of the Eretrians from Corcyra in 734 by the Corinthians, who were on their way to found Syracuse, clearly shows that the Corinthians were very aware of the strategic importance of Corcyra on the trade route to the west.

By the mid-seventh century the importance of commerce was becoming even more obvious to the Greeks, and the later colonization of the north shore of the Black Sea by Miletus, such as the colony at Olbia, *c.*645, suggests that trading motives may have been behind their foundation. At this time the cities of the Greeks in Asia Minor were being threatened by the

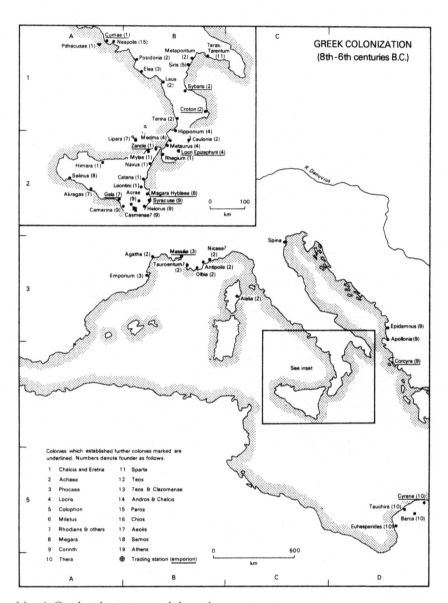

Map 1 Greek colonization, eighth–sixth centuries BC

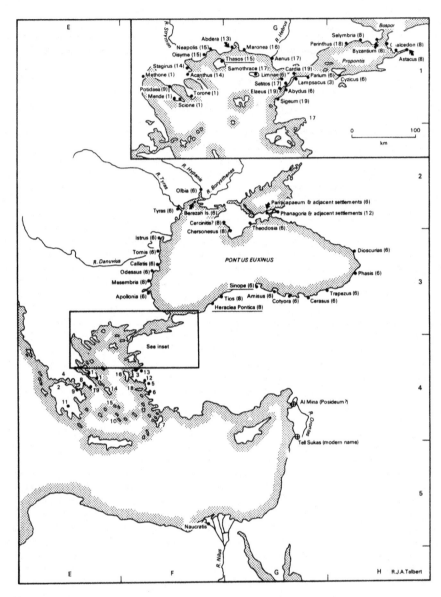

Map 1 continued

growth of the Lydian empire. Therefore access to the abundant corn supplies of the Black Sea would have done much to ease their dependence on homegrown corn, and the opportunity to import corn may have been the incentive for Miletus to send out its colonies to this area. Herodotus was very aware that these northern Black Sea colonies acted as trading centres and consequently referred to them several times as emporia (trading posts). The second wave of Corinthian colonies, founded by Cypselus and his successors (c.650–c.582: see Chapter 3) in north-west Greece at Leucas, Anactorium, Ambracia, Apollonia and Epidamnus (with Corcyra), reflect the increasing importance of commercial motives for colonization. These colonies were key staging posts on the trade route to Italy; they also provided access to the raw materials from the north-west, such as timber and flowers for Corinthian perfumes; and finally they supplied the base for Corinthian trade to increase its outlets in the interior, as can be seen from the early Greek bronzes found at Trebenishte. Finally, the Phocaeans, on the western coast of Asia Minor, provide the best example of colonization motivated by trade. They founded Massalia (modern-day Marseilles) c.600, which was poor in agricultural land but controlled the trade routes up the river Rhone, leading to commercial links with Paris, Switzerland, Germany and even Sweden. They also founded Emporion – a very revealing name – in north-east Spain at the same time as Massalia, and traded as far as Tartessus beyond the straits of Gibraltar, gaining access to tin and silver in northern Spain.

To summarize, it is probably right to see the desire for cultivable land as the primary cause of colonization, since the majority of Greeks depended for their livelihood on agriculture, and the serious social and economic problems of over-population and land-hunger did coincide with the colonizing movement in the second half of the eighth century. Trade was certainly the primary consideration in the foundation of a few colonies and an increasingly important factor in numerous others, but it is difficult to argue that it was the main cause, as this view requires unequivocal evidence that the economy of the colonies was based on trade from the beginning. Such evidence, by its very nature, is rarely available to the archaeologist.

Bibliography

Andrewes, A. *Greek Society*, ch. 6.
Austin, M. M. and Vidal-Naquet, P. *Economic and Social History of Greece*, pt 1, chs 1 and 3.
Boardman, J. *The Greeks Overseas*, chs 1, 2, 4, 5 and 6.
Graham, A. J. *CAH* vol. 3.3, 2nd edn, ch. 37.
——*Colony and Mother City in Ancient Greece*, chs 1–7.
Gwynn, A. 'The character of Greek colonization', *JHS* 38.
Murray, O. *Early Greece*, 2nd edn, chs 5–7.
Roebuck, C. *CAH* vol. 4, 2nd edn, ch. 7e.

3

THE AGE OF GREEK TYRANNY: C.650–510

The background and sources

Although tyranny existed throughout Greek history from the middle of the seventh century to the second century, 'the age of tyrants' is a term used by modern historians to refer to a period of time when many of the leading Greek cities were ruled by a tyrant, beginning with Cypselus of Corinth around 650 and ending with the fall of Peisistratus' sons at Athens in 510. This 'age of tyrants' was a transitional stage in the political development of the 'polis', bringing to an end the old aristocratic order and laying down the foundations for the middle-class, hoplite-dominated constitutions that followed the collapse of tyranny. A Greek tyrant was not necessarily a brutal ruler, as the modern sense of the word would suggest, but an individual who had seized power, usually through a military coup, and ruled as an autocrat outside the institutions of the state. The first generation of tyrants for the most part was noted for the mildness of their rule, as they depended upon the goodwill of the people to maintain their position; it was usually the second generation (most tyrannies only lasted for two generations) that showed all the hallmarks of the traditional wicked tyrant, leading to their overthrow.

The major difficulty in assessing the causes of tyranny arises from the problems of the available primary sources. The most detailed evidence for the rule of individual tyrants comes from Herodotus, whose history was written probably in the third quarter of the fifth century (450–425) and reflects the oral tradition about the tyrants that was current in the fifth century. His account of the rule of the later tyrants, such as the Athenian Peisistratids who fell in 510, is for the most part reliable, as Herodotus' birth (traditionally given as 484) was close to the events that he describes; but there are inevitably distortions, exaggeration and even a 'fairy-tale' style about the earlier tyrants, such as Cypselus who seized power around 650. Thucydides' theme was the Peloponnesian War and consequently his account of early Greek history is brief and superficial. The main history of this period was written by Ephorus of Cyme around the middle of the

40

fourth century; only fragments of his work survive, but later historians writing about early Greece used his work extensively. Ephorus' history has worth but, like that of Herodotus, should be used with caution – there is a need to sift the facts from the legends.

The evidence of the fourth-century philosophers about tyranny provides some useful insights. Plato in the *Republic* is more concerned about their (lack of) worth as a form of government, contrasting the wicked tyrant with the good king, than their history. Aristotle in the *Politics* (1310b–1315b) is far more useful in his analysis of the nature of tyranny. However, Aristotle's distinction between the tyrants of old and the tyrants of his era also causes problems – he includes Dionysius, tyrant of Syracuse from 405 to 367, among the tyrants of old, although he was a near-contemporary of Aristotle, and consequently seems to be using Dionysius' fourth-century career as a model for the seventh- and sixth-century tyrants. The contemporary evidence for the age of Greek tyranny comes from three poets: Tyrtaeus of Sparta, who explicitly reveals the importance of the middle-class 'hoplites' for the safety of the state and implicitly their growing class consciousness; Alcaeus of Mytilene, the opponent of the tyrants Pittacus and Myrsilus, whose values and prejudices help to explain the hostility that was felt towards aristocratic government; and Solon of Athens, whose poems highlight the internal problems that made tyranny inevitable, unless they were remedied. Their evidence is very useful in providing an insight into the tensions of their individual cities, but it lacks the analytical rigour of historiography and must be used with care when investigating other cities' revolutions. It is the aim of this chapter, using the above primary sources, to discuss the tyrannies of Pheidon of Argos, Cypselus of Corinth and Cleisthenes of Sicyon, where three factors – military, economic and ethnic, respectively – were prevalent in their seizure of power; the tyranny of Peisistratus in Athens and the benefits that the tyrants brought to their cities will be discussed in Chapter 6.

Aristotle is most helpful in identifying the typical characteristics of a tyrant and the means by which they came to power:

> The tyrant is installed in power from among the people ('demos') and the masses against the wealthy so that the people ('demos') suffer no injustice at their hands. This is clear from the events of history. For almost all of the tyrants have gained power from being, in a manner of speaking, leaders of the people, gaining their trust by slandering the wealthy. For some tyrannies were established in this way when their cities had already become great; but others before them came about from kings going beyond custom and aiming at more despotic rule; others arose from those who were elected to the chief office of state ... and others from oligarchies choosing one of their number to be the top official for the greatest offices of state. For, by these means, it was possible for all of them to achieve their aim easily, if only they wanted it, because they already possessed the power either of kingship or of a

particular political post. Pheidon in Argos and others became tyrants in this way when they were already kings; while the Ionian tyrants and Phalaris rose from public office; Panaitois in Leontini, Cypselus in Corinth, Peisistratus in Athens, Dionysius at Syracuse and others arose in the same way from being leaders of the people.

(Aristotle, *Politics* 1310b)

It is clear from the above quotation that the vast majority of tyrants had come from the ruling classes, but had rejected the current aristocratic government in favour of a regime which protected the people from the aristocrats, with themselves as the leader of the oppressed: hence their broad popular appeal. It is now appropriate to give concrete examples of individual tyrants and of the specific causes that allowed them to become the leaders of the people.

Pheidon of Argos: the military cause

The majority of modern historians incline to the view that the major innovation in military tactics – hoplite warfare – came about in the first quarter of the seventh century. Previously, the main defence of the state had rested upon the aristocracy that supplied the individual expert warriors, who probably rode on horseback to the battleground but fought on foot with opposing warriors of the same class: a fighting style that Homer portrays so vividly in the *Iliad*. However, the new style of fighting involved a greater number of men (often as much as a third of the citizen population), heavily armed with the same weapons and body armour, and fighting in a closely packed formation or phalanx, usually eight rows deep. In contrast to the former mode of fighting where individual courage and expertise were vital for military success, the key hoplite qualities were steadfast courage and discipline in holding the battle-line, since any uncoordinated movement, forwards or backwards, by individuals would split the tight formation and fatally weaken it. This point was emphasized by Tyrtaeus:

Those who display the courage to go into close combat in the front line, standing side by side with each other, die in fewer numbers and save those behind. But when men tremble, the courage of all is destroyed.

(Tyrtaeus fr. 11. 11–14)

It was the creation of this new fighting force, with its involvement of a greater number of citizens participating in the defence of the city, that has led many scholars to believe that there was a military cause for tyranny.

The essence of the disagreement between modern historians – whether the hoplites played a role in the rise of tyranny – revolves around the date of their introduction into Greek warfare and their effect upon tactics. One school of thought (e.g. Snodgrass) holds the view that the hoplite 'panoply' – helmet, corselet, greaves, sword, spear and shield – was introduced piecemeal over a long period of time from c.750 to c.650; and that there was a transitional stage of tactics between the former aristocratic individualistic duels and the later middle-class hoplite phalanxes. The individual warriors, initially aristocrats, but later substantial landowners, adopted individual items of the distinctive hoplite panoply as they became available in 750–650, and fought in a fairly close formation until c.650, when fighting in the closely packed hoplite phalanx became standard tactics. Consequently, hoplite warfare and the growing class-consciousness of the middle classes, which arose later as a result of the introduction of hoplite warfare, came too late to be a factor in the early tyrannies of Pheidon of Argos, Cypselus of Corinth and Orthagoras of Sicyon. In fact, it was the tyrant in power who brought about the hoplite phalanx, and not vice versa.

The other school of thought (e.g. Cartledge, Salmon) believes that there was a sudden change to hoplite tactics between 700 and 675 because, although there was on-going experimentation in the use of weapons throughout 750 to 650, the invention of the two most distinctive pieces of hoplite armour, the shield and the Corinthian helmet which appear on vases for the first time around 700, could only be effective in a closely packed hoplite phalanx. The hoplite shield was different from its predecessors in that it had a double grip, one at the centre for the forearm, and the other at the rim for the hand; the earlier shields had only a hand grip at the centre. As a result, the hoplite shield was much heavier and less manoeuvrable, much better designed for holding close to the body, for frontal defence and for pushing. This shield, when held in place, only needed half of its structure to protect the front of the hoplite, although it afforded no protection to his spear arm and right flank; its other half, to the left of the hoplite, was wasted space with regard to the holder's own defence needs. However, in a hoplite phalanx, this unnecessary space was of vital importance to and was primarily designed for the protection of the right flank of the next hoplite to the holder's left, and so on down the line. In addition, if neither phalanx broke in the first clash of front lines, the heavy shield came into its own as an offensive weapon, as reported in the hoplite battle of Delium in 424:

> But the right wing, where the Thebans were, was getting the better of the Athenians, pushing them back step by step and keeping up the pressure ... and, because of such a manoeuvre [i.e. the use of cavalry] and the Thebans pushing them on and breaking their line, the flight of the whole Athenian army took place.
>
> (Thucydides 4.96. 4–6)

In the same way the Corinthian helmet, shaped from a single sheet of bronze which covered the whole head apart from a T-shaped opening for the eyes and mouth, would only have been effective in frontal hand-to-hand fighting where the severely restricted vision and hearing were of far less importance than protection for the whole head and neck. Consequently, the hoplite phalanx made its first appearance soon after 700, was widely employed in the second quarter of the seventh century (675–650) and therefore was available to play a part in the political upheavals of the seventh century.

However, Morris has challenged the views of these two schools of thought by rejecting the whole concept of a 'hoplite reform' in military tactics. He believes that the Greeks had always fought in massed ranks, and that the weapon changes from 750 to 650 only mark an improvement in the quality of the weaponry and not a change in military tactics. It is argued that a fundamental misunderstanding of Homer and the conventions of eighth- and early seventh-century vase-painters has led to the belief that so called 'pre-hoplite' warfare only consisted of individual duels between aristocrats, with no fighting role for the rest of the people apart from throwing stones and shouting encouragement. A careful study of Homer shows that his battles were extensive in time and location, and that massed rank tactics were always employed; but that his 'freezing' of the action on different (but concurrent) individual duels, purely for literary and artistic purposes, has misled scholarly opinion on the nature of Homeric warfare. Furthermore, until the creation of the Chigi vase in *c.*660–650 which was the first to show clearly warriors in a closely packed formation, it had been the convention to portray each massed and opposing rank by the painting of the two nearest warriors, engaged apparently in individual combat. Therefore, the theory of a military cause of tyranny, which has been based on the so-called 'hoplite reform' and its use by the tyrants for political purposes, should be eliminated.

However, those scholars who do believe in a military cause of tyranny use Aristotle as further support for their view. He states that there was a direct political link between the class that was most effective in defending the state and the state's type of constitution:

> Although it is possible for one man or a few men to be superior in virtue, it is difficult for the many to be made perfect in every virtue, but they can be in the virtue of military courage, for this is found among large numbers. Therefore the class that does the fighting for the state wields supreme power in this constitution, and those who bear arms have a share in its government.
>
> (Aristotle, *Politics* 1279a–b)

He re-affirms this belief later when he stresses that, after kingship had come to an end, government passed into the hands of the aristocracy who possessed the necessary wealth to supply the cavalry that was the backbone of the state's defence, but:

> when the population of states had increased and those who possessed hoplite weapons had grown stronger, more persons came to have a share in government.
>
> (Aristotle, *Politics* 1297b)

Aristotle does not include tyranny as one of the stages in the political development of the polis, but it made its appearance soon after the invention of hoplite warfare (if this is accepted), and was in some cities the transitional stage of government between aristocratic and hoplite-dominated constitutions. The belief that the hoplites probably played the leading role in helping a tyrant to seize power by supplying the armed might that was superior to that of the aristocratic warriors is strongly implied in another quotation of Aristotle:

> In the old days, whenever the same man became leader of the people and general, they turned the constitution into a tyranny. For nearly all of the old tyrants came to power from being leaders of the people; and the reason why that happened then, but not now, is that those earlier leaders of the people were drawn from those who held the generalship.

> (Aristotle, *Politics* 1305a)

The special rapport that can exist between a general and his troops against a common enemy, seen so vividly in the last century of the Roman Republic, was seemingly utilized by the ambitious tyrant in his quest for power. The best example of this military cause of tyranny lies with the career of King Pheidon of Argos, although the evidence is often inadequate and circumstantial.

The starting-point for discussion of Pheidon's career is the shocked comment of Herodotus on him as:

> the man who carried out the most arrogant action ever of all the Greeks when he expelled the Elean presidents from the Olympic Games and presided over them himself.

> (Herodotus 6.127.3)

The mention of the Olympic Games is crucial in the attempt to pin down a date for Pheidon's activities. The late sources (Strabo, Eusebius and Pausanias) state that the Dorian Eleans presided over the games from their alleged inception in 776, but that in the seventh century (the sources do not agree on the date) the pre-Dorian Pisatans, who had been subjugated in the Dark Ages by the Eleans and were consequently an under-privileged group, seized control of the Olympic Games. The Olympic victor lists, which were published by Hippias around 400 and are considered to be reliable, record a time of Pisatan control beginning around 668, and Pausanias (6.22.2) dates the trouble at the Games to the 8th Olympiad (748), but this has been plausibly emended to the 28th Olympiad in 668. If the Pisatans gained control of Olympia in 668, it can be argued that they would have needed the help of an external military power to achieve this coup, and Herodotus' mention of Pheidon's intervention at Olympia makes him the most likely candidate. However, it is worth noting that Ephorus places Pheidon 50 years earlier, but this may be a guess, and Herodotus more than 50 years later.

If 668 is accepted as the date of Pheidon's military intervention at Olympia, then he can be linked, although not named as the commander, with the major victory of the Argive army over the Spartans at the battle of Hysiae in 669 (Pausanias 2.24.7). Hysiae is on the plain of Thyrea on the border between the territories of Argos and Sparta, and the likely cause of the conflict was the expansion of these two powers, disputing control of the plain. These are the years before Sparta's army came to be the best in Greece, but it was still a formidable force, which emphasizes the superior excellence of the Argive army in the first half of the seventh century. This sudden re-emergence of Argive status and military prowess in Peloponnesian politics is explained by Ephorus (FGrH IIA 70F115) who stated that Pheidon regained the Lot of Temenus. Legend had it that the descendants of Heracles returned to the Peloponnese in three companies during the Dark Ages and divided up their conquests by lot: one brother received Messenia, the second Lacedaimon and Temenus the Argolid. However, after Temenus' death, according to Ephorus, the Argive kingdom became weak and divided until it was reunited by Pheidon. If the legendary overlay is removed, it seems that Pheidon restored strong central government to Argos and masterminded the expansion of Argive power throughout the Argolid which led to the battle of Hysiai with Sparta.

If the above evidence (for all its limitations) is accepted, then the likely cause of Argos' brief revival of military dominance and of Pheidon's unusual constitutional position of a king turned tyrant (Aristotle, *Politics* 1310b – see above,) is the introduction of hoplite warfare. Argos either was the first state to use these new tactics or used them far more effectively than their opponents. The shield – the most distinctive piece of hoplite equipment – was called generically 'Argive' (Pausanias 8.50.1), either because it was invented in Argos or because the Argives were remembered for their outstanding skill with it. Yet more revealing is the Delphic oracle about Chalcis and Argos:

> The best of all land is the Pelasgian plain, best are the Thracian horses, Spartan women and the men who drink the water of fair Arethusa [i.e. the men of Chalcis in Euboea].
> But better still than these are those that live between Tiryns and Arcadia of the many sheep, the linen-corsleted Argives, the goads of war.
>
> (Palatine Anthology 14.73)

This oracle must be dated to the first half of the seventh century, since Sparta's pre-eminence in hoplite warfare was recognized from the late seventh century onwards. There is an illogical progression in the oracle in that it mentions the best at the beginning and then supersedes this by naming someone

46

better. Presumably the second part is a later addition to the original oracle which was occasioned by the Argives' later military superiority to the Chalcidians. Thucydides (1.15) states that the first war of any importance that split a number of Greek states into two camps was the Lelantine War between Chalcis and Eretria in Euboea, probably fought in the last 30 years of the eighth century. The victory of Chalcis earned for its soldiers the reputation contained in the first part of the oracle. Therefore it would seem that the Chalcidians were the best in pre-hoplite fighting, but that their reputation was overtaken by the Argive hoplites, who enjoyed such military success in the Peloponnese.

It is at this point that Aristotle's description of King Pheidon's seizure of power as tyrant can be explained. Pausanias 2.19.2 stated that the authority of the Argive kings had been drastically reduced as early as Medon, Temenus' grandson. The fact that political power was in the hands of the aristocracy in the early seventh century is to be expected, since it was the common situation throughout the Greek world at that time. If Pheidon was the inventor and leader of the hoplites, then it is possible that he saw his opportunity, in tyrant fashion, to make use of this new military force to overthrow the aristocratic government, and to advance his own career and the interests of his hoplite supporters. His political success with the help of the hoplites would have set a precedent for others to follow.

Cypselus of Corinth: the economic cause

The growth of trade and manufacture in the eighth and seventh centuries, encouraged by the need for raw materials, such as iron, and by the aristocrats' desire for luxury goods, and given a further boost by colonization, affected the status of the aristocracy within their communities. New ways of acquiring wealth, other than from agriculture, were now open to ambitious entrepreneurs, and they did not hesitate to grasp their opportunities. The main result was that, whereas previously birth had been the decisive factor in emphasizing the aristocracy's superiority to the rest of the community, this was being challenged by the rising importance of wealth. Many aristocrats resented this undermining of their long-held positions of power and influence by those who had acquired their wealth by trade and technology. The poetry of Theognis of Megara is a clear testimony to the bitterness that was felt by many aristocrats when wealth competed with and even surpassed birth as the distinguishing mark of social status:

> Cyrnus, we seek out thorough-bred rams, asses and horses, and everyone wants to choose from good stock. But the noble man does not hesitate to marry the low-born daughter of a low-born man, if he provides much wealth; nor is a woman ashamed to be the wife of a wealthy, low-born man, but prefers to be rich instead of honourable. For they worship wealth. The noble is married to the low-born, the low-born to the

noble. Wealth has mixed up the breed. Therefore do not be amazed, Cyrnus, that the breeding of our city is degenerating; for nobility is mixed with worthlessness.

(Theognis, *Elegies*, II. 183–92)

Although Theognis is commenting on the situation in Megara, possibly as late as the middle of the sixth century (c.550), it is clear from the political reforms of Solon, which substituted wealth for birth as the criterion for holding high office at Athens (see Chapter 5), that this change was well under way by the end of the seventh century.

Theognis' poetry suggests that in many cities any qualms that the aristocrats may have felt about inter-marrying with these entrepreneurs and sharing political power with them were assuaged by the thought of the accompanying increase in personal wealth. However, there were in some cities wealthy men who either were on the fringe of or not part of the ruling aristocracy, and who were excluded from a share in government. It is in these circumstances that the economic cause of tyranny can be perceived, which is reinforced by the implicit suggestion of Thucydides:

As Greece became more powerful and acquired still more wealth than before, tyrannies were established in the majority of cities, their revenues increased.

(Thucydides 1.13.1)

In this context it is significant that the earliest known tyranny (apart from Pheidon's) was established at Corinth, which was the wealthiest and most commercially advanced city in Greece in the archaic period.

The eighth century (799–700) had seen Corinth exploit the success of the Euboeans, who had established trading posts at Al Mina in the east and Pithecusae in the west (see Chapter 2), by being the pivotal point on this trade route of western metals and eastern luxury goods which is highlighted by Thucydides:

For the Corinthians, founding their city on the isthmus, have always had a trading centre, since the Greeks from inside and outside the Peloponnese, communicating with each other more by land than by sea in the past, had to go through their territory. So they became powerful through their wealth, as has been shown by the ancient poets, for they called the place 'Wealthy Corinth'. And when the Greeks took a greater part in sea-faring, the Corinthians obtained a fleet and removed piracy; and by providing a trading centre both by land and by sea, they made their city powerful from the resultant revenues.

(Thucydides 1.13.5)

The voyage around Cape Malea at the foot of the Peloponnese was so dangerous that traders on the east–west trade route preferred either to drag their small ships across the Corinthian isthmus or, more usually, to trade at

Corinth: thus making the city with its two harbours the most important trading centre and earning a substantial revenue from the imposition of tolls (Strabo 378). In addition, the Corinthians were prolific in their production of pottery for export, and presumably other goods that have not survived the ravages of time. The foundation of their colonies at Corcyra and Syracuse and the transportation of non-Corinthian colonists in their ships ensured that the bulk of trade and of supplies for the western colonies originated from or passed through Corinth, and was transported in Corinthian ships. Thus the growth of trade, shipping and manufacture ensured that there were many other beneficiaries, apart from the ruling aristocracy, of these wealth-creating opportunities in Corinth.

The chief cause of tyranny in Corinth was the refusal of the ruling aristocracy, unlike Megara, to admit these wealthy entrepreneurs into its ranks and give them a share in government; this situation was exploited by Cypselus and led to his tyranny, followed by that of his son Periander and his grandson Psammetichus (c.658–c.585). Corinth's rise to economic preeminence had been masterminded by the aristocratic Bacchiads who were an exclusive family, maintaining this exclusivity by forbidding marriage outside their family. Diodorus, using Ephorus as his source, states that the whole of the Bacchiads were the governing class, and that individual members of the family would take it in turn to be the king for a year. Although Corinth had benefited from their leadership, the last years of their reign appear to have been less successful. Thucydides (1.13) mentions the earliest Greek sea-battle (of which he had knowledge), which was fought between Corinth and Corcyra around 664. He gives no information about the result or the cause of the battle, and even the date is suspect. However, the main point of relevance is that Corinth was at war with one of its major colonies, which was strategically important for the western trade route. In addition, the Corinthians may have been defeated in a border war with Megarians: there is the memorial of Orsippos of Megara, dated to around 700, which praised his success in driving out hostile invaders from his homeland. The rise of Argos under Pheidon in the second quarter of the seventh century may also have caused problems for Corinth. Criticism of their foreign policy failures, exacerbated by their exclusive retention of power, inevitably led them to suppress dissent and increased their unpopularity in the last period of their rule. Thus the stage was set for their overthrow.

There are two accounts of the rise of Cypselus: one from Herodotus and one from later writers (e.g. Diodorus) but ultimately based on Ephorus. Herodotus' version is much more concerned with the oracles foretelling Cypselus' future success and his survival as a baby than about the means by which he became tyrant. Labda was a lame daughter of the Bacchiads, whom no one wished to marry due to her infirmity. Therefore she was allowed to marry outside the family and took as her husband a man of distinction in Corinthian society, Eetion. When Labda failed to conceive,

Eetion went to the Delphic oracle to consult the priestess who addressed him immediately as follows:

> Eetion, no one honours you although you are worthy of honour. Labda is pregnant and will bear a great rock. And it will fall on the ruling men and will bring justice to Corinth.
>
> (Herodotus 5.92.2)

The Bacchiads had already received an earlier cryptic oracle about their overthrow, which they had failed to decipher, but when they heard this oracle, all became clear. They attempted to kill the baby which escaped death by being hidden in a jar or chest ('cypsele') – hence the source of his name (or the legend). Herodotus tells this part of the tale in leisurely fashion, but resorts to brevity when dealing with his seizure and exercise of power. According to Herodotus, Cypselus was a violent ruler and was succeeded by his son, Periander, whose rule began mildly but soon became even more brutal than his father's.

The version of Ephorus (contained in the work of Nicolaus of Damascus, the historian of Augustus) concentrates more on how Cypselus rose to power. Having been sent abroad as a baby, he returned to Corinth in manhood and became very popular owing to his virtuous character and behaviour which contrasted starkly with that of the Bacchiads. He was elected 'polemarch' (war-leader), treated debtors with great consideration, thereby increasing his popularity, formed a faction, killed the last reigning Bacchiad and became tyrant. He exiled the Bacchiads, confiscated their property and:

> he recalled the exiles and restored citizen rights to those who had been deprived of them under the Bacchiads ... Cypselus ruled Corinth mildly, having no bodyguard and enjoying popularity among the Corinthians.
>
> (Nicolaus of Damascus FGrH 90.57)

This version, at first sight, appears more convincing than Herodotus. However, the fact that the polemarch (war-leader) in this account had only civil functions, which was the norm from the fifth century onwards, and that the other details of Cypselus' rise to power and of his treatment of his enemies reflect more accurately the internal factional strife of the fifth and fourth centuries, strongly suggests that Ephorus has grafted contemporary political behaviour onto the bare bones of the original story.

Nevertheless, there is enough in Ephorus to suggest that there is a core of truth in his version. In the first place, it emphasizes the popularity of Cypselus among the Corinthians, which was a necessary pre-requisite for any successful coup; this is in keeping with Herodotus' account of Cypselus' miraculous escape as a baby from death at the hands of his enemies, which type of story is traditionally associated with heroes not villains, and further weakens Herodotus' attempted presentation of Cypselus as a conventional brutal tyrant. Furthermore, the fact that he had no need of a bodyguard – so untypical of tyrants in general – must in all probability mean that he had the willing support of the middle-class hoplites who may even have helped to overthrow the Bacchiads. The goodwill of the people would be ensured not only by the mildness and justice of his rule, which stood in clear contrast to the later Bacchiad regime, but also by his entrepreneurial supporters who would now have access to positions of political and commercial influence. If it is right that Corinth was being less successful than before in the last years of the rule of the Bacchiads and that there was serious dissatisfaction with their direction of economic policy by these entrepreneurs, then the conduct of economic policy under the tyrants would have resolved their grievances.

In the first place, Cypselus and Periander set about exploiting the economic opportunities of north-west Greece. They founded colonies at Leucas, Anactorium, Ambracia and Apollonia, and also helped to found Epidamnus with Corcyra, which would imply that the tyrants had healed the former rift with their colony. These colonial foundations were not only protective staging posts on the western trade route to Italy, but also provided access for Corinthian manufacturers and traders to the interior of north-western Greece, which allowed them to acquire raw materials such as timber and flowers for perfume production, and to trade in Corinthian manufactured goods such as the bronzes found at Trebenishte. In addition, the friendship of Miletus, a former enemy in the Lelantine War in the last third of the eight century, was carefully cultivated to gain access to the markets of the eastern Mediterranean; and support for Athens, by judging in their favour in the dispute with Mytilene about the control of Sigeum, brought the Athenians within their trading sphere and away from Aegina's, Corinth's commercial rival. This forging of good diplomatic relations for trade purposes was also undertaken with non-Greek rulers: presents were sent to Alyattes of Lydia and Periander's successor was named Psammetichus after the king of Egypt, Psamtek.

An economic cause for the overthrow of aristocratic government at Corinth can justifiably be argued, especially as Corinth was the most commercially sophisticated city of the seventh and sixth centuries. The Corinthian outlook, with regard to manufacture, was markedly different to the rest of the Greeks.

> All the Greeks have adopted this attitude [i.e. a bias against trade and manufacture], especially the Spartans, but the Corinthians have the least prejudice towards craftsmanship
>
> (Herodotus 2.167)

It was probably due to this commercial attitude that the economic motive for tyranny was so predominant in Corinth. However, it was not only the entrepreneurial class whose economic grievances could lead to the rise of tyranny; the class of poor small farmers, who had not emigrated and whose livelihood was being threatened by the competitive imports of the new colonies, also looked to the tyrant for economic salvation. The economic problems of the poor and their effect upon the political process will be discussed in Chapter 5, which deals with Solon and his reforms.

Cleisthenes of Sicyon: the ethnic cause

Ethnic differences among the Greeks, revealed in their dialects and customs, were sufficiently pronounced to cause political problems at different times in their history. When the Athenians and their allies (mainly Ionians) were founding the Delian League in 478/7 (see Chapter 10), their choice of Delos as the League centre was highly significant since Athens, the islands and Ionia had previously held an Ionian festival there; this emphasis on their shared Ionian kinship was useful recruitment propaganda, highlighting their ethnic and cultural difference from the Dorian Spartans, who had been so unwilling to commit themselves militarily to the liberation of the Ionian Greeks from Persia. Ethnic divisions were felt yet more strongly in the Peloponnese, where the differences between the original Achaean Greeks and the Dorian invaders (see above under 'Pheidon of Argos: the military cause') were accentuated by the reduction of these pre-Dorians to a form of serfdom. The most renowned example was the 'Helots' of Sparta, whose numbers were dramatically increased in the seventh century by the Spartan conquest of Messenia, but there were other groups in a similar position: the 'naked ones' at Argos, 'the dusty-feet' at Epidaurus and the 'sheepskin-cloak-wearers' at Sicyon. However, it is also clear that many non-Dorians were admitted to citizenship by their conquerors. Apart from the three traditional Dorian tribes found throughout the Dorian states – the Dymanes, the Hylleis and the Pamphyloi – there often existed a fourth tribe, bearing a different name in different states (e.g. Aigialeis in Sicyon), which contained these non-Dorian citizens.

Although many states did achieve a degree of ethnic harmony, the evidence of the events in Sicyon under the tyranny of Cleisthenes reveals the tensions that probably existed below the surface in a number of states, as can be identified in the political struggles between the pre-Dorian Pisatans and the Dorian Eleans (see above under 'Pheidon of Argos'). Orthagoras was the founder of the tyranny at Sicyon around the middle of the seventh century, and the story of his rise to power contains the same fairy-tale elements as Cypselus' (Diodorus 8.24). Aristotle's assertion (*Politics* 1315b) that the tyranny of Orthagoras and his successors lasted for a hundred years due to the mildness of their rule, their respect for the law and their concern for their subjects' welfare is very convincing, especially as similar qualities underpinned the successful tyranny of Cypselus. Little is known about Orthagoras' immediate successor(s), but Cleisthenes (c.600–570) attracted the attention of Herodotus by his overtly ethnic policies.

When Sicyon was at war with Argos, Cleisthenes made clear his bitter hatred of Argos: he stopped the recitation of Homeric poems because they praised Argive deeds; and after his failure to remove the shrine of the Argive hero, Adrastus, from the centre of Sicyon (he was refused permission by the Delphic oracle), he persuaded the Thebans to give him the statue of Adrastus' deadly enemy, Melanippus, built a shrine to his memory and transferred to him the religious festival and honours that had previously been conducted in honour of Adrastus (Herodotus 6.67). If these actions had been the sum total of his reforms, it could be explained as jingoistic anti-Argive propaganda to unite the Sicyonians against their common enemy, but his next action was of far greater significance, since it actually emphasized rather than glossed over the internal ethnic differences within the state of Sicyon:

> Cleisthenes gave different names to the Dorian tribes (in Sicyon) so that the Argives and Sicyonians would not have the same names; and he especially mocked the Sicyonians, for he imposed upon them the names derived from 'pig' and 'donkey', omitting only the end of the words, but excluded his own tribe. He gave to them the name derived from his rule, and these were called the Archelaoi ('the Rulers'), but the rest were called 'the Pig-men', 'the Donkey-men' and 'the Swine-men'.
>
> (Herodotus 5.68)

The Orthagorid dynasty was non-Dorian, but there is no evidence that Orthagoras and his successors before Cleisthenes had felt the need to pander to such prejudice. However, it is possible that by 600 the Sicyonian tyranny was beginning to experience the increasing unpopularity that was a common characteristic of all tyrannies in their second and third generations of rule; and that Cleisthenes was deliberately stirring up hatred among his own non-Dorian ethnic group and promising privileged treatment in order to rally support behind his tyranny. Aristotle (*Politics* 1316a) quotes the events at Sicyon as an example of one tyranny replacing another, with the implication that there was a difference between Cleisthenes and Myron, his predecessor; and this may reflect Cleisthenes' use of ethnic prejudice as the crucial weapon in his pursuit of power. What is clear is that Cleisthenes was determined to present himself as the radical leader of the non-Dorians in Sicyon and that such an overtly ethno-centric position, especially at a time of war with a foreign enemy, must have promised attractive political rewards. The fact that the Dorian Spartans, after putting down the tyranny around the middle of the sixth century, did not attempt to reverse the insulting names of the Dorian tribes (they remained in force for another 60 years) is a sure sign of the strength of feeling and the influence of the non-Dorian element in Sicyon, and the need of the Spartans to retain their goodwill.

Conclusion

The limitations of the sources have made it difficult for the modern historian to identify definitively a common cause of the political phenomenon that swept most of the Greek world from around 650 to 510. Clearly the success of tyranny in one city would inspire other potential tyrants to attempt the same revolution in their own cities – we could use as a modern example the way that Mussolini's fascist movement in the 1920s acted as an inspiration in the 1930s for Hitler in Germany and Franco in Spain. In addition, tyrants were willing to help other aspirants to seize power in the hope of gaining a like-minded political ally, such as Lygdamis of Naxos who sent military aid to Polycrates in his successful bid for the tyranny of Samos. The other key factors that played an important part in the rise of tyranny appear to be military, economic and ethnic; but, whereas there is sufficiently convincing evidence to identify these factors in the establishment of a tyranny in certain individual cities, it cannot be proved that these same factors were the causes of tyranny in the other Greek cities. In the case of the cities on the coast of Asia Minor, the majority of the tyrants after 546 were imposed by the Persians as their preferred form of government for controlling the Greek subjects of their Empire; and the successive tyrannies in Mytilene on the island of Lesbos, documented in the poems of Alcaeus, reveal that competition between the ambitious aristocratic factions was the primary cause of tyranny, until Pittacus was finally elected by the people (presumably the hoplites) as their chosen tyrant (Alcaeus fr. 348). Nevertheless, the prevailing military, economic and ethnic conditions in the seventh and sixth centuries provide strong circumstantial evidence that these factors were instrumental in the rise of tyranny, to a greater or lesser degree, in the different cities throughout Greece.

Bibliography

Andrewes, A. *The Greek Tyrants*, chs 1–5.
Austin, M. M. and Vidal-Naquet, P. *Economic and Social History*, ch. 3.
Cartledge, P. 'Hoplites and Heroes', *JHS* 97 (1977).
Morris, I. *Burial and Ancient Society*, ch. 10.
Murray, O. *Early Greece*, 2nd edn, ch. IX.
Salmon, J. 'Political Hoplites?', *JHS* 97 (1977).
Sealey, R. *A History of the Greek City States 700–338* BC, ch. 2.
Snodgrass, A. M. 'The Hoplite Reform and History', *JHS* 85 (1965).

4

THE 'LYCURGAN' REFORMS AND THE RISE OF SPARTA IN THE SEVENTH AND SIXTH CENTURIES

The sources

It is a difficult task for modern scholarship to construct an accurate account of archaic (and classical) Spartan politics and society for a number of reasons. First, the Spartans did not keep written records, apart from oracles and certain lists, e.g. of kings. Second, the Spartans were extremely secretive – as noted by Thucydides, when discussing their military structure (5.68.2) – and kept most non-Spartans out of Sparta, even employing the occasional expulsion of all foreigners ('xenelasia'). Third, the Spartans deliberately created an idealized public image of Sparta, a myth (or 'mirage', as the French scholar, Ollier, termed it) of a powerful, unchanging, politically stable state, possessing 'eunomia' (good order). The myth was especially peddled in the late fifth century to conceal the deep social unrest and harsh economic pressures within the Spartan body politic, caused by a drastic reduction in the number of full Spartan citizens (about 8000 in 480 to about 2000 in the last decade of fifth century). Fourth, the eunomia of Sparta, in stark contrast to the civil war ('stasis') that erupted in numerous states (e.g. Coryra) in the Peloponnesian War (Thucydides 3.82–84), became a source of admiration in the late fifth and fourth centuries for all those – e.g. upper-class aristocrats with an oligarchic outlook, Spartan sympathisers, and philosophers – who disliked the radical democracy of Athens and preferred a state with a defined, secure political hierarchy and a compliant, regimented 'demos'. Finally, and the biggest problem of all, every change to Spartan society, no matter how radical, from the late fifth century to Roman times was always represented as 'Lycurgan', i.e. a return to the original structure as laid down by the legendary founder of the Spartan system.

The earliest literary sources are the poets Tyrtaeus (c.650) and Alcman (c.600). Tyrtaeus is useful for providing an outline of Sparta's initial conflicts with Messenia and Argos, the economic burden on the 'Helots', the troubles that the Spartans experienced in dealing with the subsequent

Messenian revolt (or the Second Messenian War – see below), and the early statement of Sparta's collectivist system of military values. Alcman's humorous, joyful, nature-loving poetry, especially when supplemented by recent archaeological finds in Sparta, puts paid to the belief that Sparta suddenly and dramatically became an austere, anti-intellectual military camp after the final conquest of Messenia. However, this marks the limits of their usefulness. Herodotus, on the other hand, for all his limitations (see Chapter 1), and despite the fact that he is not attempting to write a history of Sparta, gives valuable information about Sparta in the sixth and early fifth centuries, especially on the growth of Spartan power in the Peloponnese, and the authority, influence and policies (and the unorthodox familial relations) of the kings. Much of his knowledge was derived from discussions with politically important Spartans, although this again has to be treated carefully – his blatantly hostile treatment of King Cleomenes and his sympathetic treatment of his enemy, the deposed Demaratos who later joined the Persians against Greece as an advisor, strongly suggest that Demaratos' descendants supplied much of this information. Herodotus, although he accepted the Spartan line about Lycurgus as the great reformer (1.65), was gathering information and writing his history before the Spartan myth or 'mirage' became fully established in the late fifth century. He is chronologically our closest source to the gradual changes that were taking place throughout the sixth century in Spartan politics and society, necessitated by the extra military demands of controlling so many Helots, opposing Argos, exercising hegemony over the Peloponnesian allies and exerting influence outside the Peloponnese. It is probably in the latter half of the sixth century that the traditional hallmarks of Spartan society come into being: the emphasis on military preparedness, the minimal needs for self-sufficiency, the disappearance of the liberal arts and material luxuries, the dressing in similar fashion, and the wealthy adopting a similar lifestyle to the ordinary Spartan (Thucydides 1.6.4). Thus Herodotus is one of our most important literary sources, as he is relatively untainted by the effective state-sponsored propaganda of the later years – it was Herodotus who from the beginning saw through the Spartans' much vaunted reputation for financial honesty, revealing their readiness to accept bribes (3.148; 5.51; 6.72).

Thucydides, writing in the later fifth century, was exiled from Athens in 424 after the loss of Amphipolis, and he used this opportunity to visit the opponents of Athens to gather information for his history of the war (5.26.5). As stated above, he found it difficult to acquire the information he wanted owing to Spartan secrecy – hardly surprising as he was an Athenian, still had influential friends back in Athens and was probably asking the kind of detailed questions that the Spartan authorities had no desire to answer in a time of war, if ever, e.g. the disappearance and fate of the 2,000 'most spirited' Helots (4.80). However, there are two occasions when Thucydides seems to have put aside his usual rigour and accepted Spartan propaganda: first, that the Spartans had maintained the same constitution for more than 400 years (1.18.1); second, the detailed and vivid story about the fall of Pausanias, caused by his arrogant behaviour as leader of the Greeks, his medism and his attempt to stir up a Helot revolt (1.128–35). Thucydides' usual problem, when gathering information, stemmed from eyewitnesses giving different, conflicting accounts of the same event (1.22.3). It is possible that in the case of Pausanias, Thucydides was taken in by the unanimity of the account put forward by the Spartan authorities, who had a vested interest in proving beyond all doubt that the great victor and hero of the battle of Plataea in 479 deserved his punishment. Even so, on two occasions he uses the phrase 'it is said' (1.132.5; 1.134.1), implying some reservations about the veracity of his information.

The victory of the Spartans in the Peloponnesian War in 404 encouraged the 'Laconisers', i.e. the admirers and supporters of Sparta, to develop and enhance the myth of Sparta, especially Critias and Xenophon. Critias, an Athenian oligarch and the most ruthless of the 'Thirty Tyrants' – a narrow, repressive oligarchy that was established after the defeat of Athens by the Spartan Lysander and ruled briefly from 404–3 – played a leading role in spreading the myth of an idealized Sparta by means of distortion and invention, amply supplied by information from his Spartan supporters. Only a few fragments of his two works entitled *Constitution of the Lacedaemonians*, written in prose and verse, survive. Xenophon (see Chapter 1 for a fuller treatment), an upper-class Athenian, lived for a while in Sparta, was present with the victorious Spartan army at the battle of Coroneia in 394 (see Chapter 24), allowed his two sons to undergo the Spartan 'agoge' (education system) and enjoyed the patronage of King Agesilaos, whom he admired greatly as the living embodiment of the greatness of Sparta. His (probable) *Constitution of the Lacedaemonians* is full of uncritical praise (apart from Chapter 14) for Lycurgus whose social and economic reforms, in Xenophon's opinion, had brought about the moral qualities and outstanding courage of the empire-winning Spartans of his own day. This work is not really a constitutional history of Sparta, more a flattering description of contemporary Spartan society, education and military arrangements (including religious observance), thus explaining why so small a state had become the most powerful in Greece. Yet he must have been aware of the increasingly bitter and divisive social tension within Sparta arising from the great disparity of wealth between rich and poor Spartans, many of whom were reduced to 'Inferior' non-Spartiate status (Hypomeiones) owing to their inability to provide their compulsory contribution to their 'syssition' (dining club), the basis of full citizenship. None of this is to be found in this work, but in his *Hellenica* he describes in depth the conspiracy of Cinadon (almost certainly an 'Inferior') who in 399 allegedly planned an uprising against the Spartiates, and whose supporters consisted of Helots (presumably

Laconian), liberated Helots (Neodamodeis), 'Perioeci' and 'Inferiors' (Hypomeiones), all of whom would have happily eaten the Spartans even raw, such was the depth of their hatred (*Hell.* 3.3.4–11). The catastrophic defeat of the Spartan army at the battle of Leuctra in 371, caused mainly by this lack of Spartiate manpower, was possibly the catalyst for his one critical chapter (14), but even then the fault, in Xenophon's eyes, lies not with the admirable 'Lycurgan' system but the failure of the Spartans to adhere to it, choosing instead to be corrupted by the love of gold and the desire for foreign rule.

Xenophon's admiration of Sparta was shared by Plato, a relative of Critias and an early fourth-century philosopher, who greatly admired the Spartan *eunomia* (good order), based upon austerity and a highly regulated society. Athens, his own city, had endured stasis (civil war) in 411–10 and in 404–3, and the restored radical democracy had put to death in 399 his great hero, Socrates. His disaffection with Athens encouraged him to look to Sparta as an inspiration for his ideal state and consequently the *Republic* shows many similarities to the political and social institutions of Sparta. However, Plato is prepared to criticize Sparta and this criticism is valuable in such a mainly pro-Spartan source. In his five stages of degeneration from Aristocracy (used in its literal sense, i.e. 'rule of the best') to Tyranny, Sparta is equated with the first state of degeneration, i.e. Timocracy or Timarchia. This state is characterized by the overwhelming love of status and honour, and the ambition to achieve these leads to rivalry and splits among the ruling class. The ensuing desire for wealth and the possession of land and houses further results in wealth being concentrated within a small number of citizens (*Republic* 545a–551c). In the *Laws*, Plato is especially critical of Spartan laws on the grounds that their sole purpose is success in war, rather than peace and harmony (*Laws* 1.625–26).

This last criticism is echoed by Plato's most distinguished pupil, Aristotle, writing in the second half of the fourth century after the collapse of Sparta as an imperial power. The *Politics*, his main surviving work, is very useful as a critical counter-weight to the idealization of Sparta. It regrettable that his *Constitution of the Spartans* (similar in style to the Constitution of the Athenians, i.e. the *Ath. Pol.* – see Chapter 1) survives only in fragments. Its value as a source can be assessed by the usefulness of some of these fragments, e.g. the quotation from the Great Rhetra to be found in Plutarch's *Life of Lycurgus* 6 (see below). He agrees with Plato in criticizing the founder of the Spartan constitution for making the primary aim of his legislation conquest and war (*Politics* 1333b), but goes much further. He criticizes at length the Helot system, the excessive property power of Spartan women, the great disparity in the possession of land and wealth, the corruptibility of the 'Ephorate' and its control over most of the important areas of state policy, the defects of the Gerousia, the inherent weakness of the need to contribute individually to the dining club (syssition) as the basis of citizenship, and the inability of the financial system to fund large-scale wars (*Politics* 1269a–1271b). We also learn through him of the factional strife in early fourth-century Sparta, i.e. Lysander's attempt to abolish the kingship and King Pausanias' to abolish the Ephorate (*Politics* 1301b). Thus Aristotle's analysis, although excessively critical, is very useful, especially as he is the only source to explain, rather than merely moralize about, the cause of the defeat at Leuctra, i.e. the lack of citizen manpower ('oliganthropia'), caused by the Spartan system of land ownership and inheritance.

The evidence for archaic and classical Sparta is further complicated by the intervention of certain kings, who had a vested interest in putting forward their proposals for constitutional reform. Early in the fourth century the exiled King Pausanias wrote a pamphlet ('logos') on the constitution of Sparta and Lycurgus in his bid to regain political power, which seems to have played a major part in the idealization of 'Lycurgan' Sparta. It would seem, although this is a matter of scholarly dispute, that Pausanias favoured the abolition of the Ephorate and almost certainly quoted the *Great Rhetra* – later used by Aristotle and then Plutarch (see above) – where the 'Ephors' are conspicuous by their absence. It may also have been the case that Pausanias' pamphlet greatly influenced the kings of the third century, Agis IV (244–1) and Cleomenes III (235–222). These two kings were responsible for the so-called 'third-century revolution', and it was their reforms and their political propaganda used to justify them that have done so much to distort profoundly the history of archaic and classical Sparta for later writers and historians. By the mid-third century the distinctive 'Lycurgan' social and economic institutions, i.e. the dinner clubs (syssitia) and the state education (agoge), had broken down, and most of the Spartans were by now 'Inferiors' (Hypomeiones). These two kings in their attempts to restore Spartan power introduced many radical so-called 'Lycurgan' reforms into Spartan society, and it is these reforms, recounted fully in Plutarch's *Lives of Agis and Cleomenes*, that permeate the *Life of Lycurgus* and are foisted upon him.

Plutarch, whose Spartan Lives, especially of Lycurgus, have done so much to promote the Spartan myth for future generations, was writing in the early second century AD, many centuries after the events he describes and the sources that he employs (see Chapter 1). The numerous similarities between the reforms of Lycurgus and of the third-century BC kings are notable, e.g. Lycurgus' redistribution of all the land into equal allotments (*Lyc.* 8, 16) is similar to that of Agis (*Agis* 8) and Cleomenes (*Cleom.* 11). Plutarch's main source for the lives of these two kings was the Athenian Phylarchus, an admirer and possibly a friend of Cleomenes, who wrote a history of his age in 28 books from the death of Pyrrhus to the death of Cleomenes (272–220/19 BC). The history is dramatic and sensational in style, and treats both kings as tragic heroes in their attempts to restore Sparta's greatness, but there is enough in Plutarch's condensed version to establish the essence of their reforms and their justificatory arguments. As regards the similarities of the reforms in these *Lives* and the *Life of Lycurgus*, Plutarch either made use of Phylarchus again or made use of Sphaerus, a third-century Stoic philosopher and possibly teacher of Cleomenes. He wrote *On the Laconian Constitution* in three books but, more importantly, he acted as an advisor to Cleomenes and played a key role in the re-establishment of the agoge and the dining clubs (Plutarch, *Cleomenes* 11). Although it would be wrong to think that Plutarch relied upon only one major source for his *Life of Lycurgus*, there is still a further problem that many of his other sources are Hellenistic and thus are heavily influenced by the 'third-century revolution'. Plutarch is at his most useful when he uses sources of the fifth and fourth centuries, although he takes issue with them when critical of his inspirational, perfect lawgiver, Lycurgus, e.g. Aristotle and the failure to control the power of women (*Lyc.* 14). Although he consulted Herodotus and Thucydides, it is likely that he made extensive use of the Spartan Constitutions of Critias and Xenophon, but most of his research was centred on Aristotle and Plato, both of whom are mentioned as sources on numerous occasions. He also used Ephorus (see Chapter 1 under Diodorus Siculus), who emphasized the moral decline of the Spartans after 404 owing to the accumulation of wealth and the resultant corruption. It is likely that Ephorus in turn was influenced by the work of King Pausanias.

Plutarch also collected and made extensive use of 'Laconian Sayings' (Apophthegmata Laconica) – short, witty replies that are designed to reflect on the excellence of the Spartan character – and the *Spartan Institutions* (*Instituta Laconica*) – a description of ancient Spartan institutions and customs, probably influenced by earlier versions of Sparta's Constitution, especially those of Xenophon and Aristotle. The 'Laconian Sayings' grew in number over the centuries and can be found in the sources as early as Herodotus (e.g. 3.46 and the Samians' request for help). Unfortunately, not much historical value can be placed on their reliability and authenticity, although they are invaluable for the history of the Spartan myth. Their pointed, anecdotal, moralizing style appealed to Plutarch, who was writing biography not history (see Chapter 1) and thus used them extensively in describing Lycurgus' thinking behind his reforms, e.g. the equal division of property (*Lyc.* 8), the establishment of the dining clubs (*Lyc.* 10) and the introduction of iron spits in place of gold and silver coins as Spartan currency (*Lyc.* 9). In fact, the 'Laconic Sayings' make up the bulk of chapters 19 and 20.

Finally, mention should be made of Pausanias, a religious antiquarian, travelling around mainland Greece (and the Near East) and writing *c*.160 AD. His most famous work is the *Description of Greece* (*Periegesis tes Hellados*), a guide to the most important sites and historic places of Ancient Greece. Although born in Lydia (modern-day Turkey), he was very proud of his Greek heritage and regretted Greece's decline after the Roman conquest.

As he visits each site and describes the monuments to be seen, he also includes a discussion of the local geography, daily life, legends, etc. – in essence, a cultural history. Laconia is the subject of Book 3 and, as with the other books, he includes a synopsis of Spartan history. Although its quality is variable, there is often interesting information of genuine worth, e.g. his identification of the court that tried King Pausanias in 403 and the breakdown of the voting that led to his acquittal (3.5.2).

For the reasons given above, Plutarch and the other literary sources, although numerous, are often unreliable, especially as the dates of these sources stretch over many centuries and most are not contemporary. Consequently great care must be exercised in their use when attempting to establish concrete facts about early Spartan politics and society.

The background

The Dorians arrived in the Peloponnese around 1000 BC, and justified their conquests on the grounds that they were the descendants of Heracles and were legitimately re-claiming their former lands. The Spartan Dorians settled in the valley of the Eurotas River, situated in Laconia (also known as Lacedaimon) in the southern Peloponnese, probably in four villages ('obai'); the fifth village ('oba') of Amyclai, which was about five kilometres further south and became an integral part of the city of Sparta, was added sometime later. The Spartans then set about establishing their control throughout Laconia (and possibly south-east Messenia) by conquering the other Dorian-controlled communities, whose inhabitants came to be known, according to their status, as either the Perioeci ('those who live around') or Helots. The name Helot may have been derived from 'the inhabitants of Helos', which was a village close to the head of the Laconian Gulf, or (more likely) from the Greek word for 'those captured (in war)'.

The Perioeci were citizens in their own communities and, for the most part, possessed autonomy in the conduct of their internal affairs; but their foreign policy was controlled by the Spartans, and they were obliged to supply troops for Spartan campaigns. However, they did hold a privileged position constitutionally, as the Spartans called themselves officially 'the Lacedaimonians' (the inhabitants of Lacedaimon) and thus they considered the Perioeci communities to be part of the Spartan state, at any rate for military purposes. After the introduction of the policy which forbade the Spartans from participating in manual trades, the Perioeci became a crucial element in the maintenance of the Spartan system by supplying the necessary economic needs of the state in the form of manufacture, trade and other service industries. The Helots were the other group of inferiors, lower than the Perioeci in status and in political rights (if any), although it is difficult to know in what ways and to what degree, as later writers make no distinction between these and the Messenian Helots (see below).

By the middle of the eighth century (750) there was little to distinguish the Spartans in their political development from the other main Greek city-states: a landed aristocracy exercising power through a council. The chief difference was the continued existence of kingship, which in other states had been removed totally or had evolved into an appointed public office, and the fact that there were two kings. The Spartans also, in common with the rest of Greece, experienced the problems of over-population and of the consequent land-hunger (see Chapter 2). However, the Spartan solution – conquest in Messenia rather than overseas colonization (apart from Taras in southern Italy) – was the key factor in creating the Spartan state that was uniquely different from the other Classical Greek states of the fifth century.

The First Messenian War

This war can reliably be dated from around 730 to 710 BC, and was fought by the Spartans against fellow Dorians who lived in and owned the fertile land of Messenia in the south-west Peloponnese. The evidence for the dating of this war comes from Tyrtaeus, a Spartan poet writing around the middle of the seventh century, and the Olympic victor lists. Tyrtaeus places the war in the reign of King Theopompos, two generations before his own:

> to our king, the friend of the gods, Theopompos, through whom we captured wide-spaced Messene; Messene good for ploughing and good for planting, over which they fought – the spearmen fathers of our fathers – for nineteen years, always unceasingly and with an enduring spirit; and in the twentieth year the enemy, leaving behind their fertile lands, fled from the great heights of Ithome.
>
> (Tyrtaeus fr. 5)

In addition, the Olympic victor lists record seven Messenians from 777 to 736, but only one more subsequently; whereas the Spartans gain their first victor in 720 and dominate the lists to 576.

It is not clear whether the Spartan victory in the First Messenian War resulted in the annexation of the whole of Messenia, or just the eastern half, i.e. the fertile land in and around the valley of the river Pamisos that flows due south into the Messenian Gulf. Some of the conquered Messenians fled to different parts of Greece, almost certainly to the neighbouring Arcadians, who aided the Messenians in their revolt from Sparta during the seventh century (see below). The others were forced to work for their Spartan conquerors:

> Just like asses, worn out by their mighty burdens, they bring to their masters through wretched necessity a half of all the fruit that the land brings forth.
>
> (Tyrtaeus fr. 6)

This sudden increase in land brought immense economic prosperity to a number of Spartans, but by no means to all. There was at least one group of Spartans who were very discontented with the sharing-out of the spoils of a long and difficult war: the 'Partheniai'. It is not clear how they were different from the other Spartans, but clearly they were considered an inferior group within the body politic, and discrimination against them fomented revolution among their ranks (Aristotle, *Politics* 1306b 29–31). Colonization had been used by other Greek states as a safety valve to ease social tension (Plato, *Laws* 735f), and Sparta adopted this solution for the only time in its history by sending out the Partheniai as colonists to found Taras (Tarentum) in southern Italy in *c*.706. It would seem that their status as inferior citizens and, coming so soon after the Messenian War, their failure to acquire land were the chief grievances of the Partheniai. Their discontent has gained the most publicity in the ancient sources, but there is every reason to believe that other Spartans were also deeply unhappy at the unfair distribution of land, both in Laconia and especially in the newly acquired (or part of) Messenia.

Many of the later sources, encouraged by Spartan propaganda, played a major part in the creation of the Spartan myth – the idealization of Sparta as the perfect, well-ordered society, always free from the civil strife (stasis) that deeply scarred so many other Greek states; and the attribution of the radical political, social and economic reorganization of Sparta to the legendary law-giver, Lycurgus (see below). However, Herodotus did not accept the myth of perpetual Spartan eunomia (good order/under good laws):

> before this they were the worst governed ('kakonomotatoi') of virtually all the Greeks, having no dealings with each other or with strangers.
>
> (Herodotus 1.65)

This picture of an earlier Sparta, racked by internal discord, is further reinforced by Thucydides:

> For although Lacedaimon ... had civil strife ('stasiasasa') for the longest period of time that we know, nevertheless it acquired 'good order' earlier than any other state and has always been free from tyrants.
>
> (Thucydides 1.18.1)

The military success against Messenia and the subsequent unfair land distribution would have exacerbated the tensions which already existed in Sparta and which were manifesting themselves in other Greek states in the eighth and seventh centuries: the inequality in the size of land-holdings and the injustice of aristocratic government (see Chapter 2, especially the grievances of Hesiod of Boeotia who was writing about this time).

Events in the second quarter of the seventh century (675–650) brought these problems to a head. The Spartans, encouraged by their defeat of the Messenians, decided to challenge the power of the Argives, and attempted to seize control of the fertile Thyreatis, which was the area in the north-east Peloponnese that separated their two spheres of influence. The battle of Hysiae in 669 (Pausanias 2.24.7) resulted in a crushing defeat for the Spartans, very possibly inflicted upon them by the newly created 'hoplites' under the command of King Pheidon of Argos (see Chapter 3). Defeat in war would have increased the discontent in Sparta and would have led to renewed calls for land reform. According to Pausanias, King Polydorus who ruled from c.700 to 665 took up the grievances of the ordinary Spartan and proposed some form of land distribution, but was assassinated by the aristocrat Polemarchos before his proposals could be implemented (3.3.3). The overwhelming military defeat at the hands of the Argives and the increasing political discord within Sparta almost certainly provided the incentive for the Messenians to rise up in revolt.

The Second Messenian War

The sources are contradictory about the date of the Second Messenian War (or the Revolt of the Messenian Helots), but the combination of the events outlined above and the fact that the poet Tyrtaeus, who fought in the war, lived around the middle of the seventh century strongly suggests that the war or revolt should be dated to around 650. According to Strabo (8.4.10), the Messenians were helped by Argos, Elis, Pisa and (if an emendation to Strabo's text is accepted) Arcadia. The poetry of Tyrtaeus strongly suggests how desperate this war was for the Spartans, threatening their very existence and bringing heavy defeats:

> For you know the destructive deeds of sorrow-inducing Ares, and you have well learnt the anger of brutal war; you, young men, have often tasted flight and pursuit, and have had your fill of both.

> (Tyrtaeus fr. 11)

It is difficult to establish the length and factual details of this war, as Pausanias' main sources were writing in the aftermath of the defeat of the Spartans at the battle of Leuctra in 371 by the Thebans and the liberation of the Messenian Helots in 370–369 (see Chapter 25). These third-century BC sources, Myron of Priene and Rhianos of Bene in Crete, were more concerned with creating a mythical past of glorious Messenian resistance, based around such heroic figures as Aristomenes, and consequently most of their evidence is worthless. However, it is clear that the Spartans finally defeated the Messenians and their allies, and that the whole of Messenia was gradually pacified and brought under Spartan control, possibly as late as 600.

This would explain the remark attributed to Epaminondas, the Theban liberator of the Messenian Helots in 370–369, that he had (re-)founded Messenia after 230 years (Plutarch, *Moralia* 194B).

By 600, Sparta had emerged as the most powerful state in the Peloponnese, possessing two-fifths of its territory, and was on the threshold of acquiring greater power and influence in the sixth century (599–500). Fundamental to this success were the reforms that had been introduced at some time in the seventh century. These reforms were political, changing the constitution and emphasizing the importance of the hoplites within it; and economic and social, allocating plots of Messenian land to its citizens and creating a warrior elite of its citizens. Tradition has accredited these reforms to a single reformer, Lycurgus. Little of historical worth is known about the legendary Lycurgus, and his *Life* in Plutarch is part of the Spartan myth referred to earlier. In addition, all these reforms were not necessarily introduced by one single decree of government, and were certainly not fixed and unchanging, but developed and adapted over a period of time, although all modifications were eventually related back to Lycurgus. However, for the sake of convenience, the major reforms of the seventh century (699–600) that made the Spartans unique among the Greeks and enabled them to gain super-power status will be referred to as the 'Lycurgan' reforms.

The political reforms

The political reforms of 'Lycurgus' were vital for the Spartans' rise to power in the sixth century for two reasons: first, the resolution of their internal political problems removed the primary cause of the political upheavals that produced tyranny throughout the rest of Greece; second, the constitutional harmony between the key political forces in the state (the kings, the Gerousia and the 'damos') allowed the Spartans to direct their concerted energy against other Greek cities, as well as to exercise control over their Helots and Perioeci. In the words of Thucydides:

> For it is about four hundred years or a little more down to the end of this [i.e. Peloponnesian] war that the Lacedaimonians have enjoyed the same system of government. Having become powerful because of this, they intervened in the affairs of other states.
>
> (Thucydides 1.18.1)

The basis for these political reforms was an archaic document known as the *Great Rhetra*, which is quoted in his *Life of Lycurgus* by Plutarch, but which he almost certainly found preserved in Aristotle's lost work, *The Constitution of the Spartans*.

A 'rhetra' is the Spartan word for an enactment or decree which, according to tradition, was not written down, as was customary in fifth-century Athens. However, the *Great Rhetra* was of such immense political importance, especially to the Spartan hoplites, that its provisions were at some time written down as a guarantee that they would be respected and acted upon in the future:

> Having established a cult of Syllanian Zeus and Athena, having done the 'tribing and obing', and having established a Gerousia of thirty members including the kings, (1) season in season out they are to hold Apellai between Babyka and Knakion; (2) the Gerousia is both to introduce proposals and stand aloof; (3) the damos [Doric Greek for 'demos'] is to have the power to [in Plutarch's gloss on a badly garbled Doric phrase] 'give a decisive verdict'; ... (4) but if the damos speaks crookedly, the Gerousia and kings are to be the removers.
>
> (Plutarch, *Lycurgus* 6)

Unfortunately, the exact meaning and significance of these constitutional provisions, the dating of the document and the historical context at the time of its introduction are matters of the greatest controversy among modern scholars. Nevertheless the *Great Rhetra*, albeit in the most simplified form, laid down the powers of and the inter-relationship between three of the four main institutions of state (see below for the constitutional powers of the 'Ephors').

The kings

There were two hereditary kings from the families of the Agiads and the Eurypontids, and, although the former were traditionally the senior (Herodotus 6.51), they were constitutionally equal in authority and thus acted as a check upon each other's power. By the terms of the *Great Rhetra*, their constitutional power was diminished by being included with no special privileges among the thirty-strong aristocratic Gerousia. This is further confirmed by Herodotus who lists, apart from their social privileges, their priesthoods and their limited judicial authority (i.e. over unmarried heiresses, adoption and public roads) as their sole areas of authority in home affairs (6.57). Aristotle limited their constitutional importance to the leadership of the army on campaign:

> when he goes on a foreign expedition, he is the leader in all matters that concern the war ...; therefore this kingship is a kind of generalship which possesses full powers and is for life.
>
> (Aristotle, *Politics* 1285a 5–10)

Aristotle was undoubtedly correct in his emphasis on the supreme authority of the kings on campaign, but he did not fully appreciate their dominant influence as political leaders, especially when the kings were men of high calibre. Although their constitutional powers at home were strictly limited, the outstanding prestige that was gained from leading the Spartan army (and, later, the Peloponnesian allies) would greatly enhance the political standing and influence of the kings among the Spartan hoplites. In a society so devoted to and so respectful of military prowess, a Spartan king with a good record of success in war would win great glory and would be the focal point of the hoplites' admiration. Their influence was especially prevalent in foreign initiatives, especially if there was the possibility of a military expedition, since the king himself would be the commander-in-chief. The dynamic career of Cleomenes I (c.520–490) is amply documented by Herodotus, who assigns to him the leading, even at times the exclusive, role in the conduct of all but one of Sparta's foreign affairs. There is only one instance, to the end of the fourth century, when the Spartans adopted a policy in foreign affairs that was opposed by a powerful king: the rejection of King Archidamus' advice in 432 to postpone the declaration of war against Athens (see Chapter 17).

According to Herodotus, the Spartan kings even possessed the constitutional right to declare war:

> The Spartans have given to the kings these rights: [certain priesthoods] and to wage war against any land that they wished, and any Spartan who opposes this is liable to be put under a curse.
>
> (Herodotus 6.56)

Doubt has been cast on this statement as the evidence of the fifth and fourth centuries reveals that this power was vested in the Spartan Ecclesia (Assembly). However, it is possible that the kings did originally possess this right in theory, when they acted in concert and went on campaign together. The constitutional position may well have changed after c.506 when the clash between Cleomenes and Damaratus led to the abandonment of the invasion of Athens (see below); from then on, it was no longer allowed for two kings to campaign together, and thus it would become virtually impossible for them to exercise this shared right. Eventually the right became obsolete through lack of use.

The Gerousia

The Gerousia was the council of the two kings and twenty-eight elders ('gerontes'), the latter of whom had to be over sixty years of age, were elected by acclamation in the Spartan Assembly and – like the kings – held office for life. It is clear from the *Great Rhetra* (section 2) that the Gerousia exercised a probouleutic function, i.e. after a preliminary discussion, it prepared the agenda consisting of proposals that were to be decided and voted upon by the Assembly. This control of the issues to be discussed gave the Gerousia the greatest power and influence in policy-making. This power was further increased by section 4 of the *Great Rhetra* (often referred to as the Rider), in which the council could refuse to ratify the Assembly's decision on the grounds that the Assembly had altered the original motion, i.e. 'if the damos speaks crookedly'. According to Aristotle's commentary in Plutarch, when the Assembly began to distort the original motions by adding and removing clauses, the kings Polydorus and Theopompos added this Rider at a later date. However, it seems unlikely that the Gerousia could have exercised this power in decisions about war and peace: an assembly of warriors and retired warriors could hardly have accepted such a veto.

The Gerousia was also influential in the conduct of foreign affairs through its position as the highest law court in Sparta, which alone had the right to impose the penalties of death, exile and loss of citizen rights; even the prosecution of a king would come before the Gerousia and the five Ephors. There is far more evidence of 'political trials' in Athens, especially in the fifth and fourth centuries (see Chapter 14), but from the 490s to 378 at least seven kings and several other important military men had to face prosecutions that were in reality politically motivated, for example the prosecution of King Pleistoanax in 446/5, officially for accepting bribes but really for his perceived leniency towards Athens (see Chapter 15). It would take a brave and confident king to pursue a policy that did not command the support of the majority of the Gerousia, knowing that, in the event of failure, he was likely to be prosecuted upon his return.

The Ecclesia (Assembly)

All male Spartiates or 'Homoioi' (the Peers/the Similars), as they called themselves, were eligible to attend the Assembly (Ecclesia), which the *Great Rhetra* in section (2) authorized to be held at regular intervals, i.e. at the time of the festivals in honour of Apollo called the 'Apellai'. They had the right to elect the members of the Gerousia and the Ephors; and also had the sovereign power to ratify or reject the proposals put before the Assembly by the Gerousia. Section 3 of the *Great Rhetra*, which covers this constitutional power, is garbled, probably because of the difficulty of transcribing the passage written in an archaic Doric dialect, but Aristotle's commentary preserved in Plutarch on this particular constitutional right is very precise:

> When the people have gathered together, none of the others is allowed to put forward a motion, but the people had the sovereign power to decide upon the motion set before them by members of the Gerousia ('gerontes') and the kings.
>
> (Plutarch, *Life of Lycurgus* 6.3)

There has been much scholarly debate as to whether the Spartiates actually possessed this power of decision-making. Aristotle in the *Politics*, while discussing the democratic features of the constitutions of Carthage, Crete and Sparta, expresses the view that the Carthaginian constitution is more democratic:

> And when these [Carthaginian] kings put forward their proposals, they not only allow the people to listen to the proposals that have been decided upon by their rulers, but the people have the sovereign power to decide ('krinein'); and anyone who wants is allowed to speak against the introduced proposals, which is not possible in the other constitutions [i.e. those of Sparta and Crete].
>
> (Aristotle, *Politics* 1273a 9–13)

Some historians believe that the last clause – 'which is not possible in the other constitutions' – refers to the two powers that the Carthaginian Assembly possessed, i.e. the power to decide and the power to debate. However, if the last clause is taken to refer solely to the last power (the power to debate), then Aristotle is stating that the Spartan Assembly had the sovereign power to ratify or reject all proposals (krinein), but was not allowed to debate them. By this interpretation of the last clause, the statements in the *Great Rhetra* and in Aristotle's *Politics* can be accepted as being in agreement: the Spartan Assembly had the sovereign power of decision.

This raises a further area of scholarly debate: whether the ordinary Spartan had the right to debate. There are three viewpoints on this issue. The first (e.g. Andrewes) is that the Spartans in their Assembly possessed the right to debate the Gerousia's proposals and uses Aristotle's commentary on the Rider (section 4) of the *Great Rhetra* as supporting evidence:

> Later, however, when the people were distorting and twisting the proposals by adding and deleting words, the kings Polydorus and Theopompos inserted this clause into the rhetra: 'but if the damos [the people] speaks crookedly, the Gerousia and the kings are to be the removers'.
>
> (Plutarch, *Life of Lycurgus* 6.4)

The fact that the people were changing the proposals presupposes that there was debate, and that amendments or even counter-proposals from the floor were drastically changing the original decisions of the Gerousia; consequently Aristotle's statement above in the *Politics* (1273a) is wrong.

The second viewpoint (e.g. Forrest) maintains that there were two stages in Spartan decision-making. In the first stage, the Gerousia introduced the issue to the Assembly which was allowed to debate; when the arguments had been heard, the Gerousia would retire and frame its final proposal to reflect the prevailing majority view. The second stage would consist of the Gerousia putting its proposal for ratification without any further debate being allowed, and it is this second stage that Aristotle may have been referring to in the above quotation from the *Politics*. The third viewpoint (e.g. de Ste. Croix) holds that Aristotle's statement in the *Politics* is substantially correct, if it is accepted that no ordinary Spartan had an absolute constitutional right to speak in the Assembly, but was given the opportunity to speak if he was invited to do so by the presiding Ephor.

Aristotle, in the quotation above (Plutarch, *Lycurgus* 6.3) states clearly that no ordinary Spartan was allowed to put a motion, only to vote on the Gerousia's proposals. The Rider (section 4) was added by Polydorus and Theopompos, who invoked the authority of the Delphic oracle, because, although there was no debate, the wording of the proposals to be voted upon was being altered in the Assembly. Whenever this happened, the Gerousia now had the right to reject this alteration to its original proposal and dismiss the Assembly.

The Ephors

The Ephors are not mentioned in the *Great Rhetra* (either the post did not exist at that time or, if it did, it was a very minor post), but it is appropriate to discuss this post here, as it was the fourth major institution in the Spartan constitution. Five Ephors were elected each year from the whole citizen body and, by the fifth century, they were constitutionally the most powerful public officials. They were in charge of the day-to-day business; and were also the main executive body of state, implementing the decisions of the Assembly, at which they presided (Thucydides 1.87). They also were also in charge of private lawsuits, which they judged sitting separately (Aristotle, *Politics* 1275b); and also combined with the Gerousia in the trial of a king (Pausanias 3.5.2). They supervised the other public officials, having the power to suspend, imprison and even bring capital charges against them (Xenophon, *Constitution of the Lacedaimonians* 8.4). One of their most important responsibilities was the supervision of the agoge, the long and tough system of state education that was essential for the high standards of the Spartan army.

In the field of foreign affairs, they would receive foreign ambassadors to ascertain their business before presenting them to the Assembly. In time of war, it was their responsibility to organize the call-up of the army, deciding the precise size of the army that was needed for the coming campaign (Xenophon, *Con. of the Lac.* 11.2), and may even have possessed the power to give orders to commanders (but not the kings) in the field. When the king set out on an expedition with the army, he was always accompanied by two of the Ephors who acted as overseers. Aristotle saw the Ephors as the most powerful of the four key institutions of state, but also the most corrupt:

> For this post has total control over the greatest of Spartan affairs, but the Ephors come from the whole people with the result that very poor men often gain office who because of their poverty are often bought.
>
> (Aristotle, *Politics* 1270b)

However, he recognized that it was this post rather than power in the Assembly that kept the people content with their constitutional position in the state (1270b).

Finally, it should be made clear that two former commonly held views about the Ephors should be abandoned: that the boards of Ephors had a continuous, corporate policy; and that they were involved in a constant struggle for power with the kings. The Ephors were changed annually and (almost certainly) could not be re-elected for a second time. With regard to the first issue, there is every reason to believe that there were not only differences of opinion over policy between successive boards of Ephors, but also between individual members of the same board. There was often serious disagreement, even personal animosity, between the kings, and it is likely that each king would have his supporters among the Ephors. With regard to the second issue, the perceived conflict between the Ephors and the kings seems to derive from two sources: the monthly exchange of oaths whereby the kings swore that they would rule in accordance with the law and, if they did so, the Ephors would uphold their rule (Xenophon, *Con. of the Lac.* 15.7); and the alleged hostility during the reign of Cleomenes I. In fact, the Ephors are mentioned only twice in Herodotus' account of Cleomenes' career, and neither occasion could be construed as an example of bitter conflict. It is vital to remember that the Ephors, for all their constitutional power, only held office for one year and then returned to political obscurity, whereas the prestige of the king was long-standing. Therefore it is dangerous to deduce from the Ephors' constitutional power that they had undue influence; any Ephor who was too zealous in the exercise of his constitutional power at a king's expense was well aware that he was vulnerable to retaliation at the hands of the same king in the following years.

The most significant and politically important feature of the *Great Rhetra* was its statement that sovereign power, i.e. to 'give a decisive verdict' (section 3), was vested in the Spartan Ecclesia (Assembly). This was almost certainly the first written hoplite constitution, and was deliberately written down, unlike other 'rhetrai' (decrees), because it enshrined their rights in constitutional law. As stated earlier, the problem for the historian is to find a date and a political context for such a remarkable document. Scholarly opinion has dated the *Great Rhetra* from as early as the first quarter of the seventh century (699–675) to as late as the second half of the same century (650–600). In the same way, the political context is given as either after the success of First Messenian War (c.730– c.710), when the hoplites felt confident to assert their rights; or during the Second Messenian War (possibly being waged at some time around 660 to 650), when military defeat and war-induced hardship led to political unrest; or after the end of the Second Messenian War (date unknown), when military success led to political agitation for reform.

The fact that Sparta avoided tyranny and that the *Great Rhetra* gave the Spartan hoplites the political power, which their counterparts in other

71

states only won by supporting revolution and tyranny, makes the middle of the seventh century (c.650) the most attractive date and political context for its introduction. The Spartan aristocracy would have been deeply worried by the success of King Pheidon of Argos, quoted by Aristotle (*Politics* 1310b) as an example of a king becoming a tyrant, in utilizing the hoplites to overthrow the aristocracy in c.670; by the success of the tyrants of Sicyon and of Corinth in c.650s, Orthagoras and Cypselus, respectively; and by the recent memory of King Polydorus, who had supported the grievances of the ordinary Spartan, resulting in his assassination at the hands of an aristocrat. It was the Second Messenian War (or Messenian revolt), that occurred around the time of these tyrannies, and its all-powerful threat to Sparta's very existence, that proved to be the constitutional turning point in Sparta's history. The *Great Rhetra*, by giving sovereign power to the hoplites, was intended to resolve their political grievances, and to provide them with the incentive to save Sparta from destruction.

The social and economic reforms

The end of the Second Messenian War was very possibly the catalyst for the reform of the Spartan state. The Spartans had survived a difficult and exhausting war, and had gained or regained control of the whole of Messenia and its population. The problem now facing the Spartans was how to maintain their current military superiority over the Messenian Helots, who greatly outnumbered their conquerors. The 'Lycurgan' solution, apart from the political reform embodied in the *Great Rhetra*, was to be economic and social: the removal of the need for individual Spartiates to support themselves financially by their own agricultural labour, and the alteration of the social system to create a full-time, first-class army.

However, there is currently much scholarly debate about the nature of these changes, especially on the issues of land tenure and inheritance. The traditional school of thought believed that the Spartan authorities divided up Messenia into roughly equal plots of land ('cleroi'), and bestowed one of these plots (a 'cleros') on each citizen. In addition, each plot was assigned a requisite number of state-owned Helots, whose role was to farm the land and to pay him a portion of the agricultural produce; thus they can be viewed as 'state serfs', i.e. tied to the land and duty bound to pay rent. This agricultural produce from the cleros was directly linked with Spartan citizenship: any failure by a Spartan to contribute the required quota of food to his dining club or syssition (see below), membership of which was the criterion for full citizenship, would result in a loss of citizen rights, thus becoming an 'Inferior' (Hypomeion). Although there are some differences of opinion among scholars of the traditional school, the basic tenets underpinning their view are: first, the 'Lycurgan' land reform was a redistribution of land into equal plots; second, a Spartan had no right to alienate, i.e. to transfer, his plot to another during his lifetime whether as a gift or by sale; third, at his death, his plot had to remain undivided and he had no right to bequeath it by his will, although in all probability it passed to his elder son. To summarize this view, these plots of land were equal in size, inalienable, state-controlled and inherited by men.

There are two main sources upon which this view is based: Plutarch, *Lycurgus* (8; 16) and Plutarch, *Life of King Agis* IV (5):

> A second and very bold political act of Lycurgus was his redistribution of land. ... he persuaded them [i.e. the citizens], having pooled together all of the land, to redistribute it anew, and all to live with one another in equality and to be equal in property for their living.
>
> (Plutarch, *Lycurgus* 8.1–2)

Plutarch further states that Lycurgus allocated 9,000 lots to the Spartans, although, as Plutarch mentions, there was some disagreement among the sources about the original number (*Lyc.* 3). Later, upon the inspection of a newborn child by the elders, he says:

> If it was well-built and sturdy, they ordered the father to raise him, assigning one of the 9000 plots of land to him [i.e. the child].
>
> (Plutarch, *Lycurgus* 16.1)

Furthermore, the traditional school believes that this system of land tenure and inheritance lasted to the beginning of the fourth century until a Spartan Ephor, Epitadeus, changed the rules of inheritance:

> Nevertheless [i.e. despite Sparta's slide into corruption after 404 BC] the number of households that Lycurgus instituted was still preserved and every father still bequeathed his plot of land (cleros) to his son. But this changed when a man named Epitadeus became ephor ... he proposed a law allowing a man to alienate his property and plot of land to anyone he liked, either by gift while living or in his will.
>
> (Plutarch, *Agis* 5.2–3)

It was this seminal change, it is argued, that led to the crisis of Sparta in the early fourth century: the accumulation of wealth and land within a few hands and the consequent dire shortage of soldier citizens culminated in the shattering defeat of Sparta at Leuctra in 371, as outlined by Aristotle (*Politics* 1270a-b – see above). Even those scholars, who doubt the existence of Epitadeus and his law, still believe that the Spartan social crisis belongs to the post-404 imperial years after the defeat of Athens, caused mainly by the desire for wealth and the corruption arising from the influx of vast amounts of gold and silver.

The modern school of thought (e.g. Hodkinson) disagrees radically with the above view. First, the unreliability of Plutarch and his late sources is stressed, particularly as they are written after the third-century revolution and propaganda of Agis and Cleomenes (see above in 'The sources'). Second, the two systems of land tenure, as described in the Plutarch quotations above, are both contradictory and impracticable. The system, as described in *Lycurgus* 16.1, is one of state ownership of land, where the plot of land (cleros) is assigned by the Spartan authorities; the other (as in *Agis* 5.2–3) is a form of private ownership, where the son inherits from his father. In addition, it is highly unlikely that Sparta possessed the complex bureaucracy required to administer such a state-organized scheme of thousands of plots (*Lycurgus* 16). Furthermore, the system described in *Agis* 5.2–3 makes no provision for the granting of a cleros to the younger sons of Spartiates. Third, the earlier, more reliable sources make no mention of an equal redistribution of cleroi by Lycurgus: Herodotus does not include it in his description of the Lycurgan reforms (1.65–66); nor Xenophon in his *Constitution of the Lacedaimonians*; and Aristotle not only omits it but actually states that Phaleas of Chalcedon was the first to propose the idea of equal landholdings (*Politics* 1266a 39–40). Finally, and most importantly, the traditional school cannot adequately explain why, under this system of equal, inalienable, state-controlled cleroi, a serious decline in the number of Spartan citizens took place from the mid-fifth century at the latest, especially as this decline was linked in some way with the increasing accumulation of land by a small number of Spartiates and the increasing disparity of wealth between rich and poor, resulting in the reduction of many citizens to non-Spartiate status, i.e. 'Inferiors' (Hypomeiones).

The modern school believes that land ownership and inheritance in archaic and classical Sparta was similar to that of other Greek states, i.e. the land was privately owned and the usual rules of inheritance whereby a father bequeathed his land to his children were in force. It is also argued that land was inherited not only by the sons but also by the daughters, who may have received as much as a half portion of her brother or each of her brothers. However, their portion would probably be given not on the death of the father but as a dowry when the daughter married. It is this different system of private ownership and inheritance that explains more convincingly the continual decline of Spartan citizens from the fifth century onwards. The key source for this view is Book 2 of Aristotle's *Politics*. On the issue of the weakness of Lycurgus' legislation concerning the inequality of property ownership, Aristotle says:

> For he [i.e. the lawgiver] quite rightly made it dishonourable to buy or sell land in someone's possession but allowed those who wished to give and bequeath it ... moreover nearly two-fifths of all land is possessed by women.
>
> (Aristotle, *Politics* 1270a)

Later on in the same passage Aristotle criticizes the laws that were introduced to encourage an increase in the Spartans population:

For the lawgiver, intending that the Spartiates should be as numerous as possible, encourages the citizens to beget many children ... But it is obvious that, if many are born and the land distributed accordingly, many must inevitably become poor.

(Aristotle, *Politics* 1270b)

On the basis of Aristotle's evidence, it was possible as a typical private landowner to transfer land as a gift during one's lifetime or to bequeath it to whomever one liked. Even the sale and purchase of land is a matter of dishonour but not of illegality. Furthermore, those families of the Spartiates who followed the lawgiver's encouragement for larger families inevitably fell into poverty, as their land was divided up at their death among their sons and daughters into increasingly smaller parcels of land. However, the wealthy Spartiates, whose number is well attested throughout the classical period (Herodotus 6.61.3; Thucydides 1.6.4; Xenophon, *Lac. Pol.* 5.3), like the rich in other states, carefully planned their marriages, procreation and bequests, using these laws to consolidate their wealth and, where possible, to increase their landholdings. Thus wealthy families ensured that their children married into wealth. Families were kept small to prevent the diminution of the estate owing to too many heirs – hence the practice of one wife being shared between two men to keep the number of inheriting children small in both families. Furthermore, if the evidence of Philo, a first century AD Jewish scholar, who states that in Sparta uterine siblings (i.e. children from the same mother but different fathers) could marry (*On Special Laws* 3.4.22), is accepted, a marriage between the half-brother and the half-sister of the shared mother mentioned above would result in the inheritance and concentration of even more land. A childless Spartiate could adopt a kinsmen as his heir, thus keeping the land within the kinship group – also further evidence of the right of a Spartiate to dispose of his land as he wished.

One final quotation about land tenure must be mentioned which has caused great difficulty amongst all scholars and resists a consensus of opinion. It comes from Heracleides Lembos (fr. 373.12 Dilts), a second-century statesman and scholar, and is considered to be derived from Aristotle's lost *Constitution of the Lacedaimonians*:

To sell land is considered shameful by the Lacedaimonians, but from the ancient portion (archaias moiras) it is not allowed.

Some scholars view this source as evidence of two categories of land: private land that can be sold (although socially unacceptable) and state-controlled land – 'the ancient portion' – which it was expressly forbidden to sell. Some scholars equate this 'archaia moira' with the cleroi of Lycurgus; others that this refers to landholdings in Messenia which were given to poorer Spartans after the Second Messenian War so that they could meet the obligations of citizenship; others believe that it refers to land that has been in the possession of a Spartiate's family for many decades to differentiate it from any newly acquired land. The latest view, i.e. Hodkinson, is that this 'ancient portion' has nothing to do with land but refers to the Helots' rent, his agricultural payment in kind.

As regards the 'Lycurgan' economic and social reforms in archaic Sparta, with all the problems of the sources and the constant reinvention of the Spartan myth, it is difficult to give a definitive answer, as Plutarch does in the *Life of Lycurgus*. It seems very unlikely, however, that there was a 'Big Bang' moment when a new 'Lycurgan' system suddenly appeared ready-formed, like an Athene springing forth from Zeus' head. The fact that there was no revolution and no tyranny in Sparta strongly suggests that a consensus was reached among the Spartiates as a whole and that a collective decision was taken to adapt their economic and social (and political) institutions to meet the new demands of the seventh and sixth centuries. First, it must have been agreed at some time that every Spartan would be a hoplite citizen (usually one-third of the population in other states), whose legal duties would include daily attendance at one of the dining clubs (syssitia), where all the Homoioi (Similars/Peers) dined. Second, there must have been a distribution of some land, probably in Messenia, together with allocated Helots to the poorer citizens so that they had the means to provide their compulsory quota of food to their syssition (dining club) upon which their citizenship depended, and the opportunity to carry out their full-time civic and military duties. Finally, a social system, a common way of living (including education) was agreed upon that stretched from birth to death and in which all citizens must participate. It was this third element that was subject to change, modification and refinement over the decades of the late seventh and the sixth centuries.

Part of the social reform involved the agoge or the state military education system, which is described in detail by Xenophon (*Con. of the Lac.* 1–4) and Plutarch (*Life of Lycurgus* 14–25). Again it is not possible to give a definitive answer as to when all the different and distinctive elements of the agoge were introduced (even the term agoge may be of third century origin), although it too must have undergone changes over the decades, even centuries. Its objective was to develop the ideal qualities of a first-class soldier-citizen: patriotism, obedience, loyalty, comradeship, community spirit and uniformity. From the age of six every male child, apart from the royal heirs-apparent, was removed from his family, and joined groups of other boys in a communal life where over the next fourteen years they acquired through harsh, even brutal, training the physical strength, the discipline and the fighting skills that made the Spartans the most feared of all soldiers. Once they had served their apprenticeship in the agoge, they became 'eirenes' at the age of 20 and were then eligible to join a syssition (dining club). Each syssition would consist of roughly fifteen members (Plutarch, *Life of Lycurgus*

12) of different ages, who were expected to attend every night for the rest of their lives and share a common meal. The young Spartan man ('eiren'), once admitted, would live in the syssition for the whole of his twenties, even if married, where his older companions would complete his education by helping him to integrate into the adult Spartan life of training, fighting and dining. At a certain age, possibly 30, he became a full citizen, and was entitled to attend the Ecclesia (Assembly) and to reside with his wife. Thus the syssition and not the family, thus communal rather than private life, became the main focal point of a Spartan's existence. The result was the first full-time, professional army in Greece which not only kept the Helots subdued, but enabled the Spartans to spread their power throughout the Peloponnese in the sixth century.

The rise of Sparta in the sixth century

By the end of the sixth century (599–500) the Spartans had made throughout the Peloponnese a series of military alliances, in which they were acknowledged as the 'hegemon' (leader) of a military league, called the Peloponnesian League by modern scholars. However, due to the paucity and unreliability of the sources, it is very difficult to trace accurately the stages of the League's development. Herodotus provides the briefest of information about Sparta's expansion in the first half of the sixth century:

> In the kingship of Leon and Agasicles at Sparta, the Lacedaimonians were successful
> in their other wars, but kept on failing only against the Tegeates.
>
> (Herodotus 1.65)

Leon and Agasicles ruled from c.580 to c.560 but, with the exception of the conflict between Sparta and Tegea (see below), little is known about these successful 'other wars'. The only 'other' war that can be assigned with any confidence to this period is Sparta's intervention on the side of the Eleans, who defeated the Pisatans in c.572 and regained control over Olympia. This military alliance with Elis was intended to deter the Pisatans, who occupied the territory that bordered on north Messenia, from offering help to the Helots. The Spartans also gained a reputation as the expellers of tyrants in the sixth century (Thucydides 1.18), and it is possible that the Spartans played a part in the overthrow of the Cypselid tyranny in Corinth (c.583) and the Orthagorid tyranny of Sicyon (c.556). However, the list of Spartan-aided expulsion of tyrants from such late sources as Plutarch, *Moralia* 859c–d does not inspire confidence; and it would make more sense strategically to subdue Tegea and Argos on their northern borders before embarking on such campaigns further north.

Two powers stood in the way of the Spartans establishing their supremacy in the Peloponnese: Tegea and Argos. The Tegeates had helped the Messenian

Helots in the Second Messenian War, and would always offer them in the future either encouragement to revolt or a refuge for escape, unless stopped. The Argives had severely defeated the Spartans at Hysiai in 669 and had established themselves as one of the major powers, if not the foremost, in the Peloponnese. The Spartans chose as their first target the city-state of Tegea, the strongest and most influential of the Arcadians. This was essential due to the constant menace of an Arcadian-inspired Helot revolt, and because it would be too dangerous to launch an attack against Argos without previously ensuring that their left flank would not be left exposed to an attack by unconquered Arcadians. Therefore, in the first half of the sixth century, the Spartans set about the conquest of Tegea which, if successful, would bring the rest of Arcadia under their control.

It is clear from Herodotus' quotation above that the Spartans experienced the greatest difficulty in their attempt to subdue Tegea. According to Diodorus (Book 7 fr. 13.2) the Spartans' first campaign ended in failure when the Tegeates, aided by the Argive forces of King Meltas (grandson of Pheidon), even regained some lost territory. Far more serious was their defeat at the 'Battle of the Fetters'. So confident were the Spartans of gaining total victory, sanctioned by the Delphic oracle, that they even brought fetters with them to put on the defeated Tegeates; ironically it was the Tegeates who made use of the fetters by putting the Spartans in chains and making them farm the fields of Tegea (Herodotus 1.66). The intention of the Spartans is revealed by the fact that they brought fetters and measuring-rods on this campaign – to turn the Tegeates into Helots and to divide up their territory into more cleroi (plots of land).

The discovery at Tegea of the bones of Orestes, son of Agamemnon, and their return to their 'home' in Sparta was followed by a Spartan victory in c.550 (Herodotus 1.67–68). However, the Spartans had learned a valuable lesson from their previous defeats at the hands of the Tegeates, and now embarked on a policy of diplomacy. In place of conquest and helotization, the Spartans decided to make a military alliance with Tegea in which Sparta was the hegemon (leader). The Spartans would come to the defence of Tegea, if attacked by another state; and the Tegeates, for their part, were to supply troops for any Spartan campaign and, as can be seen from a fragment of a treaty between the two states, were to refuse any help to the Helots. It was this treaty that set a precedent for Spartan foreign policy, and led to the growth of similar military alliances with other Peloponnesian states culminating in the Peloponnesian League (see Chapter 12). The adoption of the Achaean (i.e. pre-Dorian) Orestes as a Spartan hero was a clever use of propaganda by the Spartans (presenting themselves as Achaeans rather than Dorians) to make their military leadership of the Peloponnese more politically acceptable.

This sensible diplomatic policy was put into operation during the reigns of Anaxandridas and Ariston (from c.560 onwards), and probably bears the stamp of Chilon, Ephor in c.556 and one of the 'Seven Wise Men' of Greece: 'nothing too much' was allegedly one of his famous sayings (Aristotle, *Rhetoric* 1389b). However, Herodotus again baldly states that, at the time (c.547/6) of the request for an alliance against Persia by Croesus, king of Lydia in Asia Minor:

> Most of the Peloponnese had been made subject to the Spartans.
>
> (Herodotus 1.68.6)

This could be another example of Herodotus' tendency to exaggerate; but the defeat of Tegea c.550 and the probable submission of the other Arcadian cities along with Tegea to a military alliance, in which they accepted the military superiority and leadership of the Spartans, gave Sparta control of three-fifths of the Peloponnese. Thus such a position of military strength, together with the alliance with Elis, is enough to confirm Herodotus' statement about the extent of Spartan power by the middle of the sixth century.

Argos, the old enemy, was the next target, and once again the Thyreatis, the fertile plain on the Argive side of the border with Sparta, was the chosen battleground. According to Herodotus (1.82), the Spartans had seized the land but, instead of a full-scale battle, it was agreed that 300 champions from each side would fight it out, with the disputed territory going to the winners. Both armies would retire home until the contest was concluded. When nightfall brought an end to the 'Battle of the Champions', fought c.544, two Argives and one Spartan remained alive. The two Argives, claiming victory by virtue of their superior number, returned to Argos with the news. The wily Spartan, however, stripped the arms and the armour from the dead, set up a battlefield trophy, and stayed in possession of the battleground – a symbol of victory. As both sides claimed the victory, it was left to a full-scale conflict to decide the issue conclusively: victory for Sparta. The Spartans were now undisputed masters of the Thyreatis and, if Herodotus is to be believed, also annexed the former Argive possessions along the east coast of the Peloponnese down to Cape Malea and the island of Cythera, and turned them into 'perioikic' communities.

King Cleomenes

It may have been this victory that encouraged the independent city-states of Epidaurus, Troezen and Hermione, all in the Argolid, to make military alliances with Sparta. This success against Arcadia and Argos also brought the Spartans directly into contact with the Isthmus states, and it is more likely that Corinth, Sicyon and Megara (and possibly Aegina) became part of the network of Spartan alliances in the years following the defeat of Argos rather than in the first half of the sixth century. The Corinthians had certainly become a Spartan ally by c.525, since they joined in the Spartan campaign to depose Polycrates as tyrant of Samos (Herodotus 3.39.1, 48.1). The last twenty years of the sixth century are dominated by the dynamic personality of King Cleomenes of Sparta, but the account of his reign (c.520–490) is distorted by the hostile sources used by Herodotus. It was under Cleomenes that the Spartans not only firmly established their supremacy in the Peloponnese but also, by intervening in the affairs of other states outside the Peloponnese, came to be recognized as the leaders of Greece in defence of the homeland against the Persian invasions.

Athens was to play a leading part in Cleomenes' plans for extending Spartan influence outside the Peloponnese. The assassination of Hipparchus in 514 had persuaded his brother, the tyrant Hippias, that his hopes of survival as tyrant of Athens depended upon a policy of harsh repression. One of the leading aristocratic families, the Alcmaeonids, tried to engineer Hippias' overthrow, but this was only achieved in 510 when Cleomenes used his Spartan army to support their aims (Herodotus 5.64 – see Chapter 7 for a fuller discussion). The Spartan expedition went by land which confirms that Corinth and Megara were allies of Sparta by this time, thus providing them with easy access to Attica. There is doubt as to whether Athens now formed a military alliance on the same terms as Sparta's alliances in the Peloponnese, but, at the very least, Cleomenes would have expected a pro-Spartan, oligarchic regime to be installed to maintain Sparta's growing influence. The proposal of democratic reforms by Cleisthenes was viewed with concern by Cleomenes who intervened in 508 with a small Spartan army, resulting in the exile of Cleisthenes and 700 families and in the installation of Isagoras as the leader of a narrow oligarchy.

The revolt of the Athenian demos against such an unwelcome constitution forced Cleomenes to retire in disgrace (Herodotus 5.72). Cleomenes' desire for revenge revealed Sparta's current status as the leading power of Greece:

> Cleomenes ... summoned an army from the whole of the Peloponnese, not stating the reason for its gathering, but desiring to take vengeance on the people of Athens and to establish Isagoras as tyrant.
>
> (Herodotus 5.74)

This army also included the Boeotians and the Chalcidians of Euboea, both of whom were allies of Sparta. This quotation is interesting on two accounts: first, the Spartan armed forces were so powerful that the allies felt obliged to comply with their orders, even though the objective of the campaign was not stated; second, the Spartans' claim that they expelled tyrants as a matter of principle is exposed as empty rhetoric. However, this invasion of Attica in c.506 had to be aborted at Eleusis on the Athenian borders, when the Corinthians withdrew on the grounds that they were acting unjustly by attacking Athens, to be followed by Damaratus, the other Spartan king, and the other allies (Herodotus 5.75–76).

Map 2 The Peloponnese

About two years later, although Cleomenes is not mentioned by name, the Spartans summoned a meeting of their allies and proposed the restoration in Athens of the ex-tyrant Hippias; but this was rejected on Corinthian advice by all of the delegates and the policy of launching an expedition against Athens was abandoned (Herodotus 5.91–93). This evolution from total Spartan dominance over the allies in the execution of Spartan foreign policy into the 'Peloponnesian League' in c.504 (see Chapter 12 for the constitution of the League) might seem, at first sight, to have weakened Sparta. In reality, a genuine partnership had been formed in which, because the Peloponnesian allies had been given a safeguard against Sparta acting irresponsibly, there could be closer cooperation and greater trust between the hegemon (leader) and the Peloponnesian allies. The result was the growth of the most formidable alliance in Greece which a generation later supplied the leadership and the backbone of the forces that saved Greece from Persian conquest.

81

Bibliography

Andrewes, A. 'Government of Classical Sparta', in *Ancient Society and Institutions* (dedicated to V. Ehrenberg).

——*The Greek Tyrants*, ch. 6.

Cartledge, P. *Sparta and Lakonia*, chs 8–10.

de Ste. Croix, G. E. M. *Origins of the Peloponnesian War*, ch. 4.

Finley, M. I. *The Use and Abuse of History*, ch. 10.

Forrest, W. G. *A History of Sparta 950–192 BC*, chs 3–8 and Excursus 1.

Michell, H. *Sparta*, chs 2–6.

Murray, O. *Early Greece*, 2nd edn, chs 8 and 10.

Toynbee, A. *Some Problems of Greek History*, part III, chs 2 and 3.

Wade-Gery, H. T. 'The Spartan Rhetra in Plutarch Lycurgus VI', in *Essays in Greek History*.

Bibliography for Second Edition

Cartledge, P. *Sparta and Lakonia*, ch. 14

——*Agesilaos and the Crisis of Sparta*, chs 5, 10, 21, 22

Flower, M. A. 'The Invention of Tradition in Classical and Hellenistic Sparta', in *Sparta: Beyond the Mirage*, Powell, A. and Hodkinson S. (ed.), ch. 7.

Hooker, J. T. '*Spartan Propaganda*', in *Classical Sparta: Techniques Behind Her Success*, Powell, A. (ed.)

Hodkinson, S. *Property and Wealth in Classical Sparta*, ch. 2

——'Warfare, Wealth, and the Crisis of Spartiate Society' in *War and Society in the Greek World*, Rich, J. and Shipley, G. (ed.), ch. 8

——'Spartan Society In The Fourth Century: Crisis And Continuity' in *Le IVe siecle av. J.-C, Approches historiographiques*, Carlier, P. (ed.)

Powell, A. *Athens and Sparta*, ch. 6

Rawson, E. *The Spartan Tradition in European Thought*, chs 3–5

Talbert, R. J. A. *Plutarch on Sparta*, Penguin Classics

Tigerstedt, E. N. *The Legend of Sparta in Classical Antiquity*, Book 2, chs V.1 and VII.3

5

THE REFORMS OF SOLON

The sources

The survival in later writers of Solon's poems, in which he outlines the problems that were afflicting Athens at the beginning of the sixth century (599–500) or rather his solutions to them, has supplied the historian with the best evidence of all the major political events in early Greek history. As a contemporary of the crisis, and as the leading actor in the attempts to resolve it, his evidence is invaluable. However, his pre-reform poems also reveal his concern for social justice and the well-being of the community, and thus state, in the broadest terms, his moral principles and his condemnation of the current evils: Solon clearly thought it wise, in his attempt to be accepted by both sides as the mediator in this crisis, not to publish any specific proposals or reforms that might lead to him alienating one side or the other. In his post-reform poems, there was no need to state all the details of his legislation because everyone knew them, and so he concentrated on the justice of his solutions. Therefore, the historian must deduce the particular social, economic and political grievances from a combination of, first, the poems which give some insight into Athens' problems, and, second, the actual legislation that can be identified with reasonable accuracy as Solonian.

The second source of evidence is the laws themselves. These laws were written down on wooden tablets and published so that all Athenians could have access to them. Although some modern historians have expressed doubt, they seem to have survived at least to the fourth century and probably later: Plutarch claimed to have seen fragments of them in the second century AD (*Life of Solon* 25) and there are four commentaries on Solon's laws from the fourth century onwards. However, Solon's laws were the only official law code until there was a general revision of the laws, begun in 410 and completed in 400, after the restoration of democracy at the very end of the fifth century, and it is reasonable to assume that copies were made, probably on papyrus, as the wood deteriorated. These copies would have contained Solon's laws, but they would also have been updated to include new provisions, new procedures and, as coinage came into common usage from the second half of the sixth century (550–500), the imposition of fines as punishments. Thus it is difficult to separate out the original Solonian laws. This becomes doubly difficult because public speakers in Athens were always ready to assign any law to Solon, if it improved their chances of success in the Assembly or the law courts, and thus such references have to be treated with caution.

Herodotus is of limited use, as he was more interested in and impressed with Solon's reputation as one of the 'Seven Wise Men' of the ancient world, and consequently concentrates more on his wisdom, e.g. his alleged advice to Croesus (Herodotus 1.29–33), than on his role as law-maker. Finally, there are the *Athenaion Politeia* (*Constitution of the Athenians: Ath. Pol.*), written by Aristotle or one of his pupils (see Chapter 1), a few scattered references in his *Politics*, and Plutarch's *Life of Solon*. Some scholars are very sceptical about their worth on the grounds that they are based on the work of Atthidographers, i.e. the local historians of Attica, who were very partisan in their political views, and thus Aristotle's and Plutarch's works are tainted with their political bias. However, others scholars believe that there is much to commend in these works, as the authors have made use of Solon's poems, even including quotations, and almost certainly consulted what purported to be the laws themselves.

The economic and political crisis in Athens

The problems that led the opposing sides to choose Solon as the mediator in 594 had their roots in the seventh century (699–600). That there was discontent in Athens can be seen by the attempt to establish a tyranny in c.630 by the Olympic victor Cylon who was helped by his father-in-law, Theagenes, the tyrant of Megara. The coup failed, either because the people's plight was not so desperate as to persuade them to give their whole-hearted support to a tyrant, or because they resented, due to their dislike of the Megarians, a Megarian-backed coup. Soon after this in c.621, possibly as a reaction to Cylon, Draco's Law Code was passed. Very little is known about this code of laws, and it seems very likely that the full description of its provisions in Aristotle's *Ath. Pol.* (section 4) was a later invention. It certainly dealt with the crime of homicide, and may have laid down the regulations for or even instituted the status of the 'hectemoroi' (one-sixth-parters – see below). Its frequent recourse to the death penalty as a punishment made the law code proverbial for its harshness:

> Therefore Demades later on gained fame when he said that Draco had written his laws not in ink, but in blood.
>
> (Plutarch, *Solon* 17.2)

Nevertheless, this may still be seen in retrospect as the first step on the road to democracy, as the publication of the laws curbed the power of the aristocrats to interpret the law in a purely arbitrary fashion, which had been the subject of bitter complaints by Hesiod in c.700 BC (see Chapter 2).

By 594, the civil strife between the notables ('gnorimoi') and the multitude ('plethos') had reached such a pitch that both sides were willing to appoint Solon as a mediator to resolve the economic and political crisis that would inevitably lead to tyranny, unless a solution could be found. Aristotle succinctly sums up the problems that faced Solon:

> After this [i.e. Cylon's attempted tyranny] it happened that a long period of civil strife took place between the notables (gnorimoi) and the multitude (plethos). For their constitution was in all ways oligarchic; moreover the poor and their children and wives were enslaved by the rich. They were called pelatai [see below] and hectemoroi (one-sixth parters). For, in return for this rent, they worked the fields of the rich – the whole land was in the hands of a few – and if they did not pay their rents, they themselves and their children became liable to seizure as slaves ('agogimoi'). All borrowing was based on the debtor's person as security until the time of Solon – he was the first to become the champion of the people. This slavery, sanctioned under the constitution, was to the people the harshest and most bitter feature of the regime, although they were also discontented about everything else, for they had virtually no share in government.
>
> (Aristotle, *Ath. Pol.* 2.2–3)

The use of the word 'enslaved' should not necessarily be taken literally, as it could cover any status that involved subjection or dependence on another. However, it is Aristotle's deceptively simple words about the economic problems that have led to much scholarly debate and disagreement about the nature of land tenure and of debt in pre-Solonian Athens.

The first problem is the identity of the pelatai and the hectemoroi: are these alternative names for the same class of people, or are these two separate classes? Later writers, including Plato (*Euthyphro* 4c), consider the pelatai to be the same as 'thetes', i.e. a class of free men who work for others; and Plutarch (*Solon* 13.2) equates the hectemoroi with the thetes. Thus the most probable answer is that pelatai was a general term or name to cover all types of dependent agricultural labourers; and that the hectemoroi, who were obliged to pay one-sixth of their crop, were one particular type of pelatai. A far more complex problem concerns debt, upon which Aristotle in the above quotation and other later writers concentrated: were the hectemoroi in this position because they had fallen into debt through borrowing – if so, how had this situation arisen? or should the hectemoroi be considered as a separate group, not to be associated with the 'borrowers' who, as Aristotle states above, used their own persons as security for their debt?

One theory holds that the hectemoroi were previously independent small landowners but, falling on hard times due to bad harvests, had mortgaged their land as security for borrowing. When they were unable to repay the debt, their creditors kept them tied to the land as dependent agricultural labourers, who paid them one-sixth of their crop with no specific date set to end this dependent status. The mortgaging of their land was probably marked by 'horoi' (marker stones) which Solon mentions in his poem about freeing the land (see below). Eventually many hectemoroi, who had previously found it difficult to survive even when they had full possession of their land, now found it impossible to live on five-sixths of their crop, and defaulted in their payment of one-sixth to their creditor. The result was both the loss of their land to and enslavement by their creditor, who was legally entitled to sell the former hectemoroi abroad as slaves.

Two other theories have been advanced to support this interpretation. The first centres around the introduction of coinage, which made it easier for the poor to borrow but harder to repay, especially with a high fixed rate of interest; previously, in pre-coinage days, the loan had been in the form of food, seed or farm animals, thus setting a reasonable limit to the amount of debt and making repayment a genuine possibility. The second theory is based on the dramatic growth of population in Attica in the eighth century. The division of land between too many sons (Hesiod had advised farmers to have only one son) and the consequent need to overwork the reduced land-holding to feed the increasing numbers led to soil exhaustion and a smaller yield of crops; it was this lack of sufficient crops to sustain his family that led the farmer onto the slippery slope of hectemoroi status and worse.

Attractive as this interpretation might appear, there are serious objections to it. Aristotle in the above quotation does seem to be drawing a distinction between a class of hectemoroi who pay rent as tenants, and a class of borrowers who pledge their persons as security for their loan. Plutarch is even more explicit about the distinction:

> All the people were in debt ('hupochreos') to the rich. For they either farmed their lands for them and paid one-sixth of the produce, being called 'hectemoroi' or thetes; or they took out loans on the security of their person and were liable to seizure by their creditors – some of the debtors becoming enslaved at home, others being sold as slaves in foreign countries.
>
> (Plutarch, *Solon* 13.2)

At first sight this quotation would seem to include the hectemoroi among the debtors, but the Greek word 'hupochreos' can also mean 'under obligation to', 'dependent on'; and this must be the correct translation, as Plutarch immediately makes a clear distinction between the hectemoroi who pay rent to the rich and the debtors who pledge their persons to the rich. It is also a fact that Solon in his surviving poems never mentions debt as a cause of the plight of the hectemoroi.

In addition, one-sixth of the produce seems a very small rate of return for the creditor; a half or more would be expected, as the Helots paid to their Spartan masters (Tyrtaeus fr. 6). It also seems hard to believe that all the creditors came together and agreed a uniform rate of interest rather than a variety of rates. Furthermore, this interpretation argues that the peasant farmers underwent two stages of borrowing and of default. It would be very naive on the part of the creditors to lend a second time to desperately poor peasant farmers (now hectemoroi), who had already failed to make a living with the full produce from their farms, even with the aid of the first loan; with one-sixth of their production already accounted for, the hectemoroi would inevitably default on the second loan. Finally, coinage did not become a factor in Athenian life until a generation after Solon, and small coinage, which is the usual means of transacting business among the poor, not until much later.

Other scholars, therefore, do not believe that the hectemoroi had come into existence through debt, but through hereditary serfdom. At some time in the past, the small landowners had voluntarily or semi-voluntarily accepted the status of being hectemoroi: they agreed to a quasi-feudal system, in which they would receive support and protection from the aristocrats in return for a share of their crop. This institution might go back as far as Mycenaean times when some form of conditional land tenure was standard. Alternatively, it may have arisen in the dangerous and unsettled Dark Ages (1200–900BC), or in the eighth century (799–700) when aristocratic power was at its peak and internal colonization of Attica, led by the aristocrats, was taking place due to population growth.

The most recent and radical interpretation (by Rihll) puts forward the view that the hectemoroi system was introduced as a result of conflict about the use of public land, and had nothing to do with private land. It is argued that the right of individuals to cultivate any vacant or unused public land was causing problems for the community, which was also making greater demands on this land, for example, hunting, pasturing and social events. Therefore Draco, in his law code of c.621/0, attempted to resolve this problem by establishing the hectemoroi system: the individual Athenian was allowed to cultivate public land, but compensated the community by the payment of one-sixth of the produce. The legal provision of seizure and slavery abroad upon default was included to ensure that the hectemoroi met their obligations. However, this system soon came to crisis point as a result of the rich, who controlled the law, exploiting it for their own benefit – they ignored this law in their own and their friends' cases, thereby taking control of public property; but implemented the law with its full force against others, sometimes illegally (see below).

If debt and Rihll's interpretation are put aside, then the institution of the hectemoroi had originated in the acceptance of hereditary serfdom by small landowners, but it was this system of 'conditional tenure' that the later writers did not fully understand. In a legally sophisticated society, such as

Aristotle's Athens in the fourth century (399–300), definition of ownership was relatively precise; but in archaic Athens which had no written law-code until Draco's in 621/0, and that was very rudimentary, the issue of owner-ship was not so clear-cut. The peasant farmer 'owned' his land in the sense that he tilled the soil, as his ancestors had done, bequeathed it to his sons, and retained control of it, provided he paid his one-sixth dues. On the other hand, the local aristocrat also 'owned' the land in the sense that a one-sixth share of the produce was owed to him and, if it was not paid, he had the right to enslave the peasant farmer and take over his land. It was probably this ambiguity over land ownership that led Aristotle to speak of 'the whole land was in the hands of a few'.

This hectemoroi system appears to have worked satisfactorily for a long time, but by the time of Solon it had become a major cause of tension. In addition, there was still slavery for debt. Moreover, Aristotle's division of Athens into the rich and the poor, either hectemoroi or the enslaved, is too simplistic: there must have been a class of independent landowners, some affluent, some poor, who deeply resented the current situation in Athens. It was the economic and political grievances of these groups that had made Athens by 594 so politically unstable that a mediator was required to halt the slide into tyranny. What had gone wrong?

It is clear from the poems of Solon that one of the major causes of the unrest was the greed of the rich:

> But the citizens themselves are willing in their stupidity to destroy this great city, believing in wealth. Unjust are the minds of the people's leaders who are going to endure many sufferings because of their great arrogance. For they do not know how to curb their greed ... but they grow rich; believing in unjust deeds; sparing neither religious nor secular possessions, they steal right and left for plunder.
>
> (Solon fr. 4 5–13)

In order to understand part of the worsening economic situation in Athens, it is necessary to examine the nature of debt-bondage, although this too is an area of scholarly dispute. In non-monetary agrarian societies, and this can be verified from comparable near-eastern documents, the main aim of the creditor was to acquire the debtor's labour, thus increasing his stock of dependent agricultural labour, rather than make a quick profit through the charging of interest on the loan. Many of those who needed to borrow, being well aware of the creditor's desire and knowing the harshness of the debt law, if he defaulted (i.e. liable to seizure and to sale abroad as a slave), preferred to accept the status of debt-bondsman, by which he obligated himself and his family to work in servitude for the creditor until he worked off his debt. In other words, a man who would be unable or would find it extremely difficult to meet his obligation by payment offered his labour as alternative compensation. This put the debt-bondsmen and his family in the power of the creditor but, if it is accepted that the debt-bondage relationship was entered into at the beginning of the loan and not as a result of default, he and his family were protected from being seized and sold abroad as slaves. However, there were plenty of opportunities for abuse of this relationship by the creditor, if comparisons are made with the sufferings of Roman debt-bondsmen.

The upper class's desire for expensive luxury goods, their lavish and competitive life-style and the erection of public buildings at their own expense required access to much greater wealth than before – thus producing the incentive for exploitation. Solon mentions the stockpiling of silver and gold, the international means of exchange before coinage, by which the rich could finance their extravagant living (Plutarch, *Solon* 2). Thus it would appear from Solon's poem that the rich creditors were now taking full advantage of their position of power:

> I brought back to Athens, to their divinely-built homeland, those many men who had been sold abroad, some illegally, others legally, and those who had been forced into exile through pressing debt/dire necessity [the Greek is ambiguous], no longer using the Attic tongue, as they had wandered in so many places. I also freed those at home who were in shameful slavery and trembled before their masters' moods.
>
> (Solon in Aristotle, *Ath. Pol.* 12.4)

Although Solon's words are not explicit about the treatment of the different groups of the poor, it does seem evident that many Athenians, both defaulting hectemoroi and those who had borrowed on the security of their persons, had been enslaved and sold abroad; others had fled into exile to avoid this fate. Although this penalty was sanctioned by law and this enslavement probably reflects the increasing economic pressures of population growth and exhaustion of the land on the poor, the fact that many were sold abroad illegally shows that the rich, who controlled the law, were unscrupulously exploiting their legal power to enrich themselves. In addition, the rich appear to have either treated the debt-bondsman more harshly or worsened their terms of bondage. Thus the poor had pressing economic (and legal) reasons to look to Solon as their saviour.

It is also evident from Solon's reforms and Aristotle's comment about the nature of the constitution (*Ath. Pol.* 2) that there was also serious political disenchantment. The 'Eupatridai' (the Well-born), an exclusive group of aristocratic families, had reserved for themselves the top political posts and membership of the 'Areopagus' (the aristocratic council – see below), thus ensuring a monopoly of power and thereby excluding other wealthy men from political office. In addition, the 'hoplite' middle class were virtually excluded from participation in the running of the state. The possession of political sovereignty by the hoplites in other states, such as in Sparta (see Chapter 4), must have been a source of great envy and motivation.

Finally, it may have been the case that the discontent of the hectemoroi, many of whom would have been hoplites, was not caused by economic concerns, but by their feelings of shame at their inferior, dependent status which included the humiliating threat of enslavement. The one-sixth payment was not financially demanding for many of them, but the horoi (marker stones) were a daily reminder of their political, social and economic subservience to an upper class which had little to offer in the way of protection in the age of hoplites. Thus all those outside the ranks of the Eupatridai wanted a redress of their grievances.

The reforms of Solon

An account of the economic, political and legal reforms that Solon passed to deal with the crisis is given in Aristotle's *Ath. Pol.* (6–12) and Plutarch's *Life of Solon* (15–25).

Economic reforms

The essence of Solon's economic reforms is stated in his own self-laudatory poetry:

> Did I stop before I had achieved all of the aims for which I brought the people toge-ther? May the mighty mother of the Olympian gods in the court of Time be my best witness, the Black Earth herself, from whom I removed the marker-stones (horoi) imposed in many places: previously she was a slave, now she is free. I brought back to Athens, to their divinely-built homeland, those many men who had been sold abroad, some illegally, others legally, and those who had been forced into exile through pressing debt/dire necessity, no longer using the Attic tongue, as they had wandered in so many places. I also freed those at home who were in shameful slavery and trembled before their masters' moods. These deeds I made happen, uniting perfectly together force and justice; and I carried them out as I had promised.
>
> (Solon fr. 36 in Aristotle, *Ath. Pol.* 12)

The most pressing problem was the economic and social condition of the lower classes, and Solon's overwhelming desire for social justice made this reform the centre-piece of his legislation. This part of his reform programme is explained more fully by Aristotle:

> Solon, having gained full control of Athenian affairs, set the people free both in the present and for the future by making it illegal to give loans on the security of the person, and he passed laws, and he carried out a cancellation of both private and public debts, which was called the 'Seisachtheia' (the Shaking off of Burdens) as the people shook off their heavy load.
>
> (Aristotle, *Ath. Pol.* 6.1)

Although these two sources do not give a full explanation of Solon's economic measures, a combination of both plausibly suggests that he made three major reforms. In the first place, he abolished the class of hectemoroi by removing the marker-stones (horoi). These stones were used in the fourth century as a public symbol of land being under some constraint, and presumably at the time of Solon their function was to identify the land of the hectemoroi and therefore their obligations. Solon had now 'freed' the land and given them full possession of it, thus adding substantially to the class of small landowners. In fact, it would seem from the opening lines of Solon's poem that they were the main beneficiaries of his cancellation of debts. This is not to contradict what was said above about the origins of the hectemoroi, i.e. hereditary serfdom, since 'chreos' – the Greek word that is translated by 'debt' – has a wider meaning than simply being in debt from borrowing: it is used to describe any situation where someone is dependent or under obligation, such as the payment of rent or taxes or other dues. Some scholars have found this difficult to accept, believing that the hectemoroi tilled the land of the rich and stressing Solon's words (fr. 34 in Aristotle, *Ath. Pol.* 12.3) that he did not carry out a redistribution of land. However, if it is accepted that the conditional tenure of the land led to no clear-cut identification of ownership (discussed above), then the removal of the one-sixth obligation resolved the ambiguity once and for all: the newly freed former hectemoroi were now without question the legitimate owners of the land.

The second reform, although hard to imagine in practice, set about bringing back those Athenians who had either been sold abroad or fled into exile. These Athenians would have been those identified by Aristotle (*Ath. Pol.* 2 – see above) as agogimoi, i.e. liable to seizure: hectemoroi who had failed to pay their one-sixth and borrowers who had used their own person as security. The third reform was the cancellation of debts, thus freeing the debt-bondsmen in Attica, and the prohibition of any debt that involved the pledge of the person as security. Thus no Athenian in the future could become a debt-bondsman or be sold into slavery for debt.

Political reforms

Although Solon's economic reforms were essential in order to remove the immediate danger of the crisis turning into revolution, he realized that the only hope for long-term stability in Athens was a reform of the constitution in which political power was shared equitably:

> For I gave to the people as much privilege ['power' in Plutarch's quotation in his *Life of Solon* 18.4] as was sufficient, neither removing nor increasing what was their right. I made sure that those who had power and were admired for their wealth suffered nothing unfair. I stood holding my mighty shield over both parties, and allowed neither side to triumph unjustly.
>
> (Solon fr. 5 in Aristotle, *Ath. Pol.* 12.1)

Solon, therefore, was radical in his political reforms: whereas previously the criterion for holding political power had been nobility of birth, which thus ensured the political dominance of the aristocratic Eupatridai (the Well-born), it was now replaced by wealth. However, Solon did not merely open up the top political posts to a wider spectrum of the rich, but re-organized the whole structure of political power which was to be shared out on the basis of economic status.

Solon divided up the whole people into four property classes, based on the number of measures of grain or oil and wine that were produced from the land: the 'pentacosiomedimnoi' ('the 500 Bushellers'), i.e. those whose land produced at least 500 bushels or measures of agricultural produce; the 'hippeis', producing 300 bushels or more; the 'zeugitai', producing 200 bushels or more; and the thetes (Aristotle, *Ath. Pol.* 7.3–4). Although Aristotle states that these four classes predated Solon, it is more likely that only the hippeis (mounted warriors), the zeugitai (hoplites) and the thetes (below military census) had been in existence, reflecting the military organization of Athens. Solon's innovation was to separate out the richest citizens from the hippeis as a new class, and to define precisely in economic terms the specific qualifications for each class. This precision was vital for his division of political power, as each class would have a political function within his new constitution.

The offices of state were divided among the top three classes (Aristotle, *Ath. Pol.* 7.3). The post of Treasurers of Athena was reserved for the '500 Bushellers', presumably on the grounds that their immense personal wealth would provide less temptation to defraud the state but, if they did, they also had the means to repay. The nine 'archons', who were the most important public officials, probably came from the classes of the '500 Bushellers' and the hippeis. The nine archons consisted of the 'eponymous archon', who was the top public official in civil affairs and gave his name to the year; the 'polemarch' (war-leader), who commanded the army; the 'basileus' (king-archon) who was responsible for the conduct of the state religion; and the six 'thesmothetai' who had judicial responsibilities. It would seem that all three top classes (but not the thetes) were eligible for the posts of 'poletai', who supervised public contracts and taxation and sold confiscated property; the 'Eleven', who were in charge of the state prison and were the public executioners; and the 'kolakretai', who exercised some financial functions.

Solon's replacement of aristocratic birth by landed wealth as the qualification for holding the nine archonships was designed to satisfy the political ambitions of the wealthy non-nobles. The deliberate exclusion of wealthy entrepreneurs from political power in Corinth had been one of the main reasons for the overthrow of the aristocratic Bacchiadai and the establishment of Cypselus' tyranny (see Chapter 3). This also gave them access to the most powerful body of state, the aristocratic Council of the Areopagus, as ex-archons after their year of office became life members of that institution. However, it is not clear how the nine archons were elected. Aristotle in the *Ath. Pol.* (section 8) states that the election consisted of two stages: first, each of the four tribes elected ten men; second, the nine archons were selected by lot from these forty directly elected men. However, Aristotle on two occasions in the *Politics* (1273b 40 and 1274a 16) flatly contradicts this statement, claiming that the nine archons were directly elected.

There is no way that these two statements can be reconciled, and thus it has become an issue of scholarly dispute. Those who prefer the *Politics* version argue that the use of lot for office was a key element in fifth-century 'radical' democracy, and consequently it was far too 'democratic' for Solon's carefully balanced constitution: Solon's later reputation as the 'father of democracy' has led to this reform being accredited to him anachronistically. Those who prefer the *Ath. Pol.* version stress that, even in Aristotle's fourth century, the Treasurers of Athena were still appointed by lot from the '500 Bushellers' in accordance with Solon's laws (*Ath. Pol.* 8.1 and 47.1). Therefore, a comparable use of lot for the election of archons should be accepted as a Solonian reform, and was intended to give the wealthy non-nobles a fairer chance against the better-organized aristocratic Eupatridai of gaining the archonship.

Solon also created a Boule (Council) of 400, 100 from each tribe, although Aristotle does not specify the method of election or which classes were eligible for membership (*Ath. Pol.* 8.4). The 400 councillors may have been chosen by lot in the same manner as its successor, the Cleisthenic Boule of 500; and it is reasonable to presume that the thetes were excluded from membership, thus allowing the middle-class zeugitai to be in the majority in the new council. Although there has been scepticism about the existence of this Solonian Boule of 400 on the grounds that so little was known about its function and that it was probably an invention of the Athenian oligarchs in 411 (see Chapter 23), the majority of scholarly opinion has come down in favour of accepting its establishment by Solon. It is hardly surprising that the powers of such an archaic institution had been forgotten by the fourth century; and the propaganda of a return to Solon's constitution by the revolutionary oligarchs, who in 411 set up a so-called 'Solonian' Boule of 400 as the source of their political power, could only have been so effective, if the Athenian people actually believed in the Boule's former existence. In addition, recent archaeological investigation of the site of the later Boule of 500 has uncovered a group of buildings of the early sixth century which appear to be offices, a dining-room and an open space, presumably for meetings: such a similarity to the buildings of the Boule of 500 on the very same site suggests the existence there of an earlier Boule. Finally, there is an inscription from Chios, dated 575–550, that reveals the existence of a 'people's council' (coexisting with the aristocratic council) which meets regularly, is involved in cases of appeal and carries out 'the other business of the people' (ML 8). It is tempting to believe that the Chians used Solon's Boule as the model for their council.

It is very possible that the main function of the Boule of 400 was pro-bouleutic, i.e. it held a preliminary discussion of all topics to be placed on the agenda of the 'Ecclesia' (Assembly). It was clearly intended to be a counter-balance to the power of the Areopagus, whose ranks for some years to come would still be filled with a majority of the Eupatridai (the Well-born). It was their arrogance and greed (Solon fr. 4) that had done so much to provoke this crisis:

> He thought that the city with its two councils, moored so to speak like a ship with two anchors, would be less tossed about on the sea.
>
> (Plutarch, *Solon* 19.2)

This provision that all business for the Ecclesia had to be discussed first by the Boule of 400 was probably designed to be a stabilizing factor in the constitution. This prevented the Ecclesia from being hastily summoned with little prior warning, and acted as a check, not only on the Areopagus and the archons from exerting excessive influence at sparsely attended meetings, but also on the people from passing ill-advised motions which had not been properly considered.

The lowest class, the thetes, had their position in the political structure of the state confirmed and strengthened by Solon's new constitution:

> To those of the class of thetes he only gave a share in the Assembly (Ecclesia) and the law-courts (dikasteria).
>
> (Aristotle, *Ath. Pol.* 7.3)

The thetes had probably been allowed to attend the Ecclesia before Solon's reforms, but this was based on custom not law; and it is very likely that meetings of the Ecclesia had been infrequent, and that matters of importance were rarely put before the people for their decision. Now the right to attend the Ecclesia had been enshrined in law, and it is reasonable to believe that Solon prescribed regular meetings of the Ecclesia in which the people would have the final power of decision on vital issues. However, the right of discussion was probably non-existent: voting in favour of or against a motion was almost certainly the only political right that the people had in the Ecclesia. The reference to the law courts ('dikasteria') is anachronistic, as the division of the 'Heliaea' (the People's Court) into panels of jurors belongs to the reforms of Ephialtes in 462/1, but Aristotle is probably referring to the right of the thetes to attend the Heliaea as the court of appeal (clearly stated in *Ath. Pol.* 9.1).

Legal reforms

In Aristotle's account of Solon's reforms, he highlights the three most 'democratic' features in the new constitution: first, the prohibition of debt involving the pledge of a person as security, and:

94

secondly, that it was possible for anyone who wanted to prosecute on behalf of those who were wronged; and thirdly, which is said to be the chief power of the people, there was appeal to the 'dikasterion' (the People's Court).

(Aristotle, *Ath. Pol.* 9.1)

This 'second' legal reform marked a major change in the administration of the law. Previously, only the injured party could seek justice and compensation before an Athenian magistrate, by bringing a 'dike' (a private prosecution); if, for any reason, they could not bring the case, there was no way that they could seek legal redress. Solon had now established the principle that certain crimes affected not only the wronged individual but also the public interest, and therefore that any member of the citizen public should have the right to prosecute on behalf of the state. He did this by laying a written charge ('graphe') before the magistrate, and this Greek word 'graphe' came to be used for any public prosecution (see Chapter 14).

The 'third' legal reform granted the right of appeal to the ordinary Athenians. The Appeal Court was almost certainly the Ecclesia (the Assembly) sitting as a jury court, and in this capacity was known as the Heliaea (the People's Court). However, there is scholarly dispute about how the system of appeal worked in practice. Some believe that there was no right of appeal from a magistrate's judgement, if he kept the penalty within the limit prescribed by law; in this situation the magistrate's judgement was final. But, if the magistrate wished to impose a higher penalty, he was obliged to refer the case to the Heliaea which would then decide to accept or reject the magistrate's penalty.

Others have argued more convincingly that, although there were some minor cases in which the magistrate's judgement was final, Solon in a majority of cases granted to any dissatisfied defendant the right of appeal to the Heliaea against a magistrate's judgement. The Heliaea then conducted a re-trial and passed its own judgement that over-ruled that of the magistrate. This is confirmed by Plutarch:

For Solon also gave to all those who wanted it the right of appeal to the people's court, even in the cases which he had assigned to the magistrates for them to judge.

(Plutarch, *Solon* 18.3)

Some scholars believe that Plutarch's evidence is suspect on the grounds that its marked similarity to Aristotle (*Ath. Pol.* 9) must mean that he used Aristotle as his sole source, and that any extra information is pure conjecture on the part of Plutarch. However, it is known that Plutarch did use other fourth-century evidence. Moreover, he did see the published laws of Solon (*Solon* 25), and included quotations from them (e.g. *Solon* 19); consequently there is every reason to have faith in the accuracy of his account. What is indisputable is the fact that this reform, for the first time, made the aristocratic magistrates accountable to the Athenian people for their legal decisions (Aristotle, *Politics* 1274a 15–18); and thus marked the first stage in the development of the people's control over the legal system that culminated in the reforms of Ephialtes (see Chapter 13).

Appraisal of Solon's reforms

Economic reforms

Although the abolition of enslavement for debt was an outstanding social reform and the cancellation of debts provided immediate economic relief, Solon's reforms did not remove all of the financial problems of the poor. The poorest of the former hectemoroi, even with full possession of their produce, and those who had been previously forced through poverty to become debt-bondsmen still faced the same difficulties of trying to make an adequate living for themselves and their families. Such men now found it harder to borrow, since they could no longer offer their own persons as reliable security for their debt and because creditors were wary about lending, having already suffered under one cancellation of debts. Their anger at Solon's refusal to redistribute the land, which was (in their opinion) the ideal long-term solution for their economic plight, is made clear in Solon's poem:

> They came for plunder and were filled with hopes of riches, and each one of them thought that he would find great wealth ... but now, being angry with me, they look at me suspiciously as though an enemy. This is not right. For, with the help of the gods, I accomplished all that I promised; and I did other things that were of worth. I chose neither to act with the brutality of a tyrant nor to give equal shares of our fertile homeland to the nobles and the common people alike.
>
> (Solon fr. 34 in Aristotle, *Ath. Pol.* 12.3)

Therefore, although now free in the eyes of the law, many were forced to seek the patronage of the rich, and thus became their dependants – a source of physical strength for the politically ambitious aristocrats, but a destabilizing force within the state in the years that followed Solon's archonship.

However, Solon's economic policy had long-term objectives, and was designed to create a future prosperity for the Athenian people by removing the causes that had produced, and would produce again if changes were not made, the current economic crisis:

> Seeing that ... most of the land was unfruitful and poor in quality, and that sea-traders did not usually bring in goods to those who have nothing to give in exchange, Solon turned the citizens towards skilled trades, and he passed a law that there was no need for a son, if he had not been taught a trade, to support his father.
>
> (Plutarch, *Solon* 22.1)

In addition, Solon offered Athenian citizenship to all foreign skilled trades-men who were prepared to settle permanently with their family in Athens (Plutarch, *Solon* 24.2). He also forbade by law the export of all agricultural produce, except olive oil (Plutarch, *Solon* 24.1). The long-term result of this legislation was threefold: first, it encouraged farmers to concentrate on olive oil production, which was Athens' most lucrative agricultural export; second, it encouraged those who had capital to invest in craft manufacture; and third, the growth of an industrial base in Athens provided alternative employment for those citizens who could never make an adequate living from agriculture.

It is probably in this context that Solon – if he did pass this reform and that is debatable – may have changed the weights and measures system in order to increase the Athenians' market share of foreign trade (Aristotle, *Ath. Pol.* 10). The reform of the coinage can be dismissed, as coins were not minted in Athens until a generation after Solon. However, the later coins took their names from the original weights of silver, and it is this fact that may have led later writers to associate Solon's reform of weights and mea-sures with a change in the coinage. But it is feasible to believe that Solon deliberately changed to the Euboean standard, used by Euboea and Cor-inth, in order to provide a bigger outlet for Athenian manufactured goods in their markets, especially in Sicily and southern Italy. Supporting evi-dence for this comes from the distribution of Athenian black-figure pottery which, from *c*.600 to *c*.580, is found abundantly in sites in Greece, the Black Sea, the eastern Aegean and along the trade routes to the west. However, from *c*.580 to *c*.560, there is not only a dramatic increase in the volume of black-figure pottery discovered in these same sites, but also it is found in inland Asia Minor and in large quantities in southern Italy and Sicily; by *c*.550 Attic pottery was more popular than its Corinthian coun-terpart. Thus Solon can be praised for laying the foundations of Athens' commercial success in the sixth and fifth centuries.

Legal reforms

Solon's legal reforms were without doubt his greatest success. The right of any citizen, not just the wronged person or their family, to seek legal redress in the courts marks a fundamental change in Athenian law (Aristotle, *Ath. Pol.* 8.1). Public law, in which certain actions were considered to affect the well-being of the state, was now considered to be more important and a fairer system for delivering justice in certain matters than private arbitration, which was conducted by a magistrate and only involved the parties in dispute:

> For, being asked apparently which city was the best of all to live in, Solon replied: 'The one in which those who are not wronged, no less than those who are wronged, denounce and punish the offenders.'
>
> (Plutarch, *Solon* 18.5)

The other right of any citizen, who believed that he had been treated unjustly by a magistrate, to make an appeal to the Heliaea (the People's Court) not only made the aristocratic magistrates accountable to the people but also established a role for the people in the legal system. Aristotle was correct in his assessment that this was one of the three most 'democratic' reforms of Solon: the Heliaea and the Ecclesia, the people in judicial and legislative capacities, became the twin bases of Athenian 'radical' democracy in the fifth century.

These two important legal reforms, however, would have been less effective if Solon had not also replaced the narrow, harsh law-code of Draco (apart from the law on homicide) with a comprehensive, sophisticated body of laws that embraced the many complex areas of human experience. The range of his laws, particularly at such an early stage in Athens' history, is worthy of admiration: apart from the obvious criminal and political areas of law (e.g. homicide, theft, treason and amnesty for exiles), there were also those that concerned public morality (e.g. adultery, speaking ill of the dead, bad behaviour in public places, prostitution and excessive displays of grief at funerals), family law (e.g. the rights of heiresses, the making of wills, inheritance and duties in marriage), land law (e.g. shared use of public wells, the planting of trees and boundaries), and commercial law (e.g. loans and exports). It was Solon's law-code that formed the backbone of Athenian fifth-century law and, whereas those laws which had been superseded by newer laws were removed, Solon's laws were kept on public view for many centuries as a testament to his ideal of justice for all citizens.

Political reforms

Aristotle and Plutarch describe the crisis in Attica as a class struggle between the rich nobles and the common people, but there are good grounds for believing that this view does not adequately explain the main cause of Solon's appointment as mediator. The rich and powerful land-owners were not likely to put their political dominance and their personal wealth at risk simply because the poor were discontented. It seems more likely that the nobles were afraid that someone powerful would exploit the grievances of their own dependants, draw them into his own faction and use their armed strength to become tyrant, thus destroying the nobles' power, wealth and privilege. It was this fear of tyranny that led the nobles to turn to Solon and be willing to contemplate a diminution of their power which was bound to follow from his reforms. Evidence for this view comes from Cylon's attempt at tyranny in c.630 and the expulsion and cursing of the aristocratic family of the Alcmaeonids in the aftermath, which reflect the true nature of political conflict in Athens at this time: rivalries between competing aristocratic-led factions. For the separating lines of the political divisions in Athens were not horizontal between rich and poor, but vertical, dividing powerful families or groups of families, together with their dependants, from other families with their dependants. This is confirmed by the nature of the political struggles after Solon and by Peisistratus' attempts to become tyrant. Thus a pure class struggle at the time of Solon, sandwiched between factional struggles earlier and later, seems extremely unlikely.

If this political conflict among the factions was the major problem that Solon was appointed to resolve, he failed:

> The Athenians continued to suffer from disorder in their internal affairs: some used the cancellation of debts as a cause and an excuse for their discontent (for they had been reduced to poverty), others were displeased at the great change in the constitution, and some because of rivalry amongst themselves.
>
> (Aristotle, *Ath. Pol.* 13.3)

The first cause of dissatisfaction presumably refers to the Eupatridai (the Well-born) who would have suffered financially from the abolition of payment of one-sixth of produce from the hectemoroi, although their ownership of large estates makes Aristotle's statement about poverty an exaggeration. The second cause was the reduction in the political power of the Eupatridai, which opened up the top political posts to wealthy non-nobles. Rivalries between the competing factions was the third and greatest cause of internal disorder in Athens. After Solon's departure from Athens, there was so much political conflict that no 'eponymous archon' was elected in 590/89 and again in 586/5. Furthermore a certain Damasias held onto this post for two years and two months (582/1; 581/0 and two months of 580/79), which must be seen as another attempt to set up a tyranny (Aristotle, *Ath. Pol.* 13.1–2). The decision, after the deposition of the Eupatrid Damasias, to share out the archonships between five Eupatridai, three 'agroikoi' (farmers) and two 'demiourgoi' (artisans) probably reflects a concession that was forced upon the Eupatridai by the politically ambitious non-Eupatrids, and shows that there was still tension among upper-class Athenians.

The extent of Solon's failure in his political reforms can be seen in the emergence of and rivalry between three powerful factions in the second quarter of the sixth century (575–550): 'The Men of the Coast' under the leadership of the Alcmaeonid Megacles; the 'Men of the Plain' under Lycurgus; and 'the Men of the Hills' (Aristotle, *Ath. Pol.* 13.4) or 'Men from beyond the Hills' under Peisistratus (Herodotus 1.59). This shows that the regional power-base of the aristocratic factions, supported by their dependants, was still untouched by Solon's measures. It was almost inevitable that political infighting between these factions would lead to civil unrest and eventually to tyranny. Solon tried desperately, but unsuccessfully, to warn the Athenians about approaching tyranny:

From a cloud there comes forth the strength of snow and hail, and from a bright flash of lightning there comes thunder. From powerful men comes the destruction of the city, and the people in their ignorance fall into slavery under one master. It is not easy later on to restrain a man, whom you have raised too far.

(Solon fr. 9 in *Diodorus* 9.20.2)

It was not until the tribal reforms of Cleisthenes in 508 (see Chapter 7) that the regional power of the aristocrats was finally and effectively destroyed, thus bringing the long-term political stability that Solon so desired to achieve.

Bibliography

Andrewes, A. *CAH vol. 3.3*, 2nd edn, ch. 43.
——*Greek Society*, ch. 6.
——*The Greek Tyrants*, ch. 7.
Finley, M. I. *Economy and Society in Ancient Greece*, ch. 9.
Moore, J. M. *Aristotle and Xenophon on Democracy and Oligarchy*, pt 2.
Murray, O. *Early Greece*, 2nd edn, ch. 11.
Rhodes, P. J. *A Commentary on the Aristotelian 'Athenaion Politeia'*.
Rihll, T. E. 'Hektemoroi: partners in crime?', *JHS* 111 (1991).
Stanton, G. R. *Athenian Politics c. 800–500* BC *A Sourcebook*, chs 2–3.

6

THE TYRANNY OF THE
PEISISTRATIDS AT ATHENS

The account of tyranny at Athens is covered in three stages by the literary sources – the rise of Peisistratus, his rule, and the downfall of the tyranny – but only Aristotle (or a pupil) in the *Ath. Pol.* covers all three. Herodotus concentrates on the first (1.59–64) and the third (5.55–61); and Thucydides briefly on the second (6.54.5–6) and more fully on the third (1.20.2; 6.53.3–59). The details and the nature of Peisistratus' rule are described in Aristotle's *Ath. Pol.* (16) and his *Politics* (1314a–1315b), but only in broad, general terms. However, although concrete facts are few in number, there is sufficient agreement among the sources that Peisistratus' tyranny was for the most part popular: he achieved the much-desired political stability at home by conciliating the upper class through diplomacy, and by winning the goodwill of the lower class by his economic policies.

The rise of Peisistratus

The one conspicuous failure of Solon's reforms, discussed in detail at the end of the previous chapter, was his inability to bring an end to the political unrest at Athens. The main cause of this was the conflict between the competing political factions and the personal rivalry of their aristocratic leaders. According to Aristotle, there were three major factions:

> One was the faction of the 'Men of the Coast' ('Paralioi') whose leader was Megacles, the son of Alcmaeon, and who seemed especially to be pursuing a middle type of constitution; another was that of the 'Men of the Plain' ('Pediakoi') who wanted the oligarchy and were led by Lycurgus; the third was the faction of the 'Hillmen' ('Diakrioi') over which had been appointed Peisistratus, as he seemed to be the most democratic.
>
> (Aristotle, *Ath. Pol.* 13.4)

Herodotus, much closer in time to these historical events and therefore more reliable, especially as Aristotle is clearly using (and even mentions) Herodotus as his source (*Ath. Pol.* 14.4), refers to Peisistratus' faction as the 'Men from beyond the Hills' ('Hyperakrioi'). This term is likely to be more accurate since Peisistratus' family home was at Brauron, on the east coast of Attica, and the main bulk of his supporters would have come from that region and the north-east.

Although Herodotus saw the geographical regions in Attica as the distinguishing feature of these three factions (1.59.3), Aristotle added political ideology as another. Aristotle's use of such political labels as 'middle', 'oligarchic' and 'democratic' is clearly anachronistic, and is more applicable to political conditions in the late fifth and early fourth centuries, but it is reasonable to believe that his description does reflect the basic attitudes of the three factions to Solon's reforms. The faction of the Alcmaeonid Megacles might well be viewed as 'middle' in its acceptance of Solon's legislation (or most of it), when compared to the other two factions that wished to alter it. The 'oligarchic' faction of Lycurgus, which represented the interests of the 'Eupatridai' (the Well-born) who possessed the best land in Attica and were among the richest, desired change through the abolition of Solon's reforms and a return to the pre-594 state of affairs. They resented his political reforms, which opened up the archonships (and membership of the aristocratic council, the 'Areopagus') to the non-nobles and which established the legal right of the lower and middle classes to attend the 'Ecclesia' (Assembly) and to serve as an appeal court ('Heliaea') in bringing public officials to account; and his economic reforms, which cancelled all debts and released the 'hectemoroi' from their obligation to hand over one-sixth of their produce to themselves (Aristotle, *Ath. Pol.* 13.3). The 'democratic' faction of Peisistratus probably represented the poorer farmers, including the former debt-bondsmen and hectemoroi, whose economic suffering had been removed only temporarily by the cancellation of debts, and consequently desired more radical reforms to ensure their long-term prosperity and the avoidance of debt in the future.

Nevertheless, the conflicting aims and aspirations of the supporters of the three factions were secondary; the primary cause of the political unrest was the personal ambition and rivalry of the aristocratic faction leaders in their struggle for political domination. Therefore Aristotle was right to concentrate on the post of 'eponymous archon' (chief archon) as the battleground for the competing aristocrats in the period after Solon's archonship:

> In the fifth year after Solon's archonship (590/89), they did not appoint an archon because of conflict between the factions; and again in the fifth year after this (586/5) the same thing happened for the same reason. After this same passage of time Damasias, having been chosen as archon, ruled for two years and two months until he was driven out of the archonship by force (582/1–580/79). ... Thus it is clear that the archon had the greatest power, for there always seemed to be factional conflict over this public office.
>
> (Aristotle, *Ath. Pol.* 13.1–2)

However, by the late 560s, Peisistratus had decided that he, as tyrant, offered the best hope of political stability for Athens (Herodotus 1.59.3).

The dating of Peisistratus' three attempts and periods of rule as tyrant of Athens has proved to be a thorny problem. The dates given by Aristotle in the *Ath. Pol.* are clearly wrong, and there are some inconsistencies in Herodotus' chronology; however, scholarly opinion has inclined towards the following dating. In *c*.561/0, Peisistratus made his first attempt to seize power by appearing in the main market-place in Athens, covered in self-inflicted wounds, and by claiming that he had been the subject of a murder attempt by his enemies. His request for a guard was granted by the Athenians on account of his distinguished war record, especially against Megara, and this enabled him to seize the Acropolis with their help:

> (59.6) Then Peisistratus ruled the Athenians, neither disturbing the existing public offices nor changing the laws; he governed the city in accordance with the constitution, administering it justly and effectively (60.1). Not long after this the factions of Megacles and Lycurgus united and drove him out.
>
> (Herodotus 1.59.6–60.1)

Either 560/59 or 559/8 would seem a reasonable date, after a short period of rule, for the end of Peisistratus' first stint as tyrant.

The political alliance between Megacles and Lycurgus soon collapsed, and the resultant pressure on Megacles led him to seek a pact with Peisistratus, offering his faction's support in a coup to make Peisistratus tyrant on condition that he married Megacles' daughter. After these terms were accepted, Peisistratus gained the tyranny in *c*.557/6 by the ruse of dressing up a stunningly beautiful six-foot woman in full armour; it was then claimed through messengers that she was Athene, the patron goddess of Athens, and that she herself in her chariot was delivering Peisistratus to her own Acropolis to take over the rule of Athens (Herodotus 1.60.2–5). In this way, Peisistratus became tyrant for the second time – much to the annoyance of Herodotus at the Athenians' gullibility. It would seem that Megacles was prepared to acquiesce in Peisistratus' tenure of power in the expectation that his own future grandson, the offspring of the marriage, would rule after Peisistratus' death. However, Peisistratus was determined that his grown-up sons from his previous marriage, Hippias and Hipparchus, should succeed him, and so he avoided normal sexual intercourse with Megacles' daughter to prevent conception. She kept silent about this at first, but later informed her mother. When she told Megacles, his anger at this insult to his daughter (and the impossibility of a future half-Alcmaeonid tyrant) persuaded him to bury his differences with Lycurgus and to renew their political alliance. Faced with the combined forces of these two factions, Peisistratus chose exile, possibly *c*.556/5, as Megacles' daughter was unlikely to have kept her unusual marriage arrangements from her mother for long (Herodotus 1.61.1–2).

This second failure taught Peisistratus a valuable lesson: the impossibility of seizing and holding onto the tyranny at Athens by conventional means, namely by relying on the strength of his faction and an alliance with the 'Men of the Shore'. His ambition would always be thwarted by the superior combined might of the two other factions which, owing to the unreliability of the Alcmaeonid-led 'Men of the Shore', would inevitably unite against him at some other time in the future. Therefore he realized that he needed to augment the power of his faction by acquiring troops and by forming alliances outside Attica, but that this would take time and money. During the following eleven years, Peisistratus gained considerable wealth from his involvement in the gold mines and silver mines around Mount Pangaion, near the river Strymon in Thrace (Aristotle, *Ath. Pol.* 15.2), and also won the support of powerful allies:

> He went to the area around Pangaion where he enriched himself and hired mercenaries and, coming again to Eretria in the eleventh year [i.e. after his second failure], he attempted for the first time to recover his power by force, aided enthusiastically by many others, in particular the Thebans, Lygdamis of Naxos and also the 'Hippeis' ('Knights') who had control over the government of Eretria. After winning the battle at Pallene, he captured the city and deprived the people of their weapons. He now established his tyranny on a secure footing and, taking the island of Naxos, he set up Lygdamis as ruler.
>
> (Aristotle, *Ath. Pol.* 15.2)

The mercenaries also included Argives from the Peloponnese, and the forces of Lygdamis who proved to be particularly useful to Peisistratus' cause (Herodotus 1.61.4). It is clear from the subsequent events in Naxos that a pact of mutual aid had been agreed between Peisistratus and Lygdamis.

The rule of the Peisistratids

Peisistratus ruled from c.547/6 until his death in 528/7, in which time he maintained his hold on power by a mixture of force, diplomacy in his dealings with the aristocracy and supportive policies for the poor. The forces that he had gathered by the time of the battle of Pallene were overwhelmingly superior to those of his aristocratic opponents. A number of his enemies were killed in the ensuing battle, and those of the survivors who refused to accept Peisistratus' rule departed into exile with the Alcmaeonids (Herodotus 1.64.3). Thus the immediate threat of his most irreconcilable enemies had been removed. Furthermore, in order to ensure the good behaviour of those aristocrats who were prepared to stay in Athens and collaborate with his regime, he took their children as hostages and gave them into the safekeeping of Lygdamis, the tyrant of Naxos (Herodotus 1.64.1). Finally, the disarming of the people and the retention of a force of mercenaries, paid for by tax revenues and by his income from his business interests in Thrace, provided him with the military means to enforce his will, if required.

However, Peisistratus was well aware that a repressive regime, based mainly on armed force, would provoke a violent reaction from the aristocracy and the people, and therefore pursued a liberal policy:

> For in all matters he was willing to conduct all the affairs of state in accordance with the laws, granting himself no special privilege ... and for these reasons he remained in power for a long time and, when he was deposed [i.e. before 546], he easily recovered power. For the majority of the notables and of the people favoured him, since he won over the former by diplomacy and the latter by his help in their private affairs; he was popular with both.
>
> (Aristotle, *Ath. Pol.* 16.8–9)

By not flaunting his power, Peisistratus avoided alienating the aristocrats; and by allowing them to retain their status and prestige he persuaded them to collaborate with his regime.

There is no better evidence of this than the fragment that is believed to belong to the list of eponymous archons (chief archons) which was set up in c.425 (see Table 6.1 below).

[On]eto[rides]	(527/6)
[H]ippia[s]	(526/5)
[C]leisthen[es]	(525/4)
[M]iltiades	(524/3)
[Ka]lliades	(523/2)
[Peis]istratos	(522/1)

Source: ML 6.fr.c

Thucydides (6.54.6) states that the sons of Peisistratus ensured that one of their number always held office, which must mean one of their family or political supporters; this presumably was a continuation of their father's policy. [On]eto[rides] had probably been nominated by Peisistratus before his death, and thus was allowed to hold the post of eponymous archon (chief archon). In the following year, Hippias made sure that he held office to establish his position as his father's successor as tyrant. It is the next two names that reveal the extent of the collaboration between the Peisistratids and the aristocrats. [C]leisthen[es] was the son and successor of Megacles, the Alcmaeonid leader of the 'Men from the Shore', who had fled into exile in 546 after the battle of Pallene. Herodotus (1.64.3; 6.123.1) gives the impression – based most probably on information supplied by the Alc-maeonids – that the Alcmaeonids had stayed in exile for the whole period of the tyranny, but this inscription reveals that a rapprochement between the families had taken place. In the same way, Miltiades, son of Cimon, of the distinguished Philaid family, is revealed as a collaborator. His father had also been exiled, but his dedication of his second Olympic victory, possibly in 532, to Peisistratus (Herodotus 6.103) paved the way for the recall of himself and his family.

Peisistratus showed his astuteness with regard to the aristocrats by allowing Solon's constitution to operate almost normally, or rather, almost as Solon had intended for the first time:

> Peisistratus, as was said before [i.e. 14.3], administered the state in a moderate manner and more constitutionally than as a tyrant.
>
> (Aristotle, *Ath. Pol.* 16.2)

Thus it is reasonable to believe that the archons, the Areopagus, the Ecclesia and the Boule of 400 carried out their functions, as laid down by Solon, with minimum direct interference by Peisistratus. This appearance of normality would also appeal to the aristocrats since their dignity and prestige would be publicly recognized, especially in their tenure of the archonship and membership of the Areopagus, although in reality their political power was severely curtailed. This policy of non-interference on the part of the tyrants is confirmed by Thucydides:

> These tyrants for the most part showed virtue and intelligence in their policy … and in other respects the city used the laws that had been previously enacted, except in so far as they always made sure that one of their own was among the public officials.
>
> (Thucydides 6.54.5–6)

It is clear that Hippias and Hipparchus, Peisistratus' sons, about whom Thucydides was commenting, were pursuing their father's moderate policy. There is no direct evidence that Peisistratus even confiscated the land of his exiled enemies; in fact, it is known that the property of Cimon, father of Miltiades, was left untouched during his exile (Herodotus 6.103.3), perhaps as an inducement to encourage his opponents to return. The fact that Cimon of the Philaids and Cleisthenes of the Alcmaeonids, two of the most distinguished aristocratic families in Athenian politics, and presumably other families who were politically aligned to them, returned to Athens under the Peisistratids is a testimony to the success of this policy of diplomacy and reconciliation.

The third element that was fundamental to the maintenance of Peisistratus' rule was his supportive policies for the poor:

> Moreover he lent money to the poor for their husbandry so that they might make a living from farming. He did this for two reasons: firstly, so that they did not spend

their time in the city, but would be scattered throughout the countryside; secondly, so that they would be reasonably well off and involved in their own private affairs, and consequently would neither want nor have the time to attend to public affairs. At the same time, the cultivation of the land increased the revenues, since he imposed a tax of 10 per cent ('decate') on the produce from the land.

(Aristotle, *Ath. Pol.* 61.2–4)

Solon's cancellation of debts and his ending of hectemoroi status (see Chapter 5) had only given temporary economic relief to the poor farmers, but he had done virtually nothing to provide the means to improve their financial position and thus avoid falling into debt again. Peisistratus improved upon Solon's economic reforms by lending money to the poor farmers, which provided them with positive help in a number of ways: either to invest in their land, thus increasing its agricultural output; or to support themselves in the interim period while they changed over from cereal farming to the cultivation of olives and vines; or to tide others over until the rise of employment opportunities in industry allowed them to switch from farming, for his tax on agricultural produce encouraged those with capital to diversify and invest in industry. By the fifth century, Athens had a widespread class of successful small farmers, and much of the credit for this belongs to Peisistratus.

Aristotle, revealing his pro-aristocratic bias, stresses the political motives for the tyrant's generous loans to the poor, which may have played a part in the formulation of this policy, although his motives look anachronistic, i.e. post-democratic; but the attainment of economic security by the formerly impoverished farmers was a far more important motive for the tyrant, since their resultant gratitude was a more secure way of retaining their loyalty. There is a story that on one occasion, in his many tours of Attica during which he constantly reviewed and resolved disputes, he saw a farmer struggling to cultivate a very stony patch of land. When Peisistratus asked his attendant to find out what the land produced, the farmer replied bitterly 'aches and pains' and went on to complain about the tyrant's 10 per cent tax on his meagre produce; Peisistratus immediately exempted him from all taxes (Aristotle, *Ath. Pol.* 16.6). The authenticity of this particular story may be doubted, but not Peisistratus' frequent tours of inspection around Attica which reveal his concern for the welfare of the poor. The 10 per cent tax, not very demanding in its own right, was in fact probably only a 5 per cent tax, as it was under the rule of Peisistratus' sons (Thucydides 6.54.5), since the Greek word 'decate' was probably the traditional word for any 'tax'. Furthermore, in order to improve the quality of life of the lower classes, he introduced local judges so that the administration of law would be removed from the local aristocrats, thus ensuring justice for the poor and emphasizing the superior position of the state over the aristocrats (Aristotle, *Ath. Pol.* 16.5).

The foreign policy of Peisistratus and his sons also indirectly helped Athenian prosperity: peaceful foreign relations created a favourable economic climate in which Athenians could take full advantage of the export markets:

> In general Peisistratus gave the people no trouble during his rule, but always maintained peace at home and abroad; as a result the tyranny of Peisistratus was often called the age of Cronus [i.e. 'a Golden Age'].
>
> (Aristotle, *Ath. Pol.* 16.7)

Peisistratus, unlike some other tyrants such as Cleisthenes of Sicyon (see Chapter 3), did not rely on an aggressive foreign policy to unite the people behind his rule. He had already acquired allies in Greece during the period after his second exile from Athens, namely Eretria, Thebes, Argos and Naxos; and during his tyranny an alliance was probably made with powerful Thessaly, strongly suggested by the name of his third son, Thessalos. At some point an alliance was also made with the Spartans, as revealed in the speech of Cleomenes, King of Sparta, when he was attempting to persuade his Peloponnesian allies to reinstate Hippias as tyrant of Athens (Herodotus 5.91), although this may have been formed during Hippias' rule. It would seem that Peisistratus in general preferred to secure peace by forging diplomatic links with foreign powers; but this did not prevent him from using force, when he thought that it was in Athens' or his own interests. This dual policy of diplomacy and force proved to be very effective in foreign affairs.

One of the first acts of his rule was to attack Naxos and install Lygdamis, his ally, as tyrant (Aristotle, *Ath. Pol.* 15.3). Athens' position in the Aegean and prestige among the Ionian states were further strengthened by Peisistratus' religious purification of the island of Delos (Herodotus 1.64.2) – Delos was the venue of an Ionian festival of athletics, poetry and music, in which the cities of Ionia, the islands and Athens participated (Thucydides 3.104). Sigeum, which occupied an important geographical position on the Ionian mainland close to the Hellespont, was recovered by force from Mytilene by Peisistratus who installed a son, Hegistratus, as ruler (Herodotus 5.91.5). In addition, Miltiades became the ruler of the Dolonci in the Chersonese, the peninsula on the western side of the Hellespont. Although Herodotus states that dissatisfaction with the rule of Peisistratus was an important motive for Miltiades' acceptance of the invitation of the Dolonci (6.34–35.3), it is far more likely this colony was founded with the full approval of Peisistratus, since colonists could not be removed from Athens without his consent and its important strategic position near the Hellespont, complementing Sigeum on the opposite eastern side, would have been welcomed by the tyrant. Thus a combination of peaceful relations with foreign powers and of political stability at home provided the basis for a widespread improvement in the standard of living of the Athenians during the second half of the sixth century.

The buildings and religious festivals of the Peisistratids

It is surprising that Aristotle in the *Ath. Pol.* makes no mention of the two lasting achievements of the Peisistratids: the programme of public works which also provided employment for the poorer citizens; and the encouragement of religious festivals and the patronage of the arts which emphasized the unity of Attica by reducing the importance of local cults and by focusing attention on Athens as the social, religious and cultural (as well as the political) centre of the Athenian state.

The buildings

The Peisistratids presided over the most substantial building programme in archaic Athens. However, it is difficult to establish from the architectural remains and from the uncertainty of dating by artistic style at what date the major buildings were begun or finished, and thus whether some of the building projects were begun before the tyranny or, of those that were undertaken during the tyranny, whether they should be credited to Peisistratus or to his sons. The problem is further compounded by Peisistratus' two periods of tyranny and of exile in the middle of the sixth century before he finally secured power for himself and his sons from 547/6 to 511/0. These limits on our knowledge should be borne in mind in the discussion that follows.

Although there is scholarly disagreement about the amount of building construction undertaken on the Acropolis during the tyranny and the last decade of the century, the majority of scholars hold the view that Peisistratus and his sons should receive all the credit for the sixth-century Acropolis buildings, especially as the funding of religious buildings was an effective political manoeuvre; the rebuilding of the Temple of Apollo at Delphi by the Alcmaeonids is a good example of this (see the end of this chapter). The most prestigious building was the old temple of Athena Polias, whose surviving stone rectangles on the north side of the Acropolis are known as the Dorpfeld foundations. Some scholars argue that these foundations were first laid *c.*525 when the sons of Peisistratus authorized the construction of this temple; others argue that these foundations were laid in the first half of the sixth century (599–550) for an earlier temple, which was rebuilt in the last quarter of the sixth century (525–500) on the same foundations.

The dating by most scholars of the surviving pedimental sculptures – the lions, Heracles and Triton, and Bluebeard (Hurwit, pp. 240–41) – to the 560s, combined with other religious and political events of that time, provides more convincing evidence for the earlier date. The beginning of the construction of a temple dedicated to Athena in the 560s would fit in with the introduction (or the major development) in 566 of the most important religious festival in the Athenian calendar, the Great Panathenaea, which honoured Athena as the patron goddess of Athens and emphasized the unity of the state (see next section). The 560s also saw the rise of Peisistratus as an influential political leader, who took particular care to identify himself publicly with Athena, even going so far as to claim that the goddess herself was escorting him to power in his second attempt to become tyrant (see above). Therefore it is possible that, after the decision was taken (with the probable backing of Peisistratus) to build the temple and the foundations were laid in the 560s, the political troubles of Peisistratus in the 550s slowed down its construction, and that the temple, complete with its pedimental sculptures, was not finally completed until after Peisistratus' third and final seizure of power in 547/6 – if this was the case, then this temple was renovated by his sons c.525. The other buildings on the Acropolis, which were almost certainly constructed under Peisistratus' direction, were the cult temple of Artemis of Brauron, his home district on east coast of Attica, and the first small treasury-style buildings ('oikemata').

The Agora also began to take shape under Peisistratus as the civic centre of Athens with the removal of houses and the abandonment of wells. Towards the south-west corner a large building was erected, known as Building F and dated c.550–525. It consisted of a central courtyard which was surrounded by a number of rooms on three sides. This large and imposing structure gives the impression of being both a private residence, although it is too big to be an ordinary private house, and an official public building: thus it is believed to have been the 'palace' of Peisistratus. This would be in accord with his desire to make the Athenian Agora, together with the Acropolis, the political, social and cultural centre of Attica. Two shrines were also built on the west side of the Agora in honour of Zeus Agoraios and Apollo Patroos. If their construction was intended to symbolize the union of the state, then this is further evidence of Peisistratus' deliberate policy of using religious cults to focus people's minds on Athens as the centre of a unified state (see below, Religious festivals).

The Royal Stoa, from where most of the state cults and the law courts were administered, was possibly constructed at this time on the west side. But the most ambitious project of all was the erection of the Olympieion, a temple dedicated to Olympian Zeus who was Athena's father. This was the largest temple to be attempted in Greece up to that time and, according to Aristotle (*Politics* 1313b), was begun by the Peisistratids. The undertaking was so immense that not even his sons, who some scholars believe were responsible for the project, completed its construction; this was left to the Roman emperor Hadrian c.AD 132. Peisistratus also built a temple on the eastern side of Mount Hymettos, and added a colonnade to the temple of Athena at Cape Sunium.

Peisistratus' ambitious building programme was continued by his sons and grandson:

> They [i.e. Hippias and Hipparchus] adorned their city beautifully, brought their wars to a successful conclusion, and offered sacrifices at the sanctuaries.
>
> (Thucydides 6.54.5)

They either initiated the building of the temple of Athena Polias or authorized its renovation. The original outer colonnade was replaced by a new and higher one, and the superstructure was also completely renewed. Furthermore, not only was the new so-called east pediment free-standing and executed in marble, unlike the other older pediment, sculpted in relief and executed in limestone, but also there was a dramatic new theme, namely the Gigantomachy, i.e. the battle between the giants and the gods for supremacy. Athena was given the dominant position in the pediment which shows that Peisistratus' sons were continuing his policy of emphasis on Athena and Athens. The old Propylon, the entrance to a temple, may also have been built around the same time, since it faces the temple of Athena Polias and not the Older Parthenon, whose construction was begun after the battle of Marathon in 490.

The Peisistratids also set their minds to improving the infrastructure of Athens. Hipparchus is credited with improving communications throughout Attica by setting up 'hermai' (images of Hermes, the patron god of travellers) to act as milestones on the roads (Plato, *Hipparchus* 228d). Peisistratus, the tyrant's grandson and son of Hippias, also dedicated an altar of the Twelve Gods, from which all distances from Athens were marked; it has been located archaeologically on the north side of the Agora. He was also responsible for the building of an altar of Apollo in the sanctuary of Pythian Apollo, which bore an inscription recording his dedication (Thucydides 6.54.6–7). The accuracy of Thucydides' quotation has been confirmed by the discovery of two fragments in 1877:

> This memorial of his archonship Peisist[ratos s]on [of Hippias] dedicated in the precinct of Pyth[i]an Apollo.
>
> (ML 11)

The position of the two fragments in the south-east of the city marked the location of the sanctuary of Pythian Apollo.

The sons of Peisistratus also undertook a major improvement of Athens' water supply. Two pipelines, carrying water from the hills east of Athens, were laid c.520 to run along the north and south slope of the Acropolis. The northern pipeline ended at a very large fountain-house, known as the

'Enneakrounos' ('the Nine Spouts'); and the southern one ended at another fountain-house in a residential area south-west of the Areopagus. The popularity and frequency of use of these fountain-houses are attested by their inclusion on numerous late sixth-century vases. At Eleusis, they rebuilt the 'Telesterion' (the Hall of the Mysteries) on a larger scale, and strengthened the walls of the sanctuary. This sanctuary at Eleusis was one of the most important in Attica, and its growing popularity and the increased attendance at the ceremonies during the sixth century provided a practical reason for building the larger hall. However, this building work was also motivated by a desire to compete externally with other pan-Hellenic sanctuaries and internally with the local cults throughout Attica: the celebration of the Great Mysteries stressed the unity of Attica, symbolically demonstrated by the annual pilgrimages from Athens which were attended by large numbers of Athenians (see below).

Religious festivals

Peisistratus deliberately encouraged the growth of national cults and festivals at the expense of local ones, which were dominated by the aristocrats who were his real or potential enemies. His purpose was to develop within the Athenians a sense of national identity, centred on Athena and Athens, and also to increase the prestige of the Peisistratids, domiciled at Athens, and thereby consolidate their power.

The most important of these religious festivals was the Great Panathenaea in honour of Athena, the patron goddess of Athens. There had probably been an older, simpler cult, but in 566/5 it was reorganized to consist of the Great Panathenaea in every fourth year, and a minor festival in each of the three intervening years. According to Pherecydes, who wrote a genealogy of the aristocratic family of the Philaids, the festival of the Panathenaea was founded by the Philaid Hippocleides who was eponymous archon (chief archon) at the time (FGrH 3.F.2). Eusebius, a Christian writer of the third century AD, dates the introduction of athletic contests into the Panathenaea to 566 or 565, and thus it is reasonable to believe that a major reorganization of this cult took place in Hippocleides' archonship of 566/56. It consisted of singing and dancing on the Acropolis during the night, followed by an early morning procession to the Acropolis, a sacrifice and a feast. There were also athletic and equestrian games, to which all Greek athletes were invited to compete, and very possibly singing and musical contests were introduced at this time (certainly by the time of Hipparchus).

Further evidence to support the mid-560s as the date for the reorganization of the Panathenaea comes from events elsewhere in Greece and from the political situation in Athens. Three new contests of four-yearly games, on the model of the Olympic Games, had been founded just before the Great Panathenaea: the Pythian Games at Delphi (582), the Isthmian (581) and the Nemean (573). Athens' increasing prosperity and awareness of its own self-importance were likely to act as a spur to compete as quickly as possible with these international rivals. The black-figure Panathenaic vases filled with oil from the 'sacred' olive trees, which were commissioned by the state to be awarded to the victors at the games, can be dated stylistically to this time. This is also the decade when Peisistratus was establishing himself as a major politician in the eyes of the Athenians. His ultimate aim was to become tyrant, which he attempted for the first time in 561/0, and thus he needed to maintain a high profile to win the people's goodwill. His carefully contrived association of himself with Athena and his likely public support for the construction of the temple of Athena Polias have been discussed above. In this context, it seems very significant that Hippocleides was from the Philaid family, whose centre of power was Brauron, Peisistratus' home district, and who were probably his political allies in the 560s (as they were his sons' in the 520s). Thus it can be believed that Peisistratus played a significant role in the reorganization of the Panathenaea and increased its importance during his tyranny.

The introduction and development of the City Dionysia as a national cult are not directly linked to Peisistratus by any primary source, but the fact that its growth in importance takes place during his tyranny strongly suggests his political support for and active promotion of the cult. This festival celebrated the transfer to Athens of the cult of Dionysus Eleuthereus from Eleutherae, a town on the border of Attica and Boeotia. Pausanias (1.38.8) stated that the transfer coincided with the inhabitants of Eleutherae becoming citizens of the Athenian state in order to escape from the Boeotians whom they loathed; thus political motives on the part of Peisistratus can be discerned, as well as religious reasons, for the transference of the cult. In the fifth century, the festival followed a set procedure: a couple of days before the Dionysia, the old wooden image of Dionysus was moved from its sanctuary at the foot of the Acropolis to the Academy which was situated outside the walls on the road to Boeotia; it was then brought back to its shrine in a procession just before the commencement of the main festival to commemorate its original journey; on the opening day of the festival there was a magnificent procession, escorting the bulls which were destined to be sacrificed at the altar of Dionysus' sanctuary; after the sacrifice there was much feasting and drinking; in the evening there took place the communal revelry ('komos') which consisted of men dancing and singing in the streets to the accompaniment of flutes and harps; the following three to five days were given over to the performances of tragedies and comedies, and the final judgement of the best dramatists, actors and 'choregoi' (impresarios). The core elements of the City Dionysia were the main procession, the sacrifice and feasting, and the revel (komos) in the evening, and it seems reasonable to believe these were present in the original Peisistratid festival.

113

However, there is also a link between Peisistratus and the fifth-century performances of tragedies, comedies and dithyrambs (which were songs, sung by choruses of 50 men and 50 boys, in honour of Dionysus). It is known that choral singing and dancing were common to the earliest worship of Dionysus, not only in Attica but also in Sicyon on the north coast of the Peloponnese, and probably in other parts of Greece; and it is probably from this root that the choral contests and fifth-century dramatic performances developed. Even more significant for Peisistratus is the tradition that the first performance of tragedy was undertaken by Thespis, which is recorded on the *Marmor Parium*, although the date is badly mutilated; but the *Suda*, a tenth-century AD lexicon or literary encyclopaedia, dates this event under its entry for 'Thespis' to the Olympiad 536–532, and it has been plausibly suggested that 534/3 was the actual year, six years before Peisistratus' death. Once again, the political shrewdness of Peisistratus can be observed in his active support of a national festival, which offered pageantry and entertainment in Athens to all Athenians, thus enhancing his regime's popularity. It is also worthy of note that this festival was not under the control of the 'basileus' (king-archon), the religious leader of the state, but of the eponymous archon (chief archon), whose election was controlled by the Peisistratids (see above) and who was thus subject to their political direction. Peisistratus was unlikely to have foreseen the brilliant achievements of fifth-century Athenian drama, but his patronage of the arts had provided its stimulus.

The third religious festival that bears the hallmark of Peisistratus is the Olympieia in honour of Olympian Zeus. He is believed to have instituted this festival in the second half of the sixth century as one of two means to honour Olympian Zeus; the other was the authorization of the building of the Olympieion, the largest temple of its time in the Greek mainland (see above). The date of the festival probably commemorates the anniversary of the temple's foundation, and probably consisted of the cavalry displaying skilled feats of horsemanship. Thus the celebration of public festivals with their many attendant artistic performances and the huge programme of public works were the Peisistratids' greatest achievements, for they provided an inspiration and a lasting contribution to Athens' future greatness.

The fall of the tyranny

It is clear from the primary sources that there were conflicting traditions about whether Hippias or Hipparchus was Peisistratus' successor in 528/7 and about the overthrow of the tyranny. One tradition praises the Alcmaeonids for organizing the resistance to Hippias and for helping to bring about the fall of the tyranny in 511/0. The other tradition gives the glory for ending the tyranny to the 'Tyrannicides' Harmodius and Aristogeiton, who assassinated Hipparchus at the festival of the Great Panathenaea in 514/3.

The fundamental factor in this second version is the view that Hipparchus, not Hippias, was the ruling tyrant. It also conveniently ignores the issue that the tyranny continued for another three to four years under Hippias until his expulsion in 511/0; the compiler of the Marmor Parium, a third-century inscription, even goes so far as to date the assassination of Hipparchus to 511/0. This disagreement about the effective ending of the tyranny – whether it was Hipparchus' assassination or Hippias' expulsion – and consequently about the real 'heroes' probably reflects the propaganda of the opposing political factions, especially the second version, whose objective seems to be the devaluation of the achievements of the Alcmaeonids by highlighting the fame of Harmodius and Aristogeiton.

This second version gained increasing acceptance in the fifth century to the extent that there were annual sacrifices to the Tyrannicides as heroes by the 'polemarch' on behalf of the state (Aristotle, *Ath. Pol.* 58.1), and their descendants were maintained at public expense (IG I3 131). It was Thucydides' desire to correct this (in his opinion) mistaken tradition that led him to write a digression on the fall of the Peisistratids (6.53–59) that has little to do with the main theme of that book; and the scathing tone of his digression reveals his annoyance that the second version, probably stated by the respected Atthidographer (see Glossary), Hellanicus of Lesbos, had been generally accepted by the Athenians. He stresses adamantly that Hippias was the eldest of all Peisistratus' sons and thus was his successor as tyrant (6.54.2) with which point of view Herodotus agrees (5.55.1). Aristotle, on the other hand, was the first source to put forward a compromise between the conflicting accounts by suggesting a joint rule by the sons, but even he admits that Hippias was the elder and was effectively in charge of ruling Athens (*Ath. Pol.* 18.2). However, there is good reason to believe that the existence and widespread acceptance of these two differing accounts were due to the Athenians' desire to overlook one very unpalatable fact: the lion's share of the praise for the overthrow of the tyranny at Athens belonged to the Spartans (see below).

Nevertheless there is agreement between the three main literary sources that the tyranny became harsher after the murder of Hipparchus – Aristotle, *Ath. Pol.* 19, Herodotus 5.62.2 and Thucydides:

> Hippias, now more fearful, killed many of the citizens and at the same time began to look outside Athens for a place where he might obtain safe refuge in the event of revolution.
>
> (Thucydides 6.59.2)

The fullest account of the last years of the tyranny is given in Herodotus (5.62–65). Although in error with his claim that the Alcmaeonids had been in continuous exile throughout the tyranny of the Peisistratids (see above), he is right that the focus of resistance to the tyranny was the Alcmaeonids, who must have been exiled again at some time after Cleisthenes' archonship in 525/4. Philochorus, a third-century Atthidographer, states that they were exiled by the sons and not by Peisistratus himself (FGrH 3B 328 F115), and the ruthlessness of Hippias' rule and the fearful distrust of his real or imagined enemies after his brother's assassination may well have been the political setting for their exile.

The Alcmaeonids and other exiled families, possibly in 513, made an attempt to free Athens from tyranny by force; they seized a fort at Leipsydrion in north Attica, but were heavily defeated by Hippias. They therefore decided to gain the support of the Spartans, which they did with the help of the Delphic oracle. Having undertaken the contract to rebuild the temple at Delphi, which had been burnt down in 548/7, they earned the goodwill of the oracle by using marble on its front, rather than the limestone as agreed in the contract. As a result, every Spartan consultation of the oracle met with the command from the priestess to free Athens. The first attempt by the Spartans under Anchimolios in 512/1 ended in failure due to the superiority of the Thessalian cavalry which had been summoned by Hippias in accordance with their alliance. Finally the Spartans sent a larger force under King Cleomenes which this time defeated the Thessalian cavalry and besieged Hippias and his supporters inside the Acropolis. The siege was brought to an end by the capture of the Peisistratids' sons, as they attempted to escape to safety; in exchange for the safe return of the children, Hippias agreed to leave Athens within five days. Thus ended the Peisistratid tyranny at Athens, but it would not be the last time that either Hippias or Cleomenes set foot on Attic soil.

Bibliography

Andrewes, A. *The Greek Tyrants*, ch. 9.
——CAH vol. 3.3, 2nd edn, ch. 44.
Boersma, J. S. *Athenian Building Policy from 561/0 to 405/4*, chs 2 and 3.
Forrest, W. G. *The Emergence of Greek Democracy*, ch. 7.
Hurwit, J. M. *The Art and Culture of Early Greece*, ch. 5.
Lewis, D. M. *CAH vol. 4*, 2nd edn, ch. 4.
Moore, J. M. *Aristotle and Xenophon on Democracy and Oligarchy*, pp. 227–35.
Murray, O. *Early Greece*, 2nd edn, ch. 15.
Parke, H. W. *Festivals of the Athenians*, pt 1.
Rhodes, P. J. *Commentary on the Aristotelian 'Athenaion Politeia'*, pp. 189–240.
Stanton, G. R. *Athenian Politics c. 800–500 BC A Sourcebook*, chs 3 and 4.

7

THE REFORMS OF CLEISTHENES
AND THE DEVELOPMENT OF
ATHENIAN DEMOCRACY

The sources

There are no contemporary literary sources for the reforms of Cleisthenes. Herodotus was writing about sixty to seventy years after the affair, and his history only displays a passing interest in the constitutional reforms, concentrating more on the historical narrative of events (5.66, 5.69–73.1). Aristotle's (or his pupil's) *Ath. Pol.* was written in the third quarter of the fourth century (349–325), and covers not only the historical narrative (*Ath. Pol.* 20.1–3) but also Cleisthenes' reforms in some detail (*Ath. Pol.* 21–2). The first part of Aristotle's account, describing the political rivalry of Cleisthenes and Isagoras, the intervention of the Spartan King Cleomenes in Athens and the final success of Cleisthenes, is a summary of Herodotus, and is clearly based upon his work. However, the second part that deals with the constitutional reforms contains details that are present in no other existing source, and it seems probable that his information comes from one of the fourth-century Atthidographers who wrote histories (usually biased) of Athens. The reference to the law on ostracism (*Ath. Pol.* 22) is certainly based on Androtion, an Atthidographer, and the summary of other important events in the same chapter, listed in annalistic fashion under archon-years, points again to an Atthidographer as Aristotle's source. It is reasonable to believe, therefore, that Androtion was the main source for the whole of Chapter 22 and probably for the reforms in Chapter 21.

The political background to the reforms, 511/0–507/6

It appears that there were no immediate political problems after the expulsion of Hippias the tyrant probably owing to the fact that the Peisistratids had virtually left Solon's constitution intact, apart from ensuring their control over the archonship (Thucydides 6.54.6). However, within a few years there was a serious political clash between two aristocratic-led factions, one under the leadership of the Alcmaeonid Cleisthenes and the other under Isagoras.

There is no way of knowing how many other powerful families were involved on either side or if there were other factions; but these two were certainly the dominant political forces at the time. Their struggle over the archonship – presumably the ex-archon Cleisthenes wished to prevent Isagoras' election – and therefore membership of the Areopagus, the powerful aristocratic council, is reminiscent of the rivalry and in-fighting between the aristocratic leaders and their factions in the first half of the sixth century (599–550): clearly both Cleisthenes and Isagoras regarded the post-tyranny situation as an opportunity to return to the normal pre-tyranny style of politics. This view is reinforced by the fact that there is no mention of a conflict of political principle between the two leaders, and that both the main sources state or strongly imply that they were aided by their 'hetairoi' (aristocratic supporters). Therefore the initial clash was an old-fashioned power struggle between two ambitious faction leaders in which conflicting ideologies about the nature of the constitution played no part.

The spark that ignited all the troubles was the election of Isagoras to the office of eponymous (chief) archon for 508/7 at the expense of the favoured candidate of Cleisthenes and his faction. At this point Cleisthenes adopted a new approach to strengthen his political power-base. The tyrants had already shown that the common people were a valuable political asset in any struggle for power, and Cleisthenes decided to follow their example:

> These men [i.e. Cleisthenes and Isagoras] were striving with their factions for power; and when Cleisthenes was getting the worst of it, he added the people to his faction (66.2). ... For when he had added the people of Athens, whom he had previously ignored, to his faction, he changed the names of the tribes and increased their number. He created ten 'phylarchs' (tribal leaders) instead of four, and distributed the demes among the tribes. By winning over the people he became much stronger than the rival faction (69.2).
>
> (Herodotus 5.66.2, 69.2)

Herodotus clearly held the view that political opportunism was the dominant motive behind Cleisthenes' courting of the Athenian people, but he fails to explain how Cleisthenes won over the people and how he used them against Isagoras.

The broad answer to the first question – concerning the means employed by Cleisthenes to win the support of the people – probably lies in Aristotle:

> Cleisthenes brought over the people to his side by handing over the control of the state to the common people ('plethos').
>
> (Aristotle, *Ath. Pol.* 20.2)

Cleisthenes was unlikely to have given a detailed explanation of his proposed tribal reforms which would have been very hard for the ordinary Athenian to understand due to their complexity. Therefore he probably stressed the main principle or the essence of his reforms: that in future all major political decisions would be made by the ordinary people in the Ecclesia (Assembly). He probably also said enough about the beneficial effects of the tribal reforms for those who had been recently disfranchised (see below), and thus won their backing for his proposals by raising their hopes of regaining their Athenian citizenship. The answer to the second question is more difficult; it is possible that he put the motion as a private citizen before the Ecclesia or, more probably, he enlisted the support of the 'Boule of 400' (Council of 400) whose function was to prepare motions for decision by the Ecclesia.

These proposed reforms were put before the Ecclesia shortly before or just after the election of Alcmaeon to the archonship of 507/6 – obviously from his name a kinsman of the Alcmaeonid Cleisthenes. The success of Cleisthenes' democratic legislation and the election of his political enemy's protégé to the top post proved to be too much for Isagoras – he called in King Cleomenes of Sparta.

Cleisthenes departed from Athens before Cleomenes arrived in Athens with a small force and expelled seven hundred families, picked out by Isagoras. However, Cleomenes' next move proved to be unwise:

> He then tried to dissolve the Council (boule) and entrusted the offices of state to 300 of Isagoras' faction. When the Council resisted him and was not willing to obey his orders, Cleomenes and Isagoras together with his political supporters seized the Acropolis. But the Athenians united and besieged them for two days; on the third day all those who were Spartans departed from the country under a truce.
>
> (Herodotus 5.72.1–2)

Herodotus does not make it clear whether it was the aristocratic council, the Areopagus, or the Boule of 400 that Cleomenes attempted to dissolve. The Areopagus was a very prestigious institution owing to its venerable age and the prestige of its members, and its dissolution would have been a radical step. In addition, it probably contained many members who, like Isagoras, had acquiesced in the regime of the Peisistratids, and supported or belonged to Isagoras' faction. The Boule of 400 seems a far more likely candidate for dissolution, especially if it put the motion for democratic reform to the Ecclesia (Assembly) on behalf of Cleisthenes. The surrender and departure of the Spartans and Isagoras from Athens led to the return of Cleisthenes and the 700 families from exile, to the archonship of Alcmaeon in 507/6 and to the implementation of the reform programme.

The motives of Cleisthenes

Scholarly opinion is divided about the motives that inspired Cleisthenes to pass his reforms, ranging from self-serving opportunism to high-minded altruism, with emphasis on one aspect of the reforms at the expense of others to support the respective viewpoint. However, a politician's motives are rarely simple, even when they can be deduced with reasonable accuracy, and are more likely to reflect a combination of self-interest and public-spiritedness; and this appears to be the case in respect to Cleisthenes.

Herodotus stated that Cleisthenes only added the previously ignored people to his faction when Isagoras was getting the better of him (5.69.2), and in this context a certain degree of opportunism can be suspected in his response to the problem of the new citizens. A revision of the citizen lists had taken place soon after the expulsion of Hippias and was aimed at those of impure Athenian descent who had previously looked to Peisistratus as their protector:

> Peisistratus was joined ... by those who were afraid because they were not of pure descent. Proof of this comes from the fact that, after the expulsion of the tyrants, a revision of the lists of citizens (diapsephismos) was conducted on the grounds that many possessed citizenship who were not entitled to it.
>
> (Aristotle, *Ath. Pol.* 13.5)

Two things are not clear from this: the identity of these threatened citizens, and the means by which they were disfranchised. With regard to their identity, it is possible that some of these new citizens were foreign mercenaries whom the tyrants had used to seize power in 546 and had employed throughout their regime for security (Herodotus 1.64.1; Thucydides 6.55.3); these may have been allowed by the tyrants to settle in Attica. The other new citizens were probably the descendants of those skilled artisans whom Solon had attracted to Athens by the offer of citizenship (Plutarch, *Solon* 24.4).

As for the means of disfranchisement, it is possible that the answer lies with the supposedly kinship-based 'phratries' or brotherhoods (see below for fuller discussion), membership of which was the only formal proof of citizenship before Cleisthenes' reforms. However, under the tyranny, exclusion from the phratries would not have prevented the new citizens from exercising their rights of citizenship by, for example, attending the Ecclesia. But the fall of the tyranny would have left them exposed, and the revision of the citizen rolls by the phratries, confining citizenship to members of the phratries, would have deprived them of their citizenship. Cleisthenes' decision to make membership of the 'demes' (see next section) the sole formal criterion for Athenian citizenship and his integration of the new citizens into these demes would have guaranteed their goodwill. Cleisthenes would naturally have expected their resultant gratitude to be translated into solid support for himself and his faction, especially at the time of the elections for the eponymous (chief) archon and other posts of importance.

There is also reason to suspect opportunism in the tribal reforms (see next section 7. Branches of the Alcmaeonids, and presumably their political supporters, resided in three large demes in the city of Athens, and other branches of the family in their (probable) original home on the south-west coast of Attica. Suspicions of gerrymandering for political purposes are aroused when it appears not only that these three demes were allocated to three different City 'trittyes' (thirds), but also that these three City trittyes were placed in the same three tribes as three Coastal trittyes from the south-west coast of Attica – Tribe 1 (Erechtheis), Tribe 7 (Cecropis) and Tribe 10 (Antiochis). If this was the case, then it would have resulted in the Alc-maeonid supporters and dependants being the dominant political force in two of the three trittyes in three different tribes. Thus Alcmaeonid control could be exercised in the tribal elections for the post of 'strategos' (tribal general), and on the 50 tribal councillors of the new Boule of 500. In addi-tion, if the majority of the new citizens who had their citizenship restored by Cleisthenes lived in and around the city, as is generally believed, then Alc-maeonid influence could also be exerted in most of the ten City trittyes. By contrast, his political opponents were at a distinct disadvantage because their supporters and dependants could only dominate in one out of three trittyes of the new tribes, since the other two trittyes were located in geo-graphically separate and politically non-partisan areas of Attica. Further-more, some trittyes were not geographically compact, but had demes that were geographically distant from the main locality of the trittys (see below): this was clearly designed by Cleisthenes to make it difficult for his political opponents to rally support in the trittys for the election of strategos and to influence the selection within the trittys of councillors for the Boule of 500.

Nevertheless, it is hard to believe that Cleisthenes needed to have embarked on such a complex reform if he merely desired to promote the interests of the Alcmaeonids. The history of the sixth century, including his own experience of recent events, had made Cleisthenes appreciate fully the nature of the problems that had so grievously troubled Athens: the intense rivalry of the aristocratic-led factions in their struggle for power which had caused political instability. Solon's earlier attempt to resolve this problem had failed because he had not tackled the source of factionalism: the dom-ination of the four Ionian or Attic tribes by leading aristocratic families in their own region. The origins of their domination lay in prehistory when kinship or alleged kinship was the common element that bound together the Athenians in nationality. Members of the four Ionian tribes traced their ancestry back to the four sons of Ion, the son of Apollo. Each tribe ('phyle') had a lower tier of organization, the local phratries or brother-hoods; these consisted of individual households or families ('oikoi', sing. 'oikos') and clans ('gene', sing. 'genos') in which a number of families traced their descent from a common legendary ancestor. It was in these local phratries, and therefore in the Ionian tribes, that the aristocratic clans were able to exert their political dominance due to their social status, economic strength and religious leadership, and thus maintain their hold over different regions of Attica.

The rise in the first half of the sixth century of three such aristocratic-led factions, the 'Men of the Plain', the 'Men of the Coast' and the 'Men beyond the Hills' had led to political upheavals and ultimately to tyranny, with tough consequences for the aristocratic clans in opposition to the tyrant (see Chapters 5 and 6). The ending of tyranny had led to the renewal of feuding between the aristocratic-led factions and to political instability, culminating in the exile of the clan of the Alcmaeonids and 700 families who were their political adherents. The consequences of failure in this factional style of politics had become too high a price to pay for the losers; but, more importantly, Athens would never acquire the political unity and stability that were the essential pre-conditions for becoming a state of the first rank in the Greek world. Thus Cleisthenes' reform of the demes and the tribes was designed to break the overriding regional power of these aristocratic clans and their factions by ending the formal political functions of the phratries and the old tribes; and, by means of the Boule of 500 and the Ecclesia (Assembly), to create a balanced constitution wherein the people's political power was sufficient to act as an equal counter-weight to that of the aristocracy.

The deme and tribal reforms of Cleisthenes

The deme

Local government had previously been under the control of the phratries (brotherhoods) which were dominated by the aristocratic clans (gene) for the reasons outlined above. The 'phratry' system emphasized and reinforced the power of the aristocracy because its structure was by nature hierarchical: all national directives from central government, such as on matters of taxation or military service, would be passed to the phratry leader who would be responsible for the organization and supervision of all that was required from the local community. This leadership of the phratry was hereditary and therefore undemocratic, as it was neither accountable nor open to re-election. This control of the phratries also gave to the aristocratic clans the undisputed right to decide who were and who were not legitimate Athenian citizens, since membership of the phratry was the sole formal criterion for citizenship before Cleisthenes – a power that was used with dire consequences for the new citizens after the fall of Hippias (*Ath. Pol.* 13.5 – see above). Although Aristotle emphasizes the incorporation of these new citizens into the body politic as a primary motive for Cleisthenes' deme reform, he also strongly implies that it was aimed at breaking the aristocratic monopoly of power at local level (*Ath. Pol.* 21.2–4).

Thus the reform of local government was one of the major objectives of Cleisthenes. He removed all political functions from the phratries, allowing them to continue in a purely social and religious capacity (*Ath. Pol.* 21.6). In its place he established the deme as the main political institution of local government. The demes were local communities of different sizes, similar to villages, which had probably existed in rural Attica from the seventh century (699–600), but which in the city and its suburbs had to be established for the first time by Cleisthenes; there was a total of 139 or 140 demes throughout the whole of Attica. The definitive difference between the deme and the phratry was its democratic constitution. The new leader of the deme was the 'demarch', now in all probability elected for one year by his fellow demesmen. Furthermore, all the issues that affected the deme were decided upon by the deme-assemblies, which every Athenian citizen of eighteen years or over was entitled to attend in his own deme. Each deme would also be responsible for the maintenance of its own property, of an up-to-date register of its membership and of its own cults and shrines, which were established (as well as the new tribal cults) as a new focus of loyalty for demesmen in competition with the aristocratic-dominated phratry cults.

Cleisthenes ensured that membership of a deme would not only constitute Athenian citizenship but also conceal the identity of the new citizens:

> He made those, who lived in each of the demes, fellow demesmen of each other so that they would not reveal the new citizens by calling them by their father's name, but by their deme name; this is the reason why the Athenians call themselves by their deme names.
>
> (Aristotle, *Ath. Pol.* 21.4)

Thus equality of status within the deme was made a major feature of the reform. It was also effective in weakening the local kinship organization by giving the name of a clan to the new deme with its new citizens. A good example of this is the allocation of the aristocratic name 'Boutad' to a deme, since every demesman, however humble or foreign his origins, would from now on share this name with the actual descendants of the aristocrat Boutas. So effective was this that later in the fourth century the clan of the 'Boutadai' felt the need to rename themselves the 'Eteoboutadai' ('the real descendants of Boutas') in an attempt to preserve some degree of distinctiveness. Deme membership became hereditary from the time of registration under Cleisthenes, and all future descendants retained membership of that particular deme wherever they resided in future generations.

In this way, the deme became the centre of social life but, more importantly, of political life. The deme assembly was a miniature of the Ecclesia (Assembly), and supplied the perfect training-ground for those who wished to take an active role in the decision-making of the state at a national level. In addition, membership of the deme was a pre-requisite for the position of councillor in the Boule of 500 (see below), for each deme was represented on the national council by a fixed quota of councillors in proportion to its size in 508/7. The deme was essential for the development of 'radical' democracy in the later fifth century. The experience of participating in the deme assemblies, of serving as a demarch, as a councillor in the Boule and in the courts, gradually engendered among the ordinary citizens the self-confidence and self-belief in their ability to make an effective contribution to the government of Athens. Later, as a result of this experience, came the desire to undertake the total and direct control of the government of the state by themselves.

The tribes

Cleisthenes divided the whole of Attica into three geographical areas: the 'Coast' ('Paralia'), the 'Inland' ('Mesogeia') and the 'City' ('Astu'). Each of these three areas had ten sub-divisions called trittyes (sing. 'trittys') or 'thirds', namely ten trittyes in each area, thirty in all. A trittys consisted of a number of demes, ranging from as few as one to as many as nine demes, which were usually close together geographically but not always (see below; see Map 3). Then one trittys from the Coast, one trittys from the Inland and one trittys from the City were selected and put together to form one of Cleisthenes' ten new tribes; this process was repeated for the other nine tribes – thus the 139 or 140 demes were divided among the 30 trittyes which, in turn, were divided among the ten tribes (Aristotle, *Ath. Pol.* 21.2–4).

Aristotle states that the selection of the three trittyes for each tribe was carried out by the drawing of lots (*Ath. Pol.* 24.1), but archaeological evidence concerning the size of the trittyes and the location of some of the trittyes in certain tribes (to the advantage of the Alcmaeonids – see above) suggest that a deliberate manipulation of the selection process was undertaken. Fourth-century inscriptional evidence has revealed the quota of councillors that most of the demes sent to the Boule of 500 and, although there are difficulties in assigning all the demes to their correct Coast, Inland and City trittyes, it is still clear that there was a substantial difference in the number of councillors that each trittys sent to the Boule of 500. For example, the inscription (IG II2 1750), which recorded the award of a crown for excellence to the 50 councillors of Tribe 10 (Antiochis) in 334/3, lists the quota of councillors from each of the tribe's demes; thus the quota from each of the three trittyes can be deduced with some reliability: 27 from the Coast, 13 from the Inland and 10 from the City. Most scholars agree that the ten tribes needed to be approximately equal in size, since they provided the framework for the 'hoplite' army, divided into ten tribal regiments, and for the Boule of 500, consisting of 50 councillors from each of the ten tribes. Unless all the 30 trittyes or all the trittyes in each of the three geographical areas were equal in size, selection of the trittyes by the drawing of lots would have resulted in a wide variation in the size of the tribes. This would have disrupted the effectiveness of the army due to under-strength

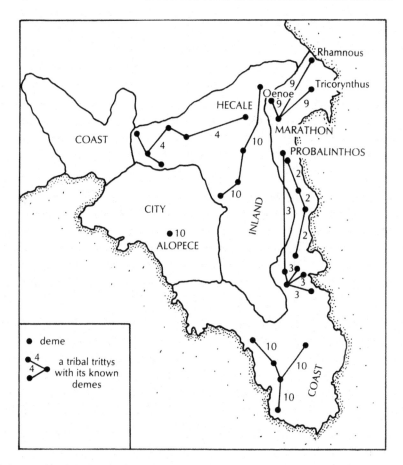

Map 3 Cleisthenes' tribal reforms

regiments, and limited the ability of small tribes to provide sufficient councillors owing to the rule that no councillor could serve more than twice in
his lifetime. Therefore, either Aristotle was mistaken, possibly because he
was influenced by the widespread use of lot in fifth- and fourth-century
democracy and assumed that it must have been used in the most fundamental of Cleisthenes' democratic reforms, or Cleisthenes claimed to be
using the drawing of lots, while secretly manipulating the allocation of the
trittyes.

Aristotle supports the view that Cleisthenes' tribal reforms were motivated
by his desire to advance the cause of democracy:

> (21.2) He first divided everyone into ten tribes instead of the old four tribes, wanting
> to mix them up so that more citizens would have a share in the running of the state

125

('politeia'). ... (21.3) The reason why he did not arrange the citizens into twelve tribes was to avoid using the existing trittyes (for the four tribes had twelve trittyes) which would have prevented the mixing up of the common people.

(Aristotle, *Ath. Pol.* 21.2–3)

Although the Greek word 'politeia' can mean 'citizenship', and therefore the above quotation could be read as 'so that more citizens would have a share in the citizenship' and be referring to his support of the recently disfranchised citizens, the chosen translation in the quotation seems more convincing as it reinforces the statement of Aristotle in his previous chapter that Cleisthenes won the backing of the people by his promise to 'hand over the control of the state to the common people' (*Ath. Pol.* 20.2). If this is correct, then Aristotle believed that Cleisthenes made the 'mixing-up' of the population the central element of his reforms to ensure greater democracy in Athens.

There is much to commend Aristotle's belief. The sixth-century rivalry and feuding between the factions had been caused by the ambitions of a few aristocratic families or clans who were able to use their dominance of certain regions of Attica as a political weapon. Cleisthenes realized that these regional power blocs, with their aristocratic leaders sustained in power by their friends and dependants through the traditional network of old loyalties and allegiances, were the greatest obstacle to political stability. Consequently, there had to be a radical reorganization of the citizen body, and therefore of the four Ionic tribes, on the grounds that the political dependence of the common people could only be broken by political separation from their aristocratic leaders. It was for this reason that Cleisthenes embarked on such a complex and artificial reform of the tribes, deliberately rejecting a much easier tribal reform programme that was at hand. He could have stopped after the reform of local government, where the emphasis on the democratic demes at the expense of aristocratic-led phratries would have led to a gradual, slower but less effective democratization of the state. He could have made use of the existing twelve trittyes of the four Ionic tribes as the basis for twelve new tribes or, alternatively, formed each of his ten new tribes by combining three trittyes from the same region. These options were ruled out, because they would have left intact the regional power of the aristocratic families and clans. Only the artificial creation of ten new tribes, virtually a re-founding of Athens, could provide the necessary fragmentation of the aristocrats' former power-base. At the same time, the 'mixing-up' of three different areas of Attica within each tribe brought a greater cohesion between different groups of Athenians, and continued the process, begun by the Peisistratids, of the unification of the state.

The creation of these new trittyes and the evidence of their distribution among the tribes add plausibility to the belief that Cleisthenes desired to separate some people and to bring together others. Control of local religious cult centres was one of the effective means by which the aristocratic families exerted their power over their dependants. Therefore it is not surprising that the deme of Hecale, a local cult centre in the home district of Isagoras, was attached to four distant demes to make the Inland trittys of Tribe 4, when its inclusion in the closer Inland trittys of Tribe 10 would have been a more natural geographical arrangement (see Map 3). In the same way, the non-allocation of the deme of Probalinthos to the Coastal trittys of either Tribe 9 or Tribe 2 reveals political manipulation, designed to split and undermine an aristocratic regional power-base. Not only did Probalinthos form the old cult-organization of the Tetrapolis with Marathon, Oenoe and Tricorynthus, but also provided the geographical link between the plain of Marathon and the plain of Brauron, the coastal trittyes of Tribe 9 and Tribe 2, respectively, which were situated in the territory from where the Peisistratids drew their strongest support. Cleisthenes' removal of Probalinthos from this Peisistratid stronghold and his allocation of it to the distant Coastal trittys of Tribe 3 served two purposes: first, it weakened the Tetrapolis by taking away one of its key constituents and, even more so, by adding Rhamnous in its place which had its own very different local cult and traditions; and second, it inserted a politically separate enclave between these two politically aligned districts (see Map 3). The introduction and encouragement of cults and sacrifices within the trittyes and the tribes offered further competition to the old phratry cults.

However, this deliberate separation and fragmentation of the regional power blocs of the aristocrats, which did so much to set Athens on the path of full democracy, were not motivated purely by altruism. As stated earlier, Cleisthenes appears to have consolidated the dominance of his own family, the Alcmaeonids, in their strongholds by his assignment of trittyes in Tribes 1, 7 and 10. Tribe 10 (Antiochis) provides a good example of this. The City trittys consisted of only one deme which, as archaeological evidence shows, was the city headquarters of the Alcmaeonids. In addition, the Coastal trittys on the south-west coast of Attica was probably their original home district and the centre of the Alcmaeonid-led faction of the Paralia (The Coast) in the first half of the sixth century (599–550): Aristotle specifically states that the three former factions took their name from the area in which they farmed (*Ath. Pol.* 13.5). Although the Alcmaeonids were the predominant political force in the City and Coastal trittyes of Tribe 10, Cleisthenes still manipulated the Inland trittys to his family's advantage by creating a long thin trittys, stretching from the borders of the City to the north-east of Attica with Mount Pendeli dividing the trittys geographically into two. The inhabitants of this trittys had very little previous experience or knowledge of each other, would experience problems in organizing themselves and, far more importantly, would find it difficult to attend tribal assemblies in Athens: such a disparate and divided trittys would offer little threat to the Alcmaeonids in tribal elections and business. Thus Cleisthenes' tribal reforms were a major, if not the most important, factor in the development of Athenian democracy, but were also a means of improving the political standing of the Alcmaeonids at the expense of their opponents.

The development of democracy

Herodotus was in no doubt that Cleisthenes was the founder of Athenian democracy, even though he was the grandson of a tyrant:

> and thus the name of the Alcmaeonids was spread throughout Greece. From this marriage [i.e. Megacles and Agariste] there was born Cleisthenes who established the tribes and the democracy for the Athenians.
>
> (Herodotus 6.131.1)

However, as Herodotus was writing in the third quarter of the fifth century (449–425) when 'radical' democracy had become established in the years after Ephialtes' reforms in 462/1 (see Chapter 13), his judgement about Cleisthenes is anachronistic since he has confused results with motive. The influential events of 511/0 to 508/7 which culminated in his reform pro-gramme reveal that he was motivated, not by a deeply held and long-standing political principle that the government of Athens should be placed fully in the hands of the common people, but by the desire to eliminate the root causes of aristocratic-led factionalism which had produced the tyranny and had provoked his clash with Isagoras. His task was to find a way of destroying this destabilizing political power of the factions, but without overthrowing the political leadership of the aristocracy (including his family), whose expertise was essential for the conduct of public affairs and the army.

His solution was twofold: to 'mix up' the people so that the old aristo-cratic families and clans lost control over their dependants; and to establish a balanced constitution in which the increased power of the people in the Ecclesia (Assembly) and the Boule of 500 would act as a check and counter-balance to the upper-class public officials, such as the nine archons, and the council of the Areopagus. The 'mixing-up' policy, based upon the reform of the tribes and the demes, underpinned his institutional reforms. The replacement of the four (allegedly) kinship tribes by ten artificial tribes, of the twelve old trittyes by thirty new ones, of the phratries by the demes as the main unit of local government, and of kinship by locality as the criter-ion for citizenship, had far-reaching political and social consequences because they undermined the regional power-bases and the consequent political dominance of the aristocratic clans. However, his creation of the City as one of the three regional areas with ten trittyes, where the top aristocratic families had their headquarters, guaranteed that aristocratic influence in all ten tribes would be strong, but not overwhelming, since it would be limited by other tribal members from two different regions of Attica except, of course, in the case of his own family.

His reform of the political institutions, blending aristocratic and democratic elements in the government of the state, produced a moderate democracy in which power was shared between the aristocracy and the common people. High office was still the preserve of the upper classes, the economic elite, since he did not abolish the Solonian property qualifications. In addition, he did not reduce the power of the archonship, which had been restored to its former level of importance upon the fall of the tyranny, and whose authority and prestige were further enhanced by the restoration of direct election by the people and the removal of interference by the tyrants (Thucydides 6.54.6). The eponymous (chief) archon was still the most powerful public official in the management of civil affairs; the 'polemarch' still held the position of commander-in-chief of the army; the 'basileus' was still in charge of state religion; and all nine archons presumably regained the judicial powers that had been given to them by Solon. All archons, after their year of office, became life-long members of the council of the Areopagus whose religious and judicial powers (see Chapter 13) appear to have been untouched by Cleisthenes – hardly surprising as he was a member of that powerful body.

Nevertheless, Cleisthenes balanced the power of the archons and the Areopagus by increasing the power and authority of the Boule of 500 and the Ecclesia. The evidence about the powers of the new Boule, which replaced Solon's Boule of 400, and about the method of appointment is very scanty, and therefore inferences have to be drawn from knowledge of its later and better-documented history. Each tribe supplied 50 councillors, with every deme supplying its quota to the tribal contingent according to its size (*Ath. Pol.* 43.2, 62.1). These tribal councillors were either directly elected by the demes or, after a preliminary selection, were chosen by the drawing of lots. It is not known whether or not the 'thetes' were eligible to stand for the Boule of 500, but the absence of state pay would have ensured the smallness of their numbers; it was the middle class who supplied most of the councillors and which was the dominant force in this institution.

The Boule of 500's chief function was probouleutic, namely to prepare the agenda for the Ecclesia by holding a preliminary discussion of all proposed legislation and policies, and then submitting them as motions for decision by the people. This control over the agenda gave the middle classes the opportunity to influence and shape the direction of Athenian policy. Although Solon's Boule of 400 had possessed this same function, the infrequent meetings and the very modest status of the Ecclesia (see below) in the first half of the sixth century and under the tyranny provided little scope for the Boule to develop into an institution of genuine importance. However, the increase in the authority of the Ecclesia under Cleisthenes directly affected the power and prestige of the Boule of 500 which cooperated with the top public officials in the running of the state. It may also, under Cleisthenes' reforms, have gained the power to receive foreign embassies in order to establish their reasons for coming to Athens (Herodotus 9.5.1); and to conduct the 'dokimasia' of the newly chosen councillors (a preliminary investigation to confirm their legal right to hold office).

Solon had opened up membership of the Ecclesia (Assembly) to the thetes, the lowest class of Athenians, and had probably confirmed its legal right to elect all the important public officials and to make the final decision on important issues such as war, peace and alliances. However, there was little scope for the Ecclesia (Assembly) to become an effective legislative body, with full sovereignty, while the aristocratic public officials and the tyrants consulted it only as a last resort. It is important to note that Aristotle did not include the control of legislation by the common people as one of Solon's three most democratic reforms (*Ath. Pol.* 9.1). Cleisthenes changed all that when he took the people into partnership and 'handed over the control of the state to the common people' (Aristotle, *Ath. Pol.* 20.2). His decision to take his proposed reforms to the Ecclesia (Assembly) for ratification via the Boule, thus directly involving the common people in the legislative process, set a precedent that henceforth all legislation would be legally valid only if approved and passed by these two institutions. It was this radical step and its political consequences for the future government of Athens, if it was allowed to become the dominant principle of political life, that compelled Isagoras to summon the Spartans.

It was about the time of Cleisthenes that the new political concept of 'isonomia' (political equality) made its appearance and continued until it was replaced in the fifth century by 'democratia' (the power of the people). There is good reason to believe that Cleisthenes used this word to define the essence of his new constitution and as a political propaganda slogan behind which the Athenian people could unite in order to secure constitutional reform. To achieve isonomia, Cleisthenes increased the legislative authority of the people: as a result there was an equal balance of power, a 'political equality', between the aristocratic public officials, who initiated policy and carried it out, if approved, and the Ecclesia and the Boule, which had the sovereign authority to pass or reject all such proposals. It is probably the case that Cleisthenes was also responsible for the new formal Athenian word for a statute, namely 'nomos' in place of the older 'thesmos'. The latter word was used to describe laws that had been imposed upon the people by the ruling aristocracy (or by the gods); whereas nomos refers to laws that became 'the norm' or 'the custom' after they had been agreed by the people in their democratic Ecclesia. The increased participation of the common people in political decision-making must have led Cleisthenes to provide for regular meetings of the Ecclesia, probably ten per year, in addition to the annual electoral assembly and to the special meetings, summoned by the public officials.

Cleisthenes, intentionally or not, was the 'father of democracy'. His reforms were primarily designed to fragment the power of the aristocratic-led factions that had plagued Athenian public life throughout the sixth century, and to end the political monopoly of the upper classes in the passing of legislation. If Aristotle is correct in assigning to Cleisthenes the introduction of the law of ostracism (*Ath. Pol.* 22.1 – see Chapter 8), whereby an Athenian could be exiled for ten years upon the vote of his fellow citizens, then this measure was also inspired by the desire for political stability and by isonomia: the people would have the opportunity to judge between the conflicting policies of aristocratic leaders, and have the power to remove the less or least favoured politician before the issue at stake spilled over into civil strife, as happened in the case of Cleisthenes and Isagoras, or even tyranny. However, the wide-ranging powers of the archons and other public officials, the restriction of these offices to wealthy citizens of the two top classes, and the retention by the aristocratic Areopagus, consisting of ex-archons with membership for life, of jurisdiction over crimes against the state and of conducting the public officials' 'euthuna' (an official review of their year in office) were considerable impediments to the realization of full democracy. Genuine 'political equality', as understood by the Athenians who voted for the reforms of Ephialtes in 462/1 and by their descendants, existed not only when all citizens, rich or poor, could participate on an equal footing with each other in deciding public policy and passing legislation, but also when they had the equal right and opportunity to hold public office themselves and to conduct the euthuna of public officials to make them accountable to the people as a whole for their official actions. Cleisthenes supplied the means for the Athenians to gain the necessary political maturity over the next half century to remove these constraints in 462/1, and thus he established the foundations for the later reforms of Ephialtes and Pericles that completed the development of full democracy (see Chapter 13).

Bibliography

Hignett, C. A *History of the Athenian Constitution*, ch. 6.

Lewis, D. M. 'Cleisthenes and Attica', *Historia* 12 (1963).

Moore, J. M. *Aristotle and Xenophon on Democracy and Oligarchy*, pp. 235–43.

Murray, O. *Early Greece*, 2nd edn, ch. 15.

Ostwald, M. *CAH* vol. 4, 2nd edn, pt 2, ch. 5.

—— *From Popular Sovereignty to the Sovereignty of Law*, pt. 1.1.

—— *Nomos and the Beginnings of the Athenian Democracy*, pt 2, ch. 3, pt 3, chs 1 and 2.

Rhodes, P. J. *Commentary on the Aristotelian 'Athenaion Politeia'*, pp. 240–62.

Stanton, G. R. *Athenian Politics c. 800–500 BC A Sourcebook*, ch. 5.

—— 'The tribal reform of Kleisthenes the Alcmeonid', *Chiron* 14 (1984).

8

ATHENIAN POLITICS FROM CLEISTHENES TO THE OUTBREAK OF THE PERSIAN WAR

The sources

It is difficult to analyse the internal politics of Athens during this period due to the fact that the available literary evidence is both scanty and non-contemporaneous. The main source is Herodotus (484–420s), but he was not an Athenian and not primarily interested in politics, so he provides only glimpses, not a continuous account, of the political issues and disagreements which were current during these years; he concentrated on the military expansion of the Persian empire and its inevitable conflict with Greece, culminating in the Persian War of 480–479. Aristotle in the *Ath. Pol.* (see Chapter 1) provides evidence for clashes between the supposed political factions in the 480s, but his account is very brief (*Ath. Pol.* 22) and his statement of motives suspect. Apart from his mention of the institution of the 'bouleutic oath' to be taken by the councillors of the Boule of 500 and the election of the ten 'strategoi' (generals), one from each tribe, his main emphasis is on the use of ostracism for political purposes. Therefore, it is a good starting-point to examine the procedure and the history of this institution.

Ostracism and its use in the 480s

Every year the issue of whether to hold an ostracism or not was placed on the agenda of the 'Ecclesia' (Assembly); if a majority of the citizens present voted in favour, it was held in the eighth prytany (the Athenian year was divided into ten prytanies). Every citizen was then given the opportunity to write down on a piece of pottery the name of the citizen whom he most desired to be removed from Attica – the Greek word for a piece of pottery or potsherd was 'ostrakon' (plural 'ostraka') and thus gave its name to the institution. A minimum of 6,000 votes had to be cast in the 'Agora' (the market-place of Athens) for the ostracism to be valid, and the person with the most votes cast against him was exiled from Attica for ten years. The ostracized person was given ten days to put his affairs in order before the ostracism was implemented. During the ten years of exile he had full control over his property and his income, and was allowed to be in contact with his family and friends, provided that he remained outside Attica. Ostracism could take place only once a year, and only one citizen could be ostracized per year. At the end of his ten-year exile, the citizen could return home and resume his full rights of citizenship.

Although most of the sources, including Aristotle (*Ath. Pol.* 22.1), name Cleisthenes as the author of the law of ostracism, a fragment of Androtion, one of the fourth-century Atthidographers (local historians of Athens) which has been preserved by a much later lexicographer Harpocration, appears to disagree:

> In his second book Androtion states that Hipparchus was a relative of the tyrant Peisistratus, and was the first man to be ostracized. The law of ostracism was first laid down at that time through suspicion of Peisistratus' supporters; for he had become tyrant when he was the leader of the people and a general.
>
> (Androtion, FGrH III B 324 F6)

However, if this passage is compared to Aristotle's (*Ath. Pol.* 22.3), the similarity of the texts is so marked that it appears that Aristotle used Androtion as his source for the institution of ostracism. Therefore it would seem that Harpocration has produced a shortened and garbled version of Androtion's text – a view that is further reinforced by his use of the unusual expression 'laid down' – and has apparently confused the first use of ostracism (488/7) with the date of its introduction (508/7). If this is so, then there is no conflict between Androtion and the other four sources (Aristotle, Vaticanus Graecus, Philochorus and Aelian).

There are two schools of thought concerning Cleisthenes' motive for introducing this law. The first holds the view that Cleisthenes was moved by a high-minded desire to bring political stability to Athens. His clash with Isagoras over the introduction of democratic reforms (see Chapter 7) had resulted in the invasion of Attica by a Spartan army under King Cleomenes who attempted to interfere directly and forcefully in the constitution of Athens. Ostracism was introduced, therefore, to prevent a potential conflict from reaching such a crisis point, as had happened in the dangerous rivalry between Cleisthenes and Isagoras, or even to thwart a renewed bid to establish a tyranny by ostracizing one of the political leaders. Aristotle in the *Ath. Pol.* (22.3) states that the example of Peisistratus, who had abused his position as popular leader and 'strategos' (general) to become tyrant, had produced among the people a suspicion of those in power, and that ostracism had been enacted to stop such an occurrence in the future. Aristotle adds further emphasis to this in the *Politics*:

133

> Whenever someone (either one man or more) becomes greater in power than is appropriate in the city or in the constitution of the state, such excessive superiority usually leads to one-man rule or oligarchy. On account of this some states have ostracism, such as Argos and Athens.
>
> (Aristotle, *Politics* 1302b)

The second school of thought believes Cleisthenes planned to use ostracism as a factional political weapon to be wielded against political enemies, weakening the opposing faction by the removal of its leader. Aristotle in the *Ath. Pol.* can also be used in support of this interpretation, as he claims that Cleisthenes' primary purpose in proposing this law was to get rid of Hipparchus (22.4); and in the *Politics* (1284b) he confirms that some states 'use ostracisms for factional purposes'.

The first opinion is to be preferred, as ostracism was not an easy weapon to use for the elimination of political opponents. There was only one opportunity provided each year, and there was the further difficulty of trying to persuade the people to vote for the holding of an ostracism. In addition, it was a risky business as the people might vote for the ostracism of the instigator and not his intended victim. There was probably a better chance of ruining the career of a political opponent by prosecuting him in the courts, as happened in the case of Miltiades at the hands of Xanthippus in 489 (see below). However, the ostracism of Hyperbolus *c.*418/7 shows that this institution, once established, could be used for 'factional purposes': his attempt to have Nicias ostracized backfired, when Nicias and Alcibiades formed a temporary coalition and directed their supporters to vote 'for' Hyperbolus. It could also be used as a fallback measure if a prosecution failed, as seems to have happened in the case of Cimon who was ostracized in 462/1 after surviving a prosecution for corruption by his opponents in 463 (see Chapter 11).

It is useful to investigate the ostracisms of the 480s and the motives alleged by Aristotle in the attempt to discover the main political issue that split the opposing factions in the last years of the sixth century and the 490s:

> The first man to be ostracized was one of his [i.e. Peisistratus'] relations, Hipparchus, son of Charmus of the deme of Collytus, on account of whom Cleisthenes had especially passed the law, wanting to exile him. For the Athenians had allowed the friends of the tyrants, all those who had not shared in their wrongdoing during the troubles, to live in the city, benefiting from the customary mildness of the people. Hipparchus was the leader and the chief of this group (22.4). ... And Megacles, son of Hippocrates of the deme of Alopece, was ostracized. For three years they ostracized the friends of the tyrants, against whom the law had been passed. After this in the fourth year, if anyone seemed to be more powerful than the rest, he was removed; and Xanthippus, son of Ariphron, was the first of those to be ostracized who were unconnected with the tyrants (22.6).
>
> (Aristotle, *Ath. Pol.* 22.4–6)

Therefore Aristotle identifies two groups who were ostracized and distinguishes between the motives for their ostracism: first, 'the friends of the tyrants'; second, those 'unconnected with the tyrants', which includes Xanthippus in 485/4 and Aristides in 483/2.

Aristotle has singled out Hipparchus, the son-in-law of Hippias the Peisistratid, as the leader and spokesman of 'the friends of the tyrants', but this alleged motive for his and the others' ostracisms does present difficulties. It seems unlikely that there was any serious or substantial support for Hippias by 488/7, as Cleisthenes' democratic reforms had been in operation for the past twenty years and the principle of 'isonomia' (political equality) had been firmly established. If tyranny was restored, these political benefits would be removed from the people. In addition, Hipparchus had been elected by the people to the top civilian political post, the eponymous (chief) 'archon', in 496/5, and he was unlikely to have achieved this position of power by standing on a pro-tyrant platform, whether explicit or implicit. Furthermore, it is hard to believe that Hipparchus was such a powerful political figure in 508/7 that he became the prime target for Cleisthenes' law. If he had been so prominent and so pro-tyranny at that time, Cleisthenes would have found little difficulty in engineering his ostracism then or soon after, while the memory of the tyrants was so fresh and the Tyrannicides, Harmodius and Aristogeiton, were being hailed as national heroes. Yet Aristotle wants his readers to believe that it was the people's 'customary mildness' that postponed Hipparchus' day of reckoning for twenty years, and presumably their forgiving generosity that rewarded him with the top archonship. Therefore, 'friends of the tyrants' seems at first sight an unsatisfactory explanation for the ostracism of Hipparchus and the other two.

However, the link between Hippias and the Persians may supply the clue to the issue that dominated Athenian politics and led to these ostracisms. In other words, it was not simply that they were 'friends of the tyrants', but friends of the ex-tyrant Hippias whose ambition to be restored to his former position of power was being actively supported by the Persians. Thus it may be that the issues of tyranny and of a cooperative policy towards Persia became connected in the minds of the people. The archaeological finds from the Kerameikos, the potters' quarter to the north-west of the Agora in Athens, reinforce this belief. Up to 1967, 1,658 ostraka had been found in the Agora and on the Acropolis, but the Kerameikos excavations unearthed a further 4,463 ostraka of which a large number date to the 480s before the destruction of Athens by the Persians in 480. These finds have been most revealing: apart from eleven ostraka for Hipparchus and 2,216 (previously fifteen) for Megacles, son of Hippocrates from the deme of Alopece, who was Cleisthenes' nephew and leader of the Alcmaeonids, 789 ostraka (previously only three) were discovered with the name Callias, son of Cratias, also from the deme of Alopece which was the city headquarters of the Alcmaeonids; four of these ostraka call him a 'Mede'

135

or 'Persian', and one ostrakon has a drawing of him in Persian clothes – he is almost certainly the third 'friend of the tyrants' who was ostracized in 486/5.

Therefore, it is possible to link the tyrant Hippias and his friends, including Hipparchus, his relative, and the Alcmaeonids and their political allies, with a policy that favoured cooperation or peaceful coexistence with Persia. If this is correct, then it was the people's mistrust of these Athenian politicians and a rejection of their policy that led to the three successive ostracisms from 488/7 to 486/5 (and probably the fourth in 485/4 – see below). Other ostraka finds from the Kerameikos provide more support for this view: Callixenos, son of Aristonymus from the deme of Xypete, and Hippocrates, son of Alcmaeonides from the deme of Alopece, were both serious contenders for ostracism in the 480s. Both were Alcmaeonids and, although unmentioned in the literary sources, were clearly men of political importance in Athens. In fact, Callixenos on the extant evidence came sixth in the unpopularity contest with 263 ostraka cast against him, and one ostrakon almost certainly calls him 'Callixenos the [trai]tor'. Thus the people seem to have developed a vendetta against the Alcmaeonids. On the basis of this evidence, it is plausible to believe that the dominant issue in Athenian politics, which split the factions in the 480s, was about the policy that Athens should adopt towards Persia and Persian expansion, namely cooperation/peaceful coexistence or resistance. The roots of this policy disagreement can be found in the events of the last years of the sixth century and the 490s, beginning c.507 with Athens' request for Persian military aid against their Greek enemies.

Athenian politics 508/7–490

In 508/7, Cleomenes, King of Sparta, invaded Athens at the request of Isagoras, exiled 700 families who were political allies of Cleisthenes and the Alcmaeonids, and tried to set up a narrow pro-Spartan oligarchy under Isagoras (see Chapter 7 for a fuller discussion). However, Cleomenes' attempt to dissolve the Boule of 400 backfired, leading to an uprising of the Athenian people in support of Cleisthenes' democratic reforms and the forced departure of his Spartan army. Such a military humiliation of the most powerful state in Greece was bound to have repercussions:

> The Athenians sent for Cleisthenes and the 700 families who had been exiled by Cleomenes; then they sent messengers to Sardis because they wanted to make a military alliance with the Persians. For they knew that they were now at war with Cleomenes and the Lacedaimonians [i.e. the Spartans].
>
> (Herodotus 5.73.1)

Cleomenes at that time was assembling an army from the whole of the Peloponnese in order to gain revenge on the Athenians and to reinstate

Isagoras. He was organizing a three-prong attack on Athens: the Spartans and the Peloponnesians were to attack Eleusis on the western border of Attica; the Boeotians were to seize Oenoe and Hysiae in the north-west; and the Chalcidians from Euboea were to raid north-east Attica (Herodotus 5.74).

It was this fear of Cleomenes' hostility that had persuaded the Athenians to seek military help from the Persians, and thus made Athenian–Persian relations a major political issue for the first time at Athens. The huge empire of Persia, under the rule of King Darius, had extended its frontiers to the very borders of mainland Greece. The Greeks on the western coast of Asia Minor had originally been conquered by Croesus the King of Lydia (560–546), but soon had come under the control of the Persians after his defeat in 546 at the hands of Cyrus 'the Great', the founder of the Persian Empire. In the last twelve years or so of the sixth century, King Darius, with the help of his generals Megabazus and Otanes, had defeated Thrace and had incorporated it within the Persian Empire, and had accepted the submission of Macedonia (Herodotus 5.18.1). Thus Persia could be viewed as a potential enemy or ally; in 506, threatened on three sides by Greek enemies, the Athenians turned to Persia as an ally.

Herodotus does not reveal the identity of the politician who proposed this military alliance with Persia, possibly due to ignorance or because he wished to protect a political reputation in the light of subsequent events. However, it is possible to believe that Cleisthenes, the leader of the Alcmaeonids, was the driving force behind this policy: his influence was at its peak, owing to the popularity of his democratic reforms, and he personally, his family and his political supporters had the most to lose if the Athenians were defeated by Cleomenes and a narrow oligarchy under Isagoras was imposed. If this is correct, then the first link was forged between the Alcmaeonids and the policy of cooperation with the Persians.

The request for a military alliance was sent to Artaphrenes, the brother of Darius and the 'satrap' (provincial governor) of Ionia and Lydia, who resided at Sardis, the main city of his 'satrapy' (province). Artaphrenes, having established who the Athenians were, was willing to give aid, but with important pre-conditions:

> He briefly summed up the situation as follows: if the Athenians were to give earth and water to King Darius, he would form a military alliance with them; but if not, he would order their [i.e. the messengers'] removal. The messengers, having discussed the issue among themselves, said that they would give earth and water because they wished to have the alliance. When these returned to their own country, they were strongly criticized.
>
> (Herodotus 5.73.2–3)

The reason for the criticism of the messengers was that the offering of earth and water was the symbol of political and military submission to Persia, and thus the Athenians were liable to pay tribute, to supply military forces when required, and to accept Persia's preferred choice of constitutional government, which at that time was tyranny, as was the case with the Greeks of Asia Minor.

This criticism of the messengers reveals naivety on the part of the Athenians, if they genuinely thought that the Persians were going to offer them a military alliance on any other terms than submission; Athens was hardly likely to be viewed as a military equal, least of all when appealing to a great empire for military help. It is worth noting that the alliance with Persia was not formally rejected by the Athenians but was ignored; either because Cleisthenes, who must have anticipated (if it was his policy) such a demand from Persia, had recognized the political danger to himself by continuing to support such a manifestly unpopular policy or, perhaps more convincingly, because the military threat to the Athenians from their Greek enemies had been removed. For the Spartan invasion had been aborted at Eleusis due to the desertion of Demaratus, Cleomenes' co-king, the Corinthians and the rest of the Peloponnesian allies (Herodotus 5.75–76; see Chapter 4 for a fuller discussion of these events). This stroke of luck allowed the Athenians to turn their attention, first, to the Boeotians who were decisively beaten in battle while on their way to join up with the Chalcidians; and, second, to the Chalcidians who were defeated in Euboea and had 4,000 Athenian settlers placed upon a confiscated part of their land (Herodotus 5.77). Nevertheless, no matter how convenient it was for the Athenians to forget the embassy to Artaphrenes at Sardis, their ambassadors had formally submitted to Persia by offering earth and water, and the Persians were not going to forget.

The next stage in the deterioration of relations between Athens and Persia was due to the exiled tyrant, Hippias, who was living at Sigeum, situated in Asia Minor at the southern end of the Hellespont. Hippias had his hopes raised of a return to Athens as tyrant by the Spartans who, after their failure in 506 to reinstate Isagoras at Athens, decided to support the restoration of Hippias. However, when the Peloponnesian allies were summoned to Sparta to discuss a proposed invasion of Athens for this purpose, once again the Corinthians came to Athens' rescue by vigorously opposing any attempt to establish tyranny anywhere. Their arguments led the Peloponnesian allies to reject the Spartans' scheme, who were forced to give up any future hopes of attacking Athens and to send Hippias back to Sigeum (Herodotus 5.91–94). But Hippias was not prepared to abandon his newly raised hopes and turned to Artaphrenes:

> When Hippias returned from Sparta to Asia, he left no stone unturned, slandering the Athenians to Artaphrenes and doing everything to bring Athens under the power of himself and Darius. While Hippias was doing these things, the Athenians, upon learning of his activities, sent messengers to Sardis, urging the Persians not to be

> won over by Athenian fugitives. Artaphrenes ordered them, if they valued their safety, to take Hippias back. When his orders were brought to them, the Athenians refused to obey. Since they would not obey, they decided to be openly at war with the Persians.
>
> (Herodotus 5.96)

Thus a state of war now existed between Athens and Persia, and this decision can probably be dated to c.501 owing to subsequent events.

The Ionian Revolt broke out in 499, initiated by Aristagoras of Miletus; he had promised to capture the island of Naxos and bring it under Persian control, but his failure and fear of punishment persuaded him that revolt was his best means of safety (Herodotus 5.30–38). The Ionians needed help from mainland Greece, if their revolt was to have any chance of succeeding, and so Aristagoras went at first to Sparta where he was rebuffed by Cleomenes (Herodotus 5.49–51). Aristagoras then appealed to Athens, stressing the kinship between the Athenians and the Milesians, and the weakness of the Persian armed forces. He had picked the right moment, for the Athenians were still angry with Artaphrenes and his demands to reinstate Hippias; they voted to send 20 of their 50-strong fleet:

> These ships were the beginning of the troubles for both the Greeks and the foreigners.
>
> (Herodotus 5.97.3)

However, the Athenians, after burning Sardis but then being defeated by the Persians, withdrew their ships and played no further part in the Ionian Revolt.

The decade of the 490s, beginning with the initial Athenian participation in the Ionian Revolt, is particularly devoid of literary sources until the battle of Marathon in 490 which is fully documented. The internal politics of Athens during this period can only be surmised, but the events of 499 suggest that the issues of Hippias and Persia had become connected, and that the dividing line between the political factions concerned future Athenian policy towards both: whether it should be cooperation with Persia and, therefore, the restoration of Hippias, or resistance. The sending and the withdrawal of the 20 ships could have been approved only by the people in the Ecclesia (Assembly), and thus there must have been a full debate on both occasions in which arguments for and against intervention on behalf of the Ionians were expressed. Those who favoured resistance must have won the day on the first occasion, when the Athenians voted to send nearly half of their navy to the Asiatic Greeks; but those who favoured cooperation with or caution towards Persia enjoyed success subsequently with the ships' recall. As the course of the Ionian Revolt unfolded from 499 to 494, this issue must have been placed numerous times on the agenda of the Ecclesia for discussion. It is into this context that the very few events, of which there is mention in the sources, are usually placed.

The first of these is the election of Hipparchus in 496/5 to the post of eponymous (chief) archon. It would seem that his kinship tie to Hippias was not the political handicap that it would have been ten, or even five, years earlier. By 496, the Persians had regained Cyprus and were in the process of launching a three-pronged attack along the whole of the western seaboard of Asia Minor. Such success would have stirred fears of retribution against Athens for taking part in the burning of Sardis. Hipparchus' election may have been an attempt to give him a position of authority in order to use his influence on behalf of the Athenians with Hippias and, through him, with Persia, possibly to explain away the initial involvement in the revolt as an error of judgement which had been quickly rectified. At the very least, his appointment would be seen as opposition to the policy of open warfare against Persia.

The defeat of the Ionian League at the sea-battle of Lade and the capture of Miletus in 494, followed by the mopping up operations in 493 brought the Ionian Revolt to an end. The failure of the revolt had two consequences of note: the return of Miltiades to Athens in 493/2 and the battle of Marathon in 490. Miltiades had been tyrant in the Thracian Chersonese (the narrow peninsula on the European side of the Hellespont), but was forced to flee by the Persian navy, which was stamping out the last remnants of the Ionian Revolt in the Hellespontine region (Herodotus 6.41). The arrival of such a powerful personality on the Athenian political stage provoked conflicting reactions. As the leading member of the powerful Philaid clan, he had cooperated with the Peisistratids, holding the post of eponymous (chief) archon in 524/3, and had gained the tyranny of the Thracian Chersonese with their support: such a link with Hippias was bound to provoke hostility in some quarters. On the other hand, his participation in the Ionian Revolt until the bitter end would have earned him popularity amongst those who favoured resistance to Persia.

Immediately upon his return, Miltiades was brought to trial by his enemies on the charge of being a tyrant in the Chersonese (Herodotus 6.104.2). It is difficult to believe that there was such a crime in Athenian law, and thus the motive for this prosecution appears to have been political. However, as Herodotus does not identify the accusers, it is not possible to know for certain whether rivalry and jealousy between the aristocratic clans or disagreement over policy towards Persia was the primary cause of his prosecution. What is certain is that his acquittal and election to the post of strategos (tribal general) were a boost for those who supported an anti-Persian policy.

In the same year as Miltiades' return and court case, Themistocles was probably elected to the post of eponymous (chief) archon. His archonship was particularly noteworthy for his development and fortification of the Piraeus:

Themistocles persuaded them to complete the walls of the Piraeus [i.e. in 479 or soon after], which had been begun previously during the year of his archonship [493/2], thinking that it was a fine site, having three natural harbours, and that the development of Athens into a naval state would be of great benefit in the acquisition of power. For he was the first man who dared to say that their future lay with the sea.

(Thucydides 1.93.3–4)

Previously the bay of Phalerum, open and indefensible, had served as the base for the navy; now the task of turning the Piraeus into the secure and fortified harbour of Athens had been begun. Prudent defence against the threat of Aegina, which was at war with Athens at different times from 505 to 481, was one motive for Themistocles' concentration on the Piraeus; the other, and probably more important, was his concern about the expansion of Persia and the likelihood of their desire for revenge. Whether this willingness to oppose Persia brought Themistocles into a political alliance with the like-minded Miltiades, it is impossible to say as there is no direct evidence. However, it must be remembered that Miltiades was a politician of the first rank due to his vast experience, while Themistocles' election to the archonship marked only the beginning of a promising political career; therefore the possibility of a political relationship between the two should be treated with great caution.

The second consequence of the failure of the Ionian Revolt was the battle of Marathon in 490. In the late 490s, the Persians set out to achieve three objectives: the reorganization of the crushed Asiatic Greeks, the consolidation of their control over the northern Aegean, and the punishment of those non-Asiatic Greek cities that had participated in the attack on Sardis. Artaphrenes mostly carried out the first objective, although it was Mardonius, the son-in-law of King Darius, who substituted so-called democracies for tyrannies as the preferred means of Persian control over the Greek cities in Asia Minor (Herodotus 6.42–43); Mardonius was also instructed to carry out the other two. In 492, he reasserted Persian control over Thrace and Macedonia, and took possession of the island of Thasos. However, his plan to march through Greece in order to punish Athens and Eretria, which had sent five ships against Sardis, was thwarted by a terrible storm as the Persians attempted to sail around the peninsula of Mount Athos in Chalcidice in the north-west Aegean; the heavy loss of ships and men led to the temporary abandonment of the third objective (Herodotus 6.44–45).

In 490, Darius appointed Datis and Artaphrenes, the son of the satrap, aided by the ex-tyrant Hippias, to complete the enslavement of Eretria and Athens. To avoid the dangers that Mardonius experienced, the large Persian force sailed across the Aegean, conquering Naxos and other islands of the Cyclades on their journey until it came to Eretria, which was burnt in revenge for Sardis and its citizens enslaved and transported to Asia (Herodotus 6.95–101). The Persian forces then landed in the bay of Marathon on the east coast of Attica and awaited the arrival of the Athenian forces. The Athenians had already asked for help from the Spartans, who replied

141

that they could not come until the full moon had passed owing to their religious practice. In the event, only the Plataeans sent help and fought alongside the Athenians. The 'polemarch' (commander-in-chief) of the Athenian army was Callimachus, who was aided in his decision-making by the ten tribal generals, the most influential proving to be Miltiades. It is clear from his speech to Callimachus in support of an immediate attack (Herodotus 6.109) that he feared the betrayal of Athens by those who favoured cooperation with or appeasement of Persia; Eretria had already shown how the issue of relations with Persia could disastrously split a Greek state (Herodotus 6.100). Callimachus' decision to risk battle ended in a decisive victory for the Athenians (Herodotus 6.111–15).

In the immediate aftermath of the battle, just as the Persians had put to sea, a flashing shield was seen:

> The Persians sailed around Sunium, wanting to arrive at the city before the Athenian army. The Alcmaeonids were accused in Athens of proposing this plan to the Persians; for, it was said, they had made an agreement with the Persians to hold up a shield for them as a signal when they were now on board (115) ... it seems remarkable to me and I do not believe the story that the Alcmaeonids would ever hold up a shield by agreement to the Persians, wanting Athens to be brought under the control of the Persians and Hippias (121).
>
> (Herodotus 6.115, 6.121)

Even Herodotus, who went to great lengths to defend the Alcmaeonids against this accusation, admitted that a flashing shield was definitely seen (Herodotus 6.124); and it is clear from the above quotation that the Persians had high hopes of capturing the undefended city. However, they were prevented by the speedy return of the Athenian army from Marathon and were forced to return to Asia. Whether the Alcmaeonids intended to betray Athens to the Persians, it is impossible to say, but Herodotus' lengthy protestations about their innocence show that many Athenians themselves believed the Alcmaeonids to be guilty, and that this belief was still current as late as the third quarter of the fifth century when Herodotus was writing. Those suspected of collaboration with the Persians and consequently considered to be 'friends of the tyrants' (Aristotle, *Ath. Pol.* 22.6) were destined to suffer in the 480s.

Athenian politics 489–481

Miltiades' reputation was at its highest in Athens due to his services at the battle of Marathon; and thus his proposal in 489 to put himself in charge of 70 ships with soldiers and money without naming the objective of his expedition but with a guarantee of acquiring great wealth for Athens was passed by the Ecclesia. In fact, he aimed to conquer the island of Paros but, after a siege of 26 days, he returned to Athens, wounded and without success. This failure provided an opportunity for his enemies to bring him down:

> After Miltiades' return from Paros, the rest of the Athenians criticized him, especially Xanthippus, son of Ariphron, who brought him before the people and demanded the death penalty on a charge of 'deceiving the Athenians' ... the people supported him in so far as they rejected the death penalty but fined him fifty talents for his crime.
>
> (Herodotus 6.136)

Miltiades died soon after this, when the wound to his thigh became gangrenous, and his son, Cimon, paid the huge fine.

Xanthippus is named as the chief prosecutor of Miltiades, and it would have been very useful if Herodotus had stated Xanthippus' motive for bringing this case. He may have been inspired by his desire for justice on behalf of the people, but his demand for the death penalty suggests bitter opposition to Miltiades and, very possibly, his policy of outright resistance to Persia. Xanthippus' marriage to the Alcmaeonid Agariste provides more evidence of a possible political alliance with the family, some of whose members may have favoured cooperation with the Persians. If this is true, then his prosecution of Miltiades was designed to weaken the opposition by removing its political leader once and for all. This seems plausible, since the dominant political issue after Marathon must have been Athens' future relations with Persia. Such a humiliating defeat at the hands of the Athenians, following on from the burning of Sardis, was bound to provoke Persian retaliation on a far greater scale. Those politicians such as Miltiades, who had always advocated resistance to Persia, would have supported a policy of preparing for the conflict by rearmament and by forming alliances with other Greek states; the others would have done their utmost to make peace at all costs with Persia and to rid Athens of dangerous warmongers.

It was in this context, when there was such a major and irreconcilable division within the state with potentially destructive consequences for Athens, that the people unleashed for the first time the weapon that Cleisthenes had forged to resolve such dangerous situations. There followed a series of ostracisms: Hipparchus, the relative of Hippias, in 488/7; Megacles, the head of the Alcmaeonids, in 487/6; almost certainly Callias, a political supporter of the Alcmaeonids (see above) in 486/5. These three were distinguished by Aristotle as the 'friends of the tyrants' (Ath. Pol. 22.6), but not Xanthippus who was the fourth to be removed in 485/4; according to Aristotle, he was ostracized because he appeared to have become too powerful and influential. There are good grounds for believing that Aristotle was wrong in alleging this motive to the people. Xanthippus was the brother-in-law of Megacles, usually the sign of a political alliance; and he conducted the successful prosecution of the anti-Persian Miltiades in 489, and may even have been his prosecutor in the first case in 493/2.

Furthermore, the numerous ostraka cast against two other Alcmaeonids, Callixenos and Hippocrates, strongly suggest that any Alcmaeonid or Alc- maeonid political ally around the middle of the 480s were the prime targets of the people for ostracism. Thus it is reasonable to believe that Xanthip- pus, in the minds of the Athenian people, was either directly associated with the perceived pro-Persian policy of the Alcmaeonids or was suspected, through his marriage connections, of being in sympathy with this policy; and it was for this reason that he was ostracized.

Many scholars have suspected that Themistocles was the mastermind behind some or all of these ostracisms, and certainly the large number of pre-480 ostraka inscribed with his name, including a find of 190 ostraka written by only fourteen hands, shows that he was sufficiently prominent and influential for his political enemies to attempt his downfall. The literary sources give no direct evidence about his political activities in the 480s until 483/2, when his proposal to build either 200 'triremes' (Herodotus 7.144) or 100 (Aristotle, *Ath. Pol.* 22.7; Plutarch, *Themistocles* 4.1–3) with the surplus from the silver mines at Laurium transformed Athens into a naval super- power. For the rest of the 480s he was the dominant politician in Athens, and held the post of 'strategos autocrator' (commander-in-chief) of the Athenian armed forces against the Persians in 480, the year of the battle of Salamis. The sources, therefore, concentrate on Themistocles when he was at the peak of his career. However, if a dramatic and sudden rise to power in 483/2 seems unlikely, then it is plausible to believe that Themistocles was politically active throughout the 480s, which is confirmed by the ostraka – many of which are linked by their location with Megacles and should be dated to his ostracism in 487/6. If he was the political opponent of the Alcmaeonids and their allies, then he in all probability supported the policy of resistance to Persia.

Themistocles has also been linked with the reform of 487/6 by which the archons were no longer appointed by direct election, but were chosen after a two-stage process: election of a larger group (possibly 100 in total, ten from each tribe) and then the use of lot among this number to choose the nine archons (Aristotle, *Ath. Pol.* 22.5). The prestige of the archonship was affected by this reform, and from that date no well-known politician is known to have held this office. Either now or soon after, the 'strategia' (generalship) became the most important and the most sought after political post in Athens. Unlike the archonship, which could be held only once in a lifetime, the strategos (general) was eligible for re-election for as many years as he retained the confidence of the electorate. This continuity of office was essential for the approaching conflict with Persia, as it ensured that men of military ability were in a position to give coherent and consistent leader- ship. It was not long before generals were also being elected for their poli- tical ability, which must have led to the transfer of some powers of the archonship to the generalship. The importance of the generalship in the

Persian Wars and in the rise of the Delian League in the 470s and 460s (see Chapter 10) increased its authority at the expense of the archonship. Themistocles was the main beneficiary in the 480s of this reform and the ostracisms, and it is for that reason that he is believed to have played a part in their implementation. Whether he did or did not, ostracism certainly provided the much-needed unity in the state by ridding Athens of Persian sympathizers, and the generalship provided the continuity of command in the vital build-up to the war with Persia.

Aristides was the last man in the 480s to be ostracized (Aristotle, *Ath. Pol.* 22.7) and, although it is not explicitly stated in the sources, the issue that probably led to his ostracism was Themistocles' naval bill. Ostensibly, Themistocles' proposal to build a new fleet was put forward to meet the threat from Aegina, but in reality he had Persia in view:

> The Aeginetans and the Athenians and the other states possessed small fleets, and most of their ships were penteconters [50-oared ships]. It was only recently that Themistocles persuaded the Athenians, when they were at war with the Aeginetans and were at the same time expecting a foreign invasion, to build a fleet with which they fought at Salamis.
>
> (Thucydides 1.14.3)

According to Plutarch (*Aristides* 2–3), there had always been great personal and political rivalry between the two politicians, but their disagreement over this issue was perceived by the Athenians to be so divisive and so potentially damaging to the state that only an ostracism could finally resolve the matter. Once again the sources fail to clarify the reason for Aristides' specific opposition to Themistocles' naval bill. Possibly he was worried that such an emphasis on sea power would weaken and undermine the quality of the Athenian 'hoplite' army. Far more likely was his fear that, if Athens' future greatness depended upon sea power, the lower class thetes, who would be the oarsmen of the ships, were bound to demand more political power than was granted to them under Cleisthenes' constitution which favoured the aristocracy and the middle classes. Themistocles, on the other hand, firmly believed that Athens' future lay on the sea, and willingly accepted the political consequences of this policy (see Chapter 11 for a fuller discussion).

Aristides' ostracism removed the last obstacle to harmony in the state, and the Athenians decided that ostracism should be suspended in order to provide a unified front to the Persian invasion. Furthermore, in 481/0, they declared an amnesty for all those who had been ostracized (Aristotle, *Ath. Pol.* 22.8), allowing them to return to Athens, admit the error of their former policies and join in defence of their homeland. All returned except Hipparchus, who was condemned to death in his absence as a traitor. The Athenians were now ready to face the sternest test in their history to date.

Bibliography

Hignett, C. *A History of the Athenian Constitution*, ch. 7.

Lenardon, R. J. *The Saga of Themistocles*, chs 3 and 4.

Lewis, D. M. *Sparta and Persia*, ch. 2.

Moore, J. M. *Aristotle and Xenophon on Democracy and Oligarchy*, pp. 241–46.

Murray, O. *Early Greece*, 2nd edn, ch. 15.

Ostwald, M. *CAH vol.4*, 2nd edn, pt 2, ch. 5.4.

Sealey, R. *A History of the Greek City States 700–338 BC*, ch. 7.

9

THE PERSIAN WAR: GREEK
STRATEGY AND THE LEADERSHIP
OF SPARTA IN 480–479

The sources

The fullest description of Xerxes' invasion of Greece is contained in the last three books of Herodotus (all source references in this chapter are to Herodotus unless otherwise stated). Although he has been criticized justifiably by modern and ancient historians for his weaknesses (see Chapter 1 for a fuller discussion), his strengths, especially when compared with later writers, are such that his account of these events should be considered reasonably trustworthy. His accuracy has often been proved by other sources, when they are available, for example, his list of the six Persian nobles who helped Darius to seize the throne of Persia in 522 compares very favourably with Darius' own list which was included in an official inscription at Behistun in Media, recording his achievements; there is only one mistake and that an explicable one. This accuracy was due to his painstaking research and interviews with many of the eyewitnesses, both Greek and Persian, of the events that he narrated. As he was writing in the third quarter of the fifth century, he had access to many of the combatants and junior officers who took part in the battles. However, his accounts of the discussions in the Greek councils of war must be treated with caution, as they must be based upon gossip and rumour, since the middle-aged chief commanders who left no memoirs were dead by the time of his research. It is also clear from his descriptions that he visited the sites of the battles of Thermopylae, Salamis and Plataea, although his understanding of strategy is very limited. It is to Herodotus' credit that Thucydides, although critical of him as a historian (Thucydides 1.20.3), generally accepts his history of the war, and adds very little extra information when referring to the Persian War, with the exception of his praise of Themistocles' qualities which was intended to contradict the anti-Themistocles traditions accepted too uncritically by Herodotus.

The other main contemporary fifth-century source is the Athenian tragedian Aeschylus, who took part in the battle of Salamis in 480 and commemorated

147

this great victory by making it the centrepiece of his play, the *Persai*, performed in 472. It is useful to use his account of the battle to supplement and compare with that of Herodotus, but clearly the major aim of the play was to celebrate, with as much dramatic skill as possible, one glorious deed in the history of the Greek resistance to the Persians, and thus sheds little light on the Persian War as a whole.

Apart from Aeschylus, Herodotus and Thucydides, the other main evidence comes from or is derived from the fourth-century writers, Ephorus and Ctesias. Ctesias of Cnidus was the court doctor of King Artaxerxes II of Persia (c.404–360) and wrote a *Persica*, a history of the Persians in 23 books. His history has not survived; a brief epitome, written by the Byzantine Bishop Photius in the ninth century, survives, and there are references to his work in Plutarch's *Life of Artaxerxes*, Strabo's *Geographia* and Diodorus' *World History*. He claimed to have used Persian royal documents (Diodorus 2.32.4) but, whatever his merit as a historian of Persian affairs during the second half of the fifth century, his account of the Persian War is filled with errors. The most glaring are the placing of the battle of Plataea (479) between Thermopylae and Salamis (both in 480), and the death of Mardonius, the Persian commander-in-chief killed by the Greeks at Plataea, at the hands of the gods in a storm that saved Delphi. His inaccuracy and untrustworthiness make not only his evidence unreliable but also those who used him as their source. Plutarch, who was particularly critical of Herodotus in his *De Malignitate Herodoti* (*About the Spitefulness of Herodotus*), used in his *Life of Themistocles* the work of a certain Phanias of Lesbos who appears also to have been dependent on Ctesias; and this may be the source of Plutarch's account of the battle of Salamis which is not based on Herodotus' narrative. In fact, Plutarch made use of many sources, and thus provides some interesting information to add to Herodotus' account, but as their information is probably derived from Ephorus, it is of doubtful value.

The most important of the fourth-century writers was Ephorus, who wrote the *Historiai*, a 'universal' Greek history in 30 books. His description of the Persian War has not survived, but it is widely agreed that Diodorus of Sicily, writing in the first century BC has followed his account closely but more briefly (11.1–19, 27–37). Ephorus clearly used Herodotus as a source, as Herodotus' name, his history and its scope are specifically mentioned (Diodorus 11.37.6); and, on many occasions, there is a marked similarity in detail. However, he was a pupil of the orator and teacher Isocrates, and shared his beliefs in the use of history and rhetoric as a means of moral improvement, namely to glorify virtue and to condemn vice. His version of Thermopylae, influenced by such rhetoric, has the Spartan King Leonidas bravely attacking the Persian camp and even entering Xerxes' tent on the night before the final destruction of the Greek forces. The differences between Ephorus' account and that of Herodotus seem to be derived, not from a separate unidentified fifth-century source, but from his attempt to rationalize the different accounts of Herodotus, Aeschylus and Ctesias. If this is the case, then Ephorus (through book 11 of Diodorus) will add very little to the content of those three sources.

Preparations for war, 484–481

Xerxes succeeded his father Darius as King of Persia in 486 and, after putting down rebellions in Egypt and Babylon, he turned his attention to Greece in 484. Under his father two attempts had been made to punish Athens (and Eretria) for taking part in the burning of Sardis in 499: the joint land and sea campaign through Thrace under the command of Mardonius in 492; and the sea-borne expedition across the Aegean under Datis and Artaphrenes in 490, culminating in the battle of Marathon (see Chapter 8). Although nominally the new campaign was against Athens, it was clear that the conquest of all Greece south of Macedon was the primary objective, and thus Xerxes had to choose between the two previous strategies. The presence of Mardonius as one of his chief military advisors and the difficulty of transporting a very large army across the Aegean probably influenced Xerxes to opt for the strategy of 492. Mardonius' strategy had been based upon a joint land and naval campaign, with the fleet and army working in concert. He had succeeded, in the aftermath of the Ionian Revolt, in restoring Persian control over Thrace and Macedon as far as the borders of Thessaly. However, the destruction of his fleet when rounding the Mount Athos peninsula in Chalcidice and the heavy casualties inflicted by the Brygi, a Thracian tribe, led to the abandonment of his plans to punish Athens and Eretria (6.43–45). Xerxes firmly believed that a repetition of the setbacks that had troubled Mardonius could be avoided.

With this in mind Xerxes set about implementing a carefully planned programme to ensure the efficient and safe movement of his troops through Thrace and Macedon. From 484 to 481 various building projects were put into operation. Three years were spent on building a canal through the isthmus of the Mount Athos peninsula so that his fleet would not have to face the dangers of rounding that stormy promontory (7.22–23). Bridges were also built over the Hellespont and the river Strymon in Thrace (7.24), and presumably over the other rivers for speed of movement. Food depots were also located on the route through Thrace and along the coast, not only to feed the Persian forces on the march through those areas (the Greek cities were expected to offer generous hospitality), but also to be a source of supplies for the troops as they advanced into Greece, if they found that the Greeks had removed or destroyed the means to sustain themselves (7.25). Roads were built and paved, where necessary, in order to cope with wheeled transport. Finally, guard-posts, inns and courier stations were established along the route to protect the Persian lines of communication and to discourage any hostile action, particularly by the Thracians, that could threaten the safety of the forces in Greece. Thus Xerxes, unlike the foolish and headstrong autocrat as portrayed in Herodotus, had been meticulous in his planning for the invasion of Greece.

In the autumn of 481, Xerxes moved the army to Sardis in order to spend the winter there in training. The size of the army and navy that Xerxes led into Greece in the following year is a very thorny problem. The figures given by Herodotus are impossibly high: the total manpower was 5,283,220 (7.186.2). The infantry was said to have been 1,700,000 (7.60.1), as well as 300,000 from those Greeks who had 'medized', i.e. had gone over to the Persian side (7.185.2); in addition there were 80,000 cavalry, apart from the camels and the chariots (7.87.1). Modern scholarship has rightly rejected these numbers and has settled on 80,000 as a reasonable estimate of his land forces. As for the navy, Herodotus has evidently used the number given by Aeschylus in the *Persai* in lines 341–43: 1,000 ships and 207 'fast ships' (7.89–95); in addition Herodotus has added 120 ships from the Greeks in Thrace and the islands off Thrace (7.185.1). Once again, this number has been reduced by modern historians to an estimate of around 600 ships. Although allowance has to be made for the patriotic zeal of the victorious Greeks in the creation of these wildly excessive numbers, it must be stressed that this was a mighty force, far bigger than anything that they had ever seen or faced in war.

When the Persian forces arrived at Sardis, Xerxes indulged in some psychological warfare:

> Having arrived at Sardis, he first of all sent heralds to Greece, demanding earth and water and requiring the preparation of dinners for the king except to Athens and Sparta. ... The reasons for sending heralds a second time for earth and water were these: he had the very confident belief that those, who had not given them at the time of Darius' sending of heralds, would give them now through fear; and he wanted to know for sure if he was right in his judgement.
>
> (Herodotus 7.32)

Herodotus' list of those states that medized by offering earth and water cannot be accepted as accurate, since it included the states of central Greece who in all probability only came over to the Persian side after the Greek defeat in 480 at Thermopylae, when there was no choice (7.132). The capture of three Greek spies at Sardis, sent by the Hellenic League to gather information on the Persian forces, gave Xerxes another opportunity to put psychological pressure upon the Greeks. Having saved them from execution, ordered by his generals, Xerxes allowed them to have a guided tour of the whole army and then to leave Sardis unharmed so that accurate information of the vast size of his army could be relayed to the Greeks, and so undermine their will to resist (7.146–47).

The impending threat of Xerxes' invasion in 481 had stirred the Greeks into action to prepare for the defence of their homeland. A conference of Greek states, including states that medized after Thermopylae, was probably convened by the Spartans, after strong encouragement by the Athenians, in Sparta (Pausanias 3.12.6). It was agreed to form the Hellenic League, as it is usually called in modern scholarship, and the purpose of which was to secure the freedom of the Greeks by resisting the Persians (7.148). A number of measures were probably decided upon at this conference: all feuds between member states should be brought to an end (7.145) – thus ending the conflict between Athens and Aegina; the command of both the army and the navy should be conferred on the Spartans (8.3); all those states who had medized voluntarily and not under compulsion should have their land confiscated (7.132); three spies should be sent to investigate the Persian army at Sardis (7.145); envoys should be sent to Argos, Syracuse, Crete and Corcyra to request military aid (7.145); and a second meeting of the new League should take place at the Isthmus in the spring of 480, when the reports of the spies and the envoys would be available, in order to decide upon Greek strategy for that year. It is believed that the 'proboulos' (delegate) of each member state, large or small, had one vote and that decisions were arrived at by a majority of votes. However, as Herodotus only mentions two formal meetings of the League, there seems to have been no provision for regular meetings. Consequently the majority of the decisions about Greek strategy were taken by the councils of war, whose mode of operation and the exercise of Spartan leadership within them will be discussed below.

Greek strategy and Spartan leadership in 480

Herodotus' figures for the size of the Greek army and navy are likely to be more trustworthy than those for the Persian forces, but should still be treated with caution. At Plataea, the main land battle of the war, he states that the Greek army consisted of 38,700 'hoplites', which is believed to be a reasonably accurate estimate, and 69,500 light-armed troops, which is considered to be less reliable (9.29–30). With regard to the navy, there is also the evidence of Aeschylus who gives the number of ships that fought at the battle of Salamis. According to Herodotus (8.1–2) the original Greek fleet at Artemisium, the first sea-battle in the war, consisted of 271 'triremes' (containing at least 150 rowers) and nine smaller penteconters (50 rowers), but this number was later increased by an extra 53 triremes (8.14): a total of 324 triremes and nine penteconters. At the battle of Salamis, Herodotus gives a total of 378 triremes and four penteconters (8.48; 8.82), but this increased number seems unlikely. The Greek fleet had suffered losses at the battle of Artemisium, and therefore the total of 310 triremes and 10 other ships, as stated by Aeschylus (Persai 339), seems more convincing. It is possible that Herodotus has given the total number of all the ships that fought at some time in the campaign without making allowances for losses.

Until the advent of the Peloponnesian War in 431, when the importance of light-armed troops was greatly increased by the need to fight in very rough and difficult terrain throughout the whole of Greece, success in war on land was almost always achieved by a state's heavily armed hoplites (see Chapter 3 for further information). The fact that all the main states of Greece relied upon these massed formations of troops ensured that they all used the same tactics and strategy. These hoplite phalanxes needed level ground to be at their most effective, since hoplite tactics were totally direc-ted towards breaking through the opposition's phalanx by the sheer weight of a coordinated charge; if these shock tactics failed initially, then hand-to-hand fighting took place until one line broke and fled. Therefore the typical offensive strategy in Greece was to invade an enemy's territory, begin to destroy the crops on their plain, and thus compel them to give battle or submit without fighting. The Persians, by contrast, had developed different tactics because their weaponry and style of fighting were designed to make best use of their Asian terrain, which was very broad and flat. Their success in battle rested mainly on their cavalry and archers, who had the mobility in an open plain to surround a phalanx and inflict devastating losses at its most vulnerable points, namely the flanks and the rear.

The land strategy of the Greeks, therefore, was shaped by this knowledge of the effectiveness of the Persian cavalry and archers, and by the Athe-nians' success at the battle of Marathon in 490. The Athenians had shown that the hoplites, owing to their heavier defensive armour and longer thrusting spears, were superior to the Persian infantry in hand-to-hand fighting; and that a position, such as the small plain of Marathon which was overlooked by hills, protecting the flanks and rear of the hoplites, and which restricted the actual fighting area owing to the proximity of the sea, marshes and the hills, not only gave protection from cavalry attacks but also offered the opportunity of launching an effective counter-attack. Con-sequently, if the Greeks were to have any chance of winning a decisive land battle, they would need to find a similar battle location which combined a secure defensive position with the potential of quickly getting to grips with the Persian infantry. The alternative, purely defensive land strategy, still shaped by the same knowledge of the strengths and weaknesses of the Per-sian army, was to defend a narrow pass where the enemy could not deploy its superior numbers, and where the shock tactics of the hoplites would bring the Persian land advance to a halt, thus causing major problems for the sustenance of the army and hopefully leading to its withdrawal.

Greek naval strategy was also shaped by contemporary tactics in sea-battles and the nature of the Persian fleet. Although the Athenians advanced the art of naval warfare in the second half of the fifth century by relying totally on ramming in the open sea, the main tactics which were employed by the

Greeks and the Persians in 480 involved boarding an enemy's ship, with or without ramming beforehand, with large numbers of heavily armed marines, who had been placed on the deck of the ship for this very purpose. This is the reason why Herodotus often mentions the capture, and not the sinking, of ships in his descriptions of the naval battles (e.g. 8.17). However, the Persians possessed a greater number of ships, superior speed and better manoeuvrability (8.10; 8.60). Therefore the Greek navy needed to fight in a narrow strait where the Persians' larger force of ships would become a handicap and their superior seamanship would be given little or no chance to display itself. In addition, such a narrow and constricted space would be more advantageous to the bigger and heavier Greek ships, when ramming prow to prow, and the ensuing fighting between the marines, when boarding the enemy ships, would favour the more heavily armed Greek hoplites. Thus there was a marked similarity between the Greek land and naval strategy and tactics. The Greeks were soon to learn that, when faced with the joint operations of the Persian army and navy, they also needed to coordinate closely their land and naval strategy.

Tempe

The second meeting of the Hellenic League took place, as agreed, in the spring of 480 at the Isthmus. The news from their envoys was very discouraging: Argos, advised by the Delphic oracle not to join the Greek alliance, had demanded impossible conditions as the price for their joining, but in fact had already formed a pact with the Persians in which they agreed to remain neutral in the coming war (7.148–52); in the same way, Gelon, the tyrant of Syracuse, demanded the leadership of either the Greek army or navy as his precondition for sending military aid, which was not acceptable, but he too was willing to medize (7.157–63); Crete, upon the advice of Delphi which was conspicuously pro-Persian, refused to send any help; Corcyra agreed to send 60 ships, which failed to arrive for the battle of Salamis, allegedly held up by contrary winds, but there was suspicion that the Corcyraeans were playing a double game (7.169).

However, a delegation had also arrived from Thessaly with both an offer of and an appeal for help:

'Men of Greece, it is necessary to guard the pass into Olympus in order that Thessaly and the whole of Greece might be sheltered from war. We are now ready to guard it with you, but you must also send a great army; if you do not send one, know well that we will come to terms with the Persians. For it is not right that we, acting alone as the defenders for the rest of Greece, should be destroyed on your behalf.'

(Herodotus 7.172.2)

This group of Thessalians who favoured the Greek cause were clearly in opposition to the Aleuadae of Larissa, who were referred to as 'the Kings of

Thessaly' by Herodotus (7.6). The Aleuadae had already allied Thessaly with Persia, probably as early as 492 at the time of Mardonius' expedition, when Persian control over Thrace and Macedon was re-established; certainly they had encouraged Xerxes to invade Greece (7.6) and were singled out by Xerxes for special praise (7.130). The Hellenic League's desire to keep northern Greece inside the alliance and to have the services of the Thessalian cavalry shaped its strategy for the beginning of the campaigning season of 480. A force of 10,000 hoplites under the command of the Spartan Euaenetus, aided by the Athenian Themistocles, was sent by sea to Halos in the Gulf of Pagasae, and marched by land to the pass of Tempe. They remained here only for a few days before they retreated back to Halos and then sailed back to the Isthmus, thus bringing about the surrender of Thessaly and northern Greece to the Persians (7.173–74).

Such a swift and embarrassing reversal of military policy needs to be explained. Herodotus states that Alexander of Macedon persuaded the Greeks to abandon Tempe by stressing the magnitude of the Persian forces and the certain destruction of the Greek expeditionary force; but he records his own belief that the chief cause of the withdrawal was the fact that Tempe could be 'turned' (i.e. troops could be marched or ferried by ship to the other end of a pass, and thus trap the defending army in the pass itself) by the Persians using a pass to the west of Tempe (7.173–74). If Herodotus' explanation is right, it does seem strange that this information was not known to the Hellenic League or that a small force was not sent first to reconnoitre the area. Furthermore, Xerxes' forces were not due to arrive at Tempe for at least two months, which makes the early despatch of 10,000 men seem unnecessary. It is possible that such a show of military force was intended to strengthen the anti-Persian faction in Thessaly and to force the pro-Persian faction into line behind the Greek cause. If this was the case, then the Greek withdrawal was caused by the absence of Thessalian unity and the fear of treachery by the supporters of the Aleuadae, for it would be impossible to defend all four passes from Macedon into Thessaly without the united support of the Thessalians. It would also seem that the Greeks had not yet appreciated the need for a joint land and sea strategy, since there was no fleet in place to protect Tempe from being turned by sea. The loss of northern Greece now made the defence of central Greece a matter of the highest importance, at least to the states north of the Peloponnese.

Thermopylae and Artemisium

The Persian army and navy, after separating at Acanthus in Chalcidice, reunited at Therma. Xerxes and the army then marched ahead of the navy through Thessaly to the Malian Gulf; the Persian fleet set out eleven days later and sailed in a single day, according to Herodotus (7.183.2), to Magnesia where it anchored at Cape Sepias. It seems most unlikely that a huge fleet could sail between ninety and one hundred miles in a single day, and thus modern scholarship has convincingly argued that Herodotus does not give a clear, accurate timetable of this and some of the subsequent events. What is clear is that Xerxes was determined that the army and navy should work closely in tandem, and this necessitated the early advance of the army to secure safe anchorage on a friendly shore for the fleet.

After the return of the Greek forces from Tempe, it was decided by the Hellenic League, shaping its strategy to match the joint operations of the Persians, to send both the army and navy to the next line of defence:

> The proposal that won the day was to guard the pass of Thermopylae. For it was narrower than the pass in Thessaly and only one [alternative translation: 'at the same time'] and nearer to their homes. They did not know that there was a path, by means of which the Greeks who fell at Thermopylae were surrounded, until they came to Thermopylae and learned of its existence from the men of Trachis. Therefore they decided to guard this pass in order to prevent the foreigner from entering Greece, and to send the fleet to Artemisium in the territory of Histiaea, for these places, being near to each other, would provide easy communication between the two forces.
>
> (Herodotus 7.175.1–2)

The aim of Greek strategy at Thermopylae and Artemisium has been much debated, but it would seem to have been based on defensive and offensive elements.

Thermopylae, if it was guarded by a sufficient number of troops, was virtually unassailable by a frontal attack, even with very superior numbers, and thus was a perfect defensive land position. The Persian army could not be defeated in such a position, but its advance could be held up indefinitely, causing severe problems for Xerxes in his need to feed his large force. Such a stalemate on the land would force the Persians to take the offensive at sea against the Greek fleet which, being less heavily outnumbered and fighting in its chosen location in order to make use of its own strengths and to negate those of the enemy, had the best chance of defeating or severely damaging the Persian navy. However, the two positions were totally inter-dependent, since defeat of either force would necessitate the withdrawal of the other. The fall of Thermopylae would allow the Persians to control the narrows of the strait of Euripus, which is only 40 yards wide at Chalcis, thus cutting off the Greek fleet's line of retreat; and the abandonment of Artemisium would allow the Persian fleet to turn the Greek army's position by sailing down the Euripus strait and landing troops in its rear. Although Artemisium is 40 sea miles from Thermopylae and does not provide easy communications, as stated by Herodotus, and was not as narrow and confined as the Greeks would have ideally wished, its strategic position was crucial. The risk of a flank attack from Artemisium prevented the Persian fleet from sailing into the Malian Gulf without first attempting to destroy the Greek fleet; and its occupation prevented the landing of Persian troops in the north of the island of Euboea, who could have marched to Chalcis and thus been in a position to turn Thermopylae and block the retreat of the Greek fleet.

The Greeks sent the following land forces, under the command of the Spartan King Leonidas, to occupy the pass at Thermopylae: 4,000 Peloponnesians, consisting of 300 Spartiates, 2,120 Arcadians, 400 Corinthians, 200 from Phleious, 80 from Mycenae and probably 900 'Helots' or 'Perioeci' (see Glossary), who were joined there by 1,000 Phocians, 1,000 Locrians, 700 Thespians and 400 Thebans – a grand total of 7,100 soldiers. The Greek fleet, under the command of the Spartan Eurybiades but ably helped by the Athenian Themistocles, was composed of 271 triremes and nine penteconters, later reinforced by 53 triremes, and was sent to occupy the position of Artemisium. This disparity between the comparatively small size of the army and the large naval forces, together with other factors, has led some modern historians to doubt that the Spartans genuinely supported the above strategy of mounting a full and effective defence of Thermopylae and central Greece, preferring privately to make the decisive stand at the Isthmus of Corinth.

Support for this view comes from this quotation – 'The proposal that won the day' (7.175.1): clearly the decision of the Hellenic League to defend Thermopylae was not unanimous. The main opposition presumably came from the Peloponnesian delegates who did not wish to send their military contingents so far north, preferring to make the Isthmus at Corinth the main line of defence. It is believed that the Spartans, although sharing this opinion, did not openly oppose this strategy, since a refusal to defend Central Greece could have led to the medism of Athens and its navy, and the fatal weakening of the Greek forces and of Sparta's claim to leadership. Furthermore, it is argued, there are three pieces of evidence which show that the Spartans knew that the army was too small to hold Thermopylae and were unwilling to send reinforcements there; but, to stop their allies in central Greece from medizing, sent the minimum possible force with no intention of reinforcing this army.

First, there was the invitation to the Locrians and the Phocians to join the Greeks at Thermopylae:

> For the Greeks themselves invited them, telling them through messengers that they themselves had come as an advance guard of the rest, and that the rest of the allies were expected to arrive any day.
>
> (Herodotus 7.203.1)

It is reasonable to believe that 'the Greeks' in the above quotation are Leonidas and the commanders of the other Peloponnesian contingents. This is clear evidence that the 4,000 Peloponnesians were only an advance guard and therefore were insufficient for the task of holding Thermopylae.

Second, the Spartan claim that they could not come at once with their full force owing to their celebration of the religious feast of the Carneia, repeated by the Peloponnesians in their celebration of the Olympic festival, was a convenient excuse to delay the sending of troops until the fall of Thermopylae (7.206). The insincerity of the Spartans and Peloponnesians is laid bare by the fact that their religious scruples did not stop them from sending some forces. Third, when the Greek army at Thermopylae lost its nerve at the arrival of Xerxes' army and the Peloponnesians wished to retreat:

> Leonidas voted to remain there and to send messengers to the cities, ordering them to send help on the grounds that they were too few in number to withstand the Persian army.
>
> (Herodotus 7.207)

All this evidence reveals the Spartans believed that the fall of Thermopylae was inevitable and therefore its defence was unwise, but political considerations dictated that they had to make some effort and give the appearance of taking the defence of Thermopylae seriously.

On the other hand, Herodotus' account of the fighting at Thermopylae and the alternative interpretation of the above evidence strongly suggest that the Greek army could have held Thermopylae indefinitely and that the Spartans were fully committed to the Thermopylae–Artemisium line of defence. The comprehensive defeat of the Persian forces on the first two days of the fighting, with only a few Greek casualties, highlights the clear superiority of the heavily armed hoplites fighting in a narrow space and contradicts the view that the Greeks had insufficient troops to hold the pass (7.210–12). The discovery of the Anopaea, the path over the mountain that could turn Thermopylae, and the need to station some of his forces there must have been a disappointment to Leonidas, but the failure of the 1,000 Phocians to defend the Anopaea was due to their incompetence, not to a lack of manpower – a more vigilant and braver force of well-armed soldiers could have successfully prevented the Persians from climbing the narrow and difficult path (7.218).

Furthermore, at the meeting of the Hellenic League, the Spartans were more likely to have supported the chosen policy of defending Thermopylae, since to give up the whole of central Greece and the island of Euboea without a struggle would have gravely damaged the Greek will to resist and increased the mood of defeatism that was felt by some of the allies. The decision of the Spartans and the Peloponnesians to delay the despatch of their main forces during the festivals of the Carneia and the Olympics was based on their confidence that an adequate number of troops had been sent to Thermopylae:

> Therefore, they sent their advance guard, not thinking that the campaign at Thermopylae would be decided so soon.
>
> (Herodotus 7.206.2)

Thus the Spartans had every intention of defending Thermopylae and, as for the festival of the Carneia, the Spartans only claimed that it was 'in the way' (7.206.1), not an insurmountable obstacle. Finally, the story of Leonidas contemplating withdrawal and his request for more troops is probably fictitious, derived from an anti-Peloponnesian source. Leonidas knew that the forces at Thermopylae and Artemisium were inextricably linked, and consequently his withdrawal would expose the Greek fleet to enormous risk (see above). Moreover, with the Persian army in front of the very pass of Thermopylae, there was no time for extra troops to be summoned and put in position before Xerxes attacked.

On the basis of the evidence and the preceding arguments, it is reasonable to believe that Thermopylae was designated as the main position for the land defence. There was no doubt among scholars that the main bulk of the Greek navy, on the basis of Herodotus' evidence, had been sent to Artemisium until the discovery of an inscription at Troezen in 1959, reproducing allegedly a 'decree of Themistocles' (ML 23). This decree is in conflict with Herodotus' account on two very important points: first, it authorizes the mass evacuation of Attica before the battle at Thermopylae; second, it orders only one hundred Athenian ships to sail to Artemisium, instructing the other hundred to remain around Salamis and the rest of Attica. In Herodotus, the evacuation of Attica was an emergency measure after the fall of Thermopylae and a matter of improvisation by individuals, not organized by the state (8.40–42); and the whole of the Athenian fleet was sent to Artemisium, with the exception of 53 triremes that joined during the three days of fighting. If the decree is authentic, then it is clear that the Athenians also had no confidence in the commitment and the ability of the Spartans to hold Thermopylae, and that the retention of a hundred triremes was designed to protect Attica from an attack by a detachment of the Persian fleet, sailing around the east coast of Euboea, while the main Persian fleet fought at Artemisium. The inscription was carved in the late fourth or early third century, and is one of a number of Persian War documents that are believed to have been forged for fourth-century political purposes. No agreement between scholars has been reached on the issue of its authenticity and therefore, for the purposes of this chapter, the account of Herodotus has been preferred.

Although it is not clear in Herodotus, the three days of fighting at Thermopylae coincided with the naval action at Artemisium. The breakthrough for the Persians at Thermopylae came on the third day, after a certain Ephialtes from Malis revealed the existence of the Anopaean path, which the Persian troops under Hydarnes exploited to turn the Greek position, after the 1,000 Phocians who had been stationed there to protect the Greek rear, had fled. Upon receipt of the news that their position was about to be turned, Leonidas held a council of war which revealed a split in the allies' opinions between retreat and resistance. Leonidas ordered the allies to retreat, with the exception of the 700 Thespians and 400 Thebans, because, according to Herodotus, he perceived that there was a lack of will to fight, and he did not want such a potentially damaging and divisive split to be made public (7.220). His decision to stay with his 300 Spartans was motivated, according to Herodotus, by the oracle which stated that Sparta's survival depended upon the death in battle of one of its kings, and by Leonidas' desire that the Spartans should gain the maximum glory from this noble sacrifice (7.220). However true this may be, there was a much more prosaic reason for Leonidas staying and engaging the Persians on the third day: the need to buy time for the other Greeks to escape. If the whole Greek force had retreated, the Persian cavalry would have soon overtaken and destroyed them. After the most dogged and the bravest resistance, the Spartans and the Thespians were annihilated, but not the Thebans who surrendered before the final Persian onslaught (7.223–25; 233). Now the whole of central Greece lay open, since the next line of land defence was the Isthmus at Corinth.

The overtaking of two and the capture of all three lookout triremes by the speedier Persian ships confirmed the Persian tactical advantage, if fighting took place in open water. However, Herodotus' account that this loss led to panic and the withdrawal of the Greek fleet to Chalcis in the Euripus strait seems unhistorical (7.183), since this would have left the Greek position at Thermopylae exposed. But there may be a kernel of truth, namely that the Greek fleet did retreat temporarily into the Malian Gulf, presumably from the terrible storm that soon arose; and the mention of the Euripus may refer to the need of the Greeks to guard against a flanking movement by the Persian fleet around the eastern side of Euboea which would cut off the Greek line of retreat down the Euripus strait. It may well be that the 53 Athenian triremes, which later joined the main fleet at Artemisium, had been given this task. The Persian fleet arrived and moored on the Magnesian coast, close to Cape Sepias, but due to their large numbers, most had to ride at anchor off the shore. A terrible storm arose that blew for three days, and inflicted major damage upon the exposed Persian fleet, but the stated losses of 400 ships (according to Herodotus) must be scaled down substantially (7.188–92). However, the reduction in Persian fighting ships did help to lessen the inequality in numbers.

After the storm, the Persians stationed their ships at Aphetae and in the safe waters of the Gulf of Pagasae. They also at some point despatched a squadron of 200 ships to sail around Euboea and attack the Greek fleet in the rear (8.7), but were destroyed by another storm, or perhaps by the three-day storm if sent earlier than in Herodotus' account (8.13–14). Although the loss of 200 is certainly an exaggeration by Herodotus, there seems no good reason to doubt that this attempt to circumnavigate Euboea took place. The Greeks launched their first attack on the same day as Xerxes first sent his army against Leonidas, but they waited until late in the day. Their tactics were presumably to catch the Persians with their ships dispersed, there being no single harbour for so large a force, defeat one division of ships, and then retreat at nightfall before the Persians could concentrate their fleet for a major battle. On the first day, the Greeks captured 30 ships (8.9–11) and on the second almost destroyed the Cilician squadron (8.14). On the third day, the Persians took the initiative and at midday went into a battle in which both sides inflicted and received heavy casualties (8.14–16). However, the news of the fall of Thermopylae meant that the Greek fleet's position was untenable; it withdrew under the cover of night to Salamis.

Salamis

There are many difficulties in Herodotus' chronology of the events leading up to the battle of Salamis, and there are serious doubts about the number of meetings of the Greeks' council of war, and about the reliability of the details and the portrayal of individuals' behaviour in these meetings. In particular, the first meeting of the Greek generals at Salamis (8.49), which was debating the possibility of retiring to the Isthmus before the Persians had even reached Athens, is still in session when it receives the news of the fall of the Acropolis – a success that took the Persians days, possibly weeks, to accomplish. In the same way, the portrayal of the Corinthians and their general Adeimantos as cowards, both in the debates in the councils of war and in the actual battle, is evidently the product of a hostile Athenian tradition that reflected the virulent anti-Corinthian feelings in Athens from 460 onwards. In fact, the Corinthians fought very bravely at Salamis, as the rest of the Greeks attested (8.94.4). However, although the greatest caution must be exercised in the use of Herodotus, what does emerge clearly from his account is the debate about the Greeks' naval strategy – whether to stay at Salamis or retire to the Isthmus where the army was hastily building a defensive wall (8.40.2).

After the battle of Artemisium, the Greek fleet put in at Salamis at the request of the Athenians so that they might evacuate their women and children to Salamis, Aegina and Troezen (8.40–41). When this was done, the Greek reserve ships joined the main fleet at Salamis. It was in Herodotus' first council of war that the arguments were put for making the Isthmus the base for the fleet:

> Eurybiades put the matter before them, allowing anyone who wished to speak to state where they thought was the most suitable place to fight a sea-battle in the territory still under their control [for Attica was already lost, but he was discussing the remaining places]. The opinions of most of the speakers were to sail to the Isthmus and fight a sea-battle for the safety of the Peloponnese – their reasons were that, if they were defeated in a sea-battle at Salamis, they would be blocked up in the island

where no help could be brought to them; whereas, at the Isthmus, they could escape
to their own people.

(Herodotus 8.49.1–2)

The identities and the arguments of the opponents of this strategy (i.e.
retreat from Salamis to the Isthmus of Corinth) are not given by Herodotus
at this point, but the opposition presumably came from the Athenians,
Aeginetans and Megarians (8.74.2).

After Herodotus' second (or extended first) council of war had allegedly
voted to retire to the Isthmus (8.56), Themistocles persuaded Eurybiades to
convene another meeting of the generals, where he put the arguments
against the Isthmus and for Salamis for the sea-battle with the Persians:

'If you take on the enemy at the Isthmus, you will fight a sea-battle in open waters
which is to our least advantage, since our ships are heavier and fewer in number. In
addition, you will lose Salamis, Megara and Aegina, even if we are successful. At the
same time their land army will follow their navy, and thus you yourselves will lead
them to the Peloponnese and put the whole of Greece at risk. But if you will do
things that I say, you will find so many advantages. First, by fighting in narrow waters
with our few ships against their many, we will win a great victory, if things in war turn
out as expected. Second, we will keep hold of Salamis where we have sent our
children and wives. Third, the thing which you most desire, you will be fighting in
defence of the Peloponnese equally by remaining here as at the Isthmus, and you will
not lead the enemy to the Peloponnese, if you are wise.'

(Herodotus 8.60.1–2)

To add force to his argument, Themistocles threatened Eurybiades that, if
the decision went against fighting at Salamis, the Athenians would leave
Greece for good and settle in Siris in Italy (8.62.2). It may have been Themistocles' blackmail that led Eurybiades, the naval commander-in-chief, to
decide to fight at Salamis, as Herodotus believed (8.63), but it is just as
likely that he, a battle-hardened commander and drawing on his knowledge
gained from the fighting at Artemisium, fully recognized the superior quality
of Themistocles' strategy.

Themistocles had devised the right strategy for dealing with the Persians.
He knew that the Persian strategy was very rigid, based almost totally on
the joint operation of the army and navy. The campaigns of Darius in
Thrace (4.89ff.) and of Mardonius in Thrace and Macedon (6.43–45) had
relied upon the same strategy, which also had been most forcefully recommended to Xerxes by Achaemenes, his brother and admiral (7.236.2), and
accepted by him. The Persian army, having devastated Attica, would not
dare advance to the Isthmus without the fleet, which would be needed to
turn the Greek land position. But the Persian fleet dare not bypass the
Greek navy, since it would expose itself either to a flank attack or, if allowed

161

to sail past unmolested, it would risk having its line of communication and supplies, especially water supplies, cut off by the Greek navy – a situation very similar to Artemisium. Therefore two options presented themselves to the Persians: either destroy the Greek fleet by attacking with the whole of the Persian navy or divide up the navy, leaving behind one large detachment to neutralize the Greek navy and sailing with the other to the Isthmus. The storms had substantially reduced the number of Persian ships, as Herodotus pointed out after the second storm:

> Everything was being done by the god in order to make the Persian navy equal to the Greek or not much larger.
>
> (Herodotus 8.13)

Their numbers had been further reduced by their losses in the fighting at Artemisium. Thus the option of dividing the fleet was a non-starter: the Persians had to fight.

Although Herodotus allows only one or two days between the arrival of the Persian fleet, the conference of Xerxes' admirals and their decision to fight, and the actual battle, most scholars believed that he has telescoped these events, and that the time-scale of these events may have been as much as three weeks. Certainly the Persians would not have been eager to fight in the narrows of Salamis, and the intervening time between the Persians' arrival and the battle may well be accounted for by their hopes of either tempting the Greeks out into the open waters to do battle or of a Greek withdrawal to the Isthmus. According to Herodotus (8.75) and Aeschylus (Persai 355–60), it was the message from Themistocles of dissension among the Greeks and their desire to flee that induced Xerxes to launch his attack. Many scholars have doubted the authenticity of this story, particularly as flight by the Greeks to the Isthmus would have suited Persian strategy perfectly. Whether the story about Themistocles' message is true or not, there were sound strategic reasons why the Persians had to attack. The sailing season was coming to an end and, if the issue was not resolved, the Persian fleet and army would be forced to retire to Thessaly for winter-quarters in order to have an adequate supply of grain. In this situation, Xerxes would have little to show for the year's campaign: the defeat of a small portion of the Greek army at Thermopylae and an indecisive outcome at Artemisium, while the bulk of the Greek forces remained intact and dangerous. Furthermore, he would have to surrender his control of central Greece, possibly having to face a repeat of Thermopylae and Artemisium, but against bigger and better prepared Greek forces. Victory at Salamis before the onset of the winter gales would lay the perfect foundation for the land campaign of 479.

Shortly after dawn the Greek fleet put out from its base to meet the Persian attack in the narrows of Salamis and, although the exact location is

a matter of scholarly dispute, the bravery of the Greek fleet flatly contradicts Herodotus' frequent statements that most of the Greeks were desperate to flee on the eve of the battle. The result was a decisive victory for the
Greeks, although this was not at first realized, since the Greeks made preparations to renew the sea-battle (8.96). Although Xerxes pretended that he
was ready to continue fighting (8.97), he had already decided that his chance
of defeating the Greek fleet had gone. He was far more worried that the
news of his defeat would encourage the revolt of the newly conquered cities
in Macedon and Thrace, and especially the Asiatic Greeks. Thus Xerxes
and the Persian navy first sailed to the Hellespont to secure the line of
retreat, and then he made his way to Sardis which he made his headquarters in order to keep a close surveillance on Ionia. Mardonius was left
in charge of the Persian army which now retired and wintered in Thessaly,
where there were abundant supplies, and prepared for a renewal of the land
campaign in 479. The refusal of the Peloponnesian naval commanders to
pursue the Persian fleet to the Hellespont, although much desired by the
Athenians (8.108–9), revealed the split between the cautious strategy of the
Spartans and the adventurous one of the Athenians that came to the fore in 479.

Greek strategy and Spartan leadership in 479

Mardonius' strategy in 479 for the conquest of Greece was devised with the
main aim of defeating the Greek army, which was still on the defensive in
an impregnable position behind the Isthmus wall, while the Greek fleet
controlled the seas. To achieve this, he formulated a primary and a reserve
strategy. Mardonius knew that a fleet was essential if he was going to turn
the Isthmus wall by landing troops in the Peloponnese (9.9.2). Therefore his
primary strategy was to win over the Athenians to the Persian side by
offering them very generous and attractive inducements on two occasions
(8.136.2–3). If the Athenians had succumbed to these blandishments, the
whole course of the war would have changed and Greece would have fallen:
a fact that Herodotus recognized and stated in the clearest and most
unequivocal terms, even though it was bound to be an unpopular opinion
in the third quarter of the fifth century (7.139).

When this strategy had to be abandoned due to Athenian patriotism, his
reserve strategy was to tempt the Greek forces to come out from behind
their defensive wall and fight a land-battle on terrain that he had chosen,
which would allow his cavalry to deliver the decisive blow against the Greek
hoplites. His major problem with the reserve strategy was the potential
operations of the Greek fleet in Ionia. He, like Xerxes, knew the extent of
the demoralization of the Persian fleet and its inability to fight an effective
sea-battle after Salamis. If the Greek fleet discovered this fact, either by
military action or by information from Ionia, then a naval offensive could
well lead to a second Ionian Revolt. In this situation, Mardonius would

have to retire with his army to protect his lines of communication and to suppress the revolt. Therefore Mardonius knew that he could not wait indefinitely to bring the Greek army to battle on his chosen terrain, but might be forced to concede this desired advantage.

Greek strategy for 479 is difficult to deduce with certainty owing to two factors: first, Herodotus describes the land campaign at Plataea in Boeotia and the sea campaign at Mycale in Ionia as two separate and independent theatres of war, and thus makes no attempt to explain their interdependent relationship in a coordinated Greek strategy; second, the tension between Athens and Sparta, reflecting their different strategic priorities, did not produce a clear-cut, definitive strategy upon which both agreed whole-heartedly. The Athenians wanted the Greek land army to forsake the Isthmus and go on the offensive, which is expressed precisely in the words of the Athenians to the Spartan ambassadors in the spring of 479:

> 'But now, as things stand thus, send out the army as soon as possible. For we reckon that the Persian army will soon be here and invading our land when it learns very quickly from our message that we will do none of the things that he wants from us. Therefore, before the Persian army comes into Attica, it is the right time for us to march first into Boeotia.'
>
> (Herodotus 8.144.5)

The Athenians had already evacuated their population and had seen their land and city devastated in 480, and consequently did not wish to undergo the same trauma in 479: hence their desire for the Greek army to advance and hold the line north of Attica in Boeotia. This Athenian emphasis on a land strategy in 479 may explain the very low profile of Themistocles, who had favoured a vigorous sea offensive at the Hellespont in the immediate aftermath of Salamis and, when thwarted, supported a naval campaign against Ionia in 479 (8.109), since the dominant Athenian politicians of 479 were Aristides and Xanthippus, in command respectively of the Athenian army and navy.

The Spartans, as Herodotus reveals in his account (derived for the most part from Athenian sources), were reluctant to pursue this offensive land strategy. The overwhelming advantage of defence behind the Isthmus wall, thus ensuring the safety of the Peloponnese, would be put in jeopardy by risking an offensive land battle in Boeotia in order to protect Attica. This of course could not be stated bluntly to the Athenians, since their fleet and their goodwill were essential to maintain the impregnability of the Isthmus wall. It is possible that the Spartans' extravagant praise of and honours to Themistocles (8.124) reflect their support for his strategy of concentrating on a naval campaign against Ionia in order to force the withdrawal of Mardonius' army from Greece without the need to fight a land battle. If this was their preferred strategy, then the gathering of only 110 Greek ships at

Aegina in the spring of 479 (8.131), compared with the 310 at Salamis in 480, could reflect the dissatisfaction of the Athenians, who may have held back their contingent from the fleet of the Hellenic League or sent only a nominal force. However, the more likely reason for the comparatively small gathering of ships at Aegina was the shortage of Greek manpower: there were insufficient troops to maintain a large army and a large navy, and therefore the strengthening of one branch of the armed forces had to be offset by the weakening of the other. In 480, Greek strategy had dictated that the main emphasis should be on the fleet, in which many hoplites had served as marines and possibly as rowers. But the Greek strategy of 479 had switched to the land which entailed the allocation of more men to the army at the expense of the navy.

It would seem, therefore, that Greek strategy for 479 was to concentrate on the defeat of Mardonius by land, but this decision did not make the Spartans enthusiastic supporters of this policy. If Demaratus, the exiled Spartan king accompanying Xerxes, is correct in his statement that the citizen-body of Sparta numbered only 8,000 in 480 (7.234.2), it is understandable, though not praiseworthy, that the Spartans, whose military super-power status depended upon the ruthless suppression of a much greater number of Helots (see Chapter 4), were reluctant to commit the bulk of their forces to such a hazardous expedition. This characteristic caution of the Spartans was noted by Thucydides who described them as:

> being traditionally slow to go to war, unless they were compelled.
>
> (Thucydides 1.118.2)

Many reasons have been put forward to explain away their failure to march out and save Attica from a second Persian invasion: the speed of the Persian advance, the need to wait for the harvest, or danger in the Peloponnese from medizing states such as Argos. Although these reasons have some plausibility, the real answer, confirmed in Herodotus' account, lies in Thucydides' astute comment above: the decision of the Spartans to advance into Boeotia was a direct result of Athenian compulsion.

Plataea

Mardonius set about implementing his primary strategy by sending the Macedonian king, Alexander, to Athens with an offer that, if the Athenians would join the Persian side they would receive very favourable terms: forgiveness for all Athenian hostile acts against Persia; the return of Attica and the gift of more territory of their choosing; internal autonomy in the conduct of their affairs; and the rebuilding of all their destroyed temples (8.140. 1–2). The report of Alexander's mission caused great disquiet to the Spartans who immediately sent an embassy to Athens. The Athenians at this

165

stage had no intention of medizing, but deliberately delayed their rejection of Mardonius' offer in order to pressurize Sparta into a land-campaign in Boeotia (8.144.5 – see quotation above). However, Athenian hopes of the Greek army advancing beyond the Isthmus wall and holding a defensive line north of Attica proved to be futile.

Upon hearing of Alexander's failure to win over the Athenians, Mardonius brought his army from Thessaly into Boeotia and then into Attica, leading to a second evacuation by the Athenians when they realized that the Spartans had no intention of protecting them. Herodotus alleges that Mardonius' motives for invading Attica were arrogance and a desire to inform Xerxes of his current success (9.2). However, he does admit that Mardonius reckoned the Athenians would be more willing to accept his repeated earlier offer, since they had been let down by the Spartans and their territory was again directly threatened with devastation (9.4). When they refused for a second time, he turned to his reserve strategy of provoking the Greeks into a land battle. Mardonius knew that his continued occupation of Attica was bound to rouse intense Athenian pressure on the Spartans to resolve the stalemate.

The Athenians, as soon as the Persians entered Boeotia and while they themselves were evacuating their families to Salamis, sent ambassadors to Sparta:

> in order to reproach the Spartans for allowing the Persians to invade Attica by not opposing them in Boeotia along with themselves, and at the same time to remind them of all the Persian promises if they would change sides. They were also to warn the Spartans that, if they did not bring help, the Athenians would find some means of helping themselves.
>
> (Herodotus 9.6)

The Spartans' excuse for their delay in protecting Attica was the celebration of the religious festival of the Hyacinthia, but Herodotus also points out significantly that the Isthmus wall was now almost complete (9.7). Even when the Spartans had received this veiled threat, the Ephors (see Glossary) were still reluctant to give a definite assurance that they would go on the offensive. However, Chileos, who was the foreigner with the most influence at Sparta but also spoke for the powerful and strategically vital Tegeans, stressed the deadly danger to the Greek cause and the futility of the Isthmus wall if the Athenians medized (9.9). The combination of Athenian blackmail and Peloponnesian pressure finally compelled the Spartans to mobilize the army of the Hellenic League and advance into Boeotia.

Upon hearing of the Greeks' mobilization, Mardonius devastated Attica for a second time and withdrew to Boeotia, for Attica was unsuitable terrain for his cavalry and he did not wish to be cut off from his main line of supplies. With Thebes as his base, he deployed his forces on the north side of the river Asopus, close to Plataea, and awaited the arrival of the Greek army under the command of Pausanias, who was acting as Spartan regent for the under-age son of Leonidas. Herodotus' account of the battle of Plataea (9.12–89) reveals that both armies, by their constant skirmishing and movements, were trying to entice the opposing side to fight on terrain that favoured their own forces: the Greeks on the south side of the Asopus and protected by the rough countryside in the foothills of Mount Cithaeron; the Persians on the north side of the Asopus in an open plain. Soothsayers on both sides had recommended remaining on the defensive (9.36–37), which led to a lengthy stalemate. Finally, Pausanias' move to the less pro-tected Asopus ridge and a complex night manoeuvre that went wrong, combined with Mardonius' fear of revolt in Ionia, induced the Persian general to cross the Asopus and attack. Pausanias held back until the Per-sian infantry was fully committed on the south side of the Asopus, and won a stunning victory with the Greek hoplites. Mardonius was killed and the Persians fled across the Asopus; those who took refuge in their fortified camp were slaughtered, while the rest under Artabazus escaped northwards and found safety back in Asia.

Mycale

Herodotus' account of Greek naval operations in 479 is given in two sec-tions, separated by his lengthy description of the events leading up to the battle of Plataea. His concentration on the land campaign at Plataea, coming after his full treatment of the naval campaign at Salamis, resulted in a less detailed account of this campaign, possibly on the grounds that it was an anti-climax after the two previous great battles. In the first section (8.131–32), Herodotus begins with the gathering of 110 ships at Aegina under the command of the Spartan King Leotychidas who, urged by conspirators from Chios to sail to Ionia, led the fleet only as far as Delos:

> For the Greeks were terribly afraid to go further, having no experience of those lands and thinking that everywhere was filled with armed men; also because they reckoned that Samos was as far away as the Pillars of Hercules.
>
> (Herodotus 8.132.3)

These reasons for stopping the naval advance at Delos, apart from the mention of 'armed men', cannot be taken seriously. However, although Greek strategy had put the emphasis on a land campaign in 479, it made sense to threaten Ionia by a forward advance, and thus put pressure on Mardonius. But it would be risky to sail closer to the enemy fleet which was still larger, even after its defeat at Salamis, than the 110 Greek ships and which could choose to fight in open waters where its speed and manoeuvrability would be to its advantage.

167

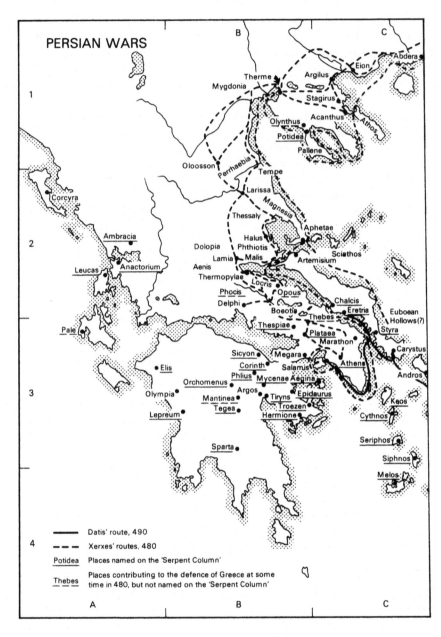

PERSIAN WARS

Datis' route, 490

Xerxes' routes, 480

Potidea Places named on the 'Serpent Column'

Thebes Places contributing to the defence of Greece at some
time in 480, but not named on the 'Serpent Column'

Map 4 Persian Wars

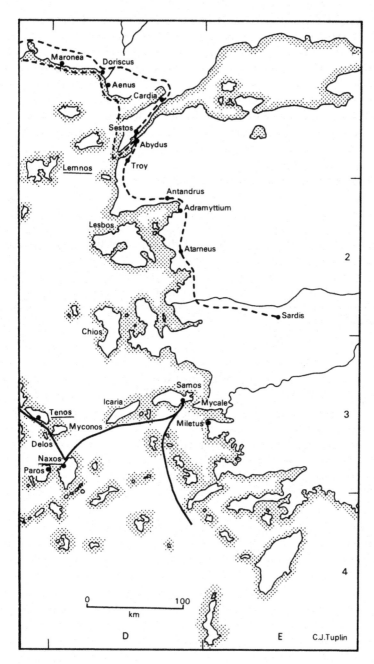

Map 4 continued

The second section (9.90–107) covers the advance of the Greek fleet across the Aegean to Samos where the Persian fleet was based and then to Mycale on the coast of Asia Minor. The key factor in the Greeks' decision to go on the offensive was the news from three Samian ambassadors that the Ionians were ready to revolt and that the Persian fleet was too demoralized to offer serious resistance (9.90.2). This was confirmed by the refusal of the Persian fleet to fight a sea-battle and its withdrawal to Mycale to be under the protection of the army (9.96). The Greeks landed and, with the help of the Ionians who deserted in the battle, won a hard-fought battle:

> In this way Ionia revolted for a second time from the Persians.
>
> (Herodotus 9.104)

The victories at Plataea and Mycale marked the liberation of Greece and the end of the defensive war. However, the revolt of the Ionians and their desire to join the Hellenic League would entail a radical change of military policy, if they were admitted: an offensive war against Persia in order to ensure their continued freedom. The reluctance of the Spartans and the willingness of the Athenians to take responsibility for the defence of the Asiatic Greeks laid the foundations for super-power rivalry and conflict throughout the fifth century.

Bibliography

Barron, J. P. *CAH vol.* 4, 2nd edn, ch. 11.

Brunt, P. A. 'The Hellenic League against Persia', *Historia* 2, reprinted in *Studies in Greek History and Thought*.

Burn, A. R. *Persia and the Greeks*, 2nd edn, pt 3.

Cartledge, P. *Sparta and Lakonia*, ch. 11.

Ehrenberg, V. *From Solon to Socrates*, 2nd edn, ch. 5.

Hammond, N. G. L. *CAH vol.* 4, 2nd edn, ch. 10.

Hignett, C. *Xerxes' Invasion of Greece*.

How, W. W. and Wells, J. A *Commentary on Herodotus vol.* 2, Appendices XX–XXIII.

Sealey, R. A *History of the Greek City States 700–338* BC, ch. 8.

10

THE DELIAN LEAGUE AND ATHENIAN EMPIRE

The establishment of the Delian League

In 478, the Hellenic League, under the command of the Spartan regent Pausanias, set about consolidating its victories of 479 and ensuring the safety of Greece by making expeditions against Cyprus and then against Byzantium (Thucydides 1.94.1–2; AE7 p. 13 – all references in this chapter are to Thucydides, unless otherwise stated). Cyprus, which was controlled by Persia and which would be a powerful base for a Persian naval counterattack in the southern Aegean, was for the most part conquered by the League forces. For similar reasons Byzantium, the gateway to the north Aegean, was besieged and captured. It was at this moment that the seeds of the Delian League (as it is called by modern historians) were sown. Pausanias, like many a Spartan removed from the strict constraints of Sparta, began to behave in an arrogant and overbearing manner towards the League's allies, resulting in their discontent with his leadership and consequently that of Sparta. The Ionians and those recently liberated from Persia approached the Athenians and, emphasizing their common Ionian kinship (see Chapter 2), asked them to become their leader (1.95.1; AE7 p. 13). Pausanias was recalled and Dorcis was sent out by Sparta as a replacement commander, but by this time the allies were committed to Athenian leadership and would not accept Dorcis' command. His return to Sparta marked the end of Sparta's official active involvement in the offensive war against Persia (1.95.2–7; AE7 p. 13).

Athens was clearly the ideal candidate for the leadership of the war against Persia. The present and future campaigns would demand a 'hegemon' (leader) who could conduct a vigorous, naval offensive, and one who was sympathetic to the aspirations of the Ionians. The Athenians' 200 ships, their Ionian kinship with many of the allies, and their support of the Ionians in 499 and in 479 made them the natural and very popular choice. But the big question was: of what should she become the leader? The Hellenic League? There was little doubt that Athens would become the hegemon in the annual elections for 477/6, especially after Sparta's withdrawal.

171

However, this leadership had little to attract the Athenians. The annual election for hegemon would give little security to the Athenians and was not a fair basis for their commitment of so many ships and men. In addition, the Peloponnesians with their votes would still have influence in deciding policy, and the Ionian mainlanders would still be excluded from membership. Consequently, the obvious solution was the establishment of an entirely new league – hence the creation in 478/7 of the Delian League.

Aims

> They made an assessment of which allied cities should provide money for the war against the Persians and which were to provide ships. They did this because a pretext for the alliance was to take revenge for their losses by devastating the Persian king's territory.
>
> (Thucydides 1.96.1; *AE*11 p. 15)

Thucydides' enigmatic choice of words – 'a pretext' ('proschema') – implies very strongly that one of the stated aims (he uses 'a' not 'the'), i.e. vengeance, was not the genuine aim. The Greek word 'proschema' has unpleasant connotations of falsehood and is normally used as a cloak for real motives or intentions. Various views have been expressed as to the reason why Thucydides used this word. One view is that, as it comes early in the 'Pentecontaetia Excursus', the purpose of which is to demonstrate the growth of Athenian power and the fear that this caused in Sparta, he believed that the Athenians from the outset deliberately intended to impose their power on the League allies. Furthermore, Thucydides' selection of events in the Pentecontaetia places more emphasis on the Athenians' suppression of their allies than their campaigns against Persia. However, such a viewpoint either credits the Athenians with remarkable and cynical foresight in 478/7 or criticizes Thucydides for using hindsight in imputing such motives to the Athenians. Another viewpoint is that the war against Persia was a pretext and that the real war that the Athenians were preparing for was against Sparta and the Peloponnesian League. However, although the sources disagree about whether the transfer of the leadership from Sparta to Athens was amicable or contentious (see below and Chapters 11 and 12), the main thrust of the League's campaigns in the 470s and 460s was against Persia and during this period the Athenians were led by the fervently pro-Spartan Cimon.

Yet another viewpoint is that the Athenians' real aim was simply and solely to gain leadership itself in 478/7 and the war against Persia was a good pretext for this. The Athenians clearly saw that their status as one of the two super-powers in Greece would be confirmed and increased by being the hegemon of a strong naval league. The example of the Spartans' dominant influence in Greek affairs owing to their leadership of the powerful Peloponnesian League was a great incentive to the Athenians to create something similar, in which they could invest their newly acquired military strength and prestige. Indeed it can be argued that this stated pretext was beneficial to both the Athenians and the Delian League allies since all the members could agree upon it, although harbouring different ideas as to what they actually wanted from the League. The Athenians, for their part, had suffered severe material loss from the two Persian occupations of 480 and 479. The allies, for their part, especially the cities on the Asiatic mainland and the neighbouring islands, fresh from deliverance from Persian domination, wanted continued freedom, as the envoys from Mytilene stated in 428 when asking for Spartan support for their revolt:

> 'We first became allies of the Athenians when you [the Spartans] abandoned us after the Persian War and they remained to see to the rest of the job. We became allies, however, not in order to subjugate the Greeks to the Athenians, but to free the Greeks from the Persians.'
>
> (Thucydides 3.10.2–3; *AE*12 p. 15)

Constitution

Both Aristotle and Plutarch (*Aristeides* 25.1; AE17 p. 17) mention an event not recorded in Thucydides:

> and he had the Ionians swear oaths to have the same friends and enemies, oaths over which they sank iron bars in the sea.
>
> (Aristotle, *Ath. Pol.* 4–5; *AE*16 p. 16)

Until recently it was believed that this sinking of iron bars signified that the alliance was to be a permanent one, i.e. the League would last until the iron bars should rise to the surface. This interpretation was reinforced by Herodotus' description of a similar action: the Phocaeans, having been forced to desert Phocaea because of the growth of the Persian Empire in the later sixth century, returned briefly and killed the Persian garrison before setting off for a new homeland. However, before leaving, they called down curses on any of their number who stayed behind in Phocaea, and then they sank a mass of iron in the sea and swore that they would never return until this iron reappeared (1.165). However, H. Jacobsen has suggested a different interpretation of this action: in other ancient Mediterranean societies the practice of taking oaths and throwing down objects is not to signify permanence but the death or exile of any person breaking the oath. In Plutarch's and Aristotle's accounts, it is the oaths that are sealed by the throwing of lumps of metal into the sea. Therefore it is possible that Herodotus misinterpreted the action of the Phocaeans, and that the meaning of Aristeides' action in 478/7 was to threaten death or exile to anyone who broke the oath 'to have the same friends and enemies' and not to suggest permanence for the League.

173

Structure

One of the most important and the most problematic of the original terms concerns the structure by which the Athenians and the allies reached their decisions about League policy. The choice lay between either a unicameral or a bicameral decision-making structure. In a unicameral structure, every member, including the hegemon, has only one vote in a single chamber – a simple majority deciding policy. In a bicameral structure, there are two chambers, consisting of the hegemon in one chamber and the rest of the allies in the other chamber. Each chamber is constitutionally equal in power to each other, and therefore a policy is only authorized when both chambers vote in favour. If one chamber opposes the proposed policy and passes a veto, then the policy is rejected. In this structure, the allies' decision would be reached by a majority verdict within their chamber.

Thucydides gives the following information:

> Delos was their treasury and it was at the sanctuary there that their meetings were held. They were leaders of allies who at first were independent and took counsel in meetings open to all.
>
> (Thucydides 1.96.2–97.1; *AE*15 p.16)

In the above quotation, the crucial section is 'who. ... took counsel in meetings open to all'. If the 'who' refers solely to the 'allies', then this would be evidence for the allies meeting separately from the hegemon to make their own decisions, thereby confirming the League as being bicameral. On the other hand, if the 'who' refers not only to the allies but also includes the subject of the sentence i.e. 'they [the Athenians]', then it suggests that the Athenians and the allies met in general meetings together to make decisions in a unicameral structure. It is clear that this source is ambiguous and can be interpreted in either way, although it is worth observing that in the original Greek the 'who' is a participle agreeing with 'the allies', thereby strengthening the claim for a bicameral institution. Further support for a bicameral structure comes from Diodorus:

> Immediately, therefore, Aristeides advised all the allies, who were holding a general meeting, to choose Delos as their common Treasury, to deposit there all the money they collected.
>
> (Diodorus 11.47.1; *AE*19 p. 17)

This source strongly suggests that the allies were having their own meeting and that Aristides, whether in an official or private capacity, was an outsider, offering advice to their deliberations.

There is one literary source, however, which strongly supports the idea that the League was unicameral. In 428, the Mytileneans, after revolting from Athens, were addressing the Spartans at Olympia in an attempt to persuade them to support their revolt by armed intervention, and were explaining how the Athenians had gained mastery over the League:

> On the other hand, our position demonstrated that those who had equal votes (iso-psephoi) did not take part in campaigns against their will, and that those whom they attacked must have done something wrong.
>
> (Thucydides 3.11.4; AE126 p. 61)

'Isopsephoi' means literally 'equal in vote' and therefore the Mytileneans were apparently stating that their vote was equal to the Athenians', which situation could only have existed in a unicameral league. However, it has been pointed out (by de Ste Croix) that this Greek word has been used elsewhere by Thucydides to mean 'having the same power of effective decision'. If this is so, then the Athenians were claiming that the Mytileneans, because they were autonomous allies and consequently had the same power as the Athenians to make their own independent decisions, must have agreed to the policy of suppressing allies in revolt, since they had the power to refuse. However, earlier in the same chapter, the Mytileneans stated:

> But since they had most of the allies under their thumb, our continuing equality was something they reasonably would find increasingly difficult to put up with. They would contrast us who alone remained their equals with the majority who had submitted to them.
>
> (Thucydides 3.11.1; AE126 pp. 60–61)

The second sentence in particular strongly suggests a unicameral organization with Mytilene having an equal vote with Athens but subsequently being outvoted by the subject-allies, who voted as the Athenians wished.

The ambiguity of the literary sources certainly causes difficulty in the attempt to establish the facts about the decision-making structure of the Delian League. However, the Athenians and the allies were hardly likely to have made their judgement in a political vacuum in 478/7. There were in Greece three other leagues, whose success or failure would probably have played a significant and influential role in the preliminary discussions leading up to the formation of the Delian League. There was the unicameral Ionian League, which operated during the Ionian Revolt (499–494) and of which many of the new Delian League allies had been members. The lack of decisive and authoritative leadership in this league led to disastrous disunity at the battle of Lade in 494 and the collapse of the revolt. There was also the unicameral Hellenic League, which was successful in achieving its aim of saving Greece from Persia, but there had been many serious, potentially destructive disagreements over policy within the League with repeated Athenian threats to desert. The third League was the bicameral Peloponnesian League with Sparta as its hegemon. This league was the backbone of the Spartans' success in Greek affairs from the second half of the sixth century onwards and was the dominant element in gaining Sparta the hegemony of the Hellenic League. A bicameral league would be attractive not only to the Athenians, with the success of the Peloponnesian League before them, but also to the Ionians, whose previous hopes of liberty had failed in a unicameral league. Finally, exactly one hundred years later, the Second Athenian League was set up as a bicameral alliance. The allies were determined that this time they would avoid the mistakes that had led to their former subjugation to Athens by a carefully drafted constitution. It is difficult to believe, if the Delian League was unicameral, thus exercising more control over the Athenians as hegemon, that the allies would give the Athenians so much extra power in the fourth century by establishing a bicameral league. What else can be said about the general meetings, apart from the issue of whether they were unicameral or bicameral? How often were they held? What were the topics of discussion? Did they have a judicial role in dealing with breaches of discipline by the League members, as the allied chamber in the Second Athenian League had? Presumably there was originally provision for a general meeting at least once a year before the beginning of the sailing season to decide upon the strategy for the forth-coming campaigning season. However, after 454 and the probable removal of the treasury from Delos to Athens, the matter becomes academic as the removal probably also marked the demise of these general meetings.

Finance

It was at that time [spring 477] that the Athenians first established the office of Hel-lenotamiai [Treasurers of the Greeks]. These were the men who received the tribute, as the money that was contributed was called. The first tribute that was assessed amounted to 460 talents. Delos was their treasury and it was at the sanctuary that their meetings were held.

(Thucydides 1.96.2; *AE*15 p. 16)

These financial regulations established the treasury at Delos, which was a centre of religious importance to the Greeks; the treasurers were called the 'Hellenotamiae' (Treasurers of the Greeks), and these officials would be Athenian, selected by and responsible to the Athenian demos. The Delian League allies would make their contribution either by paying phoros (tri-bute) or by supplying ships (1.96.1; *AE*11 p. 15). It was essential at the beginning of this great enterprise that there was no perceived unfairness in the assessment of each ally's contribution:

Wanting the burden on each city to be moderate, they asked the Athenians for Aris-teides' help, and instructed him to consider the land and income of each city and to fix the contributions according to the resources of each.

(Plutarch, *Aristeides* 24.1; *AE*20 p. 17)

Aristides, by making an assessment with which all the allies agreed, earned the title of 'Aristides the Just' (Diodorus 11.47.2; AE19 p. 17).

The first assessment of 'phoros' (tribute) was 460 talents, although Diodorus, writing much later and prone to error, made the sum 560 talents (11.47.1; AE19 p. 17). This figure of Thucydides has caused problems, as it appears to be too high when compared with other evidence. In 454/3, the Athenians probably moved the League treasury to Athens and devoted one-sixtieth of each ally's phoros to Athena as 'first fruits'; these offerings were recorded on stone and are always referred to as the 'Athenian Tribute Lists' (ATLs) by modern historians. Although these lists are fragmentary, there is confidence in accepting the figure of c.430 talents as the collection in the late 430s, when membership of the League had increased (e.g. Carystos and Aegina) and when the number of those who had converted from supplying ships to paying phoros had risen dramatically (only Lesbos and Chios still supplied ships). Therefore a figure well in excess of 460 talents would have been expected by the 430s, not a decrease. There have been various attempts to resolve this dilemma: the Athenians may have reduced the assessment in the years following 478/7; or 460 talents may have been an optimistic sum, and included the assessment not only of those who joined in 478 but of those whom the Athenians hoped would join the League; or the ATLs are unreliable, as some phoros was collected at source and not recorded on the quota lists. The most attractive solution is to accept that the ship-suppliers were assessed in a phoros equivalence (possibly one ship was the equivalent of 1 talent), and therefore the 460 talents includes cash, ships and men. Certainly, when, in the 460s onwards, ship-suppliers wished to convert to phoros-paying status, a cash equivalence was worked out (1.99.3; AE29 p. 21). It may even have been the case that Athens' naval contribution to the new League was assessed in a phoros equivalence and included in the original sum of 460 talents – if this represented a third or more, then the allies' original contribution would have been much smaller in 478, and there would be no problem about the later collection of c.430 talents as it would represent a rise. Many problems, similar to those surrounding the financial arrangements above, still exist owing to the lack of detail in Thucydides' account of the League.

From 'League' to 'Empire', 478/7–446/5

The sources

Literary

The main and best literary source for the account of the transition from league to empire from its establishment in 478/7 to the outbreak of the Peloponnesian War in 431 is Thucydides. He covers this period, which is usually referred to as the Pentecontaetia (the 'Fifty Years'), in Book 1 chapters 89–117. However, care must be exercised when using Thucydides, as he had no intention of writing a full and thorough history of the development of the Athenian Empire – that was reserved for his account of the history of the Peloponnesian War. Thucydides' main contention or, as he states it in 1.23, 'the truest cause of the war' was the growth of Athenian imperial power and the fear that this caused among the Spartans, forcing them to go to war. Thus the main purpose of the Pentecontaetia is to persuade the reader of the correctness of Thucydides' judgement about the real cause of the war. Therefore, by a process of selection and omission, of emphasis and understatement, he shapes his account of these years to demonstrate the stages in the gradual breakdown of the Athenian–Spartan relationship: the willing and harmonious change of leadership in the war against Persia in 478/7, the early Delian League campaigns against the Persians, the gradual but progressive intensification of Athenian imperial control over their allies, the campaigns and successes against Sparta's Peloponnesian League allies in the First Peloponnesian War, until finally the fear of the Spartans for their power and security became so great in the 430s that they declared war on the Athenians (1.88; AE1 p. 9).

Examples of this selection, omission, emphasis and understatement can be seen in the following: selection – the crushing of the revolt of Thasos in the 460s is highlighted to show the Athenians exercising imperial power for selfish, commercial reasons (1.100.2–101.3; AE29, p. 21 and AE39, p. 25); omission – the majority of the campaigns against Persia and the 'peace' with Persia in 449 are deliberately omitted, thus diminishing the true value of Athenian leadership in the campaigns that achieved for the Ionians freedom and security from the threat of the Persian Empire; emphasis – the arrogant behaviour of Pausanias in 478/7 is emphasized to explain the Spartans' willingness to be rid of the Persian War and to hand over the leadership to the Athenians (1.94.1–95.7; AE7, p. 13), but this does not fit in easily with his account of the Spartan fear of the Athenians in 479 and their attempt to keep the Athenians defenceless (1.89.3–1.92; AE4, pp. 10–11) – nor with the accounts of Herodotus, Aristotle and Diodorus (see Chapter 12); and finally understatement – his explanation of the Spartans' reasons for launching an expedition into central Greece to help three very small towns, resulting in them being forced to fight at the battle of Tanagra in 458/7 (1.107.2–108.1; AE39, pp. 26–27), can be called into question – an easier interpretation of the Spartans' motives, when one considers the size of the Spartan army, its presence in Boeotia (their ally), and the discontent of the Peloponnesian League at Sparta's fitful involvement in the First Peloponnesian War, is that this was a major and deliberate military campaign against Athens. However, despite these reservations and criticisms, Thucydides' account is superior to the other accounts of two later writers, Diodorus Siculus and Plutarch (for a fuller discussion of these authors, see Chapter 1). Their works rarely deal with events not covered by Thucydides but rather describe the same events in greater detail, although with differing degrees of reliability. Diodorus is particularly suspect when it comes to dating, although his main source for this period – the fourth-century historian, Ephorus – seems particularly well informed on Peloponnesian history in the fifth century.

Inscriptions

The two most useful types of inscriptional evidence for supplementing the literary works for this period are the so-called Athenian Tribute Quota Lists and the decrees passed in the Athenian Assembly. However, these decrees also have their own limitations, including the fact that they date only from the late 450s onwards, as the publication in stone of public accounts and Assembly decisions became a hallmark of the fully democratic Athens. It is generally accepted that the Athenians moved the League treasury to Athens in 454/3 and the Hellenotamiae (Treasurers of the Greeks) collected one-sixtieth of each ally's phoros every year (until 414/3 – apart from 449/8 – and again from 410/09 to 406/5) and dedicated it to Athena as 'first fruits'. These lists of annual offerings were recorded on stone and it is these records that are referred to as the 'Athenian Tribute Lists' (ATLs) by modern historians. The phoros-payers would normally pay the same annual amount of phoros in each assessment period, which would usually last for roughly four years; at the end of this period a general re-assessment of phoros to be paid would be conducted and each phoros-payer's new contribution would be assessed. These lists, although in fragmentary condition and giving only the payments of individual states, are still very useful in providing an insight into relations between Athens and her subject-allies, both collectively and on an individual basis – 'the lists serve as a barometer of Aegean politics' (Hornblower). The lists are particularly valuable when they record changes or variations from the norm, such as the unexpected appearance and disappearance of cities, especially if there is an adjustment to their phoros payment, or when there is an increase or decrease in a general re-assessment.

A good example of the first type is the island of Andros, which does not appear in lists 1–3 (454/3 to 452/1) but suddenly appears in list 4 (451/450), paying 12 talents. In list 5 (450/49) and in subsequent lists, she pays 6 talents. This unexpected appearance of Andros does highlight the limitation of the ATLs when they are the only evidence available: was Andros a ship-supplier who had decided voluntarily or had been 'encouraged' to convert to phoros-paying in 451/50? or had she, as a phoros-payer, been in revolt after Athens' defeat in Egypt in 454 but now had been forced back into line? or was she both a ship-supplier and in revolt, subsequently being crushed and forced to convert to phoros-paying? However, in Andros' case, there is literary evidence available that strongly suggests that she was in revolt. In 450, the Athenians initiated a policy of sending out 'cleruchies' (see Glossary) to disaffected allies' territory to act as unofficial garrisons and Plutarch records the despatch of one of these to Andros (*Life of Pericles* 11.5–6; AE231, p. 119). These settlers occupied a portion of confiscated land in allied territory, thus resulting in a decrease in that state's phoros – hence Andros' reduction to 6 talents in list 5 (450/49). A good example of the second type is the general re-assessment of 447/6, where as many as 30 states had their phoros reduced. Even allowing for the imposition of cleruchies in some cases, this reduction suggests that the Athenians, after their tough treatment of the subject-allies in the preceding years, were attempting to win back favour by this concession. Later, in the Archidamian War (431–421), there were two extraordinary re-assessments (i.e. not after a regular four-year period) in 428/7 and in 425/4, where the overall amount of phoros was greatly increased. This evidence from the lists reveals the increasing financial pressure that the Athenians were facing as the war progressed.

Decrees enacted in the Athenian Assembly, whether general or involving a particular city, are another valuable source for understanding Athens' relations with her allies. The main problem with this evidence is trying to find an accurate date for their enactment. In an ideal world, every decree would have in its prescript the name of the eponymous 'archon' (chief archon), who gave his name to the Athenian year. Unfortunately, this did not become a common practice until *c*.420 BC and, although there are earlier instances of the archon being named, surviving inscriptions are usually so badly damaged that their names are either missing, incomplete or impossible to read. Consequently three methods are regularly used, with varying degrees of success, to date an inscription: historical context, names of individuals mentioned in decrees and Greek lettering styles. A good example of historical context is the Chalcis Decree (ML 52; AE78 pp. 44–45). There is no easy way to date this decree on internal evidence, but in 446 the cities of the island of Euboea revolted from the Delian League, angered by the increasingly harsh imperialism of Athens in the early 440s and taking advantage of a major Athenian defeat at Coroneia (*c*.447 BC), resulting in the loss of her 'Land Empire'. Pericles soon led a force across to Euboea and crushed the revolt in 446/5. These events supply a convincing historical context for the passing of this decree against Chalcis (a city on Euboea) – a decree with exactly the same provisions was also passed against Eretria, another city on Euboea.

With regard to decrees with names of individuals contained within them, the Cleinias Decree (ML 46; AE190 pp. 102–3), which greatly tightened up the method of collecting phoros, shows the strengths and weaknesses of this approach to dating (see below in section '478/7–446/5' for the full discussion about Cleinias' possible identification, and the difference of scholarly opinion as to whether the 440s or the 420s were the appropriate historical context for this decree). The third method – Greek lettering styles – is the most problematical and is a matter of fierce academic debate. As the fifth century progressed, there was a change in the form of some letters in the Greek alphabet used in the inscriptions: the beta (b), the rho (r), the phi (ph); but most of the debate has been centred on the sigma (s) which can be written either with three bars or with four bars. One school of thought believes that the 'three-barred sigma' was used in inscriptions only up to c.445, and was replaced in later inscriptions by the 'four-barred sigma'. Therefore it is argued that similar inscriptions with the older form of sigma should be dated to pre-445. However, Mattingly has argued for a long time against this viewpoint and believes that the old-style of lettering continued to be used after c.430, and consequently Athenian imperial decrees of the early 440s should be placed in the 420s, and should be seen as the policy of Cleon and not Pericles. His case was strengthened by the inscription concerning an alliance between Athens and Segesta (or Egesta) in Sicily (ML 37). This inscription contains the 'three-barred sigma' and the old rho (r) and the archon's name '-on'. Most scholars, using the above criteria and not Mattingly's, dated this alliance to either 458/7, restoring '[Habr]on' as the archon, or 454/3 with '[Arist]on' as archon. However, laser photography has been used on this inscription and its results suggest that the damaged archon's name could be Antiphon, who was archon in 418/7, which means that the older lettering was still in use nearly 30 years after it was supposed to have died out. This does not mean necessarily that the dating of all the relevant decrees should be lowered – it means that this method of using Greek-lettering styles should be used with care. It is only when all three methods are present that there can be confidence in dating individual decrees.

478/7–446/5

The first recorded action of the Delian League was the capture of Eion:

> First [476/5] the Athenians under the command of Cimon son of Miltiades besieged and took Eion on the Strymon, which the Persians held, and enslaved it.
>
> (Thucydides 1.98.1; *AE*29 p. 21)

Apart from driving out the Persians from Greek territory, Eion commanded a very important position in the Thraceward region, which was rich in mineral wealth, offered excellent trading possibilities and even more importantly had abundant supplies of wood for the League fleet:

> Then they enslaved the island of Scyros in the Aegean, which the Dolopes inhabited, and settled it themselves.
>
> (Thucydides 1.98.2; *AE*29 p. 21)

The Dolopes on Scyros had attracted the League's attention owing to the fact that they made their living by practising piracy in the Aegean.

According to Plutarch (*Cimon* 8), Cimon soon conquered the island, established a colony there and freed the Aegean from piracy. This campaign, unlike the one against Eion, was not directed against the Persians, and shows that even at this early stage there was flexibility, at least on the part of the Athenians, in the League's aims. The League was made up of islands and coastal towns in the Aegean, and their economies were mainly dependent upon trade. The removal of piracy, the resulting free flow of trade and increased prosperity would have been greatly welcomed by the allies, but it would also be especially valuable to the Athenians, because the Piraeus was becoming the major trading centre in the eastern Mediterranean. In addition, Scyros was ideally situated on the grain route from the Hellespont to Athens.

The third recorded action of the Delian League was against Carystus, situated on the strategically important island of Euboea:

> War arose between the Athenians and the Carystians who were not supported by
> the other Euboeans, and in time a settlement was made by agreement.
> (Thucydides 1.98.3; *AE*29 p. 21)

Once again, as in the Scyros affair, the Delian League had conducted a campaign against fellow Greeks. Thucydides does not explicitly state the reason for the attack, but possibly it is implicit in his words 'who were not supported by the other Euboeans'. Carystus was a coastal town in Euboea and would have been enjoying all the political and commercial benefits of freedom from Persia and the removal of the pirates. However, unlike the other Euboean cities (and the other League allies), it was gaining all these advantages brought about by the League without contributing to the League's income. It is reasonable to assume that the 'terms', on which Carystus surrendered, were to become a phoros-paying member of the League. This incident again shows how Athens was willing to go beyond the League's original aims, especially when the action benefited themselves – Carystus was also a key city on the vital grain route from the Hellespont.

Around 471, the Athenians marked a turning point in their relations with the Delian League:

> After this they made war on the Naxians, who had revolted, and besieged and sub-
> dued them. This was the first allied city deprived of its freedom contrary to Greek
> custom.
> (Thucydides 1.98.4; *AE*29 p. 21)

Naxos was one of the original members of the League and, since it was the first member to be subjugated, Thucydides has highlighted the event. The enslavement refers to Naxos losing its autonomy and becoming a subject-ally under Athenian political control. In concrete terms, this would probably involve the establishment of an Athenian garrison, the confiscation of its fleet and the imposition of phoros-paying status (and possibly the installation of a democratic constitution). Although Thucydides gives no reasons for Naxos' revolt, it was probably a combination of Athens' increasingly high-handed behaviour and, after seven years, the growing feeling of security from Persian conquest. It would be valuable to know the feelings of the allies about this treatment of Naxos. Undoubtedly, some of the allies would have entertained the same resentment against the Athenians and would have felt great sympathy towards Naxos. Equally others, being fully aware that the Persian threat to the Aegean was far from finished, would have supported the Athenians; Naxos had been the Persians' prime target in 500 and 490 in order to gain control of the Cyclades (Herodotus 5.28–34, 6.96) and, for that reason, it was too important strategically to be allowed to secede.

> After this the sea and land battle at the river Eurymedon in Pamphylia took place between the Athenians and their allies and the Persians. The Athenians under the command of Cimon son of Miltiades were victorious on the same day in both battles, capturing and destroying some 200 Phoenician triremes.
>
> (Thucydides 1.100.1; *AE*29 p. 21)

The battle of Eurymedon c.469 was a massive victory for the Delian League, virtually removing the Persian threat from the Aegean. There were two great battles on the same day, which totally destroyed for the foreseeable future any Persian ambitions of regaining the Asiatic Greeks or the control of the Aegean. It was this success which probably affected the attitude of the allies towards the League more than any other event. The majority would have felt that the primary purpose of the League, i.e. the liberation of the Greeks from Persia, had been achieved, and consequently were reluctant to continue paying phoros or supplying ships for future campaigns. The Athenians, however, were determined that the allies should carry out their agreed obligations, and this led to them exercising a harsher and increasingly imperialistic control over the allies.

Thucydides in 1.99.1–4 (*AE*29 p. 21) gives thereafter a brief but slightly confused summary of the process, by which the Athenians transformed the League into the Athenian Empire. It is important to separate the strands of his narrative to establish the different process of subjugation for the phoros-payers and the ship-suppliers. The phoros payers after Eurymedon failed to pay their tribute, resulting in their revolt from the League. However, they were easily crushed and became subject-allies. The ship-suppliers (the islands in the League) always had a heavier burden than the phoros-payers, as they had to take part in the dangerous campaigning and had the added expense of maintaining their ships. Therefore, when the Athenians became more unpopular through their tough and insensitive leadership, the ship-suppliers reacted in one of two ways. Some such as Naxos and Thasos (see below) chose to revolt but were easily defeated by Athens' superior naval power. The others reacted as follows:

> because most of them disliked military service and absence from home, they agreed to contribute their share of the expense instead of ships.
>
> (Thucydides 1.99.3; *AE*29 p. 21)

This played into the hands of the Athenians. Whenever a ship-supplier became a phoros-payer, not only was the number of allied 'triremes' reduced but also the Athenians used the new phoros to replace those allied triremes with Athenian ones.

> As a result the Athenian fleet grew from the money that the allies brought in, and when they revolted, the allies were unprepared and short of experience in war.
>
> (Thucydides 1.99.3; *AE*29 p. 21)

Athens' action against Thasos in 465 was blatantly self-seeking and imperialistic:

> Some time later Thasians revolted. A quarrel had arisen about the trading posts on the Thracian mainland opposite and the mine, all of which they gained profit from.
>
> (Thucydides 1.100.2; *AE*29 p. 21)

Clearly both the trading posts and the mine belonged to Thasos, and the only possible cause for the dispute must have been Athens' demand for possession of them – an obvious case of commercial greed by the Athenians. This situation was further exacerbated by Athens' attempt to establish a colony at the Nine Ways on the river Strymon (1.100.3; *AE*29 p. 21), which revealed Athenian ambitions to gain control of that part of the Thraceward region. The Thasians felt that they had no other alternative but to revolt. The Athenians under Cimon won the sea-battle and began the lengthy siege of Thasos, which finally surrendered in 463. The terms imposed on Thasos were very harsh: the destruction of their defensive walls, the surrender of their navy, the payment of an indemnity, the imposition of phoros-paying status and, to complete the humiliation, the surrender of the trading posts and the mine (1.101.3; *AE*39 p. 25).

The feelings of the League allies can usually only be imagined owing to the lack of literary sources, but Diodorus, although writing much later, gives a convincing insight into their mood and their views about the nature of the Athenian leadership:

> For generally the Athenians' power was much increased and they did not use the allies fairly, as they had previously, but ruled them in a violent and overweening

manner. Many of the allies were unable to put up with this harshness, and they talked to each other about revolt, and some gave up attending the Common Meetings and made their own private dispositions.

(Diodorus 11.70.3–4; AE40 pp. 28–29)

Diodorus dates these reactions of the allies to 464/3, i.e. just as the siege of Thasos was coming to an end. Without doubt, Athens' behaviour towards Thasos had particularly shocked the allies and a majority felt oppressed by Athenian rule. However, revolt in the 460s was not a wise move as Athens was free to suppress them with ease. The outbreak of the First Peloponnesian War in 462/1, when the Athenians were fully stretched fighting the Peloponnesians, acquiring a 'Land Empire' and campaigning in Egypt, provided the ideal opportunity for the dissident allies.

Athenian foreign policy after 462/1, probably reflecting the political success of Ephialtes and the defeat of Cimon, now encompassed more ambitious goals than campaigning against Persia and gaining a greater control over the League. Alliances with Argos, Thessaly and Megara, and the campaigns against Aegina and in central Greece at Tanagra and Oenophyta, culminating in the 'Land Empire', reflect the Athenians' new territorial objectives (see Chapter 15). This warfare in mainland Greece would have roused little interest among the League allies, but they are found fighting alongside the Athenians at the battle of Aegina (1.105.2; AE39 p. 26) and at the battle of Tanagra (1.107.5–108.1; AE39 pp. 26–27). This must have caused great resentment within the League, as such warfare had little to do with the original aims of the Delian League. Even the Egyptian expedition, although more in keeping with the original aims, would not necessarily have been more attractive to the allies owing to its distance from the Aegean and the length of the campaign. Some of the allies would have seen this as an ideal time to revolt, since the Athenians would have found it very difficult to bring them back into line while fighting on so many fronts.

The defeat of the Greek forces in Egypt in 454 affected Athens' relations with the League allies, but there is disagreement about the size of the defeat and the way that the allies and the Athenians responded to it. Some modern historians (e.g. Meiggs) believe that the Athenians suffered a terrible defeat in Egypt, losing most of the 200 ships that sailed there c.460 and the majority of the 50 ships sent as a relief force. As a direct consequence of this disaster there was widespread dissatisfaction among the allies leading to numerous revolts, which forced the Athenians to intensify their rule ('arche') by adopting harsher methods of control. The basis for this belief comes from Thucydides' description of the end of the campaign:

So it was that after six years of war Greek fortunes and forces were destroyed. Of the many men involved a few were saved by marching through Libya to Cyrene, but the greatest part of the force perished.

(Thucydides 1.110.1; AE39 p. 27)

185

Thucydides' choice of language, so similar to his description of the later overwhelming defeat of the Athenians in Sicily in 413, leaves the reader in no doubt that he believed that the Athenian losses were on a massive scale. Opponents of this view, however, argue that either Thucydides was wrong about 200 ships being sent originally to Egypt from Cyprus, or he omitted to mention the withdrawal of most of the fleet, or simply he was mistaken about the scale of the defeat, having little opportunity to check his sources (being exiled from Athens in 424) and being only a child in 454.

Other historians believe that the Athenians suffered a serious setback in 454 but not a crippling disaster. It is believed that the greater part of the original 200 ships had returned to Greece after the initial victory, and that perhaps only 50 ships were left in Egypt, which were lost in the final conflict together with the majority of the 50 ships coming as a relief force. This much smaller defeat seems to have had little effect upon the Athenians' dominant control over the allies, but did lead to them carrying out a general reorganization of the League, which had been weakened by revolts (often inspired by the Persians) from early in the 450s. Evidence for this point of view also comes from Thucydides in his description of the campaigns at Megara and Tanagra. At the time of the siege of Aegina (c.459/8), the Athenians were so hard-pressed by a lack of manpower that they were forced to send the youngest and oldest of their troops to defend Megara (1.105.3–4; AE39 p. 26), but in c.457 before the battle of Tanagra:

> The Athenians marched out against them (i.e. the Spartans) in full force with a thousand Argives and contingents from the other allies to give a total force of 14,000 men.
>
> (Thucydides 1.107.5; *AE*39 p. 27)

This change in the manpower situation can be explained by reinforcements coming from Egypt. It is also suggested that a funeral 'stele', which records the names of the dead from the Erechtheid tribe, gives further support to this point of view:

> These men died in the war: on Cyprus, in Egypt, in Phoenicia, at Halieis, on Aegina, at Megara, in the same year
>
> (ML 33.1–4; *AE*42 p. 29)

If it is reasonable to assume that this list is in chronological order, then the mention of Phoenicia after Egypt can be used to argue that these men were killed on the return journey from Egypt (after the initial victory there) via Phoenicia to Athens.

Further evidence to support this view comes from Thucydides' statement that the Athenians captured 70 Aeginetan ships at the battle of Aegina (1.105.2; AE39 p. 26). The Athenian fleet must have exceeded a hundred ships at the sea-battle in order to win such a resounding victory, and it is doubtful whether the Athenians possessed the military resources to fight simultaneously on two fronts on such a large scale. The statement of Justin, who in the third century AD wrote an epitome of Pompeius Trogus' Philippic Histories, adds credence to the view that the majority of the ships had returned early in the 450s:

> Then for a short time, because they had sent the fleet into Egypt, the Athenians were weak and therefore were easily defeated, when fighting in a sea-battle. Then later after the return of their men the Athenians, increased in the strength of their fleet and army, renewed the fighting.
>
> (Justin iii. 6.6)

Finally, there is cited the evidence of Ctesias, a Greek doctor working at the Persian court c.400 and claiming to have consulted official Persian records, who states that there were only 40 ships present in the Egyptian campaign, that the name of the commander was Charitimides and that there were 6,000 survivors (63–67). On the basis of this evidence, it would seem that the Athenians had little to fear from dissident League members, and that their actions in the late 450s were more concerned with tightening-up the League and the removal of Persian influence, especially on the coast of Asia Minor. Opponents of this view, however, stress the unreliability of Ctesias and Justin – Ctesias makes serious errors and omissions in his narrative of events both in the Egyptian expedition and elsewhere in his *Persica*, and his numbers have to be treated with the greatest caution; Justin is a very late historian, and his summary of this period of Greek history is chronologically confused.

The use of epigraphic evidence becomes essential in charting the hardening of Athenian attitudes towards the allies in the late 450s and early 440s. The suppression of allied revolts in this period of time led the Athenians to infringe the autonomy of a greater number of states in a greater number of ways than had been witnessed before in the Greek world. However, there is a difference of opinion about Athens' relations with the allies in the late 450s, which is reflected in the interpretation of the Erythrae Decree, usually dated to 453/2. It is clear that there had been at Erythrae in Asia Minor a political struggle between League loyalists and medizers (supporters of a pro-Persian policy), who had gained the upper hand, revolted from the League and established a pro-Persian tyranny. The Athenians had put down the revolt, probably in 452, and the regulations, contained within this decree, impose upon the Erythraeans a democratic constitution and an Athenian military garrison. Some historians believe that the revolt was a direct result of the Athenian disaster in Egypt and therefore a tough, imperialistic solution was required. Athenian 'episcopoi' (overseers) organize the establishment of the first democratic Boule, aided by the Athenian 'phrourarch' (garrison commander), who is also given an important political role in the appointment of future 'Boulai' (Councils) at Erythrae, and there is a strong military presence:

> The [Inspectors] and Garrison Commander are to draw lots and set up the current council; in the future the council and the Garrison Commander [15] to do this not less than 30 days before the term of office expires.
>
> (ML 40; *AE*216A p. 113)

These decisions had been taken at Athens and not in consultation with the allies. Furthermore, it is the Athenians who would have the final say on internal political decisions of Erythrae:

> [25] ... and I will not drive out any of those who have stayed without the agreement of the Council of the Athenians and the People.

The alternative interpretation of these events and the purpose of the decree is that Erythrae and others had been in revolt from the early 450s, provoked by Athens' aggressive campaigns (especially the Egyptian expedition) and aided by Persian encouragement. Persia through its western 'satraps' (provincial governors) had been very active in the 450s in an attempt to regain control of the League allies on the coast of Asia Minor in order to draw the Athenians away from helping the rebel leader Inaros in Egypt. A further example of this pressure comes from the Athenian decree, passed in 451/0, which praised Sigeum on the Hellespont for its continuing loyalty and promised protection 'against anyone on the mainland' – presumably not only a reference to the Persians but also to pro-Persian Greeks (IG i.32). Therefore the installation of the garrison at Erythrae was intended more as a safety measure against any future Persian attack than as a specifically imperialist measure. In the same way, the political role of the phrourarch (garrison commander) was to vet the incoming Boule for covert pro-Persian sympathizers, who may have escaped the immediate purge after Erythrae's recovery by the Athenians. It is argued that, since garrisons were installed at Erythrae in 453/2 and at Miletus possibly in 450/49 (AE218 p. 115) but, after peace was made with the Persians in 449, not at Colophon *c.*447/6 (after its revolt had been put down – see below), the primary purpose of these military installations was to afford protection from Persia, and should not be seen as an intensification of Athenian rule. Furthermore, unlike later decrees, the Delian League allies are mentioned:

> The people are to swear the following: I will not revolt [from the Athenian People nor from the allies] of the Athenians,
>
> (ML 40; *AE*216B p. 114)

In 454/3, the Delian League treasury was probably moved from Delos to Athens either through a genuine fear for its safety after the defeat in Egypt or as a pretext to gain control of the League's finances, and the tribute lists (ATLs) begin from this period – List I records the phoros paid for the year 454/3, List 2 for the year 453/2, etc. In List 4 (451/0) and in List 5 (450/49), a significantly large number of islands appear on the lists for the first time. The reasons for this are also a source of dispute – for some historians, these islands had been withholding their phoros through discontent with Athens and were finally forced to pay up in 451/0 and 450/49 by Athenian military action; for others, these islands had still been supplying ships in the late 450s, and are recorded on Lists 4 and 5 because they became phoros-paying allies for the first time. However, there is little disagreement about Athens' final, intensive phase of imperialism from 450/49 to 446/5.

The Athenians and their allies won a decisive victory on Cyprus against the Persians (1.112.1; AE39 p. 28) c.450, and possibly in the spring of 449 a peace treaty was concluded between them. There is controversy over whether a formal peace treaty, known as the 'Peace of Callias' by its modern supporters, was signed, but it is agreed that fighting did come to an end between the two combatants at this time. Therefore the primary purpose of the League – war with Persia – had come to an end, and many allies would have entertained hopes of being released from their League obligations and Athens' increasing imperialism. The introduction of the Athenians' 'cleruchy' policy in 450, on the eve of peace with Persia, clearly shows that they had no intention of releasing their control over the allies. A cleruchy was a settlement of Athenian citizens who, while retaining their citizenship, were sent out to take over a confiscated portion of allied territory. The presence of cleruchies among dissident allies was very effective in maintaining imperial control:

> [5] In addition, Pericles sent 1,000 kleroukhoi to the Khersonese, 500 to Naxos, half that number to Andros, 1,000 to Thrace. ... [6] He did this ... , by planting settlers alongside the allies, to make them fearful and provide a guard against any revolution.
> (Plutarch, *Pericles* 11.5–6; *AE*231 p. 119)

There is no Tribute List 6 (449/8), and it is generally believed that the Athenians, with regard to the peace with Persia, declared a postponement in the collecting of phoros until a policy for the future was decided upon. Linked to this is a decree, normally referred to as the Congress Decree, which was proposed by Pericles in the spring of 449. He proposed to hold a congress, to which all the Greeks were invited to send representatives:

> to discuss: the Greek temples, which the Persians had burned down, and the sacrifices, which they owed to the gods, ... and the sea, that all might sail about with impunity and keep the peace [of Callias?]
> (Plutarch, *Pericles* 17.1; *AE*65 pp. 40–41)

Apart from an attempt by the Athenians to claim the religious leadership of Greece, the main objective of this decree was to provide a new mandate for the Delian League and for the collection of phoros. It is hardly surprising that the Spartans led the opposition to the Congress (Plutarch, *Pericles* 17.4; AE65 p. 41), since it would be held in Athens, the majority of the destroyed temples to be rebuilt were Athenian, and the freedom of the seas would be enforced for the most part by an Athenian fleet – funded in part by the Peloponnesians! It seems hard to believe that Pericles did not foresee this outcome, but the failure of the Congress to found a new league gave him the opportunity to keep the old League in operation and re-impose phoros for 448/7. As a consequence of the failure of the Congress Decree, Pericles, in c.449, proposed a decree (the evidence for which comes from a papyrus of the second century AD that appears to contain a commentary on Demosthenes' speech against Androtion) to use at once 5,000 talents and after that a further 3,000 talents, all from the Delian League funds, to finance a massive rebuilding programme of Athenian temples. The beginning of the 440s is attractive for the dating of this decree, since we know from surviving accounts that the construction of the Parthenon began in 447/6. Also, opposition to the Periclean building programme, almost certainly led by Thucydides, son of Melesias, was at its most forceful in the mid-440s (see Chapter 18).

There follows a series of exceptionally tough Athenian decrees, but the dating of two of them – the Cleinias Decree and the Coinage Decree (also known as the Standards Decree) – is a subject of intense scholarly debate (their content and possible dating are discussed at the end of this section). However, the Colophon Decree and the Chalcis Decree have been placed more confidently in c.446. After 449, the Athenians took tough, coercive action against the dissident allies who, resenting the re-imposition of phoros and Athenian imperial behaviour, revolted from the Delian League. The harshness of Athenian imperialism in this period is reflected in the Colophon Decree (ML 47; AE219 p. 115) – there is no certain date but it seems very similar in tone to the Erythrae Decree, the Miletus Decree and the Chalcis Decree, all of whose dates can be securely fixed to around this time. Colophon paid 3 talents in the first assessment period (454–450) but its absence from the Tribute Lists of 450/49 to 447/6 strongly suggests that it had been in revolt. After crushing the revolt the Athenians confiscated some of the Colophonians' territory, sent out settlers (either loyal Colophonians or Athenians) and established a democracy. Also Colophon's new phoros payment was set at 1½ talents, reflecting the new settlement on its land. The regulations, contained within the decree, are harsh:

and I will not revolt [from the Athenian People either] by word or deed, [neither I myself nor will I be persuaded to do so by anyone else], and I will love the [Athenian

People and I will not] desert and [I will not subvert] democracy [at Colophon – neither] myself nor will I [be persuaded] to do so [by anyone else]

(ML 47; *AE*219 p. 115)

The oath is far tougher than the Erythrae decree, demanding loyalty in word and deed – thus limiting freedom of speech. There is probably no mention of the 'allies' (unlike in the Erythrae Decree) which is in keeping with other decrees of this period, where the following formula was becoming commonplace: 'the cities which Athens controls', although the earliest of these decrees are honorific rather than imposing regulations.

The Chalcis Decree was probably passed in 446, after the suppression of the revolt of Euboea (ML 52; *AE*78 pp. 44–45). The Chalcidians' oath is far more detailed than the Erythraean and Colophonian oaths:

[21]. ... 'I will not revolt from the people of Athens by any means or device whatsoever, neither in word nor in deed, nor will I obey anyone who does revolt, and if anyone revolts I will denounce him to the Athenians, and [26]. ... I will be the best and fairest ally I am able to be and will help and defend the Athenian people, in the event of anyone wronging the Athenian people, and I will obey the Athenian people'.

(ML 52; *AE*78 p. 44)

Not only do the Chalcidians swear to avoid revolt in word and in deed, but even agree to betray their fellow citizens to the Athenians, if they should have rebellious ideas. In addition, the oath of loyalty is taken solely to the Athenians, and there is the explicit promise to help the Athenians in the event of an attack. In an amendment to a second decree, Athens directly interferes with the autonomy of Chalcis' judicial and political system:

[lines 70–80] Chalcidians should themselves subject their officials to scrutiny on Chalcis, just as the Athenians at Athens, except in cases involving exile, execution or loss of civic rights. On these matters there should be reference to Athens to the court of the Thesmothetai in accordance with the People's decree.

(ML 52; *AE*78 p. 45)

Athens was determined to exercise control over Chalcis by ensuring that the pro-Athenian ex-magistrates, carrying out pro-Athenian policies, were protected from prosecution and severe punishment on trumped-up charges by their political enemies – thus all cases involving exile, death or loss of citizen rights would be referred to Athens for trial (see Chapter 16 for fuller discussion).

The dating of the Cleinias Decree to either this period or to the mid-420s is a matter of scholarly dispute. This decree tightened up the collection of phoros by laying down a strict procedure for the transport of phoros to Athens:

> They are to make identification tokens for the cities to prevent those who bring the
> tribute from committing offences: the city is to write on [15] a tablet the amount of the
> tribute which it is sending and then seal it with the identification token before it sends
> it to Athens. Those who bring the tribute are to give the tablet to the Council to read
> whenever they hand over the tribute.
>
> (ML 46; *AE*190 pp. 102–3)

This system of phoros-recording tablets and identification tokens ensured
there could be no claims by phoros-payers that the correct amount had
been despatched but a part had been lost in transit. All prosecutions were
to be conducted in Athens, initially before the Boule and then before the
'Heliaea' (People's Court). There is also an expectation of Athenian officials
being present in the allied states:

> the Council and the magistrates in the cities and the Inspectors (episkopoi) should
> look after the collection of tribute every year [10] and bring it to Athens.

This decree also states, almost incidentally:

> If anyone commits an offence over the bringing of the cow or [the full set of armour],
> indictment and [punishment] are to follow the same procedure.

The implication in this section is that the decree that authorized the compulsory sending of a cow and a full set of armour (panoply) to the Great
Panathenaea, held every four years, had only been passed recently. Also,
this offence was to be treated with the same degree of seriousness as the
tribute offence.

One school of thought places this decree in the early 440s as part of the
Athenians' intensification of imperial control, when the allies, angry at
Athens' re-imposition of phoros after 449, were showing their disaffection
either by not paying it, part-paying it or by revolt. Their argument for this
dating rests on three issues: the name of Cleinias, the tribute lists of 448/7
and 447/6, and the Greek lettering on the decree. First, Cleinias who proposed this decree is not a common name in Athens, but has associations with
the family of Alcibiades, the outstanding Athenian politician in the last two
decades of the fifth century. Even more to the point, Cleinias was the name of
Alcibiades' father and he died at the battle of Coroneia in *c*.447. If this identification is correct, then Cleinias must have proposed this decree before
447 BC. Second, Tribute List 7 (448/7) has many absentees, part-payers and
late-payers, but Tribute List 8 (447/6) shows a marked improvement with
former absentees making two payments for two years, previous part-payers
making up their shortfall and some states paying in two instalments, presumably as a result of the Cleinias Decree. Third, the use of curved upsilons
(u) on this decree are not usually found on decrees passed after 430.

However, the other school of thought prefers a dating in the 420s. First, there is no proof that this Cleinias was the same man as Alcibiades' father. Second, an alternative historical context can be offered for dating this decree. As early as 428, the Athenians were struggling to keep up with the cost of the Peloponnesian War and were using up their financial reserves. In this year they held an extraordinary re-assessment (due in 426) with a significant increase in the total amount of phoros. Then, in the mid-420s, two important decrees were passed concerning phoros. The Cleonymos Decree (ML 68; AE136 pp. 64–65), which can be dated to 426/5, also improved the collection of phoros by specifically appointing Collectors in all the allied cities who were personally responsible for its collection; and the Thoudippos Decree (ML 69; AE138 pp. 66–67), which can be dated to 425/4 and therefore was another extraordinary re-assessment, authorized a threefold increase in the total amount of phoros. Furthermore, this decree (assuming the Cleinias Decree was later) is the first mention in the sources of the allies' religious obligation to supply a cow and a suit of armour at the Great Panathenaea. Therefore it is argued that the Cleinias Decree complements the Cleonymos Decree with the introduction of two new methods of tightening up the collection of phoros. Furthermore, it can be linked with the Thoudippos Decree concerning the religious obligations of the allies and should be dated soon after it. Finally, the harsh, imperialistic language with tough penalties for non-compliance is present in all these decrees and is far more in keeping with the Athens of Cleon (see Chapter 18, 'The demagogues').

The final decree, yet again with scholarly opinion split about the dating, is the Coinage Decree (Standards Decree in LACTOR 1–AE198; pp. 105–6), which has been reconstructed from various fragments found in some of the allied cities. This decree closed down allied mints and imposed Athenian silver coinage, weights and measures on all of the allies; it was to be set up in stone in the agora of each city by the local magistrates (section 8). The Athenians clearly anticipated the reluctance of all of the allies to carry this out:

[8] [The Athenians are to see to] this, if the cities themselves are not willing.

(ML 45; AE198 pp. 105–6)

The language in which it is couched is blatantly imperialistic, containing no mention of the 'allies', as in the earlier Erythrae Decree:

[9] The herald who goes is to ask them to do all that the Athenians order.

There are tough legal penalties against anyone who opposes these measures, and there is clear evidence of the widespread presence of Athenian officials in the allied cities:

[4] If there are no Athenian magistrates (archontes), the magistrates [of each city are to put into effect the provisions] of the decree.

It is not easy to establish what economic benefits this decree bestowed upon the Athenians, apart from the obvious advantages that all future phoros payments to Athens would be in Athenian silver coinage and minting fees. Certainly it would be easier for the Athenian fleet, which needed constantly to buy all kinds of supplies throughout the Aegean, if there was a uniform coinage to purchase these commodities. However, the decree did not establish a common currency, as the electrum coins (an alloy of gold and silver) of Cyzicus continued to be used in great numbers throughout the empire – also, unlike the modern euro, there were no great economic benefits arising from a common currency, since the actual (as opposed to the nominal) value of the coins was reflected in the quality and worth of their metal. This decree almost appears to be a piece of gratuitously blatant imperialism with Athens exercising control simply for the sake of it, although there would be the added political benefit of the coins serving as propaganda for the power of Athens throughout the Aegean.

Those who favour a date for this decree in the early 440s are influenced by two issues. First, having accepted the early date for the Cleinias Decree, they can see close parallels in the tone and language of the two decrees, thus suggesting a proximity in the time of their enactment. Second, one of the fragments of this decree comes from Cos and is engraved with Attic (and not Ionian) letters, suggesting that Cos was one of those reluctant displayers of the decree in its agora, and that the Athenians therefore had to have the decree engraved in Athens and then set it up themselves in Cos. The lettering on this Attic fragment displays the three-bar sigma which, it is believed by this school of thought, was not used after *c*.445 – hence a date in the early 440s. However, current scholarly opinion favours a date in either the 420s or 410s. Confidence in a pre-445 date for the three-barred sigma has been undermined (see discussion above in 'Sources' under 'Epigraphic' about the Athenian alliance with Egesta/Segesta). Of greater significance is the discovery of one of the decree's fragments at Hamaxitos in the Troad – a region in north-west Asia Minor, close to the Hellespont – which seems to have been incorporated into the Athenian Empire sometime in the 420s. Therefore this school of thought believes that this decree should be assigned a later date: either in the 420s, as it is in keeping with the harsh imperial tone of the decrees mentioned above, which were passed in the time of Cleon; or in *c*.414, as there seems to be an obvious parody of it in Aristophanes' *Birds*:

DECREE-SELLER: I am a Decree-seller, and I have come here to you to sell you new laws.
PEISETAIROS: Like what?

DECREE-SELLER: [1040] The people of Cloudcuckooland are to use these measures and weights and decrees just like the Olophyxians.

(Aristophanes, *Birds* AE199 pp. 106–7)

One of the merits of effective political satire is to use topical subject-matter – hence the argument for this date, as the *Birds* was performed in 414.

In 446, Athens' attempt to complete the transformation of the Delian League into the Athenian Empire was severely threatened by the loss of the 'Land Empire', the revolt of Euboea and the Spartan invasion of Attica under Pleistoanax. Pleistoanax's sudden withdrawal allowed the Athenians to crush the revolt of Euboea and thus snuffed out any chance of the allies breaking free from Athens' imperial control. The terms of the Thirty Year Peace in 446/5 recognized the Athenian Empire – the 'dual hegemony' of Athens and Sparta had been placed on a legal footing. Even if the Cleinias Decree and the Coinage (or Standards) Decree were not passed in the 440s, the Athenians by 446 BC had put in place all the necessary means of control by which they could govern their empire – a fleet that was virtually Athenian, the cleruchies, the garrisons, the resident Athenian officials, the imposed constitutions, the oaths of loyalty, the judicial interference and the ending of the league meetings on Delos. The big issue for the future was: would the Athenians be content with what they now controlled or would their imperial ambitions grow still greater?

Aftermath: Samos, Mytilene and Melos

Although Thucydides wished to write a comprehensive account of the events of the Peloponnesian War, the length and diversity of the war made it impractical to record everything. Thus it was necessary for him to exercise selectivity; by choosing to describe at length and in full detail a particular event or person, he was able to highlight and emphasize them as typical of a general situation that he wished to record. Thus civil war (stasis) broke out in many cities as a by-product of the Peloponnesian War, but Thucydides solves this dilemma by writing a full record of the events of the civil war in Corcyra (3.70–81), and then gives a general description of what happened elsewhere (3.82–84), but writes up no other civil war (apart from the oligarchic coup in Athens in 411 – see Chapter 23). In the same way, Cleon's tough, brutal speech against the Mytileneans and his support for the death penalty are designed to show him as the archetypal demagogue and thus typical of the politicians who dominated Athens after the death of Pericles, whereas the demagogue Hyperbolus hardly features at all. In the same way, Thucydides chose three events for full treatment: the revolt of Samos in 440/39, of Mytilene in 428/7, and the crushing of neutral Melos in 416/5. One school of thought (e.g. Finley) believes that Thucydides chose these three as examples of the progressive harshness of Athenian imperialism, coarsened by the stress of war; others believe each incident was chosen because of its specialness – Samos as the last independent ally allowed by Sparta to be crushed; Mytilene as an independent ship-supplier who chose to revolt during the war; and Melos, a neutral state, which was given the choice to determine its own fate.

Samos

The description of the revolt of Samos marks the literary end of Thucydides' Pentecontaetia (but not the historical 'Fifty Year' period which should run from *c*.480–430). The other key incidents – the alliance with Corcyra in 433 and the dispute over Potidaea in 432 – are treated separately as the grounds of complaint ('aitiai') or immediate causes of the Peloponnesian War. Thucydides' treatment of the Samian revolt is also the fullest and longest of all the incidents in the Pentecontaetia. There are probably three reasons for this: first, Samos was the last state that was allowed to have its independence removed by Athens without Spartan intervention; second, Samos was the most powerful of the independent ship-supplying allies and almost cost Athens its control of the sea; and third, the events were close enough to Thucydides' maturity to gather information directly from the combatants.

In 441/0, a war broke out between the island of Samos and Miletus, long-standing rivals, over the possession of Priene, a small city on the Ionian coast – Thucydides covers all the events in 1.115.2–117.3 (AE64 pp. 39–40). Samos was one of the three remaining independent ship-suppliers (along with Lesbos and Chios) and probably the most powerful of the three. The Milesians were defeated and turned to Athens for help. At first the Athenians adopted a softly-softly approach: they ordered the Samians to break off the war and to submit the matter to arbitration at Athens (Plutarch, *Pericles* 25.1). The Samians' refusal amounted to open defiance and forced the hand of the Athenians, who responded with such alacrity that the Samians were caught totally unprepared – presumably not expecting the Athenians to interfere in a local matter. Pericles set sail with 40 ships, subdued the island, established a democracy in place of the current oligarchy, took as hostages 50 men and 50 boys and deposited them on Lemnos, and then withdrew leaving a garrison behind. That should have been an end to it. The Athenians had behaved with restraint compared to clashes with other allies – the Samians had retained their independence, their fleet, their walls and their land.

The reaction of the Samians was one of great anger and determination to overturn the Athenian arrangements by any means. Some Samians, having fled to the mainland, made an alliance with the former oligarchic leaders and also with Pissouthnes, the Persian satrap of Sardis. They collected 700 mercenaries, rescued the hostages from Lemnos, crossed to Samos by night, seized power and revolted from Athens. To add insult to injury, the

Athenian garrison and magistrates were handed over to Pissouthnes (1.115.4–5). These Samians were determined to challenge the Athenians:

> they were defiantly determined to fight the Athenians for the supremacy of the sea.
>
> (Plutarch, *Pericles* 25.3)

Furthermore, they had the naval strength to offer a serious challenge to Athens. At the time of the oligarchic Rule of the 400 in Athens in 411 BC, the Athenian democrats, including the fleet, were based on Samos, and felt confident that their resistance from there would succeed:

> Samos was no weak city, but had indeed come extremely close to depriving the Athenians of control over the sea when it fought its war against them.
>
> (Thucydides 8.76.4; *AE*87 p. 47)

That Samos on its own could challenge Athens for control of the sea is an obvious exaggeration, although it took a fleet of over 200 ships finally to subdue Samos. However, its revolt had also inspired Byzantium to revolt (1.115.4) – there was now a real danger that such a powerful state as Samos could become a catalyst and provide the rallying point for a general uprising against the Athenians in the eastern Aegean. Furthermore, Pissouthnes appeared willing to take advantage of the unfolding events and to break the peace (whether formal or informal) between Persia and Athens in order to re-establish Persian control in Ionia and the Aegean. Thucydides mentions on two occasions that the Athenians had to divert ships away from the campaign against Samos in order to meet a perceived threat from the Phoenician (i.e. Persian) fleet – the second time Pericles himself led 60 ships to Caria in south west Asia Minor (1.116.1–3). The Samians also made an appeal for help to the Spartans and the Peloponnesians. Everything rested on the them: there would be no general uprising by the subject-allies nor would the Persian king risk a war with the Athenians unless Sparta and the Peloponnesian League joined the war effort. It was this same combination of combatants that finally defeated the Athenians in 404. The Spartans agreed to bring assistance but were stopped by the opposition of Corinth, who persuaded a majority of the Peloponnesian cities to vote against helping Samos (1.40.5; *AE*86 p. 47). That decision sealed the fate of Samos.

Although the Samians had some temporary success (1.117.1), their fleet was defeated by a combination of 160 Athenian ships and 55 ships from Chios and Lesbos, and, after a hugely expensive siege of nine months, the Samians finally surrendered:

> and they reached an agreement that they would pull down their walls, give hostages, hand over their fleet, and pay a full indemnity by regular instalments.
>
> (Thucydides 1.117.3; *AE* 64 p. 40)

The collapse of the Samian revolt also led to the Byzantines returning to subject-ally status. Although the punishment was by now standard practice, the subsequent decree is very interesting in its tone, compared to that of the Chalcis Decree:

> [15] [I will do, say and advise the Athenian people as] best [I can; I will not revolt from the people of] Athens in word [or deed, nor from the] Athenian allies. [20] [I will be faithful to] the people of Athens. [The Athenians swear:] I will do, say and [advise the people of] Samos [as best I can, and I will look after the] Samians.
>
> (ML 56; *AE*91 p. 48)

The Athenian oath is far more generous, pledging to support and look after the Samians. Furthermore, the Samians swore loyalty not solely to the Athenians (as the Chalcidians had to) but also to the allies. It seems as if the Athenians wished to acknowledge the specialness of Samos and to compensate for the removal of the Samians' fleet, their main source of military strength, by treating them less harshly than other revolting states. This policy paid off in the long run, as the Samians stayed loyal even after the Syracusan disaster in 413 when many other subject-allies revolted from Athens.

The size of the indemnity that the Samians had to repay to Athens for the cost of the war poses some problems. According to our literary sources – Isocrates, Diodorus and Nepos – the total sum was 1,200 talents. There is also a fragmentary inscription (ML 55; AE90 p. 48) that records the expenditure from the Treasury of Athena for the year 440–39: three sums are recorded with 'against the Samians' placed between the first and second sums, and 'Total' placed before a fourth sum which records a total of 1,400–1,500 talents. Some scholars believe that the first sum (128–130 talents) refers to the expenditure of subduing Byzantium, and that the second and third sums (1,276–1,280 talents) refers to the Samos. This is more than the costs stated in the literary sources but is at least closer than the 1,400+ talents. However, others have argued that there is no evidence that an expedition was ever launched to subdue Byzantium and therefore all three sums and the total should refer solely to Samos. Whatever the answer, it is interesting to note that the expenditure came from the Treasury of Athena, i.e. sacred money, and not from the Hellenotamiae, i.e. secular money. This may be the first recorded instance of wars being funded by public borrowing from temple funds.

Mytilene

Lesbos was one of the original ship-suppliers of the Delian League and by 428 was one of the two remaining independent allies who still supplied ships. There were two major cities on Lesbos, Mytilene and Methymna, and three smaller ones. Mytilene, under the control of an oligarchy, had already considered revolt before 431 but their appeal for help had been refused by the Spartans (3.13.1). In 428, Mytilene and the rest of Lesbos, apart from democratic Methymna, were secretly preparing to revolt from Athens but their plans were betrayed, thus forcing them to revolt earlier than they planned. The Athenians, after recovering from the initial shock, hurriedly sent out 40 ships, which fleet managed to blockade both harbours. However, the Mytileneans still had control of the land (3.3–6). Meanwhile the Mytileneans had sent an embassy to the Spartans, who redirected them to Olympia so that the other allies there could hear their appeal. The Mytileneans, according to Thucydides' version of their speech, explained almost apologetically that their reasons for revolt and pleas for help were not based on ill treatment by the Athenians, who had treated them with respect, but on their fears for the future and their desire for total freedom (3.9–14). The Spartans and their allies agreed to help them and allowed them to join their alliance. Unfortunately, the words of the Spartan allies were stronger than their actions: the planned second invasion of Attica failed to materialize owing to the non-appearance of the Peloponnesian allies and no help was sent to Mytilene in 428. However, the Spartans did commission a fleet of 40 ships to be sent out the following year.

The Athenians realized that the time had come for serious action: in the autumn they sent out Paches with 1,000 'hoplites', who quickly built a wall around Mytilene, thus completing the blockade of the Mytileneans by land and sea (3.18). In 427, the Spartan Alcidas and a Peloponnesian fleet of 40 ships set out, but his tardiness, lack of ambition and fear resulted in the surrender of Mytilene before his arrival (3.26; 29–33). In Mytilene the supplies of food were exhausted, and it was decided that the only hope of maintaining the revolt was to take on the Athenian hoplites in battle and thus relieve the land blockade. The oligarchs therefore gave out heavy armour to the ordinary people (used previously as light-armed troops). However, once armed, the people refused to obey the oligarchs and threatened to make an agreement with the Athenians and surrender the city, unless the oligarchs produced all the remaining food and shared it out. At this point, the oligarchs, realizing the danger to themselves if this agreement was made without their own participation, promptly came to terms with Paches: first, Athens had the right to do as she wished with the Mytileneans; second, the Athenian army could enter the city; third, the Mytileneans could send an embassy to Athens to put their case; fourth, until the return of this embassy, no Mytilenean was to be imprisoned, enslaved or killed by Paches (3.27–28). Finally, Paches sent to Athens all those Mytileneans (about 1,000 in number) who he suspected had been most involved in organizing the revolt (3.35).

Thucydides' account of the revolt of Mytilene is considerably longer (about ten times) than his account of the revolt of Samos. Yet the main purpose of this account of the military action and the speech of the

Mytileneans at Olympia is to set the scene for the main event: the speeches of Cleon and Diodotus in the Athenian Assembly. The revolt of a major ally and its ramifications, if successful, at the time of Athenian distress – the Peloponnesian invasions of Attica, the plague and the death of Pericles – is an event worthy of significant treatment in its own right. However, for Thucydides there are two more important main issues: first, the Athenians' decision, in the first meeting of the Assembly, to execute the entire population of adult males of Mytilene and to enslave all the women and children (3.36.2) was the harshest punishment to date for a revolting ally; second, in the subsequent Assembly on the next day, a debate on the issue of what was the most effective means of treating dissident allies in order to maintain the security of the empire.

Thucydides tells us that Cleon had been responsible for proposing the original motion in the first Assembly and that a ship had been dispatched that very day ordering Paches to carry out the executions at once. However, many Athenians had second thoughts. Their decision had been mainly motivated by anger: first, the Mytileneans had revolted even though the Athenians had allowed them to remain independent; second, the appearance for the first time of a Peloponnesian fleet in Ionia to support the revolt clearly implied that the revolt had been planned for a long time (3.36.2). Now, after a night of reflection:

> On the next day they were immediately filled with repentance and reckoned that the decision that they had taken was savage and unprecedented, to destroy a whole city instead of those who were guilty.
>
> (Thucydides 3.36.4)

Thus an extraordinary meeting of the Assembly was held so that the punishment of the Mytileneans could be discussed again. Thucydides tells us that various opinions were expressed, both for and against the original decision. It is almost certain, bearing in mind the sentiment above that initiated the second debate, that arguments involving humanity, pity and mercy were expressed, but Thucydides has not included them. Instead he condenses the whole debate down to two basic opposing points of view: whether the best way to control the subjects of the empire was through fear (Cleon) or through moderation (Diodotus).

Cleon wastes no time in explaining the nature of the Athenian empire:

> 'You do not realise that the empire you possess is a tyranny, exercised over those who plot against you and who are ruled against their will.'
>
> (Thucydides 3.37.2)

Cleon then stresses that Mytilene had harmed Athens more than any other city. He could understand a city driven to revolt as a result of harsh imperialism, but the Mytileneans had all the advantages of an independent city and were treated by the Athenians with the greatest honour. To talk of a revolt is a misnomer, since people revolt only when they have been mistreated. Instead it is right to talk of aggression, since they had sided with Athens' bitterest enemies and had desired Athens' destruction (3.39.2; AE129 p. 62). Furthermore, the Athenians should consider the effect of leniency on their other allies:

'Consider your allies if you impose the same punishment both on those who have been forced to revolt by your enemies and on those who have willingly revolted; who do you think will not revolt on the slightest pretext when there is freedom if successful but nothing serious, if they fail?'

(Thucydides 3.39.7)

Cleon, in the same section, highlights the financial and human costs to the Athenian state, whether successful or not in putting down revolts: apart from the campaign costs and the loss of men, even if they were successful, the city of the crushed ally would be in ruins and unable in the future to pay the phoros upon which Athenian strength depends; if they fail, the Athenians will have to face even more enemies (3.39.8; AE130 p. 62). Finally, he comes to the crux of his argument:

'Punish these men as they deserve and give a clear example to the other allies that whoever revolts will be punished with death. For if they know this, you will give more time to fighting your enemies than making war on your allies'.

(Thucydides 3.40.8)

In Cleon's opinion, the Athenian Empire was hated by the subject-allies and therefore the only secure way to maintain the empire was to instil fear: the death penalty was the most effective way to deter revolt.

The main thrust of Diodotus' argument in answer to Cleon is that expediency (i.e. that which is most useful to Athens) should underpin all decisions: he was not against the death penalty per se and would support it if it was in the Athenians' best interests (3.44.1–2). However, he strongly believed that Cleon's solution would not be useful for the Athenians when they had to deal with revolts in the future which, because of human nature, would invariably happen no matter how harsh the punishment:

'You must not make unwise decisions because of the misplaced trust in the effectiveness of the death penalty, and you must not deprive those who have revolted of the hope that they can change their minds and make up for their mistake in a very short time. [46.2] You should reflect that, as it is, if a city that has revolted decides that it is not going to succeed, it can come to terms while it is still able to pay the expenses [incurred by Athens] and pay tribute in the future.'

(Thucydides 3.46.1–2 AE131 p. 62)

This was a very effective counter to Cleon's argument about the double loss of income for Athens when a subject-ally revolted (i.e. the cost of the campaign and the crushed ally's inability to pay phoros in future). Diodotus continued by arguing that, if Cleon's method were to be adopted, every city before revolting would prepare even more carefully for it and, having revolted, would fight to the bitter end, since a short or long siege would lead to the same punishment. This would cost the Athenians even more money – a longer, costlier siege and a ruined city – because of the impossibility of reaching a settlement (3.46.2).

Diodotus then offers an allied view of the empire that directly opposes Cleon's opinion that it was a tyranny:

> At the moment in all the cities the people are your friends; either they do not join the few [i.e. oligarchs] in revolting, or, if they are forced to revolt, they become at once the enemy of those who have revolted, and when you go to war with the hostile city, you have the people, who are the majority, on your side.
>
> (Thucydides 3.47.2; *AE*132 p. 62)

Certainly it was the oligarchs who planned Mytilene's revolt, but Diodotus then brushes over the fact that the Mytilenean people, when armed, were more interested in obtaining food than surrendering the city to the Athenians (see above). However, he stresses that indiscriminate punishment of all, as proposed by Cleon, would in the future drive the people into the arms of the oligarchs. Diodotus concluded his argument by proposing that those suspected of stirring up the revolt should be tried in Athens but to allow all the others to keep their lives and live in Mytilene (3.48.1–2). Diodotus won the day, but not by many votes – a clear sign that the war was having a hardening effect upon the Athenians. When Scione in Chalcidice revolted in 423, the Athenians, on the motion of Cleon, again passed the death sentence and carried it out in 421 – this punishment was recorded in one sentence by Thucydides (5.32.1).

A ship was sent out immediately to stop Paches from carrying out the executions and arrived just in time owing to the first ship being in no hurry to deliver the harsh orders. As for the Mytileneans most suspected of stirring up the revolt, these (about 1,000) were put to death on the motion of Cleon. The Athenians then destroyed the fortifications of Mytilene, deprived them of their fleet and took possession of all the towns on the mainland that Mytilene had controlled. Finally, instead of imposing phoros, they divided all the land of Lesbos, with the exception of loyal Methymna, into 3,000 allotments: 300 were put aside as sacred to the gods and the remaining 2,700 were distributed by lot to Athenian cleruchs. However, the people of Lesbos agreed to rent these allotments, paying the Athenian allotment-holders 200 drachmas a year, and cultivated the land themselves (3.49.3–50; *AE*133 p. 63). The Chians alone remained as the only independent ship-supplying state. Their attempt to build new fortifications in the winter of 425/4 came to a swift end – on the orders of the Athenians, they promptly demolished them (4.51). However, their chance to revolt would come after the Athenian defeat in Sicily.

Melos

Melos, a Spartan colony (allegedly), was an island in the south Aegean and by 416 was the only one outside the Athenian Empire. At the beginning of the Peloponnesian War it had neutral status (2.9.4 – along with Thera), but in 426 the Athenians launched an attack on the Melians presumably to complete their domination and control of the Aegean. Owing to financial and military pressures elsewhere in the war, the Athenians were unable to do more than ravage the Melian territory and soon departed (3.91). Another possible cause of the Athenian attack was the contribution of money by Melos to the Spartan war effort in the early 420s, but this depends upon the dating of an inscription, recording contributions to the Spartan war-fund (ML 67). A possible date is about 427 at the time when Alcidas was leading the Peloponnesian fleet into the eastern Aegean to bring help to the Mytileneans in revolt (see above). However, it could equally be dated to about 405 near the end of the war as a grateful thanks offering from the surviving Melians for being restored to their state by Lysander, the Spartan commander, as he closed in on Athens (Xenophon, *Hellenica* 2.2.9). Melos also makes an appearance on the list of phoros-payers in the extraordinary re-assessment of 425/4, as recorded in the Thoudippos Decree (ML 69; AE138 pp. 66–68) – but this seems to be a wish-list on the part of the Athenians, as it also includes many other states who had never contributed phoros or had not paid for many years. However, in 416, the Athenians returned and this time they were determined to resolve the Melian issue once and for all.

The force sent against Melos included 30 Athenian ships and 1,200 hoplites, and from the allies and islanders 8 ships and roughly 1,500 hoplites, under the command of Cleomedes and Teisias (5.84.1–2) – Thucydides does not state the reason for this campaign but it is significant that allied forces are also campaigning against Melos. The generals encamped in the territory of Melos but, instead of laying waste the land immediately, they sent representatives to negotiate with the Melians:

> The Melians did not bring these men before the people but told them to tell to the magistrates and to the few what they had come for.
>
> (Thucydides 5.84.3)

Thucydides now records, uniquely in his history, a continuous point and counter-point debate between the Athenian representatives and the oligarchs

who governed Melos – hence its modern name, 'The Melian Dialogue' (5.85–113). The authenticity and the purpose of the dialogue are a matter of serious scholarly disagreement. As regards its authenticity, some scholars believe that this dialogue is mainly a product of Thucydides' imagination. First, it was a private discussion, conducted behind closed doors; second, the Melians who conducted the debate were killed soon after, and Thucydides would have had no recourse to the Athenian negotiators until after 404 when he returned from exile; third, the constant use of generalizations, e.g. the custom of the powerful always ruling the weak (5.89), would be inappropriate in this particular instance of diplomatic negotiation as well as the fact that these generalizations have constant echoes in other Thucydidean speeches, e.g. the Athenians' speech to the Spartan Assembly in 432 about the same issue (1.76.2); finally, the tough, blunt, uncompromising language and sentiments expressed by the Athenians are very untypical of standard diplomacy. However, those who accept its authenticity make the following points: first, although no one can be totally sure what Thucydides meant by 'what was the most appropriate ('ta deonta') for each speaker to give in each situation' (see Chapter 1), he does claim to stick to the general gist of his recorded speeches – 'keeping as close as possible to the general sense of what was actually said'; second, not all the Melians were killed, and he could have been given a very brief summary of the main points raised, e.g. the Melians' reliance on justice, hope and Spartan aid; third, this was not a typical public speech where diplomatic niceties were to be observed, but private negotiations where the key issues and choices – incorporation into the Athenian Empire or destruction – could be bluntly spelled out so that there was no possibility of misunderstanding.

In the same way, there is scholarly disagreement as to Thucydides' purpose in highlighting the Melos affair. On the one hand, it is believed that Thucydides wished to show the moral decline of the Athenians as the war progressed – the punishment of execution of all men of military age and the selling into slavery of all women and children was rescinded in the case of the Mytileneans in 427, but was carried out on the Melians in 415; furthermore, this progressive decline is reflected in three key speeches – from the high moral tone of Pericles' Funeral Speech at the beginning of the war (2.35–46) to the emphasis on expediency in Diodotus' speech in the Mytilenean debate in 427 (3.42–48) to the crude cynicism of the Athenian representatives in 416 (e.g. Finley). Some (e.g. Cornford) see a deliberate juxtaposition of Melos and the Sicilian disaster where the Athenians' destruction of Melos is viewed as an act of overweening arrogance (hubris) leading to their downfall (ate) in Sicily in the manner of a Greek tragedy. However, recent scholarship has moved away from this opinion, particularly pointing out that Thucydides' account is concentrated on the actual dialogue and not on the punishment which is mentioned almost incidentally, in the same brief manner as the Athenian destruction of Scione in 421 (5.32) and the Spartan slaughter of all the men at Hysiae near Argos in 417 (5.83.2). Thucydides displays no pity or revulsion over the treatment of Melos (nor Scione or Hysiae), yet the brutal, senseless slaughter of the people of Mycalessus in Boeotia, especially the killing of the boys at school, by Thracian mercenaries in 413 moved him deeply (7.2–5), suggesting that Thucydides' pity in this instance was moved by the unexpected and unplanned fate of the people of Mycalessus, but not for the Melians who were given a choice and could have avoided their fate, if they had been prudent. Very soon after, in the spring of 414, Aristophanes in the *Birds* makes a casual, passing reference to the 'Melian famine' (l.186) which seems to suggest that the fate of Melos also did little to trouble Athenian consciences.

The Melian punishment gains notoriety as the leading example of the atrocities committed under the Athenian Empire only after the end of the war and later, and this has misguidedly influenced the discussion about Thucydides' purpose in highlighting the affair of Melos. Thucydides' purpose should be searched for in the dialogue (not in the punishment) and in the context of the campaign against Melos. Unlike the Mytilenean debate, which was conducted by Athenians alone in the Athenian Assembly about the punishment of Mytilene, this was a genuine dialogue between the Athenian generals and the Melian oligarchs about whether Melos was to accept incorporation into the Athenian Empire or destruction. The fact that the Melians were neutrals (although they had given some financial help to the Spartans some years earlier (ML 67)), that they were allowed a choice in deciding their fate, that there was a point and counter-point dialogue between the combatants on this issue (unique in Thucydides rather than his typical set-piece speeches) suggest strongly that these were the main reasons for his full treatment of the Melian Dialogue. At the same time it cannot be denied that the juxtaposition of a successful attack on a small island followed immediately by a failed attack on a large one would have been another factor in Thucydides' selection. In addition, Hornblower has pointed out how the Melos affair fits in with the context of Book 5 – although the transition from the Peloponnese to an island and from complex diplomacy to open imperialism (see Chapter 20 for these events) may appear a big change of theme, in fact much of Book 5 is about bigger and more powerful states asserting their power over smaller and weaker states, e.g. the Mantineans, exploiting Sparta's weakness, had brought most of Arcadia under their control (5.29.1), and Argos was constantly attacking Epidaurus (5.53ff). Thus the Athenians' decision to impose their will upon Melos should be seen as part of this same theme, especially as Melos was a Spartan colony and the Athenians, as part of the quadruple alliance, had been recently defeated by the Spartans at the decisive battle of Mantinea (5.70–73).

The discussion takes place in private at the request of the Melian oligarchs, presumably because they feared that, if the issue was put before all of the people, they would be sympathetic to the Athenian arguments.

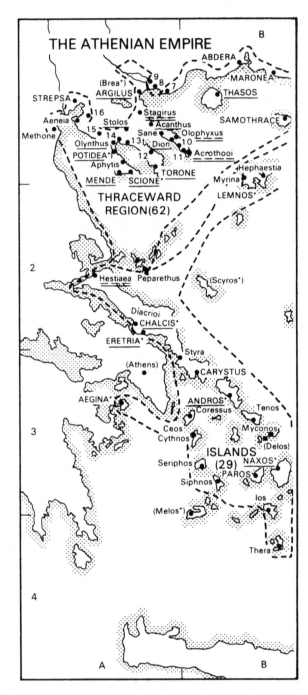

Map 5 The Athenian Empire

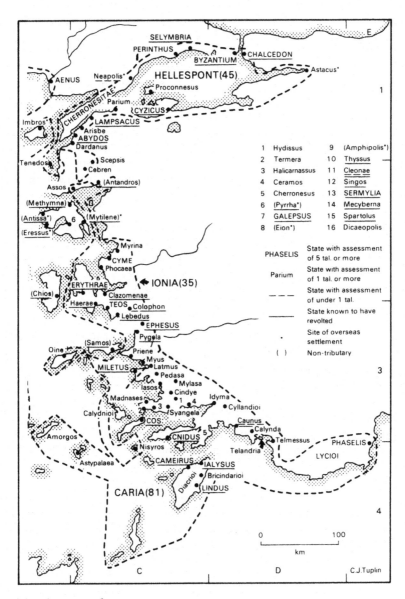

Map 5 continued

1	Hydissus	9	(Amphipolis*)
2	Termera	10	Thyssus
3	Halicarnassus	11	Cleonae
4	Ceramos	12	Singos
5	Cherronesus	13	SERMYLIA
6	(Pyrrha*)	14	Mecyberna
7	GALEPSUS	15	Spartolus
8	(Eion*)	16	Dicaeopolis

PHASELIS — State with assessment of 5 tal. or more

Parium — State with assessment of 1 tal. or more

– – – State with assessment of under 1 tal.

——— State known to have revolted

• Site of overseas settlement

( ) Non-tributary

(5.84.3; AE156 p. 72). It was probably for this reason that the Athenians' tone was harsh and their arguments blunt – it was in the interests of the ruling oligarchs to remain independent, and thus they were the least likely of the Melians to respond to gentle persuasion. Hence the need to spell out in the bluntest terms to the oligarchs the fate awaiting Melos if they chose resistance. The Athenians laid down the ground rules for the dialogue: first there would be no set speeches but a discussion of each detail, point-by-point (5.85); and second, the discussion was to be limited solely to the immediate situation, i.e. how to save the city from destruction, and therefore only relevant facts were admissible (5.87). Within these set guidelines, therefore, the Athenians would have no opportunity to justify their empire (as they usually did), and the Melians no opportunity to mention their neutrality or doing no harm to Athens in the past (5.89):

> 'We should both be aware of the other party's true position and try to get what is possible, each party knowing full well that just settlements are reached in discussions between men only when each side is equally under compulsion, and that those who have power do what that power enables them to do, and the weaker part agrees.'
>
> (Thucydides 5.89; AE157 p. 72)

By this statement the Athenians were excluding all arguments about justice because it was inappropriate to this situation. 'Just settlements' (i.e. justice) take place only when there is an equal compulsion for both sides to settle. In 421, both Athens and Sparta were desperate to make peace and thus equal compulsion led to the Peace of Nicias. However, in the present case, the compulsion was one-sided, i.e. the Melians, with a population of about 3,000 (probably 500 adult males) and their land occupied, were desperate to negotiate, whereas the Athenians with 38 ships and 2,700 hoplites, and the resources of an empire behind them, had none, apart from the desire for a quick, painless campaign. Therefore the Melians should stick to the point: the choice of incorporation within the empire or destruction.

The Melians, however, in the early part of the dialogue still try to make justice, disguised as expediency, the basis of their argument (5.90–98). The Athenians dismiss these arguments, and when the Melians reply that they, as free men, would be cowards if they submitted to slavery (5.100), they again spell out the key issue:

> 'This is not for you a contest on equal terms about honour and avoiding shame, but rather a discussion about saving yourselves and not opposing those who are much stronger than you.
>
> (Thucydides 5.100)

The Melians then offer the viewpoint that, while there is resistance, there is hope (5.102). The Athenians' response could be that of Thucydides himself – that hope for the future is a dangerous commodity in the face of present reality and often leads to irrational decisions, culminating in disaster (5.103). For the rest of the dialogue the Melians focus on two points: first, their belief that the gods will favour them because of their stand against injustice (5.104); and second, their confidence that their kinsmen, the Spartans, will come to their aid (5.104, 106, 108, 110). The Athenians attempt to disabuse them of both: first, they state that gods and men accept that it is the law of nature that men rule wherever they can, just as the Melians would if they had the same opportunity (5.105.2); second, they claim that the Spartans' foreign policy, more than that of any other state, is rooted firmly in self-interest and it is the height of folly for the Melians in their current predicament to trust in Spartan military aid (5.105.3). The Athenians' final words amount almost to a plea to the Melian oligarchs to ignore spurious ideals of honour, and to concentrate on the realities of power and the enormity of their decision for the fate of Melos (5.111).

The Athenians must have felt nothing but frustration, irritation and exasperation when the Melian oligarchs, upon reconvening after their private consultation about the Athenian proposals, restated briefly the same points as before – in fact, 5.112 is a perfect synopsis of their arguments in the Melian Dialogue. The Melians managed to hold out for some months and even had a few minor military successes, but finally surrendered in 415, and were punished as described above. Later an Athenian colony of 500 men was sent to occupy Melos (5.116). Whatever Thucydides' personal views may have been about the Athenian decision to incorporate Melos into the Empire or the severity of the punishment, one of his main concerns as a historian was to highlight the weakness of Melos and its irrational determination to resist the overwhelming might of the Athenian Empire, as portrayed in the Melian Dialogue.

Bibliography

Davies, J. K. *Democracy and Classical Greece* 2nd edn, ch. 5.

de Ste Croix, G. E. M. *The Origins of the Peloponnesian War*, Appendix 5.

Hornblower, S. *The Greek World 479–323 BC*, chs 2 and 3.

——Lactor 1, *The Athenian Empire*, pp. 17–21.

Kagan, D. *The Outbreak of the Peloponnesian War*, chs 5, 6 and 7.

Lewis, D. M. *CAH* vol. 5, 2nd edn, ch. 5, sect. II; ch. 6, sects I–III.

McGregor, M. F. *The Athenians and their Empire*, chs 4–9.

Meiggs, R. *The Athenian Empire*, chs 3–5, 6–10.

Meritt, B. D., Wade-Gery, H. T. and McGregor, M. F. *The Athenian Tribute Lists*, vol. 3, pt 2, ch. XI and pt 3, chs VI, VIII and IX.

Powell, A. *Athens and Sparta*, chs 1 and 2.

Rhodes, P. J. *The Athenian Empire*, Greece and Rome New Survey in the Classics 17, chs II and IV.

——CAH *vol. 5*, 2nd edn, ch. 3, sects I–IV.
Westlake, H. D. *Essays on Greek Historians and Greek History.*

Bibliography for second edition

Andrewes, A. *CAH vol.5*, 2nd edn, ch. 10.
——'The Mytilene Debate', *Phoenix* 16 (1962).
Bosworth, A. 'The humanitarian aspect of the Melian Dialogue', *JHS* 113 (1993).
French, A. 'Athenian ambitions and the Delian Alliance', *Phoenix* 33 (1979).
Gomme, A. W., Andrewes, A. and Dover, K. J. *A Historical Commentary on Thucydides*, vol. 5, pp. 182–88.
Hammond, N.G.L. 'The origins and the nature of the Athenian Alliance of 478/7 B. C.', *JHS* 87 (1967).
Hornblower, S. *A Commentary on Thucydides. Vol. 3, Books 5.25–8.109*, pp. 218–25.
Jacobsen, H. 'The oath of the Delian League', *Philologus* 119 (1975).
Kagan, D. *The Outbreak of the Peloponnesian War*, ch. 10.
Low, P. *The Athenian Empire*, chs 1, 4.
Powell, A. *Athens and Sparta*, 2nd edn, ch 5.
Rawlings, H. R. 'Thucydides on the purpose of the Delian League', *Phoenix* 31 (1977).
Rhodes, P. A *History of the Classical Greek World: 478–323* BC, chs 2, 5.
de Romilly, J., *Thucydides and Athenian Imperialism*, ch. 2.
de Ste Croix, G. E. M. *The Origins of the Peloponnesian War*, ch. 1 (ii).
Walker, P. K. 'Purpose and method of the Pentekontaetia', *CQ5* (1955).

11

ATHENIAN POLITICS, 478–462/1

The sources

The major source for this period is Plutarch's *Lives of Cimon and Themistocles*, since Thucydides deals with these events only in a brief, cursory fashion (1.89–102.4) as part of his short digression on the 'Pentecontaetia' ('The Fifty-Years' – see Chapter 1), and in his digression on the fall of Themistocles (1.135–38), the reliability of which has rightly been called into question (for example, how did Thucydides gain access to Themistocles' letter to the Persian king?). Diodorus gives some extra information, but his probable source was the fourth-century historian Ephorus who in turn generally relied upon Thucydides. The weaknesses of Plutarch as a historical source are discussed fully in Chapter 1, but it is worth mentioning that his main aim in the *Lives* was to portray the moral worth (or lack of it) in his subjects so as to inspire later generations (*Life of Pericles* 1–2).

As a consequence, his belief in the heroic qualities of Cimon led him to write a *Life* which is fulsome in its praise and permeated with virtually uncritical respect, especially for his conservative political ideology and his gentleness towards Athens' naval allies. It seems likely that Ion of Chios, a fifth-century playwright, poet and prose writer, and apparently an admirer of Cimon, was a major influence on Plutarch when composing the *Life of Cimon*. By contrast, Themistocles is portrayed as the clever, devious and unscrupulous politician and general, as characterized in Herodotus in the Persian War; and also as the demagogic champion of the navy and its rowers, the lower-class 'thetes', who supported his policies of 'radical' democracy and of imperialism over their naval allies, as characterized by later anti-democratic writers. It is clear that these biased stereotypes must lead to a cautious use of Plutarch, whose *Lives* must be checked where possible with the evidence of Thucydides. However, it is still possible to discern from Plutarch the underlying issues of foreign and domestic policy that divided the factions of Themistocles and Cimon in this period.

Foreign policy, 470s

The Athenian 'hawks'

In 478 there were two options available to the Athenians in foreign policy. They could use their new military power and prestige either to dominate Greece or to wage war against Persia. This was the key issue that split the political factions in Athens. In modern politics it is customary to refer to those who contend for influence over or control of foreign policy as 'hawks' and 'doves', and these terms will be used for the two Athenian factions. The hawks believed that the Persians had been beaten and, once removed from Greek territory, would no longer offer any serious threat to mainland Greece and Athens. The main danger to Athens in the future would come from Sparta and the Peloponnese. Recent history had revealed Sparta's feelings towards the Athenians. Cleomenes, King of Sparta, had intervened or attempted to intervene four times in Athenian internal affairs in the last decade of the sixth century (see end of Chapter 4). There had been a constant underlying friction between the Spartans and the Athenians in the Persian War. Far more ominous was the attempt in 479, immediately after the Persian defeat, by the Spartans to stop the Athenians from rebuilding their defensive walls, which was thwarted only by the cleverness of Themistocles (Thucydides 1.90.1–91.7; AE4 pp. 10–11). The Spartans' hostile attitude to the Athenians was motivated by fear of Athens' military strength. The majority of Spartans could never accept the existence of Athens as a new, equal and independent power and thus, the Athenian hawks believed, Sparta was bound to attack Athens to try to regain the hegemony of Greece by force. Therefore the policy of the hawks was, after removing the Persians from Greek territory, to end hostilities with them and prepare for the inevitable conflict with Sparta.

There is little doubt that Themistocles was the leader of the Athenian hawks. In 478, the Delian League was founded, which was destined to bring great glory to its commander-in-chief as he pursued a glamorous and successful naval offensive against the Persians. The obvious choice for this position was Themistocles. In 493/2, as chief 'archon', he had authorized the fortification of the Piraeus, the port of Athens, and had organized its completion immediately after the Persian Wars (Thuc. 1.93; AE4 pp. 11–12). He had been the most successful and influential politician in the 480s; in 482, he had persuaded the Athenians, against the forceful opposition of Aristides, to use the recently discovered vein of silver at Laureion to finance the construction of 100 'triremes', increased to 200 by 480, which transformed Athens into a naval super-power; and he had been the architect of the naval victory at the battle of Salamis. Yet little is heard of Themistocles until his ostracism c.471. The obvious conclusion to be drawn is that Themistocles was not interested in being commander of the Delian League. His energies in the 470s were directed towards pursuing his anti-Spartan policies.

Themistocles very probably believed that the Athenians' naval supremacy, that he had recently created, should be further strengthened at the expense of the Greeks:

> He told them ... that through the strength of their fleet they had the power not only to drive off the barbarians, but also to become the leaders of Greece.
>
> (Plutarch, *Themistocles* 4)

Even allowing for anachronism on the part of Plutarch, it is clear that Themistocles' policy meant that the Spartans, who feared Athens' sudden rise to super-power status, had to be opposed whenever and wherever they tried to increase their own power or limit that of Athens. This open opposition commenced with his deception over the issue of the rebuilding of the Athenian walls in 479 and his blunt statement to the Spartan Assembly that the Athenians would make their own decisions in their own interests and would deal with the Spartans henceforth on a basis of equality (Thuc. 1.91.4–7; *AE*4 p. 11). The Spartans, although taken aback, showed no open anger at this ruse:

> When they heard this, the Spartans did not display anger openly to the Athenians. ... But they concealed their annoyance at the Athenians for ignoring their advice.
>
> (Thucydides 1.92; *AE*4 p. 11)

Themistocles did not have to wait long for his next opportunity. The Spartans planned to gain control of the Amphictyonic Congress (a religious league for the running of the sanctuary of Delphi but possessing political influence) by attempting to expel all those states, who had not joined in the resistance to the Persians. Themistocles, seeing the ulterior motives of the Spartans, spoke against the Spartan motion and won the day:

> His stand on this occasion especially upset the Spartans.
>
> (Plutarch, *Themistocles* 20)

Throughout the 470s, Themistocles continued to pursue his anti-Spartan policies by stirring up trouble for Sparta in the Peloponnese. The Spartans' fear of and hostility towards him led them to back his political enemy:

> Cimon's position was strengthened by the support of the Spartans, as they now became bitter enemies of Themistocles.
>
> (Plutarch, *Cimon* 16)

However, the 470s saw a decline in Themistocles' political fortunes. There was still a very strong pan-Hellenic feeling in Athens after the Persian War and most of the Athenians could not be convinced of the Spartan danger. In addition, the promise of wealth accruing from the Delian League was far more attractive than a difficult and dangerous war against Sparta. Finally, c.471, the Athenians decided to ostracize Themistocles as his hawkish foreign policy and activities in the Peloponnese were becoming an embarrassment and a threat to peaceful relations between the two states. Themistocles promptly went to Argos, Sparta's deadly enemy, and brought about a coalition of anti-Spartan states in the north Peloponnese (see Chapter 12).

The Athenian 'doves'

The Athenian doves rejected this analysis of Greek super-power politics. They believed in the policy of 'dual hegemony' (joint leadership) of Greece. They argued that the Athenians and the Spartans had different spheres of influence – Athens, a sea-power, operating in the Aegean, and the Spartans, a land-power, operating in the Peloponnese – and therefore there was no need for a clash. The Persian Wars had shown that the two super-powers in general could work together and they believed that the pan-Hellenic spirit could be continued in peacetime. The goodwill that had been engendered in the Persian War would ensure that any future problems could be resolved amicably. The real enemy had to be the Persians, who had inflicted such suffering and casualties upon the Greeks. Therefore the policy of the Athenians doves was to maintain peaceful relations with the Spartans and make war on the Persians.

Cimon, the son of Miltiades, was the leader of the dove faction. He fully supported the aims of the Delian League and was probably its commander-in-chief continuously from 478/7 to 462/1. However, his commitment to peaceful relations with Sparta was based on more than expediency for Athens. He had tremendous admiration and respect for the Spartans:

> From the beginning of his career he was a great supporter of the Spartans. He actually named one of his sons Lacedaimonius ['the Spartan'].
>
> (Plutarch, *Cimon* 16)

Almost certainly he was their 'proxenos' (see Glossary), which meant that he was Sparta's main representative in Athens. Athens' friendship with Sparta was the cornerstone of his foreign policy, as this allowed the Athenians to direct their full military might against the Persians. This policy also was of great benefit in promoting Cimon's career. His greatest asset was his generalship, and the campaigns against the Persians in the 470s were the perfect arena for him to display his talents. It was said of him:

Indeed no man did more than Cimon to humble and insult the pride of the Great King himself. He did not relax his pursuit of the Persians from Greece but pressed hard on their heels … until Asia, from Ionia to Pamphylia, was totally emptied of all Persian soldiers.

(Plutarch, *Cimon* 12)

The culmination of his military success was his leadership of the Delian League forces at the battle of Eurymedon in *c*.469:

Cimon, like a top class athlete, won two victories in a single day.

(Plutarch, *Cimon* 13)

Although Plutarch exaggerates the success of Eurymedon by saying that it surpassed that of both Salamis and Plataea, this victory, on land and at sea, decisively ended the Persian menace to the Aegean. It is hardly surprising that nearly a decade of continuous military glory for Cimon gave Themistocles and his anti-Spartan policies little chance of success in the 470s.

Domestic policy, 478–462/1

There was one other issue that divided the two factions and this concerned political ideology. It is too much to say that Themistocles planned the reforms, which were introduced by Ephialtes and Pericles in 462/1; but there is strong evidence, especially if the development of Athenian demo-cratic thinking from the time of the reforms of Cleisthenes was evolu-tionary (as argued by Forrest – see Chapter 13) and not sudden, that Themistocles, perceiving this political maturing of the lower class thetes, wished to advance their political power. Thucydides (1.138) especially prai-ses his foresight, and to someone of Themistocles' (and Aristides') intelli-gence it was clear that the decision to make Athens a great naval power would have a direct bearing on the future of the Athenian constitution. Greek history had shown that political power lay with the class best able to defend the state. In the eighth and first part of the seventh centuries the aristocrats had held sway because of the state's dependence on cavalry, which only the aristocrats could afford. Then in the rest of the seventh and in the sixth century the middle-class 'hoplites' replaced the aristocrats as the defenders of the state and they, with the aid of the tyrants, gained a share in political power (Aristotle, *Politics* 1297b). Themistocles' enthusiastic sup-port for, and Aristides' opposition to, the ship-building programme in 482 strongly suggest that both men saw the implications of making Athens a great naval power dependent on the thetes. That these two men, both committed anti-Persians, on the eve of the Persian invasion of Greece should disagree so strongly that the issue could only be resolved by Aris-tides' ostracism, is clear evidence that the essence of their conflict was

215

about political ideology. Plutarch informs us of the political effects of Themistocles' naval policy:

> The result of this was that he increased the standing of the people at the upper class's expense and filled them full of confidence, with power now passing into the hands of sailors, boatswains and pilots.
>
> (Plutarch, *Themistocles* 19)

Plutarch has once again exaggerated and is describing the political situation in Athens in the second half of the fifth-century, but there is an element of truth in the growing awareness of the thetes with regard to their increasing importance to the state.

The main opposition in the 470s and 460s came from Cimon and his faction, who strongly supported the 508 constitution of Cleisthenes that had created a moderate democracy, in which political power was mainly shared between the middle-class hoplites and the upper classes. Therefore Cimon, who was a staunch supporter of the aristocratic council, the 'Areopagus', was determined to oppose Themistocles' plans for the people:

> He together with Aristides opposed Themistocles, when that man began to advance the democracy beyond its prescribed limits.
>
> (Plutarch, *Cimon* 10)

In the 470s, constitutional issues were of much less importance than foreign policy in Athenian politics, and thus Themistocles' unpopularity in foreign affairs gave him little scope to be successful in domestic policy. However, constitutional change became a major issue in the late 460s and forced Cimon into the role of the champion of moderate democracy:

> During the rest of his political career, while present, he checked and even reduced the challenges of the people on the power of the upper classes.
>
> (Plutarch, *Cimon* 15)

However, there was a fatal flaw in Cimon's domestic policy. His dynamic foreign policy led to success against the Persians (478 to 469) and to Athens' growing imperialism over the Delian League allies (469 to 462/1). This success was achieved through the naval fighting abilities of the thetes, who just like the middle-class hoplites in 508 were bound to demand recognition of this by a substantial increase in their political power. This desire for 'radical' democratic reform was anathema to Cimon and yet his foreign policy led directly to its introduction. Cimon either lacked the vital quality of foresight or hoped that a combination of personal generosity (Plutarch, *Cimon* 10) and a successful foreign policy would dissuade the people from seeking a change in the constitution.

The fall of Themistocles

Themistocles' final disgrace came at the hands of his political enemies in Athens and the Spartans. From 471 he had been travelling around the Peloponnese, helping to create an anti-Spartan coalition, which challenged the Spartans' dominance of the Peloponnese at the battle of Tegea in *c*.469 (see Chapter 12). The Spartans undoubtedly had the motive to get rid of Themistocles and the 'evidence' was at hand. Pausanias, the victor of Plataea, had allegedly spent the 470s in treacherous intrigues with the Persians and had plotted the overthrow of Sparta by promising freedom to the 'Helots' (Thuc. 1.128–35). His medism (see Glossary) was discovered and he met his death in Sparta. No exact date can be given for his death but at some time in the late 470s (or even as early as 474/3, according to Forrest) seems reasonable. According to the Spartans, when they were investigating Pausanias' case:

> certain letters and documents concerning this issue were found, which cast suspicion on Themistocles.
>
> (Plutarch, *Themistocles* 23)

The Spartans raised an outcry, claiming that this 'evidence' proved that Themistocles had shared in Pausanias' medizing intrigues and that he should be punished in a similar way. It is the time lapse between the death of Pausanias (late 470s) and the presentation of the evidence (early 460s), which creates the suspicions that this 'evidence' was manufactured, especially as the Spartans were so desperate to remove Themistocles and his troublesome influence from Peloponnesian politics. The Spartans knew, however, that it would be hard to convince the Athenians that their great war hero, although out of favour at the time, had indulged in medism. For such a charge to be successful it would need the right opportunity and support from the highest quarters in Athens.

The great victory at Eurymedon *c*.469 was the peak of Cimon's career and was the clearest vindication of the dove faction's foreign policy. It was now that Sparta had the opportunity to present their evidence, knowing full well that Cimon, their proxenos and political enemy of Themistocles, could and would use his dominant influence to back the charge of medism. We know that Cimon, either now or earlier, was willing to destroy his rival's career:

> When Alcmaeon and Cimon and many others were attacking and prosecuting him (Themistocles), Aristides was the only one who neither did nor said anything despicable.
>
> (Plutarch, *Aristides* 25)

The Athenians were persuaded and officers were sent out to arrest him and bring him back for trial. Themistocles (like Alcibiades in 415) knew that his political enemies would ensure that a verdict of guilty was passed and thus was forced, like Alcibiades, to seek protection with the enemy – in this case, ironically, with Persia as there was nowhere else in Greece that could offer sanctuary from Athenian and Spartan agents. This act naturally appeared to confirm his enemies' accusations and Themistocles' career in Greek politics was over, although he left a powerful legacy to his successors, Ephialtes and Pericles.

Athenian foreign policy, 460s

The year of 469 marked a major change in foreign policy for Cimon and the dove faction. The success at Eurymedon had virtually destroyed any chance of a Persian counter-offensive in the Aegean and many of the Delian League allies felt that the liberation of the Greeks from Persia – the chief aim of the League, for which they had joined – had been achieved. They looked forward to a rest from their labours and probably expected the League to go the way of the Hellenic League, i.e. it would still exist in name but would involve very few commitments to active service. Thucydides records their failure to understand Athenian attitudes to and intentions for the League (1.99; AE29 p. 21 – see Chapter 10). Cimon realized that the Athenians now had the opportunity to exploit the League for their own benefit and advancement, and thus began the conversion of the League into the Athenian Empire. As the ship-supplying allies became more unwilling to serve on campaigns, which Athens still insisted on conducting, Cimon (according to Plutarch) encouraged the allies to take their ease and allowed them to supply either phoros or empty ships. While the allies grew soft from easy living, Cimon filled the empty ships with Athenian sailors and made them battle-hardened. This policy soon brought results:

> The Greeks who did not take part in military campaigns became accustomed to fear and to flatter men, who were continuously at sea, who always had weapons at hand and who were thriving on constant training, and so, without realising it, they became tributaries and slaves instead of allies.
>
> (Plutarch, *Cimon* 11)

Cimon's role in this was crucial and his successful pursuit of Athenian imperial interests at the expense of the allies reflects highly on his ability to perceive and act upon policies that were advantageous to Athens.

However, there was once again a fatal flaw in this policy. The cornerstone of his foreign policy was peace with Sparta, but he failed to appreciate the fear and resentment that existed among the Spartans towards the Athenians. They had wanted to keep Athens defenceless in 479 and had only with great reluctance allowed Athens to take over the hegemony of Greece against Persia in the 470s (see Chapter 12). Now that the Persian threat to

Greece appeared to be over and the Athenians' power was growing through the suppression of their allies, so the Spartans' fear continued to grow. Sparta, being a military state, usually responded to all threats, real or imaginary, by aggression. The more eagerly that Cimon pursued his policy of crushing the allies and making them subject to Athens, so the likelihood of Spartan aggression increased. Cimon, blinded by his admiration of and trust in Sparta, lacked the foresight to appreciate this. In 465, the revolt of Thasos, instigated by Athens' commercial greed, was the incident that provoked Sparta:

> The Thasians ... appealed to the Spartans and asked them to aid them by invading Attica. Unknown to the Athenians, the Spartans promised and intended to do so.
>
> (Thucydides 1.101.1; *AE*29 p. 21)

Even though the Spartans were still allies of Athens and officially at peace, they were prepared to launch an invasion against Athens and were only prevented by the occurrence of an earthquake and the subsequent Helot revolt (see Chapter 12). Athens, even under the influence of their pro-Spartan proxenos Cimon, was still an object of profound fear.

The year of 465 marked a turning point in Cimon's career, when his popularity began to slip. After defeating the Thasians in battle, Cimon was involved in a long and unglamorous siege, which kept him out of the public eye from 465 to 463 (Plutarch, *Cimon* 14). In addition 10,000 settlers were sent out in 465 to found the colony of the Nine Ways near the river Strymon (Thuc. 1.100.3; *AE*29 p. 21). This new colony almost certainly played its part in provoking the neighbouring Thasians into revolt, as it was clear that Athens had designs on controlling that part of the North Aegean, which was strategically important and rich in natural resources. The destruction of this colony, so close to Cimon's forces, probably added to Cimon's slip in popularity. The rise of the hawks, under Ephialtes and Pericles, can probably be dated from now. Cimon's success had previously made it extremely difficult for the Athenian hawks to make headway against his faction. However, once Cimon had proved fallible, the window of opportunity opened for them to challenge his authority and to win over the Athenians to their policies – hostility to Sparta and the advancement of democracy. In 463, Cimon, upon his return from Thasos, was charged with corruption (Plutarch, *Cimon* 14). The fact that Cimon's incorruptibility was renowned and that one of the leading prosecutors was Pericles proves conclusively that this was a politically motivated trial, initiated by the hawks to test Cimon's current popularity. Cimon was acquitted but the trial showed the growing confidence of the hawks.

The overthrow of Cimon's policies came in 462/1, and the Spartans must take the major responsibility for this. The Spartans' siege of the Helots on Mount Ithome had been dragging on from 465 due to their lack of skill in conducting sieges, and they appealed to their allies, including Athens, to come to their aid (Thuc. 1.102.1; AE39 p. 25). This request caused a political storm in Athens. Ephialtes was totally opposed to the Athenians helping their rival and had hoped that the Spartans' efforts would end in failure. Cimon, however, pleaded with the Athenians to send a large force of hoplites:

> he urged them 'not to allow Greece to go lame, nor to allow their city to lose its yoke-fellow.'
>
> (Plutarch, *Cimon* 16)

Cimon won the day and was despatched with 4,000 hoplites to Ithome. However, the Spartans soon became fearful of the Athenians' presence and sent them away, alone of the allies, claiming that they had no further need of them (Thuc. 1.102.3; AE39 p. 25 – see Chapter 12). This snub at Ithome provoked a powerful backlash at Athens. The Athenians were angry at this degrading treatment and rightly held Cimon responsible for this disgrace. The hawks saw this as their moment to strike. They took advantage of the Athenians' angry mood and persuaded them to renounce their alliance with the Spartans – virtually a declaration of war – and to make a military alliance with Sparta's enemy, Argos (Thuc. 1.102.4; AE39 p. 25). The hawks also brought about the passing of the second part of their policy. While Cimon and the Athenian hoplites were still away:

> under the leadership of Ephialtes they [i.e. the people of Athens] took away from the Council of the Areopagus all its powers of jurisdiction, apart from a few, and giving themselves total authority over the law courts they turned the city into a full radical democracy, with the help of Pericles.
>
> (Plutarch, *Cimon* 15)

Cimon's foreign and domestic policies were in ruins due to the Spartan snub at Ithome. His final humiliation, ostracism in 462/1, came about as a result of his desperate attempt to restore political power to the Areopagus and the constitution of Cleisthenes (Plutarch, *Cimon* 15). The Athenians now possessed a new more democratic constitution and were set on a path of confrontation with the Spartans.

Bibliography

Bury, J. B. and Meiggs, R. *A History of Greece*, ch. 8.
Davies, J. K. *Democracy and Classical Greece*, 2nd edn, ch. 3.
Forrest, W. G. *The Emergence of Greek Democracy*, ch. 9.
——'Themistocles and Argos', CQ 10.
Hornblower, S. *The Greek World 479–323 BC*, ch. 2.

Kagan, D. *Pericles of Athens and the Birth of Democracy*, ch. 2.

Meiggs, A. *The Athenian Empire*, ch. 5.

Powell, A. *Athens and Sparta*, chs 1 and 4.

Sealey, R. *A History of Greek City States 700–338* BC, ch. 9.

de Ste. Croix, G. E. M. *The Origins of the Peloponnesian War*, ch. 5 (ii).

12

SPARTAN FOREIGN POLICY AND PROBLEMS IN THE PELOPONNESE, 478–446/5

The evolution of the Peloponnesian League

In the sixth century it had been the intention of the Spartans, building upon their success in Messenia, to attempt the conquest of the rest of the Peloponnese. However, defeat by Tegea in the middle of the century (c.550) led to a radical rethink of their policy in the Peloponnese: instead of conquest, the Spartans embarked on a policy of forming with individual states a series of military alliances, in which they would hold the 'hegemony' (leadership). These allies would swear the oath 'to have the same friends and enemies as the Spartans, and to follow the Spartans wheresoever they may lead'. The Spartans for their part would protect their Peloponnesian allies from outside attack; in return they could call upon their allies if they needed help and could summon them to participate in any military campaign in which they were engaged. This military organization, together with control of the Messenian 'Helots', was the vital element in maintaining the Spartans' supremacy in the Peloponnese. In the first place, the cultivation of Messenia by the Helots for their masters ensured that the Spartans had the necessary time and opportunity to become a first-class military state, excelling in the art of 'hoplite' warfare. This military superiority had two interrelated consequences: first, it ensured their hegemony over the other states in the Peloponnese; and second, this hegemony ensured that these allies supplied the necessary military help to suppress any revolt of the Helots, upon whom the Spartan system ultimately depended. While this virtuous (in the Spartans' eyes) circle worked successfully, the Spartans had no fears about their supremacy in the Peloponnese and therefore their status as a Greek super-power. However, if they were to lose the Helots, they would quickly lose their military superiority (having then to cultivate their own lands) and with it their hegemony over their Peloponnesian allies, as happened in the fourth century following their loss of Messenia in 370/69 (Diodorus 15.66.6) and the break-up of the Peloponnesian League in 366/5 (Xenophon, *Hellenica* 7.4.6–11 – see Chapter 25).

In the second half of the sixth century (549–500) the Spartans undertook a policy of expelling tyrants and establishing pro-Spartan oligarchies. In 508, King Cleomenes and the Spartans intervened in the internal politics of Athens, attempting to establish a pro-Spartan narrow oligarchy against the wishes of the Athenians, but were forced to withdraw in humiliating circumstances (see Chapter 4 for a fuller discussion). Therefore, in accordance with the terms of the alliances, the Spartans called upon their allies to supply their military contingents without telling them the precise objective of the expedition. It was only when the Peloponnesians reached the borders of Attica that Cleomenes' objective became clear. At this point the Corinthians refused to fight, rightly fearing that any interference in a state's government would set a dangerous precedent for them all. Their withdrawal, followed by Cleomenes' co-king Demaratus and the rest of the allies, forced the Spartans to abandon the expedition (Herodotus 5.75–76). This was the first time that the Spartans' authority to do whatever they wanted militarily and to make the allies comply with their wishes had been challenged. Soon after, the allies were invited to Sparta in order to discuss a further invasion of Attica; the majority of the allies were opposed and so the Spartans gave up their plans (Herodotus 5.91–93). This was the key turning point in the history of Sparta's relations with her Peloponnesian allies: it was from this event that the Peloponnesian League could be said to have come into existence.

Constitution of the Peloponnesian League

It is easier to establish the constitution of this League than that of the Delian League owing to the fact that Thucydides clearly shows the operation of the League's decision-making process, and states some of the major terms of agreement. It was a bicameral league with the Spartans in one chamber, i.e. the Spartan Assembly, and the rest of the allies in the other. Each chamber was constitutionally equal and therefore the veto by one chamber would prevent any proposed policy from being implemented. However, the Spartans did have one vital advantage in that they alone had the formal power to initiate policy. If the allies themselves wanted action on any particular issue, they had to persuade the Spartans to discuss and vote upon the matter in the Spartan Assembly; then and only then, if there was Spartan approval, would formal discussion be allowed in their chamber. If the Spartans in their chamber decided upon no action, then no meeting of the allies' chamber and no discussion on the issue would take place. The best evidence of the League in operation comes from the events of 432 in the build-up to the outbreak of the Peloponnesian War in 431.

By 432, relations between Corinth, Sparta's ally, and Athens had deteriorated dramatically and they had clashed in open warfare (see Chapter 17). The Corinthians wanted the Spartans and the League to declare war on the Athenians. Their first task was to encourage the Spartans to discuss the issue:

> The Corinthians therefore immediately urged the allies to go to Sparta. They, upon coming there, violently attacked the Athenians for having broken the truce and for committing injustices against the Peloponnese.
>
> (Thucydides 1.67.1)

As a result the Spartans issued an invitation to all her allies and to anyone else who claimed to have suffered from Athenian aggression (Thuc. 1.67.3). Representatives from various states came forward and put their complaints before the Spartans in their Assembly (Thuc. 1.67.4–78). It is now that the first stage of the decision-making process comes into operation:

> When the Spartans had heard the complaints made by her allies against Athens ... they, removing everyone else, discussed the present situation among themselves.
>
> (Thucydides 1.79.1)

After much discussion (Thuc. 1.79.2–86), with King Archidamus arguing against any hasty action and the 'Ephor' Sthenelaidas urging war:

> The Spartans, standing up, split into two divisions. The great majority were of the opinion that the treaty had been broken.
>
> (Thucydides 1.87.3)

The Spartans immediately informed the representatives of the allies who were present of their vote for war (Thuc. 1.87.4). These representatives returned home, and then the Spartans summoned a League Congress since:

> they [i.e. the Spartans] wanted to put to the vote the issue of whether war should be declared.
>
> (Thucydides 1.119)

The second stage of decision-making was now underway. The allies in their chamber had a general debate about the issue (Thuc. 1.119–24), in which the Corinthians played the leading role:

> The Spartans, when they had heard everyone's opinion, put the vote city by city to all the allies, who were present both great and small. The majority voted to go to war.
>
> (Thucydides 1.125)

Thus with both chambers having voted in agreement, war could now be declared. In the same way both chambers' agreement would be needed to declare peace.

All the states in the League Congress had to accept the majority verdict, even though they may have voted against the proposal. However, there existed an opt-out clause which allowed a state to refuse to comply with the majority decision – 'unless the gods or heroes prevented it' (Thuc. 5.30.3). An excellent example of this opt-out clause in operation comes from the events following the Peace of Nicias in 421. Both chambers of the League had voted in favour of the peace treaty (Thuc. 5.17.2). The Corinthians, however, had voted against acceptance in the allies' chamber because, among other things, they had not received back some of their former territory from the Athenians (Thuc. 5.30.2). This dissatisfaction led the Corinthians to refuse to accept the peace treaty and even to contemplate leaving the League. When the Spartans rebuked them for not abiding by the majority vote of the allies (Thuc. 5.30.1), the Corinthians claimed that it was impossible for them to agree to the terms of the Peace of Nicias. They claimed that they could not betray their allies in Thrace, to whom they had sworn separate oaths earlier in 432 and had given other guarantees later. Therefore they were not breaking their oaths to the Peloponnesians:

> For, having sworn guarantees in the name of the gods to those in Thrace, they would betray them if they did not stay true to their oath; the phrase used was 'unless the gods or heroes prevented it' and this seemed to them to be a situation of the gods preventing it.

> (Thucydides 5.30.3–4)

Each of these alliances was probably an individual one between Sparta and the individual state, since the League developed from these individual alliances in the sixth century. This meant that wars between individual members of the Peloponnesian League, who were not necessarily allied to each other, could and did occur, whereas in the Delian League with its oath 'to have the same friends and enemies', sworn communally by all the members, private wars were forbidden (although they did sometimes take place, for example, Samos and Miletus in 440). The alliances were permanent and no ally was allowed to secede unless it could claim that the Spartans had broken the terms of the alliance, thereby releasing the ally from its obligations to Sparta. Firm evidence for this comes from the Corinthian speech to the Spartans in 432, when they put the point that Sparta's inactivity towards Athenian aggression could lead to a mass secession from the League:

> 'Do not let your friends and kinsmen fall into the hands of their bitterest enemies. Do not drive the rest of us in despair to seek a different alliance. ... The people who break alliances are not those who join others because they have been deserted, but those who do not give the help they swore to give.'

> (Thucydides 1.71.4)

Once the fighting began Sparta completely controlled all military operations, deciding the campaigns to be fought, the strategy to be employed and supplying the generals in the field.

Sparta, 478–462/1

In 478/7, the Athenians helped to found the Delian League and took over the leadership of Greece in the war against Persia. This was bound to cause some reaction on the part of the Spartans, who had previously been the undisputed leading power in Greece and had just led the Greeks in a stunning defence of their homeland. There is an apparent conflict between the literary sources over the Spartans' reaction to Athens gaining this new position of authority. On the one hand, Herodotus believed that Athens' promotion arose from political opportunism:

> The Athenians, using the arrogance of Pausanias as an excuse, seized the leadership from the Spartans.
>
> (Herodotus 8.3)

If the Spartans perceived the Athenians exploiting this embarrassing episode for advancing their position, they are likely to have felt aggrieved at the Athenians' opportunism and fearful of their ambition. These feelings of anger and fear were given expression in a debate, recorded by Diodorus under the year 475, in which the Spartans were discussing in their Assembly a motion about regaining the hegemony of Greece by force:

> The Spartans, having let slip the leadership of the sea for no good reason, were moved to anger. ... Having convened the Gerusia, they discussed about making war on the Athenians. ... In the same way, when a general Assembly was convened, the younger men and a majority of the others were keen to recover the leadership.
>
> (Diodorus 11.50.1–3)

It is clear that a large majority were eager to attack Athens and to re-assert by warfare Sparta's position as the dominant state in Greece. It was the speech of a certain Hetoemaridas that convinced them that it was not in Sparta's interest to lay claim to the sea. He presumably realized that Sparta, owing to its unique situation with the Helots and its natural inclination towards land warfare, could not easily and safely adapt to becoming a successful sea-power.

On the basis of Herodotus and Diodorus, the Spartans resented Athens taking over the leadership of Greece and were even prepared to wage war against a fellow Hellenic League ally. On the other hand, Thucydides records a very different reaction on the part of the Spartans:

> they[the Spartans] wanted to be rid of the Persian wars, and thought that the Athenians
> were quite able to exercise leadership and were currently friendly to them.
>
> (Thucydides 1.95.7; *AE7* p. 13)

According to Thucydides, the transfer of the leadership appeared to be very amicable with Sparta being most willing to pass over the burdensome task to Athens. These sentiments reflect the attitude of Hetoemaridas in the above debate in Diodorus. However, there is no need to see a conflict between these sources, as they reveal the existence of two factions, which vied with each other throughout the fifth century for control of Spartan foreign policy. In modern politics it is customary to refer to those who contend for influence over or control of foreign policy as 'hawks' and 'doves', and these terms will be used for the two Spartan factions.

The Spartan hawks resented the Athenians' success in the Persian War, but of much greater concern was their fear of the Athenians' growing power and confidence. This fear was shown most clearly in 479 immediately after the battle of Plataea, when the Athenians were attempting to rebuild their city walls. The Spartans sent an embassy to dissuade the Athenians:

> It was partly that they themselves would rather see neither the Athenians nor anyone
> else having a wall, but more that their allies were urging them, frightened of the size
> of the Athenian fleet ... and of the daring which the Athenians had shown in the
> Persian war.
>
> (Thucydides 1.90.1; *AE4* p. 10)

The Greek dead were hardly cold in their graves and already the Spartans were less concerned with Persia and were directing their attention towards the Athenians. Athens without defensive walls would leave the Athenians totally exposed and vulnerable to a Spartan land invasion, and thus they could be blackmailed at any time to do Sparta's bidding. The Spartans had as much to fear as their allies of Athens' massive navy and daring, and would have needed very little urging to ensure Athens' vulnerability. The foundation of the Delian League and the Athenians' potential to increase their power through its leadership would have provoked even greater fear among the hawks. Fundamentally the Spartan hawks refused to accept Athens as an equal, independent super-power. They believed that the only guarantee of safety for Sparta was to possess the sole hegemony of Greece by land and by sea.

The Spartan doves on the other hand accepted the limitations on their foreign policy in Greece. They were well aware of the constant threat that the Helots posed and that a dynamic foreign policy would expose the Spartans to excessive risk. If they were to over-stretch themselves, there was every danger of their suffering a serious defeat, which would inevitably provoke a Helot revolt. A successful Helot revolt would undermine the whole basis of Spartan power and lead to its collapse. Therefore the policy of the Spartan doves was twofold: first, the Spartans must maintain their supremacy in the Peloponnese, as this guaranteed her status as an influential super-power in Greek affairs; second, they had to accept the policy of 'dual hegemony', i.e. the sharing of the leadership of Greece with the Athenians. Athens' sea power and control of the Aegean were vital for the liberty of Greece and Sparta. If the Athenians were crushed and the Delian League broke up, there would be a power vacuum in the Aegean, which Sparta as a traditional land power would find the greatest difficulty in filling. The obvious inheritor of the Athenians' position in the Aegean would be Persia, whose hopes of conquering Greece would have been greatly improved, since Greece would have been severely weakened by the loss of the Athenians' fleet.

At different times throughout the fifth century these two factions held sway over Spartan foreign policy, according to their ability to win over the Spartan Assembly to their views, and in the immediate aftermath of the Persian War there was a struggle between the hawks and doves to gain control. The hawks supported Pausanias' vigorous campaign with the Hellenic League fleet against Cyprus and Byzantium in 478 (Thuc. 1.94; *AE7* p. 13) and most probably his later activities at Byzantium and at Colonae in north-west Asia Minor (Thuc. 1.131), even though it was claimed that he was acting as a private individual. It is very possible that Hetoemaridas was a supporter of the policy of the Spartan doves, but he may have favoured a third foreign policy option that was available to the Spartans in 478, which was a less ambitious version of the policy of the hawks: the abandonment of the war at sea against Persia, but the extension of Spartan power in central and northern Greece, especially Boeotia and Thessaly. The rewards for gaining control of Thessaly were particularly attractive: first, it was wealthy and fertile (Xenophon, *Hellenica* 6.1); second, its cavalry was the best in Greece; third, it was strategically well-positioned for access to Thrace and, even more importantly, to the Hellespont through which the Athenian grain-ships – so vital for the feeding of the Athenian population – had to sail; finally, it had the presidency of and controlled the Amphictyonic Congress (a religious league whose function was to run the Delphic sanctuary but possessing political influence). The Spartans had already attempted, probably in 478, to have the medizing states of Thessaly, Boeotia and Argos expelled as members in order to guarantee Spartan domination of the Congress, but were thwarted by Themistocles' oratory (Plutarch, *Themistocles* 20). However, at some time between 478 and 476, King Leotychidas, the victor at Mycale in 479, was sent on a military expedition to Thessaly, but a massive bribe allegedly prevented him from bringing Thessaly under Spartan control. As a result he was brought before a court, exiled from Sparta and went to live in Tegea (Herodotus 6.72).

By 475, however, the aggressive foreign policy of the hawks had been discredited by the disgrace of its two most powerful advocates, Leotychidas and Pausanias, and the doves seem to have regained the initiative. Hetoemaridas had persuaded the Spartans not to go to war with the Athenians in order to regain the hegemony of Greece by force. Moreover, it was probably argued, the Persians were still a danger to Greece and the Athenians were doing a fine job by gradually removing this threat; the pro-Spartan Cimon was the dominant politician in Athens (see Chapter 11); and the Athenians were treating their Delian League allies fairly. However in c.471 serious cracks in the Delian League's unity began to appear. Naxos had revolted and, after being crushed by the Athenians, became the first subject-ally (Thuc. 1.98.4; AE29 p. 21). Then in 469 at the battle of Eurymedon Persia suffered an overwhelming defeat, which virtually removed any future Persian danger to the Aegean (Thuc. 1.100.1; AE29 p. 21). Soon after this the Delian League allies, feeling that the aim of the League had been achieved, became increasingly restless and rebellious. The Athenians' response was tough and imperialistic, putting down revolts and creating more subject-allies (Thuc. 1.99; AE29 p. 21). From 471, the Athenians' behaviour would have confirmed the worst fears of the Spartan hawks, and it would have been expected of them to demand military action to curb the growing power of the Athenians. Yet there is no recorded Spartan reaction to the Athenians' growing imperialism until 465 and the revolt of Thasos. Why was this? The clue lies in a fragment of Philochorus, a much-respected Atthidographer (see Glossary):

Athens seized the hegemony on account of the disasters that overwhelmed Sparta.

(Philochorus FGrH 328 F117)

This period in the history of Sparta and the Peloponnese is particularly difficult owing to a shortage of literary sources. However, Philochorus' mention of 'disasters' gives the historian a starting-point. It seems, from the fragmentary evidence, that by the late 470s the Spartans were facing an unprecedented challenge to their supremacy in the Peloponnese by a coalition of states, brought together by the influence of Themistocles, which would threaten Sparta's very existence. But first there is a need to identify these states and to chart the growth of their hostility towards Sparta, which culminated in the formation of this anti-Spartan coalition.

The obvious starting-point is Argos. In the past Argos had been one of the most powerful states in the Peloponnese and, as the introduction of hoplite warfare most probably took place there in the first half of the seventh century (699–650), was even the dominant state. However, the rise of Sparta after the Second Messenian War and the Lycurgan reforms eclipsed the power of Argos. Nevertheless, the Argives never forgot their former pre-eminence and resented Sparta's usurpation of their position.

Thus Argos was a traditional enemy of Sparta which was reflected in numerous battles over the generations. The most recent in this period had been the battle of Sepeia in 494, which had been a resounding defeat for Argos with a loss of 5,000 men (Herodotus 6.76–80). It was this loss of manpower that the Argives gave as their reason for neutrality in the Persian War, although there was no way that they would have ever served under Spartan leadership – so deep was their antipathy. According to Herodotus (6.83), the ruling aristocrats as a class suffered most in the slaughter at Sepeia and that the government of Argos passed into the hands of 'douloi' (slaves). This cannot literally be true but it seems possible that some important families, formerly on the fringes of power, took over the government and that 'douloi' is a term of political abuse, used by the aristocratic survivors and their descendants against them. These new families had a liberalizing effect on the Argive constitution, which became a moderate democracy – anathema to the oligarchic-minded Spartans. In 471, Themistocles was ostracized from Athens for his anti-Spartan activities (see Chapter 11) and was welcomed by the Argives (Thuc. 1.135) – no clearer sign of Argos' hostility to the Spartans in the late 470s is required.

Arcadia was also anti-Spartan by the late 470s. There is coin evidence to show that as early as the 490s an Arcadian League had been set up. The mastermind behind this was the fugitive King of Sparta, Cleomenes (Herodotus 6.74), who had been forced to flee from Sparta owing to his disgrace arising from his bribery of the Delphic oracle. The formation of this League and its threat to Sparta led to the recall of its architect to Sparta, where Cleomenes allegedly committed suicide soon after (Herodotus 6.75). However, the League was now in existence and only needed another leader to give it direction. There was also the powerful polis of Tegea in the heart of the Peloponnese and close to the borders of Laconia. Mutual suspicion existed between Sparta and Tegea, especially as Tegea had been the state that had defeated Sparta in the mid-sixth century (c.550). Tegea had been loyal in the Persian War and had fought bravely alongside the Spartans at the battle of Plataea in 479. However, by the late 470s, with the pressure from the outside invader gone, Tegea once again had reason to fear Sparta and was looking for anti-Spartan allies.

Finally, there were Elis and Mantinea. Both states had arrived late for the battle of Plataea, which seems hard to explain as there was almost two weeks of skirmishing before the actual battle was fought, unless this lateness was an excuse, similar to Argos', to avoid fighting under Spartan leadership. Each state 'synoecized' in c.471, i.e. a number of independent villages decided to unite into one bigger state, and have a shared citizenship and a common foreign policy. It was also usual that synoecism was accompanied by the introduction of a democratic constitution. The synoecism of Elis on the borders of the Messenian Helots and the synoecism of Mantinea in the heart of the Peloponnese – both now stronger and democratic – were meant to and did strike fear into the Spartans.

These five areas had one thing in common – hostility towards the Spartans in the late 470s – but they could not become a deadly threat to Sparta unless they could combine their respective strengths. It needed a remarkable politician with exceptional powers of persuasion and patience to bring about the required coalition – Themistocles. In the 470s, Themistocles had turned his back on the policy of the Delian League and had directed his attention towards (in his opinion) Athens' new enemy, Sparta. Thus he set about stirring up trouble for Sparta by encouraging this hostility among other Peloponnesian states. The reward for his patriotic efforts was to be ostracized from Athens in 471 for these anti-Spartan activities (see Chapter 11). However, he was given a warm welcome by the democratic, anti-Spartan douloi in Argos:

> He was living at Argos, though he often travelled about in the rest of the Peloponnese.
>
> (Thucydides 1.135.3)

Using Argos as his base, he now drew together the strands of the policy that he had been working on throughout the 470s. It seems likely that he was the major influence in encouraging the synoecisms and democratization of Elis and Mantinea, and in forging the anti-Spartan north-Peloponnesian coalition in the late 470s. His success was so alarming to the Spartans (even more than Cleomenes in the 490s) that they, with the help of Cimon and his supporters, engineered his condemnation at Athens in c.469/8 on the charge of medism (Plutarch, *Themistocles* 23). But it was too late. The anti-Spartan coalition of Argos, Elis and Arcadia including Tegea and Mantinea had been established.

Herodotus mentions five battles, in which Sparta was successful:

> first the battle of Plataea ...; the second the battle at Tegea against the Tegeans and the Argives; the third at Dipaea against the combined forces of the Arcadians excluding Mantinea; the fourth against the Messenians at Ithome; the last against the Athenians and Argives at Tanagra.
>
> (Herodotus 9.35)

Presumably these battles are in chronological order with Plataea in 479, Ithome in 465/4 and Tanagra in c.457. This leaves two little known battles of Tegea and Dipaea, which must have taken place between 479 (Plataea) and 465/4 (Ithome). The mention of the Tegeans, Argives and the combined forces of Arcadia as Sparta's enemies strongly suggests that the battles of Tegea and Dipaea were the actions of the north-Peloponnesian coalition against Sparta and therefore should be dated between c.471 and 465/4, i.e. between the formation of the coalition and the battle of Ithome. Forrest suggests that the battle of Tegea took place c.469 soon after the bloc was formed. The Spartans won this battle but soon had to face other problems:

Diodorus states that in 468 the Spartans could not help their ally Mycenae, which was being attacked by Argos, as 'they were involved in private wars' (11.65.4). Clearly the other members of the coalition were stretching the Spartan forces by continual attacks, thus pinning them down in defence of their homeland. Therefore, when the original question is addressed – why were the Spartan hawks not pressing for an attack against Athens' growing imperialism in the years 471 to 466 – it is clear that the Spartans' desperate problems in the Peloponnese had forced them into an isolationist foreign policy, having no time to consider Athenian actions and ambitions.

By 465, the Spartans had gained a breathing space from their troubles in the Peloponnese and turned their attention once again to international Greek politics. The Spartan hawks naturally found the situation disturbing: the Athenians were growing in power by the suppression of their allies, as exemplified by the harsh treatment of Thasos which resulted in its revolt from the Delian League (Thuc. 1.100.2; AE29 p. 21). When the Thasians were being besieged and urged the Spartans to come to their aid by invading Attica, the Spartan hawks saw this as the moment to strike:

> Unknown to the Athenians, the Spartans promised to do so and would have done so, but were prevented by the earthquake which had taken place, during which the Helots and the Perioeci from Thouria and Aithaia revolted and occupied Ithome.
>
> (Thucydides 1.101.2; *AE*29 p. 21)

Just as the Spartans were about to re-assert their importance in Greek affairs, problems in the Peloponnese forced them yet again into a policy of isolationism. The earthquake was the worst in the history of Sparta. Plutarch (*Cimon* 16) stated that the whole of Sparta with the exception of five houses was totally destroyed. It was this disaster that encouraged the Helots and the Perioeci of Thouria and Aethaea to throw off the Spartan yoke. It was only the quick thinking of King Archidamus that saved Sparta from ultimate destruction. His drawing up of the surviving Spartans into a battle-line saved the Spartans from the Helots who had descended upon Sparta (Plutarch, *Cimon* 16). Consequently the Helots withdrew to Ithome, which they used as the centre of their rebellion. Sparta's plight in 465 must also have attracted the attention of the north Peloponnesian coalition. The battle of Dipaea, waged by all of the Arcadians with the exception of Mantinea, has to be fitted in before the battle of Ithome of 465/4. Isocrates, a fourth-century rhetorician, says with almost certain exaggeration that the Spartans had to fight in one line of battle (Archidamos 99), but clearly a drastic shortage of manpower had forced the Spartans to fight in a severely depleted hoplite phalanx. Thus the destruction and loss of life in the 465 earthquake offer strong arguments for the battle of Dipaea to be placed in 465.

Having saved Sparta itself from destruction at the hands of the Helots and the north Peloponnesian coalition, the Spartans now turned their attention to subduing the Helot revolt in Messenia. This allowed the Athenians to continue their imperialist policy of crushing Thasos unhindered (Thuc. 1.101.3; AE39 p. 25). The Spartans defeated the Helots in battle but then had the difficult task of reducing them to submission in their fortress on Ithome. By 462/1 the Spartans had still failed to take the place by storm and end the Helot revolt, which was paralysing the Spartans' foreign policy. There can be no clearer proof of the Spartans' desperation than their humiliating appeal for help not only to their Peloponnesian allies but also to the Athenians (Thuc. 1.102.1–3; AE39 p. 25). After a clash in the Athenian Assembly, in which Ephialtes argued strongly but unsuccessfully against helping Sparta (Plutarch, *Cimon* 16), Cimon came with 4,000 hoplites to Ithome. However, this expedition provoked a serious disagreement between the Spartans and the Athenians, and led directly to the outbreak of the First Peloponnesian War (462/1–446/5):

> For when the place was not taken by force, the Spartans grew frightened at the bold and revolutionary character of the Athenians and also because they thought of them as alien in race. They feared that if they stayed, they would be persuaded by those on Ithome to instigate something revolutionary.
>
> (Thucydides 1.102.3; *AE* 38 p. 25)

There is doubt about the meaning of 'the bold and revolutionary character' – possibly it refers to the democratic reforms passed by Ephialtes in Cimon's absence – but there is none about the Spartans' fear of the Athenians. The difference in attitudes, values and ways of life was highlighted by their close proximity. In addition, the Athenians seem to have sympathized with the Helots' cause – fellow Greeks trying to achieve liberty. This was too much for the Spartan hawks and so the Athenians, alone of the allies, were dismissed on the grounds that the Spartans had no further need of them (Thuc. 1.102.3; AE38 p. 25). This humiliating snub at Ithome caused great anger among the Athenians and:

> as soon as they returned home put an end to the alliance which they had made with them against the Persians and to spite the Spartans made an alliance with the Argives, who were the Spartans' enemies.
>
> (Thucydides 1.102.4; *AE*38 p. 25)

This formal renunciation of membership of the Hellenic League meant that Athens and Sparta were no longer allies, and this was tantamount to a declaration of war. This was confirmed by the Athenians' military alliance with Sparta's deadliest enemy. It only needed an incident to turn the cold war into open conflict.

Sparta, 462/1–446/5

Unlike the Peloponnesian War of 431, which the Spartans waged with all their strength, the First Peloponnesian War was essentially between Sparta's allies and the Athenians. This was not due to a lack of hostility on the part of the Spartans – this had been revealed in abundance in the events at Ithome (Thuc. 1.102.1–3; AE38 p. 25) – nor lack of desire for armed conflict, but to their problems in the Peloponnese. Spartan foreign policy was always greatly affected directly or indirectly by the Helots. Since a Helot revolt threatened the very existence of the Spartan state, its suppression dominated Spartan thinking almost to the virtual exclusion of all other issues. The fact that the revolt lasted until 455 (accepting 'in the tenth year', Thuc. 1.103.1; AE38 p. 25) would on its own have severely limited Sparta's active participation in this war. However, the defection of Megara and its fortification with long walls and Athenian soldiers, in addition to the Athenian occupation of the passes over Geraneia, proved decisive for the Spartans (Thuc. 1.103.4, AE39 p. 25; 1.105.3, AE39 p. 26). Their one venture into central Greece in wartime without control of the Megarid – culminating in the battle of Tanagra in c.457 – nearly ended in disaster (Thuc. 1.107–8.2; AE39 pp. 26–27), and they did not attempt another incursion until 446, when Megara had returned to the Peloponnesian League (see below).

Although this expedition into central Greece was a risky adventure, there were sound reasons for it. If the subjugation of Doris, the 'mother country' of the Spartans, was allowed to go unpunished, Sparta's standing among the Peloponnesian allies, already unhappy at bearing the full brunt of the war without their hegemon, would have plummeted to an all-time low and may have led to further defections from the Peloponnesian League. Another motive was the hope of creating an effective opposition and threat to Athens in central Greece. Boeotia had been working towards a federal structure under the leadership of the Thebans, but their disgrace, arising from their support of the Persians in 480–479, had undermined their position in Boeotia and had arrested the growth of federalism. The Thebans therefore made an attractive offer to the Spartans:

> They thought it a good idea for the Spartans to help them to gain the hegemony of Boeotia. They promised in return for this to wage war on the Athenians by themselves so that there would be no need for the Spartans to send a land army outside the Peloponnese.
>
> (Diodorus 11.81.2)

The Spartans naturally enough saw that Boeotia, united under Theban leadership, would offer an excellent check upon Athens' growing power and would reduce the importance of the loss of the Megarid. In the event the Spartans were nearly cut off in central Greece, only just won the battle of Tanagra with heavy casualties and had to endure the ignominy of Boeotia and the rest of central Greece becoming Athens' 'Land Empire' after the battle of Oenophyta (Thuc. 1.108.2; AE39 p. 27).

The resolution of the Helot revolt in c.455 brought to an end the most difficult and dangerous period of Spartan history since the Second Messenian War in the mid-seventh century (Thuc. 1.103.1–3). From the late 470s the Spartans had faced the most sustained challenge to their military supremacy in the Peloponnese, which had been exacerbated by the ten-year Helot revolt. The lack of active warfare in Greece by the Athenians after 454 gave the Spartans the necessary respite to recuperate and to recover their strength. For the same reasons the Five Year Truce of 451–446 was also most welcome. Both the Spartan hawks and the doves probably saw this period as a valuable breathing-space before the necessary and inevitable attack upon the Athenians – the hawks rarely needed any incentive to fight, but in this situation they were joined by the doves, who viewed with alarm the Athenian 'Land Empire' which undermined the foundations of the dual hegemony. However, the Spartans' credibility among their allies and in Greece was at stake, and for that reason the attack could only be launched when they were fully confident that their renewed strength would bring victory – hence the willingness to sign a five-year truce with the Athenians. In addition, this truce allowed the Spartans to make peace with the Athenians' ally in the Peloponnese, Argos. The fact that this was a thirty-year truce and not another five-year truce clearly reveals the underlying intentions of the Spartans. In 446, they would be free to attack the Athenians without any fear of Argive intervention on the side of the Athenians, having effectively neutralized Argos.

The Sacred War in 448 was ostensibly undertaken to restore Delphi to its inhabitants, but in reality this gave the Spartans an acceptable excuse to intervene in central Greece (including Euboea) and Megara, and almost certainly spread anti-Athenian propaganda (Thuc. 1.112.5; AE64 p. 39). The swiftness of the uprising in Boeotia in c.447 and of the revolts of Megara and Euboea in 446 (Thuc. 1.113.1–114.1; AE64 p. 39) seems to be too close in time to Sparta's presence in central Greece to be coincidental. Finally, in 446, the Spartans, led by King Pleistoanax and Cleandridas, marched into Attica and trapped the Athenians behind their long walls, while the revolt of Euboea gathered strength. At this very moment, with the Athenians in dire straits, the Spartan army returned home, thus allowing the Athenians to reconquer Euboea (Thuc. 1.114.2; AE64 p. 39). This action on the part of the Spartans begs two questions: why retire when they had the Athenians at their mercy; and, even if there was no desire to destroy Athens, why retire so quickly? A siege of Athens would have helped Euboea to consolidate its revolt, especially if the Spartans had sent a garrison, and encouraged the subject-allies to gain their independence; at the very least, it would have strengthened the Spartans' bargaining position at the future peace negotiations. The answer to the Spartan 'Gerousia' was obvious – Pleistoanax and Cleandridas had been bribed to withdraw the army (Plutarch, *Pericles* 22). Money may have changed hands but it seems too simple an explanation. More convincing is the view that a deal was struck, in which the Athenians would be allowed to have a sea empire but must give up all ambitions of a land empire and also surrender its territorial possessions in the Peloponnese. In other words both spheres of influence – Sparta on land, Athens at sea – would be defined and legalized in the forthcoming peace treaty. If this interpretation is correct, then Pleistoanax belonged to the dove faction and thus was a believer in the dual hegemony. This policy fits in with that of the three Agiad kings who succeeded him, and who also believed in coexistence with the Athenians. However, a majority of the Gerousia was not convinced of the wisdom of his actions. The hawks would be angry at losing such an excellent opportunity to destroy Athens and even the non-aligned members may have felt that too many advantages had been thrown away. Thus Pleistoanax and Cleandridas were forced into exile; although their preferred foreign policy was reflected in the terms of the Thirty Year Peace (see Chapter 17).

Bibliography

Andrewes, A. 'Sparta and Arcadia in the early fifth century', *Phoenix* 6.
Cartledge, P. *Sparta and Lakonia*, chs 11 and 12.
Forrest, W. G. 'Themistocles and Argos', *CQ* 54.
Hornblower, S. *The Greek World 479–323 BC*, chs 2 and 3.
Powell, A. *Athens and Sparta*, ch. 4.
de Ste. Croix, G. E. M. *The Origins of the Peloponnesian War*, 4 (iv), 5 (v–vii) and Appendix 18.

13

THE DEMOCRATIC REFORMS OF EPHIALTES AND PERICLES, 462/1–451/0

Political background to the reforms

Themistocles' condemnation c.469/8 had deprived his faction, the Athenian hawks (see Chapter 11), of a leader to pursue their twofold policy of opposition to Sparta and the advancement of democratic reform. The success of Cimon and the Athenian doves in the first half of the 460s was decisive, which meant that his opponents had to bide their time until an opportunity should arise when they could offer an effective challenge to him and his policies. The destruction of the Nine Ways colony in 465 and the long, unglamorous siege of Thasos from 465–463 (Thucydides 1.100.2–1.101.3; AE29 p. 21; AE39 p. 25) made Cimon less popular in the eyes of his fellow Athenians, and thus it is from this time that we can date the revival of the Athenian hawks and their plans for a full democracy. The leadership of this faction had fallen to Ephialtes, son of Sophonides, who was renowned for his incorruptibility and his upright character, and to his chief assistant, Pericles. Very little is known about Ephialtes, but the fact that he was a general (Plutarch, *Cimon* 13) at some time between 465 and 463 confirms that he was an upper-class Athenian and not a poor man, as reported in later sources.

Ephialtes realized that the chief obstacle to the introduction of a full democracy was the council of the 'Areopagus', the last bastion and stronghold of aristocratic power and privilege. Almost everything about this institution was undemocratic: membership was for life and was confined to the ex-archons, who came from the two richest classes and had been chosen by lot since 487; moreover, this institution had wide-ranging powers (*Ath. Pol.* 8.4 – see below) and, even more disturbing to the 'radical' democrats, was unaccountable as a body for the exercise of these powers. One of the pillars of democracy is that no public official or public institution should be above the law but must be accountable to the people for its actions. However, Ephialtes and Pericles decided that an immediate, direct assault upon the Areopagus would not yield the required result and that there was a need for a phased attack:

First Ephialtes removed many of the members of the Areopagus, bringing them to
trial for their conduct in office.

(Aristotle, *Ath. Pol.* 25.2)

These successful prosecutions of individual Areopagites for maladministration helped to create a mood of distrust among the ordinary Athenians and
lowered the Areopagus' prestige. Then in 463 the 'radical' democrats made
their most ambitious challenge to date by bringing a charge of corruption
against Cimon, the leader of the 'moderate' democrats and the main supporter of the Areopagus (Plutarch, *Cimon* 14). All our sources attest to
Cimon's incorruptibility, and therefore Pericles' prosecution has to be seen
as a political manoeuvre to test Cimon's political standing. A verdict of
guilty would probably have paved the way for an immediate attack on the
Areopagus. However, Cimon was still sufficiently popular to be acquitted
but this case does reflect the growing confidence of the 'radical' democrats.

Cimon's success was short-lived. Although he won the debate in 462/1
against Ephialtes over the issue of supplying military help to the Spartans at
Ithome (Plutarch, *Cimon* 16), he was disgraced by the Spartans' rejection of
the Athenians and his pro-Spartan foreign policy was discredited. This was
the perfect opening for the 'radical' democrats not only to change Athenian
foreign policy but also to pass their democratic reforms:

Then Ephialtes in the archonship of Conon took away from the council [i.e. Areopagus]
all the additional powers through which it had the guardianship of the constitution,
and gave some to the Boule of 500, and others to the people and the people's jury-
courts.

(Aristotle, *Ath. Pol.* 25.2)

The fact that such an august, ancient and powerful institution could fall so
easily and so totally from political power marks the remarkable change in
the people's attitudes and confidence. Cleisthenes' reforms of 508 had given
the people the means to gain political experience, both in the 'demes' at
local level and in the Ecclesia at national level. They had matured politically
and had grown used to direct power and involvement in the political process. Therefore the position of the undemocratic Areopagus looked completely out of date in a modern, forward-looking state and thus its central
role in Athenian politics had to be removed. The proof that the Athenians were ready to govern themselves was that no new major institutions were created to take over from the Areopagus. The three key
institutions of the 'Ecclesia' (Assembly), the 'Heliaea' (People's Court)
and the Boule of 500 (Council of 500), all of which were controlled by
the Athenian people, were considered to be sufficient and effective
enough to govern Athens.

The reform of the Areopagus

The Areopagus was the main target for the reformers and in particular they planned to remove its wide-ranging legal powers and transfer them to the institutions of the people. Unfortunately the sources, which deal with the powers of the Areopagus before Ephialtes' reforms, are few in number, ambiguous and often partisan, thus requiring a certain amount of speculation. Its powers can be grouped under two headings – religious and secular.

Religious powers

The Areopagus had jurisdiction over the religious crimes of intentional homicide, wounding or poisoning with intent to kill, arson and the destruction of the sacred olive trees (Demosthenes 23.22; Ath. Pol. 60.2), and it was allowed to retain these judicial powers after Ephialtes' reforms. The Athenians, for all their political sophistication, were very conservative in religious matters and, as the 'radical' democrats' chief aim was to curtail the political powers of the Areopagus, they did not want to alienate the people by challenging their deeply held religious feelings, thus endangering their secular reforms. In addition, it is possible that part of the 'radical' democrats' propaganda to win over the people had been that the Areopagus had usurped political powers beyond its original powers over religious jurisdiction, and that their reforms were a restoration of the Areopagus' former position in the state. Therefore there was little attempt to challenge its religious status and power.

Secular powers

The secular powers which the Areopagus possessed from the time of Solon are summarized by Aristotle:

> He [i.e. Solon] ... appointed the council of the Areopagus to guard the laws, just as previously it had been the overseer of the constitution, and it was this institution that in general watched over the most and the greatest of the affairs of the city, corrected wrongdoers with full powers to fine and to punish (it deposited the fines in the treasury without writing down the reason for the fine), and tried those who conspired to overthrow the democracy, for which purpose Solon had introduced a law of impeachment 'eisangelia'.
>
> (Aristotle, Ath. Pol. 8.4)

Thus it seems that the Areopagus exercised its political powers in three main areas: guardianship of the laws ('nomophylakia'), supervision of the city's affairs with the power to impose punishments, and defence of the constitution.

With regard to the Areopagus' guardianship of the laws (nomophylakia), there is disagreement among modern scholars about what this actually entailed. Some believe, on the basis of *Ath. Pol.* 4.4, that this power gave the Areopagus only the authority to supervise public officials. However, others believe, on the basis of Demosthenes (23.62–63) and Philochorus (FGrH 328 F64), that it also gave the Areopagus the right to overrule the Ecclesia (Assembly) if it passed any illegal or undesirable legislation. Alternatively, it has been argued (e.g. by Hignett) that nomophylakia was not a specific power, but an all-embracing name, which was a summary of all the powers that the Areopagus possessed in order to ensure compliance with the law – namely, the right to hear complaints against public officials, the right to punish wrongdoers in general, and the right to try conspirators against the constitution.

Whichever theory is correct, it is clear that the Areopagus had considerable political power. Even if this power was restricted solely to the supervision of public officials, it enabled the Areopagus to exert influence over the selection, the policies and the accountability of the top public officials. The reason for this was that the Areopagus was probably involved in the three elements that constituted supervision of the public officials: first, the 'dokimasia' – the examination of public officials to see whether they were entitled to take up their post; second, the supervision of their conduct during their year of office; and third, the 'euthuna' – an investigation at the end of an official's year in office to see whether he had acted in accordance with the law. The control of the euthuna especially gave the Areopagus important political power and influence over the top public officials: first, because it was unlikely that the archons, destined to become lifelong members of the Areopagus if they passed their euthuna, would reject its advice during their tenure of office; and second, since the Areopagus had the power to accept or reject any complaints against public officials, such as the archons and generals, it thus controlled which public officials would and which would not have to undergo a euthuna.

Accountability was the watchword of Ephialtes' reforms, and thus he was determined to make all public officials accountable to the Athenian people. Although the evidence is thin, it seems that the dokimasia of the archons before Ephialtes' reforms was in two stages – first before the Areopagus, and subsequently before the Heliaea. Ephialtes removed this power from the Areopagus, and gave the first stage of the dokimasia to the Boule of 500 (*Ath. Pol.* 45.3). He also ensured that all the other public officials underwent their dokimasia before the Heliaea (*Ath. Pol.* 25.2), except for the Boule of 500, which was examined by the outgoing Boule as previously laid down by Cleisthenes in 508 (*Ath. Pol.* 45.3). Second, the right to hear complaints against public officials for misconduct during their year of office was taken from the Areopagus and given to the Boule of 500, which had the authority to try the official and to impose a fine up to a maximum of 500 drachmas

(ML 73; *Ath. Pol.* 45.1; Demosthenes 47.3); if the penalty for the crime was greater than this sum, the Boule had to pass the case onto the Heliaea (*Ath. Pol.* 45.2). Ephialtes was determined that the people should have ultimate control in all serious cases. Third, Ephialtes, because he realized that the euthuna had to be rigorous in order to root out misconduct in office, established the principle that there would be a compulsory euthuna for every public official, whether there was a complaint or not, and that it would be conducted by a panel of ten 'euthunoi' (public auditors), chosen by and from the Boule of 500 (*Ath. Pol.* 48.4–5). In addition, he probably added the 30 'logistai' (public accountants), whose task it was to investigate the accounts of all public officials who handled public funds (*Ath. Pol.* 48.3 – there were only ten in the fourth century). In this way Ephialtes wrested control of the public officials from an aristocratic body and gave it to the institutions controlled by the people.

The second power of the Areopagus was its supervision of the city's affairs with the power to punish without giving reasons. This power of arrest and of jurisdiction gave the Areopagus extensive control over the private lives of ordinary citizens, as recounted by the fourth-century rhetorician, Isocrates:

> Our ancestors kept watch over the lives of every citizen, dragging the disorderly before the Areopagus, which criticized, threatened or punished them as they deserved.
>
> (Isocrates 7.46)

Such an intrusion into the private affairs of a comparatively small, increasingly liberal community would have caused great resentment. To make matters worse, there was a lack of accountability in the exercise of this power. The essence of justice is that it should be done and be seen to be done, which was manifestly lacking when the reasons for the imposition of punishments could be ignored. After Ephialtes' reforms no other institution was given such all-pervading powers, and it was left to the responsibility of the individual Athenian to bring such matters to the Heliaea.

The third and final power of the Areopagus was: 'it tried those who conspired to overthrow the democracy' (*Ath. Pol.* 8.4). Clearly, the reference to democracy is anachronistic, reflecting the political situation in the late fifth and fourth centuries. But there is no reason to doubt that Solon did give the Areopagus the power to protect the Athenian constitution, which in his time was under threat from tyranny (Plutarch, *Solon* 19.4); Aristotle has simply stated the updated version of Solon's law. However, by the beginning of the fifth century, it appears that two changes took place: first, this criminal charge was used in a wider sense to encompass any serious crime against the state, for example, treason, misleading the people; and second, the Areopagus' power to convict was limited. It was deprived of final jurisdiction in crimes against the state, in which the penalty would be death or a very heavy punishment such as exile or loss of citizen rights. If a citizen was accused on such a charge, he would be impeached before the Areopagus. If this institution established that there was a case to answer, then the accused was brought before either the Ecclesia or (more likely) the Heliaea for final trial and verdict. Ephialtes removed this preliminary stage from the Areopagus and gave it to the Boule of 500. Any citizen could bring a charge of a crime against the state before the Boule, which would investigate the matter. If it decided that there was a case to answer, it would conduct the trial and, in the case of guilt, impose a fine up to a maximum of 500 drachmas. If the investigation revealed that the case was more serious with a greater penalty involved, then the Boule referred it to the Heliaea or, in exceptional circumstances, to the Ecclesia for judgement.

The Athenian political institutions after Ephialtes' reforms

The removal of the Areopagus' powers, which made public officials and individuals accountable to it but was not itself accountable as a body, was the essential prerequisite to the establishment of a full democracy. Ephialtes had established accountability to the people as one of the main pillars of democracy. From now on there would be a constant and regular system of calling all public officials and public institutions to give an account of their actions in office to the people or their chosen representatives. However, this on its own was insufficient, and thus the other pillar of democracy must be government by the people through the main institutions of the state. There are three branches of government, wherein power must be exercised by the people, if the constitution is to be defined as a democracy – the legislature, the judiciary and the executive. The legislature must be open to all citizens; every citizen should have an equal right to participate; all important decisions and laws must come before this body; and it must be genuinely sovereign, i.e. have the final power of decision in all policy of its choosing.

In the judiciary, the people should have the power to pass judgement in court and everyone must be equal before the law. With regard to the executive, the people should be allowed to participate in carrying out the decisions of the legislature. However, since this execution of policy and law can be conducted at any time only by a small portion of the people, it is essential that both equality of opportunity and the means (in the form of pay) to serve the state are provided. It is these criteria that must be applied to the institutions of Athens to see if Ephialtes and Pericles can be credited with the introduction of full democracy.

As mentioned above, Aristotle (*Ath. Pol.* 25) stated that the three main institutions to benefit from the demise of the Areopagus' secular powers were the Ecclesia (the people), the Heliaea (the people's jury courts) and the

Boule of 500. The Ecclesia had possessed formal sovereignty from the time of Solon, but in reality this was checked by a number of factors. It probably met only ten times a year, which restricted the number of issues that could be discussed and passed by the whole people, and which in all probability was dominated by the experienced aristocratic orators. With the exception of the most important issues, which had to be decided by the Ecclesia, the Areopagus and the top public officials had the power to take decisions between meetings. The reforms of Ephialtes radically changed this situation and confirmed in practice that the Ecclesia was the sovereign institution in Athens. All laws and policy-making came for decision before the Ecclesia, which all citizens over the age of 18 could attend. It is from now that 'isegoria' (the equal right to speak) became a reality, even if it had been legally in existence from the time of Cleisthenes. The ability of the ordinary Athenian to take a more active role and to participate more fully in the legislature was helped by the increase in the number of meetings of the Ecclesia. In the fourth century, 40 meetings per year were prescribed by law and this may date back to Ephialtes (*Ath. Pol.* 43.4–6). However, it is more likely that the previously prescribed ten meetings per year were kept but there was also a large increase in the number of extra meetings which the Athenians could summon. Thus it could be said that after 462/1:

> The people have made themselves masters of everything and control all things by decrees and by the jury courts, in which the people have the sovereign power.
>
> (Aristotle, *Ath. Pol.* 41.2)

The radical and democratic nature of Ephialtes' reforms is most revealed in the changes to the institution of the Heliaea. It had been created by Solon as a court of appeal for citizens, who were dissatisfied with the legal judgements of the aristocratic archons or the Areopagus, and was in effect the Ecclesia sitting as a law court. Ephialtes now made it a court of first instance so that it could administer justice in its own right. A panel of 6,000 jurors was selected each year by lot, very possibly 600 from each of the ten tribes (*Ath. Pol.* 24.3). This number was recognized by the Athenians as a quorum of the body politic, i.e. it was the smallest number which could be said to represent all the Athenian citizens. Therefore the 6,000 in the Heliaea were still acting as the whole 'demos' and, as they now had primary jurisdiction, there was no need for an appeal court. The Heliaea rarely sat as a court of 6,000 but was now divided up into smaller panels, known as 'dikasteria'. The supervision of the public officials in their 'dokimasiai' and their 'euthunai', and the increase in the legal business arising from the Delian League demanded a more efficient system to handle this growing amount of legal work. The use of the lot provided equality of opportunity for all those Athenians who wished to serve in the people's jury courts. However, the introduction of 'misthophoria' (state pay) at two obols a day for attendance as a juror was the other vital principle, apart from the lot, which made full democracy a reality by supplying the means for even the poorest Athenian to serve the state:

> Pericles was the first man to provide payment for jury service as a political measure to counter the private generosity of Cimon.
>
> (Aristotle, *Ath. Pol.* 27.3)

Pericles was credited with this reform, but there is doubt as to whether it was introduced in 462/1 as part of Ephialtes' reforms or soon after in the 450s. The 462/1 date is more compelling, since the enrolment of 6,000 jurors to dispense primary jurisdiction in the dikasteria would have been impossible without the introduction of pay to attract the required number. The programme of the reformers in 462/1 was wide-ranging and it should cause no surprise that Ephialtes handed over responsibility for some of the legislation to his trusted political ally. Aristides had already introduced proposals into the Ecclesia under the names of other men at an earlier date (Plutarch, *Aristides* 3) and the decree of Thoudippus (ML 69; AE138 pp. 66–67), which authorized a threefold increase in the total contributions of Athens' subject-allies in 425, was most probably inspired by Cleon, who was the dominant politician in Athens at this time and was related to Thoudippus by marriage. Plutarch states that Pericles' reform was part of the democratic programme, which was led by Ephialtes and which involved them both in the attack upon the powers of the Areopagus (*Pericles* 9) – hence 462/1 is the more likely date. Aristotle in the *Ath. Pol.* stressed that the judicial power of the people in their jury courts was the main basis for establishing political sovereignty, and this reform of the judiciary should be seen as the most far-reaching:

> For when the people are masters of the vote in court, they become masters of the state.
>
> (Aristotle, *Ath. Pol.* 9.1)

The third branch of democratic government concerns the executive which, through its public officials and boards, carries out the decisions of the people as expressed in their decrees. In Athens, the most important body of the executive (and the third main institution to benefit from the reforms of Ephialtes) was the Boule of 500. In a full democracy there is a need for a smaller body of citizens to help the legislature to be efficient in making its decisions as well as ensuring that the decrees of the legislature are implemented. Consequently, the Boule of 500 had two main functions – probouleutic and administrative. Its probouleutic power allowed the Boule to receive and discuss all proposals for inclusion on the agenda for the next meeting of the Ecclesia (*Ath. Pol.* 45.4). As the number of meetings of the Ecclesia increased after Ephialtes' reforms and consequently the number of issues to be decided, this role of the Boule became even more vital in helping the full democracy to formulate policy and make decisions. Its administrative power put it at the head of the day-to-day running of the state: apart from its own internal boards (for example, the euthunoi and the logistai), it helped and supervised the other public officials in the performance of their public duties (*Ath. Pol.* 47.1). According to Aristotle, there were 700 public officials ('archai') who had domestic responsibilities in Attica, as well as 700 (this number is suspect) overseas officials (*Ath. Pol.* 24.3). Most of these public officials were chosen by lot (one from each tribe), held office for one year only, and served on boards (usually consisting of ten members), each of which had responsibility for one specific area of public administration. Thus the Boule of 500 exercised a vital supervisory and coordinating role which was essential for the smooth running of the state. Membership of the Boule was organized on the basis of 50 men chosen by lot from each of the ten tribes (*Ath. Pol.* 43.2). Ephialtes' removal of pre-selection before the lot took place was another advance for full democracy, since it gave every citizen an equal opportunity to serve in the Boule. However, the absence of state pay meant that the middle classes still dominated as councillors in the Boule of 500 and as public officials.

Soon after the reforms were passed, Ephialtes was assassinated and the leadership of his faction probably passed to Pericles. Ephialtes had laid down the fundamental principles of a full democracy – accountability, the lot and payment for office – and it was Pericles' task to complete the democratic reforms by spreading these principles throughout the remaining institutions. Pay for serving as councillors in the Boule of 500 and as public officials (archai) was most probably introduced in the 450s. In 457, the diminished role of the archons, whose judicial role was now restricted to presidency of the dikasteria with no powers of judgement, allowed the office to be opened up to the middle-class 'zeugitae' (*Ath. Pol.* 26.2). By the end of the 450s, many more Athenians were participating in their democracy and receiving its benefits, which was one of the reasons why Pericles introduced his Citizenship Law in 451:

> In the third year after that, in the archonship of Antidotus, on account of the large number of citizens they decided on the proposal of Pericles that a man should not be a member of the citizen body unless both of his parents had been Athenian citizens.
>
> (Aristotle, *Ath. Pol.* 26.3)

With full democracy in place its financial cost could only be maintained by restricting the eligibility of those entitled to benefit from its advantages.

Bibliography

Bury, J. B. and Meiggs, R. *A History of Greece*, ch. 9.
Davies, J. K. *Democracy and Classical Greece*, ch. 4.

Forrest, W. G. *The Emergence of Greek Democracy*, ch. 9.

Hignett, C. *A History of the Athenian Constitution*, chs 4, 8 and 9.

Ostwald, M. *From Popular Sovereignty to the Sovereignty of Law*, pts 1.1 and 2.5.

Rhodes, P. J. *CAH vol.* 5, 2nd edn, ch. 4.

Roberts, J. W. *City of Socrates. An Introduction to Classical Athens*, ch. 3.

Wallace, R. W. *The Areopagus Council, to 307* BC, chs 2 and 3.

14

THE INSTITUTIONS OF ATHENIAN
DEMOCRACY

The sources

The three major institutions of Athens' democracy were the 'Boule', the 'Ecclesia' and the 'Heliaea' (also known as the 'dikasteria', when subdivided into panels of jurors). The main evidence for the workings and the powers of these three bodies comes from Aristotle's *Ath. Pol.*, the speeches of the fourth-century orators, the comedies of Aristophanes and documentary inscriptions – each of which provides some problems for the historian. The *Ath. Pol.*, although very detailed, describes the working of these institutions in the fourth century, as do the speeches of the orators; Aristophanes was comic playwright, not a constitutional historian, and his main aim was to make his audience laugh by using exaggeration and parody, not by giving accurate descriptions of the institutions in operation in the late fifth century; the documentary inscriptions come at the end of the political process, and consequently give only a partial insight into the preliminary proceedings which culminated in the law or decree contained in the inscription.

The Boule

The Boule of 500 was appointed by lot, 50 men from each of the ten tribes, with each deme within the tribe supplying its prescribed quota of tribal councillors according to its size (*Ath. Pol.* 43.2). At the same time each councillor had a substitute, also appointed by lot, allocated to them in case of illness or ineligibility to take up the post. Each appointee had to be over 30 years of age and had to undergo a 'dokimasia' (investigation) by the out-going Boule. This was a preliminary investigation to see if the new councillor was eligible to take up the post: for example, that he possessed Athenian citizenship, and was the right age (*Ath. Pol.* 45.3). The dokimasia would also ascertain if the new councillor had held this office before, as it was laid down that no man could be a councillor more than twice in his lifetime and not in successive years.

Organization

The Boule of 500 was too big and unwieldy to be in permanent session to carry out its various tasks and so it was subdivided into smaller committees, one of which would be the directing or steering committee. The Athenian year was divided into ten 'prytanies' (a period of 35 or 36 days), and the 50 councillors from each of the ten tribes took it in turn to be this steering committee for one 'prytany'. These fifty men were known as the 'prytaneis' (presidents), receiving more pay for their more onerous tasks, and the lot would be used to decide which tribe presided in which prytany. These prytaneis would eat together in the 'Tholos' ('The Round House') and it was their task to convene meetings of the Boule each day (apart from public holidays) and the Ecclesia, when appropriate. They would specify where the Boule was to meet and take charge of the agenda, specifying the topics to be discussed on the different days (*Ath. Pol.* 43.2). On each day an 'epistates' (a chief president) – who could only hold the post once in his lifetime – was chosen by lot from the 50 prytaneis. On that one day and one night he was the nominal head of the Athenian state. He would be the chairman of the Boule or even the Ecclesia, if it was in session on that day; he would also be responsible for the keys of the sanctuaries where the Athenian funds and records were kept; and finally he would be in charge of the public seal. The 50 presidents themselves were broken down into a smaller sub-committee. The epistates and one-third of the prytaneis had to be in permanent attendance at the Tholos to deal with any issue or crisis that might arise within a 24 hour period (*Ath. Pol.* 44.1).

Powers and responsibilities

The 'demos' was sovereign but it needed a smaller body not only to help the Ecclesia to be an effective policy-making institution but also to execute the wishes of the demos as expressed in its decrees and laws. The Boule was a cross-section of the demos, as every geographical area, every class and every interest was included. It was the 'polis in miniature' and thus was closely in tune with the prevailing attitudes and values of the Ecclesia. It was crucial to the working of the radical democracy of Athens, as the absence of such a body would lead to institutional anarchy; alternatively its replacement by a specialist, long-standing body would severely restrict the power of the Athenian demos by gradually absorbing the decision-making functions of the Ecclesia. The Boule had two major powers and responsibilities – administrative and probouleutic.

The Boule was placed at the head of Athenian administration and consequently its major administrative function was to aid and supervise the other public officials:

> In general, the Boule shares in the administration of the other officials.
>
> (Aristotle, *Ath. Pol.* 49.5)

248

There were numerous committees, usually consisting of ten citizens chosen by lot, specializing in one particular area of administration, such as the ten 'poletae' (sellers), who were responsible for letting out the various state contracts and leases, and the 'colecretae' (receivers), who made all the payments on behalf of the state. All these different committees were responsible to the Boule, which ensured that they carried out their duties efficiently and in accordance with the law. This supervisory and coordinating role at the heart of the administration of Athens helped to avoid a duplication and a dereliction of duties. The Boule also investigated any complaints against public officials and could fine them up to 500 drachmas:

> Most trials of officials, particularly of those who handle money, are judged by the Boule; their verdict, however, is not final but is subject to appeal to the jury-court. Private individuals also have the right to bring an impeachment ('eisangelia') against any official for illegal conduct; and in these cases also the officials can appeal to the jury-court if the Council finds them guilty.
>
> (Aristotle, *Ath. Pol.* 45.2)

The Athenians were particularly concerned that public money was properly accounted for and, as can be seen from the above quotation, they expected the Boule to exercise strict financial control. The Boule also supplied five sub-committees, chosen by lot from within its own number, which had responsibility for areas of administration that were considered too important to Athens' vital interests to be left to other bodies. There were the ten 'euthunoi' (public auditors) who reviewed an official's conduct at the end of his year in office; and (in the fifth century) the 30 'logistai' (public accountants) who checked the accounts of all officials that handled public money. These two sub-committees ensured that every action of every public official was accountable to the Athenian demos (*Ath. Pol.* 48.3–5). Two other sub-committees were involved in the crucial area of maintenance and exercise of Athens' naval power: the ten 'trieropoioi' (trireme-builders), who had authority over the construction of new warships and the necessary funds, and ten men, who were in charge of the dockyards, naval equipment and the dispatch of naval expeditions (*Ath. Pol.* 46.1). The final sub-committee consisted of the ten 'hieropoioi' (doers of sacred things), who presided at important holy ceremonies such as the consecration of first fruits at Eleusis. By its exercise of such powers described above the Boule performed the role of an Athenian Home Office.

The Boule also handled all diplomatic relations between Athens and other states, and in this respect was similar to the Foreign Office. All heralds and foreign envoys approached the Boule first in order to explain the nature of their business in Athens. In the same way Athenian envoys and generals on duty away from Athens gave their reports to the Boule, which would discuss them and put them on the agenda for the Ecclesia, if it thought fit. Whenever oaths had to be taken on behalf of the Athenian people, it was the Boule (with the Heliaea) that carried out this function:

> The Athenian Council and dikasts are to swear the oath on the following terms: 'I will not expel the Chalcidians from Chalcis.'
>
> (The Chalcis Decree [ML 52; *AE*78 p. 44])

Even more important was the role of the Boule in the assessment and collection of 'phoros' (tribute) from the subject-allies in the Athenian Empire. The Cleinias Decree, also known as the Tribute Decree, established the Boule's central role in the collection of phoros. All phoros was sealed and sent with a tablet, recording the amount of phoros, to the Boule for checking, which then had to call a meeting of the Ecclesia for the 'Hellenotamiae' (Treasurers) to report on the allies who had paid in full and on those who had defaulted. Finally it was the duty of the Boule to prosecute those defaulters, who after being warned had still not paid (ML 46; *AE*190 pp. 102–3). The phoros from the allies was the main source of Athens' income in the second half of the fifth century. Until 425, it amounted to roughly 600 talents from a total income of 1,000 talents (Xenophon, *Anabasis* 7.1.27) and, after the decree of Thoudippus in 425 (ML 69; *AE*138 pp. 66–67), roughly 1,500 talents from a total of 2,000. The above duty in the running of the Athenian Empire, together with its close working relationship the generals and the Hellenotamiae, is the perfect example of the Boule's indispensable role as the head of the administration of Athens.

The second main responsibility of the Boule was its probouleutic function, i.e. to prepare the agenda for the Ecclesia:

> It frames preliminary motions ('probouleumata') for the demos, and the demos cannot vote on any measure that has not been prepared by the Boule in this way and of which the prytaneis have not given advance notice in writing.
>
> (Aristotle, *Ath. Pol.* 45.4)

Every law or decree had to derive its existence from a 'probouleuma' (preliminary motion), which had previously been discussed in the Boule and placed upon the agenda. The subjects of these preliminary motions would be proposed by individual councillors or by public officials or by private citizens, who would usually approach a councillor and persuade him to bring up the relevant issue at a meeting of the Boule, or by the Ecclesia itself, which could instruct the Boule to bring in a probouleuma on a particular issue. The Boule at its meetings would then discuss the various issues before it, decide on the issues to be placed on the agenda for the Ecclesia and finally decide the form of each probouleuma: whether it should be a specific probouleuma – a bill worked out in full detail, recommending a course of action; or an open probouleuma – the issue simply placed on the agenda. It was essential that the legality of each probouleuma was carefully checked to ensure that it did not contravene the law; otherwise the proposer of the motion and the prytaneis, who would put the motion to the vote in the Ecclesia, would be liable to prosecution. The Boule could also pass decrees in their own right, but these covered only routine matters which needed speedy action but were not of sufficient importance to be brought before the Ecclesia.

Therefore, to summarize the Boule's role in the democracy, it played a vital role in the state's administration and was in charge of initiating business to be discussed and decided upon by the Ecclesia. Its sole concern with policy-making was its drafting of 'probouleumata' (the plural of probouleuma). However, it was here that the Boule had its one opportunity to influence state policy by casting a motion with its recommendation for a particular course of action. But every Athenian had the right in the Ecclesia to amend, reject or offer a counter-motion to that of the Boule and thus its potential influence could be nullified. Matters of a contentious nature would usually, but not always (see below under Ecclesia), be placed on the agenda as open probouleumata: it would then be left to the Athenians to decide upon a majority viewpoint and a recommended course of action after a debate in the Ecclesia. Thucydides' extensive descriptions of such key debates as those concerning the alliance with Corcyra in 433 (1.31–45) and the reply to Sparta's ultimatum in 432 (1.139–45) contain no mention of the Boule at all, let alone suggesting that it had any degree of influence in shaping Athens' policy. The Athenians created three other checks to ensure that within the Boule no corporate identity or 'esprit de corps' developed, which might tempt it to usurp power. The use of the lot in the recruitment of councillors, the rotation of office of the ten tribes' prytaneis (also decided by lot) and the limitation of one year in office (with a second year permissible but not in successive years) guaranteed that the Boule stayed the servant of the Ecclesia.

The Ecclesia

Attendance at the Ecclesia, whose meetings were held on the Pnyx, a hill near the Acropolis, was open to all Athenian citizens of eighteen years of age and above. Aristotle, writing in the second half of the fourth century, states that there were four meetings of the Ecclesia each prytany, i.e. 40 per year (Ath. Pol. 43.4–6). In each prytany there would be a Principal Assembly, known as the 'kyria ecclesia', and three others, in which some of the topics or subjects for discussion were mandatory. It seems unlikely that this prescribed number of meetings and the prescribed list of agenda topics operated in the fifth century: there were probably ten Principal Assemblies and numerous other assemblies, convened as often as the Athenians so desired; however, it is reasonable to assume that the agenda topics of the

251

fourth-century assemblies would have been the same in the second half of the fifth. Therefore Aristotle's *Ath. Pol.* is useful for discussing the range of issues that came before the fifth-century Assembly for decision:

> One meeting, the Principal Assembly ('kyria ecclesia'), is the one at which they are required to vote for the confirmation of officials if they appear to be governing well, and to deal with the food supply and the defence of the country; anyone who wishes to bring an impeachment ('eisangelia') must do so on this day; inventories of estates being confiscated must also be read and legal claims for the right of succession to inheritances and of marriage to an heiress so that everyone may have the opportunity to learn of any vacancy in an estate. (5) During the sixth prytany, in addition to the specified business, they take a vote on whether they should hold an ostracism or not; and also vote on preliminary information laid against anyone, Athenian citizen or 'metic', accused of being a sycophant, up to three cases in each class; in addition, they consider any cases where promises made to the demos have not been kept.
>
> (Aristotle, *Ath. Pol.* 43.4–5)

It can be clearly seen from the above quotation that the accountability of the public officials, especially the generals, was of paramount importance to the demos with a vote of confidence held ten times a year. However, the opportunity was also provided for any Athenian to bring an impeachment ('eisangelia') against any politically active citizen, often referred to as 'rhetores' (orators). Public officials were always directly accountable for their public actions, both in the votes of confidence in the Ecclesia and at their 'euthuna', but it was recognized that those politically active citizens, who proposed decrees in the Assembly but held no official post, also needed to be made personally accountable to the Athenian demos for their public actions. Thus one of the methods provided was the right of every Athenian citizen to impeach them in the Ecclesia for treason, which covered subversion of the democracy, betrayal, and accepting bribes to speak contrary to the best interests of the Athenian people (Hypereides Euxenippos 7–8, 29); for misleading the people by not keeping their promises (Demosthenes 49.67); or (probably) for any other crime that was not specifically covered in the existing law-code. This mechanism was designed to ensure that there could be no power without responsibility, and so acted as a deterrent to irresponsible 'demagogic' behaviour in the Ecclesia. In the sixth prytany, sycophants (see below under Heliaea), who as private prosecutors had gained a notorious reputation for unscrupulous ruthlessness, could also be indicted, and the possibility of holding an ostracism (see Glossary and Chapter 8) was made available in the same prytany. The other key issues, apart from the vote of confidence in the public officials, were the food supply and the defence of the country. Athens depended upon the importation of grain, as Attica was insufficiently fertile to feed the population, and this was intrinsically linked with the defence of the country. It was the

Athenians' loss of sea power after the battle of Aegospotamoi in 405, which resulted in the Spartans cutting off the grain imports from the Black Sea and starving the Athenians into submission in 404. Finally the Principal Assembly acted as a public information bureau for the people about such issues as confiscated property, heiresses, inheritances and probably other related issues.

> The second Assembly [in each prytany] is devoted to petitions; at this meeting anyone who wishes may lay down a suppliant branch, and then address the demos on any subject he wishes, whether private or public.
>
> (Aristotle, *Ath. Pol.* 43.6)

This Assembly meeting was given over to private members' business: it allowed the ordinary Athenian a public platform on which to raise any issue and convince his fellow Athenians that action was needed. If he managed to persuade the majority of citizens of the merits of his case, then they would instruct the Boule to introduce a probouleuma on this topic at a later session of the Ecclesia. This Assembly also ensured that the political rights of all citizens were safeguarded – any citizen, who failed to persuade a councillor to introduce his topic into the Boule for discussion and inclusion on the agenda for the Ecclesia, had the opportunity to bring it in person before the Athenian demos. The remaining two meetings were given over to three important topics:

> The other two Assemblies [in each prytany] deal with any other business; at these the laws lay down that three cases of sacred matters are to be dealt with, three cases concerning the heralds and embassies, and three cases concerning secular matters.
>
> (Aristotle, *Ath. Pol.* 4.6)

These assemblies were concerned with current affairs in the areas of religion, foreign policy and domestic issues, with precedence being given to three issues on each topic chosen by lot.

Thus the Ecclesia exercised control over every area of public business. The agenda for the assembly would be published by the prytaneis four days in advance, thus giving the citizens time to organize their thoughts and their private business. There were extra assemblies when the citizens could be convened, if for example time for discussion on an important issue ran out or there was a major rethink on a decision previously passed. An excellent example of this was the Mytilenean debate in 427, in which it had been decided that the punishment to be meted out on the revolted Mytileneans should be death to the entire adult male citizen population and slavery for the women and children. However, on the next day there was widespread disquiet at the severity of the sentence and consequently a second assembly was convened at once to discuss the matter again (Thucydides 3.36).

Procedure in the Ecclesia

The main sources are Aristophanes in his two plays, *The Thesmophoriazusae* (*Women celebrating the Thesmophoria*) and the *Ecclesiazusae* (*The Assembly Women*), and the fourth-century orators, especially Demosthenes and Aeschines. The meetings of the assembly were presided over by the prytaneis (presidents) and the epistates (chief president – see above under Boule). They were assisted by a herald, who made all the official announcements to the Ecclesia on their behalf; a secretary of the people, who read out all documents to the people; and a secretary of the Boule, who presumably took the minutes of the meeting so that all decrees and laws passed at that session could be recorded accurately, and who received all amendments and counter-motions from the floor. The procedure can be deduced from *The Thesmophoriazusae*, which contains a parody of a meeting of the Ecclesia, where, during their festival of the Thesmophoria, the women are discussing what punishment should be inflicted on Euripides for his misogyny in his tragedies. The session begins with a prayer from the herald, in which he demands silence, and prays to the gods both to help the city to act wisely and to ensure that the speakers whose advice is the best succeed (ll. 295–310). The herald then reads out the curse, which (if we remove the references to womankind, Euripides and the catalogue of women's vices) calls upon the gods to destroy anyone who plots against the people, negotiates with the Persians or plans to become or restore a tyrant (ll. 331–51). The Ecclesia is now ready for business.

The Boule had already prepared and published the agenda, which consisted of a number of probouleumata (motions), some of which had been cast either as specific motions (bills worked out in full detail, containing recommendations) or open motions (the relevant issues simply placed on the agenda). M. H. Hansen's research on the Landsgemeinde, the small cantons in German-speaking Switzerland, gives the best example of how a modern, direct democracy conducts its legislative business and gives a valuable insight into the probable workings of the Athenian Ecclesia. All specific probouleumata would be read out in turn with an immediate vote after each one by the citizens raising their hands. If the voting was unanimous in favour, then the probouleuma was immediately passed without further discussion. In this way all routine and non-contentious bills could be passed quickly, leaving more discussion time for the important or contentious issues. On the other hand, if even only one citizen voted against a specific probouleuma, then in the same way as the open probouleumata there would need to be a discussion. With the specific decrees passed, the herald would then come to the remaining probouleumata and would throw open the issue to the citizens by asking the question 'Who wishes to speak?' Once a citizen had been given permission to speak by the epistates, his rights to contribute to the legislation were total and absolute. If it was a specific probouleuma, not passed at the earlier vote, the Athenian citizen had the right to offer amendments, radically change or reject the probouleuma, or offer an alternative probouleuma to that of the Boule; if it was an open probouleuma, he had the right to offer his own specific probouleuma for consideration by the Ecclesia. After discussion, the final form of the decree with its amendments (if applicable) would be reached and the prytaneis would put it to the vote.

The role of the Ecclesia in legislation

The vital question is: Although the ordinary Athenian in theory possessed the above rights, which of the Ecclesia or the Boule in reality assumed the dominant role in the legislative process? In other words, did the Boule draft most of the decrees in detail and the Ecclesia act as a rubber-stamp in passing them, or did the Boule's probouleumata avoid controversy, leaving the real power to the Athenians to shape policy in their debates in the Ecclesia? The two main sources of how decisions were reached in the Boule and the Ecclesia are the surviving inscriptions which record the decrees passed and the debates recounted in Thucydides and Xenophon.

Let us take the inscriptional evidence first. The inscriptions from the fifth century do cause problems as the more common prescript of the decrees states: 'it was resolved by the Boule and the people' and thus it is very hard to decide from where the main initiative for the decree arose. It is easier with the fourth-century decrees as the prescript tends to follow two formulas. Apart from the above fifth-century prescript, which was still in use, there was also the following: 'it was resolved by the people'. It seems very probable that the first prescript was used when the Ecclesia passed a decree, which had previously been worked out in detail by the Boule, and used the second prescript when most, if not all, of the provisions of the decree had been worked out in the Ecclesia. However, the use of amendments in fifth-century decrees does give valuable clues. All decrees contain the name of the proposer of the decree as part of the prescript (along with the name of the presiding tribe, the epistates and the secretary of the Boule), which in itself reveals nothing; but if the amendment begins with: 'X moved this amendment to the Council's probouleuma: … ', or something similar, then the main body of the decree was drafted in the Boule and it took the main initiative. If the amendment begins with; 'X proposed this amendment to the decree of Y: … ', or something similar, then the main initiative for the decree came from the Ecclesia with the Boule simply putting the issue on the agenda in the form of an open probouleuma, as in the regulations for the establishment of the colony of Brea in c.446/5 (ML 49; AE232 pp. 119–20) or the decree of Anticles, as part of the regulations for Chalcis in 446/5 after its revolt (ML 52; AE78 pp. 44–45). Although it is not possible to identify from fifth-century inscriptions which of the two institutions was the more active in initiating legislation, it is clear that both institutions could and did play a role in shaping policy.

If the major debates that are recorded in depth in Thucydides are used as evidence, then there is no doubt that the Ecclesia assumed the main initiative in decision-making. In 433 the Athenians had to decide on the advantages and disadvantages of an alliance with Corcyra against Corinth, the consequences of which could lead to war with the Peloponnesians (1.31–45); in 432/1 the Athenians had to respond to the Spartan ultimatum (1.139–45); and in 427 decide on the fate of the population of Mytilene (3.36–49). These three examples reveal the dominance of the Ecclesia to such an extent that the Boule is not even mentioned in these events. Therefore it seems reasonable to say that the Ecclesia took the dominant role in making policy but that the Boule could exert influence over the decisions made by the people. The Thoudippus decree (ML69; AE138 pp. 66–67), which increased threefold the financial contributions of the subject-allies and whose main initiative came from the Boule, had a dramatic effect on the Athenians' income and thus their ability to wage an increasingly expensive war. However, this ability to influence could easily be blunted and removed by the ordinary Athenian citizen exerting his constitutional power in the Ecclesia.

Although the Ecclesia was sovereign, there were important legal safeguards to ensure that its power and freedom were not abused and descend into licence and lawlessness. First, no decree could be discussed and passed, unless it had already been placed on the agenda by the Boule as a probouleuma. In the second assembly in each prytany, where provision was made for any citizen to raise any private or public issue before the people, if a majority approved of it, then the issue was still referred back to the Boule to make it the subject of a probouleuma and place it on the agenda of a future meeting of the Ecclesia. Second, every amendment and alternative motion had to be in writing. Third, and most importantly, if any probouleuma was illegal or in conflict with an earlier law, then either a citizen could issue a 'graphe paranomon', i.e. a summons against someone for proposing such an illegal decree, or the prytaneis could refuse to put the probouleuma to the vote.

The best example of the Ecclesia's safeguards in operation (and being unconstitutionally overridden) comes from the trial of the six generals (eight generals were charged, but two of them had not returned to Athens) in 406, which is recorded by Xenophon. The generals had defeated the Peloponnesian navy at the battle of Arginusae but failed to pick up all of the Athenian survivors from the twelve disabled ships, which eventually sank and whose crews perished. These generals were charged with criminal negligence and the Boule proposed, as it had every right to do in cases of such public importance, that the generals should be tried in the Ecclesia. In the first meeting of the Ecclesia both the generals and their accusers gave their accounts of what happened after the battle. As it was late, the Ecclesia instructed the Boule to review the matter and to prepare a probouleuma concerning the type of trial the generals should have. At the next meeting of the Ecclesia, the Boule, under the influence of Callixeinus and with him as proposer, put forward a probouleuma that without any further speeches or evidence the Athenians should vote immediately on the generals' guilt or innocence, and that their fate should be decided by one single vote and not by six separate votes. However:

> Euryptolemus, son of Peisianax, and certain others brought a summons against Callixeinus, saying that he had made an illegal proposal ('graphe paranomon').
>
> (Xenophon, *Hellenica* 1.7.12)

This safeguard should have stopped the issue there, and the matter should have been referred to the dikasteria to rule on the legality of the Boule's probouleuma, as proposed by Callixeinus. However, a majority of the people deliberately ignored this and, after threats to Euryptolemus and his supporters that they would face the same charge as the generals, they were forced to withdraw their graphe paranomon. At this point the second safeguard came into operation:

> Some of the prytaneis said they would refuse to put such an illegal proposal to the vote.
>
> (Xenophon, *Hellenica* 1.7.14)

This action should have again stopped the progress of the probouleuma, but they in turn were threatened with being accused on the same charge as the generals and in a state of fear agreed to put the Boule's probouleuma to the vote.

There was now only one course of action left open to Euryptolemus – to put forward an alternative probouleuma to that of the Boule. He spoke in defence of the generals and:

> With these words Euryptolemus proposed a motion that the men should be tried individually under the decree (psephisma) of Cannonus; the Council's motion was that they should all be tried together on a single vote. A show of hands was taken to decide between the two motions, and at first that of Euryptolemus was carried; but when Menecles lodged an objection under oath, a second vote was taken and the Council's motion was carried. After that the eight generals who had fought the battle were found guilty and the six present were put to death.
>
> (Xenophon, *Hellenica* 1.7.34)

An objection under oath could be made, when the count was close, resulting in a recount. Later the Athenians repented of their irresponsible behaviour and in c.400 changed the rules so that the Ecclesia could not try generals in such a way. Nevertheless the events above confirm that the Ecclesia was genuinely sovereign as it even had the power to act unconstitutionally.

The Heliaea

The Heliaea, or the dikasteria as it generally became known when it was subdivided into smaller panels, was considered to be as vital as the Ecclesia for the maintenance of democracy. The main sources for the working of the law courts in Athens are Aristophanes' plays, especially *The Wasps*; Aristotle's *Ath. Pol.* and the fourth-century orators. Solon had created the Heliaea as a court of appeal, staffed by the people, which offered redress from the legal decisions of the 'archons' and the 'Areopagus'. Ephialtes' reforms in 462/1 marked a dramatic change in the demos' control of the legal system by establishing the Heliaea as a court of primary jurisdiction, dealing with the vast majority of private ('dike') and public ('graphe') cases. The demos believed that justice in a democracy would be better served by itself passing judgement in its own courts rather than by the jurisdiction of the aristocratic archons and the Areopagus. The Areopagus retained jurisdiction over intentional homicide, wounding and poisoning with an intent to kill, arson and the destruction of the sacred olive trees; the archons within a short time became merely the presidents of the courts, ensuring that the correct procedures were carried out but having no powers of judgement.

As the demos was to have direct control of the judicial process, there was a need for 6,000 jurors to be enrolled. This number was a quorum of the people, i.e. it was judged to be representative of all the citizens and was the necessary number for such procedures as ostracism. Every year 6,000 jurors ('dikastai'), probably 600 from each of the ten tribes, were chosen by lot from those who volunteered for service (*Ath. Pol.* 24.3). However, as with the Boule, an Athenian had to be thirty years of age, a limit which was probably introduced to ensure the maturity of the jurors. Aristophanes' *Wasps*, which is a comedy about how thoroughly and obsessively the jurors carried out their duties, suggests that the biggest proportion of the 6,000 consisted of old men. This vast number of jurors also made it very difficult for any criminal to tamper with the juries. However, there needed to be an incentive to attract so many men to serve and this was provided for by Pericles:

> Moreover Pericles was the first man to provide payment for jury service.
>
> (Aristotle, *Ath. Pol.* 27.3)

The pay was two obols a day, which was increased to three obols by 425. The pressure of legal business after the reforms of Ephialtes led to the breaking down of the Heliaea into smaller panels or dikasteria. There was probably a maximum of ten dikasteria, in each of which there were possibly 500 jurors, as in the fourth century. This obviously made the system more efficient by shortening the time of waiting for trial but it would be fair to say that it was no longer a judgement by the whole people as it was previously in the Heliaea. Since there was no appeal court now (or ever) in existence, miscarriages of justice by the smaller dikasteria could not be rectified:

> Procleon: 'And what's more we do these things and are not accountable unlike all the other public officials.'
>
> (Aristophanes, *Wasps* 587)

The law courts ensured personal liberty and thus, apart from a few specified crimes over which a public official could exercise jurisdiction and fine a citizen up to 50 drachmas, it was left to the ordinary individual to initiate the lawsuit, issue the summons and conduct the case in court. There were no professional lawyers, no Director of Public Prosecutions nor the police to carry out these functions on behalf of the state. Thus there was always the danger that some crimes might go unreported because of the level of commitment required in the prosecution. Therefore the Athenians decided to introduce a system of incentives for certain crimes, about which they were particularly concerned. In such crimes, for example where it was alleged that the defendant owed money to the state, the prosecutor became an 'interested party', which resulted in his receiving a percentage of the fine imposed in a successful prosecution. This proved to be too successful as it led to the rise of 'sycophants' – a class of ruthless 'professional' prosecutors – who were feared by the demos owing to their eloquence in court and their frequent resort to blackmail.

Court procedure

The first stage of a legal action was for the prosecutor or claimant to get the defendant before the correct magistrate – each one had a particular area of responsibility, for example, the chief archon dealt with family affairs and religious festivals – to make his formal accusation. To do this he had to issue a summons to a defendant in front of a witness:

> Anticleon: 'Here is another man who is coming, as it seems, to summons you and he's brought a witness as well.'
> Citizen: 'I am summonsing you for assault, old man.'
>
> (Aristophanes, *Wasps* 1415–17)

When both litigants appeared before the magistrate, the prosecutor gave the magistrate a statement of his charge and, in some criminal cases, paid his fee. In a number of private cases, both litigants would pay. The magistrate would then set a date for the 'anakrisis' (preliminary inquiry). The main purpose of the anakrisis was to clarify the exact points of dispute and what was being alleged. The magistrate would put questions to both litigants and they to each other. This was crucial for the legally untrained citizens, as it would help them to present their case in court and to establish what supporting evidence they would need to produce on the day of the trial. When the exact nature of the dispute was clear, oaths were taken and the date of the trial was fixed.

Before the trial it was the responsibility of each litigant to gather together the necessary evidence, for example a copy of the relevant law, contract. The lack of professional guidance from a fully qualified lawyer could have led to injustice, as crucial laws might not have been known or important corroborative evidence might not have been presented in court. In addition, certain evidence was inadmissible in court, i.e. that of disfranchised citizens, women and children, even though it might have had a crucial bearing on the outcome of the case. The treatment of slaves' evidence was certainly the most barbarous aspect in the presentation of evidence. It was assumed by the Athenians that slaves would naturally give untruthful testimony unless persuaded otherwise by torture:

> Indeed you [gentlemen of the jury] consider torture to be the most reliable of all tests both in private and public suits … since none of the tortured was ever proved to have made false statements gained under torture.
>
> (Demosthenes 30.37)

It must have been tempting for a slave to say whatever was necessary to bring the torture to a swift end, with little thought or care as to its veracity.

From the middle of the fifth century each juror was allotted to the same 'dikasterion' and the same magistrate for the whole year. As each magistrate dealt with specific cases, for example the 'polemarch' covered all cases concerning metics, the dikasteria became relatively specialized and therefore more effective in that area of law. However, the Athenians changed this procedure at the end of the fifth century owing to their fear about the corruption of the juries, since the litigants would know in advance which panels would be judging their case. The new system involved the drawing of lots on each day to establish which panel would be sitting with which magistrate for that day. The Athenians were more concerned in this instance with justice rather than efficiency. The litigants conducted their own cases in court and this tended to favour the eloquent and experienced litigant. Thus there arose the professional speechwriters, who for money would compose an appropriate speech for the litigant to learn by heart. In certain circumstances, close friends or relatives could be called upon to have a share in the speech making, but it was essential for the litigant to take a major part, if he did not wish to forfeit the jurors' goodwill. The litigants usually supplied witnesses to provide the bulk of the evidence appertaining to the facts. The speaker would put questions to the witness or invite him to say what he knew or confirm the speaker's statement. However, there was no possibility for the opposing litigant to cross-examine the witness and thus challenge his evidence before the jurors, as in a modern law court.

The content of the speeches was markedly different from the rigorous relevance of modern courts. The speeches were full of self-glorification and self-pity, liberally spiced with abuse of one's opponent:

> Philocleon: 'What flattery can one not hear there, addressed to a juryman? Some bewail their poverty and exaggerate their misfortunes until, in the end, they make them out to be equal to – mine. Others tell us tales, some try a comic fable of Aesop's, others crack jokes, to make me laugh and lose my anger, and if we are not persuaded by these devices, the defendant leads in his small children, his girls and his boys, by the hand and I listen. They huddle together and bleat like lambs; and then, trembling, the father on their behalf beseeches me, as if I were a god, to acquit him ... '
>
> (Aristophanes, *Wasps* 563–71)

Although this must have provided great variety and entertainment to the jurors, it was designed to stir the emotions of the jurors rather than appeal to their intellects, clouding rather than clarifying the key issues.

In both the private and the public cases the decisions of the jury were reached on the same day. This greatly speeded up the hearing of cases and prevented for the most part a backlog of cases; however, those involved with more complex cases must have experienced difficulty in presenting all of their evidence and producing arguments of sufficient depth to support their case. Aristotle informs us that four private cases were heard in one day but only one public case (*Ath. Pol.* 67.1). In private cases both the prosecution and the defence were allowed two speeches each so that both sides were given the opportunity to reply to the other side's arguments. In a public case the day was divided into three parts – the first part to the prosecutor, the second part to the defendant and the third part to the assessment of penalty, if a guilty verdict was returned. Each part of the day was fairly and carefully timed by the use of a 'clepsydra' (a water clock), whose unit of measure was 'choes' (one chous was about three minutes). Both litigants were allowed 44 choes of time to present their cases. When the speeches were finished, there was immediate voting by the jurors. It was this aspect that gives rise to the gravest doubts about the fair-mindedness of the dikasteria. There was no impartial judge or legal expert to sum up and advise the jury in its deliberations as to the relevant points of law, especially vital when the nature of the evidence is considered. In addition, there was no formal discussion between jurors before voting on the guilt or innocence of the defendant, which would have allowed those in doubt about some points of the case to have their concerns resolved, resulting in a more informed judgement.

When it came to the vote, each juror possessed a pebble (later bronze voting tokens), which he placed in one of the two urns, denoting guilt or innocence. These votes were then counted and, unlike in a modern court where a guilty verdict of the jury has to be unanimous or at times ten out of twelve jurors, conviction could be obtained by a small majority:

> Philocleon: 'I know my most dashing act. It was the time when, although only a lad, I caught the runner Phayllus, chasing/prosecuting [a pun on the Greek word] him for slander, and won the contest by two votes.'
>
> (Aristophanes, *Wasps* 1205–7)

The fact that a defendant could be found guilty by two votes out of 500, when it was evident that nearly half of the jury was convinced of the defendant's innocence, again casts doubt on the equity of these courts. However, there was a safeguard to deter malicious or trivial prosecutions – if the prosecutor failed to gain one-fifth of the votes cast, he was fined 1,000 drachmas and forbidden to bring a similar type of prosecution again (unless it was an eisangelia – see next section).

If the vote went against the defendant, the third part of the day took place, called 'the assessment of penalty'. Although certain cases had their penalty fixed by law, there was no general penal code in Athens. It was left to the prosecutor to suggest his preferred penalty and to the defendant to offer his alternative penalty. The jury then had to vote on one or other of the two suggested penalties. No compromise was allowed. Apart from the intense pressure that must have been felt by the defendant, it also meant that there was no consistency of punishment, as two people being tried on the same charge on different days could receive widely differing punishments.

For all the doubts raised, the Athenians believed that they had gained 'isonomia' (equality before the law) and that this system was far better than that which had existed before Ephialtes' reforms. Pericles in his Funeral Speech in 431/0 spoke for the mass of the Athenian people, when he said:

> in public affairs we do not break the law because it commands our great respect and we are obedient to those who hold public office and to the laws, especially those that are laid down for the protection of the oppressed.
>
> (Thucydides, *Peloponnesian War* 2.37)

The political role of the Heliaea

There were three kinds of prosecution which gave political power to the Heliaea (or dikasteria): the graphe paranomon, which was mainly used against the politically active citizens in the Ecclesia; the eisangelia or denunciation before the Ecclesia, which was mainly used against the generals, or before the Boule, which was mainly used against the other public officials; and the dokimasia and the euthuna of all public officials.

The graphe paranomon was a public charge against a citizen for proposing a decree or law, which was unconstitutional. Any person in the Ecclesia could make a 'hypomasia' (an allegation under oath) and this would lead to the suspension of the decree until its validity had been tested in the dikasteria by the prosecutor bringing the graphe paranomon against the proposer of the decree. This process could be used when, for example, a decree was being proposed that was illegal or in conflict with a previous law, or had been passed without a Boule's probouleuma, or by a citizen who had been deprived of his citizen rights ('atimia'), or if a decree in a particular instance sanctioned execution without trial for homicide, which was in direct conflict with the powers of the Areopagus. The case would be tried in a dikasterion of at least 500 (or 501) jurors, and the jury, in cases of importance, could be increased by further panels of 500. If the prosecutor won the case, then the decree was declared null and void. Therefore the dikasteria had the power to overturn the decisions of the Ecclesia. However, in this situation, the demos did not believe that it had been in the wrong in passing or trying to pass an illegal proposal but that it had been deceived by a clever orator, who accordingly should be severely punished.

The graphe paranomon was the main protection for the state against irresponsible legislation by politically active citizens, the rhetores (orators), who were not subject to the formal, statutory accountability of public officials. There is every reason to believe from the sources that it was used frequently and that most politically active citizens had to face this charge at least once in their public lives. This political power was probably ceded to the dikasteria for the very sound reason that it would lead to better decision-making. Decrees could well be passed in situations fraught with high emotion, and a referral to the dikasteria by means of the graphe paranomon provided an excellent cooling-off period for more objective consideration. Moreover, most of the jurors would probably have been present in the Ecclesia, when the proposal was aired, and would have had the time for studied reflection, aided by their own maturity. In addition, the jurors would have the whole day to consider the issue, whereas in the Ecclesia it would have been one of a number of topics on the agenda to be discussed, and the issue would be decided by an accurate count of the ballot and not by a show of hands.

If the dikasteria decided that the decree was constitutional, then the decree was presumed to be passed, giving the dikasteria constitutional power. It is revealing that in the oligarchic revolutions of 411 and 404 the graphe paranomon was suspended, as it was seen to be synonymous with democracy.

Eisangelia (impeachment) was the process by which a citizen could make a denunciation against another individual or a public official(s). The eisangelia process was used against those accused of either committing treason (subversion of the democracy, betrayal, accepting bribes to speak against the best interests of the people); or deceiving the people by not keeping their promise; or (probably) any crime that was not specifically covered in the existing law-code, for example, the Mutilation of the Hermae in 415 (see Chapter 21). Any citizen, wishing to make an eisangelia, could either wait for the Principal Assembly in each prytany, where it was a fixed item on the agenda, or could take it to the Boule, which would then put it on the agenda in the form of a probouleuma. Whoever made the denunciation was expected to deal with the whole issue from start to finish. The denouncer would put his proposal in the Ecclesia, in which he would name the denounced, the crime committed, the relevant section of the law broken (if it existed) and the punishment proposed, which was usually the death penalty. He would probably also include a recommendation as to whether the case should be tried in the Ecclesia or the dikasteria. The denouncer would then be the main prosecutor in the subsequent trial.

From the sources it is clear that this was used as a political weapon for the most part against the generals, who as elected officials exercised great power in the democracy. If a general lost a battle or failed to succeed in some enterprise and/or was a political opponent, he could be and often was denounced, not on the grounds of incompetence, because eisangelia did not recognize that as grounds for prosecution, but for treason. Cimon, in 463, was charged by his democratic opponents of having been bribed by King Alexander of Macedon not to invade and seize part of his kingdom (Plutarch, *Cimon* 14) – since Cimon's incorruptibility was so well known and documented in Plutarch, this was clearly a politically motivated charge. If a denouncer abandoned his case, then he was liable to a fine of 1,000 talents but, owing to the importance that the Athenians placed on this area of public life, he was not forbidden to bring other 'eisangeliai' in the future unlike in other criminal cases.

The final area of political involvement of the dikasteria was in the control of the public officials. Every official had to undergo a dokimasia (investigation) before he could undertake his office, to ensure that he was eligible to take up his post. With the exception of being a councillor in the Boule, the dokimasiai took place in the dikasteria, where any citizen could make an accusation against the incoming official who would have to make a defence against the charges. Whether or not an accusation was made, there was a ballot in the dikasteria which would decide if the man chosen could take up office. This was a lengthy business, as Aristotle (*Ath. Pol.* 24.3) states that there were 700 officials at home; but clearly it was viewed with great seriousness by the Athenians. Then, during an official's year of office he could be accused of maladministration and, if the punishment required a more severe penalty than 500 drachmas, once again the dikasteria would exert their control over the public officials. Finally every public official would undergo his euthuna at the end of his year of office, in which his performance in office and his accounts would be checked by the ten euthunoi and the thirty logistai (see above and Chapter 13); if there was a case to answer, the dikasteria would again be the final arbiters of the public officials. Thus it can be seen that the dikasteria played a significant political role in the fifth century, which was to increase in the next century.

Bibliography

Hansen, M. H. *The Athenian Assembly*, chs 2 and 4.
——*The Athenian Democracy in the Age of Demosthenes*, chs 6, 8 and 10.
Macdowell, D. M. *The Law in Classical Athens*, chs 11 and 16.
Ostwald, M. *From Popular Sovereignty to the Sovereignty of Law*, pt 1, ch. 1.
Rhodes, P. J. *The Athenian Boule*, chs 2 and 5.
Roberts, J. W. *City of Socrates. An Introduction to Classical Athens*, ch. 3.
Sinclair, R. K. *Democracy and Participation in Athens*, chs 3.5–6, 4 and 5.1.

15

ATHENIAN FOREIGN POLICY IN THE FIRST PELOPONNESIAN WAR, 462/1–446/5

The sources

The two main sources for this period of Greek history are Thucydides (1.102–15.1; AE39 pp. 25–28, AE64 p. 39 – all references in this chapter are to Thucydides unless otherwise stated) and Diodorus (11.71–12.7). Thucydides' narrative is very sketchy due to the fact that it is part of his digression on the so-called 'Pentecontaetia' ('The Fifty-Years'), which is in itself a brief and highly selective account of Athens' rise to power between the Persian War (480–479) and the Peloponnesian War (431–404). Although it can be reasonably assumed that most of the events are recorded in chronological sequence, Thucydides gives no specific dates; instead he makes use of phrases such as 'after this', 'soon after', 'about the same time' and 'in the third year'. Furthermore, he makes no attempt to explain the foreign policy options available to the Athenians and the reasons for their choice at different times in the war. Instead, Thucydides has given us an account of Athenian military campaigns – recording some very important ones briefly (e.g. the battle of Oenophyta) but other less important ones in detail (e.g. the defeat of the Corinthians at Megara) – and thus leaving it to the modern historian to attempt to deduce Athenian foreign policy from these campaigns. The other major weakness is the omission of important events, such as the transfer of the Delian League treasury to Athens; the pro-Persian allied revolts in the eastern Aegean during the 450s and 440s; the (formal or informal) peace with Persia in 449; and the intensification of Athenian control over their allies, all of which had an important bearing upon or reflected Athenian foreign policy.

Diodorus' account is more detailed than Thucydides, but is mainly derived from Thucydides because Diodorus, writing in the first century BC, almost certainly based his work on the history of Ephorus, who wrote in the fourth century and used Thucydides as his main source for the period 478–411. The greater amount of detail in Diodorus may be due either to Ephorus using another source, such as Hellanicus whose history of this period was criticized by Thucydides (1.97.2), or to the tendency of Ephorus to enlarge and embroider his account of events for dramatic and pro-Athenian purposes. It is for that reason that events recorded in Diodorus but not in Thucydides, such as Athenian victories and two-day battles, should be treated with great caution, especially since Diodorus can even contradict Thucydides about events that both historians recorded: for example, the Athenian defeat at the battle of Halieis (1.105.1; AE39 p. 26) is portrayed as an Athenian victory (Diodorus 11.78.1–2); and Cimon's death before the great battle of Cyprus in c.450 against the Persians (1.112.4; AE39 p. 28) is postponed until after the Athenian victory in order to glorify Cimon's achievements (Diodorus 12.3–4).

462/1–454

When the Athenians were snubbed at Ithome by the Spartans in 462/1, upon their return they left the Hellenic League, in which Sparta and Athens had been equal allies (see Chapter 12). This was tantamount to a declaration of war, which was confirmed by their alliances with Argos and Thessaly (1.102.4; AE39 p. 25). Athens' alliance with Argos, Sparta's traditional enemy, was a calculated risk, as it might have provoked the Spartans into open warfare. However, the fact that Argos was well placed geographically to cause problems for Sparta in the Peloponnese and that it had an abundant supply of 'hoplites', which the Athenians needed to strengthen their own weaker land forces, outweighed any doubts among the Athenians who had been disturbed and worried by the open display of Spartan hostility at Ithome. In the same way the Thessalian cavalry would be an excellent addition to Athens' fighting capability, if war broke out, and it would act as a counter-weight to the power of Boeotia with its pro-Spartan sympathies.

For the next few months a cold war existed between the two super-powers, but this changed in c.460:

> The Megarians also revolted from the Spartans and went over to an alliance with the Athenians, prompted by the fact that the Corinthians were winning a war over border territory. The Athenians came to hold Megara and Pegae.
>
> (Thucydides 1.103.4; AE39 p. 25)

Corinth was the leading ally of Sparta, and thus the Athenians' military support to the Megarians meant that open conflict between the two states over Megara would lead to a major war between Athens and Sparta. This momentous decision would have been taken after much discussion in the Ecclesia, and clearly possession of the Megarid – the narrow strip of land, immediately east of the Isthmus of Corinth, connecting central Greece to the Peloponnese – provided the strongest argument for the alliance with Megara and its military consequences. The cornerstone of the Spartans' strategy was always likely to be an invasion of Attica by land with their superior hoplites, but now their main offensive weapon had been blunted by Athens' control and occupation of the Megarid. The Spartans made only one attempt in this war to intervene in central Greece, while the Athenians possessed the Megarid (the Sacred War took place during the Five Year Truce), and they learned a valuable lesson from this experience (see below). However, the Athenians now had the problem of war on two fronts.

It is a fundamental tenet of war strategy that war on two fronts should be avoided. Even allowing for the confidence arising from the new, 'radical' democracy, some attempt by the Athenians to eliminate one of the two war fronts would have been expected. The obvious one was Persia, as it was further away than Sparta and, after the Delian League's crushing double victory at Eurymedon in c.469 (1.100.1; AE29 p. 21), there seems to have been less military activity against Persia in the 460s, since the Athenians were concentrating on asserting their authority over their allies (1.99; AE29 p. 21). There is a hint in Herodotus (7.151) that the Athenians may have made an attempt to negotiate a peace with the Persians at this time. Herodotus, while describing a delegation from the Argives who wanted to confirm with Artaxerxes, Xerxes' successor in 465 as King of Persia, that their mutual friendship still existed, states that at the same time an Athenian embassy including Callias was present at the Persian court 'on some business'. The problem for the historian is that no date is given and the nature of the 'business' is not stated. It could have been in 449, when many historians believe that a peace was made by the Athenians with Persia, either informally or formally, known as the Peace of Callias. If that was the 'business', it seems strange that Herodotus does not state that fact explicitly. However, there is a distinct possibility that this was an earlier attempt (c.460) at peace-making by the Athenians, which presumably failed as it was in the Persians' interest for Athens to fight on two fronts. Therefore, where diplomacy fails, military force is often used to persuade an opponent to return to the negotiating table.

In 460 or 459, the Athenians were involved in a major expedition against the Persians on Cyprus with a huge force of 200 ships (1.104.2). This campaign may have been an attempt to put pressure on the Persians to resume peace negotiations by highlighting the Athenian ability to inflict serious damage on the Persian Empire; if this was not their primary aim, then the Athenians were acting unwisely. While campaigning:

> Inaros ... led the revolt of most of Egypt from king Artaxerxes. Having made himself ruler, he called in the Athenians.
>
> (Thucydides 1.104.1; *AE*39 p. 26)

The Athenians accepted and consequently were now fully committed on two fronts. There were some good, sound reasons for getting involved initially.

Egypt was much more important to the Persians than Cyprus, and this far greater threat might have led the Persians to negotiate with the Athenians in order to remove them from this theatre of war; also, Inaros had already done most of the hard work, and it seemed that the Athenians would only be involved in a 'mopping-up' operation; and finally, even if peace with Persia did not come about, conquest of Egypt with its abundance of corn would meet Athens' needs for the future. Ultimately, however, the Athenians were drawn into an unsuccessful six-year campaign, which proved to be a very costly error of judgement in foreign policy.

For the next five to six years (460–454) the bulk of the fighting took place in mainland Greece. The Athenians lost the battle of Halieis in the Argolid, but defeated the Peloponnesians at the sea-battle of Cecryphaleia in the Saronic Gulf (1.105.1; AE39 p. 26). Then came the first major conflict of the war:

> After this, war broke out between the Athenians and the Aeginetans and a great sea-battle took place at Aegina between the Athenians and the Aeginetans, with the allies of each taking part, and the Athenians ... won, captured 70 ships, landed, and laid siege to Aegina.
>
> (Thucydides 1.105.2; AE39 p. 26)

It is worth noting that 70 ships were 'captured', which does not include those that were sunk in the battle. This sea battle deserves Thucydides' description 'great' and the Athenians must have had a very large navy, in excess of 100 ships, to gain such a notable victory over such an opponent. The Athenians now had considerable forces committed in Aegina and in Egypt, and garrisons in Megara and Pegae. The Peloponnesians, especially the Corinthians, now saw their chance to exploit the fact that the Athenian armed forces were very stretched. Three hundred hoplites were sent to the aid of Aegina, and at the same time the Corinthians and their allies made an attack on the Megarid, calculating that the Athenians would either shift troops to Megara and lose Aegina or stay put in Aegina and lose Megara owing to a shortage of troops (1.105.3; AE39 p. 26). The Athenians, although desperately short of manpower, sent out a force of the oldest (50 to 59 years of age) and the youngest (18 to 20 years of age) of the troops left in Attica, which after two battles defeated the Corinthians and kept Megara safely in Athenian hands (1.105.4–106.2; AE39 p. 26). Also at this time, clearly inspired by the success of the long walls by which they had joined the city of Megara to its nearby port of Nisaea, the Athenians commenced the building of their Long Walls from the city of Athens to the sea, one to the Piraeus and the other to Phaleron – thus making the Athenians virtually impregnable to a siege, provided they retained mastery of the sea (1.107.1; AE39 p. 26).

The events described above took place between the years 460 and 458 and, although there was active warfare between the Athenians and the Peloponnesians, Thucydides makes no mention of the Spartans. The explanation for this probably lies with the ongoing 'Helot' revolt in Messenia, which paralysed the Spartans and prevented them from carrying out their responsibilities as 'hegemon' (leader) of the Peloponnesian League and leading the campaigns against the Athenians. This changed in c.457:

> The Phocians launched an expedition against the people of Doris, who are the mother people of the Spartans, ... The Spartans sent a force of 1,500 of their own men and 10,000 allies ... to help the people of Doris.
>
> (Thucydides 1.107.2; *AE*39 p. 26)

The conquest of Doris, Sparta's mythical mother-country, was a source of great humiliation to the Spartans and thus they felt impelled to intervene, even though the regular route through the Megarid was impossible owing to the Athenian occupation. They therefore crossed the Gulf of Crisa by sea, forced the Phocians to come to terms and restored liberty to Doris. However the return journey was now fraught with difficulty, as the Athenians had no intention of allowing them an unhindered passage. The Athenians had already blocked the gulf with their fleet and intended to sink anything that tried to sail across; they also had permanent garrisons at Megara and Pegae, and had occupied the passes over Geraneia to prevent access by this route to the Peloponnese (1.107.2–4; *AE*39 pp. 26–27). Here was the clearest proof to the Spartans, if they needed it, that control of and safe passage through the Megarid were essential for any military intervention in central Greece. Now they were cut off from the Peloponnese and the longer they delayed the greater the encouragement for the Helots to strive harder with their revolt. However, the Athenians had no intention of playing a waiting game:

> The Athenians marched out against them in full force, with a thousand Argives and contingents from the other allies to give a total force of 14,000.
>
> (Thucydides 1.107.5; *AE*39 p. 27)

The battle of Tanagra (c.457) proved to be a very bloody battle with much slaughter on both sides but ended in victory for the Spartans, who then made their way back to the Peloponnese via the Megarid. Diodorus claims that a four-month truce was agreed in the aftermath of this battle, which would help to explain the Spartans' unhindered march through the Megarid (11.80.6).

It might have been expected that this bloody defeat would have crushed the Athenians' morale and enthusiasm for any immediate armed conflict but:

> Sixty-two days after the battle, the Athenians marched out under Myronides and in a battle at Oenophyta defeated the Boeotians, became masters of Boeotia and Phocis.
>
> (Thucydides 1.108.2–3; *AE*39 p. 27)

The Opuntian Locrians also handed over 100 of their richest men as hostages (1.108.3; AE39 p. 27). The Athenians had thus gained a 'Land Empire', consisting of Boeotia, Phocis and Opuntian Locris, i.e. virtually the whole of central Greece. After this (c.457) Aegina, one of Athens' major naval rivals, capitulated, surrendered its navy and became a 'phoros'-payer (1.108.4; AE39 p. 27); (c.456) the Spartans' dockyard at Gytheum was burned, Chalcis (a Corinthian foundation in Aetolia) was captured, and Sicyon, an important polis in the Peloponnese, was defeated in battle by the Athenians (1.108.5; AE39 p. 27). This phase of the war in Greece came to an end in c.455/4 with a failed attempt to restore Orestes, the exiled son of the King of Thessaly, another defeat of Sicyon under the command of Pericles and an unsuccessful siege of Oeniadae in Acarnania (1.111.1–3; AE39 p. 28). It is possible that the Athenians' conquest of Troezen and alliance with Achaea, both in the Peloponnese, should be dated to this period.

The years 460–454, marked a period of unprecedented, military successes for the Athenians in their campaigns in Greece. Corinth, Sparta's chief ally, and other Spartan allies of note (e.g. Sicyon) had been comprehensively defeated on land and at sea; Aegina had been crushed, giving the Athenians undisputed control of the Saronic Gulf; and the most spectacular of all was the acquisition of the 'Land Empire'. The Athenian objectives and their ambitions seem to have grown in tandem with their success. A Spartan land invasion in 462/1 would have been greatly feared and the Athenians' hopes of success tentative, but, in addition to the Helot revolt hampering the Spartans' war effort, the defection of Megara c.460 not only proved to be beneficial to the Athenians by denying the Spartans easy access to Attica but also gave them the confidence to pursue a dynamic foreign policy in Greece, culminating in the 'Land Empire'.

However, it has to be asked whether the 'Land Empire' was a wise foreign policy decision. The maintenance of Athenian control depended on three things: first, the Athenians had to give their full and undivided attention to it, which would require a full military occupation of central Greece; second, it was crucial that Megara remained loyal and stayed in Athenian hands, thus discouraging a Spartan land invasion; and, third, there was the need for the Helots to continue their revolt, which was paralysing the Spartans' ability to wage effective war. Ultimately the 'Land Empire' collapsed because these three preconditions could not be met: first, full military commitment to central Greece was impossible, since the Athenians also needed to conduct campaigns against the Persians and were intensifying their imperial control over the Delian League; second, the Megarians' traditional loyalty lay with the Spartans, which had only been disturbed by a temporary conflict with the Corinthians; finally, the Helot revolt came to an end in 455/4 at the latest (accepting 'in the tenth year' in Thuc. 1.103.1; AE39 p. 25), which then allowed the Spartans to turn their undivided attention to the issue of Athens' growing ambitions in Greece.

While the events described above were taking place, the Athenians were still campaigning in Egypt against the Persians. The years 460–456 saw great success for the Athenians, so much so that the Persians even tried unsuccessfully to bribe the Spartans to invade Attica in order to force the Athenians out of Egypt (1.109.2–3; AE9 p. 27). When this failed, there was only one viable alternative – a full military campaign to regain Egypt. Megabazus with a large Persian army defeated the Egyptians and their allies, drove the Greeks out of Memphis and shut them up on the island of Prosopitis, which he besieged for a year and a half. Finally in 454 he drained the canal, which left the ships high and dry, crossed over on foot, captured the island and thus defeated the Greeks. In addition, a relief squadron of 50 Greek ships, unaware of the defeat at Prosopitis, also suffered extensive damage at the hands of the Persians with most of the ships being lost (109.1–110.4; AE39 pp. 27–28).

454–446/5

This defeat in 454 was a major turning-point in Athenian foreign policy. The early years of the war had seen the Athenians embark on an ambitious policy of expansion, which had entailed fighting on more than one front and had consequently overstretched their resources. There is controversy over the size of the defeat in 454 in Egypt and its effect upon the Athenian foreign policy towards the Delian League allies (see Chapter 10). Whether it was a disaster, with the loss of over 200 ships, or a serious defeat with the loss of nearly 100 ships, it led to a major rethink in the conduct of Athenian foreign policy. The Athenians decided wisely that it was essential to concentrate on one area of foreign policy at a time in order to avoid their earlier mistakes. The first of the three areas of foreign policy that demanded action was the Delian League which, owing to a combination of allied unrest and Persian infiltration, needed to be brought fully under control; the second was Persia, which was now resurgent in confidence after the recent victory in Egypt and a potential threat to the Athenians in the Aegean; the third was Sparta, which, although needing a period of recuperation from the exhausting ten-year Helot revolt, was bound to attack at some point to restore at the very least the balance of power in Greece by helping to destroy the 'Land Empire'.

After 454, active warfare died down in Greece and this allowed the Athenians to begin to resolve the problems in the Delian League. Whether the Athenians now decided upon a policy of intensive imperialism owing to numerous revolts following their disastrous defeat in Egypt (Meiggs), or whether they were tightening up the League after revolts in the early 450s and were removing Persian influence on the coast of Asia Minor (according to the authors of the Athenian Tribute Lists), it was essential that this area of foreign policy received immediate attention, as Athens' existence as a super-power depended on the Delian League. By the late 450s, the Athenians felt secure and strong enough to tackle the next front, i.e. the Persians. An all-out military offensive, leading to a crushing victory on the scale of Eurymedon, would probably convince the Persians that there was little to be gained from continued warfare and thus persuade them to accept peace, thereby removing one of the Athenians' foreign policy problems. However, such a victory could only be gained by the full commitment of Athenian forces to the campaign, which would be very risky without some guarantee that the Spartans would not take this opportunity to stab them in the back. The need for a truce with Sparta was crucial, and the ideal man to negotiate it was Cimon, who either had been recalled earlier on the proposal of Pericles (Plutarch, *Life of Cimon* 17) or had just returned to Athens in 451 after his ten-year ostracism. A five-year truce was concluded, which would run from 451 to 446. The Athenians were now free to tackle Persia, ably led by their greatest anti-Persian general:

> The Athenians stopped fighting in Greece, but made an expedition against Cyprus with two hundred ships manned by themselves and their allies under the command of Cimon.
>
> (Thucydides 1.112.2–3; *AE*39 p. 28)

In *c*.450, although Cimon died on campaign, the Greeks won two mighty victories, reminiscent of Eurymedon, at sea and on land (1.112.4; *AE*39 p. 28). This massive defeat probably convinced the Persians of the need for peace, and negotiations between the two states led to the making of peace in 449.

The ending of the war with Persia had a direct bearing on the Delian League, originally formed in part to liberate the Greeks from the Persians, which aim had been achieved by the peace. Many of the allied cities probably hoped that the ending of the conflict and a consequent reduction in armed forces would bring an end to the Athenians' increasingly imperialistic behaviour. As for the Athenians, the decision had been taken to embark on a final, intensive period of imperialism which was to be completed by the ending of the five-year truce in 446, when a refreshed and rejuvenated Sparta was likely to take military action. Consequently the years 449–446 reveal an intensive period of imperialism by the Athenians with numerous, tough decrees, imposing the Athenians' will upon recalcitrant allies (see Chapter 10). If the timetable was adhered to, then the Athenians, with the Empire fully established and firmly in place, would be equipped in 446 to meet any Spartan hostility. However, the Spartans had no intention of making it easy for the Athenians by allowing them to execute their foreign policy in this orderly fashion:

> After this the Spartans fought the so-called Sacred War, got control of the sanctuary at Delphi and restored it to the Delphians. Then later, when the Spartans had retreated, the Athenians marched out, got control and handed it over to the Phocians.
>
> (Thucydides 1.112.5; *AE*64 p. 39)

At first sight this seems a very minor affair for Thucydides to include in his brief and highly selective digression, the so-called Pentecontaetia (see above). However, apart from the religious dimension, it can be seen from the events that followed that there were powerful, underlying political motives on the part of the Spartans. This campaign gave them access to Megara and central Greece, which would be allowed under the five-year truce, and a chance to stir up anti-Athenian feelings.

In the following year, trouble broke out in Boeotia where Boeotian exiles had occupied some places and were threatening to undermine Athenian control. The Athenians sent out a force of hoplites under Tolmides and at first gained some success against the rebels by the capture of Chaeroneia (1.113.1; AE64 p. 39). On their return:

> the Boeotian exiles from Orchomenus, together with Locrians and Euboean exiles and others who were of the same mind, attacked them at Coroneia, got the upper hand in the battle, killed some of the Athenians and took others alive. The Athenians then evacuated the whole of Boeotia
>
> (Thucydides 1.113.2–3; AE64 p. 39)

The battle of Coroneia, c.447, marked the end of the 'Land Empire' and it is relevant to point out, when making a critical assessment of Athenian foreign policy, how unwise the Athenians had been to embark on this particular policy, when one defeat had brought about the complete collapse of their control of central Greece.

This humiliating defeat had an even greater fall-out for the Athenians, as it acted as a source of encouragement for other dissident allies to throw off the Athenian yoke:

> Not much later Euboea revolted from the Athenians, and when Pericles crossed there with an Athenian army, reports came in of the revolt of Megara, of the Peloponnesians being about to invade Attica, and of the Athenians' garrison troops ... having been destroyed by the Megarians. ... Pericles quickly brought the army back from Euboea.
>
> (Thucydides 1.114.1; AE64 p. 39)

The Athenians were now facing disaster on all fronts. It was crucial to crush Euboea's revolt as soon as possible, otherwise the continued defiance of Athens by such a large island would encourage others to join in the revolt and destroy the Athenians' naval empire. In addition, the Spartans under King Pleistoanax, having taken advantage of Megara's return to their alliance, had invaded Attica and were ravaging the countryside (1.114.2; AE64 p. 39). All Pericles could do militarily was to stay behind the long walls with his army, as the inevitable defeat in a full-scale hoplite battle would bring Athens to its knees. In the event Pericles and the Spartans appear to have struck a bargain, whose terms were probably reflected in the Thirty Year Peace agreed later. This resulted in the departure of the Spartans without pressing home their military advantage (see end of Chapter 12 for possible reasons), thus allowing Pericles to return to Euboea and crush the revolt (1.114.3; AE64 p. 39).

Not long after this (446/5) the Athenians swore the Thirty Year Peace with the Spartans and their allies, which put the dual hegemony on a legal basis by attaching a list of each side's allies to the treaty and forbidding both super-powers from interfering in each other's sphere of influence. For all their successes in the early part of the war the Athenians had ended up staring defeat in the face due to mistakes in foreign policy and only survived by the withdrawal of the Spartan forces. Pericles learned some valuable lessons from the First Peloponnesian War, which helped him to shape future foreign policy decisions: Athens' power was based upon the sea and therefore the maintenance of the sea empire had to be the greatest priority for the Athenians; consequently, this naval power should not be put at risk in the future either by pursuing a land empire or by undertaking major overseas naval campaigns, while waging war in Greece. The continued possession of Aegina, allowed by the Spartans, and the consequent control of the Saronic Gulf were an added bonus; but the loss of the Megarid, allowing the Spartan army access to Attica, was a serious problem and thus some counter-measure to offset this weakness would need to be devised. Pericles believed that, if the Athenians conducted their foreign policy in accordance with these tenets, the potential disaster of 446 could be avoided in the future. As he said on the eve of the Peloponnesian War in 432/1:

> For I am more afraid of our own mistakes than the strategy of our enemies.

> (Thucydides 1.144.1)

Bibliography

Cartledge, P. *Sparta and Lakonia*, pt 3, ch. 12.
Hornblower, S. *The Greek World 479–323 BC*, ch. 3.
Kagan, D. *The Outbreak of the Peloponnesian War*, pt 2, chs 5–7.
Lewis, D. M. *CAH* vol. 5, 2nd edn, chs 5.II–6.III.
McGregor, M. F. *The Athenians and their Empire*, chs 6–10.
Sealey, R. *A History of the Greek City States 700–338 BC*, pt 2, ch. 10.
de Ste. Croix, G. E. M. *The Origins of the Peloponnesian War*, ch. 5, v–vii.

16

THE ATHENIAN EMPIRE: MEANS OF CONTROL, BENEFITS AND POPULARITY

The means of control

The basis of Athens' imperial power was the fleet. The allies were for the most part either island-cities or coastal towns, and for that reason the Athenians had the ultimate weapon in exercising imperial control. After the battle of Eurymedon in c.469 most of the ship-suppliers gradually converted to phoros-paying status to avoid military service, the expense and the strictness of Athenian leadership on campaign, resulting in the growth of the Athenian fleet:

> As a result the Athenian fleet grew from the money that the allies brought in, and when they revolted, the allies were unprepared and short of experience in war.
>
> (Thucydides 1.99.3; *AE*29 p. 21)

By 450, only Samos, Lesbos and Chios supplied ships to the League's campaigns, and even this number was soon reduced, with the reduction of Samos in 439 (Thuc. 1.117.3; *AE*64 p. 40) and Lesbos in 427 (Thuc. 3.28) – thus the Athenians had the military strength to crush any state that revolted or opposed their wishes.

This situation was made easier by the fact that they controlled a naval and not a land empire:

> Those who are subject to a land power can get the forces of small cities and fight in a body; but those who are subject to a sea power, if they are islanders, cannot unite their cities; for the sea lies in between and those who rule them have control of the sea.
>
> (Old Oligarch 2.2; *AE*108 p. 54)

The Old Oligarch, although a right-wing pamphleteer and opponent of Athens' radical democracy, is very astute in his observations of the means by which the Athenians maintained their control over the subject-allies.

Although Plutarch's statement that the Athenians kept 60 ships on permanent patrol for eight months of the year seems exaggerated owing to the
cost involved (Plutarch, *Pericles* 11), there is no doubt that an Athenian fleet
was constantly patrolling the Aegean in a policing capacity. The fear of a
sudden appearance by this fleet at any time during the sailing season in a
subject-ally's harbour would usually act as a deterrent to the anti-Athenian
faction and as a source of encouragement to the pro-Athenians. The
removal of defensive walls, at least in Ionia (Thuc. 3.33.2), whether as part
of the peace agreement with Persia in 449 or under Athenian orders, gave
the subject-allies little chance of a successful revolt.

The dominance of the fleet could also ensure good behaviour without
recourse to brute force. The economies of most of the subject-allies were
dependent on overseas exports, as well as the feeding of their populations
by grain imports, and these could easily be threatened by the Athenian
fleet:

> there is no city which does not need to import and export, and no city can do that
> unless it obeys those who rule the sea.
>
> (Old Oligarch 2.3; *AE*108 p. 54)

There were the Athenians' regulations for Methone, passed in the Archidamian war (431–421), which granted it the right to import corn from the
Athenian controlled clearing-house at Byzantium (ML 65; *AE*121 pp. 58–59).
This decree instructed the Methonians to register with the 'Hellesponto-
phylakes' (Athenian officials controlling shipping through the Hellespont) in
order to gain free access to Byzantium. A similar privilege was granted to
Aphytis near Potidaea (*AE*122 p. 59), and clearly these Athenian officials
controlled the access of other subject-allies to the Black Sea for other pro-
ducts, which was an effective means of rewarding good behaviour and punishing disloyalty. However, it must be remembered that the Athenian fleet
had removed piracy from the Aegean (Plutarch, *Cimon* 8) and kept the sea-
lanes free from this particular threat, which was of considerable benefit to the
economies of the islands and coastal towns in the Aegean.

An alternative form of military control was the presence of garrisons
among allied states. Most of the evidence for these comes from inscriptions, beginning with the Erythrae Decree, passed in *c.*453/2, after Erythrae
had been recovered by the Athenians (ML 40; *AE*216 pp. 113–14). In the
same way Miletus had revolted in the 450s, was subdued towards the end
of that decade and had to accept a garrison (*AE*218 p. 115). However, it is
likely that the Athenians had been using this method of control from the
460s as the allies became more restless. Before the peace with Persia in 449,
these garrisons could be justified on the grounds of protection for the allied
state either from an anti-democratic political faction or from Persian infiltration, but their continued existence after 449 is clear evidence of their

imperialist role. There is probably an element of truth in the report of the widespread distribution of garrisons to be found in Isocrates, although he is a propagandist pamphleteer, writing in the first half of the fourth century, and very prone to exaggeration and distortion:

> And then, when the mass of people were sovereign over affairs, we garrisoned the acropoleis of the other cities.
>
> (Isocrates 7.65 (*Areopagiticos*); AE226 p. 118)

Aristophanes in the *Wasps* (235–37; AE227 p. 118) and Eupolis in the *Cities* (fr. 233; AE228 p. 118), which were both written most probably in the late 420s, mention guard duty in Byzantium and Cyzicus, respectively; and many garrisons in the cities of Chalcidice are mentioned by Thucydides, although these were probably installed either just before or soon after the Peloponnesian War broke out.

More blatant than the garrisons as a means of controlling the allies were the 'cleruchies'. These cleruchies consisted of lower-class Athenians who, while retaining their citizenship, were sent out to take over land which had been confiscated from suspect or subdued allies. Apart from the economic and social benefits (see below), these 'cleruchs' (lot-holders) performed an important military function:

> In addition Pericles sent out 1,000 cleruchoi to the Chersonese, 500 to Naxos, half that number to Andros, 1,000 to Thrace to live among the Bisaltae ... and, by planting settlers alongside the allies to make them fearful and provide a guard against any revolution.
>
> (Plutarch, *Pericles* 11.5–6; AE231 p. 119)

Colonies were also sent out to perform a similar function, such as that founded at Brea in Thrace in *c.*445 (ML 49; AE232 p. 119–20), which can probably be identified with the above-mentioned settlement among the Bisaltae and whose military purpose was to protect Athenian interests in the Thraceward region (see Map 5, the Athenian Empire). However, it is difficult to make a clear distinction between cleruchs and colonists. It is possible that the colonists, unlike the cleruchs, gave up their Athenian citizenship; but perhaps more convincingly the term 'colonists' was applied to those who took over all the land of a tributary ally (e.g. Scyros), whereas the term 'cleruchs' was used of those who lived on confiscated territory alongside the citizens of the subject-ally. Thus the fleet, the garrisons, the cleruchies and the colonies were used whenever a show of force was necessary to intimidate and ensure acquiescence.

The Athenians defended their administration of the empire by stressing how little they relied on force – they preferred subtler, less obvious means of control by the use of political appointments. First, there was the 'phrourarch' (garrison commander). Apart from his obvious military duties in charge of the local garrison, he also played an important political role among the allied states, as shown in the Erythrae Decree:

> The [Inspectors] and Garrison Commander are to draw lots and set up the current council; in the future the council and the Garrison Commander [15] to do this no less than 30 days before the term of office expires.
>
> (ML 40; *AE*216A p. 113)

He played a leading role in the establishment of the first Council ('Boule') and the appointment of subsequent Councils. Erythrae had been in revolt in the 450s and had most probably been under the control of a pro-Persian faction (see Chapter 10). The phrourarch's political task was to vet the members of the Council to ensure that they had no political sympathies with the previous ruling faction and acted in the best interests of Athens; and to maintain a close scrutiny of all local developments.

Very similar to these were the 'archontes' (magistrates), officials sent out from Athens, who resided among the allies. They were widespread throughout the empire, as mentioned in the Coinage/Standards Decree (*AE*198 pp. 105–6) and numerous other decrees (e.g. the Miletus regulations – *AE*218 p. 115), although they did not necessarily command troops. It is worthy of note that the title phrourarch disappears from surviving inscriptions after 450/49, when peace was made with Persia, and it may be that archontes became the preferred title, avoiding the former's military connotations. Their task was to ensure that local politics reflected Athenian interests, that the 'phoros' was efficiently collected and despatched to Athens, and that the 'proxenoi' (see below) were safeguarded.

Another Athenian political appointment was the 'episcopos' (overseer), but it is more difficult to define his duties accurately, as the title was not used after the fifth century. The definition of Harpocration – a lexicographer of (possibly) the second century AD, who explained the technical terms of law and administration that were used in the speeches of the ten major Athenian orators – is very useful for supplying an insight into the role of the episcopos:

> Inspector (episcopos): Used by Antiphon in his speeches On the Tribute of the Lindians [frg.30] and Against Laispodias [frg.23]. Some men were regularly sent out to the subject cities who inspected their affairs.
>
> (Harpocration *Lexicon*, under the word 'Episcopos'; *AE*225 p. 118)

Harpocration compares them in function to the Spartan 'harmosts', who governed various states after the defeat of Athens in 404, but it seems unlikely that they were resident officials. In the Erythrae decree, quoted above, they help the phrourarch to establish the first Council but play no further part in the appointment of its successors. They seem to be visiting commissioners or trouble-shooters, who were sent out to investigate actual or potential problems in the allied states, and then report back to the Athenians. A good example of this role comes from Aristophanes' *Birds*, when the new state of Cloudcuckooland is in the very process of being founded:

> Inspector: Witness, everybody! I'm being beaten, I, an Inspector.
> Peisetairos: Shoo! Take your voting urns. Isn't it dreadful – they are already sending Inspectors to the city before we have even sacrificed to the gods!
>
> (Aristophanes, *Birds* 1031–34; *AE*224 p. 118)

The mention of the ballot boxes in the above quotation, combined with their role in Erythrae, strongly suggests that they took a leading part in the establishment of new democratic constitutions in the allied states.

Even more valuable than these Athenian appointments were the proxenoi – citizens from the allied states, who were chosen and honoured by the Athenians. The proxenoi had to repay this honour by giving active loyalty on behalf of Athens. A decree in praise of Oeniades shows in general terms how the Athenians viewed their role:

> Since Oeniades of Palaesciathos is a good man towards the city of Athens and keen to do [10] all the good he can, and does good to any Athenian who arrives at Scia-thos, he should be praised and recorded as proxenos and benefactor of Athenians.
>
> (ML 90; *AE*238 pp. 121–22)

Having been raised in the community, they had far more knowledge about local circumstances and untrustworthy individuals than the resident Athenian officials. They were usually reliable democrats and would be fully aware of those of their fellow citizens who harboured oligarchic, pro-Spartan sympathies. Their willingness to protect Athenian interests was even more valuable in the Peloponnesian War, when some allies were considering revolt and going over to the side of Sparta. In 428 the oligarchs in Mytilene were making preparations to revolt from Athens, but were compelled to advance their plans because:

> some individual Mytileneans who were of the opposite political faction and were Athenian proxenoi, told the Athenians that Mytilene was forcing the cities of Lesbos into political union, and was hurrying on all preparations for revolt in collaboration with the Spartans and their Boeotian kinsmen. They said that unless the Athenians anticipated these preparations they would lose Lesbos.
>
> (Thucydides 3.2; *AE*124 p. 60)

The premature revolt of the Mytileneans, without the necessary supplies of grain to withstand a long siege, was destined to fail – the proxenoi had proved their worth. It is hardly surprising that the first question of the episcopos, who has been sent to investigate the founding of the new polis of Cloudcuckooland in Aristophanes' *Birds*, is 'Where are the proxenoi?' (l. 1021; *AE*224 p. 117). They would be the perfect source for the vital background information that he needed in order to appraise the situation and to make his report to the Athenians.

The final means of control, which was direct interference with allied jurisdiction, was possibly the most effective – certainly much easier, safer and cheaper than the exercise of military control. This point, even allowing for right-wing bias and exaggeration, is highlighted by the Old Oligarch:

> it enables them to administer the allied cities, while staying at home, without sailing off on ships.
>
> (Old Oligarch 1.16; *AE*200 p. 107)

This judicial control operated at both state and individual level. With the demise of the Delian League synods (League meetings) probably in 454 or the early 440s, the Athenian law courts took over responsibility for judicial action involving allied states. An example of this can be seen from the Athenian decree granting protection to Acheloion, a proxenos of Athens:

> And if anyone kills [Akheloion or] any of his children [in any of the cities] that the Athenians [rule, the city is to be fined] five talents, [as in the case of] anyone killing [an Athenian. The prosecution is to be held at Athens] in the [same way as when an Athenian] is killed.
>
> (*Inscriptiones Graecae* i3 19; *AE*235 p. 121)

In the same way the Athenian law courts are central to the efficient working of the Thoudippos decree (425/4) which greatly increased the phoros payments of the allied cities. If a city that wished to appeal against its assessment of phoros, it had to make the appeal before an Athenian law-court:

> They must not [assess less] tribute for any [city] than the tribute that city [has brought in before] unless there [seems to be such shortage of resources that] that territory cannot [bring in more].
>
> (ML 69; *AE*138 p. 66)

The allied states would need to furnish the relevant proof at Athens in an open tribunal to have any chance of a reduction in phoros.

The Athenians also ensured that certain cases concerning individuals in the allied cities should be compulsorily transferred to Athens, and that the punishments should be enforceable throughout the Empire. It was essential for the Athenians to exercise a close scrutiny over all 'political' cases, i.e.

those that affected Athenian imperial interests. In some cases there was no doubt that the alleged offence was anti-Athenian and should go automatically to Athens for judgement:

> and if anyone revolts I will denounce him to the Athenians.
>
> (ML 52, Chalcis Decree; *AE*78 p. 44)

However, it was virtually impossible to define absolutely which category of cases affected Athens, and there was always the danger that anti-Athenian elements, bringing apparently non-political charges, would attempt to destroy the leaders of the democratic factions and the proxenoi upon whom the Athenians depended to maintain the loyalty and stability of the democratic regimes in the allied cities. This could be done with the aid of the allied courts, the majority of which were dominated by men of wealth and position, who in general would be anti-Athenian. Therefore the Athenians devised a system that not only protected their political allies but also ensured that their enemies were not let off or given trivial punishments by the biased local courts:

> and that they use the courts to protect some members of the people and condemn those that oppose democracy, and if all the allies dealt with cases at home, then because they are fed up with the Athenians, they would condemn precisely those who are friends of the people of Athens.
>
> (Old Oligarch 1.16; *AE*200 p. 107)

Although allowances must be made for the usual biased exaggeration of the Old Oligarch, his statement is still basically true. This was achieved by bringing all cases that involved specified penalties or specified individuals to the Athenian jury-courts. The Chalcis decree (ML 52; *AE*78 p. 44) allowed the Chalcidians to punish their own citizens except where the resulting penalty was one of exile, death or loss of citizen rights, which allowed a right of appeal to the 'Heliaea'. The Athenians could then decide if the charge against one of its supporters had been politically motivated. Later in the Empire these cases, probably also involving the penalty of confiscation of land, came automatically to Athens for judgement. The Athenians also allowed specified individuals, usually proxenoi, to bring their cases with reduced court fees to Athens, since they might not get a fair hearing in their local courts. This infringement of their autonomy was greatly resented by the allies, but was a highly effective means of control for the Athenians:

> It is this in particular [i.e. making the allies come to Athens for their court cases] that makes the allies slaves of the Athenian people.
>
> (Old Oligarch 1.18; *AE*200 p. 108)

Athenian benefits from the Empire

Political benefits

The main benefit to arise from the Empire for the Athenian poor was political power, which was summed up accurately and succinctly by the Old Oligarch:

> First of all, I maintain that it is appropriate that in Athens the poor and the common people should seem to have more power than the noble and the rich, because it is this class that provides the rowers for the fleet and on which the power of the city is based.
>
> (Old Oligarch 1.2)

Therefore their numerical strength (as much as 60 per cent of the population) and the fact that Athens' imperial power depended upon their naval prowess ensured that the poor collectively dominated Athenian politics. In other states, whose survival and power depended upon land forces, political power was usually vested either in narrow oligarchies, or in moderate oligarchies or moderate democracies, where the upper classes and to varying degrees the middle-class 'hoplites' held sway. In such states the political power of the poor was either non-existent or strictly limited. By contrast the Athenian poor had the right in the 'Ecclesia' (Assembly) to legislate and decide state policy, and the power to pass judgement in the Heliaea (People's Court):

> The people have made themselves masters of everything, and control all things by means of decrees and jury-courts, in which the people have the sovereign power.
>
> (Aristotle, *Ath. Pol.* 41.2)

Economic benefits

The Empire also brought many economic benefits to the Athenians, especially but not exclusively the poorer classes. Most of these benefits stemmed from the phoros that the subject-allies contributed. Figures are in very short supply in the literary sources, but Thucydides states that Athens at the beginning of the Peloponnesian War was receiving 600 talents a year from the allies (2.13.3). This figure can be plausibly accepted, since Xenophon also informs us that in 431 the total income of the Athenians, from both domestic and overseas sources, was 1,000 talents a year (*Anabasis* 7.1.27). If both figures are correct, then the Athenians' domestic income at the beginning of the Peloponnesian War was 400 talents. Thus in 431, 600 talents, 60 per cent of Athens' annual income, came from the allies, but this amount and percentage of income were greatly increased within a few years.

Anticleon, speaking in Aristophanes' *Wasps* (l. 660), performed in 422, claimed that Athens' total revenue was now 2,000 talents. This could be dismissed as comic exaggeration, if it were not for the evidence of the Thoudippos Decree, dated to 425 (ML 69; AE138 pp. 66–67). The cost of the war had proved to be much higher than Pericles had anticipated in 431 and consequently the allies' phoros was increased, often two- or three-fold and, in some places such as Eretria in Euboea, five-fold. The grand total of allies' contributions after 425 can be said with some certainty to have been at least 1,460 talents and perhaps as much as 1,500 talents; this coincides with Aristophanes' figure, which included the income from domestic sources. It was this massive sum of allied money – 75 per cent of Athens' total revenue – and the uses to which it was put that were the main sources of economic prosperity for the Athenian poor.

It seems reasonable to believe that the Athenians kept a standing fleet of 100 'triremes' and another 200 in dry dock ready for any emergency, and, as each trireme had a crew of 200, this would give employment to 20,000 sailors. The sources give little information about the length of and the number of ships on patrol or in practice, or the frequency of military campaigns. Plutarch (*Pericles* 11) talks of 60 triremes being on permanent patrol for eight months of the year, but this does seem excessive, and only the major campaigns, such as Eurymedon *c*.469 and Cyprus *c*.450, are mentioned by Thucydides. However, even with this lack of hard evidence, the constant use of the ships for the variety of purposes mentioned above must have given regular pay to thousands of poorer citizens (and allies) during the sailing season. Before the war of 431, the pay for an Athenian sailor was half a drachma per day, which was increased to a drachma a day at the beginning of the war. The prospect of earning pay while on campaign and of acquiring an inexhaustible supply of pay for the future was (according to Thucydides) one of the prime motives of the thetes in their enthusiastic support for the Sicilian expedition in 415 (Thuc. 6.24.3). In addition, the maintenance of this fleet would have needed a large naval infrastructure, providing employment for such craftsmen as carpenters, and other workers such as the 500 dockyard guards (Aristotle, *Ath. Pol.* 24.3; AE222 p. 116–17).

The Athenian fleet guaranteed not only the payment of phoros, which in turn paid for the fleet and the other economic benefits, but also a cheap and plentiful supply of superior grain by safeguarding the grain route from the Black Sea. The Athenians were very dependent on imported grain to feed their very large population, and the poor were always the first to suffer when there were shortages and famine. This was confirmed when the Athenian fleet was lost at Aegospotamoi in 405 and the Athenians were starved into submission in the following year. However, while their fleet and settlements protected the Black Sea corn route, the Athenians made sure that they were the first to benefit by controlling the other allies' access to grain supplies. In the Methone decree (ML 65; AE121 pp. 58–59) the

Athenians gave permission to the Methonians to import a fixed quota of grain from Byzantium without hindrance from Athenian officials. From this it is clear that other cities would need to have prior authorization and an agreed import quota from the Athenians, who would probably grant it only after their own grain requirements had been met first. Demosthenes, the fourth-century orator, mentions laws which forbade anyone who lived in Athens from bringing grain to anywhere else than Athens, and from lending money on ships carrying grain to cities other than Athens. As this was a long-standing problem for the Athenians, it is reasonable to assume that these laws were operative in the fifth century and, since the Athenians' dominance of the Aegean was unchallenged for most of that century, were far more effective in delivering cheap grain – the staple diet of the Athenian poor.

The acquisition of additional territory overseas also supplied material benefits to the Athenians by the establishment of colonies and cleruchies, which brought economic independence to the settlers. Twenty-four are known to have been founded but it is extremely difficult to identify which of these settlements were colonies and which cleruchies, and there is also doubt about whether the colonists even renounced their Athenian citizenship. Colonies were probably sent either to reinforce existing cities (e.g. Thurii), or to take over expelled or destroyed enemy cities (e.g. Aegina, Melos), or to protect areas that were strategically important to the Athenians (e.g. Brea); the cleruchies were placed on the partially confiscated territory of an existing city. These settlements were primarily aimed at improving the economic standing of the lower classes, which is clearly shown in the amendment to the Brea decree:

> [40] And the settlers to be drawn from Thetes and Zeugitai.
>
> (ML 49; *AE*135 p. 120)

The original proposal had made no specific recommendations as to which Athenians should benefit, but Phantocles' amendment made sure that the lower and the middle classes were to be the main beneficiaries. If this decree can be dated to *c*.445, then it may be that Phantocles was influenced by Pericles' cleruchy policy which was initiated in 450/49:

> He [Pericles] did this to relieve Athens of a mob that was idle and meddlesome because it had nothing to do, and to solve the people's difficulties;
>
> (Plutarch, *Pericles* 11; *AE*231 p. 119)

This was a very astute policy of Pericles, as he managed not only to export his unemployment problem and thus ease social tension, but also offered an opportunity of relative affluence. The possession of an income from such confiscated territory would usually raise the thetes to hoplite status. Even more attractive to the poor was the chance of raising their standard of living without even working for it:

> Later they did not assess Lesbos for tribute, but divided up the land … into three thousand plots. They dedicated three hundred plots as sacred to the gods, and settled Athenians chosen by lot (clerouchoi) on the other plots. The Lesbians agreed to pay these settlers 200 drachmas a year for each plot and went on farming the land.
>
> (Thucydides 3.50.2; *AE*133 p. 63)

At no point does Thucydides state or imply that this was a unique situation.

However, it was not only the poor who gained from possession of overseas land but also upper-class Athenians. It was axiomatic in the Greek world that ownership of land was restricted to citizens, except in exceptional circumstances. But there is evidence from the 'Attic Stelai' (inscribed lists of the confiscated property of those Athenians who were convicted of sacrilege in 414 after the Mutilation of the Hermae scandal – see Chapter 21) that reveals wealthy Athenians owning large tracts of territory outside Attica:

> [375–78] [Property] of Oionias son of O[inochares of the deme of Atene:] at Lelanton (in Euboea) [-] and in Diros (also in Euboea) [and in – and] in Gera[istos]: 81 1/3 talents
>
> (ML 79; *AE*239 p. 122)

The largest land holding in Attica, which was sold by auction, raised 20 talents. Oeonias' land holdings must have been extensive to raise over 81 talents, but he was not the only one to benefit. The inscription lists 19 other victims, all of whom possessed substantial tracts of land in places such as Thasos, Abydus and elsewhere in Asia Minor. There may have been disputes about how the profits from the Empire should be used (see Chapter 18), but all Athenians were united in their support of the Empire, from the 'conservative' Cimon to the 'demagogue' Cleon.

Pericles also decided to use the Delian League reserve fund on a programme of public works:

> which would excite every skill and involve every craft, it would provide employment for practically the whole city.
>
> (Plutarch, *Pericles* 12; *AE*66 p. 41)

The widespread availability of employment with regular wages was the greatest boon to the Athenian poor who did not take advantage of the overseas settlements. Evidence for the commencement of the building programme comes from a papyrus that appears to be a commentary on a speech of Demosthenes, which mentions a decree of Pericles, authorizing the immediate expenditure of 5,000 talents and a further 3,000 talents over the coming years – the Parthenon, the huge statue of Athena by Pheidias and the Propylaea (not completed) were constructed in the 440s and the 430s. It was also possible to extend pay for office, financed from League funds, to a greater number of citizens:

> From the tribute and the taxes and the allies, more than 20,000 men came to be supplied with maintenance payments.
>
> (Aristotle, *Ath. Pol.* 24.3; AE222 p. 116)

Athens (or rather its three harbours at the Piraeus), owing to its pre-eminence as a naval power and helped by the effects of the Coinage/Standards Decree, became a great trading centre, acting as a clearing house for most of the imports and exports in the eastern Mediterranean. Pericles acknowledged this in his Funeral Speech:

> On account of the size of our city all the goods from every land flow into us and we are able to enjoy foreign goods as much as our own home-produced products.
>
> (Thucydides 2.38.2)

Apart from the commercial infra-structure that arises in all great ports, providing constant employment, there was also a harbour tax – a 1 per cent duty levied on all imports and exports (Old Oligarch 1.17), which was increased to 2 per cent at the end of the fifth century (Andocides, *On the Mysteries* 1.133–34). Many small states found it economically more sensible to pay the harbour tax at the Piraeus than incur the greater expense of sailing to different cities in order to buy their essential commodities. There was also a market tax on all foreigners who traded at Athens (Demosthenes 57.34), and an annual poll tax levied on all 'metics' (resident foreigners – Xenophon, *Ways and Means* 2.1). All the sums raised from these sources were added to the Athenians' public treasury to finance the employment programme. If the money generated by tourism and the bringing of court cases to Athens is added to their total income, it can be seen that the Athenians, especially the poor, profited substantially in material terms from the Empire.

Allied benefits and the popularity of the Athenian Empire

Economic benefits

Although there is much disagreement between modern historians about the political benefits of the Empire to the allied cities, there is general agreement that the allies for the most part enjoyed economic advantages from the Empire. Most of the allies were islands or coastal towns and, because their economies were based mainly on overseas exports, their prosperity depended upon freedom of the seas. War with Persia in the first half of the fifth century meant that Phaselis in reality became the demarcation line for trading in the east Mediterranean – any ship going beyond Phaselis was liable to seizure. The peace with Persia in 449, effected and maintained by Athenian naval strength, opened up previously precluded markets, especially Egypt, which was ideally placed for taking advantage of east and west trade, bringing about a great increase in the volume of trade in the second half of the fifth century. This was also aided by the Athenians' suppression of piracy in the 470s (Plutarch, *Cimon* 8), although cities still had to obey the Athenians or lose their right to trade. In addition, cities found it easier and cheaper to buy their necessary imports at Athens rather than acquire them individually from numerous other sources of supply. Isocrates, given the caution that is necessary when using him as a source, can state with some justification:

> And under our leadership we shall find that private households gained most prosperity and cities became greatest.
>
> (Isocrates, *Panegyric Oration* 4.103; *AE*245 p. 123)

The allies' contribution to maintaining these improved economic conditions was the payment of phoros, and this was a comparatively small price to pay. Although some cities lost their fleets under compulsion, many chose to give up their navies for financial reasons, not only through dislike of overseas campaigns and tough Athenian leadership (Thuc. 1.99; *AE*29 p. 21). It cost about one to two talents to build and equip a trireme in the middle of the fifth century; and, if it managed to avoid destruction in storms, shipwreck or battle, its service life was effectively 20 years. The highest expenditure by far was the pay for the 200 sailors on each trireme – a half a talent per ship per month (with pay at half of a drachma per sailor in the mid-fifth century), increasing to one talent per ship per month at the beginning of the Peloponnesian War, when a sailor's pay was doubled. It is possible to compare the respective burdens on the allies. Lampsacus was paying ten talents as its phoros contribution from 431–428, and only twelve or thirteen states paid more than this; by contrast, in the suppression of the revolt of Samos in 440/39, the combined fleets of Chios and Lesbos, supplying 25 ships in 440 and 30 in 439 (Thuc. 1.116.2, 117.2; *AE*64 p. 40), cost them between twelve and fifteen talents per month at the lower rate of pay. The islands had always been poor in natural resources and the removal of the need to supply triremes would have brought substantial savings to their economies. It also seems most likely that the middle and lower classes even avoided this smaller burden, as the phoros payments would fall mainly on the rich.

Many individuals from the allied cities improved their standard of living by coming to live and work in Athens, which offered no barriers to 'economic migrants'. One of the biggest areas of employment was service in the fleet, as Thucydides informs us on a number of occasions (e.g. 3.16.1). Many craftsmen and those involved in the retail trade also saw greater opportunities of improving their income by leaving lowly paid jobs in their own cities and making use of the increased opportunities in Athens and the Piraeus:

> This is why in the matter of freedom of speech we have put slaves on equal terms with free men and metics [resident foreigners] with citizens, for the city needs metics because of all its industries and because of the fleet.
>
> (Old Oligarch 1.12)

These resident foreigners were known as metics and paid a poll tax of one drachma per month, known as the 'metoicion'. Although the majority would have come from the poorer classes, there was still a large number who enjoyed a middle-class income and status – 3,000 metics served as hoplites in the Athenian army in the campaign against Megara at the beginning of the war (Thuc. 2.31.2). Some of these metics became men of considerable wealth, such as the orator Lysias and his brother, who owned a shield-making factory employing nearly 120 slaves (Lysias 12.19), and whose property was sold off under the rule of the Thirty Tyrants (404–403) for 70 talents. The Athenians were very tolerant and allowed these metics to participate in Athenian festivals, go to the theatre, have access to the courts through an Athenian patron and worship their own gods in their own temples. There is a decree of 333, which gives permission to the Citians from Cyprus to purchase land in order to build a temple to 'Aphrodite', as the Egyptians had already done for Isis. Plato informs us that Apollodorus of Cyzicus, Phanosthenes of Andros and Heracleides of Clazomenae even became generals, and the last two served as public officials in another capacity (Ion 541 c–d). The only figure that allows for an estimate to be made of their number comes from the census of Demetrius of Phaleron (the pro-Macedonian ruler of Athens) of c.317, i.e. 10,000, but it is likely to have been higher when the Athenian Empire was at its greatest. The metics, therefore, made up a considerable section of the population, enjoying greater material advantages in Attica than in their native cities.

Political benefits and the popularity of the Athenian Empire

There is much disagreement between modern historians – e.g. de Ste. Croix and Bradeen – about the political benefits of the Empire to the allied cities, and consequently about the popularity of the Athenian Empire. The evidence from the allies themselves about their views on the so-called political benefits has not survived and thus we have to rely upon Thucydides as the main literary source. Thucydides harboured no doubts about the unpopularity of the Empire, with speakers (often oligarchic) constantly accusing Athens of 'enslaving' their allies. The Corinthians in 432 urged the Peloponnesian League allies to vote for war because of Athens' tyrannical behaviour:

'As for that tyrannical city that has been set up in Greece, realise that it has been set up to dominate all alike, so that it rules over some already, and is planning to rule over the others. ... and let us set free the Greeks who are already enslaved.'

(Thucydides 1.124.3)

In 428 the Mytileneans, one of the original members of the Delian League and still an independent ship-supplier, were determined to revolt because of Athens' treatment of other allies, as they explained to the Spartans:

'When we saw that they were relaxing their efforts against the Persians and increasingly enslaving the allies, we began to be afraid.'

(Thucydides 3.10.4; *AE*126 p. 60)

Statements from Athens' enemies and from allies planning to revolt may be considered possibly suspect, especially as the ruling regimes were oligarchic, but the Athenians themselves were blatant about the nature of their Empire. Cleon, who usually supported a tough policy in the control of the allies, said of the Empire in the Mytilenean Debate:

'You do not realise that the empire that you have is a tyranny imposed on subjects, who plot against you and are ruled against their will.'

(Thucydides 3.37.2)

This comment, if taken on its own, might seem to be a typical example of Cleon's harsh bluntness and tendency to exaggeration, as portrayed in the hostile sources. However, no less a 'statesman' than Pericles echoes the same sentiments:

'The empire you have now is like a tyranny: in the opinion of mankind it may seem to have been acquired unjustly, but it cannot be safely surrendered.'.

(Thucydides 2.63.2; *AE*114 p. 56)

Thucydides (1.99; *AE*29 p. 21) implies numerous revolts because of Athenian behaviour, and specifically records the revolts of Naxos, Thasos, Euboea, Samos, Lesbos and Chios – important founder members of the Delian League. When the news of Athens' disastrous defeat in Sicily in 413 became known:

> The subject states of Athens were especially eager to revolt even though it was beyond their capability.
>
> (Thucydides 8.2.2)

Thucydides clearly believed that the Athenian Empire was universally hated by both subject-allies and the rest of Greece, especially as the Athenians were prepared to use their power brutally, as in the case of Scione and Melos. Consequently, at first sight the political benefits for the allies seem to be few in number.

De Ste. Croix, however, believes that the Athenian Empire was popular with the majority of the subjects and has argued strongly, using Thucydides as his main source, that Thucydides seriously misjudged and distorted the views of the subject-allies in his portrayal of the Empire's unpopularity. The speeches in Thucydides, where the anti-Athenian sentiments are most clearly expressed, do not reflect what was actually said but are mainly a reflection of his own personal views, e.g. the speech of the Mytileneans, a part of which is quoted above, about Athens' imperialist behaviour does not reflect genuine Mytilenean opinion but Thucydides' interpretation. However, there is enough detailed evidence presented in the historical narrative of Thucydides to counteract and correct his biased views. For example, Diodotus in the Mytilene Debate, although exaggerating his point to counteract the arguments of Cleon, would have failed totally to convince his audience if the Athenian Assembly had not recognized some truth in his argument:

> 'At the moment in all the cities the people [i.e. the poor] are your friends; either they do not join the few in revolting, or, if they are forced to revolt, they become at once the enemy of those who have revolted.'
>
> (Thucydides 3.47.2; AE132 p. 62)

Furthermore, after describing in full the civil war ('stasis') in Corcyra in 427, Thucydides continues about the state of politics generally in Greece, and about how allied democrats sought out Athenian help:

> Later practically the whole of Greece was in convulsion: everywhere there was opposition between the democratic leaders who sought to bring in Athens and the oligarchs who sought to bring in the Spartans.
>
> (Thucydides 3.82.1; AE211 pp. 111–12)

The main reason for this distortion lies in Thucydides' oligarchic political outlook, shaped by political and social influences from his upper-class background. If Thucydides was not in sympathy with 'radical' democracy, as seems likely from his favourable comments about the rule of the Five Thousand in 411/0 (8.97 – see Chapter 22) and his pejorative comments on the Athenian 'demos', e.g. 'mob' (2.65.4), and if his informants within the allied cities were upper-class supporters of oligarchy, then it is possible that Thucydides mistakenly believed that the oligarchic dislike of the Athenian Empire was shared by the lower classes in the allied cities. Those with oligarchic views and states governed by oligarchies would always be fearful of Athens' radical democracy, and, although the Athenians tried to tolerate these regimes, invariably they clashed with Athens, as stressed by an Athenian oligarchic pamphleteer:

> Whenever the Athenians have tried to support the best people [i.e. oligarchs], it has not furthered their interests. It was not long before the people were enslaved in Boeotia; and when they supported the best people in Miletus, it was not long before they revolted and massacred the common people.
>
> (Old Oligarch 3.1)

Much of the tough imperialistic legislation, such as the denunciations and trials of allegedly subversive allies in Athens (Chalcis Decree; AE78 pp. 44–45), was aimed primarily at the oligarchic-minded wealthy, who looked towards Sparta or Persia in their hopes of revolt from Athens:

> For the Athenians everywhere destroyed oligarchies, the Spartans democracies.
>
> (Aristotle, *Politics* 1307b 22; *AE*214 p. 112)

Although this was an exaggeration by Aristotle about the Athenians, it is still hardly surprising in these circumstances to find a strong antipathy to the Athenian Empire among the upper class in the allied cities. They would have been Thucydides' main informants and they would have been given a sympathetic hearing by him, being himself a supporter of the Athenian 'kaloikagathoi' (see Chapter 18) and thus disliking the excesses of the demagogues and the radical democracy in their treatment of the subject-allies.

De Ste. Croix also believed that the populations of Greek states were divided strictly on class and wealth: the poor majority supporting democracy and the rich minority oligarchy. Therefore, Athens' interventions in a state's internal affairs in support of democracy would have been popular among the lower-class citizens and should be seen as a political benefit, as life would be far more agreeable in a democracy under the Athenian Empire rather than in an independent oligarchy. The reason for this lies in the nature of oligarchy, which both politically excluded and economically exploited the majority of the citizens, i.e. the poor. The philosopher Plato, who had little respect for democracy, is very candid about the failings of oligarchy:

> Oligarchy would then have this one very great defect ... from necessity it would be not one city but two, one of the poor and one of the rich.
>
> (Plato, *Republic* 8.551D)

The Old Oligarch, who unashamedly supports the cause of oligarchy, is honest enough to state its effect on the poor:

> But if you are looking for a law-abiding city [i.e. an oligarchy], the first thing you will see is that the able make laws in their own interest; then, the respectable will punish the mob and will make their own plans for the city; they will not allow madmen to become members of the Council, nor to speak in the Assembly, nor even to attend it. However excellent this might be, it would soon plunge the common people into slavery.
>
> (Old Oligarch 1.9)

Aristotle mentions a fearsome oath taken by the oligarchs in a number of cities:

> I will be hostile to the people and will plan whatever evil I can against them.
>
> (Aristotle, *Politics* 1310a 8–12)

These quotations suggest that the normal manner of self-government in a Greek city during the Peloponnesian War was not like modern consensus politics with different parties taking their turn to govern, but a bitter and violent class struggle. The poor in an oligarchy could experience extreme poverty, a lack of legal redress and deprivation of political rights. It is in this context that the words of Isocrates in his defence of the Athenian Empire have some worth:

> Second, they paid money not to save us but for democracy and their own freedom, and to avoid falling into the enormous troubles they had when they got oligarchy under dekarkhies and the rule of the Spartans [i.e. after Athens' defeat in 404].
>
> (Isocrates 12.68; *AE*14 p. 16)

Democratic constitutions in the Empire gave the poor an opportunity to participate in the internal government of their state and provided for them a better standard of living. Consequently de Ste. Croix believes that Athenian interventions would be seen and welcomed by the poor as a defence of their freedom. The payment of phoros (tribute) would be a small price to pay, especially as this burden would probably fall on the propertied classes.

Bradeen, on the other hand, takes issue with the assumptions underlying de Ste. Croix's beliefs, especially regarding his views on Thucydides. First, he does not accept that Thucydides' speeches are mainly a vehicle for his own opinions, but argues they should be seen as being mainly the authentic words and sentiments of the speakers, otherwise Thucydides' important claim to have stuck as closely as possible to the general sense of the words actually used would be meaningless (1.22). Thucydides probably heard the speeches of Pericles and Cleon in the Athenian Assembly about the nature of the Athenian Empire (quoted above), which leads to one of two conclusions. Either Pericles and Cleon did not realize the unpopularity of the Empire, resulting in Thucydides inserting these sentiments into their speeches and thus deliberately misrepresenting their views – the logical conclusion of de Ste. Croix' assumption – or that the speeches are genuine and that these politicians did acknowledge in public the Empire's unpopularity, which was reflected in the harsh imperialist tone of the decrees of the 420s.

Second, Bradeen finds it difficult to accept that Thucydides was an oligarch, rather than an aristocrat or conservative (as many of the kaloikagathoi were – see Chapter 18), but even more difficult to accept that Thucydides was the kind of man who would allow his political views to distort seriously his historical judgement. If, as de Ste. Croix argues, there is a serious conflict between Thucydides the 'editor' (the political commentator) and the Thucydides 'the reporter' (the objective reporter of events), then Bradeen argues that one of two conclusions must be reached: either Thucydides was a fool who could not recognize 'the truth' from the evidence that he was reporting (and all the other evidence he would have found as a fifth-century contemporary) – but which modern scholarship, using the same evidence, could – or else Thucydides is a completely dishonest man who deliberately distorted his history. No modern historian would accept the second conclusion (even de Ste. Croix refers to Thucydides as 'an exceptionally truthful man'), and it is difficult to accept that Thucydides, with his intelligence and experience of the range of political opinions that existed in late fifth century Athens, would have superimposed upon the citizen bodies of all the Greeks the narrow anti-Athenian views of the oligarchs.

Third, de Ste. Croix' depiction of a class struggle between poor, usually pro-Athenian democrats and wealthy, anti-Athenian oligarchs as the constant, defining characteristic of the Greek city-states is thought to be too schematic. Many of the subject-allies, e.g. in Chalcidice, would be agricultural towns with a rural population which, owing to their traditional conservatism, would have been content to live under an oligarchic constitution as their ancestors had. Furthermore, the poor were not always so dissatisfied that they sought the violent overthrow of the oligarchs:

> For the poor, who have no share in political office, are willing to remain quiet if no-one insults them nor takes away any of their possessions.
>
> (Aristotle, *Politics* 1297b)

Even in commercial cities, similar to Athens but on a much smaller scale, it is doubtful that the poor could exercise genuine democratic power, as these cities lacked the financial resources to support payment for office. More revealing are the attitudes of the people on the islands, such as Chios, Lesbos (Mytilene) and Samos – large commercial centres, possessing their own fleets – where one would expect to find a lower class, equivalent to the Athenian 'thetes', who rowed the ships and who would presumably be pro-Athenian democrats. Chios, the largest of the ship-suppliers, was an oligarchy (as far as we know) throughout the whole of the fifth century. In 424, the Athenians, fearing that the Chians were planning revolt, ordered them to demolish their new fortifications. This would have been a perfect opportunity to impose a democracy, if they had detected among the Chian lower classes a strong desire for democracy. In fact the Chians received guarantees from the Athenians that they would not change the existing state of affairs (4.51). Mytilene in Lesbos was also an oligarchy, and again it seems apparent that the lower classes preferred independence under an oligarchy with no phoros to pay and possession of their own fleet. The alternative would have been a democracy, probably imposed by armed Athenian intervention and protected by an Athenian garrison. The inevitable removal of their fleet would have put the Mytileneans in the same position as the other democratic phoros-paying subject-allies. In the revolt of 428/7, the people, having finally been given arms, threatened to surrender the city to the Athenians only if the oligarchs refused to share out the food equally (3.27–28) – an action seemingly motivated more by hunger than by loyalty to Athens or desire for democracy. In fact, it is only after the outbreak of the Peloponnesian War that violent political clashes between democrats and oligarchs, as exemplified by the stasis (civil war) of Corcyra in 427, become more frequent and Thucydides blames the war for this new phenomenon (3.82–84).

Fourth, Bradeen disagrees strongly with de Ste. Croix's insistence that the specific evidence that he quotes from Thucydides about revolts corroborates his viewpoint that the Athenian Empire was popular with and inspired the loyalty of the majority of the allied citizens. Bradeen maintains that de Ste. Croix's 'evidence' is in reality not legitimate evidence but simply a reinterpretation of ambiguous situations, with de Ste. Croix believing his analysis of the political situation to be right and Thucydides wrong. The strongest piece of evidence that de Ste. Croix provides for his viewpoint is the Mytilenean revolt and the readiness of the people to surrender the city to the Athenians once they had been given weapons by the oligarchs. To Bradeen, this is a prime example of reinterpretation, not evidence – as stated in the previous paragraph, hunger rather than loyalty could equally be put forward as the main reason for the people's willingness to surrender. In the same way, Bradeen maintains that all of de Ste. Croix's quoted examples are open to a different interpretation, i.e. that of Thucydides whose narrative agrees in general with his conclusions about the unpopularity of the Athenian Empire.

With such a difference of opinion, it is worth observing that, whereas rulers tend to share the same view of Empire, such a unitary view is not likely to be found amongst the ruled. In an ideal world the majority of allied citizens, being poor, would probably prefer to live in independent democracies, in the same manner as the Athenian demos; but for the many very small city-states such a situation was impossible, and domination by some super-power – be it Persia, Sparta or Athens – was inevitable. As de Romilly points out, fear and pressure were constant factors in shaping the policies of such states. It is in this real world that attitudes to the Athenian Empire will differ from state to state, from one group to another even within the same state, and from time to time. The attitude of many subject-allies would be shaped by pragmatism, especially in the Ionian War (413–404), when Sparta had gained a fleet and at long last challenged Athens militarily in the eastern Aegean. The presence of an Athenian or Spartan fleet close to one's harbour would provide an incentive to show support to that super-power at that moment in time, although tempered by the fear of later reprisals by the other super-power. It is for this reason that there can be no definitive answer about the popularity or unpopularity of the Empire – the fact that many subject-allies never revolted from Athens is no proof of popularity.

Some city-states, in varying degrees, would have believed that democratic constitutions, encouraged and supported by Athens, were a political benefit and would have been grateful to Athens. Obviously the proxenoi and the leaders of the democratic factions in the cities, who were generously rewarded by the Athenians, had a vested interest in their support of Athens. However, throughout most of the fifth century, many allied citizens in Ionia, accepting the likelihood of Persian conquest as the main alternative to subjugation to Athens, probably preferred Athenian control, if only as the lesser of two evils. Persia had proved to be a tough, insensitive and costly ruler of Ionia, and this, combined with their preference for tyrants as rulers in Greek cities, provoked the Ionians into two full-scale revolts. Even allowing for the glorification that is to be found in any funeral speech (which may have been written by the non-Athenian Lysias for someone else to deliver), there is a solid core of truth in the claim that:

> They [i.e. the Athenians]. ... displayed so great a power themselves that the Great King ceased to desire others' territory ... [57] no Persian ships sailed from Asia at that time, no tyrant was set up in Greece, and no Greek city was enslaved to the barbarian.
>
> (Lysias 2.56–57; *AE*244 p. 123)

In a similar way, Methone, a virtual enclave in Macedonia and constantly threatened by King Perdiccas, looked to Athens for protection and thus had a vested interest in being a loyal and willing member of the Empire. The first of the four Methone decrees authorizes the sending of three envoys to Perdiccas instructing him not to restrict Methone's use of the sea nor to lead an army through its territory without its permission (ML 65; *AE*121 pp. 58–59). Furthermore, its usefulness as a base in keeping surveillance over the city-states in Chalcidice, whose loyalty to Athens was very suspect, resulted in it receiving special privileges, e.g. it only paid the 'first fruits' (1/60) as its phoros payment, further encouraging pro-Athenian feelings – a clear sign that Athens could rule its subject-allies with a light touch. On the other hand, Amphipolis in the Thraceward district is an excellent example of a city-state that greatly resented its subject-ally status. Although founded by Athens in 437/6, it had revolted in 424/3 through a mixture of force and diplomacy employed by the Spartan commander, Brasidas (4.102–6). The Athenians were desperate to recover Amphipolis and one of the stated terms of the Peace of Nicias in 421 was the Spartan agreement to hand it back to Athens. However, the citizens of Amphipolis resolutely refused to be re-incorporated back into the Athenian Empire, even though they no longer had the protection of a Peloponnesian garrison, and even as late as 414 were still holding out and resisting Athenian attacks (7.9).

In all probability it is the viewpoint of Phrynichos, when reacting to the opinion of the Athenian oligarchic conspirators in 411 that Athens under an oligarchy would be far more attractive to the subject-allies, that best sums up the attitudes of the subject-allies to the Athenian Empire:

> For they [i.e. the allies] would not want to be slaves under an oligarchy or a democ-
> racy but would prefer to be free under whatever constitution they happened to have.
>
> (Thucydides 8.48.5)

Freedom ('eleutheria') was an emotional, deeply-rooted, instinctive feeling among the Greeks. Any restriction on an ally's freedom or independence would be viewed as 'enslavement', thus provoking opposition to Athens. For all the rational arguments of the economic and political benefits that the Athenian Empire bestowed, the subject-allies usually seized the opportunity to regain their freedom, whenever possible and whatever the economic or political cost. The subject-allies' intense dislike and resentment of the Athenian means of control in the fifth century can be seen clearly in the terms of the charter that brought into existence the Second Athenian League in 378/7 under the hegemony of Athens:

> [15] If any Greek ... wants to be an ally of the Athenians and their allies, he may do so,
> [20] being [free] and independent and under whatever constitution he chooses.
> No [garrison] will be imposed, no magistrate, nor will the allies pay tribute:
> ... neither an Athenian privately nor the Athenian state may obtain property in the lands of the allies, neither a house nor land, neither by purchase [40] nor as security, nor in any other way.
>
> (Tod 123; *AE*246 p. 124)

The memory of the restrictions on their independence, of the interference in their internal jurisdiction, of the presence of garrisons and resident

officials (archontes), of the imposition of phoros and finally of the possession of their land – whether by private ownership or cleruchies – was still
deeply ingrained in the hearts of the allies of the fourth century, never to be
forgotten. The specific provisions of this charter suggest that for the allies
the disadvantages outweighed the advantages of membership of the Athenian Empire in the fifth century. However, when their independence came
under threat from the Spartans and the Persians, the allies still recognized
and willingly accepted again the advantages of membership of a league
under Athenian hegemony, but with the crucial proviso that this time
Athenian leadership was to be carefully controlled and that their own
independence was to be legally guaranteed.

Bibliography

Bradeen, D. W. 'The popularity of the Athenian Empire', *Historia* 9 (1960).

Davies, J. K. *Democracy and Classical Greece*, 2nd edn, ch. 5.

Finley, M. I. *Economy and Society in Ancient Greece*, pt 1.3.

McGregor, M. F. *The Athenians and their Empire*, ch. 16.

Meiggs, R. *The Athenian Empire*, chs 11, 12 and 14.

Powell, A. *Athens and Sparta*, ch. 3.

Rhodes, P. J. *The Athenian Empire*, Greece and Rome New Surveys in the Classics 17, ch. 6.

Roberts, J. W. *City of Socrates. An Introduction to Classical Athens*, ch. 4.

de Ste. Croix, G. E. M. 'The character of the Athenian Empire', *Historia* 3 (1954/5), pp. 1–41, also in (ed.) Low, P. *The Athenian Empire*, ch. 11.

——'Notes on "Jurisdiction in the Athenian Empire II"', CQ 11.

Bibliography for 2nd edition

de Romilly, J. 'Thucydides and the cities of the Athenian Empire', *Bulletin of the Institute of Classical Studies*, 13, also in (ed.) Low, P., *The Athenian Empire*, ch. 12

Low, P. (ed.) *The Athenian Empire*, Part IV.

Rhodes, P. J. *A History of the Classical Greek World, 478–323 BC*, ch. 15.

17

THE CAUSES OF THE
PELOPONNESIAN WAR

> I think that the truest explanation (prophasis), but the one that was least made public, was that the growth of Athens' power and the fear that this caused among the Spartans made war inevitable. But the grounds of complaint (aitiai), which were openly stated by each side and led them to break the peace and go to war, were as follows.
>
> (Thucydides 1.23)

In these words Thucydides was attempting to single out an underlying cause of the Peloponnesian War beyond the publicly expressed grounds of complaint. His use of the words 'prophasis' and 'aitiai' has led to a dispute among historians about the actual meaning of this passage, since these words can have different meanings in different contexts – 'prophasis' can mean 'false excuse' and 'aitiai' 'true explanations'. However, the use of the qualifying words 'truest' with 'prophasis' and 'openly stated' with 'aitiai' strongly suggests that Thucydides was giving his own judgement on the real reason why Sparta went to war in 431. The Spartans would never dare to make this reason public because this was not a valid ground for breaking the peace treaty, and because it would be a shameful admission from such a powerful military state. Therefore the Spartans concentrated on the grounds of complaint, which affected their allies rather than themselves, in order to press their claims that Athens had broken the Thirty Year Peace. This is further reinforced by Thucydides' explanation of the Spartans' motives for the despatch of three embassies in the months preceding the outbreak of the war:

> During this time they kept sending embassies to the Athenians and making complaints so that they might have the best excuse to make war, if the Athenians paid no heed to them.
>
> (Thucydides 1.126.1)

However, it is important to review the events that led up to the outbreak of the war in the light of the terms of the Thirty Year Peace. In this way it will be possible to assess the accuracy of Thucydides' statement and to determine the degree of blame that each side should incur for infringing the terms of the peace treaty.

The background, 446/5–435

In 446/5, a Thirty Year Peace was agreed between Athens and Sparta on the following (so far as they are known) terms – all references in this chapter are to Thucydides, unless otherwise stated:

1) Athens had to give up control of Nisaea, Pagae, Troezen and Achaea (1.115.1).
2) There should be a list of allies of each side, and each side should keep what it possessed at the time of the treaty with the exception of those mentioned in clause 1 (1.140.2). If any ally were to revolt and be received into the other side's alliance, then the alliance which received the revolting ally would be deemed to have broken the treaty.
3) Any state not listed was deemed to be a 'neutral' and therefore was free to join either alliance, if it wished (1.35.2).
4) Neither side was allowed to make an armed attack on the other, if the latter wished to go to arbitration (1.85.2).
5) Argos, although unlisted, was exempt from clause 3. No military alliance was to exist between Argos and Athens, although diplomatic relations were allowed.
6) There may have been a clause guaranteeing the autonomy of Aegina within the Athenian Empire (1.67.2).

There is a danger with hindsight of believing that the Thirty Year Peace was doomed to end in failure, but this is to deny the skill and optimism with which it was drafted. By producing a list of each side's allies both spheres of influence had been clearly and legally defined, marking out unambiguous no-go areas. The arbitration clause was very far-sighted, and provided a mechanism to resolve by negotiation rather than a resort to war any future dispute that could not be foreseen in 446/5. There was every hope that the 'dual hegemony', now placed on a legal footing, would ensure peaceful relations between the two super-powers for the next generation. The revolt of Samos was to dispel those optimistic hopes.

In 440, Samos, one of the three remaining independent ship-suppliers, clashed with Miletus over the possession of Priene. The Athenians stepped in, resolved the dispute in Miletus' favour, changed the Samian constitution from oligarchic to democratic, placed oligarchic hostages on Lemnos, installed a garrison and returned home. However, the oligarchs who had escaped earlier, making use of Persian aid, regained control of Samos and revolted from Athens. After a long and arduous campaign, the Athenians crushed the revolt in 439, confiscated the Samian fleet, pulled down their walls, took hostages and forced them to pay an indemnity (1.115.2–117.3; AE64 pp. 39–40). The dispute with Samos should have been an internal Athenian affair, as Samos was a listed ally of Athens, but there is strong evidence that the Spartans had intended to exploit Athens' problems and launch an attack. The evidence comes from the Corinthian speech to the Athenians in 433:

> For when the Samians were in revolt and the other Peloponnesians were divided in their votes whether they should help them, we did not cast our vote against you; we clearly spoke against that, saying each state should punish its own allies.
>
> (Thucydides 1.40.5)

Corinth was referring to a debate in the allies' chamber of the Peloponnesian League, and the issue under discussion in that chamber was whether to aid Samos in its revolt from Athens. The Peloponnesian League had a bicameral constitution (see Chapter 12), in which the initiative for military action lay with Sparta. Therefore the Spartans had already held an Assembly to discuss the Samos affair and had voted for war, and thus the issue was then submitted to the allies' chamber for their decision. In the event a majority of the allies, encouraged by Corinth, voted against war, and this decision forced the Spartans to give up their plans. Thus, only six years after the signing of the peace treaty, the Spartans were prepared to break the terms of the treaty and attack the Athenians without provocation – the faction of the hawks was clearly in the ascendant, especially after the exile in 445 of King Pleistoanax, the leader of the doves (see Chapter 12 for an explanation of Spartan hawks and doves). The revelation of Sparta's hostility and readiness to ignore the treaty must have had a profound effect upon many Athenians, who probably believed that war at some time in the future was now inevitable; it only needed a few Peloponnesian allies to change their minds, when the issue was raised again, to give the Spartans the necessary mandate to wage war. To these Athenians, consolidation and prudent defence throughout the 430s had become imperative. It is reasonable to see the foundation of Amphipolis c.437/6 and Pericles' Black Sea expedition (Plutarch, *Pericles* 20) c.436 as part of these measures – the colony of Amphipolis would give the Athenians access to ample timber for their fleet, and Pericles' show of strength would ensure that the vital supply route for grain was secure.

It was the political unrest in the small polis of Epidamnus in 435 that proved to be the catalyst for the war. Epidamnus was a colony of Corcyra (modern Corfu), which in turn was a colony of Corinth. The democrats had seized power in Epidamnus but the exiled oligarchs, aided by foreign allies, were laying siege to the city. The democrats appealed to Corcyra, their mother-city, for help but the Corcyraeans refused to become involved

(1.24.5–7). The democrats then approached the Delphic oracle to ask if they should hand over their city to Corinth, which, in accordance with tradition, had supplied the leader of the Corcyraeans who were about to found the colony of Epidamnus; the Delphic oracle agreed (1.25.2–3). The Corinthians willingly accepted on the grounds that they regarded Epidamnus as belonging as much to them as to the Corcyraeans, and:

> at the same time because of their hatred of the Corcyraeans who, although they were colonists of Corinth, did not pay them respect.
>
> (Thucydides 1.25.3)

The Corinthians' hatred was fuelled by the Corcyraeans' disdain for them and their belief in the superiority of their navy, which numbered 120 ships. It was this hatred that was to be such a strong underlying motive for the Corinthians' aggressive behaviour.

The Corinthians sent out a force of troops and settlers to Epidamnus, which in turn led to the Corcyraeans besieging the city (1.26); Corinth then prepared a relief force and declared a new colony of Epidamnus, inviting people to volunteer to become new colonists (1.27). As the issue was fast slipping into armed conflict, the Corcyraeans decided to attempt to resolve the matter by diplomacy. With the backing of Sparta and Sicyon, the Corcyraeans made a generous offer to the Corinthians that, if they were not willing to give up their claims to Epidamnus and recall their troops, the whole matter should be submitted to arbitration, using as arbitrators either mutually agreed cities in the Peloponnese or the oracle at Delphi. They particularly urged the Corinthians not to start a war as this would force the Corcyraeans against their wishes to seek military help from elsewhere – a clear hint of seeking an alliance with Athens (1.28). The Corinthians refused this offer of arbitration and sent out a force of 75 ships and 2,000 'hoplites' to Epidamnus. The battle of Leucimme (435) resulted in a decisive victory for the Corcyraeans, who also gained control of Epidamnus on the same day (1.29). This should have been the end of the matter – the Corinthians, led on by ambition and hatred of the Corcyraeans, had tried to extend their power, but their adventurism had ended in failure. However, the Corinthians were not prepared to let the matter rest.

The grounds of complaint (aitiai)

Having stated the 'truest explanation' for the outbreak of the war, Thucydides then deals at length with (in his opinion) the two major openly stated grounds of complaint between the combatants – Athens' alliance with Corcyra (1.31–55) and the dispute over Potidaea (1.56–65). He also mentions the complaints of the Aeginetans who protested to the Spartans that their promised autonomy had been infringed, and those of the Megarians who referred to an Athenian decree that banned them from the ports in the Athenian Empire and the market of Athens (1.167). These four issues will be dealt with in turn.

Athens' alliance with Corcyra

Following their defeat at Leucimme in 435, the Corinthians set about building a new fleet and hiring mercenaries in order to exact revenge against Corcyra. News of these military preparations caused alarm among the Corcyraeans, and so in 433 they sent an embassy to Athens to seek an alliance. The Corinthians, fearing that the combined navies would prevent them from dealing a decisive blow against Corcyra, also sent an embassy to dissuade the Athenians from making an alliance with Corcyra (1.31). A meeting of the 'Ecclesia' was held and both sides were given the opportunity to put their case.

The Corcyraeans discussed their reasons for their previous neutrality and admitted that the present circumstances had shown how unwise this policy had been. They spoke of the Spartans' fear of Athens and their desire for war, and claimed that Corinth's attack on them was a prelude to an attack on Athens. They particularly stressed that there was no legal impediment for the Athenians in making this alliance:

> 'You will not be breaking your treaty with the Spartans, if you accept us into an alliance, since we are neutrals. For it is written down in that treaty that it is possible for any of the Greek states in that position of neutrality to join whichever side it chooses.'
>
> (Thucydides 1.35.2)

The Corcyraeans concluded by pointing out that the three strongest fleets in Greece were those of Athens, Corcyra and Corinth; and that, if the Corinthians gained control of their fleet, the Athenians would have to face their combined navies but, if they allied themselves with Corcyra, the Athenians would have overwhelming superiority in the coming war (1.32–36).

The Corinthians began their speech with abuse of the Corcyraeans, and claimed that Corinth's current war plans against the Corcyraeans were a result of the Corcyraeans' provocative behaviour over Epidamnus. The Corinthians stressed that it was not right or just for the Athenians to form an alliance with the Corcyraeans, since the clause in the Thirty Year Peace about the rights of neutral states (see peace terms above) was not meant to include a neutral state which was seeking an alliance for the purpose of waging war against a co-signatory of the treaty. The main thrust of the Corinthian argument concerned the right of a state to discipline its own allies who were in revolt:

> 'You should not establish a precedent by which you receive into your alliance those who are in revolt from the other side.'
>
> (Thucydides 1.40.5)

The Corinthians drew a parallel with their refusal to intervene against Athens, when Samos was in revolt in 440 (see p. 306), and expressed their conviction that the Athenians should pursue the same righteous course by refusing to help a Corinthian ally in revolt. They concluded that the Corcyraeans were scaremongering with their claims about the imminence of war; and that there was no certainty that war would break out, although it would not be in Athens' best interests to make Corinth an immediate enemy, even if they might become enemies in the future (1.37–43).

There was little in the Corinthian speech to assuage the Athenians' concern about the possibility of war between themselves and the Peloponnesians, and this served to add weight to that particular point of the Corcyraeans. The greatest difficulty for the Corinthians was to produce an argument to counter-act the Corcyraeans' convincing statement that the Athenians had a legal and legitimate right to make an alliance with them, as it was specifically laid down in the treaty that a neutral state was free to ally itself with whatever side it wished. The Corinthians attempted to cloud and obscure the issue by equating Corcyra's position with that of Samos. On their interpretation Corcyra was a Corinthian ally that had revolted, and thus they should have the right to discipline their recalcitrant ally without outside interference, as they themselves had argued to the Peloponnesians at the time of Samos' revolt in 440. The fallacy in the Corinthians' argument was that Corcyra, although being a colony of Corinth, was not an ally and therefore could not be in revolt – thus there was no comparability between Corcyra and Samos.

It took two meetings of the Ecclesia for the Athenians to reach their decision. In the first meeting a majority were more inclined to favour Corinth but in the second meeting:

> They decided not to make an offensive and defensive alliance (summachia) with the Corcyraeans – for if the Corcyraeans asked the Athenians to sail with them against the Corinthians, they would be breaking their treaty with the Peloponnesians – but they made a defensive alliance (epimachia) to help each other if anyone were to attack Corcyra or Athens or one of their allies.
>
> (Thucydides 1.44.1)

The main reason for granting Corcyra an alliance was the Athenians' belief that war was inevitable and their desire not to forfeit Corcyra's considerable fleet to the Corinthians. It can be argued that any form of military alliance between Athens and Corcyra was provocative, since a state of war existed between Corcyra and Corinth. However, it can also be argued that the Athenians had a legal right under the terms of the Thirty Year Peace to make a full offensive/defensive alliance, but deliberately refused this option on the specific grounds that they could be held responsible for a breach of that treaty, if the Corcyraeans should go on the offensive. In addition, the alliance was made when there were no military operations taking place, and the Corcyraeans were not planning any offensive action against Corinth. Therefore the initiative and responsibility for any future military clash would lie solely with the Corinthians, as hostilities would only break out if the Corinthians attacked Corcyra. Athens' defensive alliance was aimed at warning off Corinth, and thus preventing conflict.

The Athenians then sent ten ships and three generals as a reinforcement to Corcyra. Such a small force would have done little to calm Corcyraean fears, especially as the Corinthians were equipping a fleet of 150 ships. However, this small fleet with its large number of generals (the same number as on the Sicilian expedition in 415), including Lacedaimonius the son of Cimon and 'proxenos' of Sparta, reveals Athens' true objective: their preferred means for resolving their difficulties with Corinth was diplomacy and not military force. This is confirmed by the explicit instructions given to the Athenian generals:

> The Athenians ordered the generals not to fight a sea-battle with the Corinthians unless they should sail against Corcyra and were about to land there or at some other point in their territory – then they were to prevent it as best as possible. They gave these orders in order to avoid breaking the treaty.
>
> (Thucydides 1.45.3)

It would be interesting to know if these orders were made known to the Corcyraeans and, if they were, what their reaction was. In essence, the Athenians were ordering their generals not to fight unless the Corinthians were about to land on Corcyra or its territory, which situation would only arise if the Corcyraean fleet had already been defeated at sea – an extreme interpretation of a 'defensive' alliance.

The Corinthians decided to press ahead with their task force of 150 ships against Corcyra (1.46.1). They may have hoped that the Athenians, when it came to the crunch, would not intervene through fear of provoking a war with Sparta, or, if they did intervene, that Sparta and the Peloponnesians would come to their aid. In the battle of Sybota (433) the Athenian ships showed great restraint, offering moral support to the Corcyraeans but not joining battle with the Corinthians. However, when it was clear that the Corcyraeans had been defeated and the Corinthians were pressing on, the Athenian ships joined in the fighting. After their victory, the Corinthians set about killing the shipwrecked sailors still in the water rather than gather in their disabled ships, which was the usual practice after a sea battle. Then the Corinthians, having finally picked up their dead, sailed out again for a second battle (1.48–50.3). As the two sides prepared to engage battle, the Corinthians backed water because they had seen 20 Athenian ships (with two more generals) approaching. These had been sent out as a reinforcement by the Athenians as they feared that the original ten ships would be insufficient to save the Corcyraeans from defeat. It was now too dark for a sea battle, but on the next day the remainder of the Corcyraean fleet and the 30 Athenian ships sailed out to offer battle (1.50.4–52.1).

The Corinthians were now worried owing to their need to guard their prisoners, their lack of facilities to repair their damaged ships and the increased size of the Athenian naval forces; but there was a bigger problem, now that they had decided to return home:

> The Corinthians were afraid that the Athenians, thinking that the treaty had been broken because they had fought against each other, would prevent them from sailing away.
>
> (Thucydides 1.52.3)

The Corinthians realized how vulnerable their fleet was in this position and how the Athenians could inflict very serious damage on the grounds that a state of war now existed. However, the Athenians had no intention of escalating the conflict nor viewing the situation as a breach of the treaty, but stated clearly that the Corinthians were free to sail away unhindered, provided they made no attempt on Corcyra or its territory (1.53). Once again the Athenians were sticking strictly to the terms of the defensive alli- ance with Corcyra, and were determined to give the Corinthians no grounds to accuse them of being responsible for breaking the Thirty Year Peace – the conflict, culminating in the battle of Sybota, had been brought about by the Corinthians' determination to crush Corcyra, and they must take the main responsibility for provoking hostilities.

Athens' treatment of Potidaea

The next ground of complaint, in 432, concerned Potidaea and its inhabitants:

> who lived on the isthmus of Pallene and, although colonists of the Corinthians, were phoros-paying allies of the Athenians.
>
> (Thucydides 1.56.2)

The Thraceward region was of immense importance to the Athenians, as the foundation of the colonies of Brea and Amphipolis had confirmed. Apart from its richness in natural resources and its favourable trading position, it was the main bulwark against the eastward expansion of Macedon, which at that time was under the control of King Perdiccas. The relationship between the Athenians and Perdiccas was constantly changing from friendship to enmity, since the motivating force on both sides was expediency. At the time of the Potidaean affair, he was hostile to the Athenians due to their support of his rivals, Philip and Deucas, and consequently played an important supportive role in the revolt of Potidaea (1.57.2–5).

Potidaea became an issue of dispute because of the Athenian demands that the Potidaeans should pull down their wall on the side of Pallene, hand over hostages, and banish and not receive in the future the magistrates that Corinth usually sent each year. Without doubt these were tough demands on a state that had committed no wrong, and this harsh treatment was bound to upset the Corinthians who had retained such warm, close ties with their colony. However, it is important to look at Athenian motives for taking this action against Potidaea, as Thucydides explicitly records:

> For the Corinthians were searching for a means to avenge themselves and the
> Athenians, being fully aware of their hatred towards themselves, gave orders to the
> Potidaeans ... fearing that they, being persuaded by Perdiccas and the Corinthians,
> would revolt and cause the rest of the allies in the Thraceward region to revolt with
> themselves.
>
> (Thucydides 1.56.2)

The Athenians' treatment of Potidaea was directly provoked by the Corinthians' hatred of Athens and by their determination to find a means of retaliation because they had been prevented from crushing Corcyra; and was influenced by their fear of losing control of the Thraceward region (see Map 5, the Athenian Empire) through Corinthian incitement of the allies there to revolt.

Upon receipt of the Athenian demands, the Potidaeans sent an embassy to Athens to negotiate a retraction of their demands, but the Athenians were not prepared to compromise. At the same time:

> The Potidaeans, accompanied by Corinthians, sent an embassy to Sparta in order to
> gain help from there, if necessary ... and the Spartan authorities promised that, if the
> Athenians attacked Potidaea, they would invade Attica; and so they seized their
> opportunity, swore oaths of alliance with the Chalcidians and the Bottiaeans, and
> revolted from Athens.
>
> (Thucydides 1.58.1)

Both Corinth's and Sparta's behaviour can be condemned for breaking the terms of the Thirty Year Peace. Although Potidaea was a Corinthian colony, it was also a *listed* Athenian ally and therefore directly under the control of Athens, which Sparta and Corinth (as part of the Peloponnesian League) had legally accepted when they agreed to the Thirty Year Peace in 446/5 – clause 2: 'each side should keep what it possessed'. Even if Athens' behaviour was harsh and unjustified, Sparta and Corinth had no more legal right to intervene directly in Potidaea than they had in Samos. Their main available legal redress was to demand that the issue be submitted to arbitration, but instead the Corinthians actively urged the Potidaeans to seek military help from Sparta, and the Spartans (whether the authorities or the

Assembly) promised an invasion of Attica, thus encouraging the Potidaeans to revolt from Athens.

The Athenians had sent out Archestratos with 30 ships and 1,000 hoplites to carry out their demands, but they arrived to find that a full-scale revolt had broken out:

> Meanwhile the Corinthians, since the Potidaeans had revolted and that Athenian ships were close to Macedonia, being afraid for the place and thinking that the danger was their own responsibility, sent out volunteers of their own and, by the use of pay, sixteen hundred hoplites and four hundred light-armed troops from the other Peloponnesians.
>
> (Thucydides 1.60.1)

Therefore the Athenians sent out 40 ships and 2,000 hoplites under Callias, and, after making another cynical alliance with Perdiccas, descended upon Potidaea. There the Athenians fought a battle against the Potidaeans, the Corinthian volunteers and the Peloponnesians, resulting in an Athenian victory and the beginning of the siege of Potidaea that lasted to 429 (1.62–64).

The use of Corinthian troops in battle to support an Athenian listed ally exposes Corinth once again to the charge of acting in defiance of the terms of the treaty. However, if these Corinthian fighters were genuine volunteers and were acting independently of the state of Corinth (as many British citizens did in the Spanish Civil War in the 1930s), then Corinth can be exonerated on this issue. But the above quotation speaks of 'the Corinthians' sending out the volunteers and these 'Corinthians' must be the government of the state of Corinth. In addition, when the Peace of Nicias was signed in 421, the Corinthians refused to abide by its conditions:

> They made as their excuse the fact that they could not betray their allies in Thrace. For they had independently sworn oaths with them, when they had first revolted with the Potidaeans, and later.
>
> (Thucydides 5.30.2)

It is clear from these words that the oaths had created some form of military alliance between the Corinthians and the Potidaeans and, most probably, the Chalcidians and the Bottiaeans who had revolted together in 432, since Thucydides twice refers to the enemy forces in 432 as 'the Potidaeans and their allies' (1.63.3; 1.64.1). Oaths of alliance could not be made 'unofficially' but only between states, and therefore the Corinthians had sworn oaths of alliance with three groups of Athenian listed allies and were officially supplying military help against the Athenians – a clear breach of the treaty.

At this point in his *History*, having dealt with (in his opinion) the two main aitiai (grounds of complaint), Thucydides passes on to the events that culminated in the declaration of war by the Spartans and their allies, in the context of which he mentions the grievances that the Aeginetans and the Megarians expressed in front of the Spartans. However, modern historians believe that these grievances should also be treated as aitiai, as they had a significant bearing on the hardening of opinion on both sides in the build-up to the war.

Aegina

Aegina, situated in the heart of the Saronic Gulf and close to the Piraeus, had been an important naval power and rival of the Athenians. There had been naval clashes in the past, but the defeat of the Aeginetans, the confiscation of their fleet and their forced entry into the Delian League in c.458/7 had confirmed Athenian superiority. In 432, when the Corinthians and others in Sparta were attacking the Athenians' behaviour, they took advantage of the situation to put their complaints:

> The Aeginetans did not openly send an embassy but secretly because they feared the Athenians, and, no less than the Corinthians, played a leading role in fomenting war, claiming that they were no longer autonomous as was laid down in the treaty.
>
> (Thucydides 1.67.2)

Unfortunately Thucydides supplies no evidence as to whether the Aeginetans had a legitimate complaint against the Athenians, and it cannot be said for certain what treaty is being referred to in the above quotation. If Aegina's autonomy was one of the terms of the Thirty Year Peace, then their autonomy may have been infringed by the imposition of a garrison or by the forced referral of all serious legal cases to Athens for judgement. However, the Aeginetans only paid part of their 'phoros' in 432 and the Athenians may have taken action to recover the outstanding amount, which could have led to their complaint. Without full possession of the facts it is impossible to apportion blame to either side.

The Megarian Decree

One of the most contentious grounds of complaint among modern scholarship is the Megarian Decree, passed probably around the middle of 432. In fact, there may have been as many as four Megarian decrees but it is the 'exclusion' decree in particular, about which the Megarians were protesting to the Spartans at the time of Aegina's complaint, that is considered the most important:

> The Megarians, after stating many other grievances, complained especially about being excluded from the harbours in the Athenian Empire and from the Athenian market (agora) contrary to the terms of the treaty.
>
> (Thucydides 1.67.4)

Many modern historians believe that this was the most important ground of complaint and that the Athenians' (and Pericles') intransigence in refusing to repeal this decree makes them culpable for the outbreak of the war. This school of thought (e.g. Robinson, Hornblower) maintains that the effect of the decree was to bring economic ruin to Megara, a listed ally of Sparta, and that the destruction of the Megarian economy was an act of aggression by the Athenians. The main evidence for the economic effects of this decree comes from Aristophanes' *Achamians*, in which Dicaeopolis is reviewing the causes of the war:

> Then in anger Olympian Pericles thundered and lightened, and threw Greece into confusion by passing decrees written like drinking songs: 'that the Megarians must not stay on the land nor in the market (agora) nor on the sea nor on the mainland.' Then the Megarians, since they were slowly starving, begged the Spartans to get the decree withdrawn.
>
> (Aristophanes, *Achamians* ll. 530–37)

The fact that Dicaeopolis' statement about the starving Megarians comes immediately after the parody of the Megarian Decree argues strongly that there was a direct causal link between the two.

This view of the economic effects of the decree is supported by the clear evidence that the Athenians and their enemies were very aware of the economic stranglehold that the Athenians could exert in the Aegean through the use of their fleet. The Old Oligarch, a right-wing pamphleteer and opponent of Athenian democracy writing probably in the 420s, had said unequivocally that any state that wished to import and export freely must first submit to the rulers of the sea (2.3–11; O.O. pp. 21–23). There were also the regulations for Methone (ML 65; AE121 pp. 58–59), which granted its citizens the right to import a fixed amount of grain after they had registered with the Athenian officials who controlled the shipping through the Hellespont. This privilege could just as easily be withdrawn or withheld by the Athenians, which would have a devastating effect upon the unfortunate state. The Corinthians' first argument in their attempt to persuade the Peloponnesian League Congress to vote for war concentrated on the Athenians' ability to operate a 'closed sea' policy:

> Those of us, who have already had dealings with the Athenians, do not need to be taught to be on our guard against them. But those who live inland and not on the trade-routes must learn that, if they do not help those by the sea, they will experience greater difficulties in the transportation of their own produce to the sea and in the bringing back of imports from the sea.
>
> (Thucydides 1.120.2)

Thus the Athenians were capable of inflicting economic sanctions against their enemies, and the action against Megara should be seen in this context.

The importance of the Megarian decree as an 'aitia' can be further seen by the pre-eminence that the Spartans afforded to the issue. In their second embassy to the Athenians in 432/1, the Spartans told them:

> to withdraw from Potidaea and to allow Aegina to be autonomous. But most of all they said in the clearest terms that war could be avoided if the Athenians were to repeal the Megarian Decree.
>
> (Thucydides 1.139.1)

The Athenians' defence for passing the decree and then refusing to revoke it was that the Megarians were guilty of cultivating consecrated ground, cultivating land that did not belong to them and offering a refuge for runaway slaves (1.139). However, those who blame Athens for causing the outbreak of the war argue that this religious motive was merely a convenient pretext to disguise the real purpose of the decree, which was economic; and that, if the primary motive had been religious, then it is surprising that the exclusion decree did not specify the obvious religious meeting-places and events from which the Megarians were to be banned. On the basis of the above evidence the Athenians should be viewed as having acted aggressively against one of Sparta's allies in the passing of this decree, and their refusal to make any serious attempt to remove its economic effects on Megara made war inevitable. Thucydides' downgrading of its importance as a major ground of complaint can be explained either by his inability to understand economics or, more likely (according to Rhodes), by his patriotism and his support for Pericles' policies, which resulted in a full treatment of Corcyra and Potidaea as aitiai where Athens had a good case for intervention, but the playing down of the importance of Aegina and Megara where Athens was open to criticism.

The opposition to this view has been led by de Ste. Croix with a radical reappraisal of the decree and its effects. The cornerstone of his interpretation lies in the nature of trade in the ancient world and the fact that it was the Megarians, i.e. the citizens of Megara, that were specifically excluded. His contention is that very few citizens were involved in trade, the great majority of which was handled by foreigners or resident aliens ('metics'). These would be bringing imports into Megara for profitable sale and then, after buying Megarian produce, would be able to sell this without restriction in other places including the markets of Athens and its allies, since they were not Megarian citizens; and there is no source evidence anywhere that speaks of produce being specifically banned. The evidence from Dicaeopolis' speech in Aristophanes' *Acharnians*, which is crucial for his opponents' theory, should be treated with the greatest of caution. The purpose of a comic playwright is to entertain, and he will use every literary device available to achieve this goal including exaggeration, distortion, omission, invention and a disregard of accuracy in historical facts (see

Chapter 18 and Aristophanes' comic invention in the *Peace* that the cause of the war was Pericles' fear of losing political power over Pheidias' disgrace and thus provoking the war to save his political skin). If the whole speech of Dicaeopolis is used as evidence, instead of a passage taken out of context, it will be seen that he puts the main blame for the war on the Spartans, although stating that Athens should bear some responsibility. In addition, the whole speech is a masterpiece of literary parody – the mention of the war being caused by the mutual kidnapping of prostitutes recalls the beginning of Herodotus' *History* and his explanation of the original source of enmity between Greece and Persia; the section about the terms of the Megarian Decree plays on the words of a popular drinking song by Timocreon of Rhodes; and the whole speech has many marked similarities with the speeches of Telephus in Euripides' tragedy of the same name – and it was this literary aim, not historical accuracy, that was the driving force behind Aristophanes' speech of Dicaeopolis.

De Ste. Croix then provides historical facts as reasons why Aristophanes could refer to the starving Megarians. The Athenians invaded the Megarid twice every year from 431/0 to 425/4 with very large forces in order to ravage their land, and they also maintained a sea blockade. By 425, when the *Acharnians* was staged, the Megarians had suffered for six years from the effects of being blockaded and their crops destroyed – hence the cause of their starvation. In addition, the decree itself was only in effective operation for less than a year because, once war had broken out in 431, the Megarians and their goods would have no right of entry in a war situation. Pericles' opinion of the importance of the Megarian Decree is made clear in his last major speech before the war:

> 'Let none of you think that we are going to war over a trifle, if we do not repeal the Megarian decree, about which they especially say that there will be no war if it is repealed, and remove from your minds any thought that we have gone to war over a small matter.'
>
> (Thucydides 1.140.4)

If the decree had caused such devastating economic consequences for Megara, Pericles would have severely weakened his argument by calling the issue a 'trifle' or 'small matter', if the Athenians knew differently. Pericles held the belief that Sparta was deliberately exaggerating the importance of the decree to test the Athenians' nerve and to see if they would show weakness and give in; if they did appease the Spartans, a greater demand would soon follow as they exploited the Athenians' perceived fear of themselves (1.140–41). Thucydides shared the same view as Pericles and for that reason did not accord the Megarian Decree the status of being an aitia. Finally, there is supporting evidence that the decree could have been passed for specifically religious motives – in 352–349 the Megarians again cultivated

Athenian sacred land, and this led the Athenians to take military action against Megara; once again the cause of the conflict was religious and in this instance there could be no other ulterior motives on the part of the Athenians. This shows that the Athenians considered such behaviour as very impious and were prepared to fight over it. The Megarians, being well aware of Athenian sensitivities over this issue, may even have been urged on by the Corinthians to cultivate the sacred land in order to provoke the Athenians into a hostile reaction, and thus give cause for complaint. For these reasons, de Ste. Croix believes that the Athenians should be absolved from blame, but the Megarians (to a smaller extent) and the Spartans in particular should be blamed for exploiting the issue and making it a pretext for war.

The prelude to the war

The Corinthians had already clashed with the Athenians over Corcyra (433) and were playing an active part in Potidaea's revolt (432). So far they had acted independently, but now in the second half of 432 they decided to bring matters into the open. In fact, the Corinthians played the dominant role in the events that led up to the declaration of war. They feared that Potidaea would capitulate, so they urged their allies to send representatives to Sparta. There the Corinthians accused the Athenians of breaking the treaty and committing acts of aggression against the Peloponnese. It was on this occasion that the Aeginetans, behind the scenes, complained that they had lost their autonomy. The Spartans then issued an invitation not only to their own allies but to any other state, which claimed to have been victims of Athenian aggression, to come to Sparta to put its case. At the Spartan Assembly held for that purpose, many states made various complaints against the Athenians, including the Megarians about the exclusion decree (1.66–67). The Corinthians chose to speak last in order to capitalize on the hardening of Spartan opinion (1.68–72). The Corinthians criticized the Spartans for their constant slowness in recognizing danger and pointed out that the Athenians had exploited this lack of awareness. They urged the Spartans to take immediate action to help their allies, especially Potidaea, by invading Attica. They concluded their speech with a threat that was guaranteed to frighten the Spartans:

> 'Do not let your friends and kinsmen fall into the hands of their bitterest enemies. Do not drive the rest of us in despair to seek a different alliance.'
>
> (Thucydides 1.71.4)

The Peloponnesian League was essential in maintaining Sparta's supremacy in the Peloponnese and ensuring security from the 'Helots'. If Corinth, the most influential member of the League, were to secede and seek an alliance with Argos or even Athens, Sparta would be substantially weakened, and this could lead to a break-up of the League. The Corinthians knew how potent their threat was and the effect it would have upon the listening Spartans.

The Spartans, having removed all outsiders, continued their Assembly in order to discuss the issues raised by their allies. Most of the Spartan speakers were of the opinion that Athens had acted aggressively and that war should be declared immediately. However, King Archidamus, who would be commander-in-chief of the armed forces in the event of war, counselled caution (1.80–85). He emphasized that the war would be tough and difficult against an enemy that was wealthy, populous and maritime; and, as the Spartans needed to acquire the necessary financial and naval resources in order to wage war on equal terms, they should refrain from war for two or three years until they had remedied their weaknesses. He stressed in particular that the land invasion and devastation of Attica would not bring about a quick, easy victory. His advice in the present situation was:

'Send an embassy to the Athenians about Potidaea and about the issues, which our allies have claimed that they have been wronged, especially since the Athenians are prepared to submit to arbitration. It is illegal to attack them first, who are offering arbitration, as though they were definitely in the wrong.'

(Thucydides 1.85.2)

He suggested that the Spartans and their allies should use the time taken up with negotiations to prepare more effectively for war.

Sthenelaidas, one of the 'Ephors' (see Glossary) for that year, opposed Archidamus' appeal for a delay in declaring war in a much shorter speech, which put great emphasis on the need to defend their allies from Athenian aggression but contained no detailed arguments to counter the fears expressed by Archidamus about a long, exhaustive war. The tenor of his whole speech is effectively revealed in his final exhortation:

'Therefore, Spartans, vote for war and the honour of Sparta! Do not allow the Athenians to become stronger, do not betray our allies, but let us, with the help of the gods, advance to meet the aggressor.'

(Thucydides 1.86.5)

The force of this impassioned, patriotic appeal won the day and the Spartans voted for war. Once again Thucydides, echoing his own words in 1.23, gives his opinion of the 'truest explanation' of why the Spartans voted for war:

The Spartans voted that the treaty had been broken and that war should be declared, not so much because they were persuaded by the speeches of their allies

as because they were afraid of the further growth of Athenian power, seeing that
most of Greece was already subject to them.

(Thucydides 1.88)

The Spartans, having voted for war in their Assembly, then summoned a
League Congress for the allies to cast their votes, in accordance with the
constitution of the Peloponnesian League (see Chapter 12). The Corinthians
had already anticipated this by previously sending representatives to all the
other allies, urging them to vote for war, and again gave the last speech in
the Congress, in which they attacked the Athenians' ambitions to bring the
whole of Greece under their dominion and held out the vision of themselves
as the liberators of Greece (1.120–24). The majority of allied representatives
also voted for war (1.125). The intervening time was taken up by the Spartans
sending embassies to Athens. The first embassy demanded that the Athenians
'drive out the curse of the goddess' – a reference to impious behaviour by one
of Pericles' ancestors – which was aimed at weakening Pericles' popularity
(1.126–27); the Athenians replied in kind about the Spartans' impious treatment of Pausanias (1.128–35). The second embassy demanded the withdrawal
of the Athenians from Potidaea, the granting of autonomy to Aegina, and
principally the repeal of the Megarian Decree (1.139). Finally the third
embassy made no reference to the grounds of complaint but said simply:

'The Spartans want peace and this is possible, if you will allow independence to the
Greeks.'

(Thucydides 1.139.3)

This third embassy was viewed by many Athenians as an ultimatum, but
by others as still holding out the prospect of negotiation. In the final
Athenian debate after the third embassy, many Athenians spoke as though
the points raised in the second embassy were still on the table for discussion. However, Thucydides dismissed their views in a few words and concentrated on Pericles' speech (1.140–44), which clearly reflected Thucydides'
own analysis of the situation. Pericles expressed his belief that the Megarian
Decree was of little importance in its own right but was being used by the
Spartans to test Athenian nerve – any compromise over the decree would
be seen as fear-induced weakness and would provoke greater demands from
the Spartans; and that war was being forced upon the Athenians by the
Spartans' refusal to submit to arbitration, by their demands about Athenian
allies, and finally by their ultimatum about giving independence to the
Greeks. Pericles proposed that the Athenians should reply point by point
to the Spartan demands: first, that the Athenians would repeal the Megarian Decree, if the Spartans would exempt the Athenians and their allies
from their occasional expulsion of all foreigners from Sparta; second, as
regards giving the Greeks their independence:

'that we will give independence to the cities, if they had independence at the time of the treaty, and when the Spartans allow their own allies to have independence, which fits in with the allies' wishes and not with Spartan interests. As regards arbitration, that we are willing to submit to it in accordance with the treaty, and that we will not start a war but we will resist those who do.'

(Thucydides 1.144.2)

Pericles held the opinion that the third Spartan embassy was really demanding the dissolution of the Athenian Empire as the only meaningful condition for avoiding war, and that the Athenians should be fully informed of the real nature of the Spartans' demands. The Athenians accepted his advice and sent an embassy to Sparta, putting their counter-proposals as Pericles suggested. This was the last formal communication between the two super-powers before the outbreak of war in 431.

Athens and Sparta: the ultimate responsibility

Modern historians, like Thucydides, accept the fact that the Corinthians, whether justifiably or not, played a major role in the events that preceded the outbreak of war and in their exhortation of the allies to vote for war; however, the ultimate responsibility has to reside with the two super-powers, whose decisions made the war happen, and it is here that modern historical scholarship splits into two camps. One school of thought (e.g. Hornblower, Rhodes) believes that the Athenians should be blamed due to their relentless imperial expansion, their provocative behaviour towards Sparta's allies and the military weakness of Sparta in the late 430s. The other school of thought (e.g. de Ste. Croix) blames the Spartans due to their aggressive behaviour towards Athens throughout most of the fifth century, which was caused by their fear, resentment and overwhelming desire to crush the Athenians.

Those who blame the Athenians base their belief on the evidence of the increasing size of the Empire and the means by which it was controlled. After the battle of Eurymedon in c.469 the Athenians had concentrated more on bringing their allies under their control (1.99), so that by 446 the Athenians were in possession of an Empire. In addition, the Athenians had interfered with the autonomy of a large number of Greek states to a far greater degree than any other power by its use of garrisons, 'cleruchies', 'phrourarchs', 'archontes' and judicial control (see Chapter 16) – even Pericles and Cleon could agree upon 'tyranny' as a description of the nature of Athenian rule. The Thirty Year Peace in 446/5 had been an attempt to put the dual hegemony on a legal basis, ensuring a balance of power in the Greek world between the two super-powers. However, the Athenians were far too restless and ambitious to be constrained by these limits on their territorial possessions – a point stressed by the Corinthians in the Spartan Assembly:

> 'Therefore, if someone were to give a brief summary of the Athenians by saying that they were incapable by nature of living a quiet life themselves and incapable of allowing others to do so, he would be speaking the truth.'
>
> (Thucydides 1.70.9)

In the period after the treaty was agreed, the Athenians set about extending their power and adding to their Empire. The west had always been the traditional area of Corinthian influence, but the Athenians set about challenging their position by their foundation of the colony of Thurii in 444/3 (Plutarch, *Pericles* 11); by their help to the Acarnanians against Ambracia, a Corinthian colony, in the early 430s (2.68.7); by their alliances with Rhegium and Leontini in the 440s, renewed in 433/2; and by their alliance with Corcyra in 433 on the grounds (among others) that it was conveniently situated on the route to Italy and Sicily (1.44.3). In addition, the Athenians were strengthening their power in the Aegean in the 430s. The suppression of Samos, one of the three remaining independent ship-suppliers, and its reduction to phoros-paying subject-ally status showed clearly that the Athenians would accept no challenge to their power. There soon followed, possibly around 437/6, Pericles' Black Sea expedition (Plutarch, *Pericles* 20) that resulted in the grain route being secured by the foundation of Athenian colonies and by the display of Athenian military might to the new dynasty in the Bosporan Kingdom; and by the foundation of the strategically important colony of Amphipolis in the Thraceward region.

The second half of the 430s saw the Athenians in a war frame of mind. Callias, almost certainly in 434/3, proposed two financial decrees, which in essence imposed restrictions on public spending, especially on the building programme on the Acropolis, allowed any excess funds to be spent on the walls and the docks, and authorized the removal of treasure from the outlying temples in Attica to the Acropolis for security (ML 58). These measures were clearly taken in anticipation of war: public finance was being directed towards creating a war fund; and fear of a Spartan invasion of Attica necessitated the withdrawal of treasure from the other temples. The war between Corcyra and Corinth was essentially a private affair, and the Athenians could easily have refused to become involved, but Athenian ambitions predominated. The Athenians were also ready and willing to provoke a second clash with the Corinthians by their demands on Potidaea, which had a close relationship with its mother-city and which had done nothing to provoke such harsh treatment. The Megarian Decree may not have broken the letter of the Thirty Year Peace but its crippling effect on the Megarian economy broke its spirit; and their refusal to repeal this decree, even after the Spartans said that war could be avoided by this act, revealed the Athenians' determination to provoke a war.

The Athenians realized that their unwillingness to check their imperial ambitions would provoke war, and therefore they wished to fight the war in the most favourable circumstances for themselves – when they were in a stronger military position than the Spartans and when they could claim that they were in the right as they were victims of aggression. King Archidamus' speech (1.80–85) gives an excellent analysis of Athens' strength and Spartan weakness on the eve of the war:

'Why should we so readily start a war against these Athenians, whose land is far away and who are also the most experienced in naval matters and are the best equipped in all other ways, in private and public wealth, in ships, in horses, in arms and in a population that is greater than in any other Greek territory, and in addition have many phoros-paying allies? On what are we going to rely by rushing in unprepared? On our ships? But we are inferior in that respect. If we pay attention to them and prepare ourselves, it will take time. On our wealth? But we are even more inferior in that respect since we have neither public funds nor can we easily raise money from private sources.'

(Thucydides 1.80.3–4)

Pericles, the main advocate for the war, recognized the weakness of the Spartan position even more than most of the Spartans and explained it fully to the Athenians in the last Assembly before the war (1.141–43). The offer of arbitration was a cynical ploy, since the Spartans were bound to refuse, and therefore on the basis of the above arguments the Athenians should be blamed for the outbreak of the war.

Those historians, who apportion the greater share of the blame to the Spartans, base their belief on the Spartans' long-standing fear, their readiness to attack Athens whenever the Athenians were facing a crisis or were in a weak position, and their expectation of a quick victory in 431. Even before the Delian League had been founded, the Spartans, with the encouragement of their allies, had attempted to prevent the Athenians from rebuilding their defensive walls after the retreat of the Persians in 479 – fear of the sudden growth in the size of the Athenian navy and the daring that they showed in the war were the reasons cited by Thucydides (1.89.3–90.2; AE4 p. 10). Diodorus records a debate in Sparta (dated to 475, although 478/7 seems more likely) where the discussion was about the Spartans regaining the hegemony of Greece by force from the Athenians, and a majority was in favour of this until Hetoemaridas persuaded them that it was not in their interest to lay claim to the sea (11.50 – see Chapter 12). In 465, when the two states were still officially allies, the Spartans prepared to invade Attica while the Athenians were involved in a difficult campaign to suppress the revolt of Thasos (1.101.1–2; AE29 p. 21). Soon after this they snubbed the Athenians, who had to come to help them to put down the Helot revolt, by sending them away alone of the allies because:

the Spartans grew frightened at the bold and revolutionary character of the Athenians and also because they thought of them as alien in race.

(Thucydides 1.102.3; AE39 p. 25)

This action revealed the latent hostility of the Spartans to the Athenians and led to the First Peloponnesian War from 462/1 to 446/5.

In 440, the Spartans cynically ignored the terms of the Thirty Year Peace by voting in their Assembly to aid Samos – an Athenian-listed ally and a powerful naval state that offered a serious challenge to Athens' sea power:

> They [i.e. the pro-Athenian democratic faction in 411] also had control of Samos, which was not weak but had come very close to removing the control of the sea from the Athenians when it had waged war against them.
>
> (Thucydides 8.76.4)

In the same way the Spartans had encouraged Potidaea, another Athenian-listed ally, to revolt by promising to invade Attica, if the Athenians took action against them (1.58). They deliberately exaggerated the importance of the Megarian Decree, whose effect upon the Megarian economy was minimal, in order to have a good excuse for declaring war (1.126). Finally the third embassy, stripped of its grandiose language about the freedom of the Greeks, demanded nothing less than the dissolution of the Athenian Empire, while retaining control over their Peloponnesian allies. The Athenian offers of arbitration and repeal of the Megarian Decree (1.78, 1.144) were ignored because the Spartans preferred to settle their complaints by war. Later, in 414/3, the Spartans were prepared to admit their greater responsibility for causing the outbreak of the war:

> In the former war [i.e. the Archidamian War, 431–421] the Spartans felt that they had acted more illegally, because the Thebans had entered Plataea in peace-time, and because, although it was written down in the former treaty [i.e. the Thirty Year Peace] that they should not take up arms if the other side wished to go to arbitration, yet they themselves refused to listen to the Athenian request for arbitration.
>
> (Thucydides 7.18.2)

The Spartans were prepared to ignore arbitration and the terms of the treaty because they felt so confident of a quick and easy victory:

> The Spartans for their part found that the war had gone very differently from their expectations, when they thought that they could destroy the power of the Athenians within a few years if they devastated their land.
>
> (Thucydides 5.14.3)

The invasion of 446 and its dramatic success in bringing the First Peloponnesian War to a swift end had convinced the Spartans that a similar strategy would bring about the same result. Their hopes were buoyed up by the opinion of the rest of the Greeks:

> At the beginning of the war some thought that, if the Peloponnesians invaded their land, the Athenians might hold out for a year, others for two years or three years, but nobody thought that they could last longer than that.
>
> (Thucydides 7.28.3)

Hoplite warfare had dominated Greek military thinking for the previous 250 years, and the principle that the state with the strongest force of hoplites was destined to win wars had been continually reaffirmed in that time. The Spartans (but not King Archidamus) had failed to realize that Pericles and the Athenians were planning a totally new strategy – a mainly defensive war, avoiding pitched hoplite battles (but using sea-borne raids as the offensive element of their strategy), thus limiting the effectiveness of Sparta's main military strength.

The Athenians knew that it would be a long, hard struggle – a defensive war would inflict more damage on Attica than they could inflict in return on the enemy, and would create the unpleasantness of over-crowding behind the Long Walls every summer. It would also be a much tougher war than the First Peloponnesian War because this time the Spartans were at full strength, had no Helot problem to distract their military forces and had easy access through the Megarid to launch their annual invasions. Pericles' speech to the Athenian in 432 gives his reasons for believing in ultimate victory, but there is no mention of a quick or easy victory, rather that the Athenians 'will win through' (1.144.1). In many ways it would be extremely difficult for the Athenians to win a war by the traditional method – a land invasion of the Peloponnese, a defeat of the hoplite forces of the Peloponnesians and the taking of Sparta by storm. On the basis that no sensible power deliberately provokes a defensive war but rather is forced into war to defend itself, the Spartans should be blamed for the outbreak of the war.

Bibliography

Cartledge, P. *Sparta and Lakonia*, pt 3, ch. 12.

Hornblower, S. *The Greek World 479–323 BC*, ch. 8.

Kagan, D. *The Outbreak of the Peloponnesian War*, chs 10, 11, 13–20.

Lewis, D. M. *CAH* vol. 5, 2nd edn, chs 6.4, 9.1.

Meiggs, R. *The Athenian Empire*, ch. 10.

Powell, A. *Athens and Sparta*, ch. 4.

Rhodes, P. J. 'Thucydides on the causes of the Peloponnesian War', *Hermes* 115.

Robinson, C. E. *History of Greece*, ch. 11.

de Ste. Croix, G. E. M. *The Origins of the Peloponnesian War*, chs 1–8.

18

PERICLES AND THE NATURE OF ATHENIAN POLITICS

It is important at the outset to understand the nature of Athenian politics and of political organizations in the fifth century. There were no
political parties, in the modern sense, with distinctive political philosophies
and party structures. Political groupings in Athens centred on certain outstanding individuals – usually wealthy aristocrats, at least in the first half of
the century. The ancient writers refer to these factions as 'those around
so-and-so', and the core of a typical faction would be constituted from
relatives, close friends and immediate supporters. In a society that lacked
political parties and their organization, 'philia' (political friendship) was
absolutely crucial as the basis of political organization. However, political
success for an ambitious politician depended upon reaching out to a
wider constituency and attracting outsiders, beyond the 'philoi' (friends),
to his policies. This required good oratory, generosity to his fellow citizens,
success in military affairs and in public service, and an attractive character;
a well-judged marriage would also bring the support of another powerful
political faction. In addition, coalitions were often formed between factions usually to achieve a specific political objective – for example, although
Nicias and Alcibiades were political enemies, their factions united c.416
to secure the ostracism of Hyperbolus (Plutarch, *Nicias* 11). But these coalitions
were fleeting, for as soon as the immediate political objective had been
achieved, they would often split and form coalitions with other factions
in pursuit of a different aim. This constant flux and interaction between the
factions must be borne in mind throughout this chapter, if the personalities and political issues are to be understood. The idea that in fifth-
century Athens there existed only two or three 'parties', or that a few prominent individuals were the only important politicians, or that Pericles was the
unchallenged leader of Athens from 444/3 to his death, must be resisted,
as the literary sources concentrate solely on the prominent politicians of the
first rank, and dismiss or diminish the standing of other important
politicians, who are known from the finds of 'ostraka' (see 'ostracism' in
Chapter 7).

Pericles' early career to 444/3

Pericles first makes his mark in Athenian politics as the chief assistant of Ephialtes. His background, like the other prominent politicians of the first two-thirds of the century (499–430), was aristocratic. Xanthippus, his father, was a politician of the first rank in the 490s and the first half of the 480s; he secured the prosecution of Miltiades in 489, was ostracized in 484, but was recalled to win fame as one of the two commanders-in-chief of the victorious Greek forces at the battle of Mycale in 479 against the Persians. Agariste, his mother, was descended from the powerful and influential Alcmaeonid family. Such family connections were the ideal basis for a career in politics. In 463, Pericles prosecuted Cimon, after his return from the siege of Thasos, on a charge of corruption – he alleged that Cimon had it within his power to attack Macedonia but had been bought off by King Alexander (Plutarch, *Cimon* 14). This case was clearly politically inspired by the democratic reformers against their leading political opponent, and, although Cimon was acquitted, the trial raised Pericles' profile in Athenian public life.

Success soon came to the 'democrats' with the passing of Ephialtes' reforms in 462/1, with Pericles playing a major role in the introduction of state pay for jury service in the 'Heliaea' (Aristotle, *Ath. Pol.* 27.3). The assassination of Ephialtes soon after his reforms provided an opportunity for Pericles to advance his political career, but the view of Plutarch (*Pericles* 16) that he dominated Athenian politics for 40 years must be rejected. Athens' involvement in the First Peloponnesian War (462/1–446/5) brought to pro-minence in the 450s other men of military ability: Leocrates who defeated the Aeginetans and besieged their city in c.459 (Thuc. 1.105.2; AE 39 p. 26), Myronides who defeated the Corinthians at Megara in c.459 and the Boeo-tians at the battle of Oenophyta in c.457 (Thuc. 1.105.3–106.2; AE39 p. 26; 1.108.2–3; AE39 p. 27) and Tolmides who circumnavigated the Peloponnese and defeated the Sicyonians in c.456 (Thuc. 1.108.5; AE39 p. 27). The first reference to Pericles as a general in this war comes with his leadership of another Athenian campaign against Sicyon in c.455/4 (Thuc. 1.111.2–3; AE39 p. 28). Therefore Pericles had no monopoly of power in the 450s, and it is very likely that he, being a competent rather than an outstanding mili-tary man, concentrated on domestic politics in this decade, consolidating Ephialtes' reforms by the extension of pay for public office.

By the end of the 450s, Pericles' political standing had risen and thus provided him with the means to exercise a greater influence in the city's affairs. He was undoubtedly aware that the Athenian defeat in Egypt in 454 was due to an over-ambitious foreign policy and accepted that there was a need to fight on one front at a time. The Persians' recent success in Egypt made them the first priority, but a full-scale military offensive would leave Athens exposed and vulnerable to a Spartan attack. In these circumstances, Pericles was willing to put aside his former opposition to Cimon, who was so influential with the Spartans (see Chapter 15 and the five-year truce with Sparta, 451–446), and formed a political alliance with his faction. As a gesture of goodwill Pericles is said to have moved the decree for the early recall of Cimon from ostracism:

> Some writers say, however, that the decree for Cimon's recall was not introduced by Pericles until a secret agreement had been made between them through the help of Elpinice, Cimon's sister, that Cimon should set sail with two hundred ships and take command abroad in order to reduce the territory of the King of Persia, while Pericles should possess supreme authority at home.
>
> (Plutarch, *Pericles* 10)

If this is true, then the coalition was a division of power with each leader exercising his specialist talent and implementing his preferred policy. Cimon was free to pursue his traditional anti-Persian policy and to utilize his outstanding skills as a general, but in return he accepted the constitutional reforms of 462/1 and allowed Pericles pre-eminence in domestic policy. This political alliance may have been strengthened in the traditional manner – the marriage of Pericles' relation, Isodice, to Cimon. However, the death of Cimon, the military success against the Persians at Cyprus and the chance to end hostilities with Persia in 449 led to a major rethink by Pericles. It was his change in foreign policy and his plans for the use of the allies' 'phoros' in the post-Persian war period that led to the break-up of the coalition.

The main opposition came from a kinsman of Cimon, Thucydides son of Melesias (probably also related to Thucydides the historian). Three chapters in Plutarch's *Life of Pericles* (11, 12 and 14) are the main source for the issues of dispute between the two leaders. These chapters, especially chapter 12, are without doubt dramatically presented, and include much moralizing, rhetoric and anachronisms, but it is reasonable to accept that there is an underlying foundation of fact – the decree of Pericles (mentioned in a commentary on one of Demosthenes' speeches), authorizing the immediate use of 5,000 talents and a further 3,000 talents later on the building programme, and the commencement of the building of the Parthenon in 447, support Plutarch's account chronologically and factually. Although not mentioned by name, Thucydides is clearly the leading protagonist in the accusation against Pericles for his abuse of allied funds:

> They said: 'The Greeks must be insulted by this appalling act of arrogance and consider it to be clear-cut tyranny, when they see us covering our city with gold and beautifying it … with the tribute, taken from them by force, for the war against Persia.'
>
> (Plutarch, *Pericles* 12)

According to the above quotation, the opposition was criticizing Pericles, not about the collection of phoros nor the possession of the Empire

(Cimon had after all been the architect of its creation), but about the immorality of using allied phoros to finance an Athenian building pro-gramme. Pericles' answer to such charges was to stress that the allies paid for protection and, so long as the Athenians fulfilled this obligation, they had every right to use the surplus income for the benefit of Athens:

> 'They only supply money, which does not belong to those who give it, but to those who receive it, provided they supply the services for which they were paid. It is right, after the city has equipped itself sufficiently with the necessary resources for the war, to turn its surplus to public works ... which, inspiring every skill and setting every hand to work, would turn almost the whole city into wage-earners.'
>
> (Plutarch, *Pericles* 12)

Such a moral objection, no matter how genuinely felt, was unlikely to have won much support in the 'Ecclesia', but it may well be that the real under-lying issue was about foreign policy – Thucydides was opposing Pericles' policy of peace with Persia, and his diversion of valuable, financial resources from campaigning against the Persians.

Far more disturbing to Thucydides and his faction than the morality of the building programme and the peace with Persia were Pericles' proposals to use public funds to create economic security for the lower classes:

> Thucydides and his supporters were constantly condemning Pericles for wasting public money and destroying the national revenue.
>
> (Plutarch, *Pericles* 14)

'Misthophoria' (payment for public service) had set a precedent for pro-viding paid employment for the poor, but Pericles' proposals for the use of public funds on a massive scale to create an 'emmisthos polis' (a city of wage-earners) went much further, and was the issue that caused the greatest fear and hostility among the wealthy. The upper classes in general had come to terms with the political consequences of Ephialtes' reforms, in part because their financial and social superiority, reflected in their private benefactions and largesse to the Athenian poor, had encouraged a grateful electorate to give them a monopoly of the top political positions. Cimon was renowned for his personal generosity, offering his land's produce to all, providing daily meals and giving money donations to the poor (Plutarch, *Cimon* 10), and others of his class in the same way used their wealth to advance their political careers. But Pericles' proposals, targeting the resources of the state specifically on the needs of the poor, and removing the opportunities for public works by wealthy citizens, marked a watershed in Athenian public affairs. It is now that the beginning of class division and conflict, culminat-ing in the ideological clash (stasis) between democrats and oligarchs after Pericles' death, is first observed and is reflected in Plutarch:

For there was from the beginning a fatal flaw, as can be found in iron, giving a hint of the differences between the aims of the democratic and the aristocratic parties

(Plutarch, *Pericles* 11)

Plutarch in the above quotation was not describing the creation of two new political parties but the division of Athens on the basis of class and broad attitudes. The term 'demos' (the people) had until now covered the whole body politic, i.e. all those, whether wealthy or poor, who had the right to attend the Ecclesia, pass judgement in the Heliaea and enjoy all the benefits of Athenian citizenship; but now the term acquired political/factional overtones, and was used to describe 'the masses' or 'the common people', especially the poor. In a full 'radical' democracy this huge majority of citizens could impose its legislative will against the wishes of the upper class. This upper class – the propertied class that lived off its wealth without the need to work for a living – began to evolve a more clearly defined political identity and set of values, and to use appropriate language to reflect their superiority, moral and political, over the lower classes. Thus they often referred to themselves as the 'kaloikagathoi' ('the noble and the good', or simply 'gentlemen') as well as using other such terms as the 'beltistoi' or 'aristoi' (the best men) or the 'eugeneis' (the well-born) or the 'gnorimoi' (the notables) or the 'chrestoi' (the useful); by contrast, their contempt for the lower classes is shown in such descriptions as 'ochlos' (the mob) or the 'penetes' (the poor) or 'poneroi' (the worthless) or 'phauloi' (the vulgar) or the 'deiloi' (the cowardly) – the Old Oligarch, writing his right-wing political pamphlet probably in the 420s, fills his work with these terms (Lactor 2). It was this 'mob', using its political muscle in the Ecclesia, which was going to pass Pericles' proposed legislation and thereby assert their political and economic dominance in Athens. The building of the Long Walls had already caused concern, giving the urban lower classes military security but leaving the landed estates of the rich vulnerable to invasion; but economic security, provided by the state and Pericles, would remove the kaloikagathoi's last political advantage – the private funding of public works to gain popularity and thus election to high public office.

Equally worrying to Thucydides was Pericles' central role in this legislation and his ensuing popularity – the tyranny of the Peisistratids in the sixth century (see Chapter 6) was still remembered with fear by the upper classes, as they and their property were most at risk in a coup. Pericles' policies and tactics roused their suspicions about his ultimate intentions:

The aristocrats, seeing that Pericles was already the most important man among the citizens, wanted to set someone up in opposition to him in the city and to blunt his power so that it did not become totally one-man rule.

(Plutarch, *Pericles* 11)

Pericles' opposition to the upper class (although coming from their ranks) and his championing of the needs of the poor had, in their eyes, all the hallmarks of tyranny. The split between the two factions had now become very marked, and in these circumstances there was always a danger that this political division might undermine the stability of the state. But the Athenians possessed an effective method of resolving such political problems, and therefore in 444/3 the primacy of Pericles' policies was confirmed by the ostracism of Thucydides, son of Melesias (Plutarch, *Pericles* 14).

Pericles' career, 444/3–429

It is from the ostracism of Thucydides in 444/3 that we enter upon the period that is often called in modern scholarship 'Periclean Athens', when Pericles and his policies (according to the sources) dominated the political scene at Athens until his death in 429:

> For as long as he had the leadership of the city in peace-time, the city was wisely led and safely guarded, and it was at its greatest under him.
>
> (Thucydides 2.65.5)

Thucydides had the greatest respect for Pericles and considered his leadership, based upon his sterling qualities of intelligence, integrity, incorruptibility and strength of character (Thuc. 2.65.8), to be cast in the traditional aristocratic mould; in Thucydides' opinion, it was Pericles' less well-born and less well-bred successors, adopting methods of 'demagogy' in their ambitious pursuit of the leadership of the people, who brought about the defeat of Athens (Thuc. 2.65.10–13). However, other literary sources strongly disagree with Thucydides' assessment of Pericles:

> Socrates: 'But tell me this: are the Athenians said to have become better because of Pericles or exactly the opposite – to have been corrupted by him? I've heard that Pericles made them lazy, cowardly, talkative and greedy, by being the first to introduce state pay.
>
> (Plato, *Gorgias* 515e)

In Socrates' (or Plato's) view, Pericles was as much a 'demagogue' as his successors, and his leadership was achieved and maintained by manipulating and corrupting the demos (the common people). When Plutarch came to write the *Life of Pericles* in the first to second century AD, he was faced with two conflicting traditions, and he attempted to resolve this dilemma by dividing Pericles' career into two distinctive periods – a 'demagogic' phase until Thucydides' ostracism and a second 'statesman-like' phase until his death.

Such a sharp, dramatic change of leadership style is too simplistic to be accepted, but Plutarch is right to see the dual nature of Pericles' leadership – the factional leader, advocating popular policies to win over the support of the demos, and the loftier, aristocratic statesman, proposing policies for the good of the whole of Athens – and there is an evolution from one to another. Pericles was perhaps the first politician to realize fully the need to take the demos into account, and throughout his political career he never lost sight of the need to win over the demos in the Ecclesia. Certainly his policies and his political style in the earlier part of his career, as he struggled to make a name for himself against other aspiring politicians, could appear 'demagogic':

> Pericles' resources were insufficient for this kind of lavishness [i.e. Cimon's private generosity from his wealth] and so Damonides of Oea advised that ... since he could not compete with regard to his private wealth, he should give to the people their own property; and Pericles introduced state pay for the jurors.
>
> (Aristotle, *Ath. Pol.* 27.4)

In addition, his building programme of the 440s and its underlying motivation, i.e. his belief that it was the state's responsibility to provide full employment for the masses (Plutarch, *Pericles* 12), made him appear to many as a 'philodemos' (demos-lover – see next section). He was just as capable as Cleon of making a grandiose, extravagant gesture before the people. Thucydides had accused him of squandering public money on the building programme, and so Pericles asked the opinion of the people in the Ecclesia. When they replied that he had spent far too much, he replied:

> 'Alright then, don't let it be charged to your account but to mine, and I will have my own name inscribed on the public buildings.'
>
> (Plutarch, *Pericles* 14)

As Pericles' policies and advice over the years proved second to none, his status as a leader grew. His power of oratory, his firm grasp of complex financial and administrative details, his knowledge of Athens' resources and his incorruptibility encouraged the people to give more weight to his views, and so he evolved as the pre-eminent politician of the age with a gravitas to match. However, Thucydides' words about Pericles' dominant position within the state can give a misleading picture of Athenian politics in the 430s (although he does appear here to be commenting more on the quality of effective leadership than the nature of the constitution):

> What appeared to be a democracy was in reality the rule by the leading citizen.
>
> (Thucydides 2.65.9)

Pericles could never take the demos and its decision-making power in the Ecclesia for granted, and he had to convince them every time of the worth of his proposals. There is no better example of this than the debate in the Ecclesia after Sparta's ultimatum in 432, when Pericles had to produce effective arguments against his opponents who were in favour of revoking the Megarian Decree and attempting to find some compromise with the Spartans. His careful and perceptive analysis of Sparta's intentions and his proposals to meet Sparta's demands won the day, but it was no foregone conclusion (Thuc. 1.139.4–145). In the second year of the war, owing to their misfortunes, the Athenians sent an embassy against Pericles' wishes to Sparta to sue for peace (Thuc. 2.59.1–2), and soon after they deposed and fined him (Thuc. 2.65.3). For all his influence and power, Pericles was as accountable to the people as any other public official in the democracy. In addition, the idea that Pericles' leadership faced no opposition after the ostracism of Thucydides in 444/3 does not accord with the evidence of Plutarch and Diodorus.

The opposition to Pericles

Plutarch, in his discussion of the Megarian Decree, states that most writers blamed Pericles for preventing the decree from being revoked (*Pericles* 31). He then gives a summary of the explanations that were put forward for Pericles' motives in opposing the Megarians. However, in the rest of chapter 31 and in chapter 32, he recounts at length the most commonly accepted explanation – that Pericles' political position was so threatened by 'the opposition' attacks on his friends and himself that he deliberately provoked the Peloponnesian War by refusing any concessions over the Megarian Decree in order to save his political career. The friends concerned were Pheidias, Aspasia and Anaxagoras, who were part of Pericles' intellectual circle and had a position of influence with him. The first attack was against Pheidias, the sculptor of the cult statue of Athena for the Parthenon, who was prosecuted on a charge of stealing gold from the statue. The prosecutor was Menon, an artist working with Pheidias, but it is clear that he was acting on behalf of others:

> Some of the people were attempting through him [i.e. Pheidias] to test the mood of the people in a case that involved Pericles.
>
> (Plutarch, *Pericles* 31)

Pericles had foreseen the possibility of such a charge and had ensured that the gold could be removed from the statue for weighing, and thus Pheidias' innocence was proved.

The opposition, however, was undeterred and prosecuted Pheidias for a second time on a charge of impiety – for representing himself and Pericles as Greeks in the battle with the Amazons, depicted on Athena's shield. 'About the same time', in the crucial words of Plutarch (*Pericles* 31), the

328

comic poet Hermippos accused Pericles' mistress, Aspasia, of impiety – although the specific grounds are not clear. Immediately after this Diopeithes brought forward a decree, authorizing the prosecution of all those who did not believe in the gods or taught about the heavens – the purpose of this decree was to damage Pericles through his association with the philosopher Anaxagoras. Finally, Dracontides brought in a decree that Pericles' financial accounts in connection with the building programme should be deposited with the Boule, and that the jurors should pass judgement on Pericles with voting-ballots that had lain on the altar of Athena. Hagnon, a political ally of Pericles, persuaded the people to remove this religious element and to try the case in the ordinary, secular manner. Pericles allegedly managed to save Aspasia by an untypical display of emotion and a personal appeal in court, but he had to smuggle Anaxagoras out of the city, and:

> As he had already upset the people through Pheidias and was afraid of his own trial, he set ablaze the war that was threatening and smouldering, hoping to cast off the charges against himself and discourage the jealousy, since in the midst of great danger the city would entrust itself to him alone on account of his great reputation and power.
>
> (Plutarch, *Pericles* 32)

Diodorus has a very similar account to Plutarch's, with the variation that Pericles' case was about the misuse of imperial funds and Aspasia is not mentioned (Diodorus 12.38–39), but clearly both writers are using a common source.

Plutarch informs us that these attacks on Aspasia, Anaxagoras and Pericles happened 'about the same time' as the prosecution of Pheidias for impiety, and that Pheidias' case was directly linked with the Megarian Decree in 432 – hence the commonly believed accusation that Pericles opposed the repeal of the decree to save his political skin. Although there is some confusion about the details in each of the cases, it is generally accepted that these attacks did take place, and their chief objective was to discredit Pericles and remove him from the leadership of the people. The key question is: who was behind these attacks? If the link between the attacks and the Megarian Decree is accepted, then it has been suggested that Thucydides, son of Melesias, had renewed his opposition to Pericles in an attempt to avoid war with Sparta, since he would have returned from ostracism in 434/3. However, there is very convincing evidence that the dating of these attacks on Pericles and his friends should be placed in 438/7, and that there is no connection between the attacks and the Megarian Decree.

The main point of reference is the attack on Pheidias, as all the others are 'about the same time'. It is here that the evidence of Philochorus, a much-respected Atthidographer (fourth-century writers of Athenian histories), is crucial – he states that Pheidias' prosecution took place in 438/7 and that

Pheidias fled to Elis where he worked on the statue of Zeus (FGrH 328 F121). As Athena's statue was dedicated in 438/7, this would be the logical and most opportune time to launch a prosecution for embezzlement, and when that failed, for impiety against Pheidias. Philochorus' evidence, combined with Plutarch's, demands that the other attacks took place at about the same time, and there is strong circumstantial evidence to support this view. The investigation of Pericles' accounts, authorized by the decree of Dracontides, must refer to his position as one of the board of supervisors of Athena's statue, and as Pheidias' immediate superior. This was a concerted attack on both Pheidias and Pericles, and their handling of the financial accounts of the statue, which would explain the religious dimension of Dracontides' decree concerning the sanctified voting-tablets, since the case involved theft of sacred materials. Aspasia's prosecution is also appropriate in 438/7, one year after the suppression of the revolt of Samos. Aspasia came from Miletus, whose dispute with Samos over the possession of Priene had drawn in the Athenians that led to Samos' revolt in 440. The campaign proved to be difficult and the Athenians had to endure heavy casualties before Samos was defeated (Thuc. 1.115.2–117.3; AE64 pp. 39–40). It was widely believed that Aspasia had persuaded Pericles to intercede on behalf of Miletus, and thus her unpopularity in Athens in the immediate aftermath of the war would have been at its greatest, leaving her vulnerable to a political prosecution.

If 438/7 is accepted for the date of these attacks, then Thucydides, son of Melesias, must be discounted as Pericles' opponent since he was still ostracized. In addition, the nature of the attacks – anti-intellectual and protective of traditional religion through prosecutions on the grounds of impiety – would also suggest a different source for the opposition to Pericles than the kaloikagathoi. This direct appeal to the ultra-conservative views on traditional religion of the demos (Ephialtes in his reforms had virtually left the religious powers of the 'Areopagus' untouched, as he did not wish to alienate the demos and lose his chance to remove the Areopagus' secular powers) is much more in keeping with the style of the new politicians, the so-called 'demagogues' (see next section), emerging in the 430s. The rise, the methods and the influence of this new type of politician are the main theme of Aristophanes' *Knights*, and he particularly concentrates on 'the leather-seller' Cleon, who came to prominence in the first year of the war and who dominated Athenian politics in the 420s after Pericles' death. However, Aristophanes (*Knights* 128ff.) mentions two predecessors of Cleon – 'the oakum-seller' Eucrates and 'the sheep-seller' Lysicles who must have been politically active in the 430s, as Cleon must have been, if we are to discount a sudden, meteoric rise to fame in 431. Their opposition may have been based on Pericles' cautious (in their estimation) policy with regard to the allies and the Spartans, or their dislike of Pericles' aristocratic circle of friends, who formed 'The Establishment' and occupied the most important offices of state, or just personal ambition to replace him as the 'prostates tou demou' (leader of the people), or a combination of all three. One or more of them may be the shadowy figures, who encouraged Menon to accuse Pheidias in order to test Pericles' popularity; also the comic poet Hermippos, who prosecuted Aspasia for impiety, is found at the beginning of the war criticizing the cowardice of Pericles and supporting Cleon (Plutarch, *Pericles* 33); and oracle-mongering, as practised by Diopeithes and the author of the decree against Anaxagoras, was used on many occasions by the demagogues (Aristophanes, *Knights* 997ff.).

It would seem that Pericles' leadership emerged relatively unscathed from these attacks in 438/7, for Hagnon, his political associate, was appointed to found the vitally important colony of Amphipolis c.436 – a very prestigious appointment, reflecting the dominant influence of Pericles' faction. Thucydides the historian, even allowing for his pro-Periclean sentiments, stresses Pericles' pre-eminence in the conduct of Athenian affairs leading up to the outbreak of the war, evidence of which is reflected in the Athenians' acceptance of his advice concerning Sparta's ultimatum (Thuc. 1.145). Even after his deposition and fining in 430, possibly masterminded by Cleon:

> Not much later, as a crowd a mob habitually does, they elected him again as general, and entrusted the whole conduct of affairs to him.
>
> (Thucydides 2.65.4)

His death in 429 marked the end of an exceptional period of leadership in Athenian history, and it is likely that in the following years the inability of any one politician to achieve such a sustained dominance in the Ecclesia was a return to a more normal state of political affairs.

Finally there remains one last question: what was the original source for the charge, which had gained such widespread acceptance among later generations, that Pericles 'set ablaze the war that was threatening and smouldering' because of Pheidias' conviction and his fear for himself? Thucydides' evidence marked Pericles out as the main opponent of revoking the decree; and the source for the damning tradition against Pericles comes almost certainly from the comic poets, especially Aristophanes. The Peace of Nicias, which was signed in 421 and brought the Archidamian War to an end (see Chapter 19), had been agreed in principle when Aristophanes staged his *Peace* in spring of that year. It is in the dialogue between Hermes, the Chorus and the hero Trygaeus that a comic explanation of the cause of the war is introduced:

> Chorus: 'But where has Peace been hiding from us for such a long time? Tell us this, most kindly of the gods.'
> Hermes: 'Most wise farmers, listen to my words if you wish to hear why she departed. Pheidias, by his wrongdoing, first began the trouble. Then Pericles, being afraid

of sharing his fate and dreading your character and your ferocious temper, before he himself suffered something terrible, set the city ablaze by throwing in a spark called the Megarian Decree.'

(Aristophanes, *Peace* 601–9)

There was nothing new in 421 about the Megarian Decree and Pericles' opposition to it being an immediate cause of the war, but the specific connection with Pheidias and his prosecution does appear to have been Aristophanes' invention:

Trygaeus: 'By Apollo, I have never heard of these things from anybody, nor that Pheidias had any connection with Peace.'
Chorus: 'Nor did I until just now. That is why she (Peace) is so beautiful, because she is his relation. How many things escape our notice.'

(Aristophanes, *Peace* 615–18)

Even the imagery of fire, which is so distinctive in Aristophanes' play, has been maintained in the tradition that Plutarch recorded five to six hundred years later – a testament to the fact that a scurrilous story about a famous person is often more interesting and worth recalling than the sober truth.

The demagogues

In the 430s and especially after Pericles' death, Athens saw the rise of a new type of politician, often referred to as 'demagogues' by hostile literary sources. Their non-aristocratic background and their political methods marked them out as different from their predecessors. Traditionally, ambitious men had gained positions of political importance by the support of their philoi (friends); by judicious marriage to the daughters of other powerful political families; by military and public service, usually holding the post of 'strategos' (general); and by forming coalitions with like-minded aristocrats and their factions. Such men had the leisure, the wealth and, most of all, the organization to wield a political influence that was disproportionate to their actual numbers. The demos (the sense of being identified politically with the common people/the penetes (the poor) is to be assumed in the rest of this section), were too disparate and too disorganized to translate their superior numbers into dominance of the Ecclesia, except in exceptional circumstances when a major issue caught their attention. Otherwise, in the more routine but still important matters of state, they tended to be influenced by leaders of the organized aristocratic factions. It was the new politicians, who saw the potential of the demos and forged them into a more potent political force. Their opportunity came in the second half of the fifth century with the dramatic increase in imperial demands placed upon the Athenians, the growing confidence of the demos in the Ecclesia and

Heliaea, and the possibilities offered by 'isegoria' (equal right to speak) in shaping state policy.

The Athenians faced a formidable task in exercising control over a growing empire with its attendant responsibilities but using the political structure of a small city-state. The use of lot for the majority of offices, the limitation on tenure of office and the collegiate principle (i.e. having more than one colleague in public office with equal authority) were useful for protecting the democracy at home from its political enemies, but were unsuitable for administering a powerful empire. There was a need for some politically active citizens to provide leadership, and this was satisfied by the 'demagogues' (literally, leaders of the people) or 'prostatai tou demou' (champions of the demos). When these new leaders, some of whom had acquired their wealth from business and not only from agriculture, made direct appeals to the demos in the Ecclesia and proposed policies to their benefit (i.e. of the demos), the kaloikagathoi or 'best people' strongly disapproved, and thus the term 'demagogue' gradually acquired its derogatory meaning as a leader of the democratic faction.

The new politicians gained their position of political influence by possessing certain skills and by winning over the mass allegiance of the demos. The fundamental skill was to be an effective orator in the Ecclesia, able to put one's views with clarity and vigour, and to ward off an opponent's attacks and discredit his arguments – the term 'rhetor', meaning literally 'he who speaks', came to mean politician in the late fifth century. They had to possess a mastery of finance and administration so that they could impress the demos, who had neither the time nor the commitment to master such complex details, but who needed this information to make their decisions. In addition, the new politicians needed to have a good grasp of foreign affairs, especially knowledge of the Empire, which was supplied by their 'xenoi' (friends) in the allied cities. It was to these 'rhetores', and not to the public officials, that the demos usually looked for expert advice. However, it was the methods employed by these new politicians to gain the allegiance of the demos that provoked the greatest hostility and disdain from the kaloikagathoi and their likeminded supporters, such as Aristophanes and Thucydides. Their opposition to and prejudice against these so-called demagogues can best be seen in the career of Cleon.

Cleon seems to have inherited his wealth from his father, who had taken advantage of the wealth-making opportunities offered by the Empire and had made his money from the tanning business. This gave him the leisure to involve himself full time in the affairs of state and to acquire that mastery of detail, especially financial, that appealed to the demos. He is rightly seen as the force behind Thoudippos' Decree of 425 (ML 69; AE138 pp. 66–67), which trebled the contributions of the allies to pay for the increasing costs of waging war. He also proved later in his career to be a competent military commander by his defeat of the Spartans on Sphacteria in 425 (Thuc. 4.29–40).

If he had chosen to pursue his career in the traditional manner of the kaloikagathoi (as Nicias did, although coming from a non-aristocratic background), the literary sources may well have given him the praise that his ability warranted; but he firmly rejected, even despised, that approach to politics with its inbuilt hierarchy, conventions and its constant compromises. Plutarch (*Rules for Politicians* 806f) states that he repudiated his friends on the grounds that they could compromise his integrity in his pursuit of the right and just policy for Athens. By doing this, Cleon was turning his back on traditional philia (political friendship) to advance his political career, was giving his devotion and friendship to the demos, and aimed to become their spokesman, their protector ('prostates'). Cleon and his successors saw that it was possible to gain political power by appealing directly to the demos in the Ecclesia without the need to cultivate old-style 'friendships', form coalitions or hold public office. The allegiance of the demos became far more important for political success than the support of a narrow circle of influential men.

The development of language in a political context is useful in understanding this new approach to politics. The main source is Aristophanes, and, because he was a comic playwright and probably a personal enemy of Cleon, it is necessary to use his evidence with caution. However, even in his caricature of Cleon, who is clearly the model for Paphlagon, the servant of the old man Demos in the *Knights*, there has to be a modicum of truth to make the caricature effective. There is a recurring theme, which runs through the whole play, of Paphlagon continually expressing his loyalty and devotion to Demos in very exaggerated language:

> Demos: 'Who, Paphlagon, is harming you?'
> Paphlagon: 'I am being beaten by this man and these young men because of you.'
> Demos: 'Why?'
> Paphlagon: 'Because I love you, Demos, and I am your lover.'
>
> (Aristophanes, *Knights* 730–32)

This imagery is reinforced by the statement of the Sausage-Seller, who is Paphlagon's rival for Demos' affections:

> Whenever someone said in the Ecclesia 'I am your lover, Demos, and I love you, and I cherish you and I alone deliberate for you.'
>
> (Aristophanes, *Knights* 1340–41)

The language and ideas of aristocratic philia (friendship) have been adapted to describe the relationship with the demos, stressing that in a politician such loyalty and affection is only acceptable when directed towards the city and not to one's friends. In the same play, performed in 424, there is also in line 787 the first recorded use of the word 'philodemos' (demos-lover).

Older than this word, but parallel in its adaptation to political usage is 'philopolis' (city-lover):

> Pericles: 'And yet you are angry with a man such as me, who I think am inferior to no one in my knowledge of what is necessary and in explaining it, being a lover of the city (philopolis) and above money.'
>
> (Thucydides 2.60.5)

Loyalty to and love of the city ('polis') and the demos, and not one's circle of friends, becomes the most admirable trait in a politician and brings success in politics. As these words became common currency in the language of politics, so did their antonyms – 'misodemos' (demos-hater) and 'misopolis' (city-hater). Thus it can be deduced that politics had become far more divisive, confrontational and vicious – political opponents were now enemies of the state, constantly suspected of treason, conspiracy and tyranny.

It was probably this tough and aggressive approach to politics that led many of the kaloikagathoi to withdraw from public life who might have limited the effectiveness of these new politicians and the success of their policies, which in turn provoked Thucydides and Aristophanes to portray Cleon and the demagogues in such a lurid and derogatory manner. Thucydides had the greatest admiration for Pericles and viewed him as a politician of the old school:

> Pericles held power because through his reputation, intelligence and incorruptibility he could restrain the people while respecting their liberties.
>
> (Thucydides 2.65.8)

His description of Cleon before his speech, advocating the retention of the death penalty for all the Mytileneans in 427, could not be in starker contrast:

> He was the most violent of the citizens in every respect and at that time was the most influential among the people.
>
> (Thucydides 3.36.6)

These two politicians, epitomizing the old and the new, could not be more different in the eyes of Thucydides. It is a measure of the prejudice against and distortion of Cleon 'the demagogue' in the literary sources that when his policies, and not his style, are considered – belief in the necessity of Empire, a firm policy towards the allies, a refusal to accede to the demands of the Spartans, and genuine concern for the welfare of the demos, reflected in pay for public service and improving their standard of living – they bear a remarkable similarity to those of Pericles. In this respect at least, the Old Oligarch was not fooled by Pericles' aristocratic background or bearing – he knew a 'demagogue' when he saw one:

335

But anyone who is not one of the common people and yet chooses to live in a city governed by a democracy rather than one governed by an oligarchy, must be preparing to do wrong and have decided that a bad man can escape detection far more easily in a democratic than in an oligarchic city.

(Old Oligarch 2.20; OO p. 25)

Thus there was a change in the nature of politics in the last third of the fifth century. The dominance of the old style of politics, based on a complex web of friendships, was being superseded by a new style, which was based upon direct appeals to the demos and the forging of them into the most powerful political force in Athens. The new politician's statements of devotion to the city and the demos stressed that the clear-cut, moral duty of all politicians should be to the state and not to one's circle of friends. They also believed that all the incompetence of the upper class involved in public service should be ruthlessly exposed and punished. The kaloikagathoi intensely disliked this new style of politics and reacted in one of two ways. Some withdrew from public life, but others decided to make their philia tougher in its methods and far more political. As a result these 'friendships', which previously had been open to view and also performed social functions, became 'hetaireiai' (political clubs) that met in secret and plotted the overthrow of the democracy. Thus the stage was set for the constitutional upheavals at the end of the century (see Chapter 23).

Bibliography

Andrewes, A. 'The opposition to Pericles', *JHS* 98 (1978).

Connor, W. R. *The New Politicians of Fifth-Century Athens.*

Finley, M. I. 'The Athenian demagogues', *Past and Present* (1962), reprinted in *Democracy Ancient and Modern*, 2nd edn.

Frost, F. J. 'Pericles and Dracontides', *JHS* 84 (1964).

——'Pericles, Thucydides, son of Melesias, and Athenian politics before the war', *Historia* 13 (1964).

Gomme, A. W., Andrewes, A. and Dover, K. J. *A Historical Commentary on Thucydides*, vol. 5, sections 89–98.

Kagan, D. *The Outbreak of the Peloponnesian War*, chs 6 and 8.

Meiggs, R. *The Athenian Empire*, ch. 9.

Rhodes, P. J. *A Commentary on the Aristotelian 'Athenaion Politeia'.*

Sinclair, R. K. *Democracy and Participation in Athens*, chs 2.3 and 6.1–7.

Wade-Gery, H. T. 'Thucydides the son of Melesias', *Essays in Greek History.*

19

ATHENIAN AND SPARTAN STRATEGY IN THE ARCHIDAMIAN WAR, 431–421

There are three possible outcomes in war: victory, defeat or stalemate, but even a stalemate can be construed as a moral victory or defeat, depending upon the war aims of the combatants. Pericles realized that the Athenians had little chance of winning a decisive war in the conventional manner, i.e. an invasion of the Peloponnese and the destruction of Sparta, since the Athenian army would be destroyed by the superior forces of the Peloponnesian League:

> The Peloponnesians and their allies have the power to stand up to all the Greeks in a single battle.
>
> (Thucydides 1.141.6)

Therefore Pericles' war aim was shaped by this knowledge, which he expressed in his final speech before the outbreak of war:

> 'I have many other reasons for believing that we will win through (periesesthai).'
>
> (Thucydides 1.144.1)

The Greek word 'periesesthai' is used in two other places by Thucydides to describe Pericles' war aim (2.13.9; 2.65.7 – all references in this chapter are to Thucydides, unless otherwise stated), but there is an ambiguity about its meaning. It can be translated as 'to be superior to' or 'to survive', and for that reason 'to win through' is an effective translation. Sparta's war aim was to destroy the Athenian Empire and thus, if the Athenians could survive their attacks and retain possession of their Empire, a stalemate would ensue. However, Pericles would view this as a victory for the Athenians, whereas the failure and the consequent loss of face by the Spartans would be judged as a defeat, especially if the Spartans could be made to seem the aggressors (7.18).

Athenian strategy

With these considerations in mind, Pericles devised a defensive strategy to ensure Athens' survival:

Pericles gave the same advice as before that they should prepare for the war and bring in their property from the fields; that they should avoid battle with the enemy but come inside the city and guard it; that they should ensure the efficiency of the fleet, on which their strength depended, and should keep a firm control of the allies, saying that their power was derived from the allies' contributions of money.

(Thucydides 2.13.2)

Thucydides repeats with approval, in his obituary of Pericles and his summary of the course of the Peloponnesian War (2.65), the key elements of Pericles' defensive strategy:

For Pericles said that they would win through (periesesthai), if they pursued a defensive policy, took care of the fleet, did not extend their empire during the war and did not expose the city to danger.

(Thucydides 2.65.7)

However, there were also some important offensive elements in his strategy – attacks on the Peloponnesian fleets, whenever an opportunity presented itself; retaliatory raids against enemy territory by sea-borne forces, provided that no excessive risk was involved and that there was an easy means of escape by sea; and an annual devastation of the Megarid with large land forces, after the Peloponnesians had returned home from their invasion of Attica. This offensive part of Pericles' strategy reflected Spartan strategy, and presumably, apart from boosting Athenian morale after the destruction of Attica, was designed to emphasize Athens' lack of provocative aggression by merely responding in kind to Sparta's actions. It is not clear whether Pericles' strategy also included the building and occupation of forts in enemy territory ('epiteichismos'). Pericles does refer to this as a possible course of action, but only if the Peloponnesians should attempt it first (1.142.2–5).

This policy of epiteichismos was first put into operation in 427 (two years after Pericles' death) at Minoa opposite Megara and even more effectively at Pylos in 425, and it appears from the evidence that the years 427–424 marked a departure from the strategy advocated by Pericles. In these years Demosthenes, Cleon and other influential Athenians carried out a more ambitious offensive strategy, aiming to win the war decisively by campaigning more widely and aggressively against the Spartans and their allies, rather than waiting for the gradual evolution of a stalemate by sticking rigidly to Periclean strategy. Thucydides, in fact, is very critical of the strategy adopted by the democratic leaders who succeeded Pericles, accusing them of doing the exact opposite (2.65.7). There were undoubtedly some changes to Pericles' defensive strategy in the Archidamian War, but to speak of a complete reversal of policy is not supported by his own account of these years – it is very likely that his view in this passage was shaped by the disastrous Sicilian expedition of 415 (see Chapter 21). If Thucydides had reported (in the same extensive manner as his treatment of Pericles' strategy) the debates in the 'Ecclesia' wherein decisions about Athenian strategy would have been thrashed out, the issues of whether the strategy was changed and by whom would now be much easier to resolve. However, in the final years of the Archidamian War (424–421), there was a return to Pericles' defensive strategy owing to the Athenian failure to capture Megara, a major defeat in a 'hoplite' battle at Delium in Boeotia and the successes of the Spartan Brasidas among Athens' subjects in Thrace.

Pericles also stressed the vital importance of finance as a means of success in the coming war (2.13.2–5). This was directly linked with his strategy of keeping a firm hold upon the allies, who in 431 were providing an annual income of about 600 talents; there was also a reserve of over 6,000 talents. The Athenians also put aside 1,000 talents as a special reserve fund, which was only to be used if the city needed defending from an enemy attack by sea; in addition, the hundred best 'triremes' of each year were to be put aside for the same purpose (2.24). It is in the area of finance that Pericles can be criticized for his failure to foresee that Athens' income would be insufficient for fighting a long drawn-out defensive war. The campaign against Samos in 440/39 had cost in the region of 1,200 talents (Diodorus 28.3), and the eventual cost of the siege of Potidaea was 2,000 talents (2.70.2). Expenditure at this level would quickly drain the Athenian reserve. It was left to his successors to attempt to resolve this problem: the Thoudippos Decree, passed in 425/4, raised the allied 'phoros' payments to 1,460–1,500 talents (ML 69; AE138 pp. 66–67).

Spartan strategy

The Spartans' war aim was simply expressed and allegedly won great popularity in the Greek world:

> The good-will of men was for the most part directed towards the Spartans, especially because they declared that they would free Greece.
>
> (Thucydides 2.8.4)

The liberation of Greece could only be achieved by the destruction of the Athenian Empire (1.118.2), and this required total victory. In this way the Spartans would also remedy some of their allies' specific grievances, and protect their hegemony of the Peloponnesian League by persuading such states as Corinth to stay loyal to the League. Therefore the Spartans' strategy had to be primarily offensive in order to achieve their war aims. The cornerstone of Spartan strategy was a land invasion of Attica, which they carried out most years from 431 to 425 – there was no invasion in 429, probably through fear of the plague (2.57.1), nor in 426 when frequent earthquakes were taken as bad omens (3.89.1). These invasions would either provoke the Athenians to fight a hoplite battle in order to protect their crops, which would lead to their inevitable defeat, or destroy the crops of the Athenians, who would be starved into submission.

This 'conventional' strategy of invading an enemy's homeland with a hoplite army had been very effective in the past 250 years, and had been spectacularly successful in 446/5 when the Spartans forced the Athenians into making substantial concessions (see end of Chapter 15). Thus the Spartans believed that they could easily destroy Athenian power within a few years by ravaging their land (5.14); and this view was shared by the rest of the Greeks who believed that the Athenians might hold out for one or two years, but certainly not more than three (7.28). Even King Archidamus (see Chapter 17), who was very critical of this strategy and doubted its effectiveness to defeat the Athenians, was apparently won over to its possible success by his decision in the 431 invasion to encamp in and devastate Acharnae, the biggest 'deme' (see Glossary) seven miles from Athens. He felt confident that the combination of the young men's anger at the destruction of Attica and the pressure from the influential Acharnians who supplied 3,000 hoplites would force Pericles to risk a pitched battle (2.20). Archidamus' analysis of Athenian public opinion was correct, but he seriously underestimated Pericles' determination to maintain his strategy (2.21–22). The Spartans' biggest misjudgement in this war was their failure to realize the Athenians' ability to cause extensive damage to the Peloponnesian coastal cities by sea-borne raids.

There was also an alternative 'adventurous' strategy that was outlined by the Corinthians in 432:

'There exist for us other ways of waging war – by encouraging their allies to revolt, especially as this would deprive them of their income on which their strength depends, and the planting of forts in their territory.'

(Thucydides 1.122.1)

This meant that the Spartans had to become a naval power and be willing to fight further afield in order to support the allies in their revolt from Athens. This strategy, although it was implemented at times in the early years of the 420s, was not well supported for a number of reasons – first, it required the acquisition of the necessary finance to build a fleet and pay the crews, and only Persia could supply finance on this scale, but the price for this help would be the re-imposition of Persian control over the Asiatic Greeks; second, there was the difficulty of recruiting sailors from the Athenian Empire in time of war; and third, the Spartans were always very reluctant to commit their hoplites in far off places. The combination of the fear of the Athenian navy and the belief that it was only a matter of time before the Athenians surrendered ensured that the 'conventional' strategy predominated from 431 to 425. It was the shattering defeat at Pylos in 425 and the capture of 120 Spartiates (see next section) that tipped the balance. The inability to launch land invasions of Attica forced the Spartans to give more weight to the 'adventurous' policy, and from 424 to 422 Brasidas and his 'Helot' hoplites did much damage to the Athenians by his campaigns in the Thraceward region. However, there was a constant tension between those like Brasidas who saw these campaigns as implementing Sparta's stated war aim of liberating the Greeks (2.8.4), and the Spartan authorities who saw them as a means of putting pressure on the Athenians to make peace, and thus regain the 120 Spartiates held captive in Athens. In the end, the latter prevailed.

431–428

The outbreak of hostilities began with the attempt of Thebes, an ally of Sparta, to seize control of Plataea, an Athenian ally in Boeotia (2.1–8). The Peloponnesian forces then came together at the Isthmus under the command of King Archidamus and invaded Attica (2.10–23). The Athenians had prepared for this, in accordance with Pericles' strategy, by moving their sheep and cattle to the island of Euboea for safekeeping, and by bringing their families within the city, the Piraeus and the Long Walls for safety. The Athenians for their part sent 100 ships to conduct sea-borne raids on the coast of the Peloponnese – the offensive element in Pericles' strategy. This naval force then carried on and captured the Corinthian port of Sollium opposite the island of Leucas and handed it over to their allies, the Acarnanians; took Astacus on the Corinthian Gulf by storm and brought it into their alliance; and finally, won over the island of Cephallenia without resorting to armed conflict (2.30). These successes in north-west Greece were part of Pericles' strategy and were designed to give the Athenians the ability to hit the whole of the Peloponnesian coast with ease. It was in this context that the Athenians had earlier sent embassies to Corcyra, Acarnania, Zacynthos and Cephallenia:

> realizing that, if they were sure of their friendships with them, they could make war around the Peloponnese.
>
> (Thucydides 2.7.3)

The Athenians also expelled the Aeginetans in the same year and colonized the island themselves (2.27). However, this acquisition of territory was not in conflict with Periclean strategy, since its main purpose was defensive – gaining a greater control of the Saronic Gulf on which the Piraeus was situated and through which all their necessary imports (including grain) sailed. In the autumn of 431 Pericles led the whole Athenian army, including the 'metics', into the Megarid and, together with the fleet of 100 ships that had just returned from north-west Greece, laid waste the land – part of his parallel strategy of responding in kind to the Spartans' invasion and devastation of Attica (2.31). No attempt was made to capture Megara, as this would have involved extending the Empire and the use of manpower in holding down unwilling subjects. These Athenian invasions and devastations of the Megarid – the stretch of land between the two gulfs under Megarian control – were conducted annually until the capture of Nisaea, Megara's port on the Saronic Gulf, in 424.

The event that dominated 430 was the outbreak of the plague in Athens (2.47–55), which continued in 429 and broke out again in 426. It may have killed as many as one-third of the Athenian population, and created such despair that the Athenians, against Pericles' wishes, attempted to make peace with the Spartans, but the negotiations came to nothing (2.59). The Spartans had again invaded, but this time they stayed for 40 days (their longest stay) and were much more thorough in their devastation of Attica (2.47; 2.57). The Spartans, ever watchful to take advantage of Athenian weakness, showed enterprise by sending 100 ships to remove Zacynthos (lying opposite Elis) from its alliance with Athens – clearly Athenian success in north-west Greece and their policy of sea-borne raids were a source of fear for the Spartans. They laid waste most of the country, but could not force the Zacynthians to change sides (2.66). Pericles chose to concentrate on the east coast of the Peloponnese in 430 and conducted the campaign in person with 100 Athenian ships and 50 ships from Chios and Lesbos.

The first target was Epidaurus on the north coast of the Argolis where they laid waste the land and made an assault on the city, which was almost captured. Thucydides does not explain the reasoning behind this attempt to gain control of the city. If it was Pericles' intention to fortify it with Athenians, then this was a break with his own strategy, as Epidaurus was a large and important city, which would require considerable manpower to ensure its continued loyalty to Athens. It seems less likely that Pericles had intended this, particularly as the plague was raging in Athens. The main benefit of possessing Epidaurus was to establish short, safe communications between the Athenians and the Argives (5.53), but this only became relevant after 421 when the thirty-year peace between Argos and Sparta came to an end. If the Athenians had captured Epidaurus, it is likely that they would have sacked it in the same manner as Prasiae in eastern Laconia, after they had devastated the land of Troezen, Halieis and Hermione on the same expedition (2.56).

After the Athenians' naval forces returned from the Peloponnese, they were taken at once to Chalcidice in order to finish off the siege of Potidaea and the whole revolt in that area (2.58). This was consistent with Periclean strategy of keeping a firm hold on the allies and maintaining the flow of phoros – Chalcidice contributed about 7 per cent of Athens' income from the allies. Later in the year the Athenians sent Phormio with 20 ships to blockade the Gulf of Corinth, and thus put pressure on Sparta's leading ally (2.69). The Athenians also received the good news of the surrender of Potidaea, and thus hopes were raised of ending the revolt in Chalcidice (2.70).

In 429, the Spartans did not conduct an invasion of Attica but set about the capture by siege of Plataea (it fell in 427), probably at the insistence of their Boeotian allies and out of fear of the plague (2.71–78). The Athenians made no effort to relieve Plataea, as this would have involved a pitched battle with the Peloponnesians. However, their plans to subdue the revolt of Chalcidice came unstuck when an Athenian army of 2,000 hoplites was defeated at Spartolus with casualties of 430 (2.79). The continuing plague provided the opportunity for the Spartans to undermine Athenian control of north-west Greece. They were encouraged in this by the Ambraciots, who claimed that a Spartan joint naval and land operation against Acarnania would result in its fall and that of Zacynthos and Cephallenia; in addition, the Athenians would find it very difficult to send their fleets around the Peloponnese to attack coastal cities, and Naupactus, which occupied such an important strategic position in the Corinthian Gulf, had every chance of being captured (2.80). However, the Acarnanians defeated the land forces at Stratus which is situated close to Acarnanian–Aetolian border, and the delayed Peloponnesian fleet of 47 ships was spectacularly defeated at Naupactus by Phormio's 20 ships (2.81–84).

The campaigns of 428 appeared at the outset to be a repeat of 430: an invasion of Attica by Archidamus and a planned sailing round the Peloponnese by the Athenians. However, the news that Mytilene was attempting to take control of the island of Lesbos and revolt from Athens resulted in the Athenians despatching their fleet against Mytilene. The Mytileneans asked Sparta for help by organizing a second invasion of Attica and by sending a relief naval force to Lesbos. In the event, the second invasion failed to materialize owing to the reluctance of the Peloponnesians to forgo the harvesting of their own crops, upon which they depended. Thus the Mytileneans had to rely upon the Spartan fleet of 40 ships under the command of Alcidas, which proved eventually to be of little use owing to Alcidas' timidity (3.1–18).

427–424

Pericles' strategy had been mainly a defensive one, and in the immediate aftermath of his death in 429 his chosen strategy was maintained. However, in this period of the war there were some marked changes in strategy, initiated and executed by those Athenians who had become impatient with Pericles' limited aims and tactics; they wished to pursue a more aggressive policy, designed to strengthen Athens' offensive capability, to cause more damage to the Spartans and their allies, and thereby to win the war decisively.

It is mainly, but not exclusively, the Athenian campaigns in Sicily against Syracuse, in central Greece against Aetolia and Boeotia, and in the Peloponnese at Pylos and Cythera that reveal the success of those politicians and generals, who favoured this offensive strategy, in persuading the Athenians to accept and vote for a change in strategy.

In 427, Mytilene surrendered to the Athenians, after Alcidas' fleet from Sparta failed to arrive. More than ever this had been the moment when the Spartans had an excellent chance of trying out the effectiveness of a strategy long considered: to attack Athens while a major ally was in revolt. An earthquake and a Helot revolt in 465 at the time of Thasos' revolt and the Peloponnesians' refusal in 440 at the time of Samos' revolt had prevented its execution, but now a Spartan army was ravaging Attica, Lesbos (one of the two remaining ship-suppliers) was in revolt and, furthermore, there was for the first time a Spartan fleet of 40 ships in the eastern Aegean. However, Alcidas' timidity let down the Mytileneans, and these fine hopes of putting Athens under intense pressure came to nothing (3.25–35). The same reluctance of the Spartans to seize their opportunities was reflected in the civil war on Corcyra in the same year – once again the opportunity fell to Alcidas, who had the chance to remove Corcyra from the Athenian side, but, after an initial success against the Corcyraean navy, fled on hearing the news that Eurymedon was coming with 60 Athenian ships (3.69–81). The most imaginative move on the part of the Spartans was the foundation of the colony of Heraclea in Trachis in central Greece in 426:

> The foundation of the city seemed especially good to them for carrying on the war against the Athenians; for a fleet could be prepared to attack Euboea which was a short distance away, and it would be useful on the route to Thrace.
>
> (Thucydides 3.92.4)

There were clearly influential men at Sparta, who were also prepared to think more imaginatively about the conduct of the war, and perhaps the foundations of Brasidas' Thraceward campaign of 424–422 were being laid here.

The first change from the Periclean defensive strategy was in 427 when they responded to an appeal for help from their Sicilian ally, Leontini, which was being blockaded by Syracuse (a Corinthian colony), by sending out 20 ships. The official reason was given as a desire to help their kinsmen, but the real aims were to prevent the import of grain from there into the Peloponnese, and to make a preliminary survey as to the feasibility of the conquest of Sicily (3.86). Although there is a strong case that the first real aim was in tune with Pericles' defensive policy (see Chapter 21 for a full discussion of Athens and Sicily 427–424), the fact that 20 ships were sent with a view to exploring the possibility of future conquest was against the basic tenets of Pericles' strategy of not extending the Empire in war nor exposing the city needlessly to danger (2.65.7). In the winter of 426/5, this naval force in Sicily was increased by 40 ships – a few immediately under Pythodorus, and the rest in the spring under Sophocles and Eurymedon (3.115.5). The professed aim of wanting to end the war there more quickly (3.115.4) once again covered over the conflicting aims of those Athenians who wished to pressurize Syracuse into peace and bring back the fleet as quickly as possible for the defensive war in Greece, and those Athenians who planned the conquest of Sicily. By the time of the Congress of Gela in 424, which brought an end to the conflict in Sicily and the return of the Athenian fleet, Athenian public opinion had decisively turned in favour of conquest even while at war with Sparta, and their belief that Sicily could have been conquered resulted in the banishment of Pythodorus and Sophocles, and the fining of Eurymedon (4.65).

The second geographical area where the Athenians were pursuing a non-Periclean strategy was in central Greece. In 426 Nicias, after his failed attempt to subdue the island of Melos, landed his 2,000 hoplites at Oropus and marched them to Tanagra in Boeotia where they joined up with the whole Athenian army as pre-arranged. They fought a successful land battle against a combined force of Tanagraeans and Thebans, and then returned to Athens (3.91). The policy of avoiding land battles against the enemy had clearly been set aside, but it is the ultimate aim of this and future campaigns in this region that reveals a major break with Periclean strategy and a return to the policies of the First Peloponnesian War. The conquest of Boeotia and the revival of the 'Land Empire' (see Chapter 15) was now back on the military agenda. Soon after the battle of Tanagra, Demosthenes, who had been sent out with 30 ships to capture the island of Leucas with the help of Athenian allies in that area, decided to attack Aetolia:

> thinking in particular that he could, with the help of the Aetolians added to the mainland allies but without using the Athenians, make a land attack against Boeotia. He would go through the territory of the Ozolian Locrians to Cytinium in Doris, keeping Parnassus to the right, until he came down among the Phocians. They would probably be eager to join in an expedition on account of their long-standing friendship or if not, they could be forced into it; and Phocis was on the border of Boeotia.

> (Thucydides 3.95.1)

It seems unlikely that Demosthenes would have dared to contemplate this without the support of powerful politicians back in Athens, and its proximity in time to the attack by the whole Athenian army on Tanagra adds strength to this view. This was a major break with Periclean strategy, as it involved serious risks on the land, and success would impose upon the Athenians a massive commitment of manpower in order to hold down central Greece. However, Demosthenes was defeated in battle by the Aetolians, losing 120

Athenian hoplites (3.94–98), and this led to a postponement of this policy. In the meantime, Demosthenes managed to redeem himself later in the year when his leadership of the Acarnanians and the Amphilochians resulted in the defeat of the Peloponnesians and the Ambraciots at Olpae in Amphilochia (3.100–102; 105–14).

The attempt to bring Boeotia into the Athenian alliance was undertaken in 424. The plan of campaign contained three elements working in unison: dissident Boeotians, who favoured democracy on the Athenian model, were to seize power in different cities; Demosthenes was to lead the western Greek allies into Boeotia through its western border; and Hippocrates was to invade Boeotia from the east with the main Athenian army and seize Delium; all this was to be done on the same day so that the Boeotian army would be unable to concentrate its forces against a single enemy, especially at Delium. The anticipated result would be the rise of democratic factions within the other cities, leading to the overthrow of the pro-Spartan oligarchies, and the removal of Boeotia from its Spartan alliance (4.75–77). In the event, the plan was betrayed and Demosthenes was prevented from entering Boeotia. As a result the Boeotians were able to provide a united front against Hippocrates at Delium and inflicted the heaviest casualties (nearly 1,000 hoplites and many light-armed troops) upon the Athenians in the ten-year war (4.89–101).

The third geographical area was the Peloponnese itself where the Athenians went further than Pericles' planned sea-borne raids. In 425, Demosthenes persuaded the reluctant generals, Sophocles and Eurymedon, to establish a garrisoned fort (epiteichismos) at Pylos on the west coast of the Peloponnese, facing the island of Sphacteria. The sceptical reaction of these generals to his idea – if Demosthenes was intent on wasting Athenian money, there were dozens of other similar headlands that could be occupied, apart from that one (4.3) – strongly suggests this was an innovation, and not part of Pericles' original strategy. The Spartans' ineptitude in attempting to recover Pylos led to the capture of 120 Spartiates on Sphacteria by Demosthenes and Cleon, the loss of their fleet of 60 ships, and the humiliation of suing for peace, which the Athenians under Cleon's influence refused (4.2–41). It was this unexpected success that encouraged the Athenians to be more ambitious in their conduct of the war, which resulted in their defeat at Delium in Boeotia. In the same year as Pylos, Nicias led a force of 80 ships, 2,000 hoplites and 200 cavalry, and allied contingents in an attack on the territory of the Corinthians. A land battle was fought with half of the Corinthian army, resulting in an Athenian victory (4.42–44). Although this was a sea-borne raid, the amount of risks taken against one of the most powerful of the Peloponnesian allies in a pitched battle was non-Periclean.

In 424, Nicias and two other generals with a force of 60 ships, 2,000 hoplites and contingents of allies seized control of Cythera, an island lying off the coast of Laconia opposite Malea. He placed a garrison on the island, and then set about raiding the coast of Laconia. It was this campaign that probably gave the Athenians the best chance to win the war. The Spartans were totally demoralized by their defeat at Pylos and the loss of their Spartiates, and were convinced that the Athenians planned similar fortified garrisons (epiteichismos) in their homeland, which they would be unable to meet with their full force in one battle. They also feared that this would cause revolution against the government, which probably means that they feared a Helot revolt. All this had a devastating effect on their fighting morale:

> The many reverses of fortune, which had taken place against their expectation in such a short time, caused great panic, and they feared that another disaster of the kind that happened on the island [i.e. Sphacteria] would come upon them; and through this they became far more lacking in confidence in battle, and they thought that whatever they attempted was bound to be a failure, since their morale had collapsed due to a lack of experiencing misfortune.

(Thucydides 4.55.3–4)

The Athenians failed to capitalize on this situation, and after about seven days they set sail for home, ravaging Epidaurus Limera and Thyrea (both on the east coast of Laconia) on the return journey (4.53–57).

The other target in 424 was Megara. There had been two invasions every year from 431, in accordance with Pericles' original strategy, but now Demosthenes and Hippocrates were in secret negotiations with the democratic faction to gain control of Megara. These two generals were also involved in the attempt to gain control of Boeotia later in the same year (see above) and their tactics also included liaising with the democratic factions in various Boeotian cities. It is very tempting to see the attacks on Megara and Boeotia as part of the same policy – conquest of the Megarid (as in the First Peloponnesian War) would prevent the Spartan army from invading Attica, and this would isolate the Boeotians from their main ally, making them an easier target for conquest later in the year. The Athenians came close to success but the fortuitous presence of Brasidas saved Megara from capture, although the Athenians did capture and fortify Nisaea, the port of Megara on the Saronic Gulf (4.66–74).

The years 427 to 424 had witnessed a major change in strategy from Pericles' predominantly defensive policy. New generals, such as Demosthenes and Hippocrates, had appeared on the Athenian political scene and, backed by politicians in Athens, had set about taking the initiative in the war from Sparta and winning the war decisively. It was the failure to capture Megara and the heavy defeat at Delium, soon to be followed by Brasidas' successes in Thrace, that led to the temporary eclipse of Demosthenes and similar advocates of an aggressive war policy, and the return to Periclean defensive strategy for the remaining years of the Archidamian War.

424/3–421

After 425, the Spartans were unable to rely upon invasions of Attica as their main offensive weapon, as the Athenians had threatened to execute their prisoners from Sphacteria, if this happened. The Athenian successes in their attacks upon the Peloponnese and the territory of Sparta demanded a new strategy to ease the pressure, especially as a Helot revolt seemed to be in the offing. Therefore the appeals from cities in the Thraceward region (see Map 5, the Athenian Empire), which were still in revolt from Athens, and others that were secretly asking for help to revolt, and also from King Perdiccas of Macedonia (4.79) gave them an opportunity to throw the Athenians on the defensive and regain the initiative in the war – the Spartans were now embracing the 'adventurous' strategy. Brasidas with 700 Helots as hoplites and a force of 1,700 Peloponnesian mercenaries marched through Thessaly into Chalcidice. He soon won over Acanthus and Stagira, and impressed the locals by his revival of the claim that Sparta was fighting the war to free the Greeks (4.78–88). But it was the city of Amphipolis, which held such an important economic and strategic position, that dominated his attention. A sudden attack in the winter of 424/3 brought Amphipolis and the crossing over the river Strymon into Brasidas' hands, which caused the exile of Thucydides the Historian, the Athenian general operating in that area (4.102–7). The loss of Amphipolis caused great alarm among the Athenians, and they feared that Brasidas' moderation and his declaration of the liberation of the Greeks would lead to a widespread revolt. Brasidas showed admirable enterprise in calling for more troops to reinforce his campaign and in building triremes on the Strymon; he also won over several cities in Athos and captured Torone (4.102–16).

Brasidas, however, had badly misjudged the war aims of those who had supported the 'adventurous' strategy in the Thraceward region:

> The Lacedaimonians did not give him any help [i.e. send out another army as requested], partly because of the jealousy of the leading men, and partly because they wanted to get back the men from the island and end the war.
>
> (Thucydides 4.108.7)

The men of influence at Sparta no longer thought in terms of the liberation of Greece. At the time of disaster on Sphacteria, the main offer of the Spartans, when attempting to negotiate peace, was to restore the dual hegemony of Greece (4.17–20). There was no discussion with the Peloponnesian allies, for the Spartans were purely motivated by their own need to regain their men and were prepared to betray everyone in the pursuit of this aim. Thus the aim behind Brasidas' campaign was that, when the Spartans had a chance to make peace:

> they would be able to give back places held by themselves and receive back theirs from Athens, and bring about an end of the war for the Peloponnese.
>
> (Thucydides 4.81.2)

The Spartans knew that the success of Brasidas was causing alarm at Athens and that an offer of a one-year armistice would be well received. In this way the Spartans hoped that the Athenians would get a taste for peace and would be willing to make a longer peace, whose terms would include the return of the 120 Spartiates (4.117). There was no way that Brasidas could ultimately be successful when there was such a major conflict in aims.

It is reasonable to argue that the opponents of Brasidas were correct in their assessment of Sparta's capabilities. The support of Perdiccas of Macedonia was always suspect, which was confirmed in 423 when he made peace with the Athenians (4.128); the route through Thessaly was precarious – Perdiccas' influence prevented Spartan reinforcements from getting through Thessaly in 422 (5.12–13); and finally, there was a need for a first-class fleet, which could only be supplied by Persian gold. However, Spartan attempts to tap this source failed in the 420s through their reluctance to pay the Great King's price, which presumably was the return of the Asiatic Greeks to his dominion – it is hardly surprising that the King's letters, intercepted by the Athenians, expressed his bewilderment as to what the Spartans really wanted since each embassy said different things (4.50), but the Spartans as the self-proclaimed liberators of Greece could hardly give him a straight answer. This being the case, the Spartans were pleased with the one-year's armistice; the Athenians were also pleased to accept it, as it would put an end to Brasidas winning over other Athenian allies. Consequently they were very annoyed when Brasidas received Scione and Mende, both of which had revolted around the time of the armistice, as allies (4.120–23).

The armistice had been reasonably successful, but it was allowed to lapse mainly because of the on-going conflict in the Thraceward region. In 422 the Athenians concentrated their efforts on regaining control of this area, and sent out Cleon with an armed force to achieve this (5.2). Mende soon changed sides and Torone was captured (5.2–3). The crucial battle, however, was going to be over Amphipolis (5.7–11). Cleon's failure to capture this vital city and his death and that of Brasidas provided the impetus to make peace. The Athenians had lost their confidence of the mid-420s due to their defeats at Delium and Amphipolis; they were also worried that the defeat at Amphipolis would lead to a widespread revolt of the subject-allies and the possible collapse of their Empire. The Spartans had desired peace from the time of the disaster at Sphacteria; their hopes of a quick, easy victory by invading Attica had proved to be in vain, and now they were being

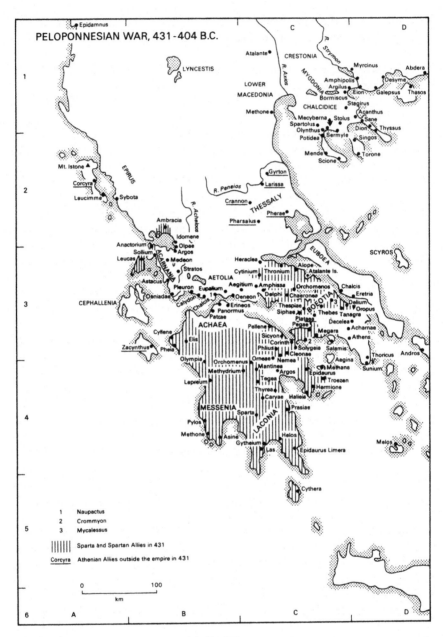

Map 6 The Peloponnesian War, 404–423 BC.

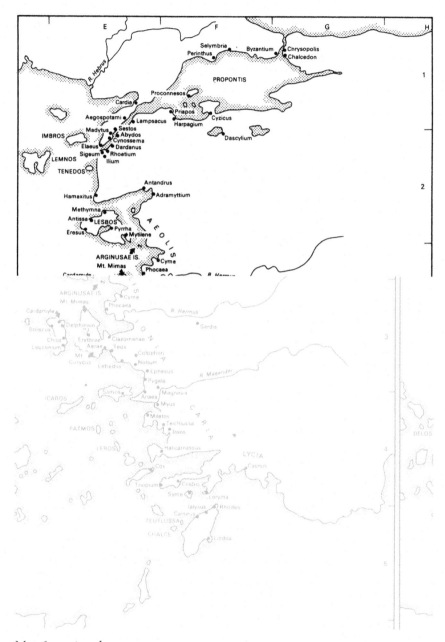

Map 6 continued

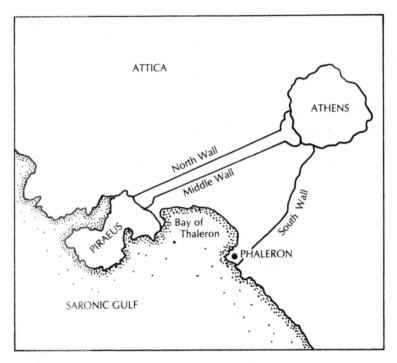

Map 7 The long walls of Athens

attacked from Pylos and Cythera; in addition, the Thirty Year Peace with Argos was coming to an end, and the Argives were acting in a bellicose manner (5.14).

The peace process was helped, first, by the deaths of the two men who most favoured the war, Cleon and Brasidas; and second, by the desire of the influential Nicias and King Pleistoanax for peace – the former, on the grounds that he wished to avoid future risk and to bring a relief from troubles for Athens, the latter, because peace would make it difficult for his political enemies, who constantly blamed him for Spartan misfortunes in the war (5.16). In 421 the Archidamian War came formally to an end with the signing of the Peace of Nicias, which was to last for 50 years (5.18–19). However, it proved to be a phoney peace or, in the words of Thucydides, 'the suspicious truce' (5.26.3 – see Chapter 20).

Bibliography

Brunt, P.A. 'Spartan policy and strategy in the Archidamian War', *Phoenix* 19.

Cartledge, P. *Sparta and Lakonia*, pt 3, ch. 12.

Cawkwell, G. L. 'Thucydides' judgement on Periclean strategy', YCS 24.

Davies, J. K. *Democracy and Classical Greece*, 2nd edn, ch. 7.

Holladay, A. J. 'Athenian strategy in the Archidamian War', *Historia* 27.

Hornblower, S. *The Greek World 479–323 BC.*

Kagan, D. *The Archidamian War.*

Lewis, D. M. *CAH* vol. 5, 2nd edn, ch. 9.2.

Westlake, H. D. *Essays on Greek Historians and Greek History*, ch. 5.

20

SPARTA, THE PELOPONNESE AND THE OUTBREAK OF THE DECELEAN WAR, 421–413

The Spartans had 'lost' the Archidamian War and needed peace in 421 more than the Athenians, especially as they were desperate to get back the 'hoplites' captured on Sphacteria in 425 (Thuc. 5.15.1 – all references in this chapter are to Thucydides, unless otherwise stated). In the first place, they had failed in their primary declared aim of liberating the Greeks from Athenian domination (2.8.4). Second, the Spartan reputation for military excellence had plummeted after their defeat at Sphacteria, leading to a drastic diminution of their prestige and authority among their Peloponnesian allies and Greece:

> For at this time Sparta had especially fallen into disrepute and was held in contempt on account of its disasters.
>
> (Thucydides 5.28.2)

Third, the cornerstone of their strategy – the annual invasions and laying waste of Attica – neither had forced the Athenians into a decisive pitched battle nor had destroyed their will to resist, even after the devastating consequences of the plague. Fourth, the Spartans had been forced to abandon this key strategy after the capture of 292 hoplites (including 120 Spartiates) on Sphacteria owing to the Athenian threats to execute them if the Spartans invaded Attica. Fifth, damaging raids from Cythera and Pylos were being directed against Spartan territory – see below. Sixth, the 'Helots' were deserting, and the Spartans feared that the loyal ones might be tempted to stage another Helot revolt (5.14.3). Finally, their Thirty Year's Peace with Argos was coming to an end in 421 or 420, and the Argives were determined to exploit Spartan difficulties and replace them as leaders of the Peloponnese (5.28.2) – a distinct possibility, since the Spartans suspected (rightly as events proved) that some of her most important allies were considering switching sides (5.14.4).

The Athenians were also keen to make peace:

The Athenians, being beaten at Delium and soon after at Amphipolis ... feared that
their allies, encouraged by Athens' failures, would spread their revolt.

(Thucydides 5.14. 1–2)

Nicias led the pro-peace supporters at Athens and, although Thucydides
ascribes personal motives to him (5.16.1), there were compelling reasons for
him to pursue this policy. As a supporter of Pericles' war aims, Nicias believed
that these had been achieved: the Athenians had 'won through' (1.144.1), had
avoided defeat, and, by wearing the Spartans down, thus disabused them of
the belief that Athens could easily be conquered. Nicias wanted a return to the
'dual hegemony', the policy that had underpinned the original Thirty Year
Peace of 446/5, the terms of which had probably been initially agreed by Pericles and King Pleistoanax of Sparta. It comes as no surprise that Pleistoanax,
having returned to Sparta from exile in c.426/5, was also enthusiastic for peace.

The Peace of Nicias and its immediate aftermath

The Peace of Nicias was finally concluded in about March 421 BC after
negotiations throughout the previous winter (5.17). Its main terms, as stated
by Thucydides (5.18–23), were as follows:

1. The treaty was to last for fifty years.

2. It was unlawful for either Athens or Sparta and their respective allies to do harm to
each other. Any future dispute was to be resolved by law or oath.

3. The Spartans were to give back Amphipolis – vital for its strategic position in Thrace,
as well as its control of mining revenues and shipbuilding timber – to the Athenians.
Furthermore, the other cities in Spartan possession in Thrace should be neutral, belonging to neither alliance, but must pay 'phoros' to the Athenians at the rate fixed by Aristides in 478/7. As regards Scione, Torone and other cities which were still in revolt and
contained besieged Peloponnesians and their allies, the Athenians were required to release
these men but were free to treat these cities as they wished – for Scione, this was to mean
the execution of all men of military age, and the enslavement of the women and children
(5.32.1). The Spartans were also to give back Panactum, a fortress on the Athenian border
which had been seized by the Boeotians, and the Boeotians' Athenian captives held in it.

4. The Athenians were to give back cities that they had captured from the Spartans. These
included Pylos (Coryphasium to the Spartans), garrisoned by Athenians and by the Messenian ex-Helots from Naupactus, who were using it as a base for guerrilla warfare against
Laconia and as a focal point for stirring up rebellion among the Helots (4.41.2–3); and
also Cythera, an island close to Laconia which was being used by the Athenians to make
frequent raids on the Peloponnese (4.55–56.1).

5. All Spartan and Athenian prisoners, including their allies, who had been captured in
war, were to be given back.

6. If any point had been overlooked in connection with this treaty, the Athenians and the
Spartans, by mutual agreement, could make alterations to it.

This treaty, even while it was being discussed, had caused great resentment among Sparta's chief allies. The Boeotians, the Corinthians, the Eleans and the Megarians opposed the terms of the treaty (5.17.2) and (presumably) voted against it. Apart from individual grievances (e.g. the Corinthians were angry that they did not get back Anactorium and Sollium from the Athenians – 5.30.2), they were particularly upset by the last clause of the treaty:

> For this clause especially threw the Peloponnese into panic, raising suspicions that the Spartans together with the Athenians were planning to enslave them. It was right, they felt, that any alteration should be made with the consent of all of the allies.
>
> (Thucydides 5.29.3)

The Boeotians, showing their growing strength and influence in Greek affairs, independently made a ten days' truce (possibly a truce renewable every ten days) with the Athenians (5.32.5). The continued refusal of this important minority of allies to accept this treaty, the refusal by the Argives to renew their former treaty, and the possible defection of their Peloponnesian allies to Argos, induced the Spartans to strengthen their ties with the Athenians by making an individual alliance with them. The Spartan thinking behind this move was that, first, the menace of a resurgent Argos would be neutralized, if it was cut off from a treaty with the Athenians (5.22.2); and second, the disaffected Peloponnesian allies would be fearful of taking action against Sparta, deterred by the prospect of having to face the combined forces of Sparta and Athens. In both instances Sparta had made a serious error of judgement. Nevertheless, a fifty-year defensive alliance was made between the Spartans and the Athenians, in which either side would come to the aid of the other if attacked. Furthermore, the Athenians agreed to send military help in the event of a Helot revolt – a major concession considering Sparta's treatment of Athens in 462/1 in the previous Helot revolt. Finally, neither city could make an alliance with a different state without the other's agreement (5.23). This swearing of a defensive alliance produced an immediate and the most major benefit for the Spartans: the return of their hoplites captured at Sphacteria (5.24.2).

This rapprochement between the two states did not last long, and, in the opinion of Thucydides, the years between 421 and 413 – 'the suspicious truce' (5.26.3) – should be seen as part of a 27-year war, i.e. the Peloponnesian War, as it is called by modern historians:

> If someone does not think it proper to consider the interval of the treaty as war, he will be making a mistake ... he will find that it is not reasonable for it to be judged as a peace, where neither party either gave back or received all that they had agreed. And, apart from this, there were violations on both sides with regard to the Mantinean and Epidaurian wars, as well as in other matters.
>
> (Thucydides 5.26.3)

The main reasons for the failure of the Peace of Nicias were: first, the Spartans' inability to carry out their obligations to Athens, by returning to Athenian control Amphipolis and a fully equipped Panactum (see below) – this resulted in the Athenians' refusal to restore Pylos and Cythera; second, the Athenians, distrusting and disillusioned with the Spartans, supported the growing challenge by Sparta's former allies, centred around Argos, to Sparta's leadership of the Peloponnese. With regard to the implementation of Peace of Nicias, lots were drawn to decide who should start this process of giving back their gains, and it fell to Sparta to return Amphipolis, the other Thracian cities in revolt and Panactum (5.35). However, the citizens of Amphipolis and the other Thracian cities were determined to stay out of the Athenian Empire, and so, faced with this intransigence, the Spartans simply removed their troops. The Spartans' failure throughout the summer of 421 to carry out this and the rest of their treaty obligations, apart from returning all Athenian prisoners in their possession, led the Athenians to suspect them of bad faith; consequently, they refused to restore Pylos and regretted returning the prisoners captured on Sphacteria (5.35.4).

The challenge to Sparta's hegemony of the Peloponnese

With regard to the threat to Sparta's leadership of the Peloponnese in the years 421–418, there were many, often fruitless, diplomatic manoeuvrings between the Peloponnesian cities as they attempted to protect themselves and to avoid isolation in the aftermath of the peace treaty. Space prevents a full description of this complex diplomacy, so only the key alliances will be included. It was the Corinthians, fearing that the Spartans along with the Athenians were planning to enslave the Peloponnese, who initiated the move against the Spartans by encouraging Argive ambitions to lead this challenge (5.27). The Argives proclaimed their willingness to receive into their alliance any city, apart from Sparta or Athens, that wished to join. The first to join were the Mantineans and their allies, who seceded from the Peloponnesian League – the first since Megara in about 460. The Mantineans had brought a large part of southern Arcadia under their control during the Archidamian War and feared that the Spartans, with the coming of the peace, would force them to give up their gains (5.29.1). The Mantinean secession acted as a spur to other states. The next to join were the Eleans, who were in dispute with the Spartans over possession of Lepreum and its territory (5.31.1–5). Then the Corinthians and the Chalcidians in Thrace joined the Argive alliance. However, the Boeotians and the Megarians, although in sympathy with their views about Sparta, did not join owing to their dislike of the Argives' democratic constitution (5.31.6). A bigger blow to the fledgling alliance was the refusal of Tegea, one of the most powerful cities, in the Peloponnese to join (5.32.3–4) – hardly surprising, since they were first in line for any future Spartan reprisals and had fought a bloody battle with the Mantineans in 423/2 (4.134). At this rebuff the Corinthians became downhearted, and throughout these three years Corinthian behaviour is notable for its timidity and vacillation.

The election of a new board of Spartan 'Ephors' in October 421 marked the beginning of the end of peaceful relations between Sparta and Athens, especially the election of Cleoboulos and Xenares, who both wanted an annulment of the Peace of Nicias (5.36.1). In the winter of 421/20 the Spartans, desperate to recover Pylos, sent an embassy to the Boeotians, begging them to hand over Panactum and the Athenian prisoners to themselves. The Boeotians agreed to this but only on condition that the Spartans made a separate alliance with them, just as they had done with the Athenians. The Spartans knew that they would be breaking the terms of their alliance with the Athenians, but so desperate were they to obtain Panactum in order to exchange it for Pylos, they readily agreed, especially those in favour of ending the treaty with Athens. (5.39.3). Once again the growing confidence of the Boeotians should be noted – no more so than their decision, without informing the Spartans, to demolish Panactum so that it could be of no military use to the Athenians. The festering problems between Sparta and Athens came to a head in spring 420. The Spartans sent an embassy to Athens to secure the return of the Athenian prisoners held by the Boeotians and to return Panactum, brazenly claiming the demolition of Panactum was really a restoration, since no hostile force could now occupy it to threaten Athens. The Athenians reacted indignantly to this sophistry and, being also very angry with the Spartans' alliance with the Boeotians and with the other unresolved treaty matters, sent them away (5.42).

This Athenian anger was exploited by the faction in Athens who had opposed the 50-year defensive alliance with Sparta, and it is here that Alcibiades makes his first appearance in Thucydides. Once again Thucydides ascribes personal motives to Alcibiades' opposition to the Spartans – his pride had been hurt because the Spartans had failed to pay him due respect but had chosen in his place to negotiate with Nicias about the peace treaty of 421 (5.43). Whether true or not, Alcibiades certainly considered an alliance with Argos to be more advantageous to the Athenians, bearing in mind Sparta's current difficulties in the Peloponnese and the opportunity to help break up the Peloponnesian League with minimal risk to Athens. Seizing the initiative, Alcibiades encouraged the Argives, Mantineans and Eleans to send envoys to the Athenians to invite them to join the Argive alliance (5.43). The Spartans, having discovered Alcibiades' plans, immediately sent a second embassy out of fear that the Athenians in their anger might agree to become a member of the Argive alliance. In addition, this embassy was to demand the restoration of Pylos as they had returned Panactum – not a wise move with the mood in Athens being so febrile.

The Spartan embassy spoke first to the Boule of 500, stating that they had come with full powers to settle all the outstanding problems between themselves and the Athenians. Alcibiades, fearing that the Athenians in the Assembly might be won over by these arguments and reject the Argive alliance, conceived a plan to discredit the Spartan ambassadors. He promised to use his influence to persuade the Athenians to return Pylos and to resolve the other matters, provided they did not admit in the Assembly that they had come with full powers to negotiate. They foolishly agreed and on the next day, having been asked in the Assembly whether they had come with full powers and having denied it, they were promptly castigated for their duplicity by Alcibiades. Only an earthquake prevented the Athenians from voting to join the Argives (5.44.2–45). This gave Nicias his last chance to avoid a split with the Spartans by persuading the Athenians to send him and others to Sparta in order to demand the restoration of Amphipolis and of an intact Panactum, and the end of their separate alliance with Boeotia. The Spartans, however, urged on by Xenares the Ephor, refused to give up their alliance with Boeotia and offered nothing new about Amphipolis and Panactum (5.46). This rebuff allowed Alcibiades' policy to prevail and a 100-year alliance was agreed between the Athenians, Argives, Mantineans and the Eleans. The alliance was mainly a defensive alliance (5.47), although it had the potential to be an offensive alliance (5.47.7). Although not formally revoked by either Athens or Sparta, the Peace of Nicias and the 50-year defensive alliance now existed only in name (5.48.1). The Corinthians, who probably had never intended to break fully with the Spartans but desired to change their foreign policy, did not join this new alliance and now began to harbour thoughts of returning to the Spartans (5.48.2–3).

The first operations of this new quadruple alliance in the summer of 419 were against Epidaurus which was pro-Spartan but probably a member of the Peloponnesian League. Its conquest would encourage Corinth's neutrality, as the territory of these two cities bordered each other, and would also greatly improve communications and the sending of troops between Athens and Argos (5.53) – at present, the Athenians had to sail around the Argolid peninsula, whereas Epidaurus was immediately opposite the island of Aegina, occupied by the Athenians (see Map 9). During this summer the Argives launched two invasions of Epidaurus in order to ravage its territory and, although the Spartans sent out two expeditions to bring aid to the Epidaurians, both were aborted on the northern frontiers of Laconia owing to unfavourable omens (5.54–55). However, in the winter of 419/8, the Spartans managed to elude the Athenian ships and sent a garrison of 300 into Epidaurus. Argive annoyance at the Athenians' negligence was allayed only by the Athenians agreeing to return to Pylos the original garrison of Messenians and Helots, who had been removed in 421 to the island of Cephallenia at the request of Sparta (5.35.7) – these could once again renew their guerrilla warfare and ravage the surrounding territory, causing great problems for the Spartans.

At the end of the winter of 419/8, the Argives launched a third invasion of Epidaurus, but failed in their attempt to capture the city. Finally, the Spartans decided to assert their power in the Peloponnese:

> The Lacedaimonians, seeing that their allies in Epidaurus were suffering greatly and that furthermore in the Peloponnese some of the states were in revolt, while others were turning against them, and thinking that, unless they swiftly took precautions, their problems would become even greater, they themselves and their helots made an expedition against Argos with their full force under the leadership of King Agis, son of Archidamus.
>
> (Thucydides 5.57.1)

The Spartans were joined by troops from Tegea and the rest of their allies in Arcadia. Furthermore, troops from their other allies in the Peloponnese (including the Corinthians) and the Boeotians also gathered at Phlius, north of Argos. The Argives were joined by the Mantineans with their allies and 3,000 hoplites from Elis, but the Athenians with their cavalry had not yet arrived. The stage was set for the greatest land battle of the Peloponnesian War, but that proved to be an anti-climax – two Argives, including Thrasyllus the general, seeing that the Argives were in a perilous situation, prevailed upon King Agis to avoid battle in return for a fair and impartial arbitration of the grievances held by Sparta against Argos and to make a treaty with a view to keeping the peace (5.49.3–4). Agis, without consultation, concluded a four-month truce with the Argives, and withdrew all his forces. Thrasyllus and Agis paid a heavy price for their diplomacy – the former was nearly stoned to death by the angry Argives who were convinced that they could have defeated the Spartans and their allies (5.60.6); the latter faced the possible destruction of his house and a large fine, having been blamed for wasting such an excellent opportunity with so many allies to crush Argos (5.63.1–4).

Alcibiades and the Athenian forces arrived soon after the departure of the Spartans, and persuaded the Argives with difficulty to resume the war on the grounds that their truce with Sparta was invalid because the Athenians had not been part of the discussions, as required by their alliance (5.61.2–3). The forces of the quadruple alliance now attacked and besieged Orchomenus in Arcadia, a Spartan ally – the citizens, fearing that they would perish before the arrival of help, surrendered and joined the alliance. However, it was now that a split opened up among the anti-Spartan allies about the next target: the Eleans wished to go against Lepreum, over which they had lost control; the Mantineans wished to go against Tegea, Sparta's most powerful ally and their most powerful rival in Arcadia. The Mantineans won the day but the Eleans angrily returned home with their 3,000 hoplites – possibly a fatal decision for the alliance in the coming battle (5.62). Desperate calls for help came to the Spartans from their supporters in Tegea, warning them that Tegea was on the point of joining the Argive alliance unless the Spartans came at once. The Spartans needed no second bidding, as the loss of Tegea could be fatal to Sparta's leadership of the Peloponnese – it also gave King Agis an opportunity to redeem himself and avoid the punishment proposed after his withdrawal from Argos. There followed the battle of Mantinea in the summer of 418 in which the Spartans achieved a brilliant victory, even though they made some potentially disastrous tactical mistakes in the battle (5.70–73), and restored their battered reputation as the foremost infantry in Greece:

> By this one action they had removed the charge, previously brought against them by the Greeks, of cowardice on account of the disaster on the island [i.e. of Sphacteria] and of a lack of judgement and of slowness in other matters; they were thought to have suffered disgrace through bad luck, but they themselves still possessed that spirit as in the past.
>
> (Thucydides 5.75.3)

It was now time for the Spartans to reap the fruits of the victory at Mantinea. The Argives withdrew from the quadruple alliance with the Mantineans, the Eleans and the Athenians, and concluded a 50-year alliance with Sparta. Furthermore the Argives agreed to have no diplomatic dealings with the Athenians until they evacuated Pylos, Cythera and Epidaurus (5.78–80.1). The Mantineans lost their confidence with the withdrawal of Argos from their alliance, and they also made a separate 30-year treaty with the Spartans in which they gave up control of the cities in Arcadia that they had conquered in the Archidamian War. It seems likely that the Eleans, now isolated, soon returned to the Peloponnesian League. Thus emboldened and exercising their restored power, the Spartans set about strengthening their grip in the Peloponnese: they established pro-Spartan oligarchies in Sicyon and Argos itself in 418 (7.81.2), and in Achaea in 417. The success of the Argive oligarchy did not last long, and the Argive democrats soon regained power and set about restoring their alliance with the Athenians (5.82.2–5). But it is doubtful whether this caused much consternation in Sparta – to all intents and purposes Argos was no longer a serious challenger for the hegemony of the Peloponnese. To rub this in, the Spartans in the winter of 417/6 invaded the Argolid; demolished the defensive long walls that the Argives were building down to the sea; conquered Hysiae, a city in Argive territory, slaughtering all the men; and returned home without any problems (5.83.1–2). The only thorn in Sparta's side was the continued occupation of Pylos by the Athenians who were still seizing large quantities of booty from the Lacedaimonians. However, in 416 the time was not yet ripe for the Spartans to react to this provocation and renounce the Peace of Nicias. That was soon to change as the politically ambitious Alcibiades, whose desire to defeat Sparta, based on an Athenian alliance with

Argos, Mantinea and Elis, had been thwarted by the battle of Mantinea, sought a new foreign policy objective to exercise his talents.

Outbreak of the Decelean War

Alcibiades' opportunity came in 415: Segesta, a non-Greek Sicilian ally of the Athenians, being hard pressed by Greek Syracuse and Selinus, sent a delegation to Athens in 416 begging for military assistance. Athens had recently concluded an alliance with Segesta, and a majority of the Athenians saw this as a perfect pretext for the conquest of the whole of Sicily (6.6.1 – see Chapter 21 for a full treatment of the Sicilian expedition). In 415, when the debate about sending help was held in the Ecclesia, Alcibiades was the foremost supporter of the expedition. Both Nicias in open debate (6.12.2) and Thucydides in his commentary (6.15.2) believed that Alcibiades' eagerness was motivated mainly by a desire to gain wealth and glory. Alcibiades was chosen as one of the three generals but, shortly before the expedition set sail, a religious scandal broke out (the mutilation of the Hermae and the profanation of the Mysteries) in which Alcibiades was allegedly implicated. He was instructed to set sail, even though he had this charge hanging over his head. While on campaign in Sicily, he was ordered to return to face trial: a likely guilty verdict and death penalty were enough to persuade him to escape into exile, finally arriving in Sparta at the Spartans' invitation (6.61).

In the winter of 415/4, the Syracusans, having suffered their first defeat in battle, sent envoys to Corinth and then to Sparta: their request was for the Spartans to be more active in open warfare in mainland Greece against Athens and to send help to Sicily (6.88.8). The Spartans, although sympathetic, were still very unwilling to break their peace treaty and alliance with Athens because of their responsibility for the outbreak of the Archidamian War:

> For in the former war (they felt) that their wrongdoing was greater because the Thebans had gone into Plataea in peacetime and, although it was stated in the previous treaty not to take up arms, if the other wished to go to arbitration, they themselves had not submitted to arbitration, although the Athenians were offering it. And because of this they believed that they deserved their misfortune and took it to heart about the disaster at Sphacteria and the other misfortunes that had befallen them.
>
> (Thucydides 7.18.2)

It was now that Alcibiades used his oratorical skills to deadly effect to the benefit of the Spartans and to the detriment of the Athenians. His intervention in the debate proved to be the catalyst that stirred the Spartans into action. First, he painted a picture of Athenian imperial aims and ambitions, deliberately exaggerated to strike fear into the Spartans: Sicily was only the first stage of conquest; this was to be followed by the conquest of the Italian Greeks, then Carthage and the Carthaginian Empire; finally, supported by these forces, a full-blown attack upon the Peloponnese to rule over the entire Hellenic world (6.90.2–3). Second, he gave them the perfect strategy for weakening and debilitating the Athenian war effort: to establish a permanent garrison at Decelea in Attica, which was equidistant from Athens and Boeotia and which easily controlled the whole of Attica, thereby denying the Athenians access to their land and forcing them to import everything by sea; to send hoplites to Syracuse; and, even more important than these, to send out a first-class Spartan general to command the forces at Syracuse (6.91.4–7). This speech removed the Spartans' previous hesitation about attacking Athens and establishing a garrisoned fort ('epi-teichismos') at Decelea; they also appointed Gylippus and ordered him to proceed at once to Sicily to organize the war effort against the Athenians there (6.93.2).

Early in the summer of 414, the Athenians removed any lingering doubts among the Spartans about the legality of attacking Athens. The Spartans had invaded the territory of Argos and had laid waste most of it. The Athenians sent 30 ships to aid Argos but, in a marked departure from the past, attacked cities on the coast of Laconia:

> The Athenians brought help to the Argives with thirty ships which most clearly of all violated the treaty with the Spartans ...; after landing at Epidaurus Limera, Prasiai and other places, they laid waste the land, and as a result they gave the Lacedai-monians the more plausible reason of self-defence against the Athenians.
>
> (Thucydides 6.105. 1–2)

This was a clear breach of the terms of the Peace of Nicias (see term 2 above) – a foolish and provocative act by the Athenians, although they may have felt emboldened by the ongoing success at Syracuse. However, by the end of summer of 414, the news from Sicily was not good – Gylippus had dramatically improved the fighting mettle of the Syracusans and had prevented the Athenians from completing the circumvallation of Syracuse. Nicias' letter to the Athenians advised either a recall of the whole expedition or the despatch of substantial reinforcements (see Chapter 21 for a full treatment of these events). The Athenians' decision in late 414 to send a second expedition in spring 413 was the final galvanizing moment for the Spartans. Although they were influenced by the Syracusans' and Corinthians' urging them to invade Attica to prevent the sending of the second expedition, and by Alcibiades' constant telling them to fortify Decelea and to prosecute the war more forcefully:

> but, most of all, the Spartans felt confident because they considered that the Athenians, having two wars – with themselves and the Sicilians, would be more easily overthrown and because they thought that the Athenians had broken the treaty first.
>
> (Thucydides 7.18.2)

Thus the Spartans were full of enthusiasm for the war, using the winter to gather materials for the building of the fort at Decelea and to prepare to send hoplites of their own and of their allies to Sicily (7.18.3–4). At the beginning of spring 413 the Spartans sent 600 hoplites, picked men from the Helots and the freedmen, to Sicily, to whom the Thebans added 300 hoplites. But their main thrust was into Attica, which Agis and the Spartans allies invaded, laid waste and in it began the building of the garrisoned fort at Decelea. It was this action that has led other ancient historians (e.g. Diodorus) to name this war from 413–404 'The Decelean War', although Thucydides explicitly rejected this title, since he considered the period of the 'suspicious peace' (421–413) as part of the Peloponnesian War. However, for the rest of this book, I shall refer to this period of warfare from 413–404 by its more common title 'The Ionian War'. It is a measure of Athenian courage or foolhardiness that, at the same time as the building of the garrisoned fort at Decelea, they still chose to send the large relief force under Demosthenes to Syracuse (7.20.1).

The total and utter destruction of the Athenian forces in Sicily in the autumn of 413 sent shock waves around the whole Greek world. Yet, just as the power of the Spartans could be destroyed only by an invasion of the Peloponnese and the breaking up the Peloponnesian League and liberation of the Helots (as was to happen in 370/69), so the Empire of the Athenians could be destroyed only by defeating their fleet in the eastern Aegean or the Hellespont and thus liberating their subject-allies there – hence the post-413 theatre of war was concentrated on naval operations in Ionia. However, the occupation of Decelea played a vital if (secondary) role in weakening the Athenian war effort. King Agis had been placed in command, and his constant excursions from Decelea meant that no part of Attica was secure or productive. All the sheep and cattle were killed, and more than 20,000 slaves – including many of the most valuable artisan slaves – escaped to Decelea. As a result there was a great loss of income both for the landowners and for the slave-owners in Athens. These financial problems were further exacerbated by the increased cost and difficulty of imports of provisions and cattle from Euboea. Previously such imports from Euboea had come quickly and cheaply by land but now that route was blocked off by the garrison at Decelea, necessitating the longer and more costly route by sea around Cape Sunium. In fact, these ongoing costs, combined with the massive financial loss of the Sicilian expedition, had crippled the Athenian economy (7.28.4). Furthermore, and a matter of vital importance, the Athenians now depended upon everything being imported by sea – consequently, if their navy were to be destroyed, they would face starvation and total defeat (as was to happen in 404). In addition, there were far more heavy demands on the military, compared to the previous short invasions in the Archidamian War – the Athenian soldiers were now forced to maintain guard duty in Athens, the Piraeus and along the Long Walls both day and night, turning the city of Athens into a garrisoned fort (7.27.4–28.2). Thucydides' summary of the effect of the constant occupation of Decelea is revealing:

> For when Decelea was fortified in this summer, first by the whole army, then by garrisons from the other cities. ... it did great damage to the Athenians and, by its devastation of property and by its destruction of men, it was one of the chief causes of the decline in Athenian power.
>
> (Thucydides 7.27.3)

However, the Spartans still had to win the war, but their tardiness and Athenian resilience allowed the Athenians to recover partially and to carry on the war until 404. Three years later in 410 it was still the same Agis, looking out from the walls of Decelea and seeing the countless grain ships sailing into the Piraeus, who complained bitterly that his success at Decelea was pointless unless the Spartans seized the sources of the grain (Xenophon, *Hellenica* 1.135). It took Persian gold to make that a reality.

Bibliography for second edition

Cartledge, P. *Sparta and Lakonia: A Regional History, 1300–362 BC*, 2nd edn ch. 12.
Hornblower, S. *The Greek World 479–323 BC*, ch. 13.
Kagan, D. *The Archidamian War*, ch. 10 and Conclusion.
Powell, A. *Athens and Sparta*, ch. 5.
Sealey, R. *A History of the Greek City States 700–338 BC*, chs 12–13.

21

ATHENS AND THE WEST, 458–413

The aims of Athenian policy in Sicily and southern Italy developed gradually over this period of time, and it would be wrong to consider the main objective of the 415 expedition (as stated by Thucydides in 6.6.1 – see below) as being the Athenians' ultimate aim from the beginning of their involvement in the west. As the situation in Greece changed from the 440s to 416, so did the desires and expectations of the Athenians, and it is convenient to chart the changes in policy aims and the reasons for them by dividing the events of this time into three chronological periods.

458/7–428

During this time the alliances that were made between the Athenians and the states in the west were almost certainly diplomatic and not military. The Athenians had to tread warily in the west in order to avoid antagonizing and provoking Syracuse – a powerful naval state and a Corinthian colony. If Athenian imperialist ambitions became too obvious, there was every chance that the Syracusans would provide military aid to the Peloponnesians, and this naval aid would provide a serious threat to Athens' naval supremacy in Greece. Therefore it is likely that the initiative for these alliances came from the states themselves, which had more to gain (so they hoped) from such an alliance by securing the support of a powerful empire against the growing ambitions of Syracuse. The Athenians, for their part, would be unlikely as an imperial power to refuse an invitation to extend their influence and gain a foothold in the west, which could prove useful at some time in the future.

The first recorded alliance was thought to have been made in the 450s with non-Greek Segesta (or Egesta) in the west of Sicily. The evidence for this comes from an inscription (ML 37), and has been dated either to 458/7 if '[Habr]on' or 454/3 if '[Arist]on' is restored as the name of the 'archon' at the time of the treaty. However, the recent use of laser photography on this inscription suggests that the damaged archon's name could be Antiphon, archon in 418/7. This later date is more convincing, since the Athenians

366

were very keen from 427 onwards to extend their influence (and even to conquer) Sicily – it was Segesta (or Egesta) that appealed for help to Athens in 416, when being hard-pressed by Syrace (see below). At some time in the 440s, possibly after 445, alliances were also made with Leontini, a close neighbour of Syracuse, and Rhegium in southern Italy. The evidence for these comes from inscriptions which record the renewal of these alliances in 433/2 (ML 63 and 64). Such alliances would usually be of at least ten years' duration, and a date soon after 445 is a distinct possibility as Syracuse's defeat of Acragas in that year had established its position as the strongest state in the west. Fear of Syracuse's territorial ambitions would explain Leontini's and Rhegium's approach to Athens for protection. However, the Athenians' defeat in the First Peloponnesian War (462/1–446/5) and the loss of their 'Land Empire' would be sufficient reasons to avoid any military commitments, and a diplomatic alliance was the most likely outcome at this time.

The Athenians' involvement in the foundation of the colony of Thurii was also motivated by the desire to extend their prestige and influence in the west. After many years the exiled citizens of Sybaris in southern Italy had attempted to re-found their city but, after five years, they were driven out again by the people of Croton. They appealed to Athens and Sparta to provide help, which the Spartans refused but which was forthcoming from the Athenians. Diodorus, whose account of these events is very muddled, places the appeal for help and the despatch of Athenians to co-habit with the Sybarites in 446/5 (12.9–11). However, there was a clash between these Athenian settlers and the Sybarites, who were driven out. Pericles then decided, in 444/3, to found, on the former site of Sybaris, the new colony of Thurii which would be open to all Greeks under the leadership of the Athenians (Plutarch, *Pericles* 11). The Athenians saw the propaganda benefits that would arise from founding a pan-Hellenic colony so soon after the First Peloponnesian War. Such a generous gesture could only bring credit to the Athenians by highlighting their desire for peaceful coexistence with their fellow Greeks, both in mainland Greece and in the west; in reality, the Athenians could not have afforded such a drain on manpower to found an all-Athenian colony after the establishment of so many 'cleruchies' and colonies in the early 440s. This policy of extending Athenian influence through diplomatic manoeuvres was maintained throughout this period until 427 when Pericles' defensive strategy for the conduct of the Peloponnesian War was challenged by other politicians, who first raised the possibility of the conquest of Sicily.

427–424

In 427 Syracuse was at war with Leontini with the full support of allies on both sides. Leontini, being blockaded by land and by sea, was in grave danger of being captured, and so their allies appealed to the Athenians in accordance with their treaty (renewed in 433/2 – see above) to send a fleet:

> The Athenians sent the ships on the pretext of their kinship, but they wanted to prevent corn being imported from there into the Peloponnese and to make a preliminary survey if they could bring Sicily under their control.
>
> (Thucydides 3.86.4)

This was a new and significant development in Athenian policy towards the west, as it marks the first known military intervention in Sicilian affairs. The fact that the Athenians decided to send 20 ships is surprising, since they were still recovering from the effects of the plague (which was to break out again just after these ships had set sail) and state funds were low after the expense of crushing the revolt of Mytilene; but a majority of Athenians were still in favour of limited intervention in Sicily. The official motive was the shared Ionian kinship between Athens and Leontini, but in reality there was a split in the underlying aims for the expedition.

Until 427, the supporters of Pericles' defensive strategy for fighting the war had held sway in the Assembly, but in 427 this strategy was challenged by others who wished to pursue a more adventurous, offensive strategy in order to win the war decisively and not simply 'to win through' (see Chapter 19). The campaigns in Greece between 427 and 424 reflect the shifting influence of these conflicting strategies, but in Sicily there was a dangerous compromise resulting in a lack of coherence and of agreement in the aims for the campaign, which was to prove especially disastrous in the 415 expedition. The first real aim was defensive and reflects the view of those who were staying true to Pericles' strategy: the Peloponnesians were not self-sufficient in grain production, and disruption of import supplies could cause shortages and lead to widespread dissatisfaction with Sparta and possible defections; more importantly, if the Syracusans were to gain control of the main producers of grain, the Peloponnesians could rely more on increased imports, and this would lead to longer and more damaging invasions of Attica. Therefore, if the Syracusans were prevented in their attempt to conquer Sicily, the Peloponnesians would still be dependent on their own harvests, and the result would be the usual shorter invasions with which the Athenians could cope. For this reason the supporters of Periclean strategy would support the despatch of military aid to their allies in the west. The second real aim to explore the feasibility of future conquest was offensive and reflects the views of those who were seeking new and dynamic policies to end the military stalemate in the war in Greece. At this stage, as only 20 ships were sent, it would appear that the supporters of a defensive strategy were the more influential.

Thucydides' account of the events in Sicily is short and disjointed, and seems to reflect his opinion that this theatre of war was relatively unimportant in the Archidamian War. In 426/5 the Sicilian allies asked the Athenians to send out more ships in support:

> The Athenians manned 40 ships in order to send them there, thinking that the war in Sicily would be brought to an end more quickly and also wanting to provide practice for the fleet.
>
> (Thucydides 3.115.4)

The number of Athenian ships committed was almost as many (a few had been destroyed earlier) as they originally agreed to send in 416. Once again the first motive reflects a split in aims: supporters of Periclean strategy wished to end Athenian commitment in Sicily as soon as possible because it removed vital military resources from the war in Greece, and thus they wanted to pressurize Syracuse into peace and bring about a withdrawal of Athenian forces; their opponents believed that such a large, superior fleet would bring the war to an end by the conquest of Syracuse and its allies. The second motive refers to the lack of trained oarsmen due to the ravages of the plague and the need for them to acquire experience in battle conditions.

Pythodorus was sent at once with a few ships, but Sophocles and Eurymedon did not arrive until the summer of 425 with the bulk of the fleet, having been involved in the events of Pylos and Corcyra. They seem to have made little impact in Sicily since Thucydides sums up their contribution in one sentence – 'they carried on the war with their allies there' (Thuc. 4.48.6 – all subsequent references in this chapter are to Thucydides, unless otherwise stated). In 424, the Congress of Gela was held in which Hermocrates the Syracusan persuaded the warring Sicilian Greek states to make peace in order to remove the presence of the Athenians, which was a menace to all Sicilians (4.58–65); however, the Athenian allies made sure that the Athenians were included in the peace settlement. The generals returned home, pleased that the aim of bringing the war to an end had been achieved and that there was now no need to worry about longer invasions due to corn imports from Sicily, since the capture of the Spartiates on Sphacteria in 425 had ended the invasions of Attica. Unfortunately for the generals, the mood of the Athenians had swung decisively in favour of conquest as the desired means to end the war in Sicily – Eurymedon was fined, and Sophocles and Pythodorus were exiled (4.65). The Athenians' probable alliance with Segesta (or Egesta) in 418/7 (see above) was a clear sign that Sicily was still in their sights. If an opportunity were to present itself in the future, conquest would be the only satisfactory outcome for the majority of Athenians.

416–413

The peace that was negotiated at the Congress of Gela did not last long, and as early as 422 Leontini had been dismantled by the Syracusans (5.4.2). In

416 Segesta was being hard pressed by Selinus and Syracuse by land and by sea, and called upon the Athenians to come to their aid by sending a fleet (6.6). This was the opportunity that so many Athenians had been waiting for:

> The Athenians were eager to make an expedition, wanting as the truest reason to conquer the whole of Sicily, but at the same time wishing to have the pretext of bringing help to their kinsmen and their other allies.
>
> (Thucydides 6.6.1)

This desire to conquer Sicily was made even more attractive by the Seges-taeans' claim that they could pay for the expedition. An Athenian delegation was sent out in 416 to check this claim, and returned in the spring of 415 with 60 talents and reports of great affluence in Segesta (6.8); these reports, however, proved to be false as the Segestaeans had cleverly conned the delegation (6.46).

The Athenians held an Assembly and, having heard the report of their delegation and the comments of the Segestaeans:

> voted to send sixty ships to Sicily with Alcibiades son of Cleinias, Nicias son of Niceratus, and Lamachus son of Xenophanes as generals with full powers, to help the Segestaeans against the Selinuntines; also to restore Leontini, if they had success in the war; and to settle the other matters in Sicily in whatever way that they thought was best for Athens.
>
> (Thucydides 6.8.2)

It is interesting that the Athenians were so circumspect in their third stated objective, which was to encompass the defeat of Syracuse and the conquest of Sicily. It is possible that they hoped to conquer Syracuse by conspiring with its pro-Athenian faction, and therefore did not wish to make this aim explicit.

Five days later the Athenians held another Assembly to discuss the quickest way of getting the expedition under way (6.8). Nicias had not wanted to be appointed to the command and felt that the Athenians were making a dreadful mistake, presumably because this expedition would put the city at risk and thus clashed with Pericles' strategy of not adding to the Empire in the time of war – so jaundiced was he with the phoney peace of 421 that bore his name. His first speech stressed the dangers that confronted the Athenians: Sparta, Corinth, Boeotia and others were still hostile and would seize any opportunity to wage war; their own allies in the Thraceward region were still in revolt and it made more sense to secure the present Empire before seeking another; Sicily, even if it was conquered, would be impossible to control; and, finally, there was the ambition of Alcibiades whose enthusiastic support for the expedition was motivated by his desire to advance his own career (6.9–14). Alcibiades responded with a bravura defence of his own character and behaviour, and then stressed that Sicilian disunity would facilitate conquest; that their enemies in Greece were demoralized and offered no threat; and, finally, the overwhelming superiority of the Athenian fleet would guarantee the security of the naval expedition (6.16–18). Alcibiades' speech was received enthusiastically by the vast majority of the Athenians, and they became even more eager for the campaign. Nicias then tried a different approach to dampen their zeal by providing an exaggerated estimate of the forces needed to undertake the expedition safely (6.20–23). However, his hopes that the Athenians would be put off by the scale of armaments and the cost produced the opposite effect: the Athenians were now totally convinced that such a huge force would make victory a foregone conclusion. As a result, the Athenians and their allies eventually set sail with 134 'triremes', 5,100 'hoplites' and more than 1,000 light-armed troops (6.43).

While these preparations were going on, the mutilation of the Hermae (square-cut stone figures topped by a head representing Hermes, found in great numbers in porches and temples) took place one night in Athens. This sacrilege greatly shocked the majority of the people, who viewed the incident both as a bad omen for the expedition and as proof of a planned coup to destroy the democracy (6.27). The investigation was widened to cover any other sacrilegious acts, and evidence was supplied of other statues being defaced, and of the Eleusinian mysteries being performed with unauthorized celebrations in private houses (6.28). Alcibiades was implicated in the wider investigation, and his political enemies exploited the situation to bring about his downfall: they deliberately linked the mutilation of the Hermae and the unauthorized celebrations of the mysteries with an oligarchic plot to destroy the democracy, and accused Alcibiades of being involved in the plot. Alcibiades fervently denied the accusation and urged the Athenians to try him at once, as it would be very unwise to send him out on campaign with the worry of such a serious charge against him. However, his enemies were effective in persuading the Athenians of the need to launch the expedition as soon as possible – thus they could engineer a more serious charge in his absence and stir up ill will against him (6.29). The expedition set sail with much pomp in mid-summer.

The campaign of 415

The first disappointment upon their arrival in Italy was the refusal of their ally, Rhegium, to join the Athenian side (6.44). This was quickly followed by the news that Segesta had only 30 talents to contribute to the war effort (6.46). With these considerations in mind it was time for the Athenian generals to hold a council of war to decide their plan of campaign. Nicias was determined to stick literally to the official objectives: they should sail to Selinus, which was the main objective of the expedition, and by force or by persuasion make an agreement between Selinus and Segesta; then sail around the island in a display of Athenian power and return home, unless they found some quick way to help Leontini or gaining some new allies (6.47). This plan was totally unsuited to the situation because it deliberately ignored the real wishes of the Athenians who wanted nothing less than conquest of Sicily. If the Athenian expedition were to return to Athens without having achieved this, it would have been sent out again with less chance of success. More than anything else this plan gives a clear insight into Nicias' cautious nature and his dislike of the whole Sicilian campaign:

> they should not put Athens at risk by wasting its resources.
>
> (Thucydides 6.47)

Alcibiades was appalled at the timidity and lack of enterprise of Nicias' plan, and believed that such a great task force should achieve something worthy of note. He recommended the use of diplomacy to win over Sicilian allies and supplies, and then proceed against Syracuse and Selinus, confident in their knowledge of whose support they could depend upon. However, they must first of all win over Messina because it was the gateway to Sicily and would make an excellent base for their army and navy (6.48). Alcibiades' plan had merit in its aim to strengthen the task force by acquiring more allies and in its recognition of the real aim of the expedition, but the element of surprise – so vital in warfare – would be lost. Clearly Alcibiades' plan was influenced by political considerations: the use of diplomacy would put his particular skills to the fore and avoided any potential military defeat that would result, with the charge still hanging over his head, in the ruin of his political career.

Lamachus had been chosen as general purely and simply on the basis of his military skills, and his plan was shaped by the immediate military situation and not influenced by politics. He advised that they should sail at once to Syracuse and fight a battle as soon as possible under the city walls as the enemy was totally unprepared:

> If they made a sudden attack while the enemy were still frightened of their coming, it would be their best chance of victory and would in every respect fill them with fear, both by the sight of the force (for it would appear at its greatest) and by the expectation of their future suffering, but most of all by the immediate danger of battle.
>
> (Thucydides 6.49.2)

Victory in battle against Syracuse would be far more successful than diplomacy in winning over allies to the Athenian cause. He also suggested as their base Megara, which was uninhabited and close to Syracuse by land and by sea. This was the plan that could have achieved success, if it had been implemented: the Syracusans had not set about the mobilization of their forces until the Athenians had reached Rhegium; they had fought no major naval battle since 453 and were facing the best navy in Greece; and their city defences were in a terrible state of disrepair. Lamachus' judgement was further justified by the early Athenian victories in 415 and the first part of the 414 campaigning season. However, to break the deadlock, he backed Alcibiades' plan.

Alcibiades' powers of persuasion failed to win over Messina, which he said was crucial for the Athenians' success, but the Athenians were well received at Naxos, and gained Catana as a base more by luck than judgement (6.50–51). At this moment came the summons for the recall of Alcibiades to face trial in Athens. His political enemies and rivals had conducted a very effective smear campaign against him, and the Athenians at home were determined to execute him. Alcibiades appeared to acquiesce in the Athenian demands but, when he reached Thurii on the journey home, he escaped and made his way eventually to Sparta (6.60–61). He was condemned to death in his absence, which gave him an even greater incentive to damage Athens.

Meanwhile, Nicias set about implementing his plan by sailing along the north coast of Sicily to Segesta and Selinus in the west of the island; there was also a successful attack on the small town of Hyccara, but an embarrassing failure at Hybla on the south coast near Gela (6.62). It was now October, and very little had been achieved in the three months or so since the arrival of the task force at Rhegium in July. Nothing in fact had been achieved in this period apart from the acquisition of Naxos and Catana as allies, which was to be expected, as they were anti-Syracuse; and the capture of Hyccara. Consequently, as Lamachus had accurately predicted, the Syracusans had put aside their initial panic and were gaining in confidence daily. Nicias' hesitation to use the forces under his command against the main foe had brought the Athenians into contempt – so much so that the Syracusans urged their generals to take the initiative and attack the Athenian base at Catana (6.63). This shamed Nicias into action and, by a false promise of betrayal by a supposedly anti-Athenian citizen of Catana, he lured the whole Syracusan army to Catana, while the Athenian forces sailed around to the Great Harbour in Syracuse. Nicias might have attempted at this moment to seize Syracuse by assault – which had been done in 461 by 600 mercenaries (Diodorus 11.76.2) – seeing as he had the whole Athenian army outside Syracuse, whose army was now at Catana, but he decided to await its return (6.64–66).

The Syracusans returned as quickly as possible to find the Athenians drawn up in an excellent position. On the next morning, the Athenians advanced to attack, catching the Syracusans unawares, and won a resounding victory by exploiting the Syracusans' lack of combat experience (6.67–71). The Athenians immediately set sail for Catana:

> For it was winter and it seemed impossible to wage war from there [i.e. Syracuse] until cavalry was sent from Athens and collected from the allies in order not to be inferior in this respect, and until money was collected from there and came from Athens.
>
> (Thucydides 6.71.2)

There is much to criticize as the campaign of 415 came to an end. Nicias had wasted four months before finally facing the enemy, which he knew that the Athenians had wanted him to attack from the outset. He could not fall back on the excuse that he was unaware of the problems to be faced in Sicily, as he gave a perfect summary of them in his second speech to the Assembly, in particular the quality of their cavalry (6.20–23). He was given a free hand by the Athenians to prepare whatever armed forces he needed, and yet he used the lack of cavalry as an excuse to postpone any further military action for another four months. If Nicias had followed Lamachus' plan and had attacked at once, the city might have fallen very quickly – compare Brasidas' sudden and devastating attack on Amphipolis in 424/3 (4.104); if not, then the cir-cumvallation (garrisoned walls or ramparts) could have been built before winter and, with Syracuse cut off from supplies and all outside help, their surrender would have been inevitable. Instead, the Athenians had revealed the areas of their military superiority and by contrast those of Syracusan weakness.

The Syracusans now had four months to rectify these deficiencies, which they did by slimming down their command structure and by introducing a vigorous training programme for their hoplites. In addition, they deci-ded, which ultimately saved Syracuse, to enlarge the line of fortifications so that any future circumvallation would have to be much longer and extend from sea to sea (6.75); this action again reflects on Nicias' lack of urgency – if he had attacked in the summer of 415, the much shorter distance to be covered would have ensured a quicker construction of the Athenian

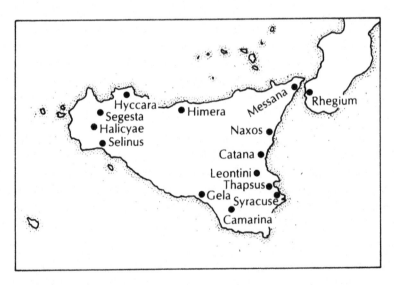

Map 8a Sicily

Map 8b The siege of Syracuse

circumvallation (6.72–75). They also requested help from the Peloponnese. The Corinthians were very willing, and the Spartans were won over by the speech of Alcibiades, who was now actively helping the Spartans: he exaggerated the Athenians' imperial plans to conquer Sicily and Carthage, before they finally turned their increased power on the Peloponnese. He advised them to send out troops, and appoint a first-class commander to organize the defence of Syracuse; and, finally, to renew the war openly against the Athenians, and to do great damage to them by permanently occupying Decelea in Attica (6.88–92). In the event, the Spartans waited another year before seizing Decelea, but sent out Gylippus whose dynamic leadership would be in such contrast to Nicias' hesitancy.

The campaign of 414

In March 414, with 650 cavalry in all from Athens, Catana and Segesta, Nicias and Lamachus initiated their strategy of circumvallation to capture Syracuse. This involved the seizure of the heights of Epipolae (see Map 8b), which was a triangular plain, stretching from its base at the walls of Syracuse in the east and rising to its apex near Euryelus in the west; the north and south sides of the triangle consisted of steep cliffs, and the easiest ascent to the plain of Epipolae was at Euryelus. The Athenian plan was to build walls between the two seas, thus cutting off supplies by land, and to maintain a sea blockade for the same purpose; if this was achieved, then the Syracusans would be starved into surrender. Nicias and Lamachus landed their hoplites before daybreak, marched at speed to Epipolae and seized control of Euryelus, easily defeating the Syracusan troops sent out to oppose them; this was immediately followed by the construction of a fort at Labdalum on the north cliff in which they stored their equipment and money (6.97). They then commenced work on the circumvallation, beginning with a fort called the Circle which was to be the hub of the two walls – one going north in the direction of Trogilus, and the other going south to the Great Harbour (6.98); the speed with which the walls were being constructed brought great dismay to the Syracusans.

The Syracusans' main defence plan was to build a counter-wall from their defences, at a right angle to the Athenian wall; if successful, there would be guaranteed access for supplies and troops from the rest of Sicily and beyond. The first counter-wall (S1 – see Map 8b) was begun from a position roughly opposite the Circle and stretched to the south cliff of Epipolae; however, Syracusan negligence and Athenian daring resulted in the capture of the counter-wall and further progress for the Athenian south wall to the Great Harbour (6.99–100). The Syracusans then constructed a second counter-wall (S2 – see Map 8b) on the lower ground between the southern cliff of Epipolae and the Great Harbour, which stretched as far as the river Anapus. There was a major battle at this second counter-wall, which was won decisively through the superior discipline of the Athenian army (6.101–2). The Athenian south wall to the Great Harbour was now completed, and it was only a matter of time before the only access to Syracuse – the north side of Epipolae – was blocked off. This on-going success brought other Sicilians, previously hesitating, into alliance with the Athenians, and demoralized the Syracusans:

> For the Syracusans no longer thought that they could win the war since no help was coming in not even from the Peloponnese, and they were discussing terms of surrender among themselves and with Nicias.
>
> (Thucydides 6.103.3)

A high price, however, was paid for this success with the death of Lamachus in the battle for the Syracusan second counter-wall; this left Nicias in sole command.

From March to June 414 the siege had been conducted with great energy under the joint command of Nicias and Lamachus, but it now suffered under the sole leadership of Nicias; slackness and complacency replaced vigour and perseverance.

It appears that a mood of over-confidence had filled Nicias and the Athenians due to the expectation that Syracuse was destined to surrender – valuable time, possibly as much as two months, was wasted on making the south wall to the Great Harbour a double one, whereas the priority should have been to finish the north wall to Trogilus in order to complete the circumvallation. There followed a catalogue of disastrous errors of judgement on the part of Nicias, which eventually allowed the Spartan commander, Gylippus, to wrest the initiative from him and to turn what should have been an impregnable position for the Athenians into one of desperation.

Gylippus set out from Laconia with four ships as an advance force and sailed to Southern Italy. Unfounded reports that Syracuse had now been completely blockaded encouraged him to attempt to save Italy from Athens. He sought help from the people of Thurii, who rebuffed him and informed Nicias of his arrival:

> But Nicias, although learning of his coming, despised the small number of his ships, in the same way as the Thurians, and having considered him to be acting more like a pirate he took no precautions as yet against him.

> (Thucydides 6.104.3)

This was Nicias' best chance to destroy Gylippus, before he had any chance to establish himself and while he was still at his most vulnerable. However, his contempt for Gylippus' four ships against the might of the Athenian navy gave the Spartan commander a breathing space. Gylippus was then allowed to slip through the straits of Messina, as Nicias had delayed in sending four ships to intercept him, and reached Himera on the north coast of Sicily, where his energy and confidence raised an army of around 3,000 men (7.1). With these he marched towards Syracuse without meeting any Athenian opposition.

Nicias must have realized that Gylippus' voyage to the north coast of Sicily was to raise an army and that the only access to Syracuse was through Euryelus, which route Nicias himself had used earlier to gain control of Epipolae. Therefore it was essential to defend the road to Euryelus in order to prevent Gylippus and his army from uniting with the Syracusans. Yet Nicias and the Athenians were taken totally by surprise by the arrival of Gylippus, who marched through Epipolae as if it was undefended (7.1–2) – this negligence was a bad blunder on the part of Nicias.

Gylippus' dynamism was revealed at once by his willingness to face the Athenians immediately in battle at their fortifications. However, the Syracusans' hoplites were so disorganized that he was forced to lead them away into more open ground. Thucydides is critical of Nicias' reaction to this retreat:

> Nicias did not lead the Athenians forward against them, but remained on the defensive by their own wall.
>
> (Thucydides 7.3.3)

This was an ideal opportunity for Nicias to defeat Gylippus, which would have destroyed his credibility among the Syracusans. The Athenians had already won four victories through their superior hoplites, and victory now would have led almost certainly to the surrender of the Syracusans, who had been on the point of holding an Assembly to discuss means of ending the war just before he arrived (7.2).

This refusal to fight cannot be explained away simply as another example of Nicias' caution, but rather as a result of fearful pessimism. For at this moment Nicias decided to fortify Plemmyrium, a promontory forming the southern side of the narrow entrance to the Great Harbour:

> He was now turning his attention more towards the war at sea, seeing that the land war, since the arrival of Gylippus, was less hopeful for themselves. Therefore, bringing across an army and ships, he built three forts; and most of the equipment was stored in them and the large boats and warships were now moored there.
>
> (Thucydides 7.4.4–5)

Apart from Nicias' personal responsibility for failing to prevent the arrival of Gylippus, which would have avoided this situation, his pessimism was unwarranted when the catalogue of Athenian success up to this moment is considered; yet, he had lost the confidence to win the all-important land war upon which the success of the whole campaign depended. Even more disturbing was the deterioration of the fighting quality of the fleet that arose from this move – the need to obtain water and supplies from further afield led to constant casualties inflicted by the Syracusan cavalry (7.4.6).

On the next day after his arrival Gylippus set about putting his plan to save Syracuse into operation. First of all, he threatened the Athenian fortifications with his army in order to divert their attention, while a detachment of troops captured the Athenian fort at Labdalum (7.3); second, he started the construction of the third Syracusan counter-wall, which was to run north of the Circle in the direction of the north side of Epipolae (7.4). As the two walls approached, Gylippus decided to attack the Athenian army, but was defeated; he accepted full responsibility for fighting the battle in a narrow space, where he could not make use of his cavalry and javelin-throwers (7.5). Gylippus then led his army out for a second battle, which resulted in the first defeat of the Athenian forces in six battles and the continuation of the counter-wall beyond the Athenian wall (7.6 – S3, see Map 8b). It was essential for Nicias to recapture this Syracusan wall; otherwise the circumvallation could not be completed and the initiative would lie with the Syracusans – one defeat in six was disappointing, but this could be reversed. However, this defeat seemed to confirm Nicias' fears about the effect of Gylippus' arrival, who was allowed to complete the counter-wall to Euryelus, thus ensuring access for supplies and the extra troops which he now intended to recruit in the rest of Sicily. The Syracusans' confidence increased dramatically; so much so that they began to train their naval crews with the intention of challenging the Athenian fleet (7.7). All this brought despondency to Nicias who, at the end of the summer of 414, sent an urgent letter to the Athenians, stressing the dangerous situation he was in, and urging either the recall of the whole expedition or the despatch of substantial reinforcements (7.8–15). The Athenians decided to send out a relief force – Eurymedon at once with ten ships, and Demosthenes in the spring with a larger force (7.16).

The campaign of 413

In the spring of 413, the Spartans decided that Athenian breaches of the Peace of Nicias justified their decision to renew the war; they invaded Attica and began to build a permanent fortification at Decelea in order to force the Athenians to fight on two fronts (7.18–19 – see Chapter 20 for a fuller discussion). However, the Athenians were still determined to offer the fullest support to the troops in Syracuse by sending out Demosthenes with 60 Athenian and 5 Chian ships, 1,200 Athenian hoplites and other forces from the islanders (7.20). Gylippus, being a first-class commander and well aware of Demosthenes' ability, decided that it was imperative to finish off Nicias' force before the arrival of Demosthenes. The first stage had to be the capture of Plemmyrium. He persuaded the Syracusans to fight a sea-battle on the following day, after he had brought his army secretly during the night around to Plemmyrium (7.21–22). The Syracusans launched their attack early in the morning with 80 triremes, which were met by 60 Athenian ships – after an initial success, the Syracusans were defeated owing to their lack of experience. But the Athenian garrisons had gone down to the shore to watch the sea battle which had been anticipated by Gylippus. He swiftly captured the three forts, which contained so much naval equipment, and established control over Plemmyrium (7.23). This was a disastrous blow for the Athenians:

> The capture of Plemmyrium was the greatest and the chief reason for the decline of the Athenian army ... and in other respects this event caused confusion and despondency in the army.
>
> (Thucydides 7.24.3)

The Syracusans now held both sides of the harbour, and the Athenian navy was hemmed in the Great Harbour by the army camp; even worse, Athenian supply lines were under constant threat from the Syracusan ships blockading the entrance to the harbour. The negligence and carelessness of the Plemmyrium garrisons were symptomatic of Nicias' failure as the commander-inchief to instil a sense of purpose and professionalism in his army.

The second stage of Gylippus' plan was to defeat Nicias' navy. The Syracusan ships were redesigned for fighting in the narrow waters of the Great Harbour: their bows were shortened and also strengthened by added timber with the intention of ramming head-on the light bows of the Athenian ships (7.36). Gylippus planned a joint attack by land and by sea to put added pressure on the Athenians. The land forces threatened the Athenian fortifications, while 80 Syracusan ships set sail against 75 Athenian ships. The first day's fighting proved inconclusive, but on the second day the Syracusan modifications of their prows proved decisive, and they won their first naval victory (7.37–41). The result of this victory convinced the Syracusans of their naval superiority and, together with their confidence in their land army, of their ability to defeat Nicias' army completely. As they prepared to deliver the final blow on land and at sea, the Syracusans suffered the greatest blow to their morale – the arrival of Demosthenes with 73 ships, 5,000 hoplites and a great force of javelin-throwers, slingers and archers (7.42).

If Thucydides' account of Demosthenes' assessment of the Syracusan campaign is accepted, he was highly critical of Nicias' generalship:

> Demosthenes, seeing the situation before him, decided that he could not waste time nor suffer the same things as Nicias had. For Nicias had caused terror when he first arrived, but when he did not attack the Syracusans at once and wintered in Catana, he became an object of contempt. In addition, Gylippus had stolen a march on him by coming from the Peloponnese with an army, which the Syracusans would not have sent for if Nicias had attacked at once, because, thinking that they had sufficient troops, they would not have realized that they were inferior and would have been blockaded by walls so that, even if they had sent for help then, it would have been much less effective.
>
> (Thucydides 7.42.3)

However, it is difficult to believe that Thucydides obtained first-hand evidence of Demosthenes' views, as the general was soon to be executed by the Syracusans. Therefore it would appear that the above quotation records Thucydides' own opinion, and reinforces his earlier implicit approval of Lamachus' original plan and his judgement that it had the greatest chance of success (6.49). Nevertheless, knowledge of Demosthenes' dynamic and decisive generalship in the Archidamian War (see Chapter 19) and of his immediate all-out attempt to seize the Syracusan third counter-wall strongly suggests that he shared the same view as Thucydides as to the root cause of the Athenian difficulties at Syracuse: Nicias' inability to prosecute the war energetically. He also totally approved of Lamachus' original strategy of an instant attack, while the enemy was in a state of terror and despair at the size of the new force. With his practised eye, he knew that the key to success had to be the capture of the Syracusan third counter-wall, which would allow the Athenians to complete the circumvallation of Syracuse and starve it into surrender:

> He thought that this was the quickest way to end the war. For he would either be successful and capture Syracuse, or he would lead away the army and not wear down the Athenian forces on campaign there nor the resources of the whole state.
>
> (Thucydides 7.42.5)

Demosthenes' attempt to capture the Syracusan counter-wall at night ended in confusion and failure (7.42–45). This defeat brought an end to the Athenian aims of the conquest of Syracuse and Sicily; they were replaced by the aim of survival. The final harrowing days of failed sea-battles, of the attempt to escape by land to Catana, of the slaughter at the river Assinarus and of Demosthenes' and Nicias' executions are described so dramatically, it is reasonable to believe that Thucydides was greatly influenced by tragedy in his presentation of these events (7.46–87). Thucydides summarized the Sicilian expedition as follows:

> This was the greatest event to have happened in the war and, as it seems to me, the greatest that we know about in Greek history – to the winners the most splendid of victories, to the losers the most disastrous of defeats, for they were totally defeated in every respect and endured the greatest sufferings – they experienced utter ruin, as the saying goes, with the loss of their army, navy and everything. Only a few from the many returned home.
>
> (Thucydides 7.87.5–6)

The causes of the Athenian defeat

Thucydides' long and detailed account of the Sicilian expedition in Books 6 and 7 reveals his own thinking that the expedition was a mistake, because it was the biggest departure from Pericles' defensive strategy. Pericles had advised the Athenians not to extend the Empire while at war (2.65.7), and both Nicias and Thucydides himself (a great admirer of Pericles) recognized that the 421 Peace of Nicias was a 'hollow peace' and that a state of war existed in truth from 421 to 414/3. It is probably for this reason that Thucydides underestimated the fact that the expedition had every chance of achieving military success, and that the chronic disunity of Sicily was a significant factor in the Athenians' favour. Instead, he emphasized the Athenian ignorance of the size of the island and its inhabitants and of the scale of the war to be fought there (6.1), even though alliances with Sicilian states stretched back to the 440s and military campaigns had been undertaken continually from 427–424.

The issue about the reason for the expedition's failure should have been clear-cut from Thucydides' detailed narrative of Books 6 and 7: he makes it abundantly clear that the serious military errors of Nicias were the chief reason for the defeat of the Athenian forces; and this judgement of Nicias' poor leadership is reinforced by Thucydides' strongly implied support for Lamachus' plan of action (6.49) and his 'reporting' of Demosthenes' damning critique of Nicias' conduct of the campaign (7.42). However, Thucydides' analysis of the failure of the Sicilian expedition has been complicated by his own statement in his review of the Athenians' achievements under Pericles and their failure under his successors:

> Many mistakes were made, as you would expect in a great city with an empire to govern, including the Sicilian expedition, which was not so much an error of judgement about the enemy, but the failure of those at home to take the right decisions (prosphora) for the forces overseas; through their private intrigues for the leadership of the people, they weakened the army in the field and brought confusion to Athens' policy by their disputes.
>
> (Thucydides 2.65.11)

It seems certain that Thucydides wrote these words after the end of the Peloponnesian War in 404 and some time after the composition of Books 6 and 7. Thucydides, in this quotation, accepts that the expedition could have been victorious, but assigns the responsibility for its failure, not to Nicias and his military blunders, but to 'those at home'. It would seem that Thucydides, writing after 404, had changed his mind about Alcibiades' military ability which he displayed so successfully in the years 411–407 during the Ionian War (see Chapter 22) on behalf of the Athenians, and had decided that Alcibiades' recall and condemnation was the crucial factor in the defeat of the Sicilian expedition by removing Athens' most talented general. Therefore, it was his political enemies at home who should bear the brunt of the blame for making the wrong decision to recall him – they had put their own personal ambitions of leading the 'demos' before the needs and the good of the state.

The evidence of Books 6 and 7 is overwhelming: poor generalship and military blunders should be accepted as the main cause of failure. Although there is a case that 'those at home' should be blamed for the quarrels over the Mutilation of the Hermae affair and the lack of wisdom in sending out Alcibiades with a charge over his head, this was not decisive. It must be remembered that Alcibiades' plan of campaign (6.48), which advocated diplomacy before any attack on Syracuse, was also lacking in vigour and contributed to the delay in the siege of Syracuse. His recommendations to the Spartans after his desertion undoubtedly did damage to the Athenians, but Decelea was not fortified for another year when Nicias' forces were already in a state of desperation; and if Nicias had built the circumvallation in 415, as Lamachus and Demosthenes believed to be the correct strategy, Alcibiades' advice about the despatch of Gylippus would have been too late to save Syracuse (see 7.42.3 above). In fact, 'those at home' are hardly mentioned after Alcibiades' condemnation, having granted full powers to the generals to conduct the campaign (6.8); they also sent out with speed all the reinforcements that Nicias requested, without complaint or criticism. Perhaps, in the final analysis, the blame for this ill-conceived expedition should be directed at Alcibiades, not for his advice to the Spartans, but for his arguments in the Athenian Assembly which were so utterly persuasive in convincing the Athenians that there was little risk:

> Our ships will guarantee our safety whether we remain, if things go well, or go away. For we will be masters of the sea even against all the Sicilians put together.
>
> (Thucydides 6.18.5)

Bibliography

Andrewes, A. *CAH vol. 5*, 2nd., edn, ch. 10.

Ferguson, W. S. *CAH vol. 5*, ch. 10.

Gomme, A. W., Andrewes, A. and Dover, K. J. *A Historical Commentary on Thucydides, Books V.25–VII*, (esp. pp. 313–16, 419–21).

Hornblower, S. *The Greek World 479–323 BC*, ch. 12.

Kagan, D. *The Archidamian War*, chs 6 and 9.

Powell, A. *Athens and Sparta*, ch. 5.

de Ste. Croix, G. E. M. *The Origins of the Peloponnesian War*, ch. VI.iii.

Westlake, H. D. *Essays on the Greek Historians and Greek History*, ch. 6.

22

PERSIAN INTERVENTION IN THE
IONIAN WAR, 413–404

In the spring of 413, possibly as the result of Alcibiades' advice (Thucydides 6.91.6 – all references in this chapter are to Thucydides, unless otherwise stated), the Spartans, under King Agis, invaded Attica and occupied Decelea, a fortified outpost equidistant from Athens and Boeotia (7.27): thus this phase of the Peloponnesian War (413–404) is often referred to as the Decelean War. The Athenians' attacks on the east coast of Laconia in 414 (6.105.2), the constant raiding from Athenian-held Pylos (7.18), and the Athenian refusal to submit these issues to arbitration convinced the Spartans that the Athenians had clearly broken the terms of the Peace of Nicias, and that they were justified in renewing the war (7.18). This permanent occupation of Decelea caused many problems for the Athenians:

> It did great damage to the Athenians and, by its destruction of property and the loss
> of men, was one of the chief causes of the decline in Athenian power.
>
> (Thucydides 7.27.3)

The invasions in the Archidamian War had only been short affairs, the longest being 40 days, but now the Athenians were permanently deprived of most of Attica; the revenue from the silver mines was lost; 20,000 slaves escaped – the majority being skilled workmen and vital for the Athenian economy; the food supplies from Euboea had to be brought in by the more expensive sea route; and, finally, there was the constant, exhausting guard-duty by day and night (7.27–28).

However, this strand of Spartan strategy, for all its debilitating effects on the Athenians, was insufficient to win the war as King Agis of Sparta so astutely observed as late as 410:

> Agis, seeing from Decelea many corn ships sailing into the Piraeus, said that it was
> useless for his troops to cut off the Athenians from their land, which had been done
> for some time now, unless some one were to seize the places from where the grain
> kept coming in by sea.
>
> (Xenophon, *Hellenica* 1.1.35)

The Spartans had to be far more adventurous and challenge the Athenians at sea in Ionia, and especially in the Hellespont: only by breaking up the Athenians' sea empire, on which they depended for revenue, and by preventing grain from the Hellespont reaching the beleaguered Athenians could the Spartans win the war. Previously, in the Archidamian War, there was little hope of this owing to the strength of the Athenian navy and a lack of finance for the maintenance of a fleet, and it was probably for this reason (as well as the desire to get back the captured Spartiates) that Brasidas' strategy in his Thraceward campaign of 424–422 was not sufficiently supported by the authorities in Sparta (see Chapter 19). The destruction of the Athenian fleet in Sicily in 413, however, had fulfilled one of the two preconditions for potential Spartan success in Ionia; the other – sufficient finance to pay the crews of a fleet that was large enough to wrest power from the Athenians in the Aegean – required the full involvement of the one power that had the wealth and the desire to destroy the Athenian Empire: Persia. Persia's financial help to the Spartans, fitful at first but more committed later, gave the Spartans the means to wage war with the Athenians in Ionia: hence 'Ionian War' is the alternative name for the war from 413–404. However, it is essential to see how the Persians were gradually drawn into the Peloponnesian War from the beginning and why the King of Persia chose to support the Spartans in the Ionian War.

Persia and the Greeks, 431–414

The Greeks on both sides had already in the Archidamian War (431–421) thought about gaining the support of Persia. King Archidamus, in his speech to the Spartans in 432, had advised the acquisition of new allies who could supply Sparta with a navy and finance, strongly hinting at Persia (1.82.1). In 431, both sides planned to send embassies to Persia (2.7.1); and in 430 a Peloponnesian embassy on the way to the King of Persia to request money and military support was handed over by the son of Sitalces, a ruler in Thrace, to the Athenians who executed these ambassadors (2.67; Herodotus 7.137). The Persians themselves were not averse to taking advantage of the Greeks when at war with each other. Pissouthnes was the 'satrap' (provincial governor) of the Persian province in south-western Asia Minor with his capital at Sardis. The 'satraps' would normally refer to the King all major matters of policy that involved his prestige or wealth, but they do seem to have had considerable independence and freedom of action. Pissouthnes had already intervened and helped the Samian oligarchs at the time of its revolt in 440 (1.115) – a clear breach of the Peace of Callias. In 430, Itamenes, a subordinate of Pissouthnes, had helped the pro-Persian faction in Colophon to seize power and revolt from Athens; and when the Colophonian exiles at Notium clashed with each other, Pissouthnes sent mercenaries to help his supporters in Notium (3.34).

Although Thucydides has little to say about Greek–Persian affairs before 412, it is clear that the Spartans were still sending embassies to the King of Persia, Artaxerxes. In 425 the Persian Artaphernes was intercepted by the Athenians at Eion on his way to Sparta. The King's translated message made interesting reading:

> many other points were mentioned but the chief point, with regard to the Spartans, was that he did not know what they wanted. Although many ambassadors had come to him, none were saying the same things. If they wished to make a definite proposal, they should send men to him with Artaphernes.
>
> (Thucydides 4.50.2)

Here was the root of the problem for Sparta. They knew that the King's price for giving military aid to Sparta would be, at the very least, the return of the Asiatic Greeks to Persian domination, and there was no way that they could agree to this without destroying their credibility as the self-proclaimed liberators of Greece – hence the Spartans' evasiveness in their dealings with the King. The disaster at Pylos and the fear of a 'Helot' revolt probably put paid to any Spartan plans of winning Persian support, as their whole attention from 425 was fixed on regaining the captured Spartiates from Athens and taking precautions against the Helots.

It was the Athenians, possibly worried by the King's message to the Spartans seeking to establish some concrete grounds for an alliance, who set about improving relations with Persia. Artaphernes was sent back to the King with some Athenian ambassadors, but when they reached Ephesus and learned of Artaxerxes' death, the Athenians returned home (4.50.3). Thucydides mentions no other negotiations, but the combination of a speech in 391 by Andocides (3.29), in which he mentions the presence of his uncle Epilycus at the negotiations that brought about a treaty and a friendship forever with Persia, and of a fourth-century copy of a fifth-century decree, honouring a certain Heraclides of Clazomenae for his help in negotiating a treaty with the King of Persia (ML 70), suggests that a treaty was signed in 424/3. This whole issue is fraught with problems, but the balance of scholarly opinion does incline towards acceptance of its authenticity and its date.

There are also convincing political reasons for this rapprochement between Athens and Persia. The Athenians' confidence of 425/4 had taken a blow with the defeat at Delium in 424 and with Brasidas' capture of Amphipolis and his success at stirring up revolt amongst their allies in the Thraceward region (see Chapter 19). If Brasidas were to gain Persian military support, he could strike at the Hellespont, Athens' lifeline in respect of the transportation of grain from the Black Sea to the Piraeus – hence the desperate need for peaceful relations with Persia. The new Persian king, Darius II (also known as Darius the Bastard) had pressing reasons for signing the treaty. Artaxerxes I had fathered one legitimate son from a Persian mother, Xerxes, but also seventeen bastard sons from concubines. The murder of Xerxes, after only 45 days as king, by one of Artaxerxes' illegitimate sons led to a power struggle. At some time in 424/3 Darius II became King of Persia, but his position was tenuous; there were the potential claims of the other bastard sons and of others of pure Persian stock, linked by blood to the royal family. In fact, Darius II's brother soon led a rebellion against him (Ctesias 50) which was followed by several others, including the revolt of Pissouthnes, the satrap in south-western Asia Minor and a grandson of Darius I, at some time between 423 and 415. The last thing that the new king wanted was to alienate the Athenians and drive them into the arms of one of his rivals. Therefore the treaty of 424/3 was of great benefit to both sides. It was, in essence, probably a renewal of the terms of the 449 Peace of Callias, but included the stronger statement of eternal friendship due to the current military difficulties of both sides. The Athenians' betrayal of this eternal friendship by supporting the revolt of Amorges, Pissouthnes' son, in 414 proved to be a fatal error of judgement.

Persia and the Greeks, 413–404

The news of the Athenian disaster in Sicily became common knowledge in Greece in the autumn of 413 and this led to a readiness among Athens' allies to revolt (8.2). This news also inspired the Spartans to throw themselves more wholeheartedly into defeating the Athenians by sea (8.2), and they commissioned the construction of 100 'triremes', built by themselves and their allies, to be ready for action in 412 (8.3). During the winter of 413/2 appeals for Spartan help came from Euboea, Lesbos, Erythrae and Chios to aid their proposed revolts from Athens.

Far more important for the eventual outcome of the war were the approaches to the Spartans by the two satraps of Persia's westernmost provinces in Asia Minor – Tissaphernes and Pharnabazus (8.5–6). Tissaphernes was the satrap of south-west Asia Minor, roughly covering the area of Lydia, with its capital at Sardis. He had gained the province from a grateful Darius II by capturing Pissouthnes, the former satrap, who had revolted from the King of Persia at some time between 423 and 415; however, he still had to contend with Amorges, Pissouthnes' son and ally of the Athenians, who had either continued or renewed the revolt after his father's capture and execution. Pharnabazus was the satrap of Hellespontine Phrygia in north-west Asia Minor with its capital at Dascylium. Their involvement in Greek affairs was due to the orders of the King of Persia, who also saw his chance to exploit the Athenian disaster in Sicily:

> For it happened that Tissaphernes had been recently ordered to exact the tribute from his own province, which he owed because he was unable to collect it on

account of the Athenians. He therefore thought that he would more easily collect the tribute by weakening the Athenians; and at the same time thought that he would make the Spartans allies of the King and thus, in accordance with the King's orders, either capture alive or kill Amorges, the bastard son of Pissouthnes, who was in revolt in Caria.

(Thucydides 8.5.5)

Pharnabazus was also under the King's orders to collect the outstanding tribute from the Asiatic Greeks, who had been paying phoros to the Athenians from 478, and wished to make use of the Spartans for this very purpose. It is clear that the Persians had never genuinely accepted Athens' right to collect tribute and had never given up hope of bringing these cities back under Persian control. The Spartans, therefore, had to choose their area of campaigning: either cooperation with Pharnabazus in Lesbos and the Hellespont, or with Tissaphernes in Chios and the southern coast of Asia Minor. In the event the Spartans, persuaded by Alcibiades' advice through the 'Ephor' Endius, made the wrong decision to work with Tissaphernes, relying upon his promise to maintain the Peloponnesian armed forces (8.6.2).

In the summer of 412 the Spartans at last galvanized themselves into action, although they soon became discouraged by the defeat of their Chios-bound fleet, at the hands of the Athenians (8.10). However, the arrival of the Spartan Chalcideus and Alcibiades with five ships, and the promise of more to come, persuaded Chios to revolt (8.14). This revolt of Athens' most powerful ally, still autonomous and the sole supplier of ships, had a profound effect upon the Athenians, who feared that Chios would be the rallying-point for all the disaffected subject-allies that wished to revolt. Therefore they voted to use the reserve of 1,000 talents, which Pericles had put aside for emergencies, to strengthen their fleet and to set about the recovery of Chios (8.15). The military campaigns of the next twelve months (summer 412 to summer 411) appear very disjointed, due partly to the unfinished revision of Book 8 by Thucydides, and partly to the piecemeal nature of the fighting. In essence, the Spartans were attempting to widen the revolt of Athens' subject-allies, and the Athenians to contain it, which resulted in both sides sending out increasingly larger fleets. Erythrae, Clazomenae, Teos, Miletus, Lebedos, Erae, Methymna and Mytilene revolted from Athens in 412 (8.14–23), although the Athenian forces, based at Samos, soon recovered Mytilene and Clazomenae.

The major reason for Sparta's inability to deliver the decisive blow to the Athenians was the duplicity of Tissaphernes over pay for the Spartan fleet. After the revolt of Miletus, the first treaty was agreed between the Spartans and their allies on one side and the King and Tissaphernes on the other (8.18). The opening clause is remarkable in what is conceded to the Persians:

Whatever territory and cities the King holds and the King's ancestors held, these are to belong to the King.

(Thucydides 8.18.1)

This, in effect, gave the Persian king control over not only Asia Minor but also Thessaly and Boeotia, which had medized in the Persian War of 480–479. The treaty also laid down that the Athenians should be prevented from collecting phoros from their cities; that the war should be waged jointly by the Spartans and the Persians, and that the consent of both allies was required in order to make peace with the Athenians. The Persians were clearly the main beneficiaries of this treaty, since, in theory, it recognized their claim over the Asiatic Greeks and beyond, and did not formally commit them to pay the Spartans. Soon after this, with the help of the Peloponnesians, Tissaphernes captured Amorges at his base in Iasos and ended the revolt, which had plagued the King and which Tissaphernes had been specifically ordered to suppress (8.28); then he caused Cnidus to revolt and installed a Persian garrison (8.31). Owing to Spartan dissatisfaction, a second treaty was soon negotiated, which was similar to the first except that the King agreed to pay the expenses of all troops in his territory at his request, and the Spartans agreed not to replace the Athenians as the collectors of tribute (8.36–37).

It was in the winter of 412/1 that Tissaphernes began his policy of weakening the Spartans by using his most effective weapon – money. Thucydides mentions Tissaphernes' reduction of Peloponnesian pay on two occasions: first, soon after the capture of Amorges, when he paid a month's payment at the rate of six obols per day per man, but proposed for the future to pay only three obols unless the King should decide otherwise (8.29); second, through the alleged influence of Alcibiades, when he decided to pay only three obols per day per man, and that irregularly (8.45). It is not clear whether these are two separate occasions, or whether both passages refer to the one and same pay reduction; either way it caused damage to the Spartans. According to Thucydides (8.45–47), Alcibiades, who had come under suspicion at Sparta and had consequently sought refuge with Tissaphernes, masterminded this policy of pay reduction. He allegedly pointed out the danger to the Persians of giving their full support to the Spartans to ensure the victory, since they, after the defeat of the Athenians, were bound to use their land and naval forces to liberate the Greeks from the Persians. He argued that the Athenians would make better allies as they would be more willing to concede sovereignty over the Asiatic Greeks to the King; and therefore it would be far better to let both sides wear themselves down and, when the Athenians were sufficiently weakened, to get rid of the Spartans completely.

As a result of Alcibiades' advice:

> Tissaphernes gave poor support to the Peloponnesians and did not allow them to fight a sea-battle, but kept saying that the Phoenician fleet would come and that they could then fight with greater superiority. Thus he damaged their cause and severely weakened the efficiency of the fleet which had been very great; and in general he made it very clear that he was not eager to wage war.

> (Thucydides 8.46.5)

The accuracy of Alcibiades' assessment of the Spartans' ultimate objectives in Asia Minor was soon confirmed to Tissaphernes at his meeting in Cnidus with the eleven Spartan commissioners, who had been sent out to organize the conduct of the war. Lichas, one of the commissioners, repudiated the two previous treaties on the grounds that acceptance of the King's territorial claims would result in Sparta offering the Greeks, including the mainland as far as Boeotia, not liberation but Persian domination (8.43). His demand for a new treaty was met by the angry walkout of Tissaphernes. Soon after this, the three cities of prosperous Rhodes revolted and joined the Spartans, thereby raising their hopes of being able to fund the war themselves without needing Tissaphernes' money (8.44).

Alcibiades' advice to Tissaphernes was designed not only to injure the Spartans, who had ordered his execution, but also to engineer his own recall to Athens. He was convinced that the democracy would never pardon him, and consequently that the establishment of an oligarchy was the essential pre-condition for his return to Athens. Therefore he started to negotiate with the officer class of the Athenian fleet at Samos, promising the friendship and support of Tissaphernes in return for the overthrow of the democracy (8.47). This proposal was welcomed enthusiastically by the Athenian upper class at Samos and in Athens who were bearing the economic brunt of the democracy's military mistakes, and accepted grudgingly by the sailors at Samos who were at least pleased at the thought of Persian pay (8.48). Phrynichus, who distrusted Alcibiades and refused to believe that the Persians would desert the Spartans in favour of the Athenians, and Peisander, two generals with the fleet at Samos, then began their machinations in early 411 to overthrow the democracy and establish an oligarchy (see Chapter 23). The Athenian Assembly (in a specially convened meeting at Colonus outside the walls) reluctantly agreed to a change in the constitution and the recall of Alcibiades, as they felt that the survival of Athens was at stake (8.53–54). Peisander was sent out to negotiate with Alcibiades and Tissaphernes (see Chapter 23 for fuller discussion).

Tissaphernes, however, had little intention of making an alliance with the Athenians, the King's long-standing enemy, especially as he wished to maintain the policy of wearing down both sides and also because he was afraid of alienating the Spartans, based so close to his satrapy. Alcibiades, realizing this and not wishing to lose face in front of the Athenian envoys, deliberately engineered an Athenian walkout. He therefore proposed increasingly exorbitant demands in return for a treaty: at first, the handing over of the whole of Ionia; and when this was accepted, then the islands off the coast; and, when there were still no objections, finally the right of the King to sail anywhere along his coast with as large a fleet as he wished. This proved to be the breaking point as it would give control of the Aegean to the Persians and expose Greece to another invasion. The Athenians walked out (8.56). Tissaphernes then returned to the Spartans, gave them pay and negotiated a third treaty, almost certainly formulated by the King himself. The King's dominion was now limited to Asia Minor to overcome Lichas' earlier objections; Tissaphernes would pay the Peloponnesian forces only until the King's fleet should arrive, after which the Peloponnesians must pay for their own ships or receive a loan from Tissaphernes (8.58).

This treaty also included, for the first time, the agreement of Pharnabazus, the satrap of Hellespontine Phrygia, and it is hardly a coincidence that the Spartans sent out a force under Dercylidas around April 411 to cooperate with Pharnabazus. As a result, Abydus and Lampsacus on the Hellespont revolted from Athens, although Lampsacus was soon retaken (8.61–62). By mid-summer the Peloponnesians were again disaffected with Tissaphernes owing to the irregularity of pay. The offer of Pharnabazus to pay for a fleet in the Hellespont and the appeal of Byzantium for help to revolt encouraged them to send a force there under Clearchus. A storm prevented most of the 40 ships from reaching the Hellespont, but the 10 ships that did arrive brought about the revolt of Byzantium (8.80). The recall of Alcibiades by the Athenians at Samos led to the belief that Tissaphernes was now in collaboration with the Athenians, and this, combined with the dissatisfaction over their lack of pay from him, provoked great anger amongst the Peloponnesians and especially among the Syracusan allies (8.83–84). Therefore, when Mindarus took over the command of the Spartans and their allies in mid-summer, mindful of the duplicity of Tissaphernes and the anger among his forces, he decided to respond to Pharnabazus' appeals and to move the main theatre of war to the Hellespont. He set out with the main fleet and reached the Hellespont where he joined up with 16 ships that had previously been sent there (8.101).

In late September or October 411 there took place the first major naval battle of the Ionian War. Mindarus with 86 ships attacked Thrasyllus and Thrasybulus, the Athenian generals, and their 76 ships at Cynossema, opposite Abydus in the Hellespont. The result was a victory for the Athenians, which did much to boost their morale after their sufferings under the rule of the Four Hundred (see Chapter 23) and the revolt of Euboea (8.104–6). Even more encouraging was the withdrawal of the Peloponnesian fleet of 50 ships from Euboea, which was still in revolt, to reinforce Mindarus' forces at the Hellespont; this same fleet was almost destroyed in a great storm as it passed the headland of Mount Athos. Four days after the battle, the Athenians crushed the revolt of Cyzicus in the Propontis (8.107).

It is at this point that the excellent history of Thucydides is broken off, and the *Hellenica* of Xenophon and the *History* of Diodorus become the main sources (referred to as 'Xen.' and 'D.S.', respectively, in this chapter) for the remaining part of the war. Although there have been modern attempts to redeem the reputation of Xenophon, the omissions, the bias and the inability to analyse deeply rightly draw unfavourable comparisons with the quality of Thucydides' work, whose detailed and analytical account of historical events has been so helpful to modern scholarship. Diodorus' history must always be used with great caution, particularly when he uses as his source Ephorus, a fourth-century historian, who was not highly rated in the ancient world. However, the discovery in 1908 of fragments of the reliable and solid 'Oxyrhynchus Historian' reveal him to be the ultimate source for Ephorus in this period; thus Diodorus' narrative to the end of the war can be considered more trustworthy than usual, while Xenophon's merits as a reliable narrative historian have been devalued even more by the discovery.

Soon after the battle of Cynossema, there was near to Abydus a hard-fought battle which was turned in favour of the Athenians by the arrival of Alcibiades with 20 ships; the Peloponnesian forces were saved from further damage by Pharnabazus' land forces (D.S. 13.45–47; Xen. 1.1.4–7). Both sides now asked their home governments for reinforcements, as they prepared for the crucial conflict about mastery of the Hellespont. Mindarus' decision to make the Hellespont the main theatre of war and to cooperate with Pharnabazus marked a significant change in Spartan strategy: instead of a slow war of attrition by picking off individual Athenian subjects, the Spartans were attempting to win the war quickly by cutting off the Athenians' grain supply and starving them into surrender. The Athenians naturally had to prevent this outcome with all their might. In March or April 410, Mindarus with 60 ships seized Cyzicus in the Propontis, but the Athenians with 86 ships, in three divisions under Alcibiades, Thrasybulus and Theramenes, lured Mindarus into a sea-battle at Cyzicus. A great victory was won by the Athenians, resulting in the death of Mindarus and the loss of the entire Peloponnesian fleet, including the Syracusan ships which were burned by their own crews to prevent them from falling into enemy hands (D.S. 13.50–51; Xen. 1.1.11–18). The Athenians then established a fortified customs station at Chrysopolis, opposite Byzantium, which ensured the safety of the grain supply and brought in much needed income by charging a customs duty of 10 per cent on all Black Sea shipping. This military success also brought about the restoration of full democracy at Athens (see Chapter 23).

The desperation of the Spartans was summed up in the typically 'laconic' despatch of Hippocrates, Mindarus' vice admiral, to Sparta:

'Ships gone. Mindarus dead. The men are starving. Don't know what to do.'

(Xenophon, *Hellenica* 1.1.23)

According to Diodorus (13.52), the Spartans even sued for peace on the terms of each side keeping what it already possessed, the withdrawal of all fortified garrisons in each other's territory and a return of captives. It would seem from the Spartans' willingness to make a separate peace that they considered the third treaty with Tissaphernes to have been rendered invalid by his failure to maintain and pay the Peloponnesian forces. The Athenians, however, flushed with confidence, once again rejected the opportunity to make peace on favourable terms, as they had in 425 after the Pylos success (D.S. 13.53).

The following three years (410–407) brought increasing success for the Athenians in the Ionian War, especially in the Hellespontine region. Although Pharnabazus was most helpful in supporting the Peloponnesian survivors from the battle of Cyzicus and ordered the construction of a new fleet (Xen. 1.1.24–25), the Peloponnesians were in no fit state to engage the Athenians at sea for a few years. The Athenians controlled most of the cities in the Hellespont and the islands, except for Chios, but Ionia and Caria were still mainly in the hands of the Spartans and Tissaphernes. Thrasyllus had been sent to Athens in the winter of 411/0 to obtain reinforcements for the Hellespontine fleet to consolidate Athenian control of this area, but it seems that the involvement of these generals, especially Alcibiades, in the establishment of the constitution of The Five Thousand (see Chapter 23) had made the Athenians reluctant to support them. In fact, Thrasyllus was sent out in 409 with a large force to Ionia with the strategic purpose of capturing Ephesus, which would have been a perfect springboard for the recovery of the cities in Ionia and offsetting the success of the Athenian generals in the Hellespont. However, Thrasyllus' forces suffered a defeat at the hands of Tissaphernes at Ephesus (Xen. 1.2.1–10), and thus, in November or December 409, they joined the Athenian forces at the Hellespont. Friction between both forces was resolved by a convincing victory over Pharnabazus at Abydus in the same winter (Xen. 1.2.15–17). There followed further successes for the Athenians in 408 with the recovery of Chalcedon and Byzantium, both at the mouth of the Black Sea (D.S. 13.66.1–4; Xen. 1.3.2–7).

By the end of 408, the Spartans were militarily in a weak position: Abydus was their sole remaining possession in the Hellespont; the Sicilian forces had been withdrawn in 409 to face a Carthaginian attack on Sicily; also Pharnabazus, who had been their most consistent supporter, was negotiating after his defeat at Chalcedon with the Athenians, and was even accompanying them on an embassy to the King (Xen. 1.3.8–9); and even Tissaphernes might have been supporting the Athenians, as he is mentioned in a decree honouring Evagoras of Salamis (IG I³ 113; SEG X 127). There may even have been another attempt by the Spartans to make peace with the Athenians (Androtion FGH324 F44). This Spartan weakness may have been the main reason for Alcibiades' and his fellow generals' willingness to return to Athens, instead of vigorously prosecuting the war in Ionia in the first half of 407. However, at this very moment, Sparta's fortunes were to change dramatically with the arrival of two powerful personalities, Lysander as the Spartan 'nauarch' (admiral-in-chief), and Cyrus, the son of King Darius II.

The turning point in Spartan–Persian relations was the return of a Spartan embassy from the King in the spring of 407 and the statement of Boiotios, one of the ambassadors:

that the Spartans had gained everything that they had wanted from the King.

(Xenophon, *Hellenica* 1.4.2)

It would seem that the King had decided to throw his weight fully and determinedly behind the Spartans to bring the war to an end. To achieve this, he had sent his younger son, Cyrus, as satrap of Lydia, Greater Phrygia and Cappadocia, and as commander of all the Persian forces in the west (Xen. *Anabasis*. 1.9.7). Cyrus had been given clear instructions from the King to wage war alongside the Spartans as vigorously as possible (D.S. 13.70.3; Xen. 1.4.3; 1.5.2–3); he said that he had also come with 500 talents and, if this was insufficient, he would use his own money to pay for the Peloponnesian fleet:

as the treaty (tas sunthekas) had laid down, there would be thirty minae [i.e. half a talent/3,000 drachmas] per month for each ship for as many ships as the Spartans should choose to maintain.

(Xenophon, *Hellenica* 1.4.3–5)

It would seem from the use of the words 'tas sunthekas' and the mention, for the first time, of specific pay rates that a treaty had been agreed between the Spartans and the King of Persia. It would seem from later negotiations that the Persians, in return, were granted the right to collect tribute from the Asiatic Greek cities, but that these cities were allowed to remain autonomous, as had previously been agreed between the towns of Chalcidice and the Athenians in the 421 Peace of Nicias (5.18.5).

Lysander, who established an excellent working relationship with the young Cyrus, asked him to increase the payment of the crews from 3 to 4 obols per day. Not only did Cyrus agree to the increase in pay, he also paid all the arrears and gave a month's wages in advance (Xen. 1.5.7). This act of generosity and good will, so different from their treatment at the hands of Tissaphernes, greatly increased the morale of the Peloponnesian sailors, but caused despondency among the Athenians, whose attempts to change Cyrus' mind through the agency of Tissaphernes proved futile (Xen. 1.5.8). The Spartans, at long last, had the necessary means to win the war at sea: a first-class commander, a large navy and regular pay. Success soon came, either late in 407 or in the spring of 406, at the battle of Notium, close to Ephesus. Alcibiades had left the Athenian fleet under the command of Antiochus with strict instructions to avoid battle, but Lysander lured him into a sea-battle and defeat (D.S. 13.71; Xen. 1.5.11–15). Although this was not a serious defeat, it destroyed Alcibiades' fragile relationship with the

Athenians; he retired in disgrace to his castle in Thrace, and thus the Athenians lost the services of their best general at the very time when they most needed him to oppose the newly invigorated Peloponnesians.

The Spartans, however, made a crucial error: Lysander was replaced as nauarch (admiral-in-chief) in summer 406 by Callicratidas; the post of nauarch was only tenable for a year. Lysander greatly resented this and made sure that there was no easy transfer of power. Instead of handing over the unused money to his successor, he returned it to Cyrus (Xen. 1.6.10); in addition, probably at his instigation, Lysander's supporters in the fleet began a whispering campaign against the new commander, stressing his inexperience compared to Lysander's (Xen. 1.6.4). There are convincing reasons to believe that the issue between the two men was not simply a matter of competitive personal ambition but of policy. Both these men were 'mothakes', the sons of Spartan fathers and 'Helot' mothers, or possibly of 'Inferiors', impoverished Spartans who had lost their Spartiate status. These mothakes, therefore, were of lower status, who hoped to attain full citizenship. Yet, Lysander and Callicratidas had risen to a position of great importance by their appointment as nauarch, which must pre-suppose political support from influential Spartans.

It would seem that relations with Persia had split Sparta into two factions: Lysander representing the faction whose policy was one of full cooperation with the Persians; while Callicratidas was representing the faction that entertained serious doubts about the wisdom and the morality of fighting alongside Persia against fellow Greeks. The Agiad kings, from Pleistoanax onwards, had supported a policy of coexistence with the Athenians; Pleistoanax had been the main Spartan advocate for the Peace of Nicias (5.16–17), and Pausanias, his son and successor in 408, did much to bring political stability to Athens in 403 and was a bitter enemy of Lysander. It is in this context that the remarks of Callicratidas, having been told by Cyrus to wait for the return of the unused money, can be understood:

> But Callicratidas, annoyed by the delay and angered at the constant visits to his [Cyrus'] doors, said that the Greeks were in a most wretched state when they have to fawn on foreigners for the sake of money; and that, if he got home safely, he would do all that he could to reconcile the Athenians and the Spartans.
>
> (Xenophon, *Hellenica* 1.6.7)

Callicratidas imposed his authority upon his forces and, with a fleet of 140 ships, captured Delphinium, the Athenian base on Chios, Teus and Methymna. He then defeated the smaller force of the Athenian general, Conon, who lost 30 ships, and blockaded him in the harbour of Mytilene (D.S. 13.76–78.3; Xen. 1.6.4–19). The Athenians sent out a relief force from Athens, amounting eventually to 150 ships, and made for Mytilene to relieve Conon. Callicratidas, who now had a fleet of 170 ships, left 50 ships to maintain the blockade of Mytilene, and sailed to the Arginusae islands to meet the new Athenian fleet. The ensuing battle in 406 was a great victory for the Athenians, resulting in the death of Callicratidas and the loss of over 70 ships (D.S. 13.97.4–99; Xen. 1.6.28–38).

The Spartan fleet had not been utterly destroyed and Eteonicus, the Spartan vice-admiral, still had roughly 90 ships but, without Persian financial support, they could not feed themselves, let alone challenge the Athenians at sea. This defeat at Arginusae and the desperate plight of the Peloponnesian navy possibly led to another fruitless attempt by the Spartans to make peace with the Athenians (Aristotle, *Ath. Pol.* 34.1), whose victorious fleet, using Samos as a base, was laying waste the territories of the pro-Spartan cities in the islands and on the mainland (D.S. 13.100.6). These pro-Spartan cities held a conference at Ephesus and decided to ask the Spartans to restore Lysander to the nauarchy; this request was further strengthened by envoys of Cyrus who also desired Lysander's reinstatement. The Spartans, faced with such a forceful demand, resolved the problem of the illegality of appointing the same man to the nauarchy twice by appointing Lysander as vice-admiral to Aracus, but making it plain that Lysander was to be in command (D.S. 13.100.8).

Lysander moved with commendable speed, assembling his fleet at Ephesus around the end of winter in 406/5, ordering the construction of new ships at Antandrus and, most important of all, visiting Cyrus at Sardis; Sparta's main need, as always, was money. Cyrus explained to Lysander how all the King's money had been spent and much more, even producing the accounts to confirm his statement, but he still provided money. In this way Lysander paid the arrears of pay to his sailors (Xen. 2.1.11–12). However, the money was insufficient in itself to bring victory, but then Lysander enjoyed a massive stroke of luck. Cyrus had executed two of his cousins for not paying the respect that was due to a king – a clear sign of his future ambitions – and was recalled by Darius II to explain his action, although the King stressed that it was more a matter of needing his presence due to his own illness (Xen. 2.1.8–9). Cyrus summoned Lysander to him and, having told him not to fight the Athenians until he had a clear superiority in ship numbers:

> he assigned to him all the tribute from the cities which personally belonged to him, and gave him the surplus money that he had.
>
> (Xenophon, *Hellenica* 2.1.14)

This massive injection of money was one of the key reasons for Lysander's success in defeating the Athenians in the final sea-battle that brought the war to an end. The other was the Athenians' execution of six of its most experienced generals after the battle of Arginusae in 406 on the grounds of failing to pick up survivors from the sea (D.S. 13.101; Xen. 1.7.1–35), and the non-appointment as generals of Theramenes, who was rejected at his 'dokimasia' (see Glossary), and Thrasybulus.

Lysander, when he was convinced that his fleet was ready, switched the theatre of war from Ionia to the Hellespont:

> in order to prevent the merchant-ships from sailing out, and to attack the cities that had revolted from the Spartans.
>
> (Xenophon, *Hellenica* 2.1.17)

He had realized, as had King Agis earlier, that the Spartans could only win the war by starving the Athenians into submission, and that this could only be achieved by cutting off their grain supply from the Black Sea. The inexperience of the Athenian generals and the skill of Lysander brought about the total defeat of the Athenian navy at Aegospotamoi, in the Hellespont opposite Lampsacus, in the late summer of 405 (D.S. 13.105–6.7; Xen. 2.1.21–29). After that, it was only a matter of time before the Athenians, blockaded on land by the forces of King Agis from Decelea and King Pausanias from the Peloponnese, and by sea by Lysander's navy, surrendered in the first half of 404:

> After this Lysander sailed into the Piraeus and the exiles returned, and they destroyed the Long Walls to the sound of flute-girls with great enthusiasm, thinking that day was the beginning of freedom for Greece.
>
> (Xenophon, *Hellenica* 2.2.23)

Cyrus' wholehearted support of the Spartans, especially in the supply of Persian gold, proved to be the decisive factor in helping the Spartans to defeat the Athenians in the Ionian War. If the Spartans had chosen to cooperate with Pharnabazus, had concentrated on the Hellespont as the main theatre of war and had displayed the necessary urgency in 413/2 to deliver the killer blow, the war would have ended much earlier. In the aftermath of Athens' surrender, the liberation of the Greeks, Sparta's rallying-cry to the Greeks in 431 against the Athenians, was exposed as a complete sham by Lysander's imposition of oligarchies and decarchies (pro-Spartan ten-men oligarchies, often supported by a garrison under a Spartan commander) throughout the former Athenian Empire and in parts of mainland Greece. As for the Persians, in the next century they were to learn to their cost the value of Alcibiades' advice to Tissaphernes, when he said that the Spartans were bound to attack the Persians, and that such a super-power, with control over the sea and land, would cause great damage to the King (8.46).

Bibliography

Andrewes, A. *CAH vol. 5*, 2nd edn, ch. 11.

Cartledge, P. *Sparta and Lakonia*, pt 3, ch. 12.
Hornblower, S. *The Greek World 479–323 BC*, ch. 12.
Kagan, D. *The Fall of the Athenian Empire*, chs 1–4, 9–13 and 15.
Lewis, D. M. *Sparta and Persia*, chs 2–6.
Powell, A. *Athens and Sparta*, ch. 5.
Sealey, R. *A History of the Greek City States 700–338 BC*, chs 13 and 14.

23

THE RISE AND FALL OF THE OLIGARCHIC MOVEMENT IN ATHENS, 411–410

The rise of oligarchy

The last recorded oligarchic threat to Athenian democracy came in c.457 after the battle of Tanagra (Thuc. 1.107.4) and, although the Athenians suspected that oligarchic plots lay behind the mutilation of the Hermae in 415 just before the Sicilian expedition set sail (Thuc. 6.27), the possibility of a successful oligarchic coup before 413 was virtually non-existent. However, after the Sicilian disaster in the autumn of 413, a number of influential factors came together which resulted in the establishment of an oligarchy in June 411. There was, first of all, the disillusionment and anger of a large number of Athenians, mainly the wealthy upper class but also among many of the more affluent 'hoplites', at the incompetence of the 'radical' democracy in its conduct of the Peloponnesian War, and the increasing economic burden upon themselves owing to the war. Second, there was the coordinated action of the upper-class political clubs ('hetaireiai') in the build-up to the coup in 411. Third, the Athenian 'demos' temporarily lost confidence in its ability, through its own democratic institutions, to win the war; this confidence was only fully restored after the resounding victory over the Peloponnesian fleet at Cyzicus in 410 (see Chapter 22). Finally, the intervention of Persia into Greek affairs led to the widespread belief that Persian support, even at the cost of giving up the democracy, was absolutely essential to avoid defeat at the hands of the Spartans.

The first key factor in the build-up to oligarchy was the change in attitude of the Athenian upper class: men of property and 'good' birth who referred to themselves as the 'kaloikagathoi' (see Chapter 18). The malicious and confrontational nature of Athenian politics after the death of Pericles in 429, personified by the so-called 'demagogues', led many of the wealthy to withdraw from active politics; but the majority of them still accepted the 'radical' democracy, while they enjoyed the economic benefits of the Empire. The outbreak of the war had placed a greater financial burden on the upper class through the ravaging of their estates by annual Peloponnesian invasions (up to 425) and the occasional imposition of a special war tax ('eisphora'). However, this financial loss was offset by the economic benefits accruing from the possession of extensive land-holdings among the subject-allies (see Chapter 16) and by their exemption from paying for the fleet, which ensured the flow of the subject-allies' 'phoros' into Athens and protected their overseas investments.

This grudging acceptance of 'radical' democracy by the upper class began to disintegrate due to the mistakes that were made in foreign policy after 415. The Sicilian campaign, a dramatic departure from the Periclean defensive strategy, was an expensive and risky campaign. After the initial expedition ran into trouble under Nicias, the demos chose to increase their stake by sending out a second lavish relief force under Demosthenes rather than cut their losses and get out of Sicily. Then the demos committed the most foolish of errors: while they were so greatly over-extended and vulnerable, they gave the Spartans the legitimate excuse to renew the war by a provocative attacks on the Peloponnese (Thuc. 7.18–26). The result was the permanent occupation of Decelea in Attica by King Agis. The loss of Attica greatly exacerbated the financial problems of the state: 20,000 slaves, including a high proportion of those employed in industry, had escaped, severely affecting economic output; the revenue from the silver mines was now cut off; all imports from Euboea had to come on the longer and more expensive sea-route; landed estates were now being constantly ravaged; military costs were being pushed up by the need to maintain guards, day and night throughout the year, to protect the Long Walls from assault by Agis' troops (Thuc. 7.27–28); and finally, the increased demand for imports to feed the vast population, now permanently domiciled behind the Long Walls, led to an inevitable rise in prices, putting more financial pressure on the state treasury which had to support the war widows and orphans:

> Expenses were not the same as earlier, but had become much greater as the war had become bigger, and their revenues were draining away.
>
> (Thucydides 7.28.4)

The loss of their estates had depleted the private wealth of the upper class, but the destruction of the fleet in Sicily was the last straw. Now there were virtually no fleet and no crews (Thuc. 8.1), and the very real danger of a mass revolt of the subject-allies (Thuc. 8.2). The potential loss of allied phoros, the cost of building a new fleet (apart from 1,000 talents emergency fund), the extra expense of subduing the subject-allies in revolt, and the need to maintain a fleet continuously throughout the year against the Peloponnesian navy in the eastern Aegean were bound to impose greater financial hardships upon the wealthy. The wealthy would have strong reasons for wanting a much more efficient conduct of war and foreign policy, and a tighter grip on state finances, but this could only be accomplished by a change in the democratic constitution. It was this disaffection with their increasing financial burden that persuaded Alcibiades to target the members of this class first, while on campaign in Samos, in order to bring about the removal of democracy and his own recall:

> The most powerful citizens, who had endured the greatest hardship, had high hopes
> for themselves of getting political power into their own hands and winning the war.
>
> (Thucydides 8.48.1)

This desire for constitutional change, however, was insufficient in itself to bring about the overthrow of democracy – it would need other factors to come into play to achieve this.

The second key factor was the bringing together of the aristocratic clubs (hetaireiai) into partnership by Peisander, at the very beginning of 411 (see below), and his direction of their coordinated efforts towards the overthrow of democracy. These hetaireiai had traditionally been social organizations, usually nothing more than upper-class dining clubs, although they did help their members at the time of elections or when a lawsuit was in progress. However, they seemed to have become more politically inclined and consequently more secretive from the 420s onwards, and it is within these clubs that the true supporters of oligarchy and the bitterest opponents of democracy were to be found. Apart from isolated acts, which were designed to frighten the demos, such as the mutilation of the Hermae (Thuc. 6.27), they had previously been too disorganized to mount a serious threat against the democracy. The arrival at Athens, either at the end of December 412 or the beginning of January in 411, of Peisander who had been instructed by his fellow conspirators to prepare the ground for the establishment of an oligarchy at Athens, changed all that:

> Peisander, having approached all the clubs ... urged them to unite and to organise a
> common policy for the overthrow of democracy.
>
> (Thucydides 8.54.4)

At some time between Peisander's departure for the court of Tissaphernes and his second return to Athens, i.e. from March or early April to the beginning of June 411, these clubs publicly advertised a programme of modifying the democracy, but secretly organized a series of assassinations which included Androcles, one of the leading politicians of the democracy (Thuc. 8.65). Far more effective was their creation of a climate of fear and distrust among the Boule of 500 and the Assembly, out of all proportion to their small numbers, so that these club members gradually intimidated these institutions into passing their preferred decisions:

> Nevertheless the Assembly and the Boule of 500 still continued to hold meetings.
> However, they discussed nothing that did not meet with the approval of the

conspirators; and not only did the speakers come from this group, but they even decided beforehand what they were going to say. None of the rest of the citizens, being afraid and seeing how widespread the conspiracy appeared to be, any longer spoke in opposition to them. If anyone did speak against them, he was immediately killed in some convenient manner.

(Thucydides 8.66.1–2)

This groundwork by the clubs was invaluable for Peisander and his oligarchic conspirators. Within a very short time of the second return of Peisander to Athens, the conspirators were able to seize power in early June 411 and establish the rule of the Four Hundred (see below).

The third key factor was the doubt of the Athenian demos itself in its capacity to conduct the war effectively. When the news of the Sicilian disaster reached Athens, the people refused to believe it, and when it could no longer be doubted, they turned on the politicians who had advocated the invasion of Sicily, conveniently forgetting that they themselves had voted for this policy. The decision that they took in the late summer of 413, although it should not be pressed too hard, marked the beginning of the anti-democratic movement:

They decided that they should put the affairs of the city on a more economic basis and that they should appoint a board of older men, who would give advice on current matters as they arose. In the immediate panic they were ready, as a democracy usually does, to put their affairs in good order.

(Thucydides 8.1.3–4)

In a time of crisis, especially in war, democracies are often prepared to put limitations on their exercise of power. Ten men were chosen to be the 'probouloi', probably one from each tribe, and it is known that Sophocles, the tragedian, and Hagnon, one of Pericles' political supporters, were members of this board. The mention of these probouloi as being 'already existing' in 411 (Aristotle, *Ath. Pol.* 29.2) suggests that there was no time limit on their tenure of office, and 40 was probably the minimum age. Thucydides does not make clear the full extent of their powers and responsibilities, but, from his words above, they may have had the power to present motions directly to the Assembly, thus replacing the probouleutic function of the Boule of 500. Alternatively, and far more likely, they worked in concert with the Boule in the drafting of motions. Aristotle argued that the existence of probouloi and a Boule in the same state was an oligarchic element in the constitution, as the probouloi would have authority over the Boule (*Politics* 1299b). Although scholarly opinion is divided on the question of whether the appointment of the probouloi was the first move in the establishment of the oligarchy in 411, it is clear that the Athenians were so troubled by the glaring deficiencies of their democracy in the conduct of the war that they were prepared to give unprecedented power and influence to a small body of elder citizens. The revolts of major allies, such as Chios, Miletus and Rhodes, the operations of the Peloponnesian fleet in the eastern Aegean and Persia's intervention on the side of the Spartans had further undermined Athenian confidence in their ability to survive. Thus, by the end of 412, the Athenians were in the right frame of mind, with effective prompting, to think the unthinkable: a change in their democratic constitution.

The catalyst for bringing the other three elements together was Alcibiades' seductive offer of bringing the Persians and their vast wealth onto the side of the Athenians. Alcibiades had already run foul of the Spartans who had issued his death warrant (Thuc. 8.45), and had fled to the court of Tissaphernes, the Persian governor ('satrap') of south-west Asia Minor, where his advice about Persia's relations with the warring Greek states was well received (Thuc. 8.46). However, Alcibiades was also planning his own recall to Athens, but presumed that there was no way that the 'radical' democracy would agree to this. Therefore, in November 412, he set about winning over the most influential men of the Athenian fleet at Samos by claiming that he had great influence with Tissaphernes and that:

> he wanted to return home and be a fellow-citizen, provided that there was an oligarchy and not the dreadful democracy that had exiled him, and he would make Tissaphernes their friend.
>
> (Thucydides 8.47.2)

A delegation of these influential Athenians crossed over from Samos to Alcibiades on the Asiatic mainland, where his legendary powers of persuasion convinced them that there was every chance of winning over Tissaphernes and the King to the Athenian side (Thuc. 8.48).

These influential Athenians, upon their return to Samos, formed themselves and other members of the officer class into a group of conspirators, and declared openly that the friendship and the money of the King were dependent upon the recall of Alcibiades and that they should not be governed by a democracy. The majority of the armed forces at Samos were angry at these conditions but grudgingly accepted them, according to Thucydides, because of the prospect of pay (Thuc. 8.48). This incident is worthy of comment for two reasons. First, this is one of the rare times that Thucydides' bias against the 'radical' democracy comes to the fore – it is just as feasible, perhaps more so, that the Athenian sailors agreed to these conditions through fear for the safety of the city and their families, rather than their desire for pay; and his use of 'ochlos' (the mob) strengthens the case of personal prejudice. Second, Alcibiades never uses the word 'oligarchy' after his first communication but, from now on, he and the conspirators talk in terms of modifying the democracy. It will be seen later in the chapter that the conspirators consisted of two groups: the 'extreme' oligarchs who adopted this language simply to deceive the demos, and the 'moderates' who believed in a more limited form of democracy.

Near the end of December 412, Peisander and other representatives were sent to Athens to carry out the agreed programme of recalling Alcibiades, overthrowing the democracy and gaining the friendship of Tissaphernes (Thuc. 8.49). According to Thucydides (8.53), Peisander immediately approached the Assembly with the conspirators' proposals, but there is other evidence (e.g. the *Lysistrata* and the *Thesmophoriazusae* of Aristophanes) which strongly suggests that Peisander did not approach the Assembly until March or early April 411. It would seem that Thucydides has telescoped the events of 411. In fact, many scholars believe that Book 8, apart from being unfinished, was also unrevised by Thucydides. There are clearly different versions of the same events in different parts of this book, which Thucydides would usually rationalize into one sequence of events; there are also virtually no direct speeches and an unusually high incidence of Thucydidean interpretation of motives, which should be treated with more caution than his statement of facts – the mention of the Athenian sailors' acceptance of Alcibiades' proposals solely through their desire for pay is a good case in point. It is reasonable to assume that Peisander used the early months of 411 explaining the conspirators' plans to oligarchic sympathizers in Athens and thereby winning their support for the planned coup (Thuc. 8.54).

In March or early April 411, Peisander put before the Assembly the conspirators' proposals about the recall of Alcibiades and an alliance with the Persians, but artfully avoided the mention of oligarchy and talked in terms of 'adopting a different form of democracy' (Thuc. 8.53). Although there was a great uproar, Peisander won the argument by concentrating on the demos' greatest fear:

> He asked each and every one of his opponents what hope they had for saving the city, when the Peloponnesian navy, confronting them at sea, was no smaller than their own, when the enemy had more allied cities on their side, when the King and Tissaphernes were supplying the enemy with money and when the Athenians themselves no longer had any, unless someone should persuade the King to change sides.
>
> (Thucydides 8.53.2)

This concentration on the enormity of the danger to Athens, combined with the argument that the Athenians could always later on change the new constitution back to the old one, won the day. Now that he had won over the Assembly, he was determined to consolidate the strength of the oligarchs. He forged the hetaireiai into a unified faction, who began their policy of intimidation and assassination after he and ten other envoys had been sent out from Athens to negotiate with Alcibiades and Tissaphernes (Thuc. 8.54).

Alcibiades, however, could not deliver his side of the bargain, as Tissaphernes preferred the policy of wearing down both sides of the Greeks (see Chapter 22). With the failure of Peisander's mission to Alcibiades and Tissaphernes, the whole raison d'être for the removal of the democratic constitution at Athens had gone. The conspirators decided to break with Alcibiades and consequently with the Persians but, having gone so far and fearing themselves to be in danger from a democratic backlash at their proposed reforms, the majority decided still to press on with their plan for changing the constitution (Thuc. 8.63). The conspirators evolved a threefold plan: to secure their position at Samos, gain constitutional control of Athens and convert the allied cities' governments into oligarchies. First, they strengthened their control over the Athenian army at Samos (possibly the hoplites as opposed to the sailors are meant here) and encouraged 300 of the most important Samians to organize an oligarchic coup on Samos; second, Peisander and five of the delegates were sent to Athens to organize the coup, but also to establish oligarchies on their journey to Athens; and third, the other five delegates were also to set up oligarchies in the rest of the Empire (Thuc. 8.63–64). The conspirators clearly believed that oligarchs in allied cities were more likely to stay loyal to Athens, even though Phrynichus had previously poured scorn on this idea (Thuc. 8.48).

Peisander arrived in Athens probably in the second half of May 411 and discovered that the hetaireiai had done an excellent job in preparing the ground for the coup. They had intimidated the Boule of 500 and the Assembly (see above) and had assassinated the conspirators' main democratic opponents. In addition, they had publicized their programme for 'adopting a different form of democracy':

> that no one should receive pay except those who were serving in the war; that no more than five thousand should have a share in the government and that these should come from those who were best able to help the state in terms of money and their persons.

> (Thucydides 8.65.3)

In other words, it would be the middle and upper classes, the hoplites and the knights, who would gain most from the constitutional reforms, and not the class of 'thetes', which supplied the rowers for the Athenian fleet. Peisander and his colleagues then summoned an Assembly and proposed that ten men (30 men in Aristotle, *Ath. Pol.* 29.2) should be given full powers to prepare proposals for the best government of Athens and present them to the people on a fixed day (Thuc. 8.67).

When this appointed day arrived (according to Thucydides' version – see next section), probably in early June 411, the commissioners made only one proposal to the Assembly which met at Colonus, outside the city walls, instead of the Pnyx – this location was possibly chosen to discourage the thetes who were unarmed from attending, while encouraging the hoplites who were and who could defend themselves if the Spartan forces under King Agis made a sortie from Decelea. The terms of the proposal were: to suspend the use of the 'graphe paranomon' (the right to prosecute someone for putting an illegal or unconstitutional motion) and to allow anyone the freedom, without fear of prosecution, to propose whatever he wanted. The failure by the commissioners to produce a more detailed set of proposals for the reform of the constitution may reflect an inability to agree among themselves on its desired form. This gave Peisander his desired opening for making a 'legitimate' proposal:

> that there should be no holding of office and payment by the state as in the present constitution; that they should choose five men as presidents who would choose 100 others, and each of this 100 men would choose three more in addition to himself; and that these, being 400 in number and having gone into the chamber of the Boule of 500, should govern with full powers to the best of their ability and should summon the 5,000 whenever they saw fit.
>
> (Thucydides 8.67.3)

This motion was passed by the Assembly and, on 9 June 411, the conspirators entered the Boule of 500's chamber, paid them off for the rest of their term of office, and established the oligarchy of The Four Hundred:

> It was not surprising that the plot, carried out by so many able men, succeeded although it was a tough undertaking. For it was difficult to deprive the Athenian demos of its liberty, especially since the tyrants had been expelled a hundred years before.
>
> (Thucydides 8.68.4)

The rule of The Four Hundred

There are two accounts of the oligarchic revolution of 411: Thucydides in Book 8 and Aristotle in the *Ath. Pol.* (29–33). Although there are certain similarities in their narrative of the events, there is a major split in the description of the constitutional reforms that were passed and the timing of their introduction. Thucydides, who was writing in exile and was a contemporary of and familiar with many of the oligarchic leaders, describes the constitutional change as a swift oligarchic coup by a group of conspirators, all of whom wanted an 'extreme' oligarchy and had no intention of introducing a 'moderate' rule of The Five Thousand, as mentioned above in 8.67.3; in fact, he makes no mention of the appointment of The Five Thousand, as he regarded their existence as totally irrelevant to The Four

Hundred in their planned government of Athens. The account of Aristotle's *Ath. Pol.* was written about a hundred years later and uses a variety of sources, including Thucydides, but also, in all probability, the work of Androtion whose father was one of The Four Hundred, which may explain why this version takes a more lenient view of the oligarchs. In this account, the reform of the constitution takes a much longer time, with the appointment of The Five Thousand and their ratification of two constitutions – one for the future and one for the present, which included the appointment of The Four Hundred.

Modern scholarship has made many attempts to reconcile these two traditions, but the commonly held view is that Aristotle's account contains much that is fictitious and reflects the contemporary propaganda of the 'extreme' oligarchs, for whom it was politically useful to pretend that The Five Thousand had a constitutional existence. Therefore, Thucydides' account is to be preferred, although it must be used with caution, as it includes his opinions about the motives of the conspirators which are open to serious challenge; in particular, his belief that there was no 'moderate' group among The Four Hundred and that such people as Theramenes were cynical, ambitious 'extreme' oligarchs who only championed the cause of The Five Thousand when The Four Hundred's rule was doomed to fall (Thuc. 8.66.1; 68.3; 89.2–4; 92).

The rule of the Four Hundred lasted just under four months, from June to September 411 (*Ath. Pol.* 31). There were three major reasons for its fall. In the first place, the Athenians had been persuaded to give up their democracy as the price that had to be paid in order to win the support and the financial backing of Tissaphernes and the King of Persia, otherwise they would be defeated by the Spartans (Thuc. 8.53.2). However, the negotiations through Alcibiades had failed to bring about a Persian alliance (Thuc. 8.56). In fact, Tissaphernes had healed his breach with the Spartans concerning a dispute over the two earlier treaties, and had signed a third treaty which greatly strengthened the Spartans' military position (Thuc. 8.58 – see Chapter 22). Therefore the main incentive for a change in the constitution had failed to materialize.

The second reason for the collapse of The Four Hundred was their treasonable intrigues with the Spartans. After Peisander's negotiations with Alcibiades and Tissaphernes had failed to win Persian support, the conspirators made it a major feature of their programme to continue the war more vigorously than the democracy against the Spartans (Thuc. 8.63). But, as soon as they seized power, they pursued a completely different policy:

> They made approaches to Agis, the King of the Spartans who was at Decelea, saying that they wished to make peace and that it was more reasonable for him to come to an agreement with them rather than the untrustworthy democracy that no longer existed.
>
> (Thucydides 8.70.2)

Agis rebuffed them at first, thinking that he could exploit the internal strife among the Athenians and bring about their surrender or that Athens would fall to a single attack. However, he had made a serious error of judgement which resulted in Peloponnesian casualties and his retirement back to Decelea. The Four Hundred were not deterred by his original rejection of their overtures, and kept sending envoys to him; upon his advice, they then sent envoys to Sparta with the same request (Thuc. 8.71).

As The Four Hundred's tenure of power became more precarious through dissatisfaction with their rule both in Athens and in the fleet at Samos, they became even more desperate to make peace with the Spartans:

> They sent Antiphon and Phrynichus and ten others as quickly as possible, fearing the situation at home and in Samos, and ordered them to make peace with the Spartans on whatever terms that were bearable.
>
> (Thucydides 8.90.2)

In addition, they were building a fortification at Eetioneia, which was part of the Piraeus. It was suspected by their opponents that, far from keeping out the democrats at Samos, its real purpose was to let in the Spartan fleet and army which was coming in the direction of the Piraeus. It was believed that The Four Hundred held the view that, if the oligarchy could not stay in power and their own lives were to be at risk from a restored democracy:

> they preferred to lead in the enemy and, having given up the walls and the fleet, to make any agreement whatsoever about the fate of the city, provided that their lives were guaranteed.
>
> (Thucydides 8.91.3)

It was this suspicion of possible treachery and a betrayal of Athens to the enemy that led the hoplites to destroy this fortification (Thuc. 8.92). When The Four Hundred were finally overthrown, Peisander and most of the remaining 'extreme' oligarchs immediately fled to Agis at Decelea (Thuc. 8.98).

The third reason for the overthrow of The Four Hundred was the internal split between the conspirators about the nature of the constitution that should replace the democracy. One faction was the 'extreme' oligarchs, which included Peisander who had proposed the establishment of The Four Hundred at the meeting at Colonus and 'was openly the most eager for the overthrow of the democracy' (Thuc. 8.68.1); Phrynichus who was a bitter enemy of Alcibiades and 'showed himself more than all the rest to be the greatest supporter of oligarchy' (Thuc. 8.68.3); and Antiphon who had masterminded the coup (Thuc. 8.68.1). They held the view that sovereign power should be vested in The Council of Four Hundred, which should be unaccountable for its decisions and actions, and whose membership should be permanent. Ideally, they wanted the Five Thousand to exist only in name but, if they had to exist, to be consulted as little as possible. Any check upon their power, even by so small a number as 5,000, was totally unacceptable:

> because they thought that sharing power with so many men [i.e. 5,000] was outright democracy.
>
> (Thucydides 8.92.11)

The other faction can be referred to as 'moderates', although their preferred constitution would cover a broad spectrum of views; they were opposed to 'extreme' oligarchy and 'radical' democracy, but some would be more inclined towards moderate oligarchy, others to moderate democracy. Therefore, to the 'moderates', the Five Thousand were the crucial element in the reformed constitution, either being the sovereign body of state or supplying all the public officials (see below for the modern controversy). The leader of this faction was Theramenes, although he is lumped among the 'extreme' oligarchs by Thucydides (8.68.4); Thucydides' hostile portrayal of Theramenes may be based on the evidence of an ex-member of The Four Hundred who fled after its fall. However, there is sufficient evidence from his later career that Theramenes was not an 'extreme' oligarch, but held a consistent view that sovereign power should be vested in the upper class and the hoplites. He played a leading part in organizing resistance to The Four Hundred and in the establishment of its successor, The Five Thousand. Although Antiphon was executed by the restored democracy, Theramenes continued to serve Athens as a general and a trierarch (captain of a 'trireme') throughout the Ionian War (413–404). When he was put on trial in 403 for opposing the brutal excesses of The Thirty Tyrants, an extreme Spartan-backed Athenian oligarchy, he made his political beliefs clear:

> 'To run the state along with those, who are able to serve it with their horses or with their shields [i.e. as cavalry or as hoplites], is the constitution that I previously thought the best, and I do not change my opinion now.'
>
> (Xenophon, *Hellenica* 2.3.48)

Theramenes' description of the constitution that he 'previously thought the best' is identical to the political manifesto published by the conspirators before the coup (Thuc. 8.65.3 – see above).

The first important reverse for The Four Hundred was the failure of the oligarchic coup in Samos. The conspirators always had their doubts about the acceptance of oligarchy by the thetes in the fleet at Samos and so, through the agency of Peisander and the oligarchic supporters in the fleet, they had encouraged 300 Samians to seize power and establish an oligarchy. In this way the conspirators hoped to cow any rebellious move by the sailors and further strengthen their hold on the government of Athens. However, the assassination of the demagogue Hyperbolus, who was living in Samos after his ostracism, forewarned the Samian democrats who appealed to the main Athenian supporters of democracy – the generals Leon and Diomedon, Thrasybulus the captain of a trireme, and Thrasyllus a hoplite. The coup failed and Samos stayed a democracy (Thuc. 8.73). Far more worrying for The Four Hundred was the declaration of support for the 'radical' democracy and of enmity to the oligarchs in Athens by the forces in Samos, now under the leadership of the newly elected generals, Thrasybulus and Thrasyllus (Thuc. 8.75–76). The recall of Alcibiades, brought about by the constant urging of Thrasybulus, his rehabilitation and his election as general by the armed forces at Samos, who believed that he could bring Tissaphernes and the Persians over to the Athenian side, deeply worried the oligarchs in power in Athens (Thuc. 8.81–82).

It was now that Alcibiades effectively split the ranks of The Four Hundred, thus fatally weakening them, by a very astute proposal. The Four Hundred had attempted to make a rapprochement with the forces in Samos by sending out a delegation, aimed at allaying their fears about events in Athens. They stressed that the change of government was to strengthen Athens in the war against the Spartans and that The Five Thousand would get their chance to share in the government. Alcibiades' reply on behalf of the forces at Samos was that he was not against The Five Thousand being the government of Athens, but he insisted on the removal of The Four Hundred and the restoration of the Boule of 500; he also approved of any financial measures that supplied better pay for the troops; and he urged them not to give in to the enemy – so long as the city was safe, there was every chance of a reconciliation between the two groups (Thuc. 8.86). This offer had the desired effect:

> Most of those who had a share in the oligarchy, who already had become dis-contented and would have been glad to get out of the business, if it could be done safely, became far more determined to do so. They now organized themselves into groups and began to criticize how the state was being run ... and they proclaimed that it was necessary for the Five Thousand to exist in reality and not just in name, and that a fairer constitution should be established.
>
> (Thucydides 8.89.1–2)

The leaders of this dissident group were Theramenes and Aristocrates, who also feared (rightly) that the 'extreme' oligarchs were plotting to betray Athens. Alcibiades' reply, by holding out the hope of a peaceful and safe compromise between the 'moderates' in Athens and the forces at Samos and by playing on their fears about the possible betrayal of Athens to Sparta, had destroyed the fragile unity of The Four Hundred.

The 'extreme' oligarchs, seeing the growing opposition to their rule, even among their own former supporters, redoubled their efforts to make peace with Sparta and built the fortification at Eetioneia (see above). However, the hoplites, who were building this fortification, rebelled against Alexicles who was a supporter of the oligarchy and was in charge of the building operation, took him prisoner, and began to destroy the wall, calling for help from all those that wanted The Five Thousand to govern (Thuc. 8.92). The Four Hundred tried to placate the hoplites by promising that they would publish the names of The Five Thousand and that, in future, membership of The Four Hundred would be recruited from this number on a rotational basis. They also agreed to hold an Assembly on a fixed day to settle the problems (Thuc. 8.93). The sighting of 42 Peloponnesian ships sailing along the coast of Salamis prevented the Assembly from being held on the appointed day and provoked great panic, again renewing the fears of the 'moderates' that The Four Hundred were about to betray Athens. The Peloponnesian ships, in fact, sailed to Oropus near Euboea and promptly defeated the hastily manned Athenian fleet which had been sent to defend Euboea (Thuc. 8.95). This revolt of Euboea, which caused even more terror and despair than the loss of the Sicilian expedition (8.96), brought about the downfall of the oligarchy; the 'moderates' now had their chance to make a better job of governing Athens.

The rule of The Five Thousand

Very little is known about this government due to the lack of literary sources, and what few facts are known are subject to disputed scholarly interpretations. The fullest account comes from Thucydides:

> The Athenians held meetings of the Assembly, including an immediate one which was summoned then for the first time to the Pnyx, as had been customary in the past, in which they deposed The Four Hundred and voted to hand over the government to the Five Thousand and as many as were able to provide their own (hoplite) weapons. They also voted that no one, on pain of being cursed, was to receive pay for any office. Other regular meetings also took place in which they voted for law-givers (nomothetai) and other arrangements for drawing up the constitution.
>
> (Thucydides 8.97.1–2)

It is not even known if this regime consisted of 5,000 enfranchised citizens. The propaganda of the original conspirators mentioned 5,000 as the maximum number of citizens who should be allowed to participate in government (Thuc. 8.65.3) but this is contradicted by the above quotation and by Aristotle (*Ath. Pol.* 29.3) who states that 5,000 was to be the minimum number. Many modern historians believe the final number was around 9,000, which was quoted in a speech by Lysias (20.13) in defence of Polystratos, one of the original members of The Four Hundred, but even this information, used in a politically sensitive trial, has to be treated with caution.

The major disagreement between scholars concerns the thetes: whether they were excluded from all political rights, or were allowed to attend the 'Ecclesia' (Assembly) and serve in the 'Heliaea' (The People's Court) as in the past before the oligarchic revolution, but were forbidden to hold public office. The weight of scholarly opinion comes down in favour of the view that, under this regime, only those of hoplite census and above had the right to vote in the Assembly, hold public office and serve as jurors in the law courts. The majority of Thucydides' evidence strongly supports this view. It was part of the original propaganda of the conspirators before the oligarchic coup (Thuc. 8.65.3); the Assembly meeting at Colonus established the part that the 5,000 were to play in the new constitution (Thuc. 67); the two *ad hoc* Assemblies, after the destruction of the fortification of Eetioneia, consisted only of hoplites (Thuc. 93.1; 93.3); these same hoplites were addressed by representatives of The Four Hundred, who promised that the names of The Five Thousand would be published and that The Four Hundred would be chosen from their number, on a rotational basis, in accordance with whatever way the hoplites thought best (Thuc. 8.93.2); and finally, after this offer was made by The Four Hundred:

> The whole body of hoplites ... agreed to hold an Assembly (ecclesia) on a fixed day in the theatre of Dionysus to resolve their differences.
>
> (Thucydides 8.93.3)

It also seems probable that the reconstituted Boule of 500, with more power than its democratic counterpart, was elected and not chosen by lot. A speech of Andocides (*On the Mysteries* 96) includes a decree of the newly restored democracy in 410 in which 'a Boule of 500 chosen by lot' is said to exist at that time – this unusual description is presumably used to emphasize its difference from the recent one of The Five Thousand.

Both Aristotle (*Ath. Pol.* 34.2) and Thucydides had high praise for this regime:

> During the first period of its rule [alternatively translated: 'For the first time, at least in my life-time'] the Athenians seem to me to have been better governed than ever before, at least in my lifetime. For there took place a moderate blending of the few and the many, and it was this that first brought about a recovery of the state from its desperate situation.
>
> (Thucydides 8.97.2)

It is tempting to see Thucydides' description of the above constitution as further support for the belief that it was only those of hoplite census and above who had full political rights. The oligarchic element in the constitution was the establishment of a property qualification as the pre-requisite for political participation; and the democratic element was that sovereignty was vested in the hoplite Assembly, and not the oligarchic Boule.

There was one very good reason why this 'moderate' constitution was destined to fail. Athens' rise to super-power status had been achieved by the strength of its navy and by the class that manned the triremes. The prosperity and ultimate safety of Athens depended upon the thetes, whose demand for full political rights to reflect their importance to the state had been met by the reforms of Ephialtes and Pericles (see Chapter 13). The new regime was committed to waging war against Sparta, but the main hope of military success lay with the thetes in the naval forces based at Samos, who had already restored the democracy in exile (Thuc. 8.75–76). It was never a long-term possibility that the thetes would accept the removal of their political rights. It had been the military defeat in Sicily and the morale-sapping campaigns against the Persian-backed Spartans in the eastern Aegean that had led to the thetes' temporary loss of confidence in their democracy. The return of Alcibiades with his confident assertion of winning-over the Persians to the Athenian side and the naval victories at Cynossema and Abydus in late 411 did much to re-establish the self-belief of the Athenian thetes. The stunning victory at the battle of Cyzicus in March or April 410, resulting in the Spartans suing for peace, was the final element that restored the full confidence of the thetes, and convinced them that they could win the war with their 'radical' democracy. In the early summer of 410 the regime of The Five Thousand was replaced and the rest of the Ionian War was conducted by the democracy until Athens was finally defeated in 404.

Bibliography

Andrewes, A. CAH vol. 5, 2nd edn, ch. 11.
——'The generals in the Hellespont, 410–407', JHS 73.
Hignett, C. A History of the Athenian Constitution, ch. 10.
Hornblower, S. The Greek World 479–323 BC, ch. 12.
Kagan, D. The Fall of The Athenian Empire, chs 1, 5–10.
Rhodes, P. J. A Commentary on the Aristotelian 'Athenaion Politeia', pp. 362–415.
——'The Five Thousand in the Athenian revolutions of 411 BC', JHS 92.
de Ste. Croix, G. E. M. 'The constitution of The Five Thousand', Historia 5.

24

SPARTAN FOREIGN POLICY, 404–387/6

In the first ten years of this period the aims of Spartan foreign policy were twofold: to succeed Athens as the leader of an Aegean-based naval empire, and to strengthen Sparta's hold on the 'hegemony' (leadership) of Greece. However, the success of the armed resistance of Corinth, Boeotia (dominated by Thebes), Argos and a revitalized Athens in the Corinthian War (395–387/6) forced the Spartans in the remaining years to give up their ambition of acquiring Athens' former naval empire and to concentrate on restoring themselves as the undisputed leaders of Greece. The decisive factor in shaping Spartan foreign policy throughout this period was Persia – Persian gold had paid for the Spartans' victory over their Greek super-power rival in 404; Persian naval success in the East Aegean and financial help to the Spartans' opponents in mainland Greece ended their imperial ambitions in Asia Minor and threatened their hegemony of Greece; finally, Persian support of Sparta in the terms of the Peace of Antalcidas (also known as the King's Peace), in return for Sparta's betrayal of the Asiatic Greeks to the Persians, ensured Spartan dominance in Greece.

The seeds of discontent and fear among Sparta's leading allies, Corinth and Thebes, were sown in the immediate aftermath of the fall of Athens in 404. Both allies had wanted the destruction of Athens, but their wishes were ignored by the Spartans who turned Athens into a puppet state by installing a brutal pro-Spartan oligarchy, known as 'The Thirty Tyrants' (Diodorus Siculus 14.3.5–7; Xenophon, *Hellenica* 2.3.2 – the abbreviations 'D.S.' and 'Xen.' will be used for these works in the rest of the chapter). The Corinthian and Boeotian mistrust of Sparta's imperial ambitions in Central Greece, exacerbated by the Spartan refusal to share the rich spoils of war, marked the beginning of passive resistance to Sparta which finally broke out into active warfare in 395, when the Quadruple Alliance of Corinth, Boeotia, Argos and Athens engaged in the Corinthian War – so called because most of the fighting on land took place around Corinth. The chief cause of this war was the growth of Spartan power over the Asiatic Greeks at the expense of Persia, and the fear that this caused among the leading states of Greece. They believed that the Spartans, if successful against the

Persians, would use their supremacy by land and by sea, on both sides of the Aegean, to establish a Spartan Empire in Greece – signs of which were evident from Sparta's aggressive behaviour in Greece during this period. Although there is a direct interrelation between Sparta's conflict with Persia in Asia Minor and that with the states of the Quadruple Alliance in Greece, it is probably easier to gain an understanding of the first period of Spartan foreign policy (404–395/4) and the causes of the Corinthian War by concentrating on the events in each region in turn.

Asia Minor, 404–394

The decisive turning-point in the Peloponnesian War (431–404) came after the signing of the so-called Treaty of Boiotios in 407 by the Spartans and Darius II, the King of Persia (see Chapter 22). Darius agreed to support the Spartan war effort far more effectively than before, sending his son Cyrus as the commander of all the Persian forces in the West (Xenophon, *Anabasis* 1.9.7) to liaise closely with the Spartans, and giving him sufficient gold to pay for the Peloponnesian fleet. It is reasonable to believe that the Spartans, for their part, recognized the Persian king's right to collect tribute from the Ionian Greeks, although they were allowed to be in some way autonomous – possibly a guarantee of no Persian garrison – provided that they paid their tribute. The Spartans probably also agreed to remove their armed forces from Asia Minor at the end of the war. The personal rapport and close cooperation between Cyrus and Lysander, the naval commander of the Spartan forces in Asia Minor, brought about the defeat of the Athenian fleet at Aegospotamoi in 405 and the Athenian surrender in 404. Then, it is believed, the Spartans removed their armed forces from Asia Minor in that year.

This did not mean, however, that the Spartans gave up all connections with the Greeks in Asia Minor. Lysander was the dominant figure in Spartan politics at this time, and his and Sparta's aim was as far as possible to take over the Athenian Empire, although there was a major difference of opinion with regard to the means of imperial control:

> Lysander established oligarchies in some cities, and decarchies in others.
>
> (D.S. 14.13.1)

'Decarchies' were brutal narrow oligarchies with political power vested in a ruling committee of ten men. It is impossible to know, due to a lack of evidence, which of the two constitutions was more widespread or how they differed in operation, but it is believed that the decarchies were more common, since they were filled with the personal supporters of Lysander (Plutarch, *Lysander* 13) who was in charge of establishing Spartan control over Athens' former subjects. These oligarchies and decarchies were usually supported by a garrison of troops under the command of a Spartan 'harmost' (controller). The surrender of Athens in 404 would have led to the removal of the harmosts and garrisons in Asia Minor, but not the decarchies. It was only in late 403 or early 402, when Lysander's influence was on the wane, engineered by his political rival King Pausanias, that the Spartan 'Ephors' (see Chapter 4) abolished the unpopular decarchies (Xen. 3.4.2). This action, far from a Spartan pullout of Persian Asia Minor, was merely the prelude to a series of military campaigns against Artaxerxes II, the elder son and successor in c.404 of Darius II.

In 404, Cyrus, although suspected of plotting to overthrow his brother, returned through the help of his influential mother to his 'satrapy' (province) in western Asia Minor, except that the cities of Ionia were now under the responsibility of Tissaphernes, the 'satrap' (provincial governor) of Caria. From 404 to 401, Cyrus made his preparations to launch his coup against Artaxerxes II. He encouraged the Ionian cities to revolt from Tissaphernes, placed garrisons in their cities as protection and secretly gathered a force of Greek mercenaries (Xenophon, *Anabasis* 1.1.6–9). Then he appealed to Sparta for help:

> Cyrus, having sent messengers to Sparta, appealed to them to be the same sort of friends to himself as he had been to them in the war against the Athenians. The ephors, thinking that his was a reasonable appeal, ordered Samius, their admiral at that time, to help Cyrus in whatever way he wanted. Indeed that man eagerly carried out whatever Cyrus asked of him.
>
> (Xen. 3.1.1)

With the active military support of the Spartans Cyrus rebelled from Artaxerxes in 401, and launched his expedition against Persia. The march of his army, the battle of Cunaxa against Artaxerxes, the death of Cyrus in this battle and the return to Greece of Cyrus' 10,000 Greek mercenaries under the command of Xenophon are recounted in Xenophon's *Anabasis* (March Up-Country). It is clear that the Spartans' military aid to Cyrus was motivated, not only by the obligation to repay a favour, but also by the expectation of a reward: the campaigns of 400–394 suggest that the addition of the Asiatic Greeks to their growing Empire was in the forefront of their minds. Instead they gained the bitter hatred of Artaxerxes.

Artaxerxes repaid Tissaphernes' loyalty by giving him Cyrus' satrapy, including the cities of Ionia. Tissaphernes' prestige and pocket had been affected by the revolt of these cities to Cyrus, and so:

> he immediately demanded that all the Ionian cities should be his subjects. But they, wanting to be free and fearing Tissaphernes because they had chosen Cyrus, while alive, instead of him, did not receive him into their cities, but sent ambassadors to the Spartans to appeal to them, as the champions of the whole of Greece, to protect

also the Greeks in Asia, so that their land might not be devastated and that they themselves might be free.

(Xen. 3.1.3)

It seems likely that Tissaphernes intended to occupy the cities of Ionia on the grounds that the Spartans had broken the so-called Treaty of Boiotios (407) by aiding the revolt of Cyrus, and therefore the autonomy of these Asiatic Greeks was forfeit. This appeal gave the Spartans the legitimate (in their opinion) excuse to intervene in Asia Minor, and so a force was despatched under the command of the Spartan Thibron who was supported by troops from the Asiatic Greek cities:

For at that time all the cities obeyed whatever order was given by a Lacedaimonian [i.e. a Spartan].

(Xen. 3.1.5)

The Spartans' ultimatum to Tissaphernes – 'not to bear arms against the Greek cities' (D.S. 14.35.6) – portrayed them as defenders of the Asiatic Greeks, and thus allowed them to install harmosts and bring the cities under their control.

The Spartans had openly declared war on Persia, and thus had committed themselves to extensive campaigning in Asia Minor, which could be successful only if large military forces (including a siege train) were deployed. Consequently the campaigns of Thibron in 400 (D.S. 14.36–37.4; Xen. 3.1.4–7) and his successor Dercylidas from 399–397 (D.S. 14.38.2–3, 39.5–6; Xen. 3.1.8–10, 1.16–2.11) were only moderately successful owing to a lack of cavalry and effective siege equipment. Dercylidas' most prominent success was to gain control of the Troad, the territory on the eastern side of the Hellespont, which had belonged to Pharnabazus, the satrap of Hellespontine Phrygia. Yet, by the end of 399, he had made truces with both Pharnabazus and Tissaphernes, which he was pleased to renew in 398, while he strengthened Spartan influence in the Thracian Chersonese, on the western side of the Hellespont (D.S. 14.38.3, 6–7; Xen. 3.2.8–10).

By 397, the Ionian cities wanted their autonomy from Tissaphernes, which had been achieved by Spartan armed intervention, to be established on a formal, legal basis. Therefore they sent an embassy to Sparta, claiming:

if Caria, where Tissaphernes had his home, were to suffer badly, he would very quickly allow themselves [i.e. the Ionian cities] to be autonomous.

(Xen. 3.2.12)

The Spartans were attracted by this strategy and ordered Dercylidas to invade Caria. In the event Dercylidas was forced to return when he heard that a large army, under the command of Tissaphernes with Pharnabazus as his second-in-command, had made a move against Ionia (D.S. 14.39.4; Xen. 3.2.14). A truce was made between both sides in order to establish the terms on which peace could be made: Dercylidas required the Persians to allow the Greek cities to be autonomous; Tissaphernes required the removal of the Greek army from what the Persians considered the King's land and of the Spartan harmosts from the cities in Asia Minor (D.S. 14.39.5–6; Xen. 3.2.20). The truce was to last until these proposals were reported to Sparta and Artaxerxes. However, both sides were preparing for an intensification of the war.

Artaxerxes was by now very worried about the Spartans' aims in Asia Minor and their capability of carrying them out. The Spartans were in possession of the former naval empire of the Athenians, but unlike them, also had the means as a formidable land power to strike deep into the King's territory in Asia Minor. It was in 397 that Pharnabazus gave the King excellent advice – to concentrate on the war at sea. If the Spartan fleet, based at Rhodes, was decisively beaten, then communications between the army in Asia Minor and mainland Greece would be cut, thus forcing the recall of this army. Artaxerxes, therefore, authorized a major naval rearmament programme, and the truces with Dercylidas and his successor King Agesilaos were designed to buy time for the build-up of this fleet. This policy was supported by Evagoras, the ruler of Salamis in Cyprus, who used his influence to secure the appointment of the very able Conon, one of the two Athenian generals to escape from the battle of Aegospotamoi in 405, as admiral of the fleet (D.S. 14.39.1). This decision by Artaxerxes proved to be the turning point in the war in Asia Minor, culminating in the naval battle of Cnidus in 394 when the Spartans were totally defeated and Persia regained control of Ionia.

But in 397, the Spartans were still confident that they could maintain their control over the Asiatic Greeks – hence Dercylidas' conditions to Tissaphernes for peace. However, news of the build-up of the Persian navy under Conon provoked the Spartans into a more ambitious foreign policy against Persia. Extra forces from the Peloponnesian League allies were summoned and the new King Agesilaos, supported by Lysander, was appointed to lead the expedition (D.S. 14.79.1; Xen. 3.4.1–3). No Spartan king had ever previously campaigned in Asia Minor, and his appointment is clear evidence of the increasing importance that the Spartans attached to Asia Minor. This campaign of Agesilaos also had major repercussions in Greece, where the major anti-Spartan cities, fearing that Spartan success in Asia Minor would lead eventually to their subjection, began to turn their thoughts to active resistance (see next section).

Agesilaos was successful in his land campaigns, causing great damage to and gaining much booty from the satrapy of Pharnabazus in 396 and 395, and inflicting an overwhelming defeat on Tissaphernes' strengthened army at the battle of Sardis in 395. This disastrous Persian failure led to the execution of Tissaphernes by order of Artaxerxes and the appointment of Tithraustes, the Grand Vizier of the whole Persian Empire, as his successor (D.S. 14.80.7). Tithraustes' offer from Artaxerxes reaffirmed the autonomy of the Ionian cities, which Tissaphernes had attempted to remove:

> The King thinks it right that Agesilaos should sail home, and that the cities in Asia should be autonomous and pay the ancient tribute to the king himself.
>
> (Xen. 3.4.25)

In other words, Artaxerxes was offering a return to the so-called Treaty of Boiotios of 407, which would result in the Spartan evacuation of Asia.

This offer was the real test of the honesty of Sparta's intentions in Asia Minor, since the cities of Ionia had only appealed to the Spartans in 400 because of Tissaphernes' intentions to violate this agreement. Agesilaos replied that he needed to refer this proposal to the authorities in Sparta; but the hollowness of the Spartans' claim to be the protectors of the Asiatic Greeks and the extent of their imperialistic aims were revealed by Agesilaos' immediate attack on Pharnabazus and by his appointment as joint commander of the army and the navy:

> The Spartans did this in the belief that, if the same man was in command of both, the land army would be much stronger, for the strength of both would be combined into one; and this would be the same for the fleet, for the army would appear wherever it was needed.
>
> (Xen. 3.4.27)

In addition, Agesilaos ordered the islands and the coastal cities to build a new force of 'triremes', which resulted in an increase of 120 ships for the Spartan fleet (Xen. 3.4.28). The Spartans' aim to increase their Empire in Asia Minor was apparent for all to see, both in Persia and in mainland Greece.

Thus it was in the interests of both the Persians and the anti-Spartan states in Greece to cooperate in their opposition to Sparta. Persia had begun this process by sending Timocrates of Rhodes in 396 with gold to persuade Thebes, Corinth, Argos and Athens to make war upon the Spartans, although they needed little persuasion (Xen. 3.5.1–2, although wrongly dated). The opening battle of the Corinthian War at Haliartus in 395 was brought about by the Thebans who tempted the Spartans into a campaign against Boeotia. The defeat of one Spartan force under Lysander, who had returned previously to Sparta, and the humiliating retreat of the other under King Pausanias led to the recall of Agesilaos and most of his forces from Asia Minor (D.S. 14.81.2–3, 83.1). Finally, the destruction of the Spartan fleet under Peisandros, who had been appointed as admiral by Agesilaos despite his lack of naval experience, by Conon and Pharnabazus at the battle of Cnidus in 394 destroyed forever the Spartans' naval empire in Ionia, the Hellespont and the Aegean islands (D.S. 14.83.4–7).

The main aim of Spartan foreign policy in the second period (395/4–387/6) was to prevent the loss of their hegemony of Greece by waging war against the coalition of Greek states, which were being aided by Persian gold and military support. It is necessary, therefore, to give an account and explanation of how Spartan imperial ambitions in Greece, in addition to (but interlinked with) those in Asia Minor, increased the fears of the main cities in Greece and finally stirred them from passive resistance (404–395) to open warfare in the Corinthian War (395–387/6).

Greece, 404–395

The realization of Sparta's imperial ambitions in Greece began with the installation of the Thirty Tyrants in Athens in 404, thus creating a Spartan puppet state, but the planning can be dated to 413 after the Athenians' disaster in Sicily:

> The Spartans reckoned that they themselves, having defeated the Athenians, would now securely dominate the whole of Greece.
>
> (Thucydides 8.2.4)

Spartan foreign policy had radically changed since 431, when they had gone to war against Athens, proclaiming the liberation of the Greeks as their objective (Thuc. 1.139.3). The Corinthians had already harboured doubts about Spartan intentions as far back as 421, when they feared that Sparta's fifty-year defensive alliance with Athens was designed to enslave the Peloponnese (Thuc. 5.27). Although the Boeotians had not shared these anxieties in 421, they were now deeply concerned by the Spartan refusal to destroy Athens, rightly thinking that Lysander would impose a rabidly pro-Spartan decarchy (in the event, a thirty-man committee) on Athens, as he had done throughout the Athenian Empire, in order to challenge Boeotian dominance in central Greece. The employment of decarchies, garrisons and harmosts, combined with the levying of tribute of over 1,000 talents per year from Athens' former subject-allies (D.S. 14.10.2), bore all the hallmarks of imperialism.

The resistance to Sparta began with the acceptance of Athenian refugees, the exiled opponents of the Thirty Tyrants, by Corinth, Megara, Elis, Argos and especially Thebes, contrary to Spartan orders (D.S. 14.6.2–3; Demosthenes 15.22; Xen. 2.4.1). Furthermore, the Thebans encouraged and helped Thrasybulus to launch his democratic coup against the pro-Spartan Thirty Tyrants in the winter of 404/3 (D.S. 14.32.1; Xen. 2.4.2–19). When King Pausanias arrived in Attica with the Peloponnesian League forces to resolve the factional strife inside Athens:

All the allies followed him except the Boeotians and the Corinthians. For these said that they would not be keeping their oaths if they were to make an expedition against the Athenians who had not broken the treaty. But they did this because they knew that the Spartans wanted to make the territory of the Athenians their own definite possession.

(Xen. 2.4.30)

This disobedience greatly angered the Spartans and, although they were not able at this time to punish the Boeotians, it was one of the Spartans' motives for attacking them in 395 (Xen. 3.5.5).

The Spartans, however, did have the power to attack Elis in 401, and thus restored Spartan supremacy in the Peloponnese (D.S. 14.34.1). Their grievances against the Eleans were that they had made an anti-Spartan alliance with the Athenians, Argives and the Mantineans after the Peace of Nicias; had prevented the Spartans from competing in the Olympic Games; and had forbidden King Agis from sacrificing there (Xen. 3.2.21–22). The Spartans imposed harsh terms upon Elis, including the establishment of a harmost and a garrison – probably the only one in the Peloponnese (Xen. 3.2.29). Once again, the Boeotians and the Corinthians showed their disapproval of this Spartan high-handed behaviour by refusing to send their quota of troops (Xen. 3.2.25).

The Spartans, apart from consolidating their hold on the Peloponnese and central Greece, were also determined to become the dominant power in northern Greece, especially in Thessaly. There is evidence that Sparta was playing a major role in c.400 in the politics of Thessaly, which at this time was a loose federation with three major centres at Larissa, Pharsalus and Pherae. In the speech 'About the Constitution' by 'Herodes', the citizens of Larissa in Thessaly were urged to join the Spartans in fighting King Archelaus of Macedon who had seized the border land between the two states. In addition, it is known from Diodorus (14.82) that a Spartan garrison had been installed at Pharsalus in Thessaly; and from Xenophon (6.4.24) that Lycophron of Pherae was a Spartan ally. Thus the Spartans were very influential and active in the three major political centres of Thessaly. Furthermore, Herippidas was sent out as a harmost in 400 to restore Spartan rule in Heraclea in Trachis, a Spartan colony (established in 426) situated in the south of Thessaly, close to Thermopylae (D.S. 14.38.4–5). This colony was strategically very important as it commanded the road into Thessaly and was an excellent base for operations against Boeotia. It is hardly surprising that the Boeotians feared this encirclement of their territory, and saw in it the Spartan desire to curb Boeotia's growing influence as an important Greek power in the aftermath of the Peloponnesian War.

The Spartan campaigns in Asia Minor under Thibron (400) and Dercylidas (399–397), although conducted officially to liberate the Asiatic Greeks from Persia (Xen. 3.1.3–4), were viewed with increasing concern by the major cities in Greece. The Athenians had already shown in the fifth century that an empire, based upon the Aegean and Asia Minor, had the potential to bring the whole of Greece under its control – as Alexander confirmed later in the fourth century. They feared that, if the Spartans were to add this same empire to their dominant position in the Peloponnese and to their military influence in central and northern Greece, it would be only a matter of time before they were all crushed: Boeotia, Corinth and Argos would be encircled by land and by sea, and the Athenians' supply of grain from the Black Sea would be cut off by the Spartan occupation of the Hellespont, as happened under Lysander in 405–404. However, the current strength of Sparta by land and by sea, the lack of finance to wage a long war and the hostility between the Boeotians and the Athenians militated against active opposition in the first few years of the 390s. It was only in 396 and 395, when the threat from Agesilaos' expedition to Asia became too powerful to be ignored and when these factors, which had limited the ability of Sparta's enemies to hit back, were resolved, that the Quadruple Alliance came together to stop Spartan expansionism.

In 396, King Agesilaos, having gained the disputed Spartan kingship in c.400 with the direct help of Lysander, was appointed to lead a military campaign in Asia Minor. No Spartan king had previously campaigned on the mainland of Asia Minor, and this clearly showed the increased importance that the Spartans were giving to this theatre of war. Furthermore, he was to be helped by Lysander who:

> wanted to campaign in person with Agesilaos in order to restore, with his help, the decarchies which had previously been established by him in the cities.
>
> (Xen. 3.4.2)

Memories of Lysander's blatant imperialism during 405–403, his likely future intentions and his influence with Agesilaos spread great alarm among the other states, especially when Agesilaos made known his intention to sacrifice at Aulis, like a latter-day Agamemnon, before leading the Greeks against Troy (Xen. 3.4.3) – thus signifying Agesilaos' belief that he could win a decisive victory over the Persians in Asia Minor. The Boeotians, the Corinthians and, for the first time since 404, the Athenians refused to send their required contingents of troops to Agesilaos. More evidence of Sparta's growing imperial ambitions beyond Greece is shown by the despatch of 30 ships to help Dionysius I, the tyrant of Syracuse in Sicily, against the Carthaginians (D.S. 14.63). The Spartans had been cultivating these political links with Dionysius I from 404, when they sent the Spartan Aretes to consolidate the tyrant's recently acquired (405) and seriously threatened position (D.S. 14.10). Thus, by 396, Spartan expansion in Greece, Asia Minor, Sicily and even Egypt (equipment and grain was sent by the rebel Pharaoh in 396 to help the Spartans in their war against Persia – D.S. 14.79) provided a greater incentive for their enemies to go to war.

The Boeotian Confederacy, dominated by Thebes, was the first to show open opposition by deliberately sending a force of cavalry to break up Agesilaos' sacrifice at Aulis (Xen. 3.4.4) – a Boeotian insult which he never forgot nor forgave.

The apparently unending chronicle of Spartan military success received its first major (and, for the campaign in Asia Minor, the most decisive) setback when the Athenian Conon, acting as a vice-admiral of the Persian fleet, brought about the revolt of Rhodes, their chief naval base, in summer or autumn of 396 (D.S. 14.79.5). This was a severe blow for the Spartans, since the loss of Rhodes prevented them from organizing a combined land and naval attack on Tissaphernes in Caria and threatened to disrupt communications between the land army in Asia Minor and Sparta. It also raised hopes in Boeotia and in Athens of mounting a successful opposition against Sparta, although a rapprochement between the two was an essential pre-condition.

Almost certainly as a result of the revolt of Rhodes, Pharnabazus, the satrap of Hellespontine Phrygia, sent Timocrates of Rhodes to give gifts of money to the leading anti-Spartan politicians in Boeotia, Corinth, Athens and Argos in order to win their support for a war against Sparta in mainland Greece (Oxyrhynchus Historian 7.2–3). This was not the cause of the Corinthian War, as Xenophon believed (3.5.1), but the offer of further financial assistance from Persia was another factor in persuading these states to adopt an actively aggressive policy towards Sparta. The Athenians were further encouraged by the continuing successes of Conon in 395 and began to revive their ambitions of regaining their naval empire. It only remained for the Athenians to bury their differences with the Boeotians, which rapprochement came about when the Boeotians successfully appealed to them for help against the impending attack on their territory by the Spartans (Xen. 3.5.8–15; D.S. 14.81.2). The main motivation for the Athenians was their fear of and need to prevent Spartan expansionism into central Greece at the expense of Boeotia.

But the Spartans had made a grave strategic blunder in their decision to launch an all-out campaign in Asia Minor before securing their military hegemony in Greece. This failure allowed the Boeotians to provoke them into a fatal conflict in central Greece. The Boeotians persuaded their allies, the Western Locrians, to levy taxes on a piece of land, which the Phocians claimed was theirs, correctly expecting Phocis to invade Locris in retaliation. This gave the Boeotians the excuse to invade the land of the Phocians who in turn appealed for military help from the Spartans:

> The Lacedaimonians happily seized on an excuse to make an expedition against the Thebans, having been angry with them for a long time ... and they reckoned that this was an excellent time to lead out an army against them and stop their arrogance towards themselves. For their campaigns were going well in Asia through the victories under Agesilaos, and there was no other war in Greece to hinder them.
>
> (Xen. 3.5.5)

Lysander was ordered to go to Phocis in order to gather an army from the Spartan allies in central Greece, and to rendezvous with King Pausanias, who was leading an army from the Peloponnese, at Haliartus on an appointed day (Xen. 3.5.6–7). It was now that the Boeotians launched their appeal for help to the Athenians. Lysander persuaded Boeotian Orchomenus to desert to the Spartan side but, instead of waiting for Pausanias, attacked Haliartus. This decision by Lysander to fight without Pausanias may well reflect a split in Spartan foreign policy: Lysander still pursuing a policy of open imperialism, while Pausanias preferred a more modest policy of ensuring Spartan supremacy in the Peloponnese and maintaining a balance of power in the rest of Greece. Lysander's rash action led to his death and the defeat of his army. When Pausanias arrived with his forces, he found the Boeotians and the Athenians lined up and ready for battle. Reflecting on the success of the Boeotians against Lysander, the refusal of the Corinthians to send their contingent, and the reluctance of the other Peloponnesians to fight, Pausanias agreed to a truce on the condition that he removed his forces from Boeotia (D.S. 14.81.2–3; Xen. 3.5.21–24).

The battle of Haliartus in 395 marked the beginning of the Corinthian War and the beginning of the end of Spartan imperial ambitions in Asia Minor. The Spartans, fearing that their enemies in Greece had become too powerful and that Sparta was in danger, recalled Agesilaos from Asia Minor (D.S. 14.83.1; Xen. 4.2.1–3). He set out in spring 394, retracing the steps of King Xerxes of Persia in 480, through Thrace, Macedon and Thessaly. The defeat of the Spartan navy by Pharnabazus and Conon in August 394 at the battle of Cnidus brought the Spartans' grandiose ambitions in Asia Minor to an end (D.S. 14.83.4–7). Although some attempts were made in 391 to renew the war there, Spartan imperial ambitions in Asia were finally laid to rest in 389/8 and confirmed in the terms of the King's Peace (or Peace of Antalcidas) in 387/6. The main aim of Spartan policy from 395–394 was to break up the Quadruple Alliance which was threatening their hegemony of Greece.

The Corinthian War, 395–387/6

The defeat of the Spartans at the battle of Haliartus in 395 and the humiliating withdrawal of the army of King Pausanias, who was condemned to death but fled into exile, were the incentive for the rallying of the anti-Spartan forces in Greece. In the summer and winter of 395/4, a Quadruple Alliance was formed by Athens, Boeotia, Corinth and Argos (D.S. 14.82.1; Xen. 4.2.1). The coalition was further strengthened by the membership of the Locrians, most of Thessaly, Euboea, Acarnania, Chalcidice and other minor states. These allies gathered their forces at the Isthmus of Corinth in the spring of 394, and in the discussion about the coalition's strategy a Corinthian suggested:

'I think that the best course of action by far is to fight the battle in Lacedaimon itself, and if not there, as near as possible.'

(Xen. 4.2.12)

It is hardly surprising that the Spartans were filled with fear and demanded the return of Agesilaos from Asia to defend Sparta (D.S. 14.83.1; Xen. 4.2.2).

The Spartans then showed commendable speed to meet this threat. They raised a Peloponnesian army under the command of Aristodamus, the acting-regent for Pausanias' under-age son Agesipolis, and marched to Nemea in the north-east of the Peloponnese; there they met the coalition's forces in a battle which resulted in a Spartan victory (D.S. 14.83.2; Xen. 4.2.16–23). Meanwhile Agesilaos, making haste from Asia by the land route, was forced to fight his way through Thrace (D.S. 14.83.3) and Thessaly (Xen. 4.3.3–9) until he reached Boeotia. His main aim, apart from bringing his considerable booty safely to Sparta, was to restore the Spartans' control in the northern half of central Greece, which would be an excellent spring-board for regaining their dominant position in northern Greece. The news of the destruction of the Spartan fleet at Cnidus spurred on Agesilaos to win the battle of Coroneia in August 394 (D.S. 14.84.1–2), and he was able to return to the Peloponnese, but only by sea, because the Quadruple Alliance controlled the Isthmus (see below).

The Spartans had won two battles, but these military successes were of little consequence as they had done nothing to relieve the Spartans' very precarious position. For they had suffered within a year a massive reversal of fortune. They had lost their naval empire in the Aegean and on the coast of Asia Minor; with the exception of Phocis and Orchomenus, they had lost control of central and northern Greece; and, far more worryingly, their supremacy in the Peloponnese, which underpinned their status as a superpower, was under threat from a coalition that included their two strongest former League allies (Boeotia and Corinth) and their deadliest enemy in the Peloponnese (Argos). They were now trapped in the Peloponnese as a result of their enemies' strategy, which was designed to bottle them up there. The Quadruple Alliance's forces had occupied the territory of Corinth, which stretched between the Corinthian and Saronic gulfs at the Isthmus, and built long walls from Corinth to its western port Lechaeon and to its eastern port Cenchreae. There was now no land passage via the Isthmus from the Peloponnese to central Greece and beyond, unless these fortifications were captured. The Corinthian War takes it name from the fighting that took place around Corinth, but in reality this theatre of war soon settled into a stalemate. The Spartans, operating from Sicyon, eventually managed to capture Lechaeon, but not Corinth itself, where the resident armed forces were always threatening, especially the lighter-armed mercenary troops of the Athenian Iphicrates who wiped out half a Spartan regiment in 390 (D.S. 14.91.2; Xen. 4.5.12–17).

The position of the Spartans in the Peloponnese was further weakened by Conon's capture of Cythera (393), the supply of Persian funds to the coalition (393) and the political 'union' of Corinth and Argos (392). Pharnabazus and Conon, having sailed around the Aegean after the battle of Cnidus in order to drive out the Spartan harmosts and garrisons, then brought the war to Spartan territory. They ravaged the coasts of Laconia and Messenia, and established a garrison on Cythera, an island off Laconia near Malea (D.S. 14.84.4–5; Xen 4.8.8). When Nicias did the same thing in 424 during the Archidamian War (see Chapter 19), it caused great panic among the Spartans who feared that the garrison would provoke a 'Helot' uprising (Thucydides 4.55.3–4). Similar feelings must have been present among the Spartans in 393, since it was only five or six years earlier that they had detected the alleged conspiracy of a certain Cinadon, who had planned to overthrow the Spartan state by forming a coalition of underdogs – Helots, emancipated Helots, Inferiors (disfranchised Spartiates) and 'Perioeci' (Xen. 3.3.4–11).

When Pharnabazus arrived at the Isthmus, his liberal gifts of Persian money improved the fighting capacity of the Quadruple Alliance's forces: the Corinthians fitted out a new navy, and Iphicrates' mercenary force was stationed permanently in Corinth from 393–389; but, most of all, the Athenians re-established themselves as a major Greek power. They rebuilt their fortifications and Long Walls (joining Athens to the Piraeus), and began to recover their former Aegean Empire, because Conon was using the Persian fleet in Pharnabazus' absence for their benefit (Xen. 4.8.9; 4.8.12). Even worse for the Spartans was the political 'union' of Corinth and Argos in 393 or 392 by which both states accepted a common citizenship (Xen. 4.4.6). The Spartans, for the last 100 years, had deliberately stirred up hostility between these two states so that, by a policy of 'divide and rule', they could ensure their own supremacy in the Peloponnese. Therefore, by 392, the Spartans were in desperate trouble and their hegemony of Greece was in danger of collapse. It was time for a major foreign policy rethink.

The Spartans realized that they had made a grave error in breaking their alliance with Persia in 400, and were now paying a high price for that folly. Therefore they decided that peace with Persia would provide the solution to their problems in Greece, but realized that they would have to make a substantial concession to win over the Persians to their side. The Spartan Antalcidas, in 392, was despatched to Tiribazus, the new Persian commander in the west (based at Sardis), in order to make an offer that Artaxerxes could not refuse:

> Antalcidas said to Tiribazus that he had come wanting peace and the sort of peace that the king wished for. For the Spartans were putting forward no claim against the king for the Greek cities in Asia, and that it was enough for them that all the islands and the other cities were autonomous.
>
> (Xen. 4.8.14)

In other words, the Spartans were prepared to betray the Asiatic Greeks and hand them over to Persia, whose possession of them would be totally secure, because there would be no Spartan army in Asia Minor, and no naval state would be strong enough, due to the autonomy of the other states in Greece, to take control of them.

The Quadruple Alliance, however, had taken steps to ensure that their representatives were also at this meeting at Sardis, but withheld their agreement to the Spartan proposals because of their fear that the autonomy clause might be used by the Spartans to weaken the members of the Alliance – the Athenians might lose control over Lemnos, Imbros and Scyros which were essential for Athens' importation of grain from the Black Sea; the Boeotian League might be dissolved, severely weakening the individual cities, especially Thebes; and the union of Corinth and Argos might be ended (Xen. 4.8.15). Tiribazus was very pleased with the Spartan peace offer, but felt that he needed to refer the matter to Artaxerxes for the final decision. The Spartans called a peace conference at Sparta with the intention of making concessions to the Quadruple Alliance over the autonomy clause (Andocides, The Peace), but the negotiations failed, for the Athenians felt that now was their best chance to regain their Aegean Empire, and possibly because they baulked at the idea of selling out the Asiatic Greeks to Persia. In the end, all the Greek discussions proved to be worthless because Artaxerxes, although gaining from the Spartans all that he had previously wanted, was so antagonistic to the Spartans owing to their earlier treacherous behaviour, especially their support for Cyrus, that he rejected the proposed peace treaty. He withdrew the pro-Spartan Tiribazus and replaced him with Strouthas, giving him clear instructions to help the Athenians against the Spartans (Xen. 4.8.17).

The Spartans renewed the war against Persia in Asia Minor by sending out Thibron, but he was soon killed by Strouthas (Xen. 4.8.17–19), and his replacement, Anaxibios, along with 12 other harmosts, was ambushed and killed by the Athenian Iphicrates in 389/8, marking the end of Spartan military involvement in Asia Minor (Xen. 4.8.34–39). The success of Iphicrates was a symbol of Athens' growing power in the immediate aftermath of the abortive peace conference in 391. The Persian money had financed the construction of a sizeable fleet, which the Athenians intended to use to lay the foundations of a second naval empire. The Athenians made alliances with Byzantium and Chalcedon, and imposed a 10 per cent toll on all ships passing through the Bosporus; they became allies of the two Thracian Kings, thus ensuring the goodwill of the Thracian coastal cities; they regained Lesbos and began collecting money from other cities in Asia Minor (Xen. 4.8.25–30). This behaviour was very reminiscent of Athens' fifth-century imperialism, which had deprived the Persian kings of their rightful (in their opinion) tribute for over 70 years. The Athenians' anti-Persian policy was made plain to see by their alliances with King Evagoras of Salamis in Cyprus (Xen. 4.8.24), and with Akoris, the ruler of Egypt (Aristophanes, *Wealth* 1.178), both of whom had revolted from Artaxerxes. This renewed spectre of Athenian imperialism brought Artaxerxes to his senses.

The Spartans perceived this to be the right moment to make another approach to Artaxerxes and sent Antalcidas, the 'nauarch' (naval commander) for 388/7, to negotiate a new treaty between themselves and Persia (D.S. 14.110.2). He was welcomed by Artaxerxes, who had realized that the revitalized Athenians were far more of a threat to his control of the Asiatic Greeks than the Spartans. Consequently he agreed to an alliance with Sparta and to the terms of the peace treaty which the Spartans wished to impose on the rest of the Greeks, but which also gave him control of the Asiatic Greeks (Xen. 5.1.25). He also reappointed Tiribazus to the command of the west, instructing him to give every possible help to the Spartans. Then Antalcidas, with more than 80 ships, including 20 from their ally, Dionysius the tyrant of Syracuse, made for the Hellespont and immediately stopped the grain ships from sailing to Athens (Xen. 5.1.28–29). This repeat of Lysander's action in 405–404 after the battle of Aegospotamoi, which had starved the Athenians into submission, was the decisive move for ending the war. The Athenians were in reality the leaders of the Quadruple Alliance, and once they were compelled to submit, there was little chance of the others continuing the war.

As a result the Greeks, having been summoned by Tiribazus, attended a meeting at Sardis in order to hear the terms of the peace that Artaxerxes was proposing:

> 'King Artaxerxes thinks it right that the cities in Asia, including Clazomenae, should belong to him, and that the other Greek cities, both small and big, should be made autonomous, except Lemnos, Imbros and Scyros. These, just as in the past, should belong to the Athenians. Whoever does not accept this peace, I will make war on them, alongside those who want this peace, by land and by sea, with ships and with money.'
>
> (Xen. 5.1.31)

The Greek representatives were then sent away to report Artaxerxes' proposals to their respective states. However, Agesilaos then used the army to ensure the acceptance of Artaxerxes' terms by Sparta's enemies in time for the formal signing of the peace.

The Thebans were very resistant to the concept of autonomy, as redefined by the Spartans, since it entailed the break-up of the Boeotian League which was the source of their strength. Agesilaos assembled the Peloponnesian League army to march upon Thebes, but had only reached as far as Tegea, when the Boeotians submitted and agreed to the terms of the peace treaty (Xen. 5.1.32–33). The Corinthians and Argos also refused at first, because in 389 they had gone a stage further than their mutual citizenship of 392 and had united into one state. However, the threat of Spartan armed intervention by Agesilaos led to the departure of the Argive garrison in Corinth, and the dissolution of the union (Xen. 5.1.34). Having sorted out the enemies of Sparta, Agesilaos was now ready for the formal signing of the King's Peace in 386.

The main beneficiary of the King's Peace was the Spartans, and for that reason the alternative name for the peace – the Peace of Antalcidas – is a better reflection of the true position. They had bargained away the Asiatic Greeks, whom they no longer had the means to control anyway, in return for the crippling of their Greek enemies. The Athenians were now prevented from acquiring a new naval empire, since all states were henceforth to be independent; the dangerous union of Corinth and Argos had been broken up, and Corinth was forced once more to rejoin the Peloponnesian League under Sparta; and, far more importantly, Thebes and the other cities of Boeotia were isolated from each other (Xen. 5.1.35–36). Thus Sparta, by the humiliation of the Boeotians, who had offered the most serious challenge from the end of the Peloponnesian War, had regained the undisputed hegemony of Greece.

Bibliography

Andrewes, A. 'Two notes on Lysander', *Phoenix* 25.
Cartledge, P. *Agesilaos and the Crisis of Sparta*, chs 6, 11, 12, 14, 17 and 18.
——*Sparta and Lakonia*, ch. 13.
Davies, J. K. *Democracy and Classical Greece*, 2nd edn, ch. 8.
Hornblower, S. *The Greek World 479–323* BC, 2nd edn, ch. 14.
Lewis, D. M. *Sparta and Persia*, chs 5 and 6.
Parke, H. W. 'The development of the second Spartan Empire', *JHS* 50.
Perlman, S. 'The causes and the outbreak of the Corinthian War', *CQ* 14.
Seager, R. 'Thrasybulus, Conon and Athenian imperialism', *JHS* 87.

25

THE 'HEGEMONY' OF THEBES, 371–362

Fifth-century Greece had been dominated by the two super-powers, Athens and Sparta, but in the first 30 years of the fourth century, Boeotia, led by Thebes, became a major force in Greek politics. After the Boeotians regained their independence from Athens in 447 at the battle of Coroneia, they restored the Boeotian League which was the source of their strength. This federal league was divided into eleven administrative constituencies, each one providing 60 members for the 660-strong federal Council which was the chief decision-making body of the Boeotians. The main executive functions of the League were carried out by a board of public officials, known as the eleven Boeotarchs, annually elected, one from each of the constituencies. As Thebes covered four of these constituencies, and thus had 240 councillors and four Boeotarchs, it naturally assumed the position of leadership within the League, although this was disputed by its main rival Orchomenus.

The power of the Boeotians had grown with the defeat of the Athenians in the Peloponnesian War (431–404), and this had caused anxiety among the Spartans. The Boeotians' passive resistance to the Spartans' growing imperialism from 404/3 became active in 395 when they joined the Athenians, the Corinthians and the Argives in a Quadruple Alliance, and fought the Spartans in the Corinthian War (see Chapter 24). However, the King's Peace (also known as the Peace of Antalcidas) in 386 had established Spartan dominance in Greece, mainly at the expense of Boeotia. The Boeotian League was dissolved, destroying the power-base of Thebes, and seemingly removing the possibility of any future challenge to Sparta's 'hegemony' (leadership) of Greece. Yet in 371, at the battle of Leuctra under the inspired leadership of Epaminondas, the Boeotians delivered the fatal blow to the Spartans that finally led to their collapse as a serious force in Greek politics. How had the position of the Boeotians changed so dramatically in that 15-year period?

The rise of Thebes, 386–371

In the years 386–379, the power of Sparta in mainland Greece seemed invincible. One of the principal terms of the King's Peace of 386 was that all states should be free and autonomous, but it was the Spartans, whether officially under the Peace or unofficially by virtue of their superior military forces, who were to be the judges of what constituted the definition of autonomy. They interpreted autonomy as the right to dissolve any grouping of cities that offered a threat to themselves or coerce any state that had the wrong kind (i.e. democratic) of constitution, while strengthening and enlarging their Peloponnesian League, which they cynically claimed consisted of 'autonomous' states. The first to suffer was the democratic state of Mantinea in Arcadia, which had been disloyal to Sparta in the Corinthian War and therefore was ripe for Spartan retribution. In 385 Mantinea was captured by a Spartan army and was broken up into its original four or five villages, which had synoecized (see Glossary) into the unified state of Mantinea c.471; a pro-Spartan oligarchy was also imposed (Xenophon, *Hellenica* 5.2.1–7 – all references in the rest of this chapter are to this work, unless stated otherwise). In 384, the Spartans ordered democratic Phlius to receive back its oligarchic exiles, but later, after a siege from 381–379, they imposed a narrow pro-Spartan oligarchy, supported by a garrison (5.2.8–10; 5.3.10–17, 21–25). In 382 the Spartans launched a major expedition against the Chalcidian League which, under the leadership of Olynthus, was growing in size and strength. In 379, Olynthus surrendered, the League was dissolved and each of its members was forced to join the Peloponnesian League (5.2.11–24; 2.37–3.1–9; 3.18–20, 26–27).

But Sparta's greatest success and most overt imperialism in this period was in Boeotia. The Spartans had ensured that extreme pro-Spartan oligarchic exiles had been restored to Thebes before the formal signing of the King's Peace in 386. In 382 this foresight came to fruition. While the Spartan Phoebidas was leading his troops through Boeotia for the campaign (allegedly) against the Chalcidian League, having plotted with Leontiadas, one of the restored Theban exiles, he suddenly seized and garrisoned the Cadmeia (the citadel of Thebes) and established a narrow pro-Spartan oligarchy under Leontiadas (5.2.25–36). Even Xenophon, who is generally so biased in favour of Sparta, was shocked by this blatant infringement of autonomy which had been guaranteed in the King's Peace (5.4.1). However, 300 anti-Spartan Thebans escaped and were given refuge in Athens. Around this time the Spartans also re-founded Plataea, which they had razed to the ground in 427 for being an ally of Athens, and strengthened their hold on Boeotia by imposing Theban-style oligarchies, backed up by Spartan 'harmosts' and garrisons, on most of the other main cities in Boeotia. Thus, by 379, Xenophon was able to write:

> Events had turned out so well for the Spartans that the Thebans and the rest of the Boeotians were completely under their power ... and their empire seemed now at last to have been well and truly established.

> (Xenophon 5.3.27)

However, it was at this Spartan pinnacle of success that the recovery of Boeotia begins.

A plot was hatched in 379 to overthrow the pro-Spartan 'polemarchs' (war-leaders), who were the chief public officials in Thebes since the dissolution of the Boeotian League. Phillidas, the polemarchs' secretary, organized the liberation of Thebes with the 300 exiled Thebans in Athens and with two Athenian generals. The exiles entered Thebes at night, assassinated the polemarchs and Leontiadas, roused the Thebans to revolt, summoned the two Athenian generals with their troops and attacked the Cadmeia where the 1,500-strong garrison under its three Spartan commanders were stationed. Having failed to get help from Plataea and Thespiae, Herippidas, the Spartan harmost, surrendered and was forced to make a humiliating retreat from Boeotia (5.4.1–13). The Spartan position, however, was still strong, as they had garrisons in the other principal Boeotian cities, but it was essential to regain control of Thebes. Therefore early in 378 King Cleombrotus was sent with a Peloponnesian army into Boeotia, but he departed after 16 days, having achieved very little there, although he left behind Sphodrias with a third of the army and money to hire mercenaries (5.4.15–18). Nevertheless his expedition did frighten the Athenians into neutrality and into the condemnation of the two generals who had helped in the liberation of Thebes (5.4.19) – this was possibly the main aim of the Spartans.

It had been one of the basic tenets of Spartan foreign policy in central Greece to encourage hostility between Athens and Boeotia so that neither could threaten Sparta. The clumsy attempt in 378 by Sphodrias, the harmost of Thespiae, to seize the Piraeus by force and his acquittal through the influence of King Agesilaos (5.4.20–33) so shocked the Athenians that they voted that the King's Peace had been broken by the Spartans (Diodorus 15.29.7); and they pressed on with making alliances with the Thebans and other states that culminated in the creation of the Second Athenian League in 378/7. It was now that the Thebans felt the confidence to start the reconstruction of the Boeotian League which was signalled by their election in 378 of four Theban Boeotarchs, the public officials of the League. The three Spartan invasions in 378 and 377 (two led by Agesilaos) and the aborted attempt in 376 under Cleombrotus had failed to conquer the Thebans, and thus their ambitions increased. In 378 the Sacred Band of 300 professional Theban soldiers was formed to be the spearhead of Boeotia's military resurgence. The Thebans defeated the troops of Phoebidas and of Thespiae in 378/7 and, as a result:

> The ambitions of the Thebans were again kindled, and they made expeditions against Thespiae and the other neighbouring cities. However, the democratic factions from these cities retired to Thebes, for narrow oligarchies had been established in all the cities, just as in Thebes.
>
> (Xenophon 5.4.46)

These narrow pro-Spartan oligarchies had proved to be deeply unpopular, and the Thebans' own moderately democratic constitution and reception of these democratic refugees helped to increase the support for the renewed Boeotian League.

The Peloponnesian League members became disaffected with Sparta's (and King Agesilaos') fixation on and failure against Boeotia, and persuaded the Spartans in 376 to direct their military efforts against the growing power of the Athenians and their new naval league. It was decided to repeat the effective strategy of 405/4 and 387/6 by starving the Athenians into submission. Therefore the Peloponnesian fleet patrolled the waters around Aegina, Ceos and Andros, so preventing the grain ships from reaching the Piraeus. However, this strategy failed miserably when the Athenians won a decisive naval battle at Naxos in September 376 (5.4.60–61). In the following year, the Athenians followed up this success by sending a fleet around the Peloponnese, at the request of the Thebans, which gained control of Corcyra and won another resounding naval victory at Alyzeia in Acarnania near the island of Leucas (5.4.64–66).

These two invasion-free years (376–375) gave the Thebans the breathing space that they needed:

> The Thebans boldly launched military expeditions against the surrounding cities and took control of them for a second time.
>
> (Xenophon 5.4.63)

The purpose of these expeditions was to restore the Boeotian League, which had been the basis of Thebes' power. According to Xenophon (6.1.1), the Thebans had restored the Boeotian League in its entirety by 375, but he is probably mistaken as Plataea, Thespiae and Orchomenus, the other principal city-states in Boeotia and long-standing rivals of Thebes, were still under Spartan control at this time. However, by 375, the restored Boeotian League had become a major force, whose new constitution (although its details in the sources are scarce) increased the power of the Thebans as the leaders. There were now only seven Boeotarchs, but Thebes still retained the right to elect four of them. In addition, many of the powers of the former Council of 660, which had been abolished, were handed over to the Boeotarchs. All citizens of the new Boeotian League were entitled to attend the sovereign federal Assembly and, as it was held in Thebes, this ensured that the Thebans were usually in the majority when policy and legislation were being decided.

The growing military prowess of the Boeotians – a clear warning to the rest of Greece – was displayed at the battle of Tegyra in 375 when Pelopidas, using the Sacred Band in conjunction with the cavalry, inflicted a defeat and heavy casualties on the Spartan garrison at Orchomenus (Diodorus 15.37.1). Such was the confidence of the Boeotians that in the same year they went on the offensive against Sparta's loyal ally in central Greece, Phocis (6.1.1). Therefore the Spartans despatched King Cleombrotus with two-thirds of the Spartan army and the same number of allied troops to defend Phocis (6.1.1). However, by the second half of 375, the Spartans were feeling the pressure: they had failed to make much of an impact against Thebes, had suffered two serious naval defeats, and were unable through a lack of manpower to help their ally, Polydamas of Pharsalus in Thessaly, against the powerful and ambitious Jason of Pherae, who was now allied with Boeotia (6.1.2–17). The Athenians too were finding the naval campaigns a major drain on finance and manpower, and shared the same deep concern about the revival of Boeotian militarism under Thebes. Thus, the request of the Persian King Artaxerxes – possibly prompted by the Spartans (Philochorus FGrH328 F151) – to renew the King's Peace of 386, for the purpose of hiring Greek mercenaries to put down a rebellion in Egypt, was welcomed by both the Spartans and the Athenians (Diodorus 15.38.1).

The major difference between the Peace of 375/4 and 386 was that it was signed by two groups of allies, led by Sparta and Athens; for the Spartans were now prepared to accept the Athenians' hegemony over their new naval league in the Aegean as the price to be paid for their cooperation against Boeotia (Nepos. Timotheos 2.3). However, there was no way that Thebes was going to accept another dissolution of the Boeotian League, and it is a sign of both Spartan and Athenian weakness and of Boeotian strength that no military action was taken when 'the Thebans' presumably agreed to the Peace on behalf of 'the Boeotians'.

The rapprochement of Sparta and Athens was the best hope of containing Boeotia, but a clash over Zacynthos and Corcyra in 373 led to renewed fighting between the two states, thus foolishly playing into the hands of the Boeotians. From 373–371 the Thebans strengthened their grip in Boeotia by crushing Plataea and Thespiae, two of their three pro-Spartan rivals, and in 371 were campaigning again against Phocis, an ally of Athens and Sparta (6.3.1, 3.5). This brought both states to their senses, and when Artaxerxes requested (possibly again prompted by the Spartans) a second renewal of the King's Peace, because the commander of his forces against Egypt had also revolted (Diodorus 15.50.4), the proposed Peace of 371 was seen as a means to curb Boeotia. King Cleombrotus was again sent with a large force to Phocis, ready to invade Boeotia, if the Thebans refused to attend the peace conference or to accept the terms of the Peace. The peace negotiations were held in Sparta, and both Sparta and Athens stressed the need for the reinforcement of the autonomy clause in the 386 King's Peace, but tacitly accepting that this clause would not be applicable to Sparta's Peloponnesian League nor Athens' Second Athenian League. But it would be applicable to Thebes and the Boeotian League; and a new clause, which gave states the right to refuse to fight against violators of the autonomy principle, would allow the Athenians to avoid military involvement while Sparta and Thebes fought it out, when the Thebans predictably refused to dissolve the Boeotian League (6.3.18).

The stage was thus set for confrontation between Sparta and Boeotia. The Spartans took the oath to accept the Peace of 371 on behalf of themselves and their allies, and the Athenians and their allies swore individually. At first the Thebans acquiesced and signed on their own behalf, according to Xenophon (6.3.19), but on the next day they demanded that 'the Thebans' should be replaced by 'the Boeotians'; in other words, the Thebans were claiming the right to sign on behalf of the Boeotian League. There was a clash between Agesilaos and the leading Theban Epaminondas:

> Agesilaos asked if it was just and equal for the cities of Boeotia to be autonomous. Epaminondas instantly and boldly asked Agesilaos in return if he thought it was just and equal for the cities of Laconia to be autonomous. Agesilaos jumped up from his seat and insisted that Epaminondas say plainly if he would grant autonomy to Boeotia; but Epaminondas only answered again in the same way, by asking Agesilaos if he would grant Laconia its autonomy.
>
> (Plutarch, *Agesilaos* 28)

Epaminondas' refusal to accept the Spartan definition of autonomy pleased Agesilaos, as he could exclude them from the Peace and declare war.

King Cleombrotus was ordered to invade Boeotia from Phocis, but at the battle of Leuctra in 371, the Spartans suffered a terrible defeat:

> The victory of the Thebans was the most famous of all those won by Greeks over Greeks.
>
> (Pausanias 9.13.11)

Four hundred Spartiates, including Cleombrotus, were killed at Leuctra – about a third of the Spartan citizen body. Although neither side knew it at the time, this battle was one of the turning points in Greek history: the Spartans, who had been so dominant in Greek politics for two and a half centuries, were about to be reduced to the status of a second-rate power. The Boeotians, under the leadership of Epaminondas and Pelopidas, were now on the threshold of becoming the most powerful state in Greece. This fact was recognized by the Athenians, who later in 371 organized a third renewal of the King's Peace; but the clause about coming to the aid of a threatened ally, previously voluntary, now became compulsory (6.5.1–2). The Thebans, by their exclusion from the Peace, were marked out as the enemy, for the Athenians, now so fearful of Theban power, were attempting to establish a balance of power with the Spartans, and this Peace was a prelude to a full military alliance between Athens and Sparta, sworn in 369 (7.1.1–14).

Theban foreign policy, 371–365

Theban foreign policy after the restoration of the Boeotian League in 378 was mainly in the hands of the seven Boeotarchs, of whom the most influential in this period were Epaminondas and Pelopidas. In the immediate aftermath of Leuctra the Thebans did little to follow up their success against Sparta, partly because they failed to realize how seriously they had weakened Sparta, partly because they still needed to consolidate the position of Boeotia in central Greece. Orchomenus, the last major opposition to the Boeotian League within Boeotia, and Phocis, the traditional enemy, were both still hostile; and there were serious concerns about the imperialist ambitions of their ally, Jason of Pherae in Thessaly. The first target was Orchomenus which, when given the choice of joining the League or being destroyed, promptly chose the former, even though its citizens would not have full citizen rights (Diodorus 15.57.1). The security of the now-unified Boeotian territory was increased by strengthening the defences along the southern coast on the Gulf of Corinth. The Spartans had previously launched sea-borne invasions of Boeotia as an alternative to land invasions through the Isthmus, but the commencement of fortifying the coastal cities and of building watchtowers and signalling stations ensured protection on the vulnerable southern flank.

Now that Boeotia had been united and fortified, there was the pressing need to take action outside the Boeotian borders in central Greece. Jason of Pherae, having brought Thessalian reinforcements at the time of Leuctra, had captured Hyampolis and destroyed Heraclea in Trachis on his return journey (6.4.27), thus giving him direct and unimpeded access to Boeotia from Thessaly. However, his probable ambition of making Thessaly into a major Greek power was brought to a sudden end by his assassination in 370. The ensuing internal turmoil and blood-letting relieved the Thebans of that threat, and they consolidated their position in central Greece by making alliances with Phocis, which, deprived of Spartan protection, was now willing to embrace the Boeotian League; with Euboea and Acarnania, both of whom deserted the Second Athenian League; and with Locris, Malis and probably Oetaea (6.5.23). Thus, by the summer of 370, the whole of central Greece, with the exception of the Athenians, had allied itself with the Boeotian League, which was now ready to adopt a higher profile in Greek affairs.

During the Theban hegemony, foreign policy was directed towards three areas: the Peloponnese; Thessaly and Macedon; and, in the second half of the decade, the Aegean. However, 'hegemony' is not a precise term to describe the power of the Thebans in this decade, since they never gained the hegemony of Greece in the way that the Spartans had in the first 30 years of the fourth century; 'pre-eminence' or 'ascendancy' is a more accurate reflection of their political position in Greece. For the Thebans made no attempt to create an empire by conquest, nor to impose direct rule on Greek cities, nor impose garrisons (except for a few special cases), nor levy tribute.

There were two reasons for this: first, their lack of manpower which prevented widespread conquest and occupation; and second, their lack of financial resources to maintain a large army for long periods of time. Epaminondas and Pelopidas recognized these constraints on Theban foreign policy, and consequently relied upon the creation of a network of alliances, in which the Boeotian League (i.e. Thebes) would be the leading ally, in order to exert Theban influence in the Peloponnese, and in Thessaly and Macedon. However, the failure of the Thebans to create a formal organization, such as the Peloponnesian League, in which a common foreign policy could be agreed, resources shared, and disputes between allies resolved, and to establish themselves as the legal and official hegemon of such an organization seriously undermined their position and led to the collapse of their ascendancy in Greece. It will be useful to consider each of the three geographical areas in turn – the Peloponnese, northern Greece (Thessaly and Macedon) and the Aegean – and finally return to the Peloponnese where Theban ambitions were checked at the battle of Mantinea in 362.

The Peloponnese: 370–365

The defeat of the Spartans at Leuctra encouraged many of the Peloponnesian states to rid themselves once and for all of Spartan domination. The first stage was 'stasis' (civil war) in Corinth, Sicyon, Argos, Phlius, Elis, Achaea and in Arcadia (especially Tegea and Mantinea), where the pro-Spartan oligarchies were being challenged by anti-Spartan democracies. The second stage was the development of anti-Spartan alliances within the Peloponnese. In 371 Mantinea re-synoecized (see 'synoecism' in Glossary) by bringing back the (four or) five villages into a unified democratic state within a rebuilt city wall (6.5.3). The probable driving-force behind this was Lycomedes, who aimed to make the Arcadians a major power in the Peloponnese. He was the architect of a new Arcadian League, formed in 370, which included most (and all of the most important) of the city-states in Arcadia (Diodorus 15.59.1). The Eleans wanted to regain Triphylia, of which they had been deprived by the Spartans c.400, and, thinking that their best hope lay with an anti-Spartan military power, allied themselves to the Arcadian League. The Argives, the traditional enemy of the Spartans, needed no second invitation to become the third member of the triple alliance – another major omission by the pro-Spartan Xenophon who conveniently ignores any institution (e.g. the Second Athenian League) or individual (e.g. Epaminondas) that outshines the Spartans.

This anti-Spartan alliance now threatened the position of dominance that the Spartans had held for the last 200 years, and was bound to provoke a

Spartan military response. The triple alliance made an unsuccessful appeal to the Athenians to join their alliance, and so approached the Thebans who voted to become allies (Diodorus 15.61.3). This alliance was the backbone of Epaminondas' Peloponnesian policy: if the Spartans could be surrounded by a ring of hostile states, then they would be cut off in the south Peloponnese and be fully committed to self-defence, thus ensuring the security of Boeotia, since all future warfare would be in the Peloponnese. In the winter of 370/69, the Thebans and their central Greek allies, under the leadership of Epaminondas and Pelopidas, led the first invasion of the Peloponnese since the Dark Ages. Having united with the forces of the triple alliance, and reinforced by the defection of the Perioeci in northern Laconia, the Thebans invaded the heartland of Sparta. They threatened the city of Sparta itself and ravaged the land of Laconia (6.5.27–32). The Spartans, although aided by Corinth, Epidaurus and a few other faithful Peloponnesian League states, could do little to prevent this humiliation.

It is doubtful whether Epaminondas aimed for the total destruction of Sparta, since its existence would be a constant source of disunity in the Peloponnese – very useful for Boeotian security. However, it was vital that the power of the Spartans was permanently reduced so that they could never again dominate Greek (and Boeotian) politics. This could only be achieved by destroying the economic base of Spartan military might through the liberation of the Messenian 'Helots':

> Epaminondas, who by nature believed in great enterprises and aimed at eternal fame, won over the Arcadians and the rest of the allies to found Messene, having been controlled for many years by the Spartans, as it was well-positioned to oppose Sparta.
>
> (Diodorus 15.66.1)

Epaminondas realized that the creation of an independent Messenian state would have two results: first, the Spartans would need to support themselves economically, thus undermining the entire military system and ending their military superiority; second, the ring of anti-Spartan states would be closed even tighter around the Spartans, thus trapping them in the south-east Peloponnese. Therefore, in early 369, Epaminondas created the state of Messene with a fortified capital at Ithome (Diodorus 15.66.6). He then returned with his forces to Boeotia, leaving behind a fatally weakened Sparta.

The Spartans turned in desperation to the Athenians, who were becoming more alarmed at the growth of Theban power, and a military alliance was concluded on the basis of equal leadership (7.1.1–14). In the summer of 369, the Arcadians, Argives and Elis again appealed to the Thebans to send an army into the Peloponnese (Diodorus 15.68.). Although the same spectacular success of the previous expedition could not be achieved and the addition of the Athenians as Spartan allies would provide stiffer resistance,

Epaminondas was determined to complete the permanent reduction of Sparta. Sparta's loyal allies along the north coast of the Peloponnese, especially Corinth, were still an important source of manpower to the Spartans and prevented easy communications between the Thebans and the triple alliance. Therefore, Epaminondas' main aim in the second invasion was either to detach them from Sparta or to put them under such intense military pressure that they would be incapable of offering military aid, thus isolating Sparta even more. Sicyon was captured and Pallene in Achaea surrendered, resulting in both states joining the anti-Spartan coalition, and the territory of Corinth, Epidaurus, Troezen and Phlius was devastated (7.1.18–22). These four cities proved to be impregnable, but such was the damage inflicted upon Epidaurus and Troezen that they no longer took part in the war on Sparta's side. Thus Epaminondas' second invasion was successful in depriving the Spartans of much-needed Peloponnesian manpower and in showing to the remaining Peloponnesian allies the inability of Sparta, their hegemon, to protect them.

In 368 the Spartans were thrown a lifeline by Ariobarzanes, the Persian 'satrap' of Hellespontine Phrygia, who lent them 2,000 mercenaries (Diodorus 15.70.2). At the same time the first cracks in the Peloponnesian triple alliance appeared. Under the influence of Lycomedes, the Arcadian League began to entertain hopes of replacing Sparta as the dominant power in the Peloponnese and to take an independent line from Thebes in Peloponnesian policy (7.1.22–25). By 368, Megalopolis ('The Big City') had been built as a major fortress to protect south-west Arcadia and Messenia from Spartan invasion, and as the new federal capital of the Arcadian League – a symbol of Arcadian ambitions. In addition, the Arcadian League accepted Triphylia as an ally, which greatly angered the Eleans, who had joined the triple alliance in order to regain Triphylia, previously removed from their control by Sparta (7.1.26).

It is in these events that the short-sightedness of the Thebans is most in evidence. If a formal league had been established with Thebes as the hegemon, there were two probable results: first, the leadership ambitions of the Arcadians would have been curtailed at the outset, thus avoiding the rivalry which led to the collapse of the anti-Spartan alliance; and second, the dispute between Elis and the Arcadian League would have been resolved, thus removing the festering grievance and source of conflict within the alliance, which finally led to the Eleans deserting and going back to the Spartans. In the event, the Spartan defeat of the Arcadians, unsupported by the Thebans and the Eleans, in the 'Tearless Battle' (so called because there were very few Spartan casualties) of 368 acted as a temporary check upon Lycomedes' ambitions; this battle showed that the Spartans were not yet a completely spent force and that the Arcadians had much to do before they could become serious challengers for the supremacy of the Peloponnese. Even more revealing, and pessimistic for the future of the anti-Spartan alliance, were the feelings of the Thebans and the Eleans after the news of the Arcadian League's defeat:

> The Thebans and the Eleans were almost as pleased as the Spartans at the defeat of
> the Arcadians – they were now so angry at their arrogance.
>
> (Xenophon 7.1.32)

By 367, the Thebans had achieved their major aim of weakening the Spartans in the Peloponnese by liberating Messenia and creating a Boeotian–Peloponnesian alliance, but this success came under threat when the Spartans yet again sought the help of the Persians. There had been a series of Persian-dictated Common Peaces (so called because the terms applied in principle to all the Greek states and not just to those engaged in hostilities), beginning with the King's Peace in 386, which had allowed the Spartans, with Persian backing, to arrange the affairs of Greece to their own satisfaction. Therefore it was essential for the Thebans to persuade the Persians to choose Thebes as their most favoured Greek ally in place of Sparta, and thus create a Common Peace that best suited Theban interests in Greece. When the Greek states' representatives attended a preliminary peace conference at Susa, Pelopidas pulled off a brilliant diplomatic coup by convincing Artaxerxes that the Thebans were the best overseers of Persian interests in Greece. As a result, the Thebans were able to dictate the terms of the peace in the King's name: the liberation of Messenia from Sparta; the independence of Amphipolis from Athens; and Elis' claim to Triphylia at the expense of the Arcadians were confirmed (7.1.33–37).

It is hardly surprising that the conference in Thebes, which was called in 366 to formalize terms of the Peace, ended in failure as the three major states refused to weaken themselves for the benefit of the Thebans (7.1.39–40). The Arcadians were especially angry over Triphylia, as they realized that the Thebans were deliberately supporting and strengthening Elis against themselves, and that the Theban hostility had been provoked by the Arcadian challenge to the hegemony of the Boeotian–Peloponnesian alliance. This divisive issue would not have arisen, if the Thebans had created a formal league with a constitutionally agreed hegemon in 370. This marked a further stage in the break-down of the alliance, but the Arcadians were not yet strong enough to declare war upon the Thebans who, in turn, did not dare to attack Arcadia directly, as it might have led to the immediate dissolution of the anti-Spartan alliance. Therefore, they found a more subtle way of bringing the Arcadians to heel.

In 366, the Thebans launched a third invasion of the Peloponnese, desiring to detach Achaea from the Peloponnesian League, but mainly to compel the allies, as required under the terms of the Boeotian–Peloponnesian alliance, to send contingents of troops to serve under the Thebans, thereby acknowledging the hegemony of Thebes (7.1.41). The Arcadians reluctantly obeyed the call to arms, for they had correctly perceived the real intentions of the Thebans in their attack upon Achaea. But the Theban pleasure at the subservience of the Arcadians was short-lived, when they requested a defensive alliance with the Athenians later in 366. The Thebans had already antagonized the Athenians by regaining control of the perennially disputed Oropus on the Boeotian–Athenian borders (7.4.1; Diodorus 15.76.1), and so the Athenians accepted the Arcadian offer of the alliance (7.4.2–3). This disturbing anti-Theban move was offset in the winter of 366/5 by the conclusion of a peace treaty between the Thebans and the Corinthians and the remaining Peloponnesian League allies, the latter having been given prior permission by the Spartans who could no longer protect their allies (7.4.6–11). It is not clear if this Peace of 366/5 was a Common Peace, as stated by Diodorus (15.76.3), but its major significance was the final break-up of the Peloponnesian League and the formal recognition by these former Spartan allies of Messene's right to independence from Sparta. Epaminondas and the Thebans had finally achieved their ultimate aims in the Peloponnese: the final and permanent reduction of Spartan power. However, this overwhelming success did not lead to a relaxation of vigilance, for the Arcadian–Athenian defensive alliance was followed by the outbreak of war between Arcadia and Elis over Triphylia (7.4.12–19; Diodorus 15.77.1–4). It was only a matter of time before Arcadia and Thebes would finally attempt to settle the issue of the hegemony of the Peloponnese on the battlefield.

Northern Greece: 369–367

Jason of Pherae, who had united Thessaly and had thus created a potential major Greek power, was assassinated in 370, which led to a power struggle for the succession and civil war. By 369, Alexander of Pherae was attempting to regain Jason's position as 'tagos' (ruler) of Thessaly (6.4.33–34). The success of Alexander again caused deep concern in Thebes, fearful for the security of Boeotia, and consequently Pelopidas did not accompany Epaminondas in his second invasion of the Peloponnese, but stayed behind at Thebes to watch the unfolding events in Thessaly. The Aleuadae, the leading aristocratic family in Thessalian Larissa (one of the three major centres in Thessaly, along with Pherae and Pharsalus), through fear of Alexander of Pherae appealed for help from King Alexander II of Macedon, who had succeeded to the throne in 370 but was being challenged by Ptolemy. Alexander of Macedon responded positively in the hope that success against Alexander of Pherae would lead the other Thessalians to give him military support against Ptolemy (Diodorus 15.61.3–4). In the event, Alexander of Macedon failed to defeat his Thessalian opponent and, due to his need to return quickly to Macedon in order to oppose Ptolemy, an appeal was made to Thebes.

The Thebans saw this as an opportunity to intervene in the affairs of Thessaly, especially to check the growing power of Alexander of Pherae:

> The Boeotians, after the Thessalians had sent for them in order to free their cities and to overthrow the tyranny of Alexander of Pherae, sent Pelopidas with an army to Thessaly, instructing him to arrange the affairs of Thessaly to the benefit of the Boeotians.
>
> (Diodorus 15.67.3)

Alexander of Macedon and the other Thessalians by their military support would ease the demands on Theban manpower, the majority of which was committed to the Peloponnese, and at the same time would be recognizing the leadership of Thebes. Pharsalus quickly joined the side of Pelopidas, whose effective campaigning forced Alexander of Pherae to seek an armistice in which he agreed to leave the Thessalian cities in peace (Philochorus FGrH 115 F409; Plutarch, *Pelopidas* 26.4). Pelopidas then (probably) reorganized and strengthened the Thessalian Confederacy, which would be both a useful ally in northern Greece and a check upon Alexander of Pherae. While still in Thessaly, Pelopidas received a request for help from Alexander of Macedon against Ptolemy. An alliance was made in which Alexander agreed to become a subject-ally and, as a token of good faith, to hand over hostages, including his brother Philip, the future King of Macedon and father of Alexander the Great (Diodorus 15.67.4; Plut., *Pel.* 26.4–8). However, there was little that Pelopidas could achieve through a lack of sufficient troops.

In 368, fresh complaints were made against Alexander of Pherae, and Pelopidas was sent to investigate, although this time without an army (Plut., *Pel.* 27.1). Pelopidas' fears were raised upon his arrival, and he began to recruit an army of mercenaries. News was then received of the assassination of Alexander of Macedon and the seizure of power by Ptolemy, leading to civil war. Even more worrying for Pelopidas and Thebes was the report that the Athenians were trying to exploit the situation by sending Iphicrates and some ships to support Ptolemy against Pausanias, another contender for the Macedonian throne; their real purpose was to get a foothold in the north Aegean and especially to regain Amphipolis. The identity of the Macedonian ruler did not matter to the Thebans provided that he was pro-Theban and anti-Athenian. Consequently Pelopidas accepted Ptolemy's offer of an alliance as a subject-ally, backed up by further hostages, so that he could check Athenian imperial aims in the north Aegean (Plut., *Pel.* 27.2–5).

Pelopidas returned to Thessaly to deal with Alexander of Pherae, but he lacked an army as his mercenaries had deserted in Macedon. His attempt to intimidate Alexander in person ended in humiliation:

> Having met Alexander the tyrant of Pherae, he was suddenly arrested along with Ismenias and placed under guard. The Thebans, having been roused to anger by these events, quickly sent 8,000 'hoplites' and 600 cavalry into Thessaly. Alexander, being afraid, sent ambassadors to Athens about an alliance. The Athenian people immediately sent him 30 ships and 1,000 soldiers under the command of Autocles.
>
> (Diodorus 15.71.2–3)

The Athenians were determined to check the growth of Theban influence in northern Greece, having failed in the Peloponnese; at the same time they were beginning a policy of imperialism in the north Aegean, centred on control of Amphipolis, which occupied most of the 360s. The Theban army, owing to poor generalship (Epaminondas had not been elected Boeotarch for 368, probably due to internal opposition to his Peloponnesian policy), was lucky to avoid a major disaster (Diodorus 15.71.5–7). However, in 367 under the leadership of the re-elected Epaminondas, the Theban army so ravaged the territory of Alexander that he sued for peace. A 30-day truce was agreed, and Pelopidas and Ismenias were returned safely to the Thebans (Diodorus 15.75.2; Plut., *Pel.* 29).

The Thebans had learnt a valuable lesson from their campaigns in Thessaly: half-hearted military intervention was going to cause serious problems. If they wished to crush Alexander of Pherae and bring Thessaly directly under their control, they would need to commit a major part of their armed forces to this theatre of war. However, this decision would involve either fighting on two fronts, thus drastically overstretching their limited manpower resources, or postponing their military operations in the Peloponnese. As the Thebans believed that the security of Boeotia was paramount and that the Peloponnese was the far more important theatre of war, they chose to stay out of Thessaly for the next three years. They knew that Alexander of Pherae, unlike Jason previously, offered no threat to their security, since the reorganized Thessalian Confederacy would act as a counter-weight to him, thereby keeping Thessaly divided and weakened. After the campaign of Epaminondas in 367, there was no fear of danger from the north.

Theban foreign policy, 364–362

The Aegean: 364

The years 364/3 marked a dramatic change in Theban foreign policy when for the first time they sought to become a major naval power in the Aegean:

> Epaminondas the Theban, who possessed the greatest prestige among the citizens, addressed them during a meeting of the assembly, urging them to gain control of the 'hegemony' (leadership) of the sea. By this speech, which he had considered over a long period of time, he showed that this attempt would be useful and possible, putting forward many arguments in support of this view and especially that it was easier for those who were superior on land to gain the command (arche) of the sea.
>
> (Diodorus 15.78.4)

As a result, the Boeotians voted to build a fleet of 100 'triremes'; to win over Rhodes, Chios and Byzantium; and to send out Epaminondas with an armed force to these three places. According to Diodorus, Epaminondas was so successful that Laches, the Athenian general who had been despatched with a large fleet to prevent the Thebans from achieving their aims, withdrew in fear, resulting in these cities attaching themselves to the Thebans (Diodorus 15.79.1).

This naval adventure was unusual for the Thebans, as they had always traditionally concentrated on being a land power. However, Diodorus' account is supported by the Athenian orator Aeschines, who stated that Epaminondas had argued in the Theban assembly that the Propylaea on the Athenian Acropolis should be transferred to the Cadmeia, the Theban citadel (2.105) – the significance of this remark was that, since the Propylaea was a symbol of the Athenian fifth-century naval empire, he was proposing a naval empire for the Thebans on the same lines. Furthermore, Isocrates, a fourth-century pamphleteer, claimed that Theban triremes were sent to Byzantium so that they might rule by land and by sea (5.53).

The most likely cause of this development in Theban foreign policy was the increasingly imperialistic behaviour of Athens. In the first half of the 360s the Athenians had set their sights on regaining Amphipolis and the Thracian Chersonese, thus attempting to re-establish their former empire in the northern Aegean and ignoring the original aims of the Second Athenian League which had been formed to protect its members from Sparta. This military activity was bound to worry the Thebans, but it was the Athenian treatment of Samos in 365 that probably sparked the Theban decision to intervene in the eastern Aegean. The Athenians had besieged and captured Samos, and then imposed an Athenian 'cleruchy' (see Glossary) on the island. 'Cleruchies' had been the most blatant and the most hated symbol of fifth-century Athenian imperialism, and had been expressly outlawed in the Charter of the Second Athenian League. This reintroduction at Samos in 365 raised the spectre of a renewed Athenian Empire. The need to form defensive alliances with major naval states to check this growth in Athenian imperial ambitions was almost certainly the prime motivation for the Theban naval policy.

In the event, the Thebans had little to show for their efforts. The most that they achieved was to detach the strategically important Byzantium from the Second Athenian League or, at least, to cause a rift between the Athenians and the Byzantines who, by 362, were interfering with the passage of the vital grain ships en route to Athens (Demosthenes 1.6; 50.6). In addition, the fact that Rhodes and Chios had attached themselves to Thebes does not necessarily mean that they revolted from Athens – the Athenians themselves became allies of the Arcadian League, which was hostile to Sparta, an Athenian ally. There is no evidence, certainly not in Diodorus, that the Thebans ever built the fleet of 100 triremes; and it is probable that Laches' retreat was caused less by fear of the Theban fleet than by fear of breaking the Peace of 366/5 if he attacked. Whatever the extent of Theban ambitions in the eastern Aegean, they proved to be short-lived due to the rapidly deteriorating situation during 364 in Thessaly and in the Peloponnese. These two areas were far more pressing for Boeotian security and far more important for Theban influence in Greek affairs. As Epaminondas must have realized, this was not the time for an ambitious naval policy.

Thessaly: 364

Alexander of Pherae had renewed his attempts to become the master of Thessaly by again attacking the cities of the Thessalian Confederacy. Their appeal to Thebes led to the despatch of Pelopidas with 300 mercenary cavalry and some Boeotian volunteers. This force, supplemented by the Thessalians, defeated Alexander at the battle of Cynoscephalae in July 364, but Pelopidas fell in the fighting. However, the victory had not achieved its object: the reduction of Alexander's growing power in Thessaly. Only decisive action on a grander scale by the Thebans could curtail the threat of Alexander. The Thebans now voted to send an army of 7,000 hoplites and 700 cavalry into Thessaly which inflicted a heavy defeat on Alexander's army:

> Alexander, having been defeated and totally crushed in a second battle, was forced by treaty to hand back to the Thessalians the cities which he had captured in war; to hand over Magnesia and Phthiotian Achaeans to the Boeotians; and in future to be the ruler only of Pherae and an ally of the Boeotians.
>
> (Diodorus 15.80.6)

In other words, Alexander had surrendered unconditionally, giving up his claim to the leadership of Thessaly and becoming a subject-ally of the Thebans. They could now retire with confidence from Thessaly in order to concentrate on the Peloponnese.

The Peloponnese: 364–362

It was the continuous war between the Arcadians and the Eleans that exposed the inner tensions within the Arcadian League, leading to its disintegration. The Eleans had allied themselves with the Spartans in 365, but by 364 they were in a desperate situation: their territory had been invaded; there had been civil war within Elis; and Olympia had been occupied by the Arcadians who had handed over the presidency of the Olympian festival to the Pisatans. The Spartans' attempt to relieve the pressure on Elis had ended in humiliating defeat at Cromnos at the hands of the Arcadians and their allies (7.4.12–32). However, this constant warfare had caused a drain on the Arcadian League's federal funds which were used mainly to pay the wages of the 'Eparitoi', the 5,000-strong full-time federal army. Therefore the Arcadian League's public officials decided to seize and use the sacred treasures of Olympia to pay the troops (7.4.33). It was this issue that revealed the underlying split between Tegea and Mantinea, traditional rivals for the leadership of Arcadia, and between the democrats and the oligarchs (Diodorus 15.82.2). The oligarchically minded Mantineans were against such an abuse of sacred money and, when the League funds became exhausted in 363 and the poorer pro-democratic soldiers in the Eparitoi were forced to leave through a lack of pay, they replaced them with more affluent pro-oligarchic supporters, thus changing the political sympathies of the army (7.4.34). The democratically minded Tegeans rightly feared that the Mantinean-led faction would seek an alliance with Sparta, and thus they appealed to Thebes for support.

Epaminondas realized that his whole Peloponnesian policy – the most important of the three areas of Theban foreign policy – was now in grave danger of collapsing. The conclusion of peace in 362 between Arcadia and Elis, without the consent of the other members of the Boeotian–Peloponnesian alliance, gave him the legal pretext to invade the Peloponnese for the fourth and last time (7.4.40). He knew that this invasion would bring about an inevitable coalition of the Mantinean-led Arcadians, Sparta and Athens (and their allies), but a victory on the battlefield over all his major Greek enemies would lead to a Common Peace (but without Persian involvement), whose terms would be dictated by the Thebans, thus guaranteeing their hegemony in Greece. Thus the battle-lines were drawn up on the plain of Mantinea in 362: on the Theban side were their allies in central and northern Greece (except Phocis which had only a defensive alliance with Boeotia), the Tegean-led Arcadians, Argives and Messenians; on the other side were the Mantinean-led Arcadians, the Spartans, the Athenians, the Eleans and the Achaeans. For the last time Epaminondas led his troops to victory, but he himself paid the ultimate price for his bravery (7.5.20–25).

The causes of the failure of the Theban 'hegemony'

Mantinea, in 362, was one of the greatest land battles in Greek history, involving over 50,000 combatants, but it resolved nothing – its result was one of widespread exhaustion and war-weariness. Immediately after the battle, with the exception of the Spartans who still refused to accept the independence of Messene, all the other Greek states agreed to the first genuine Common Peace (i.e. not involving nor dictated by the Persians) and an alliance, in which they agreed to keep what they held rather than what belonged to them (Diodorus 15.89.1–2). Although the Boeotians, led by the Thebans, were still the strongest state in Greece, the battle of Mantinea had shown that none of the traditional major powers could ever create a land empire in mainland Greece. The Thebans, even under the inspired leadership of Epaminondas and Pelopidas, lacked the wealth and manpower to become an imperial state, and their failure to create a formally constituted league of allies, such as Sparta's Peloponnesian League or Athens' fifth-century Delian League, deprived them of the organizational structure, and of the crucial extra financial and military resources that might have made the hegemony of Greece a reality.

The cornerstone of Epaminondas' policies was the establishment of the security of Boeotia from outside intervention. In his opinion, the greatest threat to Boeotia was Sparta, as it had been in the past. Therefore he decided that the most effective means of achieving this objective was to create an alliance of anti-Spartan Peloponnesian states which would keep Sparta trapped in the Peloponnese. He naturally believed that fear of the Spartans, who had dominated Greece for so long, would be the unifying factor for the allies and would produce a solid and long-lasting alliance. If there is to be criticism of Epaminondas as a statesman, it is in his failure to realize that Sparta's potential as an imperialist power had been broken forever at Leuctra in 371. The Peloponnesian allies of Thebes came to recognize this in the first half of the 360s, and thus their individual ambitions and rivalries became more important than loyal adherence to the Boeotian–Peloponnesian alliance. Epaminondas failed to find a new unifying principle, which the allies could embrace and rally behind, in the way that the Athenians, after the fear of Persia had been removed in the middle of the fifth century, had championed the cause of democracy within the Delian League (see Chapter 16).

This problem was further compounded by the failure to create a formal league, which would give new aims to the alliance after the Spartan menace had been curtailed, resolve disputes among the members, and firmly establish Thebes as the legal hegemon of the alliance. However, criticism of Epaminondas should be tempered by the fact that, although the evidence for the internal politics of Thebes in this period is scanty, he and his political ally Pelopidas do seem to have been constantly opposed by the Theban Menecleidas and his political supporters. Thus Epaminondas found it difficult to implement a coherent long-term policy for the Peloponnese due to internal disagreement over the direction of Theban foreign policy.

There was continual strife throughout Greece in the years that followed the battle of Mantinea, because no one state was strong enough to bring peace and stability: far from there being a balance of power, it was rather a balance of weakness. But in the meantime Philip II was laying down the foundations for the emergence of Macedon as the greatest super-power of all time in Greece. In 369, he had been sent as a hostage to Thebes as a token of good faith for the alliance between Macedon and Thebes (see above). Thus for three years he was able to observe at close quarters and learn from Epaminondas' exceptional ability as a military commander and as a skilful diplomat during the ascendancy of Thebes. These two qualities enabled Philip to become the master of Greece and thus the true heir to the 'hegemony' of Thebes.

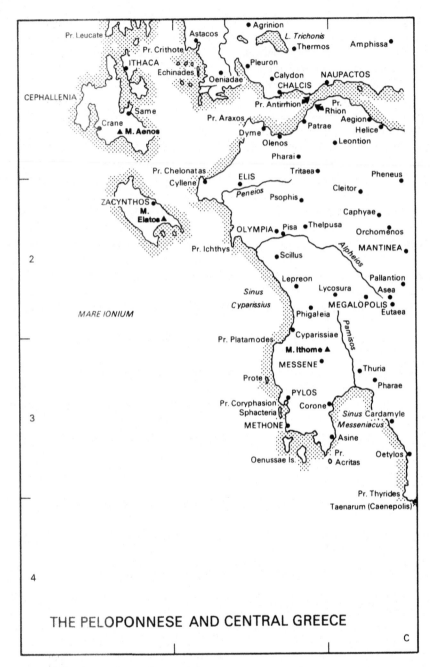

Map 9 The Peloponnese and central Greece

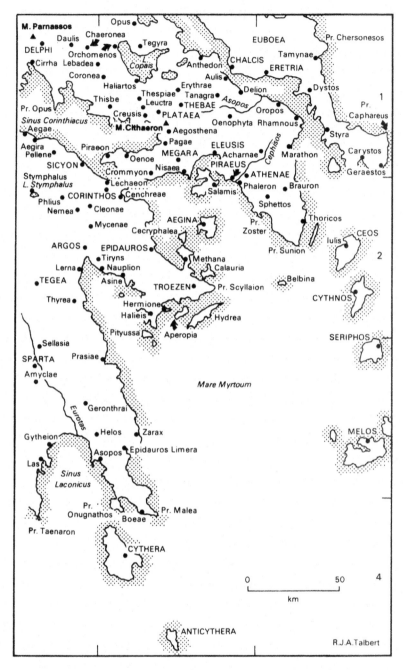

Map 9 continued

Bibliography

Buckler, J. *The Theban Hegemony, 371–362.*
Bury, J. B. and Meiggs, R. *A History of Greece*, 4th edn, ch. 14.
Cartledge, P. *Agesilaos and the Crisis of Sparta*, chs 14, 19 and 20.
——*Sparta and Lakonia*, ch. 13.
Cawkwell, G. L. 'Epaminondas and Thebes', CQ 22.
Davies, J. K. *Democracy and Classical Greece*, 2nd edn, ch. 11.
Hornblower, S. *The Greek World, 479–323* BC, chs 15 and 16.
Sealey, R. *A History of Greek City States 700–338* BC, chs 16 and 17.

26

THE RISE OF MACEDON (359–336): DIPLOMACY AND WARFARE UNDER PHILIP II

The geography of Macedonia can be divided into two parts: Lower and Upper Macedonia. Lower Macedonia, which was the heart of the kingdom, consisted of a fertile coastal plain, situated on the shores of the Thermaic Gulf in the north-west Aegean; this region was ruled by the dynasty of the Argeadae, but internal dissension within the ruling family had in the past kept it weak. Upper Macedonia to the west consisted of a number of large inland plateaux, surrounded by high mountains, which were divided politically into cantons, each governed by their own dynasties. Thus this geographically and politically divided country was exposed to attack from Thessaly and the other major Greek powers in the south, from the non-Greek Illyrians on the Adriatic coast in the west, from the Paeonians in the north, and from the Greek Chalcidians and the Thracians in the east. It is hardly surprising that the kingdom of Macedon had always been viewed throughout the previous century and a half as a pawn in the super-power rivalry of Sparta, Athens and Thebes, and before that had attracted the Persians. Consequently, the Macedonian kings needed to become adept at diplomacy, choosing and changing the alliances that were vital to ensure the safety of their kingdom. However, the accession of Philip II in 359, whether as regent for the young son of Perdiccas or as king, heralded a dramatic change in the history of Macedon and Greece, although the urgent political and military problems confronting him in 359 appeared to be the same insuperable ones that had defeated his many predecessors. But Philip was no ordinary Macedonian king.

The consolidation of Macedon in the north, 359–354

Philip came to power in the midst of yet another Macedonian crisis. King Perdiccas and 4,000 Macedonians had been killed in battle by the Illyrians under their King Bardylis (Diodorus 16.2.4–5 – all references in this chapter are to Diodorus, unless otherwise stated). But this was only one problem among many:

> About the same time, the Paeonians, who lived near Macedon, were contemptuously plundering the territory of the Macedonians; and the Illyrians were assembling great armies and were preparing to invade Macedon. In addition, a certain Pausanias, who was related to the Macedonian royal family, was planning with the aid of the Thracian king to make an attempt upon the kingship of Macedon. In the same way, the Athenians, being hostile to Philip, were attempting to restore Argaeus to the kingship, and had sent Mantias as general with 3,000 hoplites and a sizeable naval force.
>
> (Diodorus 16.6.2)

The immediate objective of Philip was survival. He bribed Berisades, one of the Thracian Kings, in order to withdraw his support of Pausanias and the Paeonians in order to stop their ravaging the kingdom of Macedon. At the same time he conducted a massive reorganization and thorough training of the Macedonian army, laying the foundations for that formidable force, which would be one of his two instruments of foreign policy (16.3.1–6).

Philip also set about winning over the Athenians by diplomacy. He knew that the Athenian support of Argaeus was motivated simply by their single-minded desire to regain Amphipolis, and therefore he withdrew the Macedonian garrison from Amphipolis and declared it autonomous (16.3.3). This astute move was designed to give the impression that he had recognized Athens' claim to Amphipolis, thus making the Athenians lukewarm in their backing of Argaeus. Although accompanying Argaeus with 3,000 mercenary troops to the port of Methone in Lower Macedonia, Mantias, the Athenian commander, took no part in his march to Aegae, the old capital of the Macedonian kingdom, where Argaeus attempted but failed to win over the inhabitants to his cause. He was defeated on his return journey to Methone by Philip who:

> having captured some of our [i.e. Athenian] citizens, let them go and restored all their losses to them. He also sent a letter in which he stated that he was ready to make an alliance and renew his father's friendship with us.
>
> (Demosthenes 23.121)

Philip's generous treatment of his Athenian prisoners, his defeat of Argaeus and his willingness to make a treaty on favourable terms to the Athenians won the day:

> Philip sent ambassadors to Athens and persuaded the Athenian people to make peace with him by giving up all claim to Amphipolis.
>
> (Diodorus 16.4.1)

The Athenians were now removed from the list of Macedon's immediate enemies.

Philip then exploited the situation in Paeonia where the king had just died; a military expedition in 358 defeated the Paeonians in battle and brought them under Macedonian control (16.4.2). Philip was now ready for the Illyrians who had seized a large part of Macedonia. A decisive victory over the Illyrians and their King Bardylis led to their total withdrawal from Macedonian territory (16.4.3–7). In 358, Philip advanced into Thessaly (Justin 7.6.8). Thessaly in the 370s had risen to its greatest position of Greek power and influence under the dynamic leadership of Jason of Pherae who, before his assassination in 370, had planned to take control of Macedon (Xenophon, *Hellenica* 6.1.11). Philip's objective was to secure Perrhaebia in north Thessaly, since his Macedonian kingdom, without control of this buffer state, was always vulnerable to an invasion from the south. It was at this time that Philip married a Larissan woman to strengthen his diplomatic ties with one of the three most important political cities of Thessaly, and the news of the assassination of Alexander of Pherae, the Thessalian 'tagos' (ruler), eased the threat from the south.

The security of Macedon, both internal and external, was also strengthened by a series of politically motivated marriages. Between 359 and 357, Philip seems to have married Phila, the daughter of the ruler of Elimiotis, one of the cantons of Upper Macedon; Audata, the daughter of Bardylis, the King of the Illyrians; Philinna of Larissa in Thessaly; and Olympias, the Greek daughter of the Molossian ruler of Epirus, who became Philip's queen and gave birth to Alexander in 356 (Athenaeus 13.557b–d). Thus, by 357, Philip had consolidated his power over the cantons of Upper Macedon and, for the first time in its history, was close to creating a unified Macedonian state – only the Greek colonies of Pydna and Methone on the coast lay temporarily outside his control. In addition, his military victories and marriages in the north, west and south had secured these borders of Macedon. It now remained to make safe Macedon's eastern flank.

Philip's first target in 357 was Amphipolis: situated on the banks of the river Strymon, this former Athenian colony controlled the main access to and from Thrace and the Hellespont, and, if brought under control, would afford protection to the eastern side of Macedon. The citizens of Amphipolis appealed for help to the Athenians, who took no action, because a secret deal had apparently been agreed between the Athenians and Philip to exchange Pydna, an Athenian stronghold in Lower Macedonia, for Amphipolis (Demosthenes 2.6; Theopompos FGrH 115 F30). Philip did not hand over Amphipolis to the Athenians after its surrender (16.8.2), but found reasons to delay the transfer. At this point the Olynthian-led Chalcidian League, which had been revived after its dismemberment in 379 by Agesilaos (see Chapter 24), because it feared Philip's territorial ambitions after his success at Amphipolis, sought an alliance with Athens. But the Athenians rejected this offer, partly because they at this time had too many problems with their naval allies (see below), and partly because they did not wish to alienate Philip and lose their chance to regain Amphipolis.

Philip knew that a combination of Athens and the Chalcidian League alliance would be a grave threat to his newly acquired kingdom, and thus he needed to calm the fears and win the goodwill of the Olynthians and the Chalcidian League concerning his military activities, and to keep them hostile to Athens. Potidaea in Chalcidice was still under the control of the Athenians, who had sent out colonists as recently as 361, and thus was a source of danger in the heart of the Chalcidian League. In addition, there had always been conflict between Macedon and the Olynthians about the possession of Anthemous on their shared borders. Therefore Philip made an alliance with Olynthus which was very favourable to them (16.8.3–5):

'Do you not think that the Olynthians would have listened in annoyance if someone had spoken ill of Philip at that time when he was handing over Anthemus to them, which all the former kings of Macedon had claimed, when he was giving them Potidaea and throwing out our settlers, when he was stirring up hostility towards us and giving them the opportunity to enjoy the land of Potidaea?'

(Demosthenes 6.17)

The capture of Pydna, one of Athens' two strongholds in Lower Macedon, around the same time as that of Potidaea ensured war with Athens (16.8.3–5), but his generosity towards the Olynthian-led Chalcidian League had gained a valuable anti-Athenian ally for Macedon, and had given him the opportunity to extend Macedonian influence into Thrace without hindrance. The Chalcidian League would come to regret their being deceived by Philip's apparent friendship.

The Athenians tried to check Philip's advance *c*.356 by making an alliance with the kings of Illyria, Paeonia and western Thrace (GHI 157), but he defeated these three, one by one, and forced them to join him in alliance (16.22.3). A clear understanding and dating of Philip's relations with the three kings of Thrace are not easy to achieve owing to the scantiness of sources; however, Philip appears to have won a victory at this time over Cetriporis, the King of western Thrace, who was reduced to the status of subject-ally. About the same time Philip set his sights on Crenides, which had been founded by Thasos in 360. He easily gained control of it, increased its population and renamed it Philippi after himself. The attraction of this city was its gold and silver mines which eventually produced 1,000 talents per year, thus greatly increasing Philip's financial strength, his ability to hire mercenaries and his lavish bribes to politicians in other states (16.8.6). In 355, Philip attacked Methone, the last Athenian outpost in Lower Macedonia, and captured it in the following year after a siege in which he lost an eye (16.31.6).

By 354, Philip had consolidated his position of authority within a unified Macedon; had secured Macedon's borders by warfare and alliances, especially with Olynthus and the Chalcidian League; had gained safe and unthreatened access to the Aegean Sea; and had a well-trained and battle-hardened army. The success of Macedon in the north during the years 359–354 was due not only to Philip's exceptional diplomatic and military abilities, but also to the weakness in the 350s of the traditional major powers of Greece: Sparta, Athens and Thebes. Sparta had not recovered from the loss of Messenia at the hands of Epaminondas and the Thebans (see Chapter 25), and in this period was more concerned with restoring a position of influence in Peloponnesian politics. The Athenians had become embroiled in the Social War (357–355), i.e. a war against their allies – a number of their allies in the Second Athenian League, having become disaffected with Athenian imperialistic behaviour, had seceded from the League under the leadership of Rhodes, Chios and Byzantium. Two naval defeats at the hands of the rebels persuaded the Athenians to make peace in 355 and to recognize the independence of those who had seceded, thus considerably weakening Athenian naval power. Finally, Thebes' long-standing hostility to Phocis came to a head in the Third Sacred War (355–346), which drained Theban resources. It was this war that gave Philip his opportunity to intervene in the mainstream of Greek politics and establish Macedon as the leading power in Greece.

The rise of Macedon in Greece, 353–346

The origins of the Sacred War lay with the Theban desire to re-assert their authority in central Greece, after their humiliating expulsion from Euboea in 357, and their hostility towards the Phocians, who had refused to join Epaminondas' last invasion of the Peloponnese in 362. The chosen weapon was the religious Amphictyonic League, whose function was to care for the temple of Apollo at Delphi (as well as the temple of Demeter near Thermopylae). This League consisted mainly of central and northern Greek states, but the Thebans, after their settlement of Thessaly by force in 364, controlled 16 of the 24 votes in the Council, which carried out the business of the League. Therefore, in 357, the Thebans manipulated the Amphictyonic Council to condemn the Phocians for cultivating Delphic sacred land and to impose a hefty fine on them. When the Phocians failed to pay, the Council ordered the land of the Phocians to be confiscated and dedicated to Apollo. Faced with such punitive action, the Phocians, in 356, under the leadership of Philomelus formed alliances with Thebes' enemies, Athens and Sparta, and seized Delphi with its treasure (16.23–24; 27.5).

In 355, the Amphictyonic League declared a sacred war against the Phocians, who were now surrounded by enemies: in particular, the Boeotians, the Locrians and the Thessalians. The need to hire a large mercenary army to confront these enemies led the Phocians to 'borrow' money from the sacred treasury of Delphi, which outraged Greek opinion, especially when the 'borrowing' became very frequent and the huge sums of money became impossible to pay back (16.29). After initial successes against the Locrians and the Thessalians, the Phocians were heavily defeated by the Boeotians at the battle of Neon in 354, and Philomelus was killed (16.30–31.4). However, the Phocians were far from finished: they chose Onomarchus as their new commander-in-chief, who again raided the Delphic treasury to strengthen his army. With this new army he defeated the Locrians and gained control of Thermopylae (16.33). He also capitalized upon the old rivalry between Pherae and the rest of Thessaly, which the Thebans had attempted to end in 364 (see Chapter 25). Onomarchus won over the rulers of Pherae to the Phocian cause (16.35.1), thus kindling their hopes of regaining control of Thessaly as in the days of Jason of Pherae. The Thebans and the rest of the Thessalians turned for help to their former ally in the north – Macedon (16.35.1; Justin, *Philippica* 8.2.1–2). In this way Philip became a combatant in the Sacred War.

The entry of Philip with an army into Thessaly led the rulers of Pherae to summon help from the Phocians, who sent a force of 7,000 men under Onomarchus' brother, Phayllus. The defeat of this Phocian force resulted in the despatch of the main Phocian army under Onomarchus who defeated Philip in two battles and forced him to withdraw from Thessaly (16.35.1–2). Philip's defeats in 353 had been caused by being outnumbered in troops, which he remedied in the following year, when he returned to the attack. The Thessalians appointed him 'archon', a post which was held for life and gave the post-holder command of the Thessalian armed forces and control of the state's revenues (Justin 11.3.2) – a great increase in Philip's power. In 352, Philip and the Thessalians won a decisive victory at the mighty battle of the Crocus Field against the joint forces of Phocis and Pherae: Ono-marchus and 6,000 mercenaries were killed, 3,000 were captured, and the rulers of Pherae handed over their city to Philip and retired to Phocis with their mercenaries (16.35.3–6; 37.3).

The whole of Thessaly was now under the power of Philip, but he saw that an opportunity existed to increase his prestige and to extend his influence into central Greece by following up his victory and conquering the Phocians, the 'sacrilegious temple-robbers' of Delphi. He marched to Thermopylae, which commanded the entrance into central Greece, but arrived too late. The pass at Thermopylae had already been occupied by the Phocians under Phayllus, the mercenaries of Pherae, and the Athenians who, on this rare occasion, had moved swiftly to oppose Philip (16.38.2; Demosthenes 4). Philip had no alternative but to accept that it was impossible to force the pass:

> Since the Athenians were preventing him from going through the pass, he returned to Macedon, having increased his kingdom by his deeds and by his respect for the god.
>
> (Diodorus 16.38.2)

But Philip had also learned a valuable lesson for the future: the strategic importance of seizing the pass at Thermopylae in order to create an effective threat to his enemies in the south.

As he had been thwarted in the south, Philip turned his attention again to Thrace. In late 352, he was attacking Heraeum Teichos, which was on the shores of the Propontis, the small sea that connects the Hellespont to the Black Sea (Demosthenes 3.4). By this time he had taken over the kingdom of Amadocus, who had ruled in central Thrace, and was now threatening Cersebleptes, who ruled eastern Thrace (Dem. 1.13). However, Cersebleptes was saved from suffering the same fate as Amadocus by a combination of Philip's illness (Dem. 3.5) and the support of Athens. The price for this Athenian help had been the transfer of the Thracian Chersonese, apart from Cardia, to the Athenians, who established a 'cleruchy' (see Glossary) in the city of Sestos – vital for safeguarding the grain fleets through the Hellespont. Nevertheless Cersebleptes, even with Athenian help, was still vulnerable, and therefore the surrender of his son as a hostage was aimed at winning Philip's goodwill, thereby (he hoped) securing his own position. In 351 and 350, Philip appears to have taken little or no action against the Greek cities, but this was to change in 349, when the sole threat to Macedonian power in the north – Olynthus and the Chalcidian League – became Philip's next target.

The Olynthian-led Chalcidian League had become more fearful of Philip and, in 352, made peace with Athens and were discussing the possibility of an alliance (Dem. 23.109). This was a breach of their alliance with Philip, and such a threat on the very borders of Macedon sealed the fate of the Chalcidians. If the Chalcidians had been willing to accept subject-ally status, as the Thessalians had, they might have escaped their fate, but their disloyalty provoked the ruthless side of Philip's nature:

> When Philip was 40 stades from the city of the Olynthus, he said that one of two
> things must happen: either they must stop living in Olynthus or he in Macedon.
>
> (Demosthenes 9.11)

Philip declared war in late 349, and successfully besieged the cities in the Chalcidian League one by one, leaving Olynthus to the last. Despite desperate appeals from the Olynthians and probably three relief expeditions from the Athenians (Philochorus 328 frs 49–51; Demosthenes, *Olynthiacs* I–III), he had won his war by September 348. Philip was true to his word, for he totally destroyed Olynthus and the Chalcidian cities that had resisted him, and sold the Olynthian citizens into slavery (16.52.9, 53.1–3; Dem. 9.26). Chalcidice was now incorporated within the Macedonian state, and the land distributed to Philip's supporters.

One of the reasons for Athens' failure to be more effective in opposing Philip in 348 was the revolt of Euboea, which was of vital strategic importance to Athens. If Euboea were to be occupied by Philip, he could turn the pass at Thermopylae; land troops in Boeotia; link up with the Thebans, his allies in the Sacred War; and invade Attica by land. He may even have inspired the Euboeans to revolt, but this depends upon the possibly corrupt reading of 'Philip' in the speech of the Athenian politician, Aeschines (3.87). Nevertheless it was typical of the man, always seeking to extend Macedonian influence and undermining his opponents.

The first steps in the peace process between Philip and the Athenians, culminating in the Peace of Philocrates in 346, began in 348. The Athenians, because of the loss of Euboea, their fears for their continued control of the Thracian Chersonese and the desperate state of their economy, were ready to consider peace. It is hard to say why Philip was so willing. Possibly, the conclusion of peace and an alliance with Athens was the first stage in his planned domination of Greece, as he had done previously with the Olynthian-led Chalcidian League when he was attempting to establish Macedonian dominance in the north. Possibly, he desired to remove the Athenians from the Sacred War and from their alliance with the Phocians so that he could achieve his two immediate objectives: first, increased prestige and influence in Greek affairs by ending the Sacred War; and second, membership of the Amphictyonic League, thereby gaining the previously withheld Greek recognition of Macedon's 'Greekness'.

It is very difficult to give an accurate account of the events and their chronology in the run-up to the Peace of Philocrates. The main reason for this is that most of the evidence comes from two speeches of Demosthenes (18 and 19) and two from Aeschines (2 and 3), bitter political enemies, delivered a number of years after the swearing of the Peace. By 343, when the first pair of speeches was delivered (i.e. Demosthenes 19 and Aeschines 2), it was patently clear from the advantages that Philip had acquired from the Peace that its ratification had been a grave error of judgement. Unfortunately, both Demosthenes and Aeschines had encouraged the Athenians to accept the Peace, and therefore each wished to distance himself from the responsibility of having recommended the Peace. Furthermore, as they were deadly political opponents, each wished to blacken the other's name and reputation. As a result the speeches are full of gross distortions of the truth, biased interpretation of the events for political advantage and blatant lies. It is for this reason that the following account has to be treated with caution.

The first peace initiatives came to nothing, possibly because the Athenians, who at first were keen to enter negotiations, became disinclined after Philip's harsh treatment of Olynthus (Aeschines 2.12–17). Throughout 347, Philip was active in putting pressure on the Athenians: he raided the Athenian settlers on the islands of Lemnos, Imbros and Scyrus, conducted military operations in Thrace (Aeschines 2.72) and once again became involved in the Sacred War. The Phocians had deposed Phalaecus from the generalship (although he still kept control of a considerable number of mercenaries), and appointed three others in his stead. Their successful campaign in Boeotia, resulting in their seizure of several important cities, especially Orchomenus, forced the Thebans to appeal to Philip (16.56.2–3, 58.1):

The king, happily witnessing their difficulties and wanting to humble their pride over Leuctra [see Chapter 25], sent a few soldiers, guarding against one thing only: that he did not appear to be disregarding the plundering of the (Delphic) oracle.

(Diodorus 16.58.3)

Philip had sent only sufficient troops to check the advance of the Phocians, but not enough to conquer Phocis, as he wanted the glory and the resultant prestige for personally ending the Sacred War and punishing the 'temple-robbers'.

Philip's repeated offer of peace and an additional request for an alliance in 347 was reasonably well received by the Athenians, but they had not at this point given up hope of resisting Philip, which they had done so successfully in 352. Early in 346 (this dating is a matter of scholarly dispute), the Athenians voted to hold a Greek congress at Athens to discuss the defence of Greece against Philip (Dem. 19.303–6). In addition, when the Phocians (apart from Phalaecus) appealed for military support upon receipt of the news that Philip and the Thessalians were planning to march south, the Athenians and the Spartans sent forces to occupy Thermopylae (Aeschines 2.132–34). However, the Athenians were forced into making a sudden and dramatic change of policy.

Their appeal to the Greeks to form an anti-Philip coalition evoked a lukewarm response: none offered any support (Aesch. 2.79). Far more devastating was the news that Phalaecus had refused to hand over Thermopylae to the Athenian and Spartan forces, and had ordered them home (Aesch. 2.133–34). The Athenians suspected, almost certainly correctly, that Philip and Phalaecus had been negotiating in secret, whereby Phalaecus would hand over Thermopylae to Philip in return for lenient treatment of himself and Phocis for their 'sacrilegious' behaviour. The consequence of this would be the exposure of Attica and southern Greece to invasion by Philip's forces and the Thebans: the Athenians now had an urgent need, in March 346, to enter into serious discussions with Philip for peace.

The first Athenian embassy to Philip was sent in March 346 (Aesch. 2.18). Philip presumably agreed to send Macedonian representatives to Athens to negotiate terms, and agreed to make no attack upon the Chersonese while the peace negotiations were in progress. Philip then set out to attack Cersebleptes, the last remaining king in Thrace (Aesch. 2.82). After the Athenians, in consultation with Philip's representatives, had agreed to the terms of the peace and to an alliance, a second embassy was sent to Macedon in order to receive the oaths of Philip and his allies to the Peace. There is no better example of Philip's deviousness in diplomacy than in the events that followed. First, he deliberately delayed swearing the oath, presumably on the grounds that not all of his allies were present. In the meantime, he pressed on and further reduced the kingdom of Cersebleptes, Athens' ally (Aesch. 2.89–90; Dem. 19.156). Second, when the second Athenian embassy was joined by other embassies from the Thebans, the

459

Thessalians, the Phocians and the Spartans, whose purpose was to discuss with Philip the settlement of the Sacred War (Justin 8.4.1–3), Philip made sure that he saw each delegation separately. The Thebans and the Thessalians wanted him to take over the hegemony of Greece and punish the hated Phocians (Justin 8.4.4–5). The Phocians, backed by their Athenian and Spartan allies, were begging Philip not to settle the issue by warfare (Justin 8.4.6–7):

> Having heard each of the two embassies and having made them swear on oath that they would betray his reply to no-one, he secretly promised his support for each of them in the war; and that he would come and bring help to them; and he ordered both sides not to prepare for nor fear war.
>
> (Justin, *Philippica* 8.4.11)

His purpose was to convince all of them that he would give his full backing to their preferred outcome of the Sacred War.

Philip succeeded brilliantly in winning over the goodwill and the trust of the two embassies, but at the same time did not reveal his true intentions:

> 'Phalaecus, the tyrant of Phocis, distrusted us and the Spartans, but trusted Philip. But was he the only man who did not foresee the outcome? What were your own public feelings in this matter? Did you not all reckon that Philip would humble the Thebans, witnessing their audacity and not wanting to increase the power of men whom he did not trust? ... Were not the Theban ambassadors themselves in despair and afraid? Did not the Thessalians laugh at all the rest, saying that the expedition was for their benefit?'
>
> (Aeschines 2.135–36)

In reality, Philip's only sensible option was to back the Thessalians and the Thebans: he needed the continued support of the Thessalians, who were deadly enemies of the Phocians, and their excellent cavalry; and he would have lost all prestige within Greece and the Amphictyonic League, which was still dominated by the Thebans, if he had sided with the temple-robbers.

The key to winning the Sacred War was possession of Thermopylae. Once again Philip proved too wily for his opponents. He had almost certainly been negotiating with Phalaecus who 'trusted Philip', but he needed to bring his army within close striking distance of Thermopylae without frightening the Athenians into fortifying the pass. The means of deception was the small town of Halus on the gulf of Pagasae, which Philip had been besieging for a number of months. Philip was sufficiently convincing to persuade the embassies that his military build-up was directed against Halus. Consequently, when he did advance southwards with his army, accompanied by the embassies, their suspicions were allayed – especially those of the Athenians, as he finally swore the oath to the Peace of Philocrates at Pherae in southern Thessaly, very close to Thermopylae (Dem. 19.158). By the time that the Athenian second embassy had reported to the Athenian Assembly, Philip had gained control of Thermopylae, and the whole of central and southern Greece lay open to his armies: the Athenians were in no position to resist him militarily, and reaffirmed the Peace of Philocrates and the Athenian–Macedonian alliance.

Philip made a truce with Phalaecus, who was allowed to retire with his mercenaries to the Peloponnese. The Phocians immediately surrendered to Philip, thus bringing the Sacred War to an end – the first of his objectives (16.59.2–3). Philip left the final settlement to the Amphictyonic League, although it is certain that he manipulated its decisions behind the scenes. The League passed a decree which granted Philip and his descendants League membership – the second of his objectives – and gave Macedon the two votes that had previously belonged to Phocis. The Phocians were allowed to keep their land, but all their cities were destroyed; they were only allowed to live in small villages. In addition, they were ordered to pay 60 talents every year to Delphi until they repaid all their debt (16.60.1–2). Far more galling for the Athenians was the restoration of Theban power in central Greece: the important Boeotian cities of Orchomenus and Coroneia, previously captured by the Phocians, were given back to the Thebans, who also benefited from the drastic reduction of the state of Phocis (16.60.1; Dem. 19.325).

After holding the prestigious post of president of the Pythian Festival:

> Philip returned to Macedon, not only having gained a reputation for piety and superb generalship, but also having made considerable preparations for the increase of power that was destined to be his. For he wished to be appointed the commander-in-chief of Greece and to wage war against the Persians.
>
> (Diodorus 16.60.4)

There are doubts whether Philip was already planning a Panhellenic crusade against the Persians as early as 346. On the other hand, it would help to explain, first, his desire for an alliance with the Athenians, who possessed the best navy in Greece, which was vital for such an enterprise; and, second, his decision not to invade Attica, when Athens was so vulnerable to attack after his seizure of Thermopylae. However, there could be no doubt about one thing: Macedon under Philip was now the strongest power in Greece.

The further rise of Macedon in Greece, 346–338

The Peace of Philocrates lasted from 346 to 340, but throughout that time Demosthenes, although an original supporter of the Peace, employed all his energy and eloquence to bring about its collapse. He had been convinced since 351 that Philip was a dangerous threat to Athens in particular and was intent upon the subjection of Greece. Thus, at every opportunity, he high-lighted Philip's infringements of the Peace, and gradually won the Athe-nians over to his policy of open warfare with Philip. It is difficult to assess accurately how justified or how exaggerated were Demosthenes' accusations against Philip for his alleged breaches of the Peace, since most of the evidence comes from the very speeches of Demosthenes who had a vested interest in damning every action of Philip. The leadership of the policy of peaceful cooperation with Philip was held by Aeschines, but he gradually lost ground to Demosthenes. From 346–345, Philip was concerned with internal reforms within Macedon (Justin 8.5.7) and delivering yet another defeat to the Illyrians (16.69.7). However, his actions in 344 provided ample scope for Demosthenes and his supporters to stir up Athenian animosity against Philip.

In 344, Philip conducted a reorganization of Thessaly by dividing it up into four 'tetrarchies', each with its own governor. Immediately Demos-thenes complained bitterly about the Thessalians' loss of freedom (Dem. 9.26), even though the Thessalians had already elected Philip as archon (leader) of Thessaly for life in 352 (see above). Demosthenes was even more perturbed when he heard that Philip was sending help to the citizens of Messene, Argos and Megalopolis (Dem. 6.9, 15). It would seem that the Spartans yet again were trying to restore their position of influence within the Peloponnese, and that Philip's demand that the Spartans should renounce their claim to Messenia was the result of an appeal for help from the Peloponnesians (Dem. 6.13). Demosthenes, fearing the growth of Macedonian influence in a new area of Greece, was sent on an embassy to dissuade these Peloponnesian states from allying themselves with Philip (6.19–26). He failed to win them over, because he did not appreciate that such states, having for very many years been under the control of Sparta, saw Philip as the guarantor of their continued freedom and independence (Polybius 18.4.1–11). They did not consider, as Demosthenes did, that the freedom of Greece was directly linked with Athenian power, especially as the Athenians were allies of the hated Spartans.

In 344, an embassy arrived in Athens, probably sent jointly by Philip and by the Messenians and Argives, to discuss the situation in the Peloponnese. This gave Demosthenes the chance to deliver his powerful Second Philippic in which he accused Philip of plotting against the whole of Greece (Dem. 6.2). It is not known what was the resultant decision of the Athenian Assembly, but it seems likely that an embassy was despatched to Philip to complain about the unfair terms of the Peace of Philocrates. In 343, Philip sent an embassy to Athens, led by Python of Byzantium, in an attempt to preserve his good name and to maintain peaceful relations with the Athenians:

'Therefore Python urged the public speakers not to find fault with the Peace, because it was not good policy to end it. But if they were not satisfied with any of the terms in the Peace, they should put forward amendments since Philip intended to do all that you [i.e. the Athenians] had voted for. But if these men slander him, but do not put forward proposals with the result that the Peace continues to exist but the distrust of Philip does not stop, you should ignore such men.'

(Demosthenes 7.22)

The Athenians, however, did not respond generously to this offer. They proposed two amendments: first, that both sides should retain, not the territories that each held when the Peace was sworn (Dem. 7.26), but those which lawfully belonged to them (Dem. 7.18); and second, that the Peace of Philocrates should not be binding solely upon Athens and Macedon and their respective allies, but should be a Common Peace, namely a peace to include all the Greek states and to guarantee their freedom and autonomy by armed intervention against any aggressor (Dem. 7.30–31). Hegesippus, a member of Demosthenes' anti-Philip faction and the probable author of Demosthenes' Seventh Speech, was sent to Macedon to deliver the Athenian answer.

Philip was very displeased with the first amendment, as this was an implicit claim by the Athenians of their legal right to regain their colony of Amphipolis, which was crucial to Macedon, both as a protection to its eastern flank and as the base for advancing into Thrace. Philip took his time, and did not reply until the following year. In the meantime, in the winter of 343/2, he intervened in the kingdom of the Molossi in Epirus, deposed the king and replaced him with Alexander, the brother of Olympias, one of Philip's wives. He then advanced to Cassopia, just north of Acarnania, captured three small cities, and handed them over to Alexander (Dem. 7.32). In this way Philip consolidated the kingdom of the Molossi and therefore the south-western border of Macedon from outside attack. This military action strengthened the hand of Demosthenes who capitalized on the anti-Philip mood of the Athenians. He had already played his part in 343 in the downfall of Philocrates, the original proposer of the Peace (Aeschines 2.6) and had only just failed to secure the condemnation of Aeschines (Plutarch, *Demosthenes* 15.3). He now portrayed Philip's actions against Cassopia as a planned attack on Ambracia (Dem. 7.32).

In 342, Philip made one last attempt to resolve his difficulties with Athens by diplomacy. He rejected outright the Athenian claim for Amphipolis, which was a non-starter from the beginning and which the Athenians had not possessed since 424 (Dem. 7.18). However, he was willing to accept the second amendment and be a willing participant in a Common Peace which he hoped would show his commitment to peace in Greece (Dem. 7.33). But Demosthenes and his faction were now dominant in Athens; the scathing and belligerent Seventh Speech, delivered by either Demosthenes or Hegesippus, rejecting all his proposals and offers of arbitration, was the turning point in Philip's relations with Athens. Diplomacy had failed, because

463

the Athenians had refused to trust him under this Peace and were not prepared to negotiate seriously in the formulation of a new peace, in which he
could allay their fears. Now it would have to be war.

In mid-342, Philip once more turned to Thrace. According to Diodorus,
his aim was to deal with Cersebleptes who was continually attacking and
ravaging the territory of the Greeks in the Hellespont (16.71.1). Without
doubt Philip had decided once and for all to finish off Cersebleptes, who
had defied him since 352, and he quickly defeated and expelled the Thracian King (Dem. 12.10). But Philip's aims must have been more far-reaching
than the expulsion of Cersebleptes, since he continued to campaign for the
next two years before he attacked Perinthus in 340 (see below). His campaigns
took him beyond the river Hebrus into the far north of Thrace, and his marriage to the daughter of the King of the Getae in that region marked his success against that tribe. Philip incorporated much of Thrace into his enlarged
kingdom, possibly turning it into a Macedonian province under the
authority of a Macedonian general (17.62.5; Arrian, *Anabasis* 1.25). The
northern parts of Thrace were turned into dependent client-kingdoms. It
would seem, therefore, that Philip had planned the conquest of the whole
of Thrace, and it is very possible that his main aim in this Thracian campaign
was to secure his northern flank from Macedon to the Hellespont in preparation for his attack upon Persia.

Meanwhile the Athenians were enjoying some success at Philip's expense
in Euboea. In 348, the Euboeans had managed to gain independence from
Athens, but internal rivalry between the contenders for the tyranny of both
Eretria and Oreus gave Philip the opening to intervene in that island. In
c.342, Cleitarchus, the tyrant of Eretria, appealed to Philip for help against
his political rival and on three separate occasions received military aid
(Dem. 9.58). Philistides, the tyrant of Oreus, also received Macedonian
military backing to shore up his position (Dem. 9.59–62, 65). The presence
of pro-Macedonian tyrants in Euboea, which was strategically important for
Athens (see above), and the fear that Macedonian influence might spread
throughout the island, drove Demosthenes and the Athenians into action.
Demosthenes forcefully denounced Philip's infiltration of Euboea in his
Third Philippic and, in 341, the Athenians formed an alliance with Chalcis,
one of the most important cities in Euboea. A combined army of Athenians
and Chalcidians overthrew both tyrants, thus removing a grave source of
danger to Athens' borders (Philochorus FGrH 328 fr. 159–60).

War finally broke out in 340, when Philip and Athens clashed in the
Propontis, the small sea that connects the Bosporus to the Hellespont.
There had already been tension in 341: the Athenian commander, Diopeithes, had attacked Cardia, which was an ally of Philip, but was claimed
by the Athenians as part of their territory in the Chersonese. Philip's offer
to submit the dispute to arbitration was rejected by the Athenians, and
therefore he supplied troops to protect Cardia from attack (Dem. 12.11).

464

Diopeithes, in retaliation, attacked places in Thrace that belonged to Philip (Dem. 12.3; 8.8–9). In July 340, Philip attacked and besieged the city of Perinthus on the Propontis, which, according to Diodorus, was opposed to him and favoured the Athenians (16.74.2), although a more likely reason was its failure to supply troops to Philip's campaign against Cersebleptes. However, help in the form of money, supplies and mercenaries was sent to Perinthus by the Persian satraps in that region on the orders of the Persian king, who was increasingly disturbed by the growth of Macedonian power on his western border (16.75.1; Dem. 11.5). Perinthus was further helped by Byzantium which also sent soldiers and generals (16.75.2). Therefore Philip also attacked and besieged Byzantium which was strategically far more important, since it commanded the Bosporus, the narrow strait that controlled access to and from the Black Sea.

This military operation caused the greatest fear among the Athenians because Philip, if he gained control of Byzantium, could prevent the Black Sea grain ships from reaching Athens, thus starving them into submission. The Athenians acted swiftly. They put aside their former hostility to the Byzantines, made an alliance, sent out a naval force and secured control of the sea around Byzantium (16.77.1). At the same time Byzantium's other allies, Chios, Rhodes and Cos also sent help. Philip's willingness to use diplomacy in his dealings with Athens was at an end:

'These are my complaints against you. Since you have begun the aggression and, on account of my restraint, are already making more attacks on my interests and are harming me with all your power, I will justly resist you and, calling upon the gods as witnesses, I will take issue with you.'

(Demosthenes 12.23)

The Athenians responded to Philip's declaration of war, delivered in September 340, by destroying the stone that recorded the Peace of Philocrates and by manning a fleet under the command of Phocion (Philochorus FGrH 328 fr. 55).

Philip soon realized that his siege of Byzantium and Perinthus, with their superb natural defences and with the increased reinforcements, would be long and arduous. Always the realist, Philip broke off both sieges: the conquest of that part of Thrace would have to wait. Athens was the real enemy, not Byzantium, which was far more likely to capitulate if Athens was defeated; in addition, there was still unfinished business in the north. Philip spent the winter of 340/39 advancing even further northwards than before, and, upon reaching the banks of the river Danube, he defeated the nomadic Scythians and married the daughter of their king, thus removing any possible threat to Macedon and Thrace from the north (16.1.5). Philip was now ready for the final reckoning with the Athenians.

A dispute in the Amphictyonic League between the Athenians and the Locrians provided Philip with the opportunity to intervene in central Greece. The Locrians of Amphissa were accused by the Athenians of cultivating sacred land and of charging tolls at Cirrha, the port of Delphi. As a consequence, a fourth Sacred War was declared and Philip, who controlled most of the votes in the Amphictyonic Council, was chosen as the leader of the League's forces against Amphissa (Dem. 18.143–52; Aesch. 3.113–31). This appointment was important for Philip, since his passage through Thermopylae had been blocked by the Theban seizure in 339 of the town of Nicaea that controlled the pass at Thermopylae (Philochorus FGrH 328 fr. 56b). Philip moved south with his Macedonian and Thessalian forces, and bypassed Thermopylae by going directly from Thessalian Lamia to Doris, north of Amphissa. However, in a lightning move, he suddenly captured Elatea in Phocis, situated near the Boeotian border and on the main route to Thebes (Aesch. 3.140). Tension between Philip and Thebes had already been in evidence from the seizure of Nicaea by the Thebans, who were traditional allies of the Locrians and also resented Philip's ascendancy in the Amphictyonic League. Philip's fortification of Elatea was a veiled threat to the Boeotians to stay loyal to their alliance with Philip.

The news of Philip's capture of Elatea, only two days' march from Attica, caused panic among the Athenians (Dem. 18.169–70). An Athenian embassy, including Demosthenes, was despatched to Thebes to attempt to negotiate a military alliance with the Boeotians against Philip. In Thebes they found Philip's embassy requesting the Boeotians as his allies to either join in his attack on Athens or give him free passage through Boeotia (Dem. 18.213). It is a tribute to Demosthenes' eloquence and Boeotian courage that the Boeotians decided to risk all by allying themselves with Athens. During the winter of 339/8, both sides stayed on the defensive with some minor skirmishing, but the Athenians used this time in winning over the support of Achaea, Corinth, Megara, Euboea, Acarnania, Leucas and Corcyra for the show-down with Philip (Dem. 18.237).

It was well within Philip's power to bring the issue to a quick decision by forcing a battle with the Athenians and Boeotians before they received reinforcements from their new allies – thus it is probable that his decision to delay battle was motivated by his preference to resolve the situation by diplomacy. His planned invasion of Persia would have a much greater chance of success, if he did not leave behind in Greece a deep-seated bitterness and implacable hostility towards himself by conquered opponents, as Agesilaos and the Spartans had discovered to their cost in the 390s (see Chapter 24). However, his offer of peace terms, although favourably received by the Athenian general Phocion (Plutarch, *Phocion* 16.1) and by the Boeotarchs, the elected leaders of the Boeotian League, was vehemently rejected by Demosthenes, denouncing as a traitor any man who brought forward Philip's peace overtures for discussion in the Athenian and Boeotian Assemblies (Aesch. 3.148–51). Demosthenes carried the day and both sides met at the battle of Chaeroneia in August 338: Philip's overwhelmingly decisive victory made him the master of Greece.

The Macedonian hegemony of Greece, 338–336

Although the Athenians and the Boeotians feared the worst, Philip had no intention of destroying his enemies. His ultimate aim was to attack Persia; to succeed in this undertaking, he needed the political cooperation and the military support of the Greeks. The means would be a newly constituted league, the so-called League of Corinth, which would formally recognize the Macedonian hegemony of Greece. However, before this could be implemented, he had to deal with the states that had opposed him. His toughest treatment was reserved for the Thebans.

Philip's harsh punishment of the Thebans is reminiscent of his unforgiving treatment of the Olynthian-led Chalcidian League (see above). These two allies, towards whom he had acted generously but who had subsequently betrayed his trust by allying themselves with Athens, felt the full force of his displeasure. The Thebans were obliged to pay ransoms for the return of their dead and those who had been captured at Chaeroneia (Justin 9.4.6); a Macedonian garrison was installed in the Cadmeia, the citadel of Thebes (16.87.3); the Theban opponents of Philip were either executed or exiled, and the pro-Philip Theban exiles were restored to power (Justin 9.4.7–8); Plataea and Orchomenus, which had been destroyed by the Thebans, were either rebuilt and repopulated (Pausanias 9.1.8, 37.8) or planned for the future (Arrian, *Anabasis* 1.9.11). There is a possibility that the Boeotian League – the source of Theban power – was dissolved, but the evidence suggests that Philip allowed it to continue: Arrian (see beginning of Chapter 27) mentions the Boeotarchs, the leading officials of the League, in 335 (*Anabasis* 1.7.11).

By contrast, the Athenians were treated with remarkable leniency. Admittedly, the Second Athenian League was dissolved, but this was not a serious blow, as it had already been severely weakened by the secession of many of the strongest allies (Pausanias 1.25.3). On the other hand, the Athenians were allowed to keep their 'cleruchies' (see Glossary) on Samos, Lemnos, Imbros, Scyros and Delos (Aristotle, *Ath. Pol.* 61.6, 62.2), and were also given Oropus, the much disputed town on the Athenian–Boeotian borders, which at that time had been in the possession of the Boeotians (18.56.6–7). It was also a great relief to many Athenian families, when Philip restored the 2,000 Athenian captives without requiring a ransom (Justin 9.4.4; Polybius 5.10.4). Philip made it clear that he had no intention of attacking Athens by initiating a peace treaty and an alliance with the Athenians, to which they readily agreed (16.87.3). Such generous treatment must be linked with Athens' powerful navy, which was essential for his planned invasion of Asia Minor, and with Athens' influential position within Greece: a grateful and compliant Athens would be a major asset in his new Greek league.

Little is known of Philip's treatment of his other opponents, but it is very likely that peace treaties were also signed with them, with the deliberate

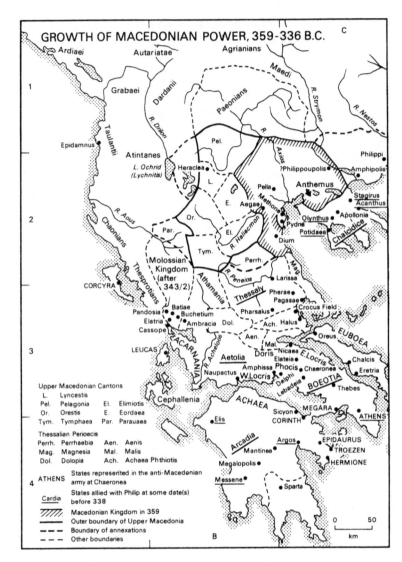

Map 10 Growth of Macedonian power, 359–336 BC

exception of Sparta. This was probably accompanied by his sympathizers and supporters within these states gaining control of their respective governments – thus smoothing the way for acceptance of his future proposals about Greece. Macedonian garrisons were used sparingly, being placed in key strategic positions to maintain his grip on Greece: Ambracia in the west, Chalcis in the east and Corinth in the south (17.3.3; Deinarchus 1.18). The last of his preliminary operations was in the Peloponnese, where he

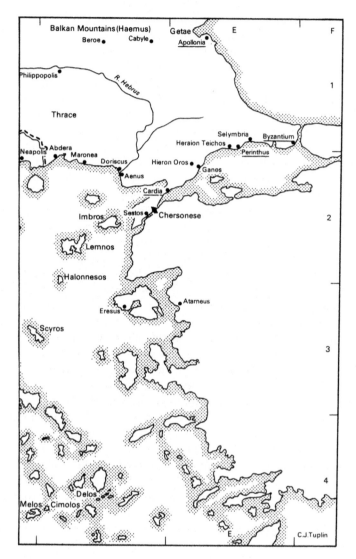

Map 10 continued

ravaged Spartan territory and resolved long-standing territorial disputes by
giving Spartan frontier districts to Tegea, Megalopolis, Argos and Messenia
(Polybius 9.28.6–7; Pausanias 8.7.4; Tacitus, *Annals* 4.43). In this way he
won the goodwill of these states, and removed the source of tension that
had led to the break-up of the Boeotian–Peloponnesian alliance and the loss
of Theban influence in the Peloponnese (see Chapter 25) – another lesson
that he had learned from his close observation of Theban foreign policy in

469

the 360s. Now Philip was ready to place the Macedonian hegemony of Greece on a constitutional and legal footing.

In mid-337, a congress, to be held at Corinth, was announced to which all Greek states were invited to send representatives, possessing the power to take decisions on behalf of their states (16.89). At this congress, the so-called League of Corinth was established with its own constitution; Sparta refused to attend, because once again the independence of Messene was implicitly accepted by its right to participate. The main evidence for the constitution comes from a damaged stone, which records the terms of a general Greek peace with Philip (GHI 177); and from Demosthenes' speech 'On the Treaty with Alexander' (17), delivered in 331/0, in which he cites alleged infringements of the constitution by Alexander. Many of the terms were typical of the Common Peaces that had been sworn throughout the fourth century: for example, the guarantee of each state's right to freedom and autonomy, and a sanctions clause, i.e. the right to take military action against those who broke the terms of the Peace. However, there were two significant differences, arising from the fact that a league had also been created.

First, a 'synod' (meeting) of all member-states was established (Aesch. 3.161), which had the power to pass decrees that were binding on all members and to exercise jurisdiction. Second, the position of 'hegemon' (leader) was formally established, who also had the authority under the sanctions clause to intervene directly against any state that broke the Peace (Dem. 17.6, 17.19): this provided Philip with the legitimate right, backed by the League, to suppress any action perceived as anti-Macedonian. It is clear from this particular stipulation in the constitution that Philip intended to use the League as the means to control Greece. At the second meeting of the League, Philip was elected as 'general of Greece with full powers', and he began to organize a Greek expedition against Persia (16.89.3; Justin 9.4). In 336, an advanced force was sent to Ephesus under the command of two of Philip's generals, Parmenion and Attalus (16.91.2). Philip was making preparations to follow with a much larger force when he was struck down by an assassin's dagger.

Philip's outstanding achievements have not always been fully appreciated in the past. This is probably due to three reasons: first, the brilliance of his son; second, the main surviving record of his life and actions comes from Demosthenes, his arch-enemy; and third, the fragmentary nature of Theopompos' *Philippica*, which was the first general Greek history centred on the exploits of an outstanding individual. But Philip is worthy of the highest praise. By a combination of adroitness in diplomacy and superiority in warfare, he welded Macedon into a permanently unified state, thus avoiding the usual internal convulsions and civil war that followed the death of a Macedonian King; and he had put Macedon at the centre of Greek politics – Macedon, previously considered semi-barbarian and of marginal importance to the former traditional super-powers of Greece. He had laid the political and military foundations of Macedon's supremacy over Greece, which enabled Alexander to dedicate most of his short life to the acquisition of eternal fame by the conquest of Persia. If he had lived, perhaps he may have gained the title of 'Philip the Great'.

Bibliography

Bury, J. B. and Meiggs, R. *A History of Greece*, 4th edn, ch. 16.

Cawkwell, G. *Philip of Macedon*, chs 3, 5–9, 11–12.

——'The peace of Philocrates again', CQ 28.

Griffith, G. T. 'The Macedonian background', in *Alexander the Great*, Greece and Rome Supplement vol. 12, no. 2.

Griffith, G. T. and Hammond, N. G. L. *Macedonia vol. 2*.

Hornblower, S. *The Greek World 479–323 BC*, 2nd edn, ch. 17.

Perlman, S. *Philip and Athens*.

Ryder, T. T. B. Introduction to *Demosthenes and Aeschines*.

ALEXANDER'S GENERALSHIP AT THE BATTLES OF THE RIVER GRANICUS (334), ISSUS (333) AND GAUGAMELA (331)

The assassination of Philip in summer 336 postponed the invasion of the Persian Empire for two years. When Alexander ascended to the Macedonian throne, he was immediately threatened by enemies on all sides. His first immediate task was to remove all potential challengers for the kingship which he did with alacrity (Plutarch, *Moralia* 327). His second was to establish himself in his father's place as commander-in-chief of the Greeks for the planned military campaign against Persia: his swift march through Greece resulted in his election to this post by the League of Corinth (Diodorus 17.3–4). Alexander's third task was to ensure that Macedon was safe from an attack by the traditionally hostile Illyrians on its western border, and that there was no danger of a Thracian revolt in his rear, while waging war in Asia: his successful campaigns in 335 against the Triballi, the most rebellious of the Thracian tribes, and against the Illyrians put an end to these problems (Arrian, *Anabasis* 1.1–6). In the same year the sack of Thebes after its uprising served as a warning to all the Greek states that Alexander would deal ruthlessly with any opposition (Diodorus 17.13–14). Alexander was now ready in the spring of 334 to invade the Persian Empire: he crossed the Hellespont and, before coming to land, cast his spear into the Asian soil, thus asserting his claim to Asia by right of conquest (Diodorus 17.17). His victory in three great battles at the River Granicus (334), at Issus (333) and at Gaugamela (331) turned his claim into fact.

The sources

It is a difficult problem to give an accurate account of these battles due to the fact that the surviving accounts are written by historians, who lived long after the events that they describe. In addition, the contemporary or near-contemporary sources that they used are noted for their bias and their exaggeration. The most reliable account, with reservations, is the *Anabasis* of Arrian (A.A. for the rest of this chapter), who wrote in the second century AD. His main sources were the near-contemporary accounts of two eyewitnesses of Alexander's military successes: the Macedonian Ptolemy, Arrian's principal source (A.A. 6.2.4), one of Alexander's senior officers and, after Alexander's death, the ruler and first king of Egypt; and Aristobulus of Cassandreia, a junior officer, possibly an engineer or architect. Ptolemy's concentration on military matters gives Arrian's account more credibility, but he does exaggerate his own role in military operations and his services to Alexander, while denigrating those of his personal enemies. Aristobulus must also be handled with caution, as he is so flattering to Alexander and so protective of his reputation. To complicate matters further, both these writers made use of the works of the Greek Callisthenes, a relative of Aristotle, who had been employed by Alexander specifically to give a glowing and heroic account of his achievements. Nevertheless, Ptolemy's military expertise and Arrian's military experience as a Roman governor have combined to produce a generally reliable and clear description of these battles.

Modern scholarship uses two terms to denote the two different traditions of Alexander's reign: the 'official tradition' and the 'vulgate'. The 'official tradition' refers to Ptolemy and Aristobulus, who were the main sources for Arrian's *Anabasis*. The 'vulgate tradition' is contained in the 17th book of Diodorus Siculus (D.S. for the rest of the chapter), writing nearly 300 years after Alexander's death, and the Roman Quintus Curtius Rufus, writing in the first century AD, both of whom used the Greek Cleitarchus as their main source. Little is known about the personal life of Cleitarchus apart from the fact that he lived in Alexandria under Ptolemy in the late fourth or early third century. His literary work is highly critical of Alexander, possibly due to his dislike of the Macedonians, and was noted in antiquity for its cavalier treatment of the truth and its fondness for sensationalism, such as the information that Alexander set fire to Persepolis, after the suggestion was made at a drunken party by Thais, an Athenian prostitute, to avenge Xerxes' destruction of Athens in 480 (Curtius 5.7.3–11; D.S. 17.72). Finally there is Plutarch's *Life of Alexander*, which made use of a very wide range of sources, including all those mentioned above, and therefore should be treated separately from the two main traditions.

Alexander's army

The precise numbers of infantry and cavalry that accompanied Alexander, when he marched to the Hellespont in 334 to begin the invasion of the Persian Empire, is a tough problem to resolve. Plutarch (*Alexander* 15.1) noted that estimates ranged from 30,000 infantry and 4,000 cavalry (Aristobulus' figures) to 43,000 infantry and 5,500 cavalry (the figures of Anaximenes, a fourth-century historian and rhetorician). Arrian, who was most probably using Ptolemy as his source, states that Alexander had not many more than 30,000 infantry and over 5,000 cavalry (A.A. 1.11.3). Only Diodorus gives a detailed breakdown of the size of the different army units (D.S. 17.17):

Infantry:
12,000 Macedonians
7,000 Greek allies
5,000 Greek mercenaries
7,000 Balkan troops (i.e. Odrysians, Triballians, and Illyrians)
1,000 Agrianians and archers
Total
32,000
Cavalry:
1,800 Macedonians (i.e. the 'Companions' – see below)
1,800 Thessalians
600 Greek allies
600 Thracians, 'Prodromoi' ('Fore-runners') and Paeonians
Total
5,100

However, there is a further complication with Diodorus: the sum total that he gives for the cavalry is 4,800, even though the correct total, based on his own figures, should read 5,100.

It is possible to have confidence in the figure of 32,000 infantry, since it accords with the totals which were given by Arrian ('not much more than 30,000') and Diodorus in his detailed analysis; and which have probably been rounded down by Aristobulus. Anaximenes' total of 43,000 infantry can probably be explained by his inclusion of the earlier expeditionary force, which was sent by Philip in 336 under the command of Parmenion, and consisted of at least 10,000 men (Polyaenus 5.44.4). As for the size of the cavalry contingent, it has proved to be impossible for modern scholarship to reconcile the conflicting figures with any certainty.

The cavalry

The strongest and most prestigious troops of the Macedonian army were the heavily armed cavalry: the 'Companions' ('hetairoi'). These 1,800 men were divided into eight 'ilai' (squadrons), consisting of 225 men (A.A. 3.11.8); one of these squadrons was the 'Royal Squadron', the elite group that fought alongside the King. In 331/0, when 500 extra troops were added, each squadron was divided into two 'lochoi' (companies). The overall commander of the Companion Cavalry was Philotas, son of Parmenion, who was Alexander's most experienced general (A.A. 3.11.8). Philotas was executed in 330 for allegedly plotting against Alexander, who divided the command between two 'hipparchs' (commanders of the cavalry) because:

he did not want one man, not even his dearest friend, to be in charge of so many cavalry, especially since they were the most renowned and the most formidable of the whole cavalry.

(Arrian, *Anabasis* 3.27.4)

In 327, the command structure of the Companion Cavalry was again modified so that there were at least six, but in all probability eight hipparchs – this can be inferred from Alexander's campaigning in 327, since Arrian states that he was accompanied by four hipparchs and half of the Companions (A.A. 4.22.7, 24.1).

The Companion Cavalry wore a metal helmet, corselet and a short metal or leather kilt, and were heavily armed with a lance, made of tough cornel-wood and possessing a blade at each end, and a curved slashing sword. The lack of saddles and stirrups prevented the cavalryman from using his lance in the traditional, later manner, i.e. putting the whole weight of his body behind the lance, since he would have quickly become unseated; instead he used it as a stabbing spear. The Companion Cavalry rode into battle in a wedge-shaped formation, its apex facing the enemy, so that they had the flexibility to swing quickly to the right or left, and charge into any gap that appeared in the enemy's line. As the main strength of the Persian forces rested on their cavalry, it was the vital task of the Companion Cavalry to shatter the Persian cavalry by punching a hole in its formation by a full-blooded, concentrated shock-attack. When the Persian cavalry was driven off, the Companion Cavalry could then attack the Persian infantry in the flank and the rear. Finally, they could pursue and finish off the fleeing infantry in the open plain.

The rest of Alexander's cavalry consisted of non-Macedonians, of whom the elite were the 1,800 heavily armed Thessalians. These had been tradi-tionally the best horsemen in Greece, and their fighting worth was recog-nized by Alexander, who placed them on the left wing of his battle-line as a balance to his Companion Cavalry on the right. Their body armour and curved, slashing swords were similar to those of the Companion Cavalry, but they were also armed with two short spears: one was used as a javelin, the other either as a second javelin or as a stabbing spear, according to cir-cumstances. Alexander also employed six other squadrons, each consisting of 150 men: one of Thracians, one of Paeonians and four of 'Prodromoi' ('Fore-Runners'). The non-Greek Thracians and Paeonians were armed with javelins, but the Prodromoi carried much longer lances than the rest, simi-lar to the long 'sarissa' (pike) of the Macedonian phalanx (see below), which they had to hold with both hands, while controlling their horses with only their legs. All these cavalry units came from territories which either had been incorporated within the Macedonian state or were under the direct control of Alexander. The rest of the Greeks in the League of Corinth supplied only 600 cavalry.

The infantry

The backbone of the infantry was the Macedonian phalanx, the 'pezetairoi' ('Foot-Companions'). These had been established as a regular body of troops by one of the predecessors of Philip, but it was he who turned them into a formidable fighting force. They were divided into six battalions ('taxeis'), each one consisting of 1,500 men, making a total of 9,000 men (A.A. 3.11.9). At the battle of Hydaspes in 326, there were seven battalions (A.A. 5.11.3, 12.1ff.), which were possibly formed when reinforcements were sent to Alexander in Susa (A.A. 3.16.11). The Macedonian soldier in the phalanx was not as heavily armed as the Greek 'hoplite', since he had no corselet to protect his breast and possessed a smaller shield, which probably was suspended from his neck to cover his left side. The reason for this was that his main weapon was the very long sarissa, probably about 5½ metres in length in Alexander's time (6½ metres in the second century – Polybius 18.29), which needed both hands to be free in order to hold it. As a result, the 'sarissae' of the first three or four ranks projected beyond the front line of battle, creating a wall of spear-points. The sarissae of the remaining ranks (it is not clear if the phalanx consisted of eight or sixteen ranks) were held upright to afford some protection from the enemy's missiles. The main function of the phalanx was to hold its ground in the centre of the battle-line and keep the enemy's centre engaged, while Alexander and the Companion Cavalry on the right wing destroyed the enemy's left wing and then joined in the attack on the enemy's centre from the side and rear.

The elite of the Macedonian infantry were the 'hypaspists' or 'shield-bearers', organized into three battalions, each with 1,000 troops (A.A. 4.30.5). There was even an elite within these battalions, one bearing the name of 'agema' or 'the Royal Footguard'. These 3,000 hypaspists were placed immediately on the right of the phalanx in the battle-line to protect its exposed, open right flank. It is not clear from the sources how they were armed, but Arrian strongly implies that they were more lightly armed by including them among the other light-armed troops, the archers and the javelin-men, and contrasting them with the heavily armed troops of the phalanx (A.A. 2.4.3). The fact that Alexander used them frequently for forced marches and other special operations adds support to this view. The final components of the Macedonian infantry were two battalions of archers, one Macedonian, the other Cretan; and the highly valued and much-employed 1,000 non-Greek Agrianians, whose equipment was based upon that of the 'peltasts', the 5,000 Greek mercenaries in Alexander's invasion force – the javelin, the long sword, the small shield and the light body-armour. The remaining 7,000 Greek troops were heavily armed hoplites, who were mainly used for garrison duty and maintaining Alexander's lines of communication. In contrast, the Persian infantry wore hardly any protective body-armour, were armed with short spears and relied mainly on the bow, thus putting them at a great disadvantage in hand-to-hand fighting.

The battle of the River Granicus (334)

The opening battle of Alexander's campaign in Persia took place in 334 at the River Granicus, which flows in a northerly direction into the Propontis or Sea of Marmara. Darius III, the King of Persia, sent reinforcements, but left the strategy and the direction of the battle to his local 'satraps' in western Asia Minor and to Memnon, a Greek commander in his employment. Memnon's advice to avoid a pitched battle and to rely upon a 'scorched earth' policy, so that Alexander would be forced to abandon his campaign due to a lack of supplies, was rejected by the satraps as too defeatist (A.A. 1.12.9–10). However, his stated concern about the Macedonian superiority in infantry persuaded them to adopt a defensive strategy: they drew up their forces on the east bank of the Granicus, thus ensuring that Alexander would have to cross the river to engage forces – a very difficult and dangerous enterprise.

The sources

It is in the description of this battle that the widest divergence is found between the 'official tradition', Ptolemy and Aristobulus, and the 'vulgate', Diodorus. There has been some scholarly support for Diodorus' account (e.g. Bosworth), but it has been in the minority due to the serious problems arising from Diodorus' version of events. First, he claims that there were 100,000 Persian infantry, which is a gross exaggeration (D.S. 17.19.5); second, he places Alexander's attack at dawn, which is at variance with all the other sources (D. S. 17.19.3); third, he states that Alexander was allowed to cross the river unopposed and draw up his battle formation – thus negating the key element in the Persian satraps' defensive tactics (D.S. 17.19.3). Finally, Diodorus' battle consists of two distinct and separate phases, namely a cavalry battle (D.S. 17.19.6–21.4) followed by an infantry battle (D.S. 17.21.5–6) – thus ignoring the fundamental principle of Alexander's battle tactics, which coordinated the use of the cavalry and the infantry as a combined striking force. On these grounds, Arrian's account has found more favour with modern scholarship.

The deployment of the armies

According to Arrian, when the Macedonian forces arrived in the afternoon at the Granicus, Alexander and Parmenion had a discussion about the best course of action. The authenticity of this debate is suspect, but it does lay out clearly the advantages and disadvantages of fighting this battle. Parmenion, a very experienced commander, outlined clearly the tactical problems of going on the offensive and the strategic results of a defeat:

> 'It seems to me that we will be taking a very great risk if we attack now, because we cannot lead the army across the river in line-abreast on a broad front. For you can

477

see that many parts of the river are deep, and that the banks are steep, even cliff-like. As a result, when we emerge, we will be in loose order and in column [i.e. not line abreast], which is the weakest formation, and the enemy cavalry, drawn up in massed formation, will strike hard at our phalanx. This disaster at the beginning will cause difficulties for the present and will be very damaging to the outcome of the whole war.'

(Arrian, *Anabasis* 1.13.4–5)

However, Alexander had decided upon the tactics to overcome the specific doubts and fears of Parmenion.

In Arrian's account, the Persians had 20,000 (probably exaggerated) cavalry, drawn up along the high edge of the bank, and 20,000 infantry, consisting mainly of Greek mercenaries, drawn up on a ridge behind the level ground that stretched from the river-bank (A.A. 1.14.4 – see Map 11). In recounting the battle formation of Alexander's forces, Arrian makes no mention of the 7,000 Greek allied infantry, the 5,000 Greek mercenaries nor of the 7,000 Balkan troops. However, the Persian defensive tactics and Memnon's remark about the Macedonian superiority in infantry (A.A. 1.12.9) strongly imply that these Greek forces were present, most probably held in reserve, ready to be brought into the action if the first attack faltered or failed. Alexander placed the phalanx, the six battalions of his 'Foot-Companions', in the centre. On the right of the phalanx stood the three battalions of hypaspists; on their right came a combined force of cavalry – the light-armed Prodromoi and Paeonians, and one squadron of the Companion Cavalry under its squadron commander, Socrates; on their right came the remaining squadrons of Companion Cavalry under Philotas; and finally, on the extreme right wing, the Agrianians (the javelin-men) and the archers. Alexander was in command of the right half of the army, including three battalions of the phalanx to the right. On the left of the phalanx stood the Thracian cavalry; to their left were the Greek allied cavalry; and on the extreme left wing the Thessalian cavalry was positioned. Parmenion was the commander of the left half of the army, including the three battalions of the phalanx to the left.

The battle

The decision of Alexander to attack that very afternoon, almost immediately after his arrival at the Granicus, gave the Persians no time to rearrange their two battle-lines. However, the prominence of Alexander in his white-plumed helmet on the right wing with his Companions persuaded the Persians to reinforce their left wing in order to oppose him (A.A. 1.14.4). Alexander began the battle by ordering an assault force, consisting of the Royal battalion of hypaspists, the Prodromoi, the Paeonians and Socrates' squadron of

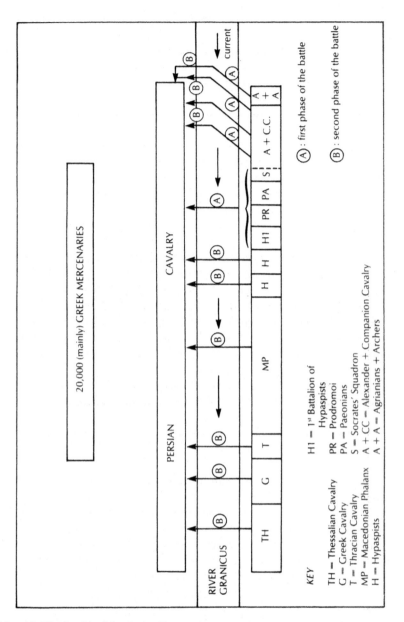

Map 11 The battle of the River Granicus

the Companion Cavalry, to make a frontal attack on the enemy line opposite them (A.A. 1.14.6). He also ordered his right wing to enter the river
but, to the surprise of the Persians, he did not make straight for the enemy
line, but led his forces across the river at an oblique angle. It is the direction
of this manoeuvre that has caused disagreement in modern scholarship.

The standard translation of Arrian's description of the movement of
Alexander and the Macedonian right wing has been as follows:

> He himself, leading the right wing to the sound of trumpets and shouts to the God of
> War, enters the stream, continually extending his line of battle at an angle in the
> direction, where the current was pulling them [i.e. downstream], so that the Persians
> would not attack him as he emerged in column, but so that he himself might attack
> them, being as far as possible in deep formation.
>
> (Arrian, *Anabasis* 1.14.7)

Thus, it is argued, Arrian believed that Alexander and his right wing moved
in the direction of the current, i.e. to the left, in order to attack the Persian
left-centre. It is difficult to make military sense of such a move, since it
would involve two groups of Alexander's forces attempting to cut across
each other in the midst of a fast-flowing river, and yet expecting to keep in
formation. Furthermore, it is extremely difficult to stay in formation when
advancing in the same direction as a river current, as it would tend to sweep
the troops along in a disorderly fashion.

A different interpretation (by Hammond) of Alexander's manoeuvre is
based on an alternative translation of the key passage in Arrian:

> continually extending his line of battle at an angle at this/that point, where the current
> was pulling them, so that the Persians ...

It is argued that an unstated but implicit antecedent 'at this point' ('tautei')
or 'at that point' ('ekeinei') should be placed before 'where the current was
pulling them'. If this translation is accepted, then Arrian was stating that
Alexander and his right wing entered the river and were advancing against
the current, i.e. to the right. This interpretation is supported by the only
other source that recorded Alexander's sideways movement across the
river:

> While crossing the Granicus, Alexander outflanked the wing of the Persians, as they
> were about to attack from a higher position, by means of himself leading the Mace-
> donians upstream (or 'towards the water/flow').
>
> (Polyaenus 4.3.16)

Polyaenus emphasizes that the movement of Alexander and the right wing
was upstream, i.e. to the right, in order to outflank the Persian left wing.

Furthermore, it is easier for an armed force to keep its balance and there-fore its battle-formation by advancing against a current. Arrian himself, in the speech given to Parmenion (see above), stresses this specific point: the vital importance of keeping in formation as the Macedonians mounted the opposite riverbank. This could only be achieved by crossing at an oblique angle to the right against the current. Consequently, Polyaenus' evidence strengthens Hammond's translation of Arrian, and his view on this issue should be preferred.

While Alexander and the right wing were carrying out this manoeuvre, the initial assault force had engaged the enemy. There were heavy casualties on the Macedonian side, because the steepness of the riverbank made it difficult to mount and the Persians, towering above them, had an easy target for their javelins (A.A. 1.15.1–2). As this first assault began to falter, Alex-ander stopped the move to the right and ordered his right wing to launch a frontal attack. Alexander, at the head of the Royal Squadron of Compa-nion Cavalry, forced his way onto the bank, where a violent and furious cavalry battle took place (A.A. 1.15.3–8). The superior quality of Alex-ander's Royal Squadron and their longer spears, even against greater num-bers, enabled him to establish a bridgehead on the east bank, thus allowing the other squadrons of Companion Cavalry to join him. Just as deadly to the Persian cavalry was the presence of the Agrianian javelin-men and archers, who had outflanked them. Interspersed with the Macedonian cavalry, they wreaked havoc by attacking the Persian horses. Gradually the Persian cavalry began to be pushed back, but the turning point in the battle came further down the Persian line of battle:

> But when the Persian centre had given way, then both of the cavalry wings also broke, and the rout was complete.
>
> (Arrian, *Anabasis* 1.16.1)

Although not mentioned in Arrian's account, the Macedonian phalanx in the centre and the Thessalian cavalry and the others on the left had pre-sumably crossed the Granicus to confront the Persian centre and right wing, while the other recorded action was taking place. The long sarissae of the phalanx achieved the key break-through in the centre, resulting in the flight of the whole Persian cavalry.

Alexander then led his forces against the 20,000 (mainly) Greek mercen-aries, drawn up on a ridge as the Persian second line of defence. They were attacked in the front by the Macedonian phalanx, and on the flanks and in the rear by the Macedonian and allied cavalry. Arrian states unconvincingly that this highly trained, very experienced and numerous army of mercen-aries was quickly over-whelmed and massacred, and that there were only 2,000 survivors, who surrendered unconditionally (A.A. 1.16.2). Plutarch's account is much more realistic: a tough and bloody battle, which resulted in more casualties for Alexander than were sustained in the fighting with the Persian cavalry (Plutarch, *Alexander* 16). Plutarch, citing Aristobulus as his source, gives the Macedonian losses as 25 cavalry and 9 infantry (Plut. *Alex.* 16), whereas Arrian gives 25 Companion Cavalry, more than 60 of the rest of the cavalry and about 30 infantry (A.A. 1.16.4) – remarkably and suspiciously low.

Alexander had gained his first success in the Persian campaign and was now free to march through Asia Minor. The victory at the River Granicus had been achieved by the superior fighting qualities of the Macedonian army and by Alexander's generalship. He had displayed confidence in his own judgement by rejecting Parmenion's advice to delay the battle until the following morning; and decisiveness by launching an immediate attack upon the Persians. He also showed outstanding organizational ability by coordinating both light and heavy cavalry and light- and heavy-armed infantry into an effective single attacking force. In addition, he revealed flexibility and originality in adapting tactics to meet a particular situation, when he ordered his right wing to move across the river at an angle to outflank the Persian left wing and to mount the opposite bank in line of battle. There was also that vital sense of timing – knowing exactly when to strike to inflict the maximum damage on the enemy – when he attacked the Persian left wing just as the first assault force, whose objective was to pin down the Persian cavalry on the left, had begun to falter and was being pushed back into the river.

Finally, he possessed that outstanding quality that endears every general to his troops and is so vital for army morale: personal courage. He led his army from the front and faced the same danger as the humblest soldier. In fact, Alexander was nearly killed three times in this battle: first, when he was hit on his helmet by the axe of Rhoesaces (A.A. 1.15.7) or of Spithridates (Plut., *Alex.* 16); second, when he was about to be struck from behind by Spithridates' sword, but was saved by 'Black Cleitus', one of the Royal Squadron of the Companion Cavalry (A.A. 1.15.8; Plut., *Alex.* 16); and third, when his horse was killed beneath him by a sword thrust from one of the Greek mercenaries (Plut., *Alex.* 16). It is hardly surprising that the Macedonian army held Alexander in the highest esteem and affection.

The battle of Issus (333)

In November 333, Darius led his army over the Amanus mountains and placed his army in the rear of Alexander's forces on the north side of the River Pinarus, situated close to Issus on the Gulf of Alexandretta, which forms the right-angle between Asia Minor and Phoenicia. The identification of the Pinarus has been a matter of scholarly dispute, but the majority opinion inclines towards the Delai Chai rather than the Payas, which is further south. There are two main grounds for this belief: first, the steep banks of the Payas would have made Alexander's cavalry charge impossible;

and second, the gradual deployment of Alexander's army from marching line of column into its final battle-formation, as he advanced northwards, could only have taken place in the terrain between the Payas and the Delai Chai.

The sources

The clearest account of the battle comes from Arrian (2.6–11), who made use of the 'official tradition', Ptolemy (mentioned by name in A.A. 2.11.8) and Aristobulus. However, there is also the fragmentary narrative of the contemporary historian, Callisthenes himself, which can be recovered from Polybius' detailed criticism of that writer's account (12.17–22). Although critical of Callisthenes' work, Polybius concedes that Callisthenes' account was generally accepted, and even ranks him among the most learned of the old historians (6.45.1). In addition, Polybius' summary of Callisthenes' account strongly suggests that Arrian's main sources, Ptolemy and Aristobulus, agreed with and, in all probability, made use of Callisthenes' work. Although Callisthenes has his failings – exaggeration of the Persian forces and inaccurate estimates of distances – his account, and therefore Arrian's, can be generally considered as reliable. Quintus Curtius (3.8–11) also seems to be drawing on the same tradition for much of his information about the build-up to the battle and thus, apart from his usual dramatic and sensational treatment of events, helps to provide a consistent picture of events. However, his version differs radically from Arrian's about the fighting around Darius and Darius' behaviour in the battle, and it would seem that he, together with Diodorus (17.32–36), was following a different tradition for this stage of the battle.

The deployment of the armies

The size of the Persian army under Darius can only be guessed, since the numbers given by all the sources are clearly exaggerated: 600,000, including 30,000 Greek mercenaries and 60,000 Cardaces, a specialized group of infantry, possibly similar to peltasts (A.A. 2.8.8); 400,000 infantry and 100,000 cavalry (D.S. 17.31.2); and 310,000 in total (Quintus Curtius 3.2). All that can be said with confidence was that Alexander must have been outnumbered, since he organized his forces in such a way as to avoid being outflanked. When news of Alexander's approach was brought to Darius, he sent the whole of his cavalry and some light-armed troops across the Pinarus in order to draw up his battle-formation in safety. He placed the Greek mercenaries, his best infantry troops, in the middle to confront the Macedonian phalanx; on either side of them he placed the Cardaces (A.A. 2.8.6), in front of whom were posted archers (A.A. 2.10.3). Behind these he placed the rest of the Asiatic infantry, a mixture of heavy- and light-armed troops as a reserve force (A.A. 2.8.8). Furthermore:

He also stationed about 20,000 troops on the mountain on their left against Alexander's right wing, and some of these were actually positioned to Alexander's rear.

(Arrian, *Anabasis* 2.8.7)

These had been placed on the foothills of the Amanus mountains, in advance of his line of battle. Their role was, defensively, to prevent the Persian left wing from being outflanked and, offensively, to outflank Alexander's right wing.

Having deployed his infantry, Darius recalled the cavalry from the southern side of the Pinarus:

and placed most of them on the right wing, next to the sea opposite Parmenion, because the terrain there was suitable for horses.

(Arrian, *Anabasis* 2.8.10)

Darius had now covered the whole coastal plain from the sea to the mountains with his forces. He now took his place in the centre with his 3,000-strong Royal Cavalry Guard, presumably behind the Greek mercenaries. His battle-plan is revealed by Curtius:

Darius wanted to make it an issue between the cavalry, since he believed that the phalanx was the main strength of the Macedonian army.

(Quintus Curtius 3.11.1)

Darius, without necessarily realizing it, was intending to imitate Alexander's tactics by using his cavalry on the Persian right to defeat and rout Alexander's left wing, and then attack the phalanx in the flank and the rear.

Alexander marched northwards with his infantry in front and his cavalry behind them but, when he reached the coastal plain that gradually became broader, he deployed his infantry in a widening line of battle as he advanced, at first 32 men deep, then 16, then 8 (Polybius 19.6, 21.1), keeping the right flank close to the mountains, and the left close to the sea (A.A. 2.8.2). Finally there was enough room to deploy his cavalry: he positioned the Companion Cavalry on the immediate right of the hypaspists, next the Thessalians and presumably (there is a missing section in Arrian's text) the Prodromoi and the Paeonians on the extreme right wing; he sent the allied Greek cavalry to Parmenion to take up position on his left wing (A.A. 2.8.9). However, when Alexander drew closer to the Pinarus and saw Darius' final battle-formation, he made some key changes to his line of battle. He quickly realized that he had to strengthen his left wing, since the bulk of the Persian cavalry had been drawn up on the Persian right next to the sea. Therefore he removed the Thessalians from the Macedonian right and trans-ferred them to the left, but he ordered them to carry out this manoeuvre behind the front line so that the Persians would not see what was happening.

In addition, he placed the Thracian javelin-men and the Cretan archers between the reinforced cavalry on the left wing and the phalanx in the centre (A.A. 2.9.1, 9.3 – see Map 12).

Alexander now had to reorganize his right wing to fill the space made by the withdrawal of the Thessalians and to defend his right flank from the Persians positioned on the foothills of the Amanus Mountains. He placed the archers under Antiochus on the immediate right of the hypaspists, thus moving the Companion Cavalry further right, and closed up the line by moving the Pro-dromoi and the Paeonians leftwards to link up with the Companion Cavalry (A.A 2.9.2). As for the Persians in the foothills of the mountains:

> He drew up the Agrianians under Attalus, some of the cavalry and some of the archers at an angle towards the mountain in his rear with the result that, on his right wing, his line of battle was split into two prongs, one facing Darius and all of the Persians on the opposite side of the river, the other facing those Persians who had been stationed on the mountain to the Macedonian rear.
>
> (Arrian, *Anabasis* 2.9.2)

In other words, Alexander's right wing formed a right-angle to prevent an encircling movement by that force of Persians. The Greek mercenaries were drawn up as a reserve behind the phalanx.

The battle

As he advanced, Alexander decided to test the mettle of the Persians in the foothills by launching the Agrianians and some archers against them. The result was an easy victory for the Macedonians, who drove the Persians in flight to the summit, thereby excluding them from any further part in the battle (A.A. 2.9.4). With the threat to his right flank virtually removed, Alexander carried out the final reorganization of his battle-formation (see Map 12):

> Since the battle-line on his right wing did not seem solid enough to him, and because the Persians seemed to be greatly outflanking him here, he ordered two squadrons of the Companion Cavalry ... to go from the centre unobserved to the right wing. He also brought over the archers [i.e. those on the right of the hypaspists], some of the Agrianians and some of the Greek mercenaries [i.e. from the second line] to the right wing, and thus extended his battle-line to outflank the Persian left wing.
>
> (Arrian, *Anabasis* 2.9.3–4)

The two squadrons of Companion Cavalry were presumably sent to join the Prodromoi and the Paeonians to provide depth at that part of the line. Alexander was now in an excellent position: by driving off the Persians from the foothills and by extending his right wing, he had effectively cut off

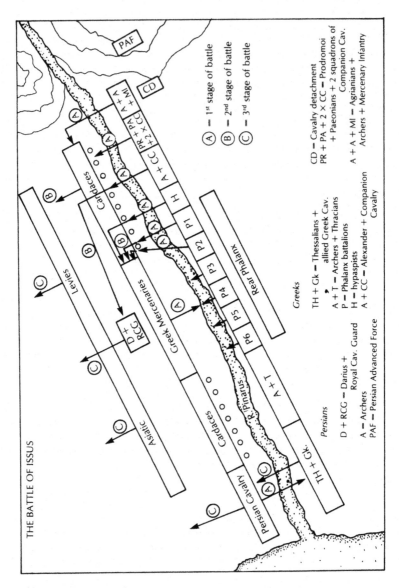

Map 12 The battle of Issus

the Persian left wing on the north side of the Pinarus from its advance force on the south side in the hills. Alexander decided that a detachment of 300 cavalry (possibly with the remaining Agrianians) was sufficient to keep watch on the hill-men (A.A. 2.9.4).

The battle began either when the Persian cavalry charged across the river against the Macedonian left wing (Quintus Curtius 3.11.1; Polybius 12.18.11) or when Alexander led the Companion Cavalry in a charge against the Cardaces on the Persian left wing (A.A. 2.10.3). The shock of Alexander's frontal attack with the cavalry, aided by the Agrianians and the other Greeks working around the flank, broke the resistance of the Cardaces on the left, who fled in disorder (A.A. 2.10.3–4). However, the Macedonian centre quickly ran into trouble:

> The Greek mercenaries with Darius attacked at the point where the Macedonian phalanx had split and come apart on the right. The cause of this was that, when Alexander had plunged very swiftly into the river and, fighting at close quarters, was forcing back the Persian forces placed there, those in the Macedonian centre had not attacked with the same speed, and finding the river banks steep in many places, were unable to maintain a regular and unbroken line. And it was at this point that the Greeks attacked the Macedonians, where they saw the line of battle especially broken.
>
> (Arrian, *Anabasis* 2.10.4–5)

It would seem that the hypaspists and the two right-sided battalions of the phalanx had quickly followed Alexander and the Companion Cavalry against the Cardaces on the Persian left. However, the remaining four battalions of the phalanx had to contend with a more difficult part of the river bank and with Darius' Greek mercenaries, who were first-class, battle-hardened soldiers. As a result, the Macedonian line came apart and the Greek mercenaries were skilfully exploiting this, by pushing the Macedonians back into the river and inflicting heavy casualties on them – the battalion commander, Ptolemy, and 120 of the phalanx perished (A.A. 2.10.6–7).

The situation in the centre was saved by the hypaspists and the two right-sided battalions who, having swiftly completed the rout of the Cardaces on the Persian left, turned half-left and attacked the Greek mercenaries in the flank with great success (A.A. 2.11.1). According to Arrian and the 'official tradition', Darius fled as soon as his left wing broke (A.A. 2.11.2), whereas the 'vulgate' sources of Diodorus (17.34.2–7) and Quintus Curtius (3.11.7–12) describe hard and bloody fighting around Darius, who fled only when his death or capture was imminent. These two traditions cannot be reconciled. However, the 'vulgate' tradition seems more convincing: first, because Callisthenes, the ultimate source of the 'official tradition', habitually portrays Darius as a coward and thus influenced Arrian (A.A. 2.10.1, 11.4; 3.14.3, 22.4); and second, because the casualties among the Royal Cavalry Guard,

Darius' bodyguard, would have been sustained only while Darius was still there to be defended (A.A. 2.11.8). If Darius had fled so soon into the battle, they also would have made an immediate escape to safety.

Meanwhile, on the Macedonian left wing, a desperate cavalry fight was taking place. The squadrons of heavy Persian cavalry, with man and horse protected by rows of armour-plating, had already overcome one squadron of Thessalian cavalry which, having retreated and regrouped, had launched a ferocious counter-attack (Quintus Curtius 3.11.13–15). When the news of Darius' flight reached the Persian cavalry, already suffering at the hands of the Thessalians, they also turned and fled (A.A. 2.11.2). There is no mention of the Cardaces, who were posted next to the Persian cavalry, but they also presumably fled at the same time as their cavalry. Alexander pursued the Persians until nightfall, adding to their casualties; having stormed Darius' camp, he captured the Persian king's mother, wife and son, and other Persian noble ladies (A.A. 2.11.9).

This was a much greater victory than the one that Alexander had achieved at the Granicus River. Apart from the same qualities of generalship that he had displayed at the Granicus, Alexander also showed coolness under pressure, when he discovered that his enemy was to his rear and had cut off his line of retreat. More deserving of praise was his tactical ability to assess almost instantaneously the enemy's strengths and weaknesses, and to rearrange his own battle-formation to take advantage of this assessment, even as he was advancing into battle. Finally, although obviously flushed with victory but still in pain from a sword wound in his thigh, he nevertheless found time to visit the Macedonian wounded (A.A. 2.12.1) – such was the close bond between general and his soldiers.

The battle of Gaugamela (331)

Darius had paid the penalty at Issus for fighting a battle in a confined space, where he could not make use of his superior numbers. In his final encounter with Alexander in the autumn of 331, Darius had chosen the wide plain of Gaugamela (in Mesopotamia, near the river Tigris) in order to make full use of his numerical superiority and to provide the most suitable terrain for his cavalry, on whom he placed his best hopes of victory. The sources give widely divergent numbers for Darius' infantry: 1,000,000 (A.A. 3.8.6), 800,000 (D.S. 17.53.3), 400,000 (Justin 11.12.5) and 200,000 (Quintus Curtius 4.12.13). These numbers have clearly been greatly exaggerated to increase the glory of Alexander's victory. It is impossible to give an accurate estimate, which in any case would be a fruitless exercise, since all the sources agree that the Persian infantry played a negligible part in the battle. There is a similar problem with the figures for Darius' cavalry; but, whereas the 200,000 of Diodorus (17.53.3) and 100,000 of Justin (11.12.5) can be readily discounted, the 40,000 of Arrian (3.8.6) and the 45,000 of Curtius (4.12.13) are sufficiently close and reasonable enough to be accepted with caution. What can be said with certainty is that they greatly outnumbered Alexander's cavalry. The newest addiction to Darius' army was the 200 scythed-chariots, each drawn by two or four horses (D.S. 17.53.1–2).

Deployment of the armies

Darius' battle-formation comes from a Persian document which, according to Aristobulus, was captured after the battle (A.A. 3.11.3). The Persian army was drawn up in a straight line of varying depth. Darius commanded the centre and was protected by 50 chariots in the very front, followed by a mixture of cavalry and infantry divisions, including archers and about 6,000 Greek mercenaries. Behind Darius' centre was stationed the reserve infantry force in formation. The main fighting strength – the cavalry – was placed on the wings, where Bessus commanded the Persian left wing with the best cavalry (Persians, Bactrians and Scythians) and Mazaeus the Persian right. In addition, 100 chariots were posted on the left, facing Alexander's stronger right wing, and 50 on the right. This arrangement of Persian forces gives an insight into Darius' battle-plan (see Map 13). The chariots were intended to disrupt the formations of the Macedonian phalanx and cavalry squadrons by launching full speed attacks. However, the key to success lay with the cavalry, which was to outflank and envelop the two Macedonian wings, and, after crushing them, to attack the Macedonian centre in the flanks and the rear.

Alexander's army consisted of 40,000 infantry and 7,000 cavalry (A.A. 3.12.5). He drew up his front line of battle in his favoured attacking formation: the Companion Cavalry were stationed on the right wing; next to them, from right to left, came the three battalions of hypaspists with the Royal Footguard on the immediate left of the Companion Cavalry; the six battalions of the phalanx occupied the centre; and on the left wing came the Greek allied cavalry, stationed next to the phalanx, with the Thessalian cavalry on the extreme left (A.A. 3.11.8–10). However, it was his assignment of the other troops that reveal Alexander's quality as a field commander. He arranged the rest of his troops to offset the dangers posed by Darius' battle-plan. In the first place:

> He also drew up a second line so that the phalanx could face both ways. He gave orders to the commanders of this force to turn about-face and receive the enemy's attack, if they saw themselves being encircled by the Persian army.
>
> (Arrian, *Anabasis* 3.12.1)

Having ensured the safety of the front line in its rear, he needed now to protect its flanks. To achieve this, he placed flank-guards at both ends of the front line, but stationed roughly at an angle of 45 degrees to the front line:

> in case it became necessary to extend the front line or to close up the phalanx.
>
> (Arrian, *Anabasis* 11.12.2)

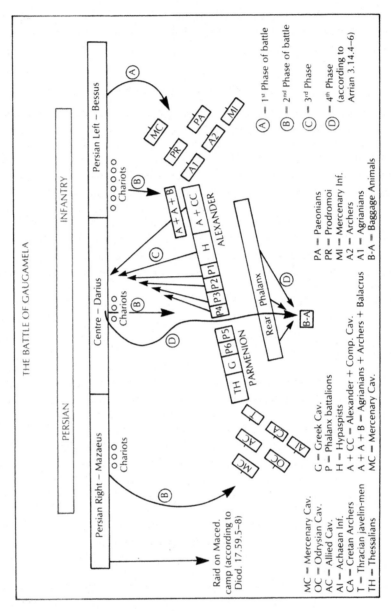

THE BATTLE OF GAUGAMELA

PERSIAN

INFANTRY

Persian Right – Mazaeus

o o o
Chariots

Persian Left – Bessus

Centre – Darius

o o o o o
Chariots

o l o o
Chariots

o l o o
Chariots

A + A + B

A + CC

ALEXANDER

H
P1
P2
P3
P4

Rear Phalanx

TH G P6 P5

PARMENION

B-A

MC

OC

CA

AI

T

MC

PR

AI

PA

A2

MI

Raid on Maced.
camp (according to
Diod. 17.59.5–8)

MC = Mercenary Cav.
OC = Odrysian Cav.
AC = Allied Cav.
AI = Achaean Inf.
CA = Cretan Archers
T = Thracian javelin-men
TH = Thessalians

G = Greek Cav.
P = Phalanx battalions
H = Hypaspists
A + CC = Alexander + Comp. Cav.
A + A + B = Agrianians + Archers + Balacrus
MC = Mercenary Cav.

PA = Paeonians
PR = Prodromoi
MI = Mercenary Inf.
A2 = Archers
AI = Agrianians
B-A = Baggage Animals

Ⓐ = 1ˢᵗ Phase of battle
Ⓑ = 2ⁿᵈ Phase of battle
Ⓒ = 3ʳᵈ Phase
Ⓓ = 4ᵗʰ Phase
(according to
Arrian 3.14.4–6)

Map 13 The battle of Gaugamela

Thus, the flank-guards had an in-built flexibility, being ready either to swing forward in order to join the Companion Cavalry in an offensive capacity or to swing back to close up the sides of the front and rear lines, and thereby create a defensive 'square'.

These flank-guards were arranged by Alexander into two roughly triangular-shaped wedges (see Map 13), each unit at first facing the Persian front line, but ready to face away from the Macedonian centre so that they could attack the Persian cavalry in their exposed flank, whenever they tried to envelop the Macedonian wings (A.A. 3.12.4). Each wedge consisted of a combination of infantry and cavalry units, drawn up into three rows. On the right wing, the bottom row consisted of three units – half of the Agrianians (next to the Companion Cavalry), the Macedonian archers and the veteran mercenaries; the middle row consisted of two units – the Prodromoi and the Paeonians; and the mercenary cavalry under Menidas formed the point of the wedge. On the left, the bottom row contained the Thracian javelin-men (next to the Thessalian cavalry), the Cretan archers, and the Achaean mercenary infantry; the allied Greek cavalry and the Odrysian cavalry comprised the middle row; and the Greek mercenary cavalry under Coeranus were the point (A.A. 3.12.4–5; Diodorus 17.57.4). Finally, Alexander stationed the other two halves of the Agrianians and the Macedonian archers, together with a force of javelin-men under Balacrus, in front of the Companion Cavalry to act as their shield and to tackle the scythed-chariots.

The sources

The sources vary considerably on the details of this battle, but it is possible to give a reasonably accurate description by combining their accounts, since they concentrate on different parts of the battle. Arrian concentrates entirely on the action of Alexander's right wing, and thus provides no record of the fighting on the Macedonian left wing, which was under the command of Parmenion. Diodorus, however, gives a detailed description of the combined attack of the Persian cavalry and scythed-chariots, under the command of Mazaeus, on the Macedonian left wing (17.58.2–5); and of the Persians' attack on the Macedonian camp, after they had successfully out-flanked the Macedonians (17.59.5–8). Curtius' detailed account is careless and muddled, and, since he is apparently using the same sources as both Arrian and Diodorus, it is a safer course to follow their accounts of the battle.

The battle

When Alexander's army took the field, his right wing was in line with the Persian centre. Therefore he ordered his army to advance to the right in an oblique or slanting battle-line to reduce the considerable overlap of the Persian left wing (A.A. 3.13.1; D.S. 17.57.6). It was this rightwards movement that provoked the battle because Darius, fearing that Alexander would pass beyond the specially levelled ground for the scythed-chariots, ordered some of his cavalry squadrons in front of the Persian left wing to ride around the Macedonian right wing to stop its rightward advance. Alexander's response was to send the mercenary cavalry under Menidas (the point of the flank-guards' wedge on the right – see Map 13) against them. However, Menidas' force, being greatly out-numbered by the Scythian and Bactrian cavalry squadrons, was driven back by their counter-charge (A.A. 3.13.2–3). At this point Alexander launched the Paeonians, the mercenary infantry under Cleanor, and most probably the Prodromoi (their later 'second' charge at A.A. 3.14.1 marks the resumption of Arrian's account of the fighting on the Macedonian right wing, after he had described the attack of the scythed-chariots). So successful were these Macedonian reinforcements that Bessus, Darius' commander of the Persian left, was forced to send in the rest of the Bactrian cavalry, possibly as many as 8,000 (Quintus Curtius 4.12.6). The fighting in this area of the battle was long and hard, culminating eventually in success for the Macedonian right flank-guards (A.A. 3.13.4).

Very soon after Bessus had engaged Alexander's right wing, Darius ordered the rest of the Persian front-line to engage the enemy (A.A. 3.14.1). The scythed-chariots proved to be very ineffectual: the force of Agrianians and Balacrus' javelin-men, stationed in front of the Companion Cavalry on the Macedonian right, drove them back with heavy casualties; those that did manage to reach the Macedonian phalanx were allowed to pass harmlessly through the opened ranks, and were overpowered in the rear (A.A. 3.13.5–6). Mazaeus, Darius' commander on the Persian right wing, launched his cavalry squadrons and scythed-chariots against the 'refused' Macedonian left wing, commanded by Parmenion, and the left flank-guards. He may also have sent 2,000 Cardusii and 1,000 Scythians around the Macedonian left flank to attack the Macedonian camp itself (D.S. 17.59.5–8). However, there are doubts whether this attack ever took place, since it is linked with the entertaining, but certainly fictitious, story of the refusal of Darius' mother to be rescued from the camp, and because these Persian units were known to have been stationed on the Persian left wing (see below).

Darius' main hope of defeating Alexander lay with his cavalry on both wings, whose role was to surround and envelop the Macedonian wings. However, by sending reinforcements to help Bessus against the Macedonian right wing, Darius made a fatal mistake:

> But when the [Persian] cavalry, which was sent to bring aid to those who were encircling the right wing, had to some extent broken their own front line of battle, Alexander, having turned towards the gap and having made, as it were, a wedge of the Companion Cavalry and the phalanx that was drawn up on this side, led them at full speed and with a loud battle-cry against Darius himself.
>
> (Arrian, *Anabasis* 3.14.2)

Alexander had learned from the battle of Issus that he had to deliver the knock-out blow against Darius himself, as this would lead to the collapse of Persian resistance. By committing his right wing flank-guards to attack in stages, he had drawn the Persian left wing and then, far more importantly, the Persian centre-left into a concentrated attack on his right, thus creating the gap which offered direct access to Darius. In addition, he had kept the Companion Cavalry removed and protected from the initial fighting in order to preserve their attacking strength. Then, at this key moment, he and the Companion Cavalry wheeled to the left, forming the point and the right-hand side of an inverted 'v'-shape wedge, while the hypaspists and the four nearest battalions of the phalanx formed the left-hand side, and together they charged into the opening in the Persian line. After some fierce hand-to-hand fighting, first Darius and then the Persian centre broke into flight (A.A. 3.14.3; D.S. 17.60.2–4). At this point Bessus and the Persian right wing, seeing the collapse of the centre, presumably also withdrew from the battle (A.A. 3.14.3).

Most scholars have been in general agreement, although expressing differences of opinion about some of the details, about the action on the Macedonian right wing and Alexander's thrust against Darius in the Persian centre-left. However, the events on the Macedonian left wing and the last stages of the battle are a major source of disagreement, because of the divergent narratives of the official tradition and the 'vulgate'. The first point of disagreement concerns a Persian attack that was launched through a gap in the Macedonian front line:

> But the battalion [of the Macedonian phalanx] under Simmias was no longer able to join with Alexander in his pursuit, but had brought its phalanx to a halt and was fighting where it had stopped, because it was reported that the Macedonian left wing was under severe pressure. At this point where the Macedonian line of battle had split, some Indians and Persian cavalry burst through the gap right up to where the Macedonian baggage animals were.
>
> (Arrian, *Anabasis* 3.14.4–5)

According to Arrian, Alexander's 'v'–shaped wedge consisted only of the four nearest battalions of the phalanx, for the remaining two had to check their advance in order to help the Macedonian left, thus creating a gap between the fourth and fifth battalions. Arrian then states that the Persians, who raced into this gap, attacked the baggage animals and the Macedonians guarding them, but were defeated by the Macedonian second line of battle which turned about-face and attacked them in the rear (A.A. 3.14.6).

In the 'vulgate' version of Diodorus and Quintus Curtius there is no mention of a gap appearing in the Macedonian phalanx and no break-through by Indians and Persians. However, they both describe an attack on Alexander's camp. Diodorus records Mazaeus' dispatch of a force of

Cardusii and Scythians, who rode around the Macedonian left wing without contact and successfully attacked the camp, although they failed to persuade Darius' mother to gain her freedom from Alexander (17.59.5–8). Quintus Curtius also describes a large-scale attack on the Macedonian camp (Quintus Curtius 4.15.5–10). Clearly the 'official tradition' and the 'vulgate' are recording two separate traditions. Furthermore, the sources disagree upon the identity and the nature of the camps, which also affects the interpretation of events in the battle.

Alexander's four-day fortified camp (A.A. 3.9.1), which was about 16 miles from the battlefield, can be excluded from consideration, although it is precisely this camp where Darius' mother was most likely to have been based. But Arrian mentions a make-shift night-camp, 3–4 miles from the battlefield (A.A. 3.9.3–4); whereas Curtius mentions two camps of which the second was the main fortified camp, which was the object of the Mazaeus' planned attack (Quintus Curtius 4.12.17, 12.24). In Arrian's account, there is even doubt whether the Indians and Persian cavalry actually attacked the Macedonian make-shift night-camp: first, since it was an unlikely thing for a fleeing force to do; and second, because it would have taken the Macedonian second battle-line one to two hours to cover the 3–4 miles, and this time-scale is not in keeping with Arrian's narrative. It seems more likely that Arrian was referring to the baggage-park, which contained the baggage animals and their handlers and which was situated close to the battlefield. On the basis of the above evidence, it is impossible to reconcile these two conflicting traditions.

The second major area of disagreement concerns Parmenion's appeal for help to Alexander, which is mentioned by all the sources, although they disagree about Alexander's response. According to Arrian, Alexander, having received Parmenion's message, turned back from his pursuit of Darius, but upon his arrival discovered that Parmenion and the Macedonian left wing had triumphed (A.A. 3.15.1, 15.3). Plutarch's account is in substantial agreement with Arrian, although he records Alexander's irritation with Parmenion (Plutarch, *Alexander* 33.9–11). Quintus Curtius also appears at first sight to agree with Arrian's and Plutarch's version, when he states that Alexander received Parmenion's message at some distance from the battlefield (Quintus Curtius 4.16.3); but later he says that Alexander halted his pursuit at the river Lycus, partly because it was late in the day, and partly because he believed that his left wing was in danger (Quintus Curtius 4.16.16–19). This strongly suggests that Alexander never received Parmenion's message, and this accords with Diodorus:

> As a great slaughter was taking place and because the strength of the Persians was proving hard to withstand, Parmenion sent some of his cavalry to Alexander, urging him to bring help as soon as possible. These carried out their orders swiftly, but upon discovering that Alexander had gone far from the battlefield in pursuit, they went back having failed to give him the message.
>
> (Diodorus 17.60.7)

The Diodorus version of the unsuccessful appeal seems more convincing, since it would be extremely difficult to identify Alexander in the dust and the confusion of battle (Quintus Curtius 4.15.32–33; D.S. 17.60.4), let alone reach him when he was already in full pursuit of Darius. The different version of Arrian and Plutarch probably derives from Callisthenes, who displays an anti-Parmenion bias throughout his work (an example of which can be seen in Plutarch, *Alexander* 33.10).

The final encounter in the battle was the clash between Alexander and the Companion Cavalry, returning from their pursuit of Darius, and the Parthians, Indians and Persians as they were fleeing. This tough and difficult encounter resulted in the death of 60 of the Companion Cavalry (A.A. 13.15.1–2). There has been an attempt to identify this group with the Indians and the Persians, who had broken through the Macedonian phalanx and attacked the baggage animals (according to Arrian); it is argued that they were now attempting to escape in the direction of the main Persian flight, when they met the returning Alexander and the Companion Cavalry. This seems unlikely, for Arrian does not mention any Parthians among the original group, and he states that only 'some Indians and Persian cavalry' broke through, most of whom were killed by the Macedonian second line of battle (A.A. 3.14.5–6). It is far more likely that these were Darius' cavalry squadrons, including the elite squadron of the Royal kinsmen, who had been stationed on the Persian centre and centre-right and were eventually broken by the Macedonian phalanx. As they fled from the battlefield, they ran into Alexander and the Companion Cavalry, as they were returning to help Parmenion.

This was possibly Alexander's greatest victory against Darius. At the battle of Issus, the battlefield had favoured Alexander – a fact recognized by Darius:

> For some had persuaded Darius that, with regard to the battle of Issus, he had lost it due to the narrowness of the battlefield, and Darius agreed wholeheartedly.
>
> (Arrian, *Anabasis* 3.8.7)

Alexander had now proved without the slightest shadow of doubt that he could defeat the Persians on any battlefield. His positioning and arrangement of his flank-guards and his staged introduction of them into the battle reveal that Alexander had no equal as a field commander in the mastery of tactics. In particular, his use of the 'v'-shaped wedge, which brought about the collapse of the Persian centre-left, Darius' flight and the Macedonian victory, was outstanding in its originality and marked a major advance in the art of warfare. Alexander had truly won the kingdom of Persia by right of conquest.

Bibliography

Bosworth, A. B. *Commentary on Arrian's History of Alexander*, vol. 1, pp. 114–27 (Granicus); pp. 198–219 (Issus); pp. 285–313 (Gaugamela).

Brunt, P. A. *Arrian's Anabasis*, vols 1 and 2 (Loeb), Introduction and Appendixes.

Burn, A. R. 'Notes on Alexander's campaigns, 332–330', *JHS* 72.

——'The generalship of Alexander', *Greece and Rome*, vol. 12.

Fuller, J. F. C. *The Generalship of Alexander the Great*, pt 2, ch. 6.

Griffith, G. T. 'Alexander's generalship at Gaugamela', *JHS* 67.

Hammond, N. G. L. *Alexander the Great: King, Commander and Statesman*, 2nd edn, ch. 2, 4–6.

——'The Battle of the Granicus River', *JHS* 100.

Hornblower, S. *The Greek World 479–323 BC*, ch. 18.

Marsden, E. W. *The Campaign of Gaugamela*, ch. 4.

Tarn, W. W. *CAH vol.* 6, ch. 12, sects 3, 4 and 7.

GLOSSARY

agora

A market-place; the civic centre of any town, very similar in function to the Roman forum.

apoikia

A colony; but it was also a totally independent settlement, which had its own government and whose inhabitants were citizens of the colony and not of its mother-state.

archon

This was the name given to the top public officials in Athens before the advent of full democracy in the fifth century. There were the 'eponymous archon', who gave his name to the Athenian year; the 'polemarch' (war-leader), who was in charge of the army; the 'basileus' (king-archon), who was in charge of the state religion; and the six 'thesmothetai', who had judicial responsibilities.

archontes

These were Athenian officials who were resident in the cities of the Athenian Empire; it was their role to ensure that local politics reflected Athenian interests, that the 'phoros' was collected and despatched to Athens, and that the Athenian 'proxenoi' (see below) were protected. They were often in charge of small garrisons of troops and were widely spread throughout the Empire.

Areopagus

The aristocratic council in Athens, membership of which was restricted to ex-archons after their year of office. Ephialtes removed its political powers in 462/1.

Atthidographers

The collective name given to those historians who wrote an 'Atthis', a history of Athens.

Boule

A Council; in Athens, after the reforms of Cleisthenes (508/7) the Boule consisted of 500 citizens. It had two main tasks: first, to prepare the agenda for the Ecclesia; second, to supervise the administration of the state.

cleruchy

This was a settlement of Athenian citizens who, while retaining their citizenship, were sent out to take over a confiscated portion of allied territory.

Common Peace

This name was given to a series of peace treaties in the fourth century, in which the terms were applicable to all Greek states and not just those who had been in conflict. The first one was the King's Peace (also known as the Peace of Antalcidas) in 386. These Common Peaces were Persian-backed and allowed the Persians' favoured Greek ally (Sparta in the 380s and 370s, Thebes in the 360s) to impose their will on Greece, using as a pretext their position as 'protectors' of the Peace.

decarchy

A ruling oligarchy of ten men. These pro-Spartan decarchies were set up in the cities of the Athenian Empire by the Spartan commander, Lysander, in the last phase and in the immediate aftermath of the Peloponnesian War (431–404).

deme

Local communities, about 140 in number, which became the basis of political organization in Athens after the reforms of Cleisthenes. Each deme had its own Assembly and officials, including an elected 'demarch' (deme-leader); they also had to maintain a register of citizens, since membership of a deme was a necessary requirement for citizenship – every citizen was identified by his deme name as well as his father's name.

demos

This term has a wide variety of meanings: first, the whole adult male citizen body; second, the common people or the poorer citizens, thus being differentiated from the rich, the aristocracy, etc.; third, the democrats who were in opposition to those who supported other constitutions, usually oligarchs; finally, the Athenian people in the Ecclesia.

dokimasia

A preliminary investigation of an incoming public official with regard to his eligibility to take up a public office.

Ecclesia

The Assembly; the meeting of adult male citizens. It was the sovereign body of state in Athens, regularly meeting four times a month.

Ephor

Five Ephors were elected annually from the whole Spartan citizen body and, by the fifth century, were the most powerful institution in Sparta.

episcopos

An overseer; these were Athenian visiting commissioners who were sent out to the cities in the Empire to investigate internal problems and then to report back their findings to the Athenian people. They were also involved in the establishment of democratic constitutions among the allied cities.

euthuna

The examination of a public official's record and financial accounts at the end of his year of office.

Gerousia

The Spartan council, consisting of the two kings and 28 elders, which prepared the agenda for the Spartan Assembly, acted as a criminal court and was influential in the formation of Spartan foreign policy.

harmost

A controller; a Spartan officer who was sent with a garrison to control cities that had revolted from the Athenian Empire.

hegemon

The leader; this term is usually applied to a state which held the leadership ('hegemony') over a number of subordinate allied states.

Heliaea

The People's courts. From Solon to Ephialtes this institution was the Athenian Ecclesia meeting in a judicial capacity as a court of appeal. After Ephialtes' reforms its 6,000 jurors ('dikasts') were granted primary jurisdiction. Because of the pressure of legal work, the Heliaea was broken down into smaller panels of jurors known as 'dikasteria' (singular – 'dikasterion').

Helots

The Helots were Greek state-owned serfs who lived in Messenia and Laconia. They had been conquered by the Spartans, and were compelled to farm their land and pay a portion of the agricultural produce to their absentee Spartan landlord, thus allowing the Spartans to devote themselves to the arts of war.

hoplite

Heavily armed Greek soldiers whose strength and effectiveness lay in fighting in a closely packed formation or phalanx. As these warriors had to supply their own armour and weapons, the hoplite army was mainly recruited from the middle classes.

medism

The term applied to individuals who supported pro-Persian policies, and to states which accepted Persian rule.

ostracism

This was the banishment of a prominent citizen from Attica for ten years. The Athenian Assembly was given the opportunity every year to decide if it wished to hold an ostracism and, if it decided to hold one, citizens voted for the candidate of their choice by writing his name on a piece of pottery ('ostrakon'). The candidate with the highest number of votes recorded with his name was ostracized.

Perioeci

This term means 'those who live around', and refers to the non-Spartan and non-Helot inhabitants of Laconia and Messenia in the Peloponnese. These communities possessed internal autonomy, but their foreign policy was controlled by the Spartans and they were obliged to supply troops for Spartan campaigns. They were important to the Spartan military state, since they supplied the traders and manufacturers – the Spartans were forbidden to engage in such economic pursuits.

phoros

Contribution or tribute; when the Delian League was founded in 478/7, those allies who did not supply ships paid phoros as their 'contribution' to the war effort against Persia. However, when the Athenians turned the League into an Empire, it was this 'tribute', supplied by the vast majority of the subject-allies, which was the financial basis of the Athenian Empire.

phrourarch

A garrison commander; such men were in command of garrisons of Athenian soldiers, who were stationed in allied territory. They also had political duties and thus were one of the means by which the Athenians controlled their empire.

polis (plural: poleis)

An independent, self-governing, Greek city-state, each one possessing its own citizenship, law code, coinage, festivals, etc.

proxenos

A citizen of one state who served as a representative of another state, while still residing in his own state.

satrap

This was the name given to a Persian provincial governor, who was in charge of a 'satrapy' (province). Although they owed allegiance to the Persian king, they had and exercised a great deal of independence.

strategos

A general; ten generals were elected annually by the Athenian people, and the 'strategia' (generalship) was open to re-election. Apart from their military duties, the generals were very influential in the shaping of the policies of the Athenian Assembly.

synoecism

This is the name given to the joining of several communities into one city-state ('polis').

thetes

The lowest class of the four Athenian economic classes, as laid down by Solon, which supplied the rowers for the Athenian imperial fleet.

trireme

The standard warship of the fifth century, which had three banks of rowers and was equipped with a ram in the bows.

tyrant

This term was originally used in the seventh century to describe an individual who had seized power unconstitutionally, but did not necessarily reflect the nature of the rule. However, by the fifth century, it had gained its pejorative meaning of an autocratic, brutal ruler.

zeugitai

Literally, 'those who possessed a team of oxen'; they were the third of Solon's economic classes, and served as hoplites in the Athenian army, since they could afford to pay for their own armour and weapons.

BIBLIOGRAPHY

Anderson, J. K. (1974) *Xenophon*, London: Duckworth.

Andrewes, A. (1952) 'Sparta and Arcadia in the early fifth century', *Phoenix* 6.

——(1953) 'The generals in the Hellespont, 410–407', *Journal of Hellenic Studies* 73.

——(1956) *The Greek Tyrants*, London: Hutchinson.

——(1962) 'The Mytilene Debate', *Phoenix* 16.

——(1966) 'Government in Classical Sparta' in *Ancient Society and Institutions* (dedicated to V. Ehrenberg), Oxford: Blackwell.

——(1971) *Greek Society*, London: Penguin.

——(1971) 'Two notes on Lysander', *Phoenix* 25.

——(1978) 'The opposition to Pericles', *Journal of Hellenic Studies* 98.

——(1982) *The Cambridge Ancient History* vol. 3.3, 2nd edn, Cambridge: Cambridge University Press.

——(1992) *The Cambridge Ancient History* vol. 5, 2nd edn, Cambridge: Cambridge University Press.

Austin, M. M. and Vidal-Naquet, P. (1973) *Economic and Social History of Greece*, London: Batsford.

Boardman, J. (1980) *The Greeks Overseas*, 2nd edn, London: Thames & Hudson.

Boersma, J. S. (1970) *Athenian Building Policy from 561/0 to 405/4*, Groningen: Wolters-Noordhoff.

Bosworth, A. (1993) 'The humanitarian aspect of the Melian Dialogue', *Journal of Hellenic Studies* 113.

——(1980) *Commentary on Arrian's History of Alexander*, vol. 1, Oxford: Oxford University Press.

Bradeen, D. W. (1960) 'The popularity of the Athenian Empire', *Historia* 9.

Brunt, P. A. (1953–54) 'The Hellenic League against Persia', *Historia* 2.

——(1965) 'Spartan policy and strategy in the Archidamian War', *Phoenix* 19.

——(1976) *Arrian's Anabasis*, vols. 1 and 2, London and Cambridge, Mass.: Loeb.

Buckler, J. (1980) *The Theban Hegemony, 371–362*, London and Cambridge, Mass.: Harvard University Press.

Burn, A. R. (1952) 'Notes on Alexander's campaigns', *Journal of Hellenic Studies* 72.

——(1965) 'The generalship of Alexander' in *Greece and Rome*, vol. 12, Oxford: Oxford University Press.

——(1984) *Persia and the Greeks*, 2nd edn, London: Duckworth.

Bury, J. B. and Meiggs, R. (1975) *A History of Greece*, 4th edn, London: Macmillan.

Cartledge, P. (1977) 'Hoplites and heroes', *Journal of Hellenic Studies* 97.

——(1979) *Sparta and Lakonia*, London and Boston: Routledge & Kegan Paul.

——(1987) *Agesilaos and the Crisis of Sparta*, London: Duckworth.

——(2002) 'Spartan wives: Liberation or licence', *Classical Quarterly* 31; reprinted in Whitby, M. (ed.) *Sparta*, Edinburgh: Edinburgh University Press.

Cawkwell, G. L. (1972) 'Epaminondas and Thebes', *Classical Quarterly* 22.

——(1975) 'Thucydides' judgement of Periclean strategy', *Yale Classical Studies* 28.

——(1978) 'The peace of Philocrates again', *Classical Quarterly* 28.

——(1978) *Philip of Macedon*, London and Boston: Faber & Faber.

Connor, W. R. (1971) *The New Politicians of Fifth-Century Athens*, Princeton, New Jersey: Princeton University Press.

——(1984) *Thucydides*, Princeton, New Jersey: Princeton University Press.

Crawford, M. and Whitehead, D. (1983) *Archaic and Classical Greece*, Cambridge: Cambridge University Press.

Davies, J. K. (1993) *Democracy and Classical Greece*, 2nd edn, Hassocks: Harvester.

Dover, K. J. (1973) *Thucydides*, Oxford: Greece & Rome New Surveys in the Classics, vol. 7.

Ehrenberg, V. (1968) *From Solon to Socrates*, 2nd edn, London: Methuen.

Ferguson, W. S. (1953) *Cambridge Ancient History vol. 5*, Cambridge: Cambridge University Press.

Finley, M. I. (1975) *The Use and Abuse of History*, London: Chatto & Windus.

——(1981) *Economy and Society in Ancient Greece*, London: Penguin.

——(1985) 'The Athenian demagogues', *Past and Present* 1962, reprinted in *Democracy Ancient and Modern*, 2nd edn, London: Chatto & Windus.

Flower, M. (2002) 'The invention of tradition in Classical and Hellenistic Sparta' in Powell, A. and Hodkinson, S. (eds) *Sparta: Beyond the Mirage*, Swansea: Classical Press of Wales.

Forrest, W. G. (1960) 'Themistocles and Argos', *Classical Quarterly* 10.

——(1968) *A History of Sparta 950–192 BC*, London: Hutchinson.

——(1972) *The Emergence of Greek Democracy*, London: Weidenfeld & Nicolson.

French, A. (1979) 'Athenian ambitions and the Delian Alliance', *Phoenix* 33.

Frost, F. J. (1964) 'Pericles and Dracontides', *Journal of Hellenic Studies* 84.

——(1964) 'Pericles, Thucydides, Son of Melesias, and politics before the war', *Historia* 13.

Fuller, J. F. C. (1958) *The Generalship of Alexander The Great*, London: Eyre & Spottiswoode.

Gomme, A. W., Andrewes, A. and Dover, K. J. (1945–81) *A Historical Commentary on Thucydides*, Oxford: Clarendon Press.

Graham, A. J. (1964) *Colony and Mother City in Ancient Greece*, Manchester: Manchester University Press.

——(1982) *The Cambridge Ancient History vol. 3.3*, 2nd edn, Cambridge: Cambridge University Press.

Griffith, G. T. (1947) 'Alexander's generalship at Gaugamela', *Journal of Hellenic Studies* 67.

——(1965) 'The Macedonian background' in *Alexander The Great*, Greece & Rome vol. 12, No. 2, Oxford: Clarendon Press.

Griffith, G. T. and Hammond, N. G. L. (1979) *Macedonia*, vol. 2, Oxford: Oxford University Press.

Gwynn, A. (1918) 'The character of Greek colonization', *Journal of Hellenic Studies* 38.

Hammond, N. G. L. (1967) 'The origins and the nature of the Athenian Alliance of 478/7 BC', *Journal of Hellenic Studies* 87.

——(1980) 'The Battle of the Granicus River', *Journal of Hellenic Studies* 100.

——(1988) *Cambridge Ancient History vol. 4*, 2nd edn, Cambridge: Cambridge University Press.

——(1989) *Alexander the Great: King, Commander and Statesman*, 2nd edn, Bristol: Bristol University Press.

Hansen, M. H. (1983) *The Athenian Ecclesia. Collection of Articles 1976–83*, Copenhagen: Museum Tusculanum Press.

——(1989) *The Athenian Ecclesia 2. Collection of Articles 1983–89*, Copenhagen: Museum Tusculanum Press.

——(1991) *The Athenian Democracy in the Age of Demosthenes*, Oxford and Cambridge, Mass.: Blackwell.

Hignett, C. (1952) *A History of the Athenian Constitution*, Oxford: Oxford University Press.

——(1963) *Xerxes' Invasion of Greece*, Oxford: Oxford University Press.

Hodkinson, S. (1989) 'Inheritance, marriage and demography: Perspectives upon the success and decline of Classical Sparta' in Powell, A. (ed.) *Classical Sparta: Techniques Behind Her Success*, London: Routledge.

——(1993) 'Warfare, wealth, and the crisis of Spartiate society' in Rich, J. and Shipley, G. (eds) *War and Society in the Greek World*, London: Routledge.

——(1994) '"Blind Ploutos"?: Contemporary images of the role of wealth in Classical Sparta' in Powell, A. and Hodkinson, S. (eds) *The Shadow of Sparta*, London and New York: Routledge.

——(1996) 'Spartan society in the fourth century: Crisis and continuity' in Carlier, P. (ed.) *Le IVe siecle av. J.C.: Approches historiographiques*, Paris: de Boccard.

——(1997) 'The development of Spartan society in the Archaic period' in Mitchell, L. and Rhodes, P. J. (eds) *The Development of the Polis in Archaic Greece*, London: Routledge.

——(2000) *Property and Wealth in Classical Sparta*, London: Duckworth.

Holladay, A. J. (1978) 'Athenian strategy in the Archidamian War', *Historia* 27.

Hooker, J. T. (1989) 'Spartan propaganda' in Powell, A. (ed.) *Classical Sparta: Techniques Behind Her Success*, London: Routledge.

Hornblower, J. (1981) *Hieronymus of Cardia*, Oxford: Oxford University Press.

Hornblower, S. (1983) *The Greek World 479–323 BC*, London and New York: Methuen.

——(1987) *Thucydides*, London: Duckworth.

——(2008) *A Commentary on Thucydides, vol. 3, Books 5.25–8.10*, Oxford: Oxford University Press.

How, W. W. and Wells, J. (1928) *A Commentary on Herodotus vol. 2*, 2nd edn, Oxford: Oxford University Press.

Hurwit, J. M. (1985) *The Art and Culture of Early Greece, 1100–480*, Ithaca and London: Cornell University Press.

Jacobsen, H. (1975) 'The oath of the Delian League', *Philologus* 119.

Kagan, D. (1969) *The Outbreak of the Peloponnesian War*, Ithaca and London: Cornell University Press.

———(1974) *The Archidamian War*, Ithaca and London: Cornell University Press.

———(1987) *The Fall of the Athenian Empire*, Ithaca: Cornell University Press.

———(1990) *Pericles of Athens and the Birth of Democracy*, London: Guild.

Lenardon, A. J. (1978) *The Saga of Themistocles*, London: Thames & Hudson.

Lewis, D. M. (1963) 'Cleisthenes and Attica', *Historia* 12.

———(1977) *Sparta and Persia*, Leiden: E. J. Brill.

———(1988) *Cambridge Ancient History vol. 4*, 2nd edn, Cambridge: Cambridge University Press.

———(1992) *Cambridge Ancient History vol. 5*, 2nd edn, Cambridge: Cambridge University Press.

Low, P. (ed) (2008) *The Athenian Empire*, Edinburgh: Edinburgh University Press.

McGregor, M. F. (1987) *The Athenians and their Empire*, Vancouver: University of British Columbia.

Macdowell, D. M. (1978) *The Law in Classical Athens*, London: Thames & Hudson.

Marsden, E. W. (1964) *The Campaign of Gaugamela*, Liverpool: Liverpool University Press.

Meiggs, R. (1972) *The Athenian Empire*, Oxford: Oxford University Press.

Meiggs, R. and Lewis, D. M. (1969) *A Selection of Greek Historical Inscriptions to the End of the Fifth Century*, Oxford: Oxford University Press.

Merritt, B. D., Wade-Gery, H. T. and McGregor, M. F. (1949–53) *The Athenian Tribute Lists*, Princeton, New Jersey: American School of Classical Studies.

Michell, H. (1952) *Sparta*, Cambridge: Cambridge University Press.

Moore, J. M. (1983) *Aristotle and Xenophon on Democracy and Oligarchy*, 2nd edn, London: Chatto & Windus.

Morris, I. (1987) *Burial and Ancient Society*, Cambridge: Cambridge University Press.

Murray, O. (1993) *Early Greece*, 2nd edn, London: Fontana Press.

Ostwald, M. (1969) *Nomos and the Beginnings of Athenian Democracy*, Oxford: Oxford University Press.

———(1986) *From Popular Sovereignty to the Sovereignty of Law*, Berkeley, Los Angeles: University of California.

———(1988) *Cambridge Ancient History vol. 4*, Cambridge: Cambridge University Press.

Parke, H. W. (1930) 'The development of the second Spartan Empire', *Journal of Hellenic Studies* 50.

———(1977) *Festivals of the Athenians*, London: Thames & Hudson.

Pelling, C. B. R. (1980) 'Plutarch's adaptation of his source material', *Journal of Hellenic Studies* 100.

Perlman, S. (1964) 'The causes and outbreak of the Corinthian War', *Classical Quarterly* 14.

———(1973) *Philip and Athens*, Cambridge: Cambridge University Press.

Pickard-Cambridge, A. W. (1953) *Cambridge Ancient History vol. 6*, Cambridge: Cambridge University Press.

Powell, A. (1988) *Athens and Sparta*, London: Routledge.

Rawlings, H. H. (1977) 'Thucydides on the purpose of the Delian League', *Phoenix* 31.

Rawson, E. (1969) *The Spartan Tradition in European Thought*, Oxford: Oxford University Press.

Rhodes, P. J. (1972) *The Athenian Boule*, Oxford: Oxford University Press.

———(1972) 'The Five Thousand in the Athenian revolutions of 411 BC', *Journal of Hellenic Studies* 92.

——(1981) A *Commentary on the Aristotelian 'Athenaion Politeia'*, Oxford: Clarendon Press.

——(1985) *The Athenian Empire*, Oxford: Greece & Rome New Surveys in the Classics 17.

——(1987) 'Thucydides on the causes of the Peloponnesian War', *Hermes* 115.

——(1992) *Cambridge Ancient History vol. 5*, Cambridge: Cambridge University Press.

——(2003) *A History of the Classical Greek World: 478–323 BC*, Oxford: Blackwell.

Rihll, T. E. (1991) 'Hektemoroi: Partners in crime?', *Journal of Hellenic Studies* 111.

Roberts, J. W. (1984) *City of Socrates. An Introduction to Classical Athens*, London: Routledge and Kegan Paul.

Robinson, C. E. (1957) *A History of Greece*, London: Methuen.

Roebuck, C. (1988) *Cambridge Ancient History vol. 4*, Cambridge: Cambridge University Press.

de Romilly, J. (1963) *Thucydides and Athenian Imperialism*, Oxford: Blackwell.

——(1966) 'Thucydides and the cities of the Athenian Empire', *Bulletin of the Institute of Classical Studies*, 13; reprinted in Low, P. (2008) (ed.) *The Athenian Empire*, Edinburgh: Edinburgh University Press.

Russell, D. A. (1973) *Plutarch*, London: Duckworth.

Ryder, T. T. B. (1975) 'Introduction' in *Demosthenes and Aeschines*, London: Penguin Classics.

Salmon, J. (1977) 'Political hoplites?', *Journal of Hellenic Studies* 97.

Seager, R. (1967) 'Thrasybulus, Conon, and Athenian imperialism', *Journal of Hellenic Studies* 87.

Sealey, R. (1976) *A History of the Greek City States 700–338 BC*, London: University of California.

Sinclair, R. K. (1988) *Democracy and Participation in Athens*, Cambridge: Cambridge University Press.

Snodgrass, A. M. (1965) 'The hoplite reform and history', *Journal of Hellenic Studies* 85.

Stanton, G. R. (1984) 'The tribal reform of Kleisthenes the Alcmaeonid', *Chiron* 14.

——(1990) *Athenian Politics c.800–500 BC: A Sourcebook*, London and New York: Routledge.

de Ste. Croix, G. E. M. (1954–55) 'The character of the Athenian Empire', *Historia* 3; reprinted in Low, P. (2008) (ed.) *The Athenian Empire*, Edinburgh: Edinburgh University Press.

——(1956) 'The constitution of The Five Thousand', *Historia* 5.

——(1961) 'Jurisdiction in the Athenian Empire II', *Classical Quarterly* 11.

——(1972) *The Origins of the Peloponnesian War*, London: Duckworth.

Talbert, R. J. A. (1988) *Plutarch on Sparta*, Penguin Classics.

Tarn, W. W. (1953) *Cambridge Ancient History vol. 6*, Cambridge: Cambridge University Press.

Tigerstedt, E. N. (1965–78) *The Legend of Sparta in Classical Antiquity*, 2 vols. and Index vol., Stockholm, Goteborg and Uppsala: Almqvist & Wiksell.

Toynbee, A. (1969) *Some Problems of Greek History*, Oxford: Oxford University Press.

Wade-Gery, H. T. (1958) 'The Spartan Rhetra in Plutarch Lycurgus VI' in *Essays in Greek History*, Oxford: Blackwell.

——(1958) 'Thucydides the Son of Melesias' in *Essays in Greek History*, Oxford: Blackwell.

Walker, P. K. (1955) 'Purpose and the method of the Pentekontaetia', *Classical Quarterly* 5.

Wallace, R. W. (1989) *The Areopagus Council, to 307* BC, Baltimore and London: Johns Hopkins University Press.

Wardman, A. E. (1971) *Plutarch's Methods in his Lives, Classical Quarterly* 21.

Westlake, A. D. (1969) *Essays on Greek Historians and Greek History*, Manchester: Manchester University Press.

WEBSITES

Wikipedia: http://en.wikipedia.org/wiki/Main_Page

A good starting point for basic (and more, in some cases) information on the widest range of Greek history topics. Effective links within a topic and suggested reading.

Perseus: http://www.perseus.tufts.edu/hopper

An excellent site for the whole range of the Ancient World. Click on 'Collections and Texts' and then on 'Greek and Roman Materials' to gain access to all the ancient Greek literary sources, both in Greek and in English. Click on 'Art and Archaeology Artifact Browser' for access to a superb photographic collection of sites, buildings, sculpture, vases, coins, etc.

Internet Ancient History Sourcebook: http://www.fordham.edu/halsall/ancient/asbook.html

A very useful website. It has a section on primary sources and how to use them under 'Studying History'. It also has translations of six of the major Greek history authors, including Pausanias, under 'Greece: Major Historians: Complete Texts'. Finally it has links to specific topics and primary source translation under such themes as 'The Age of Tyranny', 'Sparta', etc.

Ancient Greek Cities: http://www.sikyon.com/index.html

A brief overview of the history, art, monuments, etc., of Athens and Sparta, and seven others (e.g. Sikyon, Argos).

INDEX

Revising for AS and A2 level exams?

Visit www.routledge.com/textbooks/AlevelClassics

From here you can access resources for books in our *Aspects of Classical Civilisation* series, all of which can be used in preparation for AS and A2 level exams.
  You can:

- Visit the syllabi breakdown to find out which sections of each book will help you with particular modules
- Browse the first 30 pages of each book for free, and find other books which cover AS and A2 level topics
- You will also find image galleries with maps and timelines, glossaries of difficult terms and links to other useful websites.

Related titles from Routledge

Ancient Greece
Social and Historical Documents from Archaic Times to the Death of Alexander

Matthew Dillon and Lynda Garland

In this revised edition, Matthew Dillon and Lynda Garland have expanded the chronological range of Ancient Greece to include the Greek world of the fourth century. The sourcebook now ranges from the first lines of Greek literature to the death of Alexander the Great, covering all of the main historical periods and social phenomena of Ancient Greece. The material is taken from a variety of sources: historians, inscriptions, graffiti, law codes, epitaphs, decrees, drama and poetry. It includes the major literary authors, but also covers a wide selection of writers, including many non-Athenian authors. Whilst focusing on the main cities of Ancient Greece – Athens and Sparta – the sourcebook also draws on a wide range of material concerning the Greeks in Egypt, Italy, Sicily, Asia Minor and the Black Sea.

Ancient Greece covers not only the chronological, political history of Ancient Greece, but also explores the full spectrum of Greek life through topics such as gender, social class, race and labour. This revised edition includes:

- Two completely new chapters – "The Rise of Macedon" and "Alexander 'the Great', 336–323" BC
- New material in the chapters on The City-State, Religion in the Greek World, Tyrants and Tyranny, The Peloponnesian War and its Aftermath, Labour: Slaves, Serfs and Citizens, and Women, Sexuality and the Family

It is structured so that:

- Thematically arranged chapters arranged allow students to build up gradually knowledge of the Ancient Greek world
- Introductory essays to each chapter give necessary background to understand topic areas
- Linking commentaries help students understand the source extracts and what they reveal about the Ancient Greeks

Ancient Greece: Social and Historical Documents from Archaic Times to the Death of Alexander the Great (third edition), will continue to be a definitive collection of source material on the society and culture of the Greeks.

Hb: 978-0-415-47329-3
Pb: 978-0-415-47330-9

Available at all good bookshops
For ordering and further information please visit: www.routledge.com

Related titles from Routledge

Aspects of Roman History 82BC–AD14
A Source-based Approach

Hilary Swain and Mark Everson Davies

Aspects of Roman History 82BC–AD14 examines the political and military history of Rome and its empire in the Ciceronian and Augustan ages. It is an indispensable introduction to this central period of Roman History for all students of Roman history, from pre-university to undergraduate level.

This is the first book since H.H. Scullard's From the Gracchi to Nero, published two generations ago, to offer a full introductory account of one of the most compelling and vital periods in the history of Europe. Aspects of Roman History 82BC–AD14:

- Brings to life the great figures of Pompey, Caesar, Antony, Cleopatra and Augustus, and explores how power was gained, used and abused
- Covers the lives of women and slaves, the running of the empire and the lives of provincials, and religion, culture and propaganda
- Offers both a survey of the main topics and a detailed narrative through the close examination of sources
- Introduces students to the problems of interpreting evidence, and helps develop the knowledge and skills needed to further the study of ancient history

Written by experienced teachers, *Aspects of Roman History 82BC–AD14* is an invaluable aid to note-taking, essay preparation and examination revision

Hb: 978-0-415-49693-3
Pb: 978-0-415-49694-0

Available at all good bookshops
For ordering and further information please visit:
www.routledge.com

Aspects of Roman History AD14–117
Richard Alston

Aspects of Roman History charts the history of the Roman Imperial period, from the establishment of the Augustan principate to the reign of Trajan, providing a basic chronological framework of the main events and introductory outlines of the major issues of the period. The first half of the book outlines the linear development of the Roman Empire, emperor by emperor, accenting the military and political events. The second half of the book concentrates on important themes which apply to the period as a whole, such as the religious, economic and social functioning of the Roman Empire.

It includes:

- a discussion of the primary sources of Roman Imperial history
- clearly laid out chapters on different themes of the Roman Empire such as patronage, religion, the role of the senate, the army and the position of women and slaves
- designed for easy cross-referencing with the chronological outline of events
- maps and illustrations
- a guide to further reading.

Richard Alston's highly accessible book is designed specifically for students with little previous experience of studying ancient/Roman history. *Aspects of Roman History* provides an invaluable introduction to Roman Imperial history, which will allow students to gain an over-view of the period and will be an indispensable aid to note-taking, essay preparation and examination revision.

Hb: 978-0-415-13236-7
Pb: 978-0-415-13237-4

Related titles from Routledge

The Greeks
An Introduction to Their Culture
Robin Sowerby

The Greeks has provided a concise yet wide-ranging introduction to the culture of Ancient Greece since its first publication. In this new and expanded second edition the best-selling volume offers a lucid survey that:

- covers all the key elements of Ancient Greek civilization from the age of Homer to the Hellenistic period
- provides detailed discussions of the main trends in literature and drama, philosophy, art and architecture, with generous reference to original sources
- places Ancient Greek culture firmly in its political, social and historical context
- includes a new chapter on 'Religion and Social Life'.

The Greeks now contains more illustrations, a chronological chart, maps and suggestions for further reading as well as a new glossary. *The Greeks* is an indispensable introduction for all students of Classics, and an invaluable guide for students of other disciplines who require grounding in Greek civilization.

Hb: 978-0-415-46938-8
Pb: 978-0-415-46937-1

Available at all good bookshops
For ordering and further information please visit:
www.routledge.com

Lightning Source UK Ltd.
Milton Keynes UK
UKOW05f2000260117

292973UK00015B/256/P